EASTERN STANDARD TIME

To my parents Bailing and David, my sister Christine, and to Jen Wana, for putting up with me...so far.—J.Y.

•

To my mom, dad, and the rest of the Gan clan, including, of course, my nephews Mitch and Max.—D.G.

•

To mom, dad, Gregor, and Schuyler.—T.H.

•

Thanks to Nathaniel Wice and Stephen Daly, Norman Wang, Rosana Chang, Barbara Lowenstein, Madeline Morel, Eileen Cope, Chris Coffin, Peter Strupp, and a numberless list of others.

•

Special thanks to Luciana Chang, whose tireless efforts got us through the long home stretch. We told you it would be worth it!

EASTERN STANDARD TIME

A Guide to Asian Influence on American Culture: from Astro Boy to Zen Buddhism

**Jeff Yang,
Dina Gan,
Terry Hong,
and the staff of
A. Magazine**

A Mariner Original
Houghton Mifflin Company
Boston New York 1997

cover image: *Astro Boy*: © 1963 NBC Films, renewed 1991 Suzuki Associates International, Inc.
Distributed in North America by The Right Stuf International, Inc.

For information about permission to reproduce selections from this book, please write to:
Permissions
Houghton Mifflin Company
215 Park Avenue South
New York, New York 10003

For information about this and other Houghton Mifflin trade and reference books and multimedia products, visit The Bookstore at Houghton Mifflin on the World Wide Web at:
http://www.hmco.com/trade

CIP data is available

ISBN 0-395-76341-X

Printed in the United States of America

10 9 8 7 6 5 4 3 2 1

Editors
Jeff Yang (J.Y.)
Dina Gan (D.G.)
Terry Hong (T.H.)

Assistant Editor
Kenneth Li (K.L.)

Research Assistant
Wendy Cheung (W.Ch.)

Senior Contributors
Wei Ming Dariotis (W.M.D.), Nan Kim (N.K.), Eleanor Lim-Midyett (E.L.M.), Eunice Lin (E.L.), Gene Chung-Ngai Moy (G.C.M.), Miryam Sas (M.S.), Temujin (T.), Martin Wong (M.W.)

Contributors
Yuan-Kwan Chan (Y.K.C.), Gloria Chang (G.C.), Richard Chang (R.C.), Gilbert Cheah (Gi.C.), Derrick Chen (D.C.), Joanne Chen (J.C.), Evelyn Ch'ien (E.C.), James Cho (Ja.C.), John Choi (Jo.C.), Jerome Chou (Je.C.), Stephen Chung (S.C.), Jason Cohn (J.Co.), Anthony M. Gallegos (A.M.G.), Nito Gan (N.G.), Erick Gonzales (E.G.), Rod Gonzalo (R.G.), Noell Howard (N.H.), Chiu-Huey Hsia (C.H.H.), Todd Inoue (T.I.), Hank Kim (H.K.), Lisa Mitsuko Kitayama (L.M.K.), Claudine Ko (C.K.), Henry Lam (H.L.), Karen Lam (K.M.L.), Grace Lee (G.L.), Leslie Lee (L.L.), Marie G. Lee (M.G.L.), Soyoung Lee (S.L.), Terence Lee (T.L.), Alvin Lu (A.L.), O.P. Malik (O.P.M.), Ameena Meer (A.M.), Ashraf Meer (As.M.), Andrea Moed (An.M.), Eric Nakamura (E.N.), N. Rain Noe (R.N.), Lynn Padilla (L.P.), Felicia Paik (F.P.), Tricia Paik (T.P.), Kamran Pasha (K.P.), Natasha Rafi (N.R.), Angelo Ragaza (A.R.), Jayne Riew (J. R.), Joanne Rim (Jo.R.), Hugh Son (H.S.), Kevin Sun (K.S.), Fumiko Takagi (F.T.) , Emma Teng (E.T.), Sofia Theophilus (S.T.), Nelson Wang (N.W.), Oliver Wang (O.W.), Alice Woo (A.W.), Amy Wu (Am.W.), John Yee (Jo.Y.), Cynthia Yoon (C.Y.), Debbie Yuan (D.Y.)

Designers
Barabara Love Ong-Shen
Mannar Wong

Picture Editor/Production Manager
Luciana Chang

Production Assistant
Rosana Chang

Photographers
Henry Chen, *still life*
Melissa Cooperman, *photojournalism*

Illustrators
Shino Arihara, *watercolor*
Mike Quon, *line art*

Copy Editor
Anna Lee

**"Oh, East is East and West is West,
and never the twain shall meet,
Till Earth and Sky stand presently
at God's great Judgment Seat."**

—Rudyard Kipling,

"The Ballad of East and West"

Introduction

When Rudyard Kipling wrote "The Ballad of East and West" in 1889, he was merely repeating conventional wisdom. After all, among most residents of the West, it was accepted fact that Asians were godless heathens who practiced none of the refinements of art and philosophy enjoyed by cultured people. Meanwhile, among inhabitants of the East, it was considered a fundamental truism that the white devils of the West were hairy barbarians, unschooled in the ways of civilized man. In short, conventional wisdom said that East and West were as compatible as, say, ham and hot fudge.

Of course, this wouldn't be the first time that conventional wisdom was proven to be an utter crock. The reality is that East and West have never been as far apart as those of either hemisphere might have imagined or wished. Trade in Asian spices and textiles fueled Western exploration and built the British Empire. It was the East's most drinkable export, tea, that America's erstwhile revolutionaries dumped to symbolize their indignance toward the Crown. Asian immigrants worked the orchards of California, the canefields of Hawaii, and the mines and boomtowns of the old frontier. And yes, America's railroads ran on the aching backs of Chinese workers, who were lured by tales of gold, and who found instead bitter labor.

Those looking further back into America's history might find that, for all intents and purposes, America was Asian before it was American; the ancestors of the continent's original inhabitants were Siberians who made the long, cold journey across the Bering Strait some 11,000 years ago, seeking (as would later generations of Asian immigrants) a better way of life. According to some anthropologists, lost fishermen from Japan were cast ashore in Ecuador around 3000 B.C., thus becoming the first non-natives to "discover" the New World. Meanwhile, the Chinese have their own pre-Columbus discovery myth: they claim that Hui Shen, a Buddhist monk living in the 5th century A.D., sailed to Mexico, lived there for 40 years, and returned to tell the tale. And when the Great Navigator finally did embark upon his fabled voyage in 1492, he was searching not for unknown territories, but for a new sea route to India.

Today, at the turn of the millennium, America is more Asian than ever: a place where ramen is slurped on the run, curry is consumed in a hurry, and General Tso's Chicken rules the roost at every corner take-out; where Sonic and Super Mario duke it out on home video screens, and John Woo and Jackie Chan reign supreme in Hollywood. As the examples in this book should make eminently clear, in 20th century America, the twain of East and West have not only met—they've mingled, mated, and produced myriad offspring, inhabitants of one world, without borders or boundaries, but with plenty of style, hype, and attitude.

In Beijing, they're wearing Levis and drinking Coke; in New York, they're sipping tea in Anna Sui. While Pizzicato Five is spinning heads in the U.S., Metallica is banging them in Japan.

Paging Earth and Sky; please report at once to God's great Judgment Seat.

—*Jeff Yang*

ART AND DESIGN

"You can see the Asian influence in the Vietnam Memorial: the sensitivity to the landscape, the simplicity, the basic philosophy of the design. It doesn't dictate how you should think—it asks and provokes you. In that sense it's very Eastern. It wants you to come to your own personal resolution. My works are not overtly loud; they move on an intimate level. They're more like a book, a one-on-one dialogue between the person seeing the work and the work itself."

—Vietnam War Memorial designer Maya Lin

Japan's Designer Plants: Bonsai and Ikebana

In nature, a tree can live for centuries and grow to hundreds of feet. Now, imagine that same tree spending its decades in a six-inch ceramic pot. This is the miracle of miniaturization known as *bonsai,* an art form that translates literally from the Japanese as "miniature tray landscape." Most historians place the origin of bonsai in the 15th century. Though associated with Japan, the technique of dwarfing potted trees is thought to have been brought there from China by a Buddhist monk. Still, whatever its origin, the art has been filtered through Japanese aesthetics, and in turn has acquired a mystical significance for its American admirers. "The art of bonsai lies not in what the plant is, but in what it *suggests,*" says George Hull, author of the book *Bonsai for America.*

As an artistic concept, bonsai is focused on the recreation of an aspect of the natural landscape, carefully refined and scaled to miniature proportions; it is believed that by having such miniature versions of nature about one's dwelling, the bonsai owner brings peace and harmony to his or her physical and spiritual surroundings. Such is the paradox of bonsai: it is nature reduced, tamed, and controlled by man—a painstaking exercise in artificiality that is nevertheless meant to denote cosmic harmony.

Bonsai trees are difficult to care for, and—having been tamed and miniaturized—will turn brown and die with little notice. Those seeking a slightly less frustrating form of the Japanese agricultural aesthetic might turn to *ikebana,* the delicate arrangement of cut flowers and plants.

Ikebana evolved in 15th century Japan from the Chinese Buddhist ritual of the "flower offering," which migrated to Japan in the 7th century.

Derived from *ikeru* ("to keep alive") and *hana* ("flower"), ikebana came into its own as an art form in the latter part of the 15th century, establishing a style of composition from which all later schools of Japanese flower arrangement are derived.

Generally speaking, the art of ikebana consists of the arrangement of a set of branches or floral stems (known as the *shushi*) to create a harmonious and thought-provoking pattern. In the school of ikebana most commonly practiced today, there are three stems in the shushi, ordered by length: The longest is known as the *shin,* the stem of middle length is called the *soe,* and the last and shortest is called the *hikae.* While the placement of these three stems may seem random to the casual eye, in fact every bend, twist, and angle is carefully planned according to a blueprint known as the *kakeizu.* After the shushi are set in place, subordinate stems, blooms, and leaves (known as *jushi*) are often arranged around them,

THE MAKING OF A BONSAI

Looking to create your own midget tree? Here's how:

1 Carefully deliberate over the shape and color of the pot you plan to use. In order to create the desired aesthetic and philosophical effect, here are some hints: a deep pot represents a precipice; a flat pot creates the atmosphere of a plain or field; a brown pot implies uncultivated land; a blue pot represents water; and a yellow pot suggests the scenery of yellow trees or an autumn field.

2 Once you've chosen your vessel, select your tree. Trees are chosen for their longevity and the smallness of their leaves and branches. For this reason, the most popular trees are pine, plum, cherry, azalea, and Japanese maple. Be reasonable: You will have little luck attempting to bonsai a giant sequoia.

3 Time to choose a style. There are about 10 recognized principal styles and many more variations. A sampling:

a. The "coiled style," in which the trunk twists and winds to create the effect of an ancient tree, gnarled but vigorous.

b. The "clinging-to-rock style," which strives to mimic nature by planting trees on a rock.

c. The "slanting style," in which—you guessed it—the tree leans over to one side.

d. The "cascading style," which features a bent-over tree, giving the weeping-willow effect.

e. Now that you've made your pot, tree, and trunk-style decisions, you can begin the excruciating and neverending process of tending to the tree. The process is simple: Wire and trim. The tree is bent into position (gently; snapping the trunk produces the aesthetically displeasing "dead bonsai" effect) and wired into place, so that as it grows it will assume the trunk formation selected; meanwhile, in order to prevent it from attaining the size of your house, its roots and branches must be constantly limited through trimming.

4 Reduce the root system.

5 Limit the branch system.

6 Repeat steps 4 and 5 constantly. Don't give up—you'll have to work at it for a good 10 years to attain your desired effect. (Less elaborate bonsai may require fewer years, but the operative term is years, not months or days.)

7 Pass the plant on to your offspring, reminding them to water it carefully so that it doesn't dry out. With a potential life expectancy of at least 200 years or so, it'll make the perfect family heirloom.

8 Take a well-deserved rest.

to lend color and fullness to the finished work.

In contrast to the vivid hubris sometimes displayed in Western flower arrangements, ikebana teaches the quiet (and humble) appreciation of time itself. A philosophy lesson in a vase, it seeks to cultivate a sensitivity to growth as an elastic continuum: It celebrates both the fading and the blossoming of the flower. In ikebana, a perfect leaf might be cut to resemble a torn one, so as to represent decay. A flower's bud might be considered more beautiful than one in full bloom, because ikebana finds within the bud "the energy of life's opening toward the future."

And this may be the reason for its time-tested popularity both in Japan and, more recently, throughout the world: ikebana offers sanctuary from the world of fast food and fax machines, showing that a rose is never just a rose—and that nothing lasts, or is lost, forever.

I LIKE IKEBANA

Ikebana was once taught to Japanese women as a necessary accomplishment, a critical step in "finishing." Upper-class women, that is—who could afford the requisite private master. As ikebana itself teaches us, however, times change: Now the art has been introduced throughout the world as something to be appreciated by both sexes, and as a skill that can be taught in classrooms, rather than solely through private tutorial. A disclaimer: This democratization hasn't made it easier to learn. Ikebana is, in fact, so monstrously elaborate that its rules are outlined (in excruciating detail) in a tome of 12 large volumes—an epic that has as yet gone untranslated into English. So:

1. Don't expect to be able to learn about ikebana in one handy, thumbnail lesson.

2. Take some time to ponder the essences of growth, change, death, and rebirth.

3. Now learn some fundamentals. Modern ikebana pieces fall into two general classifications, based on the type of container used to hold the work: Pieces which use shallow dishes are known as *moribana,* and pieces which use long, narrow vases are called *nageire*. Moribana give the illusion of plants springing forth from the soil; a spiked plate known as the *kenzan* is used to keep the shushi and jushi upright. Nageire, which are more obviously arrangements of cut flowers and branches, are held in place by twists and manipulations of the plant matter itself, or, if necessary, with supports made of cut branches. Once the type of container to be used is chosen, the next thing to do is to determine the flow of the piece. This depends on the orientation of the shin: A strong, upright shin indicates a "masculine" line; a shin that is angled produces a graceful, "feminine" line. (Any thoughts regarding the implicit sexism in all of this can be forwarded to Japan, circa 1400 A.D.)

4. Now that you're fluent in the basic terms, get thee to a library, enroll in a school, or best yet, find yourself a willing guru. This won't be easy, and mastering ikebana will take years. However, if you've truly absorbed the aforementioned essences (step 2), you'll have the patience required to learn, and learn well. —T.

Brush Painting

Long before Western artists were engaging in surrealism or abstract art, Chinese painters understood that the only way to represent the true beauty of an object, landscape, or person was to show its essence—to express its spirit (its *qi*; 👁**243**). As a result, Chinese painting is in some ways the most liberating of disciplines; it is, in others, the most rigid, since its rules of stroke, shape, and composition have been established for eons.

Both painting and calligraphy have their roots before the beginning of recorded Chinese history. The Chinese were using brushes for both painting and calligraphy from as early as the 16th century B.C., as evidenced by surviving Neolithic pottery works, decorated with simple painted patterns. The Zhou dynasty (1000–200 B.C.) produced the first wall paintings and murals, examples of which have survived to today. By the Han dynasty (200 B.C.–200 A.D.) and onward, full-fledged brushwork was abundant, especially after the invention of paper in the 1st century.

THE TWO SCHOOLS

In spite of its long history of changing styles and philosophies, almost all brush painting falls into two main categories:

KU LE or KU FA: The "contour" or "bone manner" style. The style is defined by carefully drawn outlines in varying shades of black ink, which delineate the basic structure of the form.

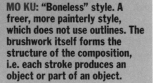

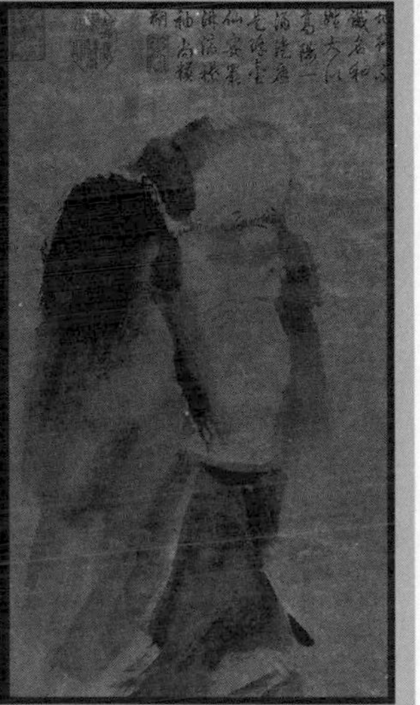

MO KU: "Boneless" style. A freer, more painterly style, which does not use outlines. The brushwork itself forms the structure of the composition, i.e. each stroke produces an object or part of an object.

THE "FOUR TREASURES"

According to Chinese tradition, these are the "four gems" of brush painting and calligraphy:

Brush: Tradition has it that Meng Tian (d. 209 B.C.) invented the brush. The earliest calligraphic brush yet discovered dates back to the Warring States period (480–222 B.C.), but brushes were used as early as the 3rd century B.C. to apply designs on pottery. The two main types of brushes are hard-fur (*jian hao*) and soft-fur (*rou hao*), each of which also falls into two categories: *dakai bi* for writing large characters, and *xiao kai bi* for writing letters or documents. The brush is held vertically between the thumb and index finger, with the middle and ring finger used to guide the hand, and the fingers lightly closed. Calligraphers say that when the brush is held properly, one can place an egg in the hollow of one's hand.

Ink and inkstone: Ink from the Far East has always been carbon-based. The invention of carbon-based ink is attributed to Cang Jie (697–597 B.C.); the first inkmaker to actually be documented is the calligrapher Wei Tan (179–253 A.D.). Chinese ink is a superior product, valued for its smoothness and balanced tone. It has a translucent quality, is waterproof, and does not fade with age. Calligraphy ink is prepared by rubbing the ink stick (usually a decorated ingot of solid ink) against a special inkstone, while adding water from a small dripper.

Paper: [👁**233**] Calligraphers once used both silk [👁**303**] and paper, but paper eventually became preferred. Even today, the best paper is considered to be Xuan paper, produced in the city of Xuan in Anhui Province, where two families have handed down its secrets for centuries. —T.H.

THE SIX CANONS

These simple principles, set forth by Xie Hou in the 5th century A.D., define the philosophical foundation of brush painting.

1 QI YUN SHENG DONG: "Spirit or life-force." The most important of the Six Canons: the artist must strive to represent the intangible "breath" of the subject through his painting.

2 KU FA YANG PI: "Bone structure." The artist must strive to use strong strokes, as strong strokes create a strong painting.

3 YING WU XING XING: "Resemblance." The artist must strive to create a likeness of forms found in nature (though not necessarily in a photorealistic manner).

4 SUI LEI FU CAI: "Coloring." Black is considered a color in brush painting, and much of its dynamic texture rests in the enormous range of black shades used. When colors other than black are used, they must conform with those found in nature.

5 QING YING WEI QI: "Composition." All elements of a work must be balanced, with one another and with the white space of the complete piece.

6 CHUAN YI MOU XIE: "Copying classical works." The artist must learn by repeatedly trying to duplicate the works of the great masters. Through copying, the artist is able to create a foundation from which to add expressions of individual creativity.

Calligraphy

The Seven Periods of Development in Chinese Brush Arts

THE FIRST PERIOD: the Neolithic Age to the end of the Han dynasty. The beginnings of brush and pigment work.

THE SECOND PERIOD: 3rd to 6th centuries A.D. Painting and calligraphy are, by this period, entrenched as serious art. The "Six Canons" are set forth by the artist Xie Hou.

THE THIRD PERIOD: 7th century to beginning of 10th. This period marks the beginning of a division in painting styles: colorful, elaborate figures and landscapes versus works that substantially utilize black ink.

THE FOURTH PERIOD: 10th to 13th centuries. These three centuries mark the full flowering of landscape art. During the Sung period, paintings become heavily influenced by literary themes.

THE FIFTH PERIOD: the Yuan Dynasty (1279-1368), founded by Mongol conquerors. This is considered a definitive period for Chinese art: painting moves toward landscapes in ink only, often combined with original poetry and calligraphy.

THE SIXTH PERIOD: the Ming Dynasty (1368-1644), which represents the restoration of native Han Chinese rule. This period represents a continuation of literary-inspired paintings.

THE SEVENTH PERIOD: the first 100 years of Qing Dynasty (1633-1911). Paintings during this period predominantly reflect a pursuit of antiquity, i.e. art inspired by ancient examples.

Throughout history, only three civilizations have produced true, original calligraphy—the Arabs, the Chinese, and Western European civilization. The most marked difference between these three was the historical social position of the calligrapher: In both the traditional Arab and Western societies, the calligrapher was always "in service," providing a skill for a patron, the Church, or a client. Only in Asia did the calligrapher emerge as a revered independent artist, whose work was honored as a discrete form of creative expression. Part of the reason for this may lie in the fact that, unlike Arabic script or the Western alphabet, Chinese characters are pictograms, rooted in images from nature rather than phonetically represented sounds [👁**219**]; as a result, the Chinese written language is as much an art form as a tool for communication.

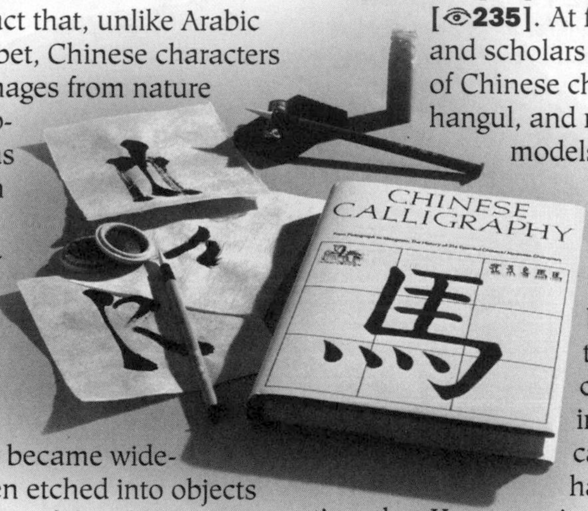

HISTORY AT THE TIP OF A BRUSH

Calligraphy in China

Before the art of calligraphy became widespread, characters were often etched into objects for decorative purposes; some of the oldest artifacts date back to 3000 B.C. when bones were inscribed with characters for the purposes of divination[👁**224**]. As written language developed and the number of characters grew, Chinese writing became increasingly sophisticated. In the 3rd century B.C., when China was for the first time united under the Emperor Qin Shi Huang Di (259–210 B.C.) existing writing systems were collated to create an all-encompassing 10,000 character script, allowing the proper recording of official data. By the 3rd century A.D., a simplified set of the character script had been devised, and the introduction of paper [👁**233**] had led to a flourishing of calligraphic art. Later, a "running script" was developed, allowing a new ease of brush movement and giving calligraphers greater creative freedom. Even today in China, calligraphy is still the most highly regarded of the "Three Perfections"—the others being poetry and brush painting [👁**4**].

Calligraphy in Korea

By the 7th century A.D., Chinese characters had become the official script of the Korean court, and remained so until the legendary King Sejong (reigned 1418–1450 A.D.) invented and instated *hangul,* a simple phonetic Korean alphabet [👁**235**]. At first, Korean calligraphers and scholars wrote using a combination of Chinese characters and Korean hangul, and relied on Chinese stylistic models, changing their forms as Chinese calligraphers came in and out of fashion. Individual Korean styles did not begin to develop and become popularized until the 19th century; in the 20th century, one of the most important trends has been calligraphy using only hangul, representing the first time that Korean artisans have attempted to create a purely indigenous calligraphy.

Calligraphy in Japan

As with the majority of its artistic and expressive forms, Japan first came into contact with calligraphy and the Chinese writing system via Korea—most likely through Japan's invasion and occupation of Korea (307–567 A.D.). Calligraphy as an art form first emerged during the Nara period (710–974 A.D.), during which time a considerable number of Chinese monks, who were also accomplished calligraphers, came to Japan. The first important Japanese calligraphic practices focused on the copying of Buddhist sutras; not until the Heian dynasty (794–1185 A.D.) did Japanese calligraphy develop its own unique tradition. —T.H.

Daruma

Need some luck in your life? Consider purchasing a *daruma*. These black, red, and white roly-poly dolls with fearsomely painted faces and two wide eyes are traditionally used in Japan as charms, and while no one's saying they'll change your life, fortune and happiness have been staked on stupider things in the past.

The daruma is a direct descendant of the children's toy known as the *okiagari koboshi* (literally, "the little priest who stands up"). For those of you who know your playthings, the okiagari koboshi was the original Weeble: with its rounded, weighted bottom, it too wobbles but doesn't fall down. The okiagari koboshi was popular as a toy during the 16th century, but had at the time no luck-bringing or wish-fulfillment function.

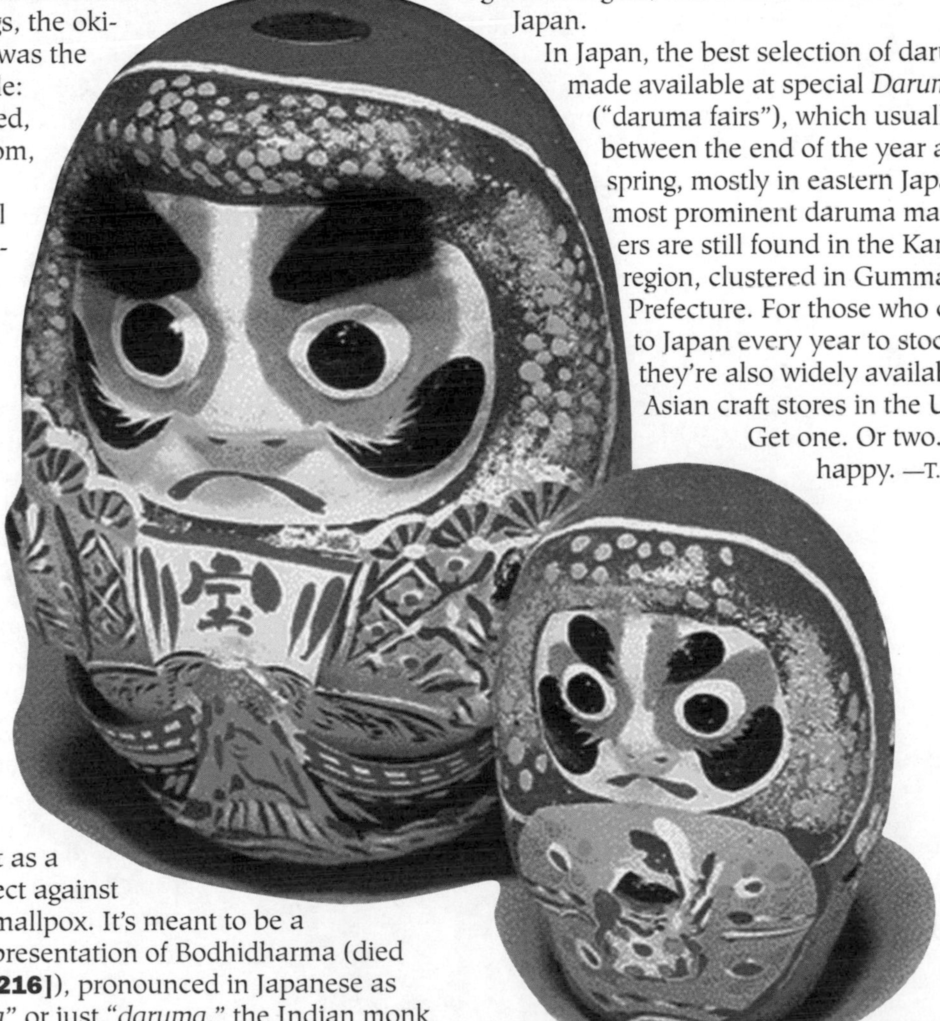

The daruma in its present form dates to the Edo period (1600–1868), where it was believed to act as a charm to protect against the dreaded smallpox. It's meant to be a cute, goofy representation of Bodhidharma (died circa 532; [👁**216**]), pronounced in Japanese as "*bodai daruma*" or just "*daruma*," the Indian monk who is believed to have brought Buddhism, not to mention kung fu, to China. The daruma's rotund, limbless form is due to the fact that, after meditating in a cave for nine years, the monk lost the use of his arms and legs. (After nearly a decade of inactivity, you'd resemble a Weeble too.)

Today, daruma are wish-fulfillment charms used to ask the Bodhidharma for a successful harvest, a good test score, victory in an election, and so on—a custom which first developed in the silk-producing Kanto region, and is now common throughout Japan.

In Japan, the best selection of daruma is made available at special *Darumaichi* ("daruma fairs"), which usually happen between the end of the year and early spring, mostly in eastern Japan. The most prominent daruma manufacturers are still found in the Kanto region, clustered in Gumma Prefecture. For those who can't get to Japan every year to stock up, they're also widely available in Asian craft stores in the U.S.

Get one. Or two. Be happy. —T.H.

DOING DARUMA

If you've got a deep and secret wish—whether it's getting Ms. Right to agree to a first date, being accepted into a prestigious university, or hoping your enemy gets hit by lightning—these easy steps should hasten your progress toward your goal:

1 **Purchase the daruma of your choice. You'll know which one to get; it'll be the one gently calling out your name.**

2 **Using black ink or paint, fill in one of its large white eyes while thinking of your goal.**

3 **Place this precious vehicle of fortune in your family shrine. (If you don't have one, or if you're not Buddhist, put it on your mantelpiece. If you think it's hideous and want to tuck it somewhere out of the way, that's okay too. Bodhidharma is a forgiving guy.)**

4 **Keep on wishing. Hard.**

5 **Once your wish comes true—and, of course, it will, if you wished hard enough—paint in the other eye so that it matches the first. That locks in the wish, and completes your daruma. If you have <u>another</u> wish, you'll have to get another doll.**

Fans

Fans—the heat-busting, not the sports-watching variety—had their origin in China some 5,000 years ago. Of course, the requisite quaint legend exists surrounding the invention of the hand-held fan. Apparently, while the rather practical-minded daughter of a distinguished mandarin was celebrating the Lantern Festival, she felt suddenly faint from the heat, so she took off the mask she was wearing at the time and did the obvious—held it close to her face and moved it back and forth to create a slight breeze. The other court maidens saw her example and immediately began to relieve themselves in the same way. Is this truth or fiction? Believe what you want.

Stories aside, the original fans were made of leaves, bound grasses, or feathers (especially peacock plumage), fixed to a wood or bone handle; they were used to cool the face, encourage fires, and for various ceremonial purposes. Eventually, the technique of stretching silk [👁**303**] and later, paper [👁**233**] across a rigid wire frame to create a flat, paddle-shaped fan was developed, and screen fans largely replaced the bound-feather variety.

Chinese screen fans were first introduced to Japan during the Nara period (710–794 A.D.), where they were called *uchiwa*. Less than a century later, the Japanese improved on the Chinese original by inventing the folding fan, called the *ogi*—a pleated, decorated leaf of paper, mounted on a semicircular frame of thin, flat sticks. Folding-fan technology migrated back to China, where it was quickly adopted by the Chinese (with a certain amount of disgruntlement at having been outdone by their island cousins yet again); from there, in the 14th century, the fan traveled to Europe. By the 15th century, thanks to the efforts of peripatetic Portuguese traders, fans were ubiquitous, and European demand seemed limitless. To increase the efficiency of manufacture, fan parts were often imported from China and assembled domestically in Europe.

By the 17th and 18th centuries, France had become the leading manufacturing center of fans, which had became an essential part of the genteel wardrobe. They had become increasingly intricate, using materials that included vellum, fabric, and lace, and designs that featured printed, hand-colored, embroidered, and even lacquered decor. Fan handles were most often made of mother-of-pearl; folding-fan skeletons were constructed from ivory, mother-of-pearl, or fancy wood, and held in place with silk ribbons or thread.

Fashion dictated that a woman—that is, a lady—had to have a different fan for every outfit; a lady was never fully dressed without her fan, which served not just as a fashion statement, but also as a means for discreet flirtation. Entire books were written purporting to teach the "language of the fan," lest a knot-headed male not understand female signals of fannish desire. (To offer even greater flirting flexibility, ingenious craftsmen created "lorgnette fans" with built-in eyeglasses, and "domino fans" with carved-out eyeholes.)

By the 20th century, inventors had engineered mechanized fans that did a much better job of cooling, and the arrival of the air conditioner virtually ended the era of the fan-as-utilitarian-instrument. Bereft of its practical use, the popularity of the hand-held fan largely faded by the end of the 19th century. However, the fan retained its value as a flirtation device—and the continuing popularity of Southern epics like *Gone with the Wind* may someday lead to a revival of the demure, but naughty "social" fan. Certainly there are gentlemen (and not-so-gentle men) for whom a smoky, half-hidden look over a folded-paper half-moon might be an incomparable aphrodisiac. And with a more subtle use of her fannish wiles, might Scarlett not have gotten Rhett to give a damn? —T.H.

Eiko Ishioka

Best Costume Design, 1992/65th Academy Awards

Eiko Ishioka is perhaps the most prominent Japanese graphic designer of the last decade. Multitalented and multifaceted, her works can be found in advertising, on stage, in video, on film, and around the world.

Ishioka was born in Japan on July 12, around 1939. Her father was a pioneering graphic designer, who became Eiko's first source of inspiration. He didn't, however, encourage this interest, advising her to go into a noncompetitive, "feminine" area of design, like making dolls or shoes. Ishioka didn't listen, going on to study graphic arts at the Tokyo National University of Fine Arts and Music. Upon graduating in 1961, she went to work in the advertising division of Shiseido, Japan's oldest cosmetics company. Then, in 1970, Ishioka received international acclaim with her poster design for Japan's Expo '70, an event that showcased the nation's most noteworthy artistic and technological achievements. One year later, Ishioka began her legendary affiliation with Parco, a chain of Japanese department superstores. Ishioka singlehandedly created and maintained the company's public image through a series of groundbreaking posters that rarely had anything to do with the fashions available at Parco. Instead, Ishioka's work was about women, fashion, society, and sometimes about nothing in particular; these bold visual statements quickly established the company as one of Japan's major trend giants, especially among the all-important young consumer market.

In 1971, Ishioka became the first woman to be elected to the Tokyo Art Directors Club. One sour peer announced that it was her gender which made her newsworthy; had she been a man, her election would never have drawn media attention. He'd later have to eat his words: Ishioka was no novelty, and attention would follow her like bees to honey. In 1979, Ishioka designed the posters for Francis Ford Coppola's wrenching *Apocalypse Now* [**116**]. Ishioka also designed the Japanese edition of Eleanor Coppola's book, *Notes,* which detailed the difficult making of *Apocalypse Now.* Then, in 1983, Ishioka wrote and designed the elegant book *Eiko on Eiko*—which, for the first time, introduced her genius to an international English-speaking audience. Despite their common work, Ishioka and Coppola did not meet face to face until 1984, when the director arrived in Japan to produce Paul Shrader's *Mishima,* for which Ishioka did the production set designs. The film won a Special Jury Prize at Cannes, and Eiko and Francis were off to a rich collaborative future. In 1985, Ishioka did the surreal sets for another Coppola work, *Faerie Tale Theatre*'s video production of the story of Rip Van Winkle. Then came *Dracula.* While Ishioka's specific credit is that of costume designer, the ambiance of the film was largely of her creation. It was her costumes, inspired by everything from Australian frilled lizards to Buddhist figurines, that served as the production's visual core; so successful were her designs that they resulted in editorial spreads in *Vogue, Harper's Bazaar,* and *Mirabella.* Of course, there's far more to Ishioka than her work with Coppola. Other projects include the 1988 Tony Award–winning Broadway hit, *M. Butterfly,* by David Henry Hwang [**28**]; the cover for Miles Davis's album *Tutu,* which won her a Grammy; and the Issey Miyake [**296**] fashion show, which she transformed into a theater event that played for six packed performances. Rarely has an artist been successful in as many media as has Eiko; rarer still has an artist's work been so influential. —T.H.

Overlooked Facts:

EIKO, MEET OSCAR— Upon winning her Best Costume Oscar, Eiko admitted that she was pretty sure she'd won from the very beginning: "I don't know what I would have done if I hadn't won. There are tens of thousands of people in Hollywood who have struggled for a long time to succeed in the business. I won an Oscar for my first big movie, for which I am thankful Coppola gave me the opportunity. I really enjoyed the experience but at the same time feel guilty for getting an Oscar so easily."

OSCAR: EIKO WHO?—When Eiko actually examined the award she received, she found out that her name had been misspelled.

Quirks:

A HARSH MISTRESS—She's so demanding that she's been known to make her collaborators and workers cry; people are willing to put up with her wrath because the end results are undeniably worth the tears and frustration.

Quotable quote:

"Male rivals used to say I was only famous because I was a woman, a novelty. I promised myself then that I would become so obviously special in my field that they would have to shut their mouths."

THE MASTER BUILDERS OF JAPAN

Arata Isozaki

An architect of international repute, whose designs are in almost every corner of the world. His work represents a myriad of structures of every type and varying scale, including museums, cultural complexes, offices, homes, Olympic stadiums, libraries, country clubs, city halls, stage sets, exhibitions—even visionary cities. As for his designs in the U.S., Isozaki is probably best known for the playful Museum of Contemporary Art in Los Angeles and the giant, mouse-eared "Team Disney" building, headquarters for the Florida Disney operations in Lake Buena Vista, Florida.

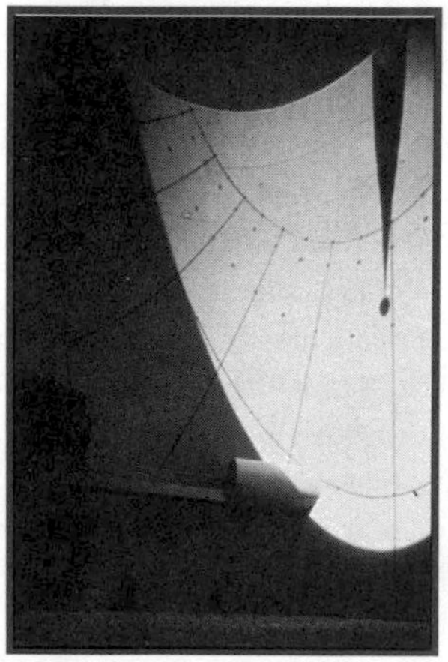

Building Japanese: Japanese Architecture in America

American architects have long been drawn to Japanese style because of its simplicity, functionality, and the serenity and calm it provides. As a result, from San Francisco to New York City and in many a suburb in between, Japanese architectural motifs have made a deep impression. Since the 1870s, Americans from coast to coast have fashioned gardens, homes, and office buildings after Japanese models; creative inspirations have ranged widely from ancient Asuka-period monasteries to late-20th-century earthquake-resistant designs. The common aesthetic threads between them: Clean proportions, the elimination of unnecessary elements, and a sense of harmony with the natural surroundings—drawn from Buddhist notions of simplicity and the need for oneness with one's environment.

Take a stroll through any U.S. neighborhood, and chances are you'll see a Japanese-style gate or a spare, yet tastefully decorated, rock garden. Meanwhile, simple interiors with hardwood floors and moveable-screen walls have become both the fashion and comfort of the day. In fact, Japanese style is so ubiquitous in American construction today, we often fail to recognize their origins. We no longer think of triangular roofs, stone-in-grass walkways, and wood-paneled floors as Japanese; we think of them as American. And, as is the case with so many things Asian—now they are.

BUILDING ON EASTERN TIME
A brief history of Japanese-style architecture in the U.S.:

1876 The Philadelphia **Centennial International Exhibition** features a Japanese dwelling and tea house, which are at first derided, but, with the passage of time, eventually admired.

1869 **Frank Lloyd Wright**, the foremost member of the **"Chicago School"** of architects, is born. Wright is drawn to Japanese architecture because it corresponds with what he comes to call "organic architecture." Throughout his career, Wright designs hundreds of homes and buildings that replicate Japanese form, philosophy, and structure.

1893 At the **World's Columbian Exposition** in Chicago, a Japanese "phoenix villa," or *hoho-do*, is constructed for display. It attracts the attention of architects from across the the nation, but especially those working locally in Chicago, like Wright

The Japanese American Historical Plaza at Waterfront Park in Portla

and his Chicago School.

1939 The New York **World's Fair**: Japanese architects erect a Shinto shrine–styled building to commemorate the 150th anniversary of the inauguration of President George Washington; vacation homes loosely modeled after this building soon dot the American countryside.

1949 New York's **Museum of Modern Art** features an exhibit of a contemporary Japanese house, citing its "unique relevance to modern Western architecture."

"Japanese art and architecture have organic character. Their art is more nearly modern than [that of] any European civilization alive or dead."
—Frank Lloyd Wright

THE HOUSE OF THE RISING SUN

If you're looking to build a home the Japanese way—and why not?—keep the following guidelines in mind.

1 **Above all, remember that a house is more than just a building.** Every structure must relate to its neighbors and to the natural environment. So, before you build, examine your location and build with your surroundings in mind. One good, if non-Japanese, way of ensuring that your home harmonizes with the energy of the terrain is to follow the principles of feng shui [👁226].

2 **The Western obsession between "indoors" and "outdoors" is just a state of mind:** your home is not meant to be a fortress-like barricade between you and the world, but a frame that helps you adapt to the world, and vice versa. Thus, natural lighting, "open" rooms and terraces, and large windows are a must. The design of your home should put you in a position to appreciate your environment without being buffeted by the elements.

3 **Keep it simple.** A minimum of ornament (using predominantly natural textures and colors) and strong but clean proportions will prevent your house from becoming a distraction. The following are some design touches to consider:

Indoors...
- silk screens
- sliding wood panels
- wood-paneled floors
- straightforward, geometric building plans—e.g., triangular roofs; long, rectangular hallways

And out...
- open, uncluttered courtyards
- gardens with rock, trees, and a single stream
- arching bridges
- shrines and open pavilions —R.C.

Minoru Yamasaki

The chief architect of New York City's 110-story twin towers at the World Trade Center, which at the time of their completion in 1974, were the world's two tallest buildings.

Tadao Ando

One of the world's most respected contemporary Japanese architects. Working in a strictly modern idiom, Ando's work is characterized by its minimalism; nearly all of his work is marked by its austere concrete surfaces and simple, organizing geometry. While most of his work has been built in Japan, the extensive publication of his work, combined with his lectures and exhibitions, and his professorships at such prestigious universities as Columbia, Harvard, and Yale have made him an architect of international reputation.

Paper on Fire: Graphic Design in Japan

Simple, yet striking; tightly controlled, yet visually astonishing. From page layout to packaging, Japanese design has long been considered among the best—and certainly the most forward-thinking—in the world. Longer, perhaps, than you might realize: One could say that Japanese design has been on the cutting edge since as early as the 17th century, when, during the Edo period (1600-1868), color woodblock handbills were used as advertisements for such retail outlets as dry goods stores and kimono shops. These woodblock one-sheets were the mercantile counterparts of the more artistically motivated ukiyo-e prints [👁**24**], and often the same artists who created the latter began as artisans who crafted the former.

With the advent of the Meiji Restoration in 1868 (when Japan was opened to western trade, and vice versa), advertisements for the first time migrated from free-standing handbills into newspapers and magazines. A Japanese graphic aesthetic began to take shape, informed by the strengths and limitations of the earlier woodblock posters; it featured strong lines and simple shapes, brightly displayed in color. (This aesthetic would deeply influence American modernism from the late 19th century onward; [👁**14**].)

In the years following World War II, graphic designers banded together to combine their creative powers employed by print media to influence, even direct the whims of popular culture. That impact remains strong. Today, combined with near-obsessive attention to surface detail, Japanese design maintains an artful, sophisticated image in America, aiding the sale of cosmetics, electronics, liquor, and other high-end Japanese goods. —An.M.

PAPER TIGERS: A Timeline of Japanese Graphic Design

1850 — Nariakira Shimazu, Lord of Satsuma, creates the Japanese national flag. A simple red circle on a white field, it remains the best-known Japanese graphic today internationally—though not, unfortunately, the best loved.

1876 — The Philadelphia Centennial Exposition provides the first mass American encounter with the Japanese graphic arts, in the form of ukiyo-e prints. American artists are inspired by the prints' compositional sophistication and use of flat tones, adding momentum to the new American poster movement.

1901 — The Tokyo School of Art opens Japan's first design department, where students learn to work in emerging formats such as newspaper advertising and department store posters.

1916 — The Tokyo-based cosmetics company Shiseido hires a full-time graphic design staff to produce posters and packaging for its products. Shiseido becomes an early leader in high-design advertising with a definitively cosmopolitan edge—a position which it retains to this day.

1946 — The postwar U.S. occupation government legislates coeducation in higher learning, enabling the training of the first female graphic designers in Japan—including Eiko Ishioka [👁8] and Harumi Yamaguchi.

1950s AND 60s — Japan's postwar economic boom gives rise to its first generation of internationally known commercial graphic designers. Some of their most recognized designs include Yusuku Kamekura's geometric posters for the camera company Nikon, Kenji Itoh's shutter-"C" logo for photographic and business machine giant Canon, and Tadashi Ohashi's finely illustrated graphics for Kikkoman soy sauce.

1960 — Toyko hosts the World Design Conference, and graphic design from Japan begins to reach a truly global audience; during the '60s, a number of Japanese poster designers develop international reputations and become greatly in demand in the West.

1964 — The Olympic Games come to Tokyo. Design coordinator and art director Masaru Katzumie and his team of young designers win international praise for the creation of signs and graphics that communicate across language barriers, including innovative pictograms representing the various sports.

1960s AND 70s — A second, more widely known generation of designers perfects a newly contructivist graphic style marked by the use of flat, geometric shapes. While exploring new techniques such as airbrushing, many designers return to using images of traditional culture, which had formerly been considered "provincial." For the first time, Shiseido ads feature more Asian women than Europeans.

1980s AND 90s — Mostly through the advertising of Sony, Suntory, Shiseido, and others, Japanese graphics continue to gain visibility in America. Much of this work is characterized by rich, textured surfaces, rendering the play of light on stone, metal, and the ubiquitous black matte finish of consumer electronics [👁**176**]. Widely copied by American designers, such work makes use of and encourages advances in computer printing and photomanipulation technology..

Maya Lin

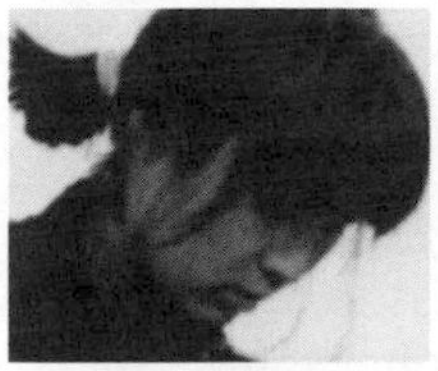

Though decades have passed, Maya Ying Lin is still best known as the 21-year-old Yale undergraduate wunderkind who won the national competition for the Vietnam Veterans Memorial in Washington D.C. in 1981. Her design: two highly polished walls of black granite, set in a "V," inscribed with the names of the 58,000 dead or missing veterans of the Vietnam War.

Lin was born October 5, 1959, in Athens, Ohio to the late Henry Huan Lin, a well-known ceramics artist and former dean of fine arts at Ohio University, and Julia Chang Lin, a professor of Asian literature at Ohio University. Before deciding on architecture as a career, Lin considered biology. Fortunately for those who have been uplifted by her work, she found herself unenthused by her prospects as an undergrad bio major, and set her sights on more monumental goals.

After graduating from college, Lin briefly taught high school, and then entered the Yale University School of Architecture, where she studied with sculptor Richard Serra and master architect Frank Gehry. Finding her formal education lacking when it came to non-European cultures, she also apprenticed with Japanese architect Fumihiko Maki, an experience that she says taught her an admiration for the Japanese approach to design and construction **[👁9]**.

That education in simplicity and minimalism proved critical to her unexpected and overwhelming success: At 21, Lin became an international celebrity by winning a competition over 1,441 candidates for the design of the Vietnam War Memorial with her solemn, yet striking, "Wall of Remembrance."

With her victory, however, came unwanted notoriety, which led to a year of shuttling back and forth between New Haven, Connecticut, and Washington, D.C. to defend her design against detractors who threw at her slurs of every kind: She was too young; she was the wrong race; she was the wrong gender; she did not understand the scope of the project. Some of her loudest opponents were such notable public figures as H. Ross Perot, Phyllis Schlafly, Tom Wolfe, and then–Interior Secretary James Watt.

In the end, both Lin and her design survived, and in spite of Lin's successive triumphs, the Wall undoubtedly remains her signature work. And, as something of a rebuke to her critics, in the decade-plus since its erection, the Vietnam Veterans Memorial has become the best-known, and certainly the most visited, work of contemporary art in the U.S., as well as one of D.C.'s most popular tourist sites, attracting more than 2.5 million visitors a year.

After the media frenzy of "the Wall," Lin reemerged in the public limelight with her first major commission—a monument to a different kind of battle, the Civil Rights Memorial in Montgomery, Alabama. Upon its completion in 1989, Lin announced that she was retiring from memorial making.

Since then, Lin has had other significant commissions, including "The Women's Table" (1993), a salute to the women students of Yale University; "Eclipsed Time," a clock in the vaulted ceiling of Manhattan's Pennsylvania Station; "Groundswell" (1994), Lin's version of a Japanese Zen Garden, built of recycled glass as part of the Wexner Center for the Arts in Columbus, Ohio; and "Wave Field," an undulating quadrangle of green inserted as part of the aerodynamics complex at the University of Michigan. She's also had her own one-woman show, aptly titled "Maya Lin: Public/Private" which opened in 1993 at the Wexner Center.

In 1995, Lin burst into the headlines once again, this time as subject of Frieda Lee Mock's cinematic biography, *Maya Lin: A Strong Clear Vision,* which, in a cloud of controversy, won an Oscar for best documentary feature. Lin was no doubt uncomfortable to be back in the spotlight—and worse yet, for a project not her own. —T.H.

Overlooked Facts:

EDIBLE, BUT UNFORGETTABLE—Design of "The Wall" began in Lin's senior year studio class at Yale, which focused on funerary architecture. Citing her habit of using three-dimensional models rather than drawings, Lin remembers, "I think the Vietnam memorial was first laid out in mashed potatoes or something."

AN UNEXAMINED CAREER—Although Lin holds a Masters of Architecture from Yale and has completed all her internship requirements, she has yet to take the registration exam to become a professional architect. Citing a busy schedule, Lin also says that being registered would not change the way she works anyway. As far as actual architecture projects, Lin surprisingly has not done very many. She designed the interior loft spaces for the Museum of African Art in New York. Her first and only from-the-ground-up building was a private one-bedroom house in the hills of Williamstown, Massachusetts.

Quirks:

DO NOT DISTURB—Lin, a notoriously private person, lives and works in a home studio four flights above New York's Chinatown, identified only by "Lin" on the doorbell. She also owns a house in Vermont. She's proud to tell you that her number is unlisted, and that the only way to get in touch with her is to know someone who knows her.

S A M U N O G U C H I

Overlooked Facts:

SETTING THE STAGE—Beginning in 1935, for three decades Noguchi created sets and props for the productions of modern dance legend Martha Graham. He also designed sets for Ruth Page, Erick Hawkins, Merce Cunningham, and George Balanchine.

NEITHER HERE NOR THERE—In January 1942, Noguchi organized an activist group of Japanese American creatives, the Nisei Writers and Artists Mobilization for Democracy. In March of the same year, he voluntarily entered the Japanese internment camp at Poston, Arizona, with the hope of improving the lives of the internees [👁31]. He left, discouraged, after seven months. After the war, Noguchi designed the railings for two bridges into the Peace Park at Hiroshima, completed in 1952 [👁320]. In 1952, he was invited to design a memorial for the Peace Park itself, but at the last minute his design—Memorial to the Dead, Hiroshima—was rejected by the city committee...because he was an American.

Quirks:

LOVE STORIES—Noguchi was seductive and energetic, if a bit self-absorbed. He had a number of long-term romances including one marriage to Japanese movie star Yoshiko Yamaguchi, which lasted about four years.

Isamu Noguchi

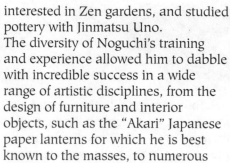

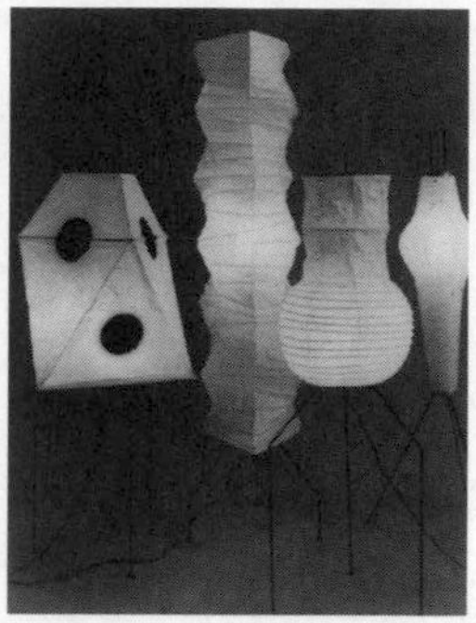

Known at various times in his childhood as Sam Gilmour and Isamu Gilmour, the man who would become one of the great modern sculptors of our time settled on the name Isamu Noguchi as he embarked on his career as an artist.

He was born November 17, 1904, in Los Angeles, California, to Leonie Gilmour, a Bryn Mawr graduate and aspiring writer, and Yonejiro Noguchi, a Japanese poet who had arrived in the U.S. hoping to gain recognition for his works in English. In New York, seeking editorial and linguistic help, Noguchi met Gilmour. Dore Ashton, Noguchi's biographer, writes: "Their romance, which for Noguchi [Sr.] at least was particularly expedient, lasted long enough for Gilmour to become pregnant. By the time Isamu was born...his father had gone to London to impress the literary establishment...and had returned to Japan." Isamu's relationship with his father remained troubled throughout the older Noguchi's life.

After moving to Japan with his mother in 1906, Noguchi was sent back to America alone at the age 14 to attend the renowned arts school, Interlaken, in Indiana. When the school was closed for wartime use, the school's founder placed him with a Swedenborgian minister, who raised him until he reached college age. Noguchi entered Columbia University in 1922, intending to study medicine. With his mother's encouragement, however, he took a sculpture class at the Leonardo da Vinci Art School in New York, and in 1924 left Columbia to concentrate on art.

In 1927, Noguchi was awarded the Guggenheim Fellowship; he used the money to travel to Paris, where he assisted the great sculptor Brancusi. In 1930, after his one-man show in New York, Noguchi traveled to Beijing and studied brush painting with Chi Pai Shih. He then went to Japan, where—snubbed by his father, who asked him not to use the name Noguchi—he became interested in Zen gardens, and studied pottery with Jinmatsu Uno.

The diversity of Noguchi's training and experience allowed him to dabble with incredible success in a wide range of artistic disciplines, from the design of furniture and interior objects, such as the "Akari" Japanese paper lanterns for which he is best known to the masses, to numerous exterior designs for plazas, gardens, and public spaces. Among his most acclaimed and prominent projects are the gardens for UNESCO headquarters, Paris (1958); the Billy Rose Sculpture Garden for the Israeli Museum in Jerusalem (1965); and the Horace E. Dodge Fountain and Philip A. Hart Plaza in Detroit (1979). He also designed the Sunken Garden for the Beinecke Rare Book and Manuscript Library at Yale University (1964), and a playground for children near Tokyo (*Kodomo no kuni*, 1966), among many others.

In the last two decades of his life, Noguchi commuted between his studio in Shikoku, Japan and a converted warehouse in Queens, New York. The latter has been transformed into the Isamu Noguchi Garden Museum, and houses an extensive retrospective of his work; his studio in the town of Mure, Shikoku also maintains a garden and display of his works.

Noguchi died in December 30, 1988, but not before receiving a generous trove of honors—including the National Medal of Arts in 1987 and the Third Order of the Sacred Treasure from the Japanese government.

More lasting and important than any of these awards is the serene simplicity of the aesthetic that he brought to the eyes (and under the feet) of the masses. His assertion that sculpture must exist as an integral part of the surrounding environment has had an overwhelming influence on modern design philosophy, and the objects and spaces that he designed with this harmony in mind continue to uplift and enlighten their users today. —M.S.

"Oriental" Style: Japonisme and Chinoiserie

Republic Bank, NYC's Chinatown

Odd things happen when Eastern arts meet Western tastes. The two separate but related vogues for "Oriental" handicrafts, Chinoiserie and Japonisme, have made a lasting mark on Western design, in fields ranging from furniture-making to architecture. Chinoiserie, the Western vogue for the Chinese and Chinese-inspired, had its start in the 17th century, when the opening of standardized trade routes to the East precipitated an incoming flood of objets d'art that quickly found an eager audience among Western decorators and knickknack collectors—particularly in France, where style *a la Chine* quickly became the rage at King Louis XIV's court at Versailles. Of course, while elite fans of Chinoiserie built collections of actual Eastern relics, in general the phenomenon had less to do with authentic Chinese style than with Western invention, featuring design motifs drawn from an imagined idea of the "Chinese manner" that ranged from the farcical and grotesque (e.g., monkeys dressed as Mandarins), to the romanticized and pastoral.

Chinoiserie reached its peak during Europe's 18th century Rococo period, and continued to evolve through the 20th century, though, by the 19th century, it was overtaken by stylistic competition from another Eastern source: Japonisme.

The forced "opening" of Japan in 1868 brought Western tastes, fashion, and culture into the formerly isolated island nation; it also led to the first substantial introduction of things Japanese to the West. Not surprisingly, Europeans and Americans were instantly seduced by the array of novelties and collectibles available by open trade, and a new phenomenon was born: the aesthetic fad that French art critic Philippe Burty dubbed "Japonisme."

Unlike Chinoiserie, which was mainly fueled by the interest of collectors and patrons, Japonisme was a movement that first developed among artists themselves. French graphic artist Felix Bracquemond (1833–1914) introduced Hokusai's woodblock prints **[👁24]** to Parisian society, leading to a frenzy of Japan-inspired artistic endeavors. Notably, James McNeill Whistler (1834–1903), best known among laypeople for painting his mother, was one of the earliest artists to incorporate Japanese motifs into his work, while living as an expatriate in Paris.

Japonisme would be crucial in the development of Modern Art, influencing Impressionism (1870–1890), Post-Impressionism (1880s–early 1890s), Neo-Impressionism (1880–1900), Art Nouveau (1880–1914), the Nabis (1890s), and Abstract Expressionism (mid 1940s–1950s). In particular, the bold composition and geometrical elements of *ukiyo-e* woodblock prints served to move Western art away from representation and towards greater abstraction. Other stylistic swipes from ukiyo-e included the use of dramatic foreshortening and aerial perspectives; asymmetry and truncated compositions; a minimalist spareness and emphasis on patterning; the incorporation of text into painting; and the use of visible calligraphic brushstrokes.

The Japonisme phenomenon—both as a stylistic influence and as an ornamental style, in which Japanese artifacts were used for decorative purposes—continued to be popular well into the 20th century, until the outbreak of the World War II destroyed its appeal. Since then, however, Japan has regained its hold as a primary aesthetic influence on the West, particularly in architecture **[👁9]** and graphic design **[👁11]**—not to mention fashion and home furnishing **[👁26]**. These days, of course, Western fascination with Japan is tempered with equal and opposite paranoia. So, even as urban drones decorate their homes with futons, folding screens, and matte-black consumer electronics, their corporate bosses are decrying Japan's killer competitiveness. How inscrutable. —E.T.

DRAGONS 'R' US

Objects created in the "Chinese manner" tend to be playfully—even garishly—decorative and patterned in geometrical shapes. Do these in any way resemble authentic Chinese designs? Not often, but (like Japonisme) Chinoiserie is less about imitating a culture than constructing one from scratch. Still, if you're bent on decorating the pseudo-Chinese way, here are some things to remember:

1 "Ornament" equals "Orient," so go wild with asymmetrical designs, grotesque repeated motifs, and pseudo-Chinese decorative elements.

2 Use rich, exotic materials, but never leave well enough alone—if you've got a gorgeous mahogany cabinet, make sure you carve it to such a degree that its grain is almost unrecognizable. When in doubt, paint it bright red with gold trim.

3 If you're building a house, use pseudo-Chinese architectural motifs like pagoda cresting, upswept roofs, and fret and latticework. And, since a house without a garden is like a rickshaw without a coolie, dot your back lot with winding pathways and streams, gentle slopes, and strategically placed follies—all of which should follow the principle of "sharawadgi," an invented term for the Chinoiserie aesthetic of "contrived irregularity."

4 And indoors? Decorate your new "Imperial Palace" with appropriately Chinese-ish ceramics, cloisonne, lacquerware, fans, and tapestries. Your friends will be impressed.

Nam June Paik

Overlooked facts:

SYNTH AND SENSIBILITY—Paik is the inventor, with Japanese engineer Shuya Abe, of the "videosynthesizer." The invention, which allows anyone to generate video images using simple controls, universally influenced the first generation of video artists.

LAYING DOWN THE ROAD—During the 1970s, Paik coined the term "electronic superhighway" and predicted the emergence of cable television stations. Meanwhile, a paper he wrote on the future of electronic media for the Rockefeller Foundation has been credited with securing seed money for the first video departments in major museums in the U.S.

HOME VIDEOS—Paik isn't the only acclaimed video artist in his family; his wife, Shigeko Kubota, is also an accomplished and accoladed innovator in the field.

Quirks:

JOHN TESH, EAT YOUR HEART OUT—A critic once called Paik the "world's most famous bad pianist," a distinction in which the artist took immense pride.

COLLEGE FOR ONE—In the mid-'60s, Paik founded the University for Avant-Garde Hinduism, of which he remains the sole member and participant.

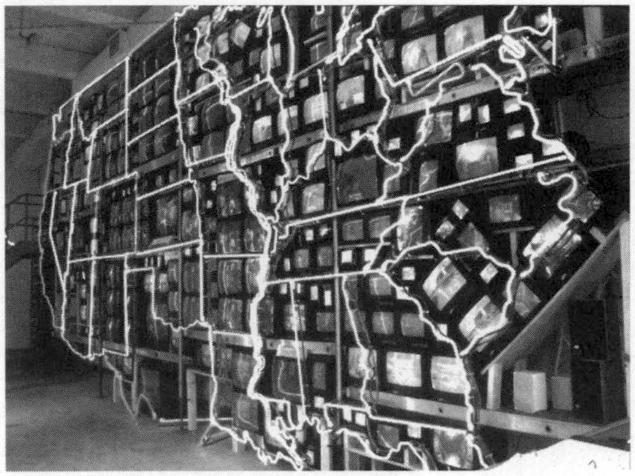

Electronic Superhighway, *1995*

In 1963, Nam June Paik was the first artist to use television as a medium, rigging magnets to distort the pictures of 13 TV sets in an exhibition held in Wuppertal, Germany. In the ensuing decade, video art took off, as TV and video technology rapidly advanced and became steadily cheaper and more accessible. Since then, he's rightly been called the "Father of Video Art."

Paik was born in Seoul, Korea, in 1932, to a well-to-do family that was forced to flee the Korean War in 1950. The youngest of five children, Paik moved with his family first to Hong Kong, then Tokyo. Although Paik was to break ground for art appropriate to the TV generation, he says he spent his own childhood as a bookish, shy boy who became a Marxist at age 13. He attended the University of Tokyo, where he studied philosophy, aesthetics, and Western music. After receiving his degree in 1956, Paik went on to do graduate work at the University of Munich and the Conservatory in Freiberg. During his years in Germany, Paik got a solid grounding in music theory which would later influence his video work.

Upon moving to New York, Paik immersed himself in the underground art community, and, in the late 1950s and early '60s, became a proponent of the neo-Dada, anti-high-art Fluxus movement. Paik was already extremely active in New York performance-art "happenings" before becoming a video pioneer; late at night, however, he would return home to his apartment to read up on the nascent videorecorder industry, dismantle dozens of television sets, and study TV circuitry inside and out. His hobby led him to create works incorporating and subverting the new technology; today, the video art he pioneered has burgeoned into a broad and resonant genre.

Two individuals, both key collaborators, have influenced Paik's work more than any others. The first was avant-garde composer John Cage, whom Paik met in 1958. Paik was inspired by Cage's interest in moving music toward the direction of the theater, and both shared an irrepressible delight in the absurd. They often collaborated until Cage's death at age 80 in 1992. Another was co-conspirator and musician Charlotte Moorman, said to have been the leading interpreter of Paik's work. A classically trained cellist, Moorman left a career with the American Symphony Orchestra to perform Paik's works, which combined video installations and experimental music. Moorman, who had been quietly battling cancer for decades, died at age 58 in 1991. She left behind and enduring legacy, however: *TV Cello* and *TV Bra for Living Sculpture,* both performed by Moorman, were among the most visually memorable of Paik's creations. In the latter, a contraption made up of two three-inch TV sets were strapped across Moorman's chest and wired to her cello, so that her playing generated images on the tiny screens. The work brought Paik closer to two of his goals as an artist: to "humanize electronics" and to bring sex—a major influence in every other art form—to classical music.

Paik has reached other, more worldly goals as well; not only has he been publicly recognized as the visionary he set out to be, but his works—once considered impossibly experimental—are now important parts of collections all over the world, iincluding the Pompidou Center in Paris and the Whitney Museum of American Art in New York. Meanwhile, his installations, such as the 429-monitor *Information Wall* at Chase Manhattan Bank's Metrotech Center in Brooklyn, New York, have also been commissioned as permanent lobby art. —N.K.

I.M. Pei

One of the undisputed grand masters of modern structure design, Ieoh Ming Pei's fame is so great that just the single syllable of his last name is enough to inspire recognition, and in some cases reverence. Born in April 26, 1917, in Guangzhou, China, to Tsuyee Pei, a well-to-do banker, and his wife Lien Kwun, he was educated in China by Protestant missionaries, and then left for the U.S. at age 17 to study architecture at the University of Pennsylvania. Unfortunately, the program there emphasized drawing, in which Pei thought he was unlikely to excel; after a mere two weeks, he transferred to the Massachusetts Institute of Technology to study engineering instead. Luckily, professors there recognized his talent and put him back on the architecture track. He received his B.A. with honors in 1940, and decided to return to China; however, by that time Japan had invaded, and Pei's father advised him to remain in the U.S. He began a master's in architecture at Harvard in December 1942, but soon took time off to volunteer for the National Defense Research Committee. His assignment? Ironically, developing plans for how to *destroy* buildings.

Pei finished his Harvard degree in 1946, still intent on returning to China. By this time, however, the Communists had taken over, and Pei realized he would never be able to return as a Chinese national. Remaining for a time at Harvard as an assistant professor, academia soon lost its interest, and in 1948, hungry for real action, Pei began his architecture career with a bang—assuming a post created for him as director of architecture at Webb & Knapp, a New York real estate development corporation. By 1955, he was out on his own, forming I.M. Pei & Associates, now Pei Cobb Freed & Partners.

Pei first became a household name with his design for the East Wing expansion of the National Gallery in Washington, D.C. Like much of Pei's later work, the project proved to be controversial, and his design was attacked as wildly extravagant. But once the ribbon was cut on the building on May 30, 1978, Pei's detractors recanted. The American Academy and Institute of Arts and Letters subsequently elected him as the first architect to serve as its chancellor. Then, in June 1979, Pei received the American Institute of Architects' gold medal, the highest of awards possible from his peers.

After that, the clients lined up in droves. The client whose job proved to be the most challenging—and highest profile—was French President Francois Mitterand. His job? Designing an expansion to the legendary Louvre. Once Pei's designs were announced, controversy erupted that made the hubbub that had followed his East Wing work look like schoolyard taunting. Critics and historiographers alike bemoaned his modernist, radial-triangular pyramids, which they declared would ruin the classic lines of the timeless museum. Still, the plans were approved, and the Louvre's new additions debuted to the public in November 1993. Critics later concluded that the pyramids actually work: after all, attempting to mimic the existing edifices would have been the height of presumption, whereas the sleek geometry of Pei's structures highlight their more ornate neighbors.

Pei has severely cut back his workload, though he still goes to his Manhattan offices regularly, and maintains the vigor that, over a half-century, created such masterpieces as the John F. Kennedy Library (1964–79) and New York's Jacob K. Javits Convention Center (1979–86). Pei's legacy continues—and will continue long after he himself passes on. —T.H.

The Rock and Roll Hall of Fame and Museum

Overlooked Facts:

LATE FOR HOME—In 1983, Pei was awarded the Laureate of the Pritzker Architecture Prize, an honor equivalent in stature (in the field of architecture, anyway) to the Nobel prize. He took the $100,000 award, and used it to establish a scholarship fund for Chinese students to study architecture in the U.S. The catch: These students must return to China to practice their profession—something Pei himself regrets not being able to do until 1978, when he was commissioned to create the Fragrant Hill Hotel in Beijing.

Quirks:

ROCK 101—When Pei was first approached to do the Rock and Roll Hall of Fame and Museum in Cleveland, he thought it was a joke—he was hardy an expert in the genre, or even a fan. But the tenacious rock 'n' roll folks wooed him, and when they finally convinced him, they had to give him a crash course in blues progressions and the heavy back beat. But nothing too challenging...or too loud: The Hall of Fame's trustees took him to the centers of rock history, including Nashville, Memphis, and New Orleans, and even got him to go to a Paul Simon concert.

Pagoda

The pagoda, or *ta* in Chinese and *to* in Japanese, is a Buddhist architectural monument which marks the burial site of a Buddhist relic, or the tomb of a monk. As one might expect, early forms of the pagoda first appeared in China around the time of the arrival of Buddhism from India, in 68 A.D.

Physically, the pagoda is a multistoried, towerlike structure of superimposed stories with overhanging roofs, usually made of wood or stone, built up from a square, circular, or polygon-shaped foundation. Its origins are in the merger of an ancient Indian structure, the *stupa* (which in India literally means "heap," since it consisted of brick and stone piled on top of a tomb to mark its place), with the Chinese multistoried tower, which was square in plan, constructed of timber and topped with a wooden spire. The oldest Chinese pagoda still standing today dates back to the early 6th century A.D., although concrete evidence of pagodas built as early as the 3rd century exist; because the earliest pagodas were constructed of wood, examples did not, for the most part, survive the test of time.

As the Buddhist religion spread during the 6th century, from China into Japan by way of Korea, the pagoda spread as well, soon becoming a major defining form in Japanese religious architecture.

By the 11th century, the octagonal-based *ta*, featuring interior galleries and built-in stairs (an idea which dates back to the middle of the 5th century) began to appear in profusion, becoming the "benchmark" pagoda of the period. This octagonal format was essentially the first "pagoda" as the structure is known today, and, in fact, is responsible for the generalized Western name for the *ta*: in Cantonese, the words for "eight-cornered *ta*" sound like *pa kou ta,* or, slurred together, "pagoda."

Over its millennium-and-a-half history, details of the pagoda have changed, but its basic shape and its monumental function have remained constant—in the East, at least. As the European infatuation with Asian goods and phenomena developed during the 16th century, the shape of the once-exotic pagoda became an almost familiar form in the West. Europe's most famous pagoda may be the one built at London's Kew Gardens by Sir William Chambers, the noted British architect and author of 1757's *Designs of Chinese Buildings, Furniture, Dresses, Machines, and Utensils*. Of course, what he created had little to do with a genuine attempt to understand the Asian structure (you'll certainly find no relics, Buddhist or otherwise, under Chambers's pagoda). In the West today, pagodas are generally associated with Chinese architecture, and mimicked as a decorative motif for "oriental" structures ranging from mall take-out food stalls to ATMs.

Oh, and that whirring sound you hear? Thousands of deceased Buddhist worthies rotating rapidly in their graves. —T.H.

A Chinese pagoda in its natural habitat

A phone kiosk in New York's Chinatown

Ceramics and Porcelain

Earth, water, and fire: These are the basic elements of pottery, one of man's oldest modes of handiwork, and a keystone of human civilization. Seven-thousand-year-old pottery has been discovered in the Near East, and the earliest examples from China date back to the Neolithic period, that is to say, at least 5000 B.C. At first made for utilitarian purposes such as the storage and preparation of food, pottery quickly evolved into a visible and concrete manifestation of cultural attitudes and aesthetics—as well as of interchange between cultures.

In general, the term pottery refers to baked clay vessels and the techniques by which they are created (the term "ceramics" is a synonym). There are three basic types of pottery: earthenware, stoneware, and porcelain. All are made from clay, mixed with water and fired in an oven, and their differences depend on the type of clay used and the temperature at which it is baked, which in turn determines the hardness of the final product. Porcelain is most brittle form of pottery, while stoneware—per its name—is the hardest.

Today, such modern commodities as Mercedes convertibles, Armani suits, and Tiffany rings are arguably the ultimate universal status symbols. But at one point in history, the delicate ceramic known as porcelain reigned as the object of material desire in both East and West.

Porcelain originated in China (which is why it's often called, well, "china"); true porcelain was probably being made there by the beginning of 11th century, though porcellaneous ceramics (i.e., pottery having the translucent and brittle properties of porcelain but not containing its definitive ingredients) were produced as early as the Tang dynasty (618–906 A.D.).

For centuries, China remained the world's greatest producer of porcelain, establishing a brisk trade in porcelain works with Europe until 1640, when China underwent its disruptive transition from the Ming to the Manchu Qing dynasty.

Japan, which had learned Chinese techniques, then took over as Europe's principal supplier of porcelain—until the 1740s, when Europeans, after much trial and error, managed to develop a domestic porcelain industry of its very own.

PORCELAIN'S PROGRESS

A timeline of Western ceramics

1575: Medici "porcelain" debuts—the first in Europe, though it is a soft-paste rather than a true porcelain.

1708: At Meissen in Dresden, Saxony, Europe's first true porcelain is created.

1738: In Savannah, Georgia, the first documented American porcelain is made.

1744: In Bow, England, the first bone china is made.

1750s: The ceramics factory at Worcester, England, is founded—the only one among seven mid-18th-century English porcelain factories still functioning today

1756: The Sèvres, France, factory is founded, producing soft-paste porcelain; as Germany's Meissen factory declines, Sèvres becomes Europe's foremost ceramics manufacturer.

1827: Philadelphia's Tucker factory, America's first successful porcelain maker, is founded.

1844: The birth of Hugh Cornwall Robertson, a master potter who, after seeing the Centennial Exposition (below), begins a bold attempt to recreate lost Chinese glazes, especially the brilliant sang-de-boeuf (in French, "cow's blood") shade of red. He also duplicates grey-white Japanese "crackle glaze."

1876: The Philadelphia Centennial Exposition became the first chance for Americans the work of Japanese craftsmen.

1880: The establishment of Cincinnati's Rookwood Pottery, one of America's most important and prolific art pottery workshops. Rookwood bears a strong Japanese influence; among its in-house decorators was Kataro Shirayamadani.

1883: The renaissance of the Royal Copenhagen factory, first established in 1775, as artist Arnold Krog develops new decorative styles inspired by Japanese masters.

1903: The founding of Detroit's Pewabic Pottery, another major factory whose works show a strong Asian influence. Pewabic gained recognition through the patronage of Charles Lang Freer, a notable collector of East Asian arts. Though Pewabic shut its doors in 1961, it reopened 1968, and remains open to this day.

1906: The Lenox China Company is founded—the only important U.S. porcelain manufacturer from this period still in existence today.

CHINA, NO BULL
The Elements of Porcelain

Porcelain refers generally to a type of ceramic that is highly vitrified (i.e., glassy) and translucent, and that is usually white in color. Composed, like other ceramics, of clay and water fired in a kiln, it gains its special qualities both from the use of particularly fine clays (and possibly the addition of other ingredients) and from the use of extremely high temperatures in its firing. There are three major types of porcelain:

- **true (or hard-paste) porcelain**, which is made of a combination of kaolin, a white refractory clay, and petuntse, a feldspathic stone, fired at 1280°C and higher
- **soft-paste porcelain**, a mixture of sand, alum, sea salt, gypsum, soda, and nitrate that looks just like true porcelain; traditionally associated with French works
- **bone china**, made of an ash of burned animal bones added to basic true porcelain ingredients; its introduction is credited to English master potter Josiah Spode II, and it has been the standard English porcelain since early 19th century.

Porcelain imported from the Far East was often named or categorized according to its decorative features. Some common porcelain styles include:

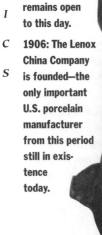

from China:

blue-and-white: white porcelain with an underglaze decoration in cobalt blue, a pigment originally imported from Persia; first made in the Yuan dynasty (1260-1368), but the products exported to the West were mostly made during the Ming dynasty—including the infamous "Ming vases" used as many a comedy sketch macguffin.

kraak porselein: a blue-and-white porcelain made for export to both Southeast Asia and Europe in early 17th century; the term derives from the Dutch word for Portuguese "carracks," the boats in which porcelain was transported from China

from Japan:

Imari ware: porcelain produced in Arita in Japan's Kyushu Province, and shipped from the port at Imari; Imari works included both blue-and-white and polychrome enameled ceramics. Particularly popular were objects in the Kakiemon style, which were later copied at Meissen and other major European porcelain factories.

POTTERY TODAY

Modern ceramics in the West owes much of its aesthetic to traditions originating in Asia. In 1940, the publication of *Potter's Book* by the English master potter Bernard Leach, who spent 12 years learning and training in Japan, led to a direct infusion of Japanese method and design theory to the ceramist's art in the West. *Potter's Book* was particularly popular in America, becoming a ceramist's must-read well into the 1960s. Among Leach's teachings were Japanese techniques of stoneware (high-fired pottery) and glaze; he also evangelized on the importance of chance occurrence in pottery (the stray touch or turn that changes the shape of a work on the wheel) and of freedom from constraints, both theories attributable to his study in Japan. In the late '40s Japanese ceramist Shoji Hamada emerged as one of the key figures in post-war pottery. Hamada introduced new decoration methods and aesthetics to artisans in the U.S., derived from those of the famous 18th century Japanese master potter Kenzan. The following decade heralded the arrival in the U.S. of Hamada's countryman Toshiko Takeazu, one of the most influential of the many Asian or Asian-trained potters who came to the U.S. to practice their art after the war. He experimented with and refined a limited repertoire of forms to what some would call perfection, including the teapot, the wine bottle, the two-spouted bottle, and the double vase. —S.L.

Oriental Rugs

A note on cultural sensitivity: Rugs are about the only thing you can appropriately call "oriental," since the term "oriental rug" commonly refers to carpets whose origin might be anywhere in the Islamic Near and Middle East, China, or China's satellites—that is to say, a region that spans the entire East, or "orient." (Besides which, rugs are slower to take offense than people. [336])

Most of the world's oldest oriental rugs date to the 13th and 14th centuries. However, in the late 1940s, the excavation of the Scythian tombs of the Altai Mountains in Siberia led to the exhumation of a number of rugs, well preserved in ice, dating back to the 5th century B.C. Archaeologists puzzle over this find, since no evidence of knotted-pile rugs has been found spanning that 700-year lapse.

Regardless of when the art of oriental rugmaking began, it continues today to be one of the few art forms still performed entirely by hand—using age-old patterns and employing techniques that have been virtually untouched by the advance of progress. It's this labor-intensive manufacturing process, in addition to the fine craftsmanship involved and the dramatic beauty of the final product, that has made oriental rugs coveted throughout time and throughout the world. —T.H.

Turkish		Turkish rugs have been collected and valued longer than any others. They generally feature all-wool construction, lustrous pile dyed in primary colors, and repetitive designs, often of native flowers.
Caucasian		The Caucasus is the region bordered by the Black Sea to the west and Caspian Sea to the east. Caucasian rugs show the influence of Chinese art and symbols on the Islamic world, featuring large-scale repeated bold patterns, brilliant colors, and symmetrical knots in woolen pile on an all-wool foundation.
Persian/Iranian		The great 16th and 17th century Persian rugs were the standards to which all of the carpet-weaving world aspired, but by the 19th century, the Iranian weaving industry had adapted to Western needs, creating a widely used system of standard sizes, and creating product of greater density and coarser weave—to accommodate the barbaric Western habit of wearing street shoes inside the house.
Turkoman		The world-famous "red rugs" of Central Asia were woven by the nomadic Turkoman tribes, who used the madder plant to create a huge variety of red and red-brown hues. Usually of odd, small sizes and peculiar shapes, Turkoman designs are characterized by the use of patterns called *gul,* a medallion-like motif representing particular tribal groups, generally octagon-shaped and appearing in repeated rows.
Indian		During the 17th century, Indian artisans provided strong competition as a source for carpets woven in imported Persian designs. Today, because of drastic changes in Iran's industrial economy (mainly as a result of the boom in international petroleum demand), India has quickly taken over as heir to the Iranian/Persian weaving tradition. Indian rugmaking still generally adheres to the Persian model, with the exception of carpets woven in 17th and 18th century, which followed court designs of the Mughal empire.
Chinese		Knotted-pile rugmaking began in China during the 13th century, presumably introduced by Mongols. Before then, artisans used fine silks to produce woven floor coverings. Traditional motifs include repeating geometric patterns, such as the Buddhist symbol for "long life," which, unfortunately, was reversed and used by the Nazis as their emblem, the swastika.

Roots of the Rug

The ancient cradle of knotted-pile rugmaking was Turkestan, a region where many semi-nomadic tribes—including the Uighur, Tadshik, Uzbek, Kazak, and Kirghiz—not to mention Mongolians and Chinese, roamed and lived for over 2,000 years. From Turkestan, the techniques of rugmaking spread West into the Balkan states and South into the Middle East, as well as East into China. Turkoman products began to appear in the West in the late 19th century; many ended up in the U.S., particularly in New England. Ironically, the few surviving examples of older Turkoman rugs are actually some of the youngest examples of ancient rugmaking—and today, there are virtually no rugs of significance being produced in Turkestan.

CARPETING THE GLOBE

Beginning in the 15th century, the oriental carpet flew west, becoming a decorative staple in better European homes by the early 16th century. Of course, only the most wealthy could afford them. Oriental rugs appeared so often in the works of European artists that styles of carpets were endowed with the names of their frequent painters: for example, the "Holbein rugs" or the "Lotto carpets." As a final point of irony, Catholic clergymen often used these hand-woven treasures as ecclesiastical decor. And what of the fact that the carpets were woven by devout Muslims? Shuffled under the rug, so to speak.

The Sanrio Also Rises: Hello Kitty, Inc.

The Rise and Rise of Sanrio Inc.

1960: Sanrio is founded by Shintaro Tsuji.

1963: Sanrio employee Yuko Sakiyama creates Hello Kitty, Little Twin Stars, My Melody, and Tuxedo Sam. The world will never be the same.

1975: Tsuji begins publishing STRAWBERRY NEWS, a Japanese magazine for kids, beginning his move toward a multimedia Kitty empire.

1976: Sanrio comes to America, and sets off a frenzy among girls aged zero through 12.

1983: Tsuji opens stores in Europe and Mexico, as well as corporate headquarters in Brazil, Germany, and Switzerland to join the one in Japan and the U.S.

1985: Kitty and her pals, heretofore limited to over-the-counter display, leap onto the small screen with a series of home videos in Japan (now available in the U.S., dubbed into English).

1988: Sanrio displays shocking bad taste—and lack of sensitivity—when it releases its "Sambo" character, a heinous African stereotype. Merchandise featuring the blackface cartoon is immediately pulled from shelves, at the cost of $15 million and the voluntary institution of company cultural awareness programs in the U.S. and Japan.

1988: Keroppi bounces onto the scene, bringing boys into the big

She's small! She's white! She has no mouth! And these days, she's...everywhere. We're talking, of course, about Hello Kitty, that feline avatar of sugary sweetness who serves as the flagship character of Sanrio's happy family. Kitty isn't just for little Asian girls anymore; these days you'll see her adorning the gear of skateboarders, punk rockers, riot grrrls, ravers, anime freaks, artists, and even parents. Heck, if Sanrio has its way, *everyone* is a potential Kitty customer.

Of course, the quintessential cute cat wasn't always on top of the dog-eat-dog world of pencil boxes and scented erasers. Sanrio was founded in Japan in 1960 by Shintaro Tsuji, a novelist by trade who had the idea to open a boutique offering simple gift items "to help a giver express his or her feelings to others." While the store was modestly successful, it wasn't until 1963, when Tsuji had graphic artist Yuko Sakiyama create a family of cartoon characters to enhance his line of gifts, that Sanrio went supernova.

Today, Sanrio is a publicly traded megacorporation, with $1.2 billion in annual worldwide sales, 648 company-owned stores, 600 licensed shops, and 3,600 retail accounts around the world—including the United States, where Kitty and her friends have gone from kiddie-cult to marketing monster over the course of just two decades.

Sanrio opened its San Jose headquarters and its first U.S. boutique in 1976, debuting the slogan they still proclaim with glee—"Small Gift, Big Smile!" Since then, Sanrio has rapidly expanded its wholesale and retail operations, both by licensing the right to sell Sanrio products to independent franchisees and through the creation of "Sanrio Worlds" within the outlets of large American toy chains, like F.A.O. Schwarz, stocking any or all of the 3,000 available items in the U.S. Sanrio catalog (over *11,000* Sanrio-branded items are available in Japan). By adding products every season and introducing new characters regularly, Sanrio has continued to creep into mainstream outlets, and sales have grown steadily ever since. These days, in California, the epicenter of American trends, nearly every mall has a Sanrio Surprises or Gift Gate store doing brisk business, selling nothing but products adorned with Hello Kitty and her friends.

THE SANRIO HALL OF FAME

HELLO KITTY (1963): A white, tiny-eyed, bewhiskered cat, with no mouth and a red bow above one ear. According to Sanrio's official bio, Kitty was born and lives in London, where she lives with her parents and her twin sister, **Mimi**. Both kitties are eternally in the third grade, when they're not travelling the world "making friends." Kitty's hobbies include music, reading, and making new friends. Quotable Kitty quote: "You can never have too many friends."

KIKI and **LALA**, the **LITTLE TWIN STARS** (1963): Innocent cherubs with squat bodies and pink and blue hair, usually depicted nestled among giant, five-pointed stars. The angelic Adam and Eve of Sanrio's Character Town.

WINKIPINKI (1995): A plaid-wearing cat who, unlike most felines, doesn't eat fish. Unlike her adventuresome friends Kitty and Mimi, Winki is more of a stay-at-home creative type—she has an active imagination, and is often depicted toting a sketchbook and daydreaming about picnics and flowers. According to Sanrio's description, she was born in a flower garden "just around the time when the tulips were blooming." Her best friends, besides the flowers, are "the fish in the nearby pond," (which she doesn't eat, of course), and her non-anthropomorphic pet terrier. Winkipinki's combination of earthy goodness and

loopy dreaminess makes her an ideal spokeskitten for a blissed-out generation of recyclers.

POCHACCO (1989): Pochacco's color schemes—maroons and forest greens—are the most masculine of the Sanrio family. Like Dottie, Pochacco, according to Sanrio, lives in New York, where he's "known as the best soccer and basketball player on his street." However, his real passion is skateboarding, which he "learned as a very young puppy in his home town in Brazil, where he was born." Despite being a "health-conscious pup," Pekkle has a soft spot for banana ice cream.

SPOTTIE DOTTIE (1990): A fashionable dalmatian with a red bow (or sometimes a pair of sunglasses) behind one lop ear. She's somewhat more realistically rendered than her pals; while Keroppi the frog, for instance, could just as easily be a gnome or space alien, Dottie is a dog—no bones about it. According to Sanrio's bio, Dottie lives in "one of the world's great fashion capitals—New York City." Dottie's dad is a firedog with the city fire department, which no doubt makes it difficult for her to maintain her stylish lifestyle.

PEKKLE (1990): A carefree duck with a snappy raffish air—and a girlfriend, **Ruby**, Pekkle was born in the city of Cairns in Australia. According to Sanrio, "Pekkle is very loyal. He'll do almost anything to defend his friend's honor. He's an unlikely sort of hero, surprising many who know him for his laid back attitude." Throw another shrimp on the barbie, Pekkle, ol' chum.

TUXEDO SAM (1963): Sam, a formally dressed, gumdrop-shaped penguin, is the most somber figure in the Sanrio family, due to his blue-tone pigmentation; perhaps this is because he seems to have been back-burnered by Sanrio, with little by the way of new product in recent years.

PIPPO (1993): According to Sanrio, Pippo is an urban swine—he lives in a "small apartment across the street from a large park." (Perhaps to fend off admirers, Sanrio does not give his address.) His biggest flaw? An inquisitive curiosity, which "sometimes...gets him into a little trouble, but mainly it just helps him discover new things and make new friends." Meanwhile, the resurgent pop-culture popularity of pigs in recent years (*Babe*, Wilbur from *Charlotte's Web*, Arnold of *Green Acres*) seems to put Pippo in good odor.

KEROPPI (1988): This goggle-eyed frog is usually seen winking one eye, jumping, and playing sports with his amphibious friends of Donut Pond. According to Sanrio, he has a girlfriend—or is that girlfrog?—named Keroleen. Sanrio also says that he's "one of the most intelligent and adventurous of all his friends," and calls him "the leader of the group." Clearly a frog with a future. The first character designed to appeal to both sexes, Keroppi seems to have caught on in a big way—he's acquired cachet among fashion victims, and has a broad, unisex base. *The New York Times* even labelled him the "New Hot Character." Fasten your seat belt, Kitty; it's going to be a bumpy ride...

BAD BADTZ MARU (1995): Ornery Badtz Maru is best described as a gangsta penguin, with a spiky 'do and seen-it-all eyes. Part of Sanrio's crafty response to its growing popularity among the nightclub demimonde, Badtz Maru seems designed to appeal directly to those with a more roguish sense of fashion and morality. As long as there are curfews and kids to break them, Badtz seems like a keeper. —J.Y. & M.W.

fun Sanrio consumer family.

1989: Sanrio decides to debut Pochacco, a soccer-playing pup designed to appeal to Y chromosomes.

1991: Kitty goes Klub Kid! Twentysomethings join the kult of kute, donning Kitty baby-tees and toting Keroppi lunchboxes as handbags, transforming Sanrio from elementary-school accessory king into essential grunge 'n' techno gear supplier.

1993: Sanrio opens its monster U.S. flagship store in San Francisco, featuring over 5,000

branded gift items on three floors, with over 6,000 square feet of gaudy rainbow-and-pastel selling space.

1995: Sanrio goes cyber, with a series of screen savers and CD-ROMs starring Kitty (Hello Kitty Big Fun Deluxe) and Keroppi (Keroppi Day Hopper), produced by Big Top Productions.

1996: The company reaches worldwide sales of $1.2 billion, with $75 million of that in the U.S. alone. Each character brand grows 10 to 15 percent in sales volume per year.

Taj Mahal

The Taj Majal—history's greatest and most enduring testament to true love—was built in 1648 by the Mughal emperor Shah Jahan to exalt the earthly remains of his beloved wife, the Empress Mumtaz Mahal. The monument's name, which translates approximately as "Crown of the Palace," is believed to be an abbreviated version of "Mumtaz Mahal"—which, as yet another indication of the high regard Jahan gave to his royal lady, means "Exalted One of the Palace." Situated on the banks of the serene River Yamuna in the North Indian city of Agra, 125 miles south of New Delhi, the Taj Mahal—one of the "Seven Wonders of the World"—is considered to be the pinnacle of Indian Muslim architecture. Some 18,000 devotees can worship at a time within its elaborate walls, and over 1.5 million tourists make the sojourn to the Taj every year, making it India's most popular tourist destination. Over the last few decades, there has been growing concern over the destructive effects of the already dangerously high levels of pollution in Agra, which were recently compounded by the erection of a major oil refinery nearby. A shame indeed: Jahan had intended for the Taj to be unique, irreplaceable, and eternal. After the structure was completed—thanks to the labor of 20,000 craftsmen who worked for over 20 years—legend has it that Shah Jehan ordered the architect's hands cut off and his eyes gouged out, so he would never be able to duplicate the masterpiece.

Ironically, this hasn't stopped numerous sharp individuals from creating sometimes impressive, sometimes ridiculous replicas of the Taj: Over the years, the glorious tomb and love-gift has, unfortunately, transformed from a symbol of adoration into an icon of kitsch.

Reflections of the Taj: the Indian memorial meets Atlantic City's pleasure dome

1930: An eccentric and wealthy Englishman erects the first American Taj, on the corner of Avenida de La Vereda and Camino del Arroyo in Ojai, California; the builder's motives are somewhat less impressive than those behind the original (he was hoping to establish some sort of cosmic bond with a local Ojai guru/philosopher, who basically wanted nothing to do with him). Even with four bedrooms and four baths, three kitchens, a living room, and drawing studio, the Taj California doesn't quite measure up to its Indian counterpart; nevertheless, tourists flock to its doors.
1930s: Billionairess Doris Duke models her Indo-Persian palace in Hawaii on the island of Oahu after the Taj. She was inspired to do so after visiting the original on her honeymoon in 1935. The palace lasts longer than the marriage: She divorces her husband less than a decade later.
1950s: The "Walk-O-Wonders" tourist spectacle, located in the parking lot of the Great Western Shopping Center in Columbus, Ohio, debuts, featuring design-scale model replicas of the Taj and the other Six Wonders. The venture only survives to the early '70s—less than the two decades it took to build the original.
1980s: Sonoma County developer and resort owner Bill Harlan builds a custom-designed, intricately detailed Taj Mahal houseboat. Within its resplendent 4,500 square feet, the floating mansion boasts twin onion-shaped domes, a third-level meditation pavilion, a sauna, a wine cellar, an all-black bedroom (one of four) with padded walls, two kitchens, four fireplaces, and of course, an elevator. After five years of keeping it afloat, Harlan eventually puts his masterpiece on the market for $3 million, The palace finally sells in 1995 for a mere $795,000.
1990: Nothing, of course, comes closer to winning the ultimate kitsch award than the $1 billion Taj pseudo-replica built by mogul Donald Trump: the Trump Taj Mahal casino resort in Atlantic City. With its gaudy domes and minarets, life-sized stone elephants, walls of marble and gold, gushing fountains, and $14 million worth of Austrian crystal chandeliers, Trump's dump misses resembling the elegant original structure by at least a million neon lights. However, its 120,000-square-foot gaming floor is the largest in the world—and the thunder of the rolling of thousands of craps dice probably drowns out the sounds of the gentle weeping of Mumtaz Mahal's ghost. —T.H.

UKIYO-E

You may not be familiar with the term *ukiyo-e*, but you've probably seen it: Stylized prints of beautiful women, Kabuki-faced caricatures, landscapes of rushing waves or faraway Mt. Fuji—once printed on delicate silk or paper and collected by connoisseurs, now recycled for use as sushi-bar decor and dorm-room posters.

Ukiyo-e, which translates as "pictures of the floating world," was the predominant artistic genre of Japan's Edo period (1600–1868). It consisted of woodblock prints, available as single sheets, scrolls, greeting cards, and book illustrations. Although popular throughout Japan, the most characteristic ukiyo-e were produced in Edo (now Tokyo) between 1680 to the 1850s. By the 19th to early 20th century, Western artists like Edouard Manet, Edgar Degas, Mary Cassatt, and James Abbott McNeill Whistler, had incorporated ukiyo-e's decorative style and two-dimensional structure into their own art, contributing to the development of a phenomenon later known as "japonisme" [👁**14**]. The two great masters of the form—whose works are still visible on T-shirts everywhere—were Hokusai and Hiroshige.

HOKUSAI: THE MAD PAINTER

Hokusai (born Tokitaro) was the greatest master of ukiyo-e, and the creator of the celebrated series of woodblock prints, *Fugaku sanjurokkei* ("Thirty-Six Views of Mt. Fuji")—the most famous of which is *Beneath the Waves off Kanagawa.* Otherwise known just as Hokusai's *Waves,* to the Western world, this world-famous piece is virtually synonymous with Japanese art, and has become one of the most duplicated images in history.

Hokusai was born in 1760—probably in the Warigesui section of the Honjo district of Edo. He began studying at the age of 18 at the studio of ukiyo-e painter Katsukawa Shunsho, who was best known as a portraitist specializing in the faces of actors. Hokusawa remained there until Shunsho's death in 1792, whereupon he applied and was passed over for the head position of the Katsukawa School; from then on, he stopped painting actor portraits. Instead, his work moved away from typical ukiyo-e style toward one that was personal and idiosyncratic.

After successfully creating an illustration for a verse anthology, Hokusai began to establish himself in the late 1790s as a designer of special-order single-sheet prints and album illustrations, known as *surimono.* He found immediate success in the genre and his work quickly became a source of imitation among contemporary artists.

Hokusai was hardly limited in his media, of course. In 1804, Hokusai painted a 2,600-square foot half-length picture of Bodhidharma within an

A TIMELINE OF THE FLOATING WORLD

EARLY 1600s: Popular paintings, then called fuzokuga, for the most part depict scenes and people from the pleasure districts of Osaka, Edo, and Kyoto. Their lifestyle is dubbed ukiyo, or "the floating world"—a carefree kind of life—and subsequently, the pictures are named ukiyo-e.

1660s–1680s: Shunga, or sex manuals (literally "spring pictures"), are the earliest printed—rather than painted—ukiyo-e. Although they often depict illicit love scenes, couples are rarely shown in complete nudity. Other common subjects: courtesans in the casual act of combing their hair or reading, serving as studies in the drapery of the kimono. A related form is the bijin-e, or the "beautiful woman picture."

LATE 17th CENTURY: Ukiyo-e production, originally centered in the Kyoto-Osaka region, moves to Edo, where single-sheet prints become the popular medium, often mounted on scrolls for display. While early ukiyo-e depict scenes from popular books, the most successful are those illustrating scenes from Edo's pleasure quarters, depicting the adventures of the tsujin—the gentleman dandy.

EARLY 18th CENTURY: Two schools of ukiyo-e develop during the beginning decades of the new century: The first, called the Torii School, closely parallels the new theatrical form called Kabuki; Torii School ukiyo-e help to popularize Kabuki through prints featuring performers in full makeup, enacting popular

scenes. The second, the Kaigetsudo School, continues to feature paintings of elegant, regal courtesans.

1745: Artists begin using non-black pigments, the most striking of which is a safflower-derived shade of red. These colored prints are called benzuri-e.

1764: Multiple-pigment, Technicolor ukiyo-e arrives. By 1766, color becomes the norm.

1770: Ukiyo-e for the first time represents its subjects as distinctive individuals (rather than as generic characters).

1770s: Collaborations between writers of kyoka (a type of comic verse) and ukiyo-e artists become popular.

1790s: Surimono, single-sheets combining ukiyo-e with kyoka or haikai (a form of poetry similar to haiku) become dominant.

LATE 18th CENTURY: This period is marked by rapid changes in style, especially in the manner that subjects are depicted: tall, elegant figures are replaced by short, hunched figures, actors' faces are grotesquely exaggerated, and so on.

1820s AND ON: The landscape ukiyo-e emerges, made famous by Hokusai and Hiroshige.

MEIJI ERA (1868–1912): Japan faces radical westernization following the opening of its ports, and, in its native country the popularity of ukiyo-e fades away. Ironically, now that once-isolated Japan is newly accessible to the West, ukiyo-e becomes a collectible of choice for European enthusiasts.

Edo temple. Between 1814 and 1834, Hokusai produced the 13-volume *Hokusai manga* ("Sketches by Hokusai"), a series of picture books filled with humorous sketches and cartoons. In 1831, Hokusai returned to the landscape as his subject, creating woodblock prints of waterfalls, bridges, birds, and ghosts—the images that would become his trademark series, "Thirty-Six Views of Mt. Fuji." In 1834, Hokusai's subsequent book illustration masterpiece, *Fugaku hyakkei* ("One Hundred Views of Mt. Fuji"), was published in full. And, in 1835, publication began on Hokusai's last important series of prints, meant to accompany the poetry anthology, *Hyakunin isshu uba ga etoki* ("Illustrations of the One Hundred Poems"); unfortunately for his admirers past and present, after 27 works were finished, the series was interrupted and never resumed.

Hokusai died in 1849, leaving behind a treasury of images that remain as breathtaking today as when he first created them. He also left another legacy, and one that—in Japan—rivals or exceeds the first in influence: the burgeoning manga industry, which has budded off from Hokusai's humorous woodblock prints into a publishing phenomenon unmatched anywhere in the world [👁46].

HIROSHIGE: THE LAST GREAT MASTER

Like Hokusai, Hiroshige specialized in landscapes, and is particularly known for his series *Tokaido gojïsantsugi* ("Fifty-Three Stations of the Tokaido Road"), which captured picturesque scenes along the highway between Edo and Kyoto.

Hiroshige was born Ando Tokutaro in 1787, in Edo's Yoyosugashi district (now Yaesu). At the age of 24, Hiroshige joined the studio of Utagawa Toyohiro, a ukiyo-e painter best known for his *bijinga,* or portraits of beautiful women. Soon after his debut at the studio, Tokutaro was given the pseudonym Hiroshige, which he would use throughout his career.

In the spring of 1818, Hiroshige published a series of book illustrations, believed to be his first signed works. Later that year, his first surimono began to appear; these works were generally regarded as undistinguished.

Bemused at the indifferent reception to his work, Hiroshige began to produce "bird-and-flower paintings," considered one of the three broad categories of classical East Asian art (the others being figure painting and landscape painting). His paintings were narrow works with calligraphic inscriptions and seals, printed in full color. With these, Hiroshige found instant success, and he continued to produce them throughout his career, eventually completing nearly a thousand. Hiroshige also produced many horizontal landscape prints, of which more than a thousand were views of his home city of Edo, a subject that he began depicting around 1830—inspired by his peer Hokusai.

By the early 1830s, Hokusai had firmly established himself with the success of his celebrated series "Thirty-Six Views of Mt. Fuji." That success did not go unnoticed: In 1832, Hiroshige was invited to join a shogunal expedition to Kyoto. The trip, which took Hiroshige on the Tokaido route from Edo to Kyoto along the Pacific Coast, inspired a series of prints which would become "Fifty-Three Stations of the Tokaido Road." Produced from 1833-34, the series is considered Hiroshige's signature achievement. (Although the series is named "Fifty-Three Stations," it contains 55 individual scenes, as the 16th station, the mountain village of Kambara, is depicted in two different scenes.)

It would fall to Hiroshige, one of the great lights of the ukiyo-e period, to usher the era out. His *Meisho Edo Hyakkei* ("One Hundred Famous Views of Edo"), produced between 1856 and 1859, depicted an age that was about to disappear, overshadowed by a new age of social change and unstoppable Westernization—a final farewell to a world sinking beneath the waves of progress. —T.P., T.H.

The Urban Nest:
A striver's guide to decor the Japanese way—from futon to tatami

So you've made it to the city. You're on your way. But life at the bottom of the urban ladder isn't easy—and it certainly isn't cheap. Still, that doesn't mean you have to live with cinder-block bookcases and particle-board furniture. The Japanese, who've lived with unimaginably cramped housing and scarce resources for generations, have come up with a number of attractive (and largely affordable) furnishing alternatives you might want to consider. Not that this is any secret to metro dwellers: You'll find most of the following in a store near you, and yes, they'll probably deliver...

THE FUTON

This traditional Japanese bedding originally consisted of two separate parts: the *shikibuton,* a mattress stuffed with raw cotton, and the *kakebuton,* a thick, quilt-like bed-cover. First used in the 16th century, futons were (and still are, in households that have not adapted to Western sleeping arrangements) laid out at night, then rolled up and put away during the day. Futons made for Western consumption are a somewhat different beast: they're thicker (up to eight inches, as opposed to two or three inches for the Japanese variety) and are intended to be more or less permanent fixtures; an eight-inch futon mattress is nearly impossible to roll up in any case. (Westerners also dispense with kakebuton, preferring to use standard sheets and bedding.) One thing to remember: Since Western futon mattresses are rarely moved, they should always be placed on a slatted frame, rather than directly on a flat surface or the floor. This allows air to circulate through the mattress, keeping it from compacting into a rock-hard slab.

THE PAPER LANTERN

Tired of the harsh glare of your 300-watt halogen? Why not shed a gentler light on the situation with a paper lantern, based on traditional Japanese *bombori* or *andon* designs? Bombori are hexagonal lanterns fixed on a pole base, designed for portability and outdoors use, but easily adapted as a permanent interior fixture; andon are square, squat lanterns that usually rest on four legs, and are traditionally decorated on all four sides with cutout designs. Both originally used candles or oil for illumination—a tricky thing, considering that the lamps are usually made of flammable paper and wood—but electrified versions are now quite common. Isamu Noguchi's brilliant, unconventional designs [👁13] also inspired a plethora of nontraditional offerings, combining the simple appeal of the originals with a modernist flair.

THE SHOJI SCREEN

Transform your one-room studio into a classy—and flexible—multi-use miracle with these cool, crisp, wood-and-paper panels. The *shoji* screen, which had its origin during Japan's Heian period (794-1185 A.D.), was traditionally made with delicate rice paper, which offers sublime translucency at the expense of durability; American versions use tougher oiled paper or thin plastic. Either way, shoji screens are a terrific away to divide an open space while allowing the diffusion of light and the circulation of air.

TATAMI MAT

Like shoji, *tatami*—the straw-and-woven rush mats traditionally used as a floor covering in Japan—originated during the Heian period. Back then, they were used in isolated units, placed where necessary to allow comfortable kneeling; by the time of the Muromachi period (1333-1568), the floors of many residences were completely covered in tatami. The use of tatami continues to this day in Japan, though most homes restrict tatami to bedrooms or sitting rooms.

In a rather odd quirk, however, Japanese apartments are still measured according to the number of mats it would take to cover their floors: since tatami are standardized by region (the exact measurements are different from Tokyo to Kyoto, but all tatami are close to six feet by three feet in size), rental notices will frequently advertise a "six-mat" or "eight-mat" room for let. Tatami mats in Japan are generally made of a bulky straw backing with a thin cover of woven rushes; unless you have the wherewithal to cover your entire room, these won't do you much good. However, thin, rollable "tatami" mats composed only of the woven rush material are widely available in the U.S., and make an attractive and natural—and cheap—covering for hallways and entryways. —J.Y., C.-H.H.

BOKS AND LITERATURE

"I have a theory of my own about what this art of the novel is, and how it came into being. To begin with, it does not simply consist of the author's telling a story about the adventures of some other person. On the contrary, it happens because the storyteller's own experiences of men and things, whether for good or ill—not only that he has passed through himself, but events which he has only witnessed or been told of—has moved him to an emotion so passionate that he can no longer keep it shut up in his heart....Viewed in this light, the novel is seen to be not as is usually supposed, a mixture of useful truth with idle invention, but something which at every stage has a definite and serious purpose."

—*Lady Shikibu Murasaki, author of* The Tale of Genji, *on the nature of the novel*

Asian American Literature: "Foreigners" at Home

Though their great-grandparents may have been U.S. citizens from birth, many Asian American writers still confront the issue of being perceived "foreign" to various degrees, both socially and in the literary world. When does the term Asian American cross over into simply being "American"? Certainly burgeoning sales figures alone don't necessarily determine passage into the cultural mainstream. Though writers like Maxine Hong Kingston and Amy Tan have had tremendous mainstream success, at times they've also been presented as examples of how the market hankers for the exotic—the identifiably and comfortably foreign. This is ironic, because the stories they tell, of immigrant hope and despair in a New World, of difference and diversity, and confronting the ghosts of memory, are in many ways the most American ones of all. —T., W.M.D.

Author/ Birthdate	Works include:	Defining work (and why)	Synopsis
Frank Chin (1940, in Berkeley, CA; he's a self-proclaimed "fifth-generation Chinaman"; lives in Los Angeles, CA)	**Anthologies** (co-editor): *Aiiieeeee! An Anthology of Asian American Writers* (1974), *The Big Aiiieeeee!* (1991). **Drama:** *The Chickencoop Chinaman* (1972), *The Year of the Dragon* (1974). **Fiction:** *Donald Duk* (1991), *Gunga Din Highway* (1994)	***Aiiieeeee!*** Named ironically for the shout (of pain or rage) emitted by the caricature Asians of martial arts movies, it was the first major anthology of Asian American literature published in U.S., and was largely responsible for introducing the concept of an "Asian American" literature to mainstream America. Still one of most referred-to texts in ethnic literature today.	"Chinamen are made, not born, my dear. Out of junk-imports, lies, railroad scrap iron, dirty jokes, broken bottles, cigar smoke, Cosquilla Indian blood, wino spit, and lots of milk of magnesia." (from his play *The Chickencoop Chinaman*)
Philip Kan Gotanda (1951, in Stockton, CA; lives in San Francisco, CA)	**Drama**: *The Avocado Kid* (musical, 1980); *Song for a Nisei Fisherman* (1981); *The Wash* (1987; also film, 1988); *Yankee Dawg You Die* (1988); *Day Standing On Its Head* (1993); *The Ballad of Yachiyo* (1995)	***The Wash***. Gotanda's exposition of the shifting values of a Japanese American community is accomplished with economy through a tight focus on the changing dynamics in a single family. This play is frequently taught in college courses on Asian American literature, and has been made into a PBS *American Playhouse* film, currently available on videotape.	Nobu: "Place is a dump, mama. Neighborhood's no good. Full of colored people. Mexicans... Masi: ... (mimicking Nobu) "I don't like 'Hakujin'–white people make me nervous. So you don't like white people, you don't like black people, you don't like Mexicans. So who do you like? Huh? '*Monku, monku, monku.*'" (*monku*="complain") (*The Wash*)
Garrett Hongo (1951, in Volcano, HI; lives in Portland, OR)	**Numerous poems and the poetry collections**: *Yellow Light* (1988) and *The River of Heaven* (1989). **Anthology** (editor): *The Open Boat, Poems from Asian America* (1993)	***The River of Heaven*** was awarded the Lamont Poetry Prize of the Academy of American Poets and was a finalist for the Pulitzer Prize in poetry.	"What I did, I won't excuse, except/ to say it was a way to change,/ the way new flows add to the land,/ making things new, clearing the garden. (from "The Unreal Dwelling: My Years in Volcano" from *The River of Heaven*)
David Henry Hwang (1957, in Southern CA; grew up in San Gabriel, CA; lives in Los Angeles, CA and New York, NY)	**Drama:** *FOB* (1981); *Dance and the Railroad* (1982); *The House of Sleeping Beauties* and *The Sound of the Voice* (1983); *M. Butterfly* (1988); *1000 Airplanes on the Roof* (with Philip Glass, 1988); *Bondage* (1992); *Face Value* (1993); *The Golden Child* (1996)	***M. Butterfly***—the first major Asian American work mounted on Broadway (where it made its world premiere!); it was a huge commercial success, grossing over $35 million, and garnered multiple awards, including the Tony Award for Best Play.	"Consider it this way: what would you say if a blond homecoming queen fell in love with a short Japanese business man? He treats her cruelly, then goes home for three years, during which time she prays to his picture and turns down marriage from a young Kennedy. Then, when she learns he has remarried, she kills herself. Now, I believe you would consider this girl to be a deranged idiot, correct? But because it's an Oriental who kills herself for a Westerner–ah!–you find it beautiful." (*M. Butterfly*)
Gish Jen (1955, in Queens, NY; lives in Boston, MA)	**Fiction:** *Typical American* (1991); *Mona in the Promised Land* (1996)	***Typical American***—Jen's acclaimed debut comic novel about the adventures of Ralph Chang, who comes to the U.S. in search of an American Ph.D. and finds his American dream in a fried-chicken palace.	"'We are family,' echoed Helen. 'Team,' said Ralph. 'We should have name. The Chinese Yankees. Call Chang-kees for short. "Ball games became even more fun...'Let's go Chang-kees!' This was in the privacy of their apartment...the one time they went to an actual game, people had called them names and told them to go back to their laundry." (*Typical American*)

Author/ Birthdate	Works include:	Defining work (and why)	Synopsis
Cynthia Kadohata (1956, in Chicago, IL; lives in Los Angeles, CA)	**Fiction:** *The Floating World* (1988); *In the Heart of the Valley of Love* (1992)	***The Floating World,*** her critically lauded and commercially successful coming-of-age debut novel.	"The floating world was the gas station attendants, restaurants, and jobs we depended on, the motel towns floating in the middle of fields and mountains...We were stable, traveling through an unstable world while my father looked for jobs." (*The Floating World*)
Maxine Hong Kingston (1940, in Stockton, CA; lives in Berkeley, CA)	**Fiction:** *The Woman Warrior: Memoirs of a Girlhood Among Ghosts* (1976); *China Men* (1980); *Tripmaster Monkey: His Fake Book* (1989)	***The Woman Warrior: Memoirs of a Girlhood Among Ghosts.*** It's one of the most taught works on college campuses nationwide—a personal memoir of growing up as the child of immigrant Chinese parents in a mostly white society.	"I liked the Negro students (Black Ghosts) best because they laughed the loudest and talked to me as if I were a daring talker too. One of the Negro girls had her mother coil braids over her ears Shanghai-style like mine; we were the Shanghai twins." (*Woman Warrior*)
Gus Lee (1946, in San Francisco, CA; lives in Colorado Springs, CO)	**Fiction:** *China Boy* (1991); *Honor and Duty* (1994); *Tiger's Tail* (1996)	***China Boy,*** Lee's successful autobiographical debut novel, was a six-month bestseller, a Literary Guild selection, and one of the *New York Times* Best 100 for 1991	"I was special. I was trying to become an accepted black male youth in the 1950s—a competitive, dangerous, and harshly won objective. This was all the more difficult because I was Chinese." (*China Boy*)
Amy Tan (1952 in Oakland, CA; lives in San Francisco, CA)	**Fiction:** *The Joy Luck Club* (1989; film, 1993), *The Kitchen God's Wife* (1991), *The Hundred Secret Senses* (1995). Children: *The Moon Lady* (1992); *The Chinese Siamese Cat* (1994)	***The Joy Luck Club*** is the most commercially successful novel ever written by an Asian American writer, and one of the most successful novels ever, regardless of author ethnicity.	"My mother believed you could be anything you wanted to be in America. You could open a restaurant. You could work for the government and get good retirement. You could buy a house with almost no money down. You could become rich. You could become instantly famous." (*The Joy Luck Club*)
Shawn Wong (1949, in Oakland, CA; lives in Seattle, WA)	**Fiction:** *Homebase* (1979); *American Knees* (1995). **Anthologies** (co-editor): *Aiiieeeee!*; *The Big Aiiieeeee!*	At the time ***Homebase*** was published, it was the only novel in print by an American-born Chinese American author. Many might argue, however, that Wong's most recent novel, *American Knees,* is his most important work, because it is one of the few Asian American novels that deals frankly with sex and relationships between Asian Americans.	"And today, after 125 years of our life here, I do not want just a home that time allowed me to have. America must give me legends with spirit. I take myths to name this country's canyons, dry riverbeds, mountains, after my father, grandfather, and great-grandfather. We are old enough to haunt this land like an Indian who laid down to rest and his body became the outline of the horizon." (*Homebase*)
Hisaye Yamamoto (1921, in Redondo Beach, CA; lives in Los Angeles, CA)	**Short story collection:** *Seventeen Syllables and Other Stories* (1988); numerous short stories in anthologies, literary journals, magazines	***Seventeen Syllables and Other Stories*** contains Yamamoto's best-known short works. As the editors of *Aiiieeeee!* wrote, "Technically and stylistically, hers is among the most highly developed of Asian American writing."	"Hilltop House also phones when another Asian patient turns up. So I call her and learn that she is from Japan. I have to rummage in the back of my mind for words I haven't used in years, but manage to get the information that she and her brother have come to this country together. They are getting on well until her brother falls in love with and marries a white girl. Whether from feelings of abandonment or not, she decides to kill herself." (from "Eucalyptus" in the Jessica Hagedorn–edited anthology *Charlie Chan is Dead*)
Laurence Yep (1948, in San Francisco, CA where he still lives)	**Fiction** (mostly for young adults): *Sweetwater;* (1973); *Dragonwings* (1975); *Child of the Owl* (1977); *Dragon of the Lost Sea;* (1982); *The Rainbow People* (1989); *The Lost Garden* (1991); *The Star Fisher* (1991); *Tongues of Jace* (1991); *Dragon's Gate* (1993); *Hiroshima: A Novella* (1995); *Later, Gator* (1995);	***Child of the Owl.*** This work, like all of Laurence Yep's novels, whether they fall into the category of science fiction, children's literature, or fantasy, accomplishes the difficult task of being equally engaging for children and adults alike. Yep's rendition of a historically specific moment in Chinese American history is also notable as one of the few literary works which concerns itself with the nontraditional coming of age of a young woman.	"I knew more about race horses than I knew about myself—I mean myself as a Chinese....Maybe it was because I thought of myself as an American and all Americans were supposed to be white like on TV or in books or in movies, but now I felt like some mad scientist had switched bodies on me like in all those monster movies, so that I had woken up in the wrong one." (*Child of the Owl*)

Asian American Literature
Immigrant Words

America as a foreign land. Leaving behind comforts of the homeland for the "New World"—the promising yet forbidding unknown. The allure and pursuit of the American dream. These are the common threads that bind Asians who have made America their new home, and gone on to write about it. Each of these immigrant authors dips into the shared well of struggle, aloneness, and the drive for an America that sometimes lives up to its myth, and sometimes remains a dream confined to the imagination.

Here are a few of the many authors who made the journey across the Pacific to America, and lived to tell about their experiences. —R.C.

Author/ Birthdate	Came to the U.S./ Died (if deceased)	Works	Memorable quote
Younghill Kang (1903 in Song-Dune-Chi, Korea)	1921, at age 18; December 11, 1972 in Satellite Beach, FL	*The Grass Roof* (1931); *The Happy Grove* (1933); *East Goes West* (1937)	"And New York's rebellion called to me excitedly, this savagery which piled great concrete block on concrete block...the great nature-severed city with diamonds of frozen electric phenomena—it fascinated me, the Asian man." (*East Goes West*)
Carlos Bulosan (1913 in Binalonan, Luzon, Philippines)	1930, at age 17; September 11, 1956 in Seattle, WA	*Chorus for America* (1942); *Letters from America* (1942); *The Voice of Bataan* (1943); *The Laughter of my Father* (1944); *America is in the Heart* (1946); *The Sound of Falling Light* (1960); *The Cry and the Dedication* (published as *The Power of the People* in 1986); contributed to numerous magazines and anthologies	"I came to know afterward that in many ways it was a crime to be a Filipino in California." (*America is in the Heart*)
Louis Chu (1915 in Toishan, China)	1924, at age nine; February 27, 1970 in New York, NY	*Eat a Bowl of Tea* (1961)	"And now that she had married Wang Ben Loy and come to New York, the greatest and most beautiful city in all the world, she should be happy, very happy...But today her frustrations and heaviness of heart dwarfed even the discomforts of her illness from the plane." (*Eat a Bowl of Tea*)
Theresa Hak Kyung Cha (1951 in Pusan, Republic of Korea)	1963, at age 12; murdered November 5, 1982 in New York, NY	"Exilee Temp Morts" in *Hotel* (1980); *Dictee* (1982). **Edited:** *Apparatus* (1980). **Videos:** *Secret Spill* (1974); *Mouth to Mouth* (1975); *Permutations* (1976); *Re Dis Appearing* (1976); *Passages, Paysages* (1976), *Exilee* (1980)	"From A Far What nationality or what kindred and relation what blood relation what blood ties of blood what ancestry what race generation." (*Dictee*)
Jessica Tarahara Hagedorn (1949 in Manila, Philippines)	1963, at age 14	*Dangerous Music* (1975); *Pet Food & Tropical Apparitions* (1981), *Dogeaters* (1990); *Danger and Beauty* (1993); has also written several plays and theater pieces. **Edited:** *Charlie Chan is Dead: An Anthology of Contemporary Asian American Fiction* (1993)	"and leaving you/again and again/for america/the loneliest of countries/my words change.../ sometimes/i even forget english." (*Dangerous Music*)
Bharati Muhkerjee (1940 in Calcutta, West Bengal, India)	1961, at age 20	*The Tiger's Daughter* (1971); *Wife* (1971); *Darkness* (1985); *The Middleman and Other Stories* (1988); *The Sorrow and the Terror: The Haunting Legacy of the Air India Tragedy* (1987); *Jasmine* (1989); *The Holder of the World* (1994)	"I could not admit that I had accustomed myself to American clothes. American clothes disguised my widowhood. In a T-shirt and cords, I was taken for a student. In this apartment of artificially maintained Indianness, I wanted to distance myself from everything Indian." (*Jasmine*)
Chang-Rae Lee (1966 in Seoul, South Korea)	1969, at age three	*Native Speaker* (1995; Lee's debut was a broadly acclaimed bestseller, and winner of the prestigious PEN Hemingway Award for Best First Novel.)	"Despite how well he spoke...I kept listening for the errant tone, the flag, the minor mistake that would tell of his original race." (*Native Speaker*)

Asian American Literature:
The Japanese Internment

On March 18, 1942, President Franklin Roosevelt signed Executive Order 9066, which allowed for the exclusion of Japanese Americans from the West Coast, under the argument that this was a military imperative after the bombing of Pearl Harbor. Thousands of Japanese Americans were routed from their homes, losing businesses, heirlooms, and ties to friends and community. Internees were housed in horse stalls at racetracks and fairgrounds for up to a year, before they were moved to the hastily constructed camps. Even for those who were not segregated from their families, the internment brought a degradation of family life. Things as simple as the inadequacy of living quarters (with as many as four families sharing a room) and the mess-hall style of eating discouraged the family structure which had been the strength of Japanese American communities.

A young internee

While interned, Japanese Americans were still expected to contribute to the war effort, and they did—first by farming, and later by volunteering en masse for service in the Armed Forces. The 100th Infantry Battalion and the 442nd RCT, which were composed entirely of Nisei (second-generation Japanese Americans) from the mainland internment camps and among the Japanese Americans of Hawaii, are still renowned for their heroism: The 442nd suffered more casualties, and was more decorated, than any other comparable military unit in the war. In total, nearly 10,000 Hawaiian and 1200 mainland Nisei volunteered for the draft, all in answer to a dubious loyalty questionnaire, devised in February 1942 to distinguish "trustworthy" from "untrustworthy" internees. Among the items in this questionnaire were the infamous Questions 27 and 28. The former asked if the internees were willing to fight in the U.S. armed forces against the Japanese Army. Since the Issei (first generation) were still Japanese citizens (in many cases, as a result of anti-Asian immigration policies), and many of the Nisei were still angry over their own nation's betrayal of their citizenship, inevitably many were inclined to answer "no." Question 28 asked if the respondents would rescind any allegiance to the Japanese government and swear unqualified allegiance to the U.S. government. Because the Issei were not allowed access to U.S. citizenship, such an affirmation would have left them stateless. For the Nisei, the question posed a different problem. Would they be admitting they had an allegiance to Japan if they forswore it? Those who answered "no" to either question were arrested and segregated to the special camp at Tule Lake. They were called "No-No Boys," and they lived under a shadow of suspicion long after the war.

No evidence was ever revealed that indicated that Japanese Americans were anything but loyal to the U.S. The most damning evidence that racism, rather than military imperative, was at the root of the internment is the simple fact that thousands of Italian and German Americans were never shipped off to camps—though both of their ancestral countries were also at war with America.

The end of internment was mandated by the War Department on December 17, 1944. The closing of the camps left Japanese Americans with another dilemma. Families were further scattered and broken up as people went wherever they could to find jobs, schools, and housing that would take them—often far from their original homes on the West Coast. Although the financial losses they suffered were great, the emotional losses were greater. The repercussions of these years continue to haunt even generations born after the experience.

In recent years, many Japanese Americans have found literature to be a way of understanding as well as chronicling the events of the War years. Even during the internment, writers like Hisaye Yamamoto recorded the psychological effects of camp life in poetry and prose. John Okada's *No-No Boy* was written shortly after the internment's end, in the 1950s. Later, the social movements of the late '60s and early '70s provided an opportunity for individuals and the community as a whole to begin telling their stories. Michi Weglyn's sociological examination of the camps, and Jeanne Wakatsuki Houston's memoirs were published, breaking the dam of emotion and repressed memory; they have since been followed by a rich outpouring detailing almost every aspect of camp life. From children's books, which convey the profound impact the internment had on family life, to poetry written in traditional Japanese forms but conveying the American reality of life behind barbed wire, these works tell of the lives of Japanese Americans before, during, and after one of the most terrible and tragic events in American history. What these works reveal is that, for a community betrayed by its own government, life would never be the same again. —W.M.D.

The Classics of Asian Literature

Most Westerners would be surprised to hear that China's name for itself, *zhong guo*, literally means the "Middle Kingdom"—reflecting China's traditional belief that it, and it alone, is at the center of the cosmos. After all, that's a position Westerners tend to reserve for themselves. As a result, the "classics" of literature in the West are generally restricted to European, Greco-Roman, and, occasionally, American works. Here's a short introductory list of Asian works that by all rights should join them. —T.H.

Work, Author, Date	English Translation	Synopsis	Significance
Shi Qing (China) attributed to Confucius, 6th century	*The Book of Songs*	Anthology of 305 poems. Believed to have been compiled by Confucius and later given canonical status during the Han dynasty. The collection ranges from simple courtship songs to ritual hymns and dynastic legends.	Considered to be the fountainhead of all Chinese poetry
Xiyu Qi (China) Wu Chengen, ca. 1506-1581	*Journey to the West* or *The Story of Monkey*	An epic about the monk Xuan Zhang's pilgrimage to India to retrieve certain sacred scripts critical to the growth of Buddhism in China. He is accompanied by a simian guardian Sun Wugong (Monkey), a half-pig and half-human figure Chu Pacheng (Pigsy), and morose monk Xia Wuqing (Sandy).	This 100-chapter narrative, one of the most popular traditional Chinese works, is among the most-adapted in modern media.
Hung Lou Meng (China) Cao Xueqin (Cao Chan), died in 1763	*Dream of the Red Chamber* or *The Story of the Stone*	The story of the Jia family, threatened with downfall due to the profligacy of its male members. Baoyu, who is looked upon as a rare promising successor of the family line, falls in love with his orphaned distant cousin, Lin Daiyu, causing family conflict. The novel has 120 chapters, of which 80 are based on Cao's manuscript (the concluding inferior 40 were posthumously added by another writer).	This allegorical account of the decline of a great family is considered to be the greatest realistic novel in Chinese literature.
Manyoshu (Japan) Various, especially Yakamochi Otomo, late 8th c.	*Ten Thousand Leaves*	This expansive anthology expresses considerable range in its subject matter; its scope includes simple love poems, ballads, eulogies, and gloomy expressions of separation anxiety.	The earliest surviving collection of Japanese poetry.
Genji Monogatari (Japan) Shikibu Murasaki, early 11th century	*The Tale of Genji*	A very long romance, running to 54 chapters, describing the court life of 10th-11th century Heian Japan. It revolves around the life and loves of the nobleman known as the "Shining Prince," or Genji; a vaguely nostalgic work, in that, to the novel's characters, the good days are considered to be in the past.	A great masterpiece of Japanese literature. Many also argue that it is the world's first novel.
Chun Hyang Chun (Korea) Anonymous, end of 19th century	*The Tale of Choon-Hyang*	A love story of a young couple from different social standings: Yi Mong-Ryong is the son of a prominent administrator of Nam-Won, while Choon Hyang is a *kisaeng* (singing and dancing girl) of low birth.	A popular work derived from *pansori* (a song genre). Representative of the national literature; has been frequently adapted for both stage and film.
Kim Van Kieu (Vietnam) Nguyen Du, 1875	*The Story of Thuy Kieu*	The story is about the trials of Thuy Kieu, a young woman who is constantly in despair over her life. She believes that she is doomed to the miserable existence of a courtesan due to some sin she committed in a past life.	The best-known Vietnamese narrative poem.
Mahabharata (India) According to legend, its author was the sage Yyasa; dating is unclear.	*The Mahabharata*	Consisting of 110,000 couplets or 220,000 lines, it is perhaps the largest compendium of its kind in the world, incorporating many religious poems, didactic passages, myths, and legends. The text is the story of the descendants of Bharata, the founder of the great Indian families of the past.	The major encyclopedic source for Indian civilization. Known in the West via Peter Brook's six-hour stage-play interpretation.
Ramayana (India) Possibly composed by sage Valmiki; ca. 250 AD	*The Ramayana of Valmiki*	One of the two great epics of India, the other being *The Mahabharata, The Ramayana* cycle centers on the story of Rama, a virtuous prince and incarnation of Vishnu [👁232].	Exemplifies fundamental values and forms the basis for many later religious texts.
Bhagavad Gita (India) Unknown, ca. 300 A.D.	*The Bhagavad Gita: Krishna's Counsel in Time of War* or *Song of the Lord*	A philosophical interlude which constitutes a part of the *Bhishma-parva* section (section six) of *The Mahabharata*, but is read as a discrete text. In the section, the battlefield of Kurukshetra is described; Arjuna begins to doubt his own motives, and learns from the teachings of Krishna.	A central text of Hindu devotion; the classic statement of Hindu social ethics. Significant as a philosophical synthesis of many aspects of Indian thought.

Asian "Gaijin": Westerners born in Asia

From Rudyard Kipling to Marguerite Duras, the unique perspective of Asian-born Caucasians has for decades attempted to unlock the mysterious gates to the Orient...from the inside. Out of this bizarre cultural juxtaposition—the between-worlds status of being neither native nor tourist—some writers have managed to make careers, even win Nobel Prizes. While this literature ostensibly attempts to bring East and West closer together, unfortunately, it has often instead reinforced difference. —E.L.M.

Author/ Born; Died	Novels include	Short fiction and other writings	Nobel Prizes and other distinctions	Notable quote
Rudyard Kipling (born 1865 in Bombay, India; died 1936)	*The Light That Failed* (1890); *The Naulahka: A Story of West and East* (1892); *Captains Courageous: A Story of the Grand Banks* (1897); *Kim* (1901)	*The Courting of Dinah Shadd and Other Stories* (1890); *Mine Own People* (1891); *The Jungle Book* (1894); *The Second Jungle Book* (1895)	Nobel Prize in Literature, 1907; several posthumous Hollywood films of his works, including two Disney adaptations of *The Jungle Book*, one animated, one live.	"You'll never plumb the oriental mind,/And if you did it isn't worth the toil./Think of a sleek French priest in Canada;/Divide by twenty half-breeds. Multiply/By twice the Sphinx's silence. There's your East,/And you're as wise as ever" (From "One Viceroy Resigns")
Pearl S. Buck (born 1892 in Hillsboro, West Virginia; moved at five months to Chinking, China; died 1973)	*East Wind: West Wind* (1930); *The Good Earth* (1931); *Sons* (1932); *The Mother* (1934); *A House Divided* (1935); *Dragon Seed* (1942); *China Sky* (1942); *The Townsman* (1945, as "John Sedges"); *Imperial Woman* (1956)	*Far and Near, Stories of Japan, China, and America* (1947); *East and West* (1975); also wrote numerous works of nonfiction and children's literature	Nobel Prize in Literature, 1938; screen adaptation of *Dragon Seed* starred Katherine Hepburn as (gulp!) a Chinese woman **[👁118]**.	"To the Chinese the dragon is not an evil creature, but is a god and the friend of men who worship him. He holds in his power prosperity and peace. ...In the Hsia dynasty two dragons fought a great duel until both disappeared, leaving only a fertile foam from which were born the descendants of the Hsia. Thus the dragons came to be looked upon as the ancestors of a race of heroes." (*Dragon Seed*)
George Orwell (born Eric Arthur Blair 1903, in Motihari, Bengal–now Bihar, India; died 1950)	*Burmese Days* (1934); *A Clergyman's Daughter* (1935); *Keep the Aspidistra Flying* (1936); *Coming Up for Air* (1939); *Animal Farm* (1945); *1984* (1949)	No published short works of fiction (though he wrote many essays and short nonfiction pieces); wrote numerous works of nonfiction and essays	No Nobel, but *Animal Farm* and *1984* have been adapted for the screen.	"Ma Hla May came across to the bed, sat down on the edge and put her arms rather abruptly around Flory. She smelled at his cheek with her flat nose, in the Burmese fashion. 'Why did my master not send for me this afternoon?' she said. 'I was sleeping. It is too hot for that kind of thing.' 'So you would rather sleep alone than with Ma Hla May? How ugly you must think me, then! Am I ugly, master?' 'Go away,' he said, pushing her back. 'I don't want you at this time of day.' 'At least touch me with your lips, then. (There is no Burmese word for 'to kiss.') All white men do that to their women.'" (*Burmese Days*)
Rumer Godden (born 1907 in Sussex, England; moved to India at nine months)	*Chinese Puzzle* (1936); *Black Narcissus* (1939); *Gypsy, Gypsy* (1940); *The River* (1946); *The Peacock of Spring* (1975); *The Dark Horse* (1984); *Coromandel Sea Change* (1990)	No notable short fiction works; wrote numerous works of juvenile fiction and nonfiction	No Nobel, no big-screen adaptations.	"There is an Indian proverb or axiom that says that everyone is a house with four rooms, a physical, a mental, an emotional and a spiritual. Most of us tend to live in one room most of the time but, unless we go into every room every day, even if only to keep it aired, we are not a complete person." (*A House with Four Rooms*)
Marguerite Duras (Born Marguerite Donnadieu in 1914 in Gia Dinh near Saigon, Vietnam; died 1996)	Works translated into English include: *The Sea Wall* (1952); *The Square* (1959); *Moderato Cantabile* (1960); *The Sailor from Gibraltar* (1966); *The Vice-consul* (1968), *The Lover* (1985); *The North China Lover* (1992)	No notable short fiction works; wrote numerous articles, plays, and screenplays including *Hiroshima Mon Amour* (1959)	No Nobel, but *The Lover* was filmed (under protest from Duras) by Jean-Jacques Annaud, who cast Hong Kong star Tony Leung Kar-Fai **[👁83]** in the titular role, and nymphet Jane March in the author's role.	

"O i ntal" Exp ssions:
Asia In Western Pop Lit

The women are dewy-eyed demoiselles in need of salvation by the right hairy-chested foreigner...or diabolical Dragon Ladies, hiding steel claws in their silken elbow-length gloves. The men are stolid, self-sacrificing drones for whom honor is worth more than life...or evil tyrants with menacing eyebrows and a taste for world domination. And the settings! Tropical paradises, bamboo jungles, ancient cities, ruined temples—a dizzying Disneyland of exotic kitsch. This is the world of contemporary literary orientalia, as defined by the likes of Sax Rohmer and Eric Von Lustbader. The *shogun* of this colorful genre, however, is undoubtedly the late James duMaresq Clavell (1925-1994), who set the standard for sultry prose and lurid imagery—not to mention historical inaccuracy and obtuse plotting—with works like *Tai-Pan*, *King Rat*, and yes, *Shogun*. While critics and academic purists castigated him for his abuses, the readers who purchased his books at drugstores and airport gift shops everywhere couldn't get enough, making him one of the top-selling authors of our time.

Clavell, like his literary kin, owed his success to his canny ability to provide a thrilling vantage point from which the West can view Asia's evil twin, the inscrutable Orient. His sensibility was likely influenced by his life experiences: While serving in the British Army during World War II, he spent time in a Japanese prison camp. After receiving a discharge due to a leg injury suffered in a motor accident, Clavell went—as did many would-be writers in the postwar boom—to Hollywood, where he was responsible for scripting movies such as *The Fly* (1958) and *The Great Escape* (1963). During the great screenwriters' strike of 1960, he turned to novel-writing, and scored the first of his many successes with *King Rat* two years later.

Two decades after his jump into the breathy world of the page-turner, his career came full circle, bringing him back into Hollywood with a bang, as his best-selling *Shogun* was made into a television mini-series. An estimated *120 million* people tuned in to watch the exploits of Will Blackthorne, the English "*anjin-san*" (pilot, an anachronism) in *shogun* (military governor) Toranaga's court—and in many cases, learned all that they would ever know about "Japanese" culture and history.

Clavell no doubt relished the irony, pondering the fate of his former captors...while laughing all the way to the bank. —G.C.M.

Title Author	Venue	Europeans or Americans are:	Asians are:	Notable facts
Fu Manchu series (Sax Rohmer, 1910s)	London...and the exotic Orient, of course	Superheroes like Nayland Smith or the good Dr. Petrie, saving the world from The Ultimate Evil.	Fu Manchu, the world's smartest and most ruthless man—resplendent in razor-slash eyebrows and three-inch fingernails. Also see: The Ultimate Evil.	Despite the top-line mention of Mr. Fu in the books' titles, all the action revolves around the deeds of the white protagonists. You just can't judge a book by its title.
Tales of Chinatown (Sax Rohmer, 1916-1922)	A dark, fantastic, and wholly non-factual Chinatown	Puppetmasters pulling the strings.	Marionettes shakin' it for the man.	None. For would-be page-turners, these are rather pedestrian.
Charlie Chan series (Earl Derr Biggers, 1920s)	Honolulu, Hawaii, and various world hotspots of that era	Foils for the Great Oriental Detective, with dialogue along the lines of "Great Scott! What now, Chan?"	Plump, mincing effeminate characters whose inscrutable nature and recondite powers of observation enable them to solve all manner of crimes, major and minor.	The Chan books were adapted for the screen numerous times, with a series of unconvincing white men in the lead (most famously Warner Oland). Keye Luke played Chan's "Number One Son"; Luke would later play the ancient master in the later yellowface classic, *Kung Fu*.
Mr. Moto series (John Marquand, 1930s)	United States	Foils for the Great Oriental Detective, with dialogue along the lines of "Great Scott! What now, Moto?"	Plump, mincing effeminate characters whose inscrutable nature and recondite powers of observation enable them to solve all manner of crimes, major and minor.	Plump, mincing, effeminate Peter Lorre played the eponymous hero in the movies—again, in yellowface.

Title Author	Venue	Europeans or Americans are:	Asians are:	Curious facts
Anna & the King of Siam (Margaret Langdon, 1944)	Thailand	A civilizing savior-figure (that is to say, Anna) with many redeeming feminist values complicated by issues of race and colonialism.	Recalcitrant, totalitarian heathens with hordes of wives and children.	The 1951 musical *The King & I* was a big hit for Rodgers & Hammerstein.
Tales of the South Pacific (James Michener, 1947)	The South Pacific	French planters and natives try to get along with the U.S. Navy; all are vying against the Japanese.	Scheming protocapitalists.	The 1949 musical *South Pacific* was a big hit for Rodgers & Hammerstein. (Note: Michener was one of Oscar Hammerstein's neighbors.)
Sayonara (James Michener, 1954)	Japan	Not around, ultimately, when you need them.	Tragic figures in yet another *Madame Butterfly* remix. Guess how it ends.	The book won a Pulitzer Prize for Michener.
King Rat (James Clavell, 1962)	Changi Prison, near Singapore, 1945	Victims and victimizers, forced together by cruel circumstances at the hands of those dirty Asians.	Conniving, lust-filled, murderous creeps. A novel about colonialists fighting other colonialists; the Japanese are strangely invisible.	Clavell's literary debut.
Tai-pan (James Clavell, 1966)	Hong Kong, 1841	Freebooting corporate bandits (Dirk Struan and company).	Conniving, lust-filled, murderous creeps.	In contrast to the book's version, history tells us that the British took Hong Kong by force, while pushing drugs into China.
Shogun (James Clavell, 1975)	Tokugawa Japan, 1600	Freebooting corporate bandit turned victim/victor (Blackthorne); scheming Jesuit politicos.	Conniving, lust-filled, murderous creeps.	It sold 3.5 million copies and was on *The New York Times* bestseller list for 32 weeks. Unlike Michener's best-sellers, a 1990 musical version was an utter flop—perhaps because Rodgers and Hammerstein, being dead, had nothing to do with it.
Noble House (James Clavell, 1981)	Hong Kong, 1962 and other world hotspots	Freebooting corporate bandits (various Struans and Gornts).	Conniving, lust-filled, murderous creeps.	A sequel to *Tai-Pan*, with the British still there, still doing much the same thing, but with more cast members.
Gai-jin (James Clavell, 1993)	Yokohama, 1862, on the eve of the Meiji Era	Freebooting corporate bandits (yet more Struans and Gornts); victims (Angelique Richaud et al.).	Conniving, lust-filled, murderous creeps.	Oops! Didn't get all the stereotypes! Back to Japan to tie *Shogun* & *Tai-pan* together.
Jian (1985), ***Shan*** (1987) (Eric van Lustbader)	Modern day Hong Kong, China, and various world capitals	Freebooting corporate and government agents.	Jake Maroc, a biracial Chinese American and would-be shaper of China's destiny; otherwise, conniving, lust-filled, murderous.	Nothing. Absolutely nothing. A *Noble House* wannabe with more sex and violence.
The Ninja series (1980-present, Eric van Lustbader)	Modern-day world hotspots	Freebooting corporate agents.	Nicholas Linnear, a biracial Japanese American financier by day...ninja by night. Otherwise, conniving, lust-filled, murderous.	Disgusting, yet phenomenally successful attempt to capitalize off of '80s ninja-mania [👁**109**] Frighteningly, *The Ninja* has been translated into 23 languages.
Rising Sun (**1992**, Michael Crichton)	Los Angeles, California	Hapless victims of Japanese trickery; hard-bitten cops seeking to put an end to said Japanese trickery; prostitutes turning tricks for the Japanese	Conniving, murderous, lust-filled creeps.	Disgusting, yet phenomenally successful attempt to capitalize off of '90s Japanophobia. The film version, featuring Sean Connery and Wesley Snipes, was also phenomenally successful.
Chung Kuo series (David Wingrove, 1990-)	The world, but not as we know it	Paranoid, oppressed victims of the "yellow horde," a European "elite" stealthily manipulating their way into control and overthrow of the system	The novels are set in a dark 23rd century where the Chinese have taken over the Earth. Ooh. Scary. The Chinese are portrayed as conniving, murderous, and above all, corrupt. In short, creeps.	Amazingly xenophobic and reactionary science fiction. Now up to the fifth book in the series—collect 'em all!

The Lotus Butterfly and Other Myths: Asian Sex Manuals

The Orient has long been perceived by the West as a bastion of erotic mystery. Based on this perception, it's no wonder that a number of Asian "sex manuals" have gained notoriety among Western readers. The question is: Are these works genuine "how-to" guides intended to titillate the passionate reader—or are they didactic works meant to illustrate the type of licentious behavior that moral readers should *not* emulate?

Commentators make a strong case for the latter. Take the best known treatise, *The Kama Sutra of Vatsyayana*. Only the second of its seven sections deal exclusively with sexual intercourse; the other six instruct the reader on such topics as "how to win a wife" and "proper wifely conduct." After all, it was written by a moral religious student. Then again, not *all* Asian sex manuals are meant to serve as primers on moral conduct; for instance, the *The Tao of Sex: An Annotated Translation of the 28th Section of the Essence of Medical Prescriptions (Ishimpo)* is a comprehensive exploration of the most beneficial ways to engage in sexual intercourse—albeit in a scientific, almost clinical manner. A final word of caution, from the preface to *The Plum in the Golden Vase:* "He who reads the *Plum in the Golden Vase (Chin P'ing Mei)* and responds with a feeling of compassion is a Bodhisattva; he who responds with a feeling of apprehension is a superior man; he who responds with a feeling of enjoyment is a petty person, and he who responds with a feeling of emulation is no better than a beast." —E.L.M.

Work, Author,Date	Original Language / English translations	Famous Love Scene / Recommended sexual positions	Gymnastic rating	Will you enjoy this?
The Kama Sutra of Vatsyayana Vatsyayana c. 4th c. A.D.	Sanskrit: 1. *The Kama Sutra of Vatsyayana.* Richard Burton and F.F. Arbuthnot, trans. (London: George Allen and Unwin Ltd., 1963).; 2. *The Complete Kama Sutra.* Alain Daniélou, trans. (Park Street Pr. Inner Traditions, 1994); 3. *Anne Hooper's Kama Sutra: Classic Lovemaking Techniques Reinterpreted for Today's Lovers* (London: Dorling Kindersley, 1994).	**"Splitting the Bamboo"**–The woman places one of her legs on her lover's shoulder, and stretches the other out, then alternates the placement of her legs, all while engaging in coitus.	**6**. Some limberness required on the part of the female, and a fair amount of endurance on the part of the male.	According to the book's authors, **yes**; the woman may find this particularly stimulating. (The man stands the risk of getting kicked in the head.)
The Tao of Sex compiled by Tamba Yasuyori c. 982-984 A.D.	Japanese (but based on several ancient Chinese sources): *The Tao of Sex: An Annotated Translation of the 28th Section of the Essence of Medical Prescriptions* (Ishimpo). Akira Ishihara and Howard S. Levy, trans. (Yokohama: Shibundo, 1968).	**"The Dragon Turns Over"**: The woman lies down facing directly upwards; the male lies on top of her, his thighs pressing on a mat. The woman raises her vagina and thereby receives the jade stalk. He prices her grain seed and attacks her from above. He moves about leisurely, eight shallow and two deep.	**2**, but the description is opaque enough to cast doubt on this rating. It is a distinct possibility that "pricing grain seed" may require some agility, or perhaps numerical skills.	**Not entirely clear.** However, according to the book, the male's "vigor flourishes" and the woman is "flustered and pleased, and her joy is like that of a songstress."
The Plum in the Golden Vase, The Scoffing Scholar of Lan-ling (Author pseudonym) c.. 1618 A.D.	Chinese: 1. *The Golden Lotus.* Clement Egerton, trans. (4 volumes) (London: Routledge & Kegan Paul, 1972); 2. *The Plum in the Golden Vase.* David T. Roy, trans. (Princeton: Princeton University Press, 1993).	In perhaps the most infamous scene of the novel (Chapter 27), Ximen Qing plays the game **"Striking the Silver Swan with a Golden Ball"**–he ties his fifth wife Pan Jinlian to a grape arbor trellis, and attempts to cast plums into her vagina.	**9**. Don't try this at home.	**No.** Even should you find a willing companion, the trellis-hanging, juice-spattered female will probably break a limb. Men who derive erotic pleasure from basketball are a suspect lot, anyway.
The Carnal Prayer Mat Li Yu 1657 A.D.	Chinese: *The Carnal Prayer Mat* Patrick Hanan, trans. (New York: Ballantine Books, 1990).	**"The Releasing of the Butterfly in Search of Fragrance"** –The woman sits on the Lake Tai rock with her legs apart while the man sends his jade whisk into her vagina and moves it from side to side seeking the heart of the flower.	**5**; more, depending on exactly where the "heart of the flower" is.	**Yes.** If the Lake Tai rock is comfortable, and the man's jade whisk up to the task, this could be quite pleasurable.

Asian Travel Diaries: Asia Through the Eyes of Visitors

Although travel diaries documenting sojourns through Asia have been around since even before Marco Polo's Far Eastern explorations, they seem to have become more popular within the last decade. While such works offer varied and vivid observations on the myriad landscapes, cultures, and peoples of Asia, travel diaries often also relate Asian perceptions of the West and *its* culture. As Pico Iyer explains in his collection of travel essays, *Video Night in Kathmandu,* "I went to Asia, not only to see Asia but to see America, from a different vantage point, with new eyes."

While the "new eyes" of travellers in Asia are necessarily connected to an old (and subjective) brain, travel diaries can nevertheless be a valuable means of vicarious exploration...if taken with a world-weary grain of salt. —E.L.M.

Author/ Nationality	**Work(s)/ Date of Travel**	**Travel Route/ Places Visited**	**Synopsis**	**Quote/Notable Moment**
Mark Twain American	*Following the Equator* (1987)	Vancouver-Australia-New Zealand-India-South Africa	Through his signature humorous but ironic style, Twain relates lively anecdotes from his travels, framed by his disdain for the imprint of Western imperialism in countries such as India.	En route to a Hindu betrothal ceremony, Twain describes Bombay streets at midnight: "We seemed to move through a city of the dead...everywhere on the ground lay sleeping natives...stretched at full length and tightly wrapped in blankets, heads and all."
S.J. Perelman American	*Westward Ha!* (1947)	People's Republic of China-Hong Kong, Macao-Singapore-Malaysia-Thailand-India-Egypt-Italy-France-England	Perelman's work is an irreverently humorous account of his 1947 *Holiday* magazine-sponsored around-the-world jaunt with caricaturist Al Hirschfeld.	During Perelman's stop in Malaysia, he and his companions embark on a tour of the largest rubber plantation in Johore. He comments: "There ought to be some kind of insurance policy available, whereby the traveller could protect himself against visiting a rubber estate. Unless your name is Harvey Firestone, it is doubtful whether the sight of twelve thousand acres of future hot water bottles will affect you as the Grecian urn did Keats."
Paul Theroux American	*The Great Railway Bazaar: By Train through Asia* (1975)	England-France-Italy-Yugoslavia-Turkey-Iran-Afghanistan-India-Burma-Thailand-Cambodia-Vietnam-Japan-Russia	Despite the somewhat lofty air which he assumes in his various ports of call toward the inhabitants of these localities and their cultural practices, Theroux's work is largely responsible for the breakthrough in the commercial success of travel accounts.	Travelling along the only road between Hue and Danang in Vietnam, Theroux observes the shelters of sentries, flying red and yellow banners. A typical banner reads, "Greet the peace happily, but don't sleep and forget the war."
Pico Iyer British	*Video Night in Kathmandu: And Other Reports from the Not-So-Far East* (1985)	Bali, Tibet, Nepal, People's Republic of China, the Philippines, Burma, Hong Kong, India, Thailand, Japan	A series of travel essays, Iyer's work puts a new twist on the conventional travel diary by looking at how "America's pop-cultural imperalism" has spread throughout Asia.	As Iyer traverses Asia in the fall of 1985 and witnesses the masses of people who flock to view the opening of *Rambo II: First Blood,* he comes to the conclusion that "Rambo had conquered Asia....But there seemed a particular justice in his capturing of Asian hearts and minds. For Rambo's great mission, after all was to reverse the course of history and single-fisted, to redress America's military losses in the theaters of Asia."
Ian Buruma British	*God's Dust: A Modern Asian Journey* (1987)	Burma, Thailand, The Philippines, Malaysia, Singapore, Taiwan, South Korea, Japan	Perhaps the most politically oriented of notable travellers through Asia, Buruma tries to make sense of the dilemmas, cultural confusion, and search for both meaning and national identity of Asian nations in the context of the new modern world order.	On former Philippines president Ferdinand Marcos and his wife Imelda: "[Imelda] exemplifies the Filipino trait of wishing to be taken seriously, while doing everything in her power to prevent one from doing so. For the same reason it is hard to see the Marcos couple as tragic. Pathetic yes, but not tragic. They wish to appear tragic, but the tragedy so quickly turns to comedy, to a dream world peopled by Ted Koppel, communists, and General MacArthur."

Chinese Literature: Writing 'Bout the Revolution

Many China scholars describe the 10-year period between 1966 and 1976—infamously known as the "Great Proletarian Cultural Revolution"—as a lost decade, in which little if no advancement was made in economics, science, literature, or the arts. In terms of literary production, an involuntary silence was imposed on writers and intellectuals who, for fear of political backlash, were afraid to voice their true feelings and opinions.

As a scholar of both Chinese literature and culture, Perry Link explains in *Stubborn Weeds*–his seminal work on post–Cultural Revolution literature–that "literature became so politically bowdlerized that actual reader preferences were frightened almost entirely out of sight." Due to China's closed-door policies, little if anything was known in the Western world about what went on in the People's Republic during this tumultuous period. But with the death of Mao Zedong in 1976 and the arrest of the "Gang of Four," headed by Mao's wife Jiang Qing, shortly thereafter, the strict literary deep-freeze in China suddenly experienced a major thaw. The thaw produced two major types of literature: 1. "Scar" or "wound" literature (*shanghen wenxue*) which attempts to document the terrors of those times, initiated by Lu Xinhua's 1978 *Scar*, which relates the ruin of a family at the hands of the political pressures of the Cultural Revolution; 2. Personal accounts written by victims and former participants of Mao's Cultural Revolution. —E.L.M.

"SCAR"-RED WRITERS	
Bei Dao (Zhao Zhenkai)	Considered by many to be China's finest poet, Zhao (under the pseudonym Bei Dao) wrote *Waves* (1979, trans. 1987), a fiction collection that relates the disillusion and despair among China's "lost generation."
Liu Binyan	Liu's collection of reportage works, *People or Monsters?: And Other Stories and Reportage from China after Mao* (1979-81, trans. 1983), successfully exposes the widespread corruption among both low-level and high-ranking cadres during the Cultural Revolution.
Wang Anyi	One of the most popular Chinese woman writers of her time, Wang explores the repercussions of the Ten Lost Years on members of her generation in *Lapse of Time* (1980–1984, trans. 1988).
Wang Meng	Known for his experimentation with modernist techniques, Wang wrote *The Butterfly and Other Stories* (1970s and '80s, trans. 1983), an anthology of short fiction composed of characters, situation, plots, and techniques that are emblematic of the 30 turbulent years following the 1957 anti-Rightist movement.
THE PERSONAL SIDE	
Liang Heng	The account Liang wrote with Judith Shapiro, *Son of the Revolution* (1983), relates the strain which surprise search raids and the Big Character Posters denouncing both his reporter-father and his Public Security Bureau cadre-mother placed on his family.
Yue Daiyun	Yue wrote *To the Story: The Odyssey of a Revolutionary Chinese Woman* (1985), which leads the reader through Yue's tumultuous relationship with the Communist Party as an intellectual beginning with the birth of the PRC up until the end of the Cultural Revolution.
Gao Yuan	Yuan's *Born Red* (1987) is a chronicle of the author's first hand experience as a Red Guard during the Cultural Revolution during which Chinese youths were often called upon to denounce their teachers and publicly disown their parents in order to display Party loyalty.
Nien Cheng	Cheng's *Life and Death in Shanghai* (1987) relates the early raids and struggle sessions perpetrated by Red Guards due to Cheng's connections with Shell, her confinement and torture in the No. 1 Detention House, and her final release and quest for justice.
Feng Jicai	One of China's leading contemporary writers, Feng wrote *Voices from the Whirlwind: An Oral History of the Chinese Cultural Revolution* (1991), a series of interviews with various people about their experiences during the Cultural Revolution. Among Feng's subjects are a former Red Guard whose sister was raped when she was sent down to the countryside, and a physician who agreed to kill both her parents and herself in order to end their persecution but was unable to end her own life before the Guards discovered her.
Anchee Min	Min's coming-of-age novel, *Red Azalea* (1994) relates the controversial sexual awakening of the protagonist in a lesbian relationship against the backdrop of the sexually repressive atmosphere of the Cultural Revolution. Min escaped to America with the assistance of actress Joan Chen, with whom she became friends when both were young actresses in Shanghai.

Introduction to Modern Chinese Fiction 101 (In Translation)

In the preface to his 1971 work, *A History of Modern Chinese Fiction,* 2nd ed., now retired Columbia University professor C.T. Hsia writes, "At a time when modern China has become in this country a subject of intensive study, it is a matter of some surprise that its literature has been permitted to suffer comparative neglect." Almost 25 years later, no major modern Chinese author has yet managed to become a household name in the United States.

While images of the 1989 Tiananmen Square massacre remain permanently etched upon the memories of most Americans, few people are aware that China has a rich legacy of student activism. In China, students have long served as the voice of protest against unfair government policy and as the social conscience of the nation. On May 4th, 1919, students demonstrated at Tiananmen Square against the terms of the Treaty of Versailles, and ignited an iconoclastic intellectual movement which sought to explore different forms of Western cultural and political models. It was during this famed May 4th Era that Modern Chinese Fiction was conceived.

Generally regarded as the father of Modern Chinese Fiction and the greatest of modern Chinese writers, Lu Xun abandoned his study of medical science in order to address the spiritual ills of his fellow countrymen through the promotion of a new type of literature. When asked to contribute some of his work to the then-in-vogue *New Youth* magazine, Lu Xun expressed some of his doubts as to the efficacy of fostering reform through literature: "Imagine an iron house without windows, absolutely indestructible, with many people fast asleep inside who will soon die of suffocation. But you know since they will die in their sleep, they will not feel the pain of death. Now if you cry aloud to wake a few of the lighter sleepers, making those unfortunate few suffer the agony of irrevocable death, do you think you are doing them a good turn?"

Despite this warning, ever since Lu Xun, many modern Chinese authors have attempted to awaken the sleepers in the iron house to the social and political ailments which exist in China. Only a few of these cries by modern Chinese authors have been heard across the ocean in the West.

Below is a list of translated works by May 4th authors that might likely be found on the syllabus of any introductory survey course on Modern Chinese Literature at universities throughout America: —E.L.M.

Author	Definitive translation	Date published in Chinese	Synopsis
Lu Xun	*The Complete Stories of Lu Xun.* Yang Xianyi and Gladys Yang, trans. (Bloomington: Indiana University Press, 1981.)	Includes translated works from both Lu Xun's first collection of stories, Call to Arms, published in 1923, and his second collection of stories, Wandering, published in 1926.	Demonstrative of the author's ability as an innovator in literary forms, this anthology lodges a powerful indictment against Chinese tradition and exposes the hypocrisy and cruelty which Lu Xun felt to be endemic among his fellow compatriots.
Yu Dafu	*Nights of Spring Fever and Other Writings.*	Contains stories published between 1923 and 1935.	Yu's stories explore the psychological trauma and sexual repression experienced by young Chinese.
Shen Congwen	*The Chinese Earth.* Qing Di and Robert Payne, trans. (New York: Columbia University Press, 1982).	Contains stories published between the mid-1920s to mid-1930s.	Shen's stories focus on the picturesque customs of the Miao tribes indigenous to Western Hunan.
Ba Jin	*Family.* Sidney Shapiro, trans. (Prospect Heights, IL: Waveland Press, 1989)	Family is the first part of the long trilogy called Turbulent Currents first published in China in 1931.	Ba Jin's novel relates the struggle of women and May 4th youth for liberation from the oppression of the traditional Confucian family system.
Lao She	*Rickshaw Boy.* Evan King, trans. (New York, 1945); Rickshaw, the novel of Lo-T'o Hsiang Tzu. Jean M. James, trans. (Honolulu: University of Hawaii Press, 1979.)	Published originally in serial form from September 1936 to May 1937.	An engaging account—amidst a very vibrant Beijing backdrop—of a man's struggle to acquire his own rickshaw, a quest which results in his ultimate demise .
Ding Ling	*Miss Sophie's Diary.* W.J.F. Jenner, trans. (Beijing: Panda Books, 1985.)	Contains works of short fiction published from 1928-1941.	While the title work in this anthology is famous for its bold exploration of a young woman's sexual desires, the other works in the volume demonstrate Ding's commitment to revolutionary, Leftist politics.

Chinese Literature:
After the Fall-Post-Tiananmen Square

During the months preceding June 4, 1989, a sense of hope permeated the literary air in China. Writers, artists, and intellectuals gushed about the Democracy Movement, imagining a future "in which a hundred flowers would bloom, a hundred schools of thought contend," though perhaps they might have taken warning from earlier periods of creative and political reform in China—which invariably ended in repression and disaster. The Misty Poets, known for their obscure, imagistic, and avant-garde verses, grew bolder in their challenges of collective mentality. Literary reporters and fiction writers also joined the movement.

But then tanks rolled into Tiananmen Square and soldiers shot students in cold blood. The crackdown had begun, and those writers who had hailed freedom became targets. Many fled China and became exiles; others were imprisoned by the state; still others were executed.

A substantial number of writers were silenced by the events of June 1989, resulting in what is known as *chouti wenxue*, or "drawer literature." This term describes all of the manuscripts which, once written, were left in drawers, unsubmitted to publishers.

But the Tiananmen incident also prompted a new wave of writing, especially among those in exile. These writers sought to stake out new territory, free from societal and political pressures. They also actively sought a different, non-Chinese audience. As prolific critic and translator Howard Goldblatt notes, post-Tiananmen writers grew "more interested in mocking the government and socialist society than in trying to reform them, more concerned with the reception of their work by the international community than with their status in China."

> "Tiananmen prompted a new wave of writing, especially among those in exile. These writers staked out new territory, free from societal and political pressures. They also sought a non-Chinese audience."

What resulted was a blossoming of writing that challenged more than just the governmental establishment. Dark works flowed from disillusioned pens, envisioning apocalyptic futures and exploring previously taboo subjects such as murder, kinky sex, and distinctly anti-Confucian family relations (such as incest). While some have maintained their optimism for China's future (such as post-Misty poet Bei Ling), others (such as Bei Dao and Su Tong) have aimed to expose the seamy underbelly of China's past and present.

Some critics have attacked the new Chinese writing as pandering too much to Western tastes; however, critic Goldblatt notes that contemporary Chinese writers "speak to the rest of the world precisely because they no longer care to speak *for* China." Indeed, today's Chinese writers have effectively cast off the previous generation's mold as state-supported "literary workers." They now have moved into a room, however painful or bitter, of their own. While the future of China remains unclear, the future of Chinese literature looks unmistakably bright. —R.C.

A Post-Tiananmen Literary Sampling

LITERARY REPORTERS

JIA LUSHENG, even before Tiananmen,was questioning government policies, living with and writing about the underclass in Chinese society. After Tiananmen, Jia wrote a critique of the Chinese government (Who Will Take Charge?, 1991) that was officially banned, yet became a black-market bestseller.

LIU BINYAN, known as China's foremost journalist, is one of the founders of baogao wenxue, or literary reportage. His works include China's Crisis, China's Hope (1990); Tell the World: What Happened in China and Why (1989); A Higher Kind of Loyalty (1990).

POETS

BEI DAO (Zhao Zhenkai), founder of the famous underground literary magazine Jintian ("Today"), is one of the leading poets of the 1980s and the 1990s. [👁38]

ZHANG ZHEN, once involved with the Poetry Society at Fudan University, is currently a graduate student in Comparative Literature at the University of Iowa.

BEI LING has been actively involved in human rights and democracy movements in China; he encountered many difficulties on a 1993 return trip to China while trying to distribute Tendency Quarterly. Currently working on Underground, a personal memoir.

FICTION WRITERS

MO YAN, author of Red Sorghum (1987; 1993 in U.S.; also a film by Zhang Yimou 👁102), The Garlic Ballads (1989, 1995 in U.S.), and numerous short stories.

Can Xue, the foremost woman fiction writer of her generation, wrote Dialogues in Paradise (1989), Old Floating Cloud: Two Novellas (1991), as well as numerous short stories.

SU TONG, author of Raise the Red Lantern: Three Novellas (1993 in U.S.; also a film by Zhang Yimou [👁103]) and Rice (1995). Su was an editor for Zhongshan, a literary magazine in China.

Chinese Pulp Fiction:
Jin Yong and The World of the Sword

Somewhere deep in China's mythical past, in the strange space between fantasy and history, there existed an age known as the *jiang hu*.

The jiang hu—literally in Mandarin, "rivers and lakes," but meaning the "martial world"—was a time of astounding supernatural forces and Machiavellian intrigue, where wandering men and women of the sword staged epic battles for honor, for power, and for the sheer love of war. In countless *wuxia xiaoshuo* ("warrior novels"), the jiang hu' s heroes and monsters have thrilled young and old alike throughout Asia. Wuxia xiaoshuo remain among the most popular books published in Asia today—the equivalent of American pulp fiction, only with white-haired warrior queens and renegade swordsmen rather than hardboiled detectives, grizzled cowboys, and space-faring star explorers. These tales of the jiang hu, with their grim and flamboyant depiction of the liquid fickleness of life in a world

where the only thing to be trusted is the edge of a blade, have also inspired some of Hong Kong' s most fantastic works of the silver screen.

The greatest contemporary writer of wuxia xiaoshuo is undeniably Louis Cha Liang Yong, who, under the pen name "Jin Yong," wrote a dozen novels of the jiang hu that have become enduring bestsellers in China, Hong Kong, Taiwan, and even, through translations, Korea and Southeast Asia. "Wherever there are Chinese people, wherever there is a Chinatown," said Hong Kong critic Stephen Soong, "you will always find the novels of Louis Cha."

Cha was born in 1924 in Zhejian, China. After graduating from college and then law school, he trained as a diplomat, but decided instead to pursue a career as a journalist, taking a job as a writer for Shanghai's *Ta Kung Pao* newspaper. Sent by the paper to Hong Kong, he began to grow bored with reporting, and turned to reviewing films, then screenwriting. Finally, in 1955, Cha wrote the first installment in the work that would become *Book and Sword: Gratitude and Revenge*—his first novel as "Jin Yong." Serialized in the *Xin Wan Bao* newspaper, it proved immensely popular. Cha-as-Jin Yong penned a dozen more wuxia books over the next 13 years—after 1959, serializing them in a paper he founded called the *Ming Pao Daily*. He finished the last of his novels, *The Deer and the Cauldron*, in 1972, after which he swore never to write a wuxia book again. His vow stands unbroken, but his legacy continues on. —J.Y.

A JIN YONG READER

Book and Sword: Gratitude and Revenge (1955)—Set during the Qing Dynasty, *Book* concerns the exploits of Chinese rebels seeking to overthrow the Manchu.

Sword Stained with Royal Blood (1956)—Another story set during the struggle against the Qing, this was considered by Cha to be one of his most problematic works, and was later revised, all (in his opinion) to no avail. His readers haven't been as critical.

Flying Fox of Snowy Mountain (1959)—One of Jin Yong's shorter works, it tells the fantastic tale of the brave adventurer Flying Fox. Followed later by a longer and better-known prequel. This is one of the few Jin Yong novels to have been translated into English.

The Eagle-Shooting Heroes (1976)—The first part of a grand trilogy set during the fall of the Sung Dynasty, when the Mongols were massing on China' s borders, *Heroes* tells the story of the warrior Kuo Tsing, his lover Huang Yung, and the four great martial arts masters: Ouyang Feng the "Evil West," Huang Yau-shi the "Sinister East," Hung Chi-kung the "Northern Beggar," and Duan Qixing, the "Emperor of the South."

The Great Eagle and Its Companion—(1959) Set a decade after *Eagle-Shooting Heroes*, by the start of *Great Eagle*, the Mongols have invaded and Kuo Tsing and his wife are attempting to hold the city of Shang Yang against the hordes. The main protagonist, Kuo' s adopted son Yang, is the blood son of one of Kuo' s greatest enemies.

The Young Flying Fox (1960)—The prequel to Cha's earlier Hu Fei book, this novel tells of the early years of Flying Fox and of a feud between Hu's clan and two other families over the ownership of a pair of powerful swords.

Heaven's Sword and Dragonslayer Saber (1963)—The finale of the trilogy that began in *Eagle-Shooting Heroes*, *Sword* begins 90 years after the Mongol invasion of China, and is the epic tale of the Ming Cult' s battle to retake the throne, using the power of two magical swords and an all-powerful martial arts technique.

Demi-Gods and Demi-Devils (1963-7)—Set in 1094 A.D., during the Northern Song Dynasty, *Demi-Gods* is an intricate (some would say incomprehensible) tapestry of power struggles between martial artists whose abilities are virtually supernatural in prowess.

Ode to Gallantry (1966)—A book of short stories constituting a tour through the world of Chinese chivalry.

The Proud Smiling Wanderer (1963)—Probably Cha's best-known work, the novel is the tale of a wandering swordsman caught up in a struggle over a mystic scroll.

The Deer and the Cauldron (1969-72) —The last (and perhaps best) of Jin Yong's wuxia works, *Deer* was something of an anomaly—serving almost as a satire and refutation of the principles of the jiang hu. Rather than a brave warrior, the hero, Wei Xiao Bao, is the son of a prostitute whose only goal is to someday own his own brothel. Through his native guile and trickery, he instead rises to become the friend and first advisor of the Manchu Emperor Kang Xi.

Japanese Literature:
The Gen-Xers

If the world were about to end, the hip urban youth who populate the novels of the new generation of Japanese writers would probably just shrug their shoulders, release a jaded sigh, and light a last cigarette. Propelled constantly into bizarre situations, skating from significant chance encounter to significant chance encounter, riffing through understated dialogues laden with foreboding or unspoken resonance, the characters in this latest generation of Japanese novels operate in the odd and manic world of the megacity; surrounded by electrical appliances and references from American culture, they nonetheless eat *soba* noodles and frequent the particular kind of dingy bars that exist only in certain neighborhoods in *shitamachi* (downtown) Tokyo. And even when they venture outside of their magical Tokyo reality to make a foray into a foreign land, there's something about these characters—the way they behave and the things they believe—that marks them indelibly as a part of the fictional world generated by Japan's post-bubble literati.

These writers, deeply influenced by American fiction, have begun to return the favor—flowing into our reading and writing world in translation at ever-increasing speed, casting blasé glances over their shoulders, and stepping carelessly into the traffic of our literary culture. —M.S.

Name	Best-known work in U.S./ Date (of English trans.)	Plot	Memorable moment	Other works in translation	Grunge factor
Haruki Murakami	*A Wild Sheep Chase* (1989)	The narrator, a world-weary loner, meets a woman with bewitchingly erotic ears; she accompanies him to the north of Japan (Sapporo) in search of a mysterious supernatural sheep.	**Ear and wow:** "Those ears had me in their thrall. They were the dream image of an ear. The quintessence, the paragon of ears. Never had any enlarged part of the human body (genitals included, of course) held such strong attraction for me. They were like some great whirlpool of fate sucking me in...The supple flesh of the earlobe surpassed them all, transcending all beauty and desire."	*Hard-Boiled Wonderland and the End of the World* (1991); *Dance, Dance, Dance* (1994, a sequel to *A Wild Sheep Chase*); *Wind-Up Bird Chronicles* (forthcoming); *Norwegian Wood* (two volumes)	See below
	The Elephant Vanishes (1993)	A collection of stories of seemingly ordinary, disaffected, young white-collar workers drawn into strange experiences: for instance, attacking a McDonald's and stealing 30 Big Macs.	**Asian Orange:** The woman who knows how to mime peeling a bowl of mandarin oranges (she goes on to "pick up one imaginary orange, then slowly peel it, pop pieces into her mouth, and spit out the pulp one section at a time, finally disposing of the skin-wrapped residue") so convincingly that the narrator feels "the reality of everything around me being siphoned away." ("Barn Burning")		**2.** Murakami's stories are less kinky than curious—he has a fascination with the sudden protrusions of the uncanny into the lives of otherwise ordinary (even drab) individuals.
Banana Yoshimoto (real name: Mihoko Yoshimoto)	*Kitchen* (1993; sold two million copies in Japan, and almost that many abroad)	An orphaned schoolgirl moves in with a fellow student and his transsexual father-turned-mother, Eriko. A lyrical story of family, the comforting hum of appliances, and a girl's thoughts about love.	**The Japanese have a name for it:** Perhaps the most memorable thing about Yoshimoto's books is the phenomenal worship of them by her readers, which the media has dubbed "Bananamania."	*N.P.*; *Lizard*	**5.** Banana's grunge is the kind that can be removed with tile cleanser: "I love seeing incredibly dirty kitchens to distraction...so dirty your slippers turn black on the bottom."

Name	Best-known work in U.S./ Date (of English trans.)	Plot	Memorable moment	Other works in translation	Grunge factor
Eimi Yamada (Amy Yamada)	*Trash* (1994)	Koko, a Japanese woman living in New York with her older black alcoholic boyfriend and his son, tries to sort out her failing relationship, and eventually breaks out of it in search of new love.	**Wistful mist:** When Koko puts a dab of perfume on the backs of her knees, even though by this time the relationship is so far gone there's no chance her boyfriend will notice it.	None (yet)	**8.** The title says it all.
Ryu Murakami	*Almost Transparent Blue* (1977)	Drugs and sex. Orgies, genitalia, saliva, rotten food, heroin, rock bands, and vomit. One tends to forget the plot.	**The pause that refreshes:** When—briefly—the body fluids let up, for a moment of lyrical relief: "The fragment of glass...was a boundless blue, almost transparent. I stood up, and as I walked toward my own apartment, I thought, I want to become like this glass. And then I want to reflect this smooth white curving myself. I want to show other people these splendid curves reflected in me."	69 and the film *Tokyo Decadence* (based on his novel *Topaz*)	**10.** The *Washington Post* described it as follows: "Bugs and mucus, cheesecake and semen, rain and runaways—all lovingly described."
	Coin Locker Babies (1995)	Two babies (Hashi and Kiku) are rescued from coin lockers, where their mothers had abandoned them, and are adopted as brothers. An uncanny, at times tender, at times terrifying saga of their growing up and their doomed destiny.	**Crocodile snock:** When Anemone, the odd beautiful model who becomes Kiku's lover, buys pounds of meat to feed her beloved pet crocodile.		**9.** Hashi, the musician brother, gets frustrated with his voice, and snips off the tip of his tongue with scissors.
Masahiko Shimada	*Dream Messenger* (1993)	A Japanese American mother hires a former beauty queen and a novelist with writer's block to search for her long-lost son. The story switches off between their story and the son's (he's the dream messenger of the title): he grew up working at a "rental family" service, and now does similar work on a freelance basis.	**Inside the outside:** When the son, Masao (a.k.a. Matthew), meets the writer Shimada himself during the course of the story, and finds out he is the main character in the writer's work in progress.	Short stories "Momotaro in a Capsule" and "A Callow Fellow of Jewish Descent," in the anthologies *Monkey Brain Sushi* and *New Japanese Voices.* (These compilations also contain brief samplings from other, as yet untranslated, Gen Xers.)	**6.** One of the clues the mother gives detectives searching for her lost son is the size of four moles on his buttocks

Japanese Literature: Recollections of Things Past

The following authors are the grand old men of Japanese literature (now all dead, of course)—the ones through whom Westerners first discovered that there was such a thing as modern Japanese literature. Unlike their Johnny- (and Jenny-) come-lately Gen-X fellows, their world is one in which the predominant drink is tea, not Coke; where women haven't yet doffed kimono in favor of thigh-high miniskirts, and *koto* music has not yet been replaced with the grimy blare of *Nirubana* and *Paru Jamu*. Though they wrote at a time when Japan was undergoing rapid changes toward Westernization, their intimate descriptions of fading Japanese traditions have just the note of nostalgia (*natsukashisa*) to make them perfect fodder for Western readers who were looking for a touch of the "exotic Orient."

Of course, from Nobel Prize winner Yasunari Kawabata's *Snow Country,* about the relationship between a wealthy businessman and a country geisha in a Japanese hot spring resort, to, say, Mishima's *Confessions of a Mask,* in which a young man awakens to his homosexuality, there is already a world of difference. But for many American readers, their works, brought into English by translators like Edward Seidensticker and Donald Keene—along with classics like *The Tale of Genji*)—gave us our first impressions of Japanese literature, and sparked American imaginings of Japanese aesthetics, love, art, and life.

On the other hand, Japan's emergence into and immersion in the things of the West didn't necessarily inspire a sense of boundless optimism in these authors: three of them, Tanizaki, Mishima, and Kawabata, died by their own hand—Kawabata only four years after winning the Nobel Prize. —M.S.

Name/ Born; Died	Major works in translation	Sample entrance exam question and answer	Notable moment
Mori Ogai (1862–1922)	*Vita Sexualis*; *The Wild Geese*; *Youth and Other Stories*; *Woman in the Crested Kimono (from Shibue Chusai)*	**Q: Why does the love affair between Okada and Otama in *The Wild Goose* never even begin?** A: Because of the accidental killing of the wild goose.	In *The Wild Goose*: Okada unintentionally kills the goose by throwing a stone. He and his fellow students go off to cook and eat the goose, just at the moment when the woman (Otama) has decided to approach Okada and reveal her love. She can't approach him with the other students there, and the next day Okada must leave for Germany—thus ending the one source of hope in the woman's sad life. In the mind of the narrator, the dead goose is clearly identified with the woman herself.
Natsume Soseki (1867–1916)	*Botchan*; *I Am a Cat*; *Kokoro*; *Grass on the Wayside*; *The Three-Cornered World*	**Q: How does *Kokoro* begin?** A: "I always called him sensei."	When sensei writes his testament to his student, he describes the passing on of his story in a rather gory manner: "Now, I myself am about to cut open my own heart, and drench your face with my blood. And I shall be satisfied if, when my heart stops beating, a new life lodges itself in your breast."
Yasunari Kawabata (1899–1972)	*Snow Country*; *The Izu Dancer*; *Thousand Cranes*; *Palm of the Hand Stories*	**Q: What is the opening line of Kawabata's *Snow Country*?** A: "The train came out of a long tunnel..."	Perhaps the most resonant image in *Snow Country* is the description of the reflection of the female protagonist's face in the window of the train, superimposed with the evening landscape passing by outside.
Yukio Mishima (1925-70)	*Confessions of a Mask*; *The Temple of the Golden Pavilion*; *Spring Snow*; *The Sound of the Waves*; *Five Modern Noh Plays*	**Q: Why did the stuttering acolyte in *Temple of the Golden Pavilion* burn down the Kinkakuji temple?** A: Because he was obsessed and tormented by the mystery and power of its overwhelming beauty.	When, in *Confessions of a Mask,* the protagonist comes upon a picture in an art book of the martyrdom of St. Sebastian, and, gazing at the blood oozing from the saint's arrow-wounds, he is aroused to masturbate for the first time.
Jun'ichiro Tanizaki (1886–1965)	*Naomi*; *The Key*; *The Makioka Sisters*; *Some Prefer Nettles*; *Diary of a Mad Old Man*; *In Praise of Shadows*; *The Reed Cutter*	**Q: What is a toilet? (according to *In Praise of Shadows*, the toilet is the most aesthetic aspect of Japanese architecture)** A: "No words can describe that sensation as one sits in the dim light, basking in the faint glow reflected from the *shoji*, lost in meditation."	In *Naomi*, when the protagonist discovers that the way his girlfriend makes her skin so white and pure in the way that obsesses him is by shaving the tiny dark hairs off her shoulders and back.

Overlooked facts:

INTO THE WOODS, AND OUT AGAIN—After World War II, Oe was left with little desire to attend university, dreaming instead of becoming a forest ranger. But regulations required rangers to read Latin, a course no school in Oe's region taught. He shrugged and took French instead—a decision that led to literary and academic pursuits, and eventually, the Nobel.

Quirks:

MAYBE THIS IS WHY HE WANTED TO BE A RANGER?—During the Occupation, Oe's teachers instructed him on the importance of the kiss in American culture, suggesting that he should make it an object of study. Oe thus took to his beloved woods, where he practiced smooching with a young, beautiful...oak tree.

THANKS, BUT NO THANKS—Although it is customarily awarded to Japanese Nobel laureates, Oe refused the Japanese government's Imperial Culture Award, since he identifies himself with the periphery of Japanese culture. In his letter to the Prime Minister declining the award, Oe wrote, "I have only two pockets, a Swedish pocket, which is now full, and the other pocket. I want to be at liberty to choose what goes into it, and your medal is too big for my pocket."

Kenzaburo Oe

Kenzaburo Oe, winner of the Nobel Prize for Literature and one of Japan's greatest living writers, was born in 1935 in Ose, a small village on Shikoku, an isolated, southern island of Japan. While still a child of eight, Oe became mesmerized with two books: *The Adventures of Huckleberry Finn* by Mark Twain and *The Wonderful Adventures of Nils* by Swedish writer Selma Lagerlof. (He especially admired Huck Finn, who, according to Oe, chose to "go to hell" rather than betray his friend and runaway slave, Jim. Not only did these books enthrall his young mind with literature but also made Oe want to "run away from [his] family to sleep in the forest." This arboreal infatuation would follow Oe all his life.)

Oe entered Tokyo University in 1954 to study French literature, and there worked closely with mentor Kazuo Watanabe, a scholar of French Renaissance thought who translated the works of François Rabelais into Japanese. In 1958, while still a university student, he won the Akutagawa Prize, Japan's preeminent literary award for new writers, for a short story entitled "The Catch." In 1959, Oe graduated with honors, writing his thesis on Jean-Paul Sartre.

A year later, he married Yukari Itami, the sister of Oe's high school friend—the celebrated film director Juzo Itami; the marriage continues to be a committed partnership, despite having been marked with tragedy. In 1963, the couple had their first child, a son named Hikari ("light" in Japanese), who suffered brain damage due to an operation for a cerebral hernia following his birth in 1963.

Oe's struggle to accept his son's disability provided the spiritual and artistic inspiration for him to overcome a psyche and writing jaded by the desperate shadow of World War II. His son's birth sparked what he calls his second period, a stage in which Oe says he attempted to use his writing as a bridge: "to start from personal matter, and then to link it up with the society, the state, and the world."

Meanwhile, Hikari Oe, too, has managed to bridge his disability through art: Though he speaks with the vocabulary of a three-year-old, he composes classical music, and has released two CDs of his compositions. Seiji Ozawa, musical director of the Boston Symphony and neighbor of the Oe family when in Tokyo, says he often unwinds with a Hikari CD on concert nights.

In 1994, Oe received the Nobel Prize in Literature. The citation lauded him as a writer who "with poetic force creates an imagined world where life and myth condense to form a disconcerting picture of the human predicament today." Oe has said that he wishes to write one final book, before turning himself to other pursuits. Through much of his career, Oe wrote to give voice to his son who could barely speak. But now that Hikari has discovered his voice through music, Oe says he no longer needs to champion his son's silence. For the next five years, Oe plans to read widely, exploring new structures of literature, and then write his last work, the story of his life. —N.H.

Manga

In America, comic books may be just a passing fancy—a distraction for adolescent boys desperately awaiting the arrival of puberty. Not so in Japan, where comics are read in thick, dictionary-size volumes by men, women, and children of all ages. In fact, manga in Japan is by far and away the most popular form of printed media, with top-selling *Shonen Jump* selling over 5 million copies a week—five times more than the most popular non-manga periodical in Japan. Collectively, over 2.3 billion manga are sold each year, many of which are handed from schoolchild to schoolchild, or thumbed through in public places like noodle shops and hair salons. It's no wonder then that some analysts say that, in Japan, comics are more influential than newspapers or TV. But, perhaps fortunately for the literacy of the Japanese people, manga isn't as limited in subject matter and format as American comics; cartoon art both amplifies and sweetens material that might otherwise be tedious, so manga are regularly used to teach history and classic literature, train businesspeople, and spread public service announcements. "Time is limited, and society is moving so fast," says Noboru Nakano of Shueisha, the publisher of *Boys Jump* and a wide variety of other manga titles. "Manga are easier than reading a book. If you can convey the same thing by pictures, why not?"

Why not indeed? Of course, manga is far from being dominated by educational works. The ranks of manga intended to entertain or titillate are legion, and most readers of manga are seeking much the same thing as comic-fans around the world—escapist release. The rough translation of manga is "irresponsible pictures," and, though the roots of the manga tradition lie in the satirical woodcuts created by ukiyo-e masters such as Hokusai [👁**24**], up until the late 1940s, manga was dominated by basic, unsophisticated gag-panel art. In 1947, however, the manga world—and thus Japan—was changed forever, by the release of a work called *Shin-takarajima,* or *New Treasure Island.* The work was a narrative epic with 200 pages of action, drawn in in a bold, cinematic style inspired by American cartoon animation—the first modern manga book. Despite the poverty of postwar Japan, it sold well over 400,000 copies. The artist who created it, and who would subsequently invent the billion-dollar manga industry, was a man named Osamu Tezuka.

Tezuka was born in Toyonaka City in Osaka, Japan in 1928; despite being urged into medical studies by his parents, he was an incessant doodler, and resolved early in his life to someday follow his dream of becoming a comic artist. After graduating from Osaka University and practicing as a physician for several years, he began drawing a weekly strip for the *Mainichi Daily* newspaper, before abandoning his medical career in favor of full-time work as a comic artist. After his resounding success with *New Treasure Island,* he launched a series called *Jungle Emperor* (1951), about a lion cub training to become king of the jungle. This would later find Western stardom in animated form as *Kimba the White Lion*. As popular as that series was, its successor was even more of a smash: a 1952 series about a boy robot in the far future, known and beloved in America as *Astro Boy* [👁**65**]. That year also marked Tezuka's move from Osaka to the bustling capital of Tokyo, where he attracted a following of young artists who sought to learn at his feet—among them such masters as Reiji Matsumoto (*see sidebar*) and the team known as Fujiko-Fujio, who created the astoundingly successful kiddie comic *Doraemon*.

Over his career, Tezuka personally drew over 150,000 pages of comics, and completed over 500 manga titles—an astounding total. When he died of stomach cancer on February 9, 1989, all of Japan was shocked. The artist known as the "God of Manga" had, after all, single-handedly fueled the growth of Japan's number-one entertainment medium, while creating hundreds of popular cartoon characters and stories, shaping the industry with his work, and inspiring successive generations

MANGA MASTERS

AKIRA TORIYAMA—Born in 1954, Toriyama graduated from high school in 1974 with a focus in graphic design. In 1977, he debuted as a manga artist with the publication of a one-shot story named "Wonder Island" in Shonen Jump. Then, in 1980 he created his first monster hit: the wacky science-fiction series Dr. Slump. Dr. Slump ran for nearly five years in the comics, and from 1981 through 1986 on TV. Due to Slump's success, Toriyama joined manga's elite ranks—earning over $2.4 million a year from sales of the comic, the series, and merchandizing. In 1984, while Dr. Slump was still hot, Toriyama began a gargantuan new series called Dragonball—perhaps the most popular manga series ever. It has lasted for over a decade in the comics and on TV and has spawned a billion-dollar merchandising industry [👁58].

REIJI MATSUMOTO—Matsumoto, the artist whose character designs brought Space Cruiser Yamato [👁64] to life, was born in 1938, the son of an Air Force officer. Despite early promise, Matsumoto remained lost in obscurity until 1972, when his work Otoko Oidon ("I Am a Man") was published in Shonen Magazine. It became a smash success, lifting Matsumoto out of the manga ghetto (he'd previously been supporting himself by penning girls' romance comics). It was Matsumoto's brilliant work on Yamato that made him a manga hero, however. Over time, it became one of Japan's most popular series ever, on TV and in manga form. And in 1979, the

show made its debut on U.S. television, where it brought a generation of American children to the stars.

RUMIKO TAKAHASHI—Born in Niigata, Japan in 1957, Takahashi is arguably Japan's most beloved living comic artist, with such classics as Urusei Yatsura, Maison Ikkoku, and Ranma 1/2 to her credit. You certainly won't get any argument if you call her one of the most successful: Takahashi has nearly 50 million copies of her works in print, and is reputedly one of the wealthiest single women in Japan.

CLAMP—CLAMP differs from the artists above in three major ways. First of all, CLAMP is not a person, but a team of four young women: Nanase Okawa, Mokona Apapa, "Mick" Nekoi , and Satsuki Igarashi. Secondly, CLAMP's most popular works are shojo manga, or comics for girls. And thirdly, CLAMP is a prime example of a unique phenomenon in Japanese comics: the dojinshi artist. Dojinshi are amateur works that often feature well-known characters, appropriated for use in new (and sometimes scandalous) situations. CLAMP began in dojinshi, but soon broke through as professionals, creating such popular works as Rg Veda, Tokyo Babylon, and, most recently, Magical Knight Rayearth; all three have been adapted as anime, and Rayearth is a standout smash that has been considered for broadcast in America. As the quartet is still in their 20s, it's clear that CLAMP has a lock on the manga future.

of artists with his style and success. A year after his death, in 1990, the National Museum of Modern Art in Tokyo paid its first-ever tribute to manga art with "The Osamu Tezuka Exhibition." Soon after, in Takarazuka (a city best known for its all-female musical theater revue), a museum was constructed in his honor, which drew over 400,000 visitors in the first six months. Through such tributes—and countless reprints and reruns—the God of Manga has lived on to inspire future generations of artists, animators, and dreamers.

THE PEN AS LENS

In addition to being substantially longer and more involved than Western comic books, with some series lasting hundreds of volumes and involving story arcs covering dozens of issues, manga has a unique look and structure. Panels are shaped for effect, and regularly distorted or exploded by action extending beyond the panel frame. Sound effects are prominent, with even such otherwise silent activities as thinking and feeling represented by its own distinctive noise. Comic figures range from the crude and only vaguely human to the deliberately realist, though unrealistically large eyes, hair, and other prominent bodily characteristics are common. However, the greatest innovation of manga (and the one which has had the most influence on Western comics) is its cinematic style; since Tezuka's inspiration was the medium of animation, the art form he pioneered is similarly dynamic. The pen-and-ink "camera" of the manga artist holds on foreground objects (a glass of water, a landscape) as conversation takes place "off-screen"; it can "pan" across a background, pull in for "closeups," achieve rapid-cut "montages," and otherwise perform acts heretofore limited to film. Manga artists have reinvented sequential art along a new and exciting paradigm, and Western comic creators have since learned and adapted these techniques as well. The result? Comics on both sides of the Pacific have never been better.

Lum **(Urusei Yatsura)**

Ranma 1/2

THE SOUNDS OF MANGA

The quirkiest element of manga may well be the range of sound effects it incorporates for every action, no matter how small, unusual, or complex. The rule seems to be that if it can be drawn, then it can make a noise that can be rendered in florid kana characters. Here are some examples:

burun—the sound of breasts being exposed by the release of a bra
bushuu—the sound of gushing blood
doki doki waku waku—the sound of a heart pounding
gata gata—the sound of trembling
kacha—the sound of a door opening
noro noro—the sound of moving slowly
pachi pachi—the sound of clapping
peko peko—the sound of bowing humbly
suru suru—the sound of noodles being slurped
ta ta ta—the sound of footsteps —J.Y.

Salman Rushdie

Born in India, on June 19, 1947—the eve of India's independence from British Colonial rule, Salman Rushdie was sent at the age of 14 to boarding school in England; after the completion of his education and the partition of India, he joined his family in the new Pakistan, and then lived for a time in Nicaragua. Rushdie eventually returned to England, where he began a career as a successful advertising copywriter. This, of course, was just an hors d'oeuvre before his true literary profession came to light. He debuted with *Grimus* (1975), and followed with *The Jaguar Smile: A Nicaraguan Journey* in 1977. Then, in 1981, he won Britain's prestigious Booker Prize for *Midnight's Children*, which in 1993 was subsequently chosen as the best book to have won the Booker since the award's inception in 1969. Without a doubt, *Children* is one of the most insightful novels written on India's turbulent time of independence and partition.

Unfortunately for Rushdie, the best known—and least read—of his books continues to be *The Satanic Verses*. Like many of his novels, it is told in a particularly South Asian style of magical realism, interweaving *The Arabian Nights* with traditional Indian folk tales and themes derived from the politics and culture of his countries—India, Pakistan, and Britain.

Written in an irreverent, fragmented style, *Verses* begins with the explosion of a hijacked plane over London, which triggers a magical journey for the two main characters through history and fantasy. An exploration of good and evil, the book is also an unsubtle attack on religious fundamentalism—which brought out fundamentalist Islamic groups in droves, and prompted riots, bookstore bombings, death threats, and more.

In 1989, the Ayatollah Khomeini of Iran announced that the book defamed the prophet Muhammad and the Qura'an and issued a fatwah, or "decree," that called for Rushdie's death as a heretic. The Ayatollah wasn't kidding around—he even threw in a $5 million bounty for the devout soul who rang Rushdie's bell. Rushdie had no choice but to go into hiding.

As of 1995, Salman Rushdie is still in hiding under the protection of the British government, despite his years of criticism of that institution. While moving constantly from safehouse to safehouse, surrounded by SWAT teams, Rushdie continues to publish. His recent books include the children's work *Haroun and the Sea Stories* (1990), the nonfiction *Imaginary Homelands: Essays and Criticism, 1981–1991* (1991), *East, West* (1995), and *The Moor's Last Sigh*. (1996).

In addition to being a prolific writer of fiction, essays, and journalism, Rushdie (not a little motivated by his own plight) has recently emerged as a champion of human rights. And, although the media has largely forgotten his plight, he remains very much a man on the run. —A.M.

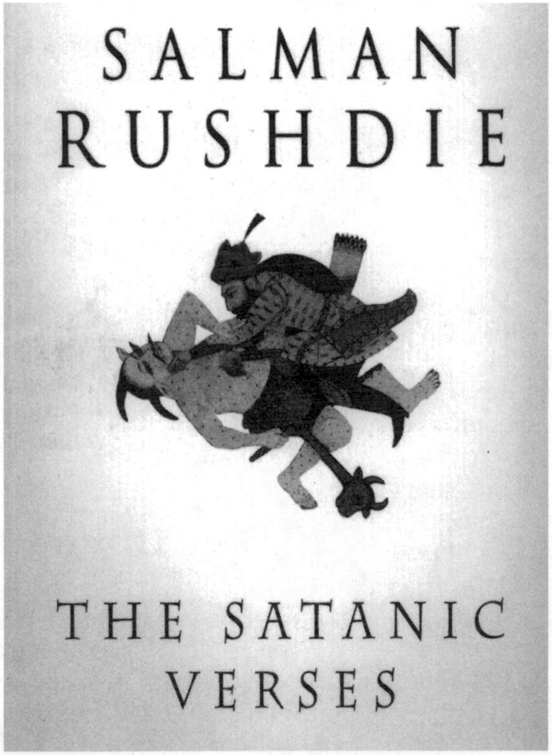

Overlooked facts:

HE'S NOT THERE—The biggest "overlooked fact" about Rushdie, of course, is his exact physical location. He's in hiding, with security provided by the British government. But he does make the occasional, unscheduled appearance. You just never know where...or when.

Quirks:

BUM RUSHDIE SHOW—He's infamous for his incredibly rapid brain, his arrogance, and a reputation for showing up at the glamorous International PEN Award dinners in "battered jeans and decaying green sneakers."

DEATH ON DELIVERY—In the midst of all the controversy surrounding his Satanic Verses in 1988, Rushdie's aunt telephoned his mother to tell her she should have drowned him at birth.

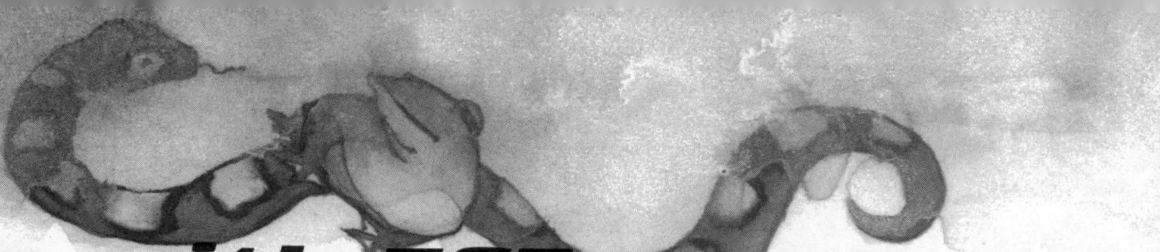

Read Along with EST: Myths, Tales, and Legends to Scare Your Children With

Noble woodcutters, enchanted princesses, and very, very lucky youngest sons—whether your fairy tale is Grimm or Goose (or even of another continent entirely), the cast of characters seems to remain largely the same, and so do the moral messages. After all, where else will kids learn the importance of telling the truth, sharing with others, and refusing apples offered by kindly old crones?

Of course, the stories themselves may differ, and understandably so, since the origin of most folk tales, myths, and legends (regardless of their ethnic roots) is in the oral tradition, with stories passed down from one generation to the next, until eventually someone thinks to record the gem for posterity. As a result, details change from family to family, province to province, and region to region.

With that caveat, however, the following are a few of the more popular, timeless stories told in Asia to entertain the young—while teaching them how to straighten up and fly right... —T.H.

"The Twelve Animals of the Zodiac" (China)

Once upon a time, in order to help his people keep track of time, the Emperor (in some variations, it's Buddha) decided to hold a contest on his birthday: The first 12 animals to win a race across the great river would be represented as the symbols of the great 12-year cycle. The rat and cat, who at the time were the best of friends, decided to journey together. They were helped by the kindly ox, who offered to carry them across the water. On the way, the rat tricked the cat, pushing him into the water. Once across, the rat leapt off the ox's shoulders and became the first to finish the contest, all the while touting his own cleverness. The other animals eventually came across, the last one being the wet and furious cat—who arrived too late to be included as one of the 12. Upon hearing that he would not be one of the chosen animals, the cat lunged at the rat, beginning their mortal feud, which still lasts to this day. And even today, the rat, now ashamed of how he won the race, hides all day and only comes out under the cloak of night.

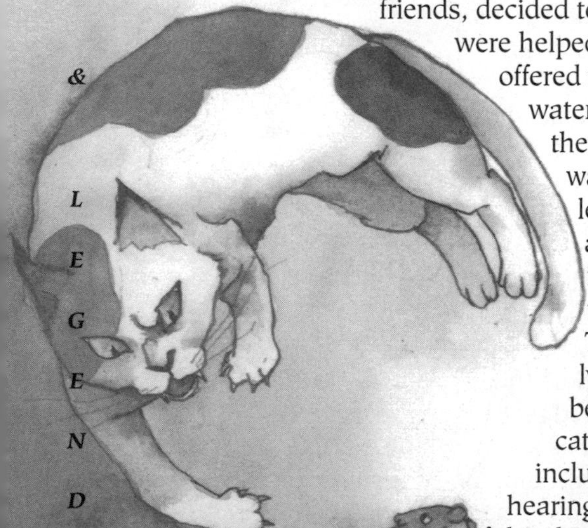

THE RIGHT LESSON: *Unfair gains will not go unpunished.*
THE WRONG LESSON: *You can't depend on your friends when you really need them.*

Walk into any Chinese takeout restaurant during the first few months of the New Year (the western New Year and Chinese New Year don't coincide, of course,so they keep the "New Year" paraphernalia out for a while to cover both calendar systems), and beneath your teacup and the inevitable disposable wooden chopsticks will be a paper placemat reminding you that it's the Year of the Rat, or the Dragon, or the Rabbit. And depending on which year you were born in, you'll also read all about your own personality...just in case you haven't already realized your strengths and weaknesses. [👁224]

"The Opium Flower" (India)

Long, long ago, there lived a holy man whose only companion was a tiny mouse, to whom he granted the power of human speech. One day, the mouse graciously asked the holy man for another favor. Tormented daily by a cruel cat, the mouse wished to be transformed

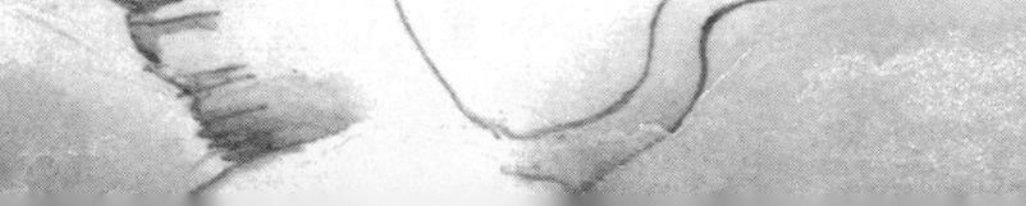

into a cat so he could fight his enemy on an equal basis. The holy man immediately turned him into a cat. A few days later, the cat asked the holy man to turn him into a dog, in order to defend itself against a pack of wild dogs. So the cat became a dog. Still the dog was not happy, returning to request transformation into a monkey, so that it could more easily climb trees to gather luscious fruits from high branches. Then the monkey wanted to become a boar, so it could laze around all day in the wet mud. And then the boar wished to become a proud elephant decorated with jewels, to bear the king on its back. But the king gave the proud elephant to his queen, and the elephant thought her unworthy of his royal back. The elephant realized that it could only be happy if it could be the queen of the world. Patiently, the holy man explained that he could not create a king and kingdom, without which the elephant could not be queen of the world, so the holy man transformed the elephant into a young woman so beautiful that someday a king might fall in love with her and make her his queen. Indeed, the king happened upon the holy man's garden, fell instantly in love with the holy man's beautiful young "daughter," and took her as his queen. In the palace courtyard, the new queen caught a glimpse of her own reflection in an open well, and became so enamored with her own beauty that she fell in and drowned. Heartbroken, the king returned to the holy man, asking him to bring her back to life. But the holy man explained that his "daughter" had lived out her destiny. To console the king, the holy man promised that in the well would grow an exquisite white flower, the poppy, whose seeds, if abused, would make men suffer through all of the beautiful woman's incarnations: he would in turns be as meek as a mouse, as sly as cat, as combative as a dog, as wily as a monkey, as dirty as a boar, as ignorant as an elephant, and as demanding as a queen. Thus did opium come to be.

THE RIGHT LESSON: *Be careful what you wish for...it might come true.*

THE WRONG LESSON: *Holy men can change animals into people.*

An elaborate predecessor to today's War Against Drugs advertisements, this curious installment in the "How Things Came to Be" genre of myths may be a bit overdetermined for small children to understand; besides, they'd probably just ask too many questions about opium. A Chinese version of this myth (which apparently has a counterpart in African legend) involves a humble stonecutter who toils in the mountains, until an all-powerful deity takes mercy on him and offers to change him into something with an easier lot in life. The stonecutter accepts the offer, and then requests transformations into more and more lofty items—a soaring lark, a great eagle, an emperor, the sun, a thundercloud—until he demands, finally, to be transformed into the towering form of the mountains themselves, since they are more powerful even than the crashing rain, the flashing lightning, and the wailing winds. The deity shrugs in exasperation and gives him his final demand. And so he is satisfied...until he becomes aware of a sharp pain in his foot, and notices a little stonecutter chip-chip-chipping away at his base...

"The Crane Maiden" (Japan)

Long, long ago in a remote village, a poor but honest man set out to town to buy food with his last few pieces of money. Along the way, however, he came upon a beautiful crane caught in a trap. Deciding to free the helpless bird, he was surprised by the hunter who'd set the trap, whereupon he paid for the crane's life with the last of his money. Rather than taking it home and eating it—as others of empty pocket and stomach might do—he immediately let the bird fly free. He returned home empty-handed, told his wife what happened, and received praises for his kindheartedness; once again, the couple

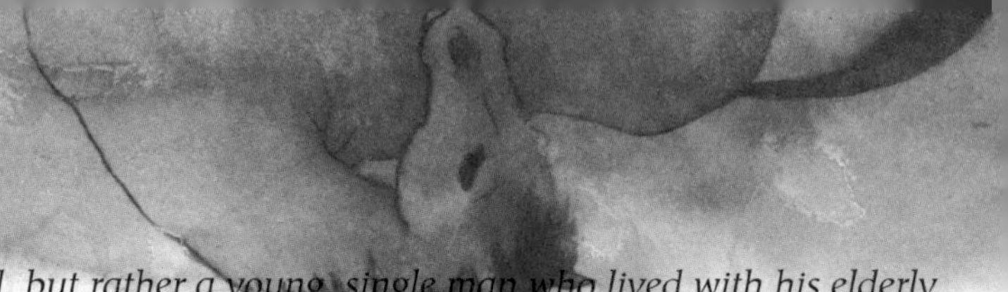

went to sleep hungry. The next morning, however, a mysterious and beautiful young woman appeared at their door, asking to be taken in. The kindly old couple, always willing to share despite having little to spare, welcomed her, and she soon became a beloved part of their household. After spending some time with the couple, she asked to use their loom, to help out with the wife's weaving. However, claiming shyness, she asked to be left completely alone while performing her work. She disappeared into the weaving room, and reemerged a few days later with a stunning piece of cloth, which she gave to the elderly couple to sell. The old man was able to sell the cloth for a tremendous amount of money, giving the couple cause to rejoice. The young woman then promised to make another piece, this time even more spectacular—but, in order to do so, she would have to be left completely alone for a full week. Concerned about the girl, the couple were not able to restrain themselves from peeking into the room on the final day of the week, thinking that she surely would need food or rest. But when they looked in, they saw instead the crane, pulling out her feathers to weave the magnificent cloth. The young woman was then forced to reveal that she was indeed the crane that the man set free, and that she had returned in the guise of a woman to repay his kindness; however, now that the couple knew her true identity, she could no longer stay with them. But before she left forever, the young woman gave the couple the new cloth, instructing them to sell it—giving them enough money to live comfortably for the rest of their lives.

THE RIGHT LESSON: *Curiosity killed the cat. (Or, in this case, chased away the crane.)*

THE WRONG LESSON: *Young women can live without food or water for a week.*

Another variation of the story says that the kind old man was actually not that *old, but rather a young, single man who lived with his elderly mother. So when the young woman appeared at his door, she asked him to take her as her wife; the man's elderly mother recognizeed a good soul and urged her son to marry her. This, of course, makes the young crane-woman's departure at story's end all the more poignant. (Some versions even have the crane maiden giving birth to a half-human/half-crane child, which transforms into a baby crane and flies off with her, leaving the poor young man completely alone...)*

"The Three Royal Tests" (Philippines)

Long, long ago, a powerful king had a daughter whom he loved above all things. As she grew older, he realized that soon she would have to marry. But the daughter, who did not want to leave her father, was not at all interested in finding a husband. The king gently explained that he would someday pass on, and that she must have a husband to take care of her. As a dutiful child, the daughter reluctantly agreed, and left the choice of husband to her wise father. The king put out a call to all eligible men, proclaiming that the man able to pass the king's three royal tests would be the one to win the princess' hand. The two most promising suitors were a handsome prince and a powerful magician. The first test was to bring back the enchanted pearl necklace from the bottom of the sea. The prince quickly asked the help of his friend, the King of the Sea, and retrieved the precious gift. The frustrated magician could do nothing but snarl. The two then set out to accomplish the second task—to bring back seven petals of a rare flower that only grew atop a faraway mountain. On the way, the prince met an old woman carrying a very heavy load and—being a kind person—he insisted on helping her, even though it meant clambering back down the mountain. The magician, meanwhile, raced toward the goal, chuckling at the prince's naive generosity.

Meanwhile, the old woman, recognizing a good soul, revealed herself as the beautiful fairy guardian of the rare flower; she told him that she could only give the petals to a true-hearted person, unlike the magician, who had denied the old woman help and rushed on. She granted the prince the prize, and he happily returned to the palace. (Sometime later, the magician returned, sweaty, flowerless, and, if possible, even more angry.) The third and most difficult test was to bring back the Volcano God's magic cane, which would give wielder the ability to bring rain. Again the magician rushed off, while the kind prince stopped to assist an old man who had difficulty walking. In gratitude, the old man led him to the Volcano God's brother, who in turn helped him get the magic cane. Furious beyond belief at being stymied once again, the magician used his powers to try to prevent the prince from returning to the palace with the final prize, sending horrendous obstacles into his path. The prince was forced to give up—and sadly returned to his own kingdom with a broken heart.

THE RIGHT LESSON: *Be a good soul and you'll be rewarded—but you can't always get what you want.*
THE WRONG LESSON: *You should always marry whomever your father chooses, regardless of how stupid the criteria used for choosing them.*

This is a rather bizarre fairy tale to tell a young listener, though, to be fair, it probably offers a more realistic vision of reality than other fables. There are more optimistic versions in which the prince gets his princess in the end. And certainly, those happy ending versions are the ones kids enjoy...even if they fail to teach an important practical fact about life.

"The Naughty Frog" (Korea)

Once upon a time, there lived a very naughty frog. Although he wasn't an evil frog, he had a hard time obeying his mother: Whenever she asked him to do something, he always did exactly the opposite. One day, the mother frog felt her death approaching, and, in preparation, she asked the son to bury her in the river—thinking of course that he would do the opposite, and bury her in the mountains, where her body would be safe on solid ground. Once she passed away, however, the naughty frog realized with great guilt how bad he had been, and decided to fulfill at least his mother's last wish. As a result, he buried her body in the river. Now, every time it rains, the frog cries and croaks, desperately worried that his mother will be washed away.

THE RIGHT LESSON: *Not obeying your parents while they're alive can have tragic consequences.*
THE WRONG LESSON: *Frogs have nuclear families and engage in complex burial rituals.*

Depending on the gender of the child being told the story, the frog child becomes a he or a she. It's an equal opportunity tale: As a result, any boy or girl can be made to feel horrible whenever he or she does something going against his or her parents' wishes, which (in Asian families) is not an uncommon event.

"The Story of Tam and Cam" (Vietnam)

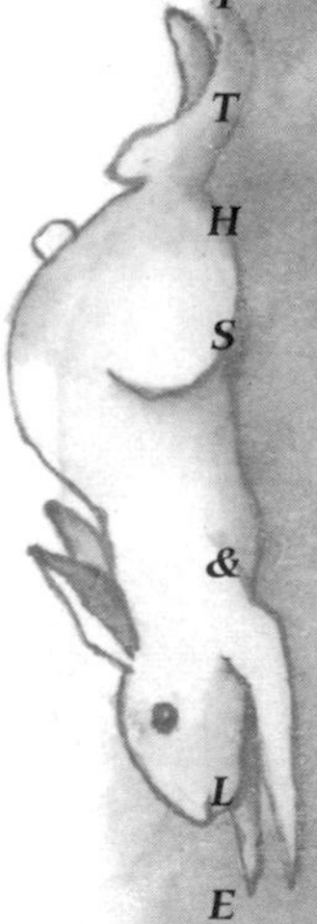

Once upon a time, there lived a beautiful young girl, Tam, who lost her mother at a young age. Her father remarried a beautiful (if nasty) woman who had a daughter of her own, Cam. Tam was a kind and gentle girl, always serving her stepmother's whims without question. Cam, on the other hand, was wicked and spoiled. Meanwhile, the stepmother made life for Tam as difficult as possible. On the night of the grand town ball at the royal palace, the stepmother came up with a nearly impossible task for Tam to finish before she would be allowed to go to the ball. But with the help of the Goddess of Mercy, Tam made it to the event, where she was the most beautiful guest of all. Discovered by her stepmother and Cam, she ran out, dropping a slipper behind her in her hurry. The next day, the palace sent out word that the one whose foot the slipper fit would become the next queen of the kingdom. Tam fit the bill perfectly and she married her

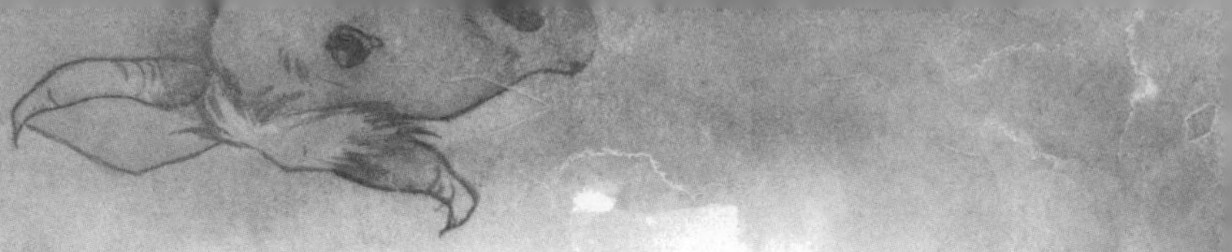

king. Of course, she should have lived happily ever after. Not so! After becoming the queen, she still returned home to fulfill her filial duty to her parents, where she was brutally murdered by the jealous stepmother. Broken-hearted, the king was persuaded to take Cam as his next queen. But Tam's forlorn spirit refused to fade away, and she returned to life as the king's favorite songbird, only to be killed off again by a jealous Cam; she was then reborn again as a young girl who quietly served an old, needy woman. Some years later, the king happened on the old woman's hut, saw the girl, and instantly recognized her as his own beloved (first) wife. The lovers were gloriously reunited, but once again nasty Cam tried to kill off her half-sister. Finally, the gullible Tam became aware that Cam was a bad person, and in the end, Cam died, the victim of her own devices. And Tam and the king lived happily ever after, after all.

THE RIGHT LESSON: *True love conquers all, even death.*
THE WRONG LESSON: *All stepmothers and step-siblings are horrible, murderous people.*

For obvious reasons, this tale has been called the "Vietnamese Cinderella" story (similar variations are also told in Korea and Japan). Of course, while Cinderella's trials ended with her marriage to the man of her dreams, poor Tam has a rougher life, and the lesson taught here is (like the story of the Three Royal Tests above) a grimly pragmatic one. Again, cultural differences breed interesting diversity in folk tales...

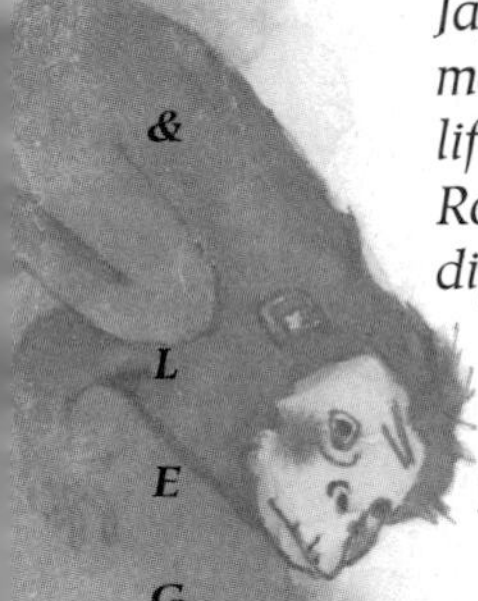

"The Inevitable Marriage" (Thailand)

Once upon a time, there was a wealthy young boy who lived with his elderly mother. One day, a famous fortuneteller passed through the town and told the boy three things: that he would marry a slave's daughter, that this daughter was still an infant, and that for now, his wife-to-be was in a lower station in life than the boy. Although the boy was not an evil soul, he didn't like the fortuneteller's predictions. He realized that the newborn daughter of one of his mother's slaves must be the child to whom Fate had decreed he be betrothed. Determined to change his future, he attempted to kill the child as it slept. However, the knife he dropped above the sleeping child did not fatally injure her, and the mother was able to save her daughter's life. As time passed, the boy's family fell upon hard times and lost its fortune. The slave woman was set free, and she traveled away with her family to find a new life. After the death of his parents, the boy, having grown to young manhood without training in proper job skills, was forced to leave his home, and after much hardship was accepted as an apprentice by a wealthy merchant. The merchant admired the young man's hard work and diligence, and he came to have deep respect for the young man. One day, the lad met his patron's daughter—an exquisite young woman, who immediately inspired feelings of adoration in the young man. The merchant was delighted that his favorite apprentice should love and be loved by his daughter, and the two were soon happily wed. On their wedding night, the husband noticed a small scar on his lovely wife's neck and asked about its origin. She told him the story she had heard from her mother, about how she had been the child of a slave and was nearly killed by the son of her mistress, who had been told that he would someday marry her. The husband then realized his wife's identity and finally accepted that Fate cannot be avoided.

THE RIGHT LESSON: *Fate cannot be changed.*
THE WRONG LESSON: *Slavery is okay, as is murder, so long as you're rich.*

Similar versions of this story also exist in the Philippines and Malaysia. Again, Western audiences might find this tale a strange one—and certainly not one that would be told to children, considering that it involves attempted infanticide (which ultimately results in reward).

FILM AND TELEVISION

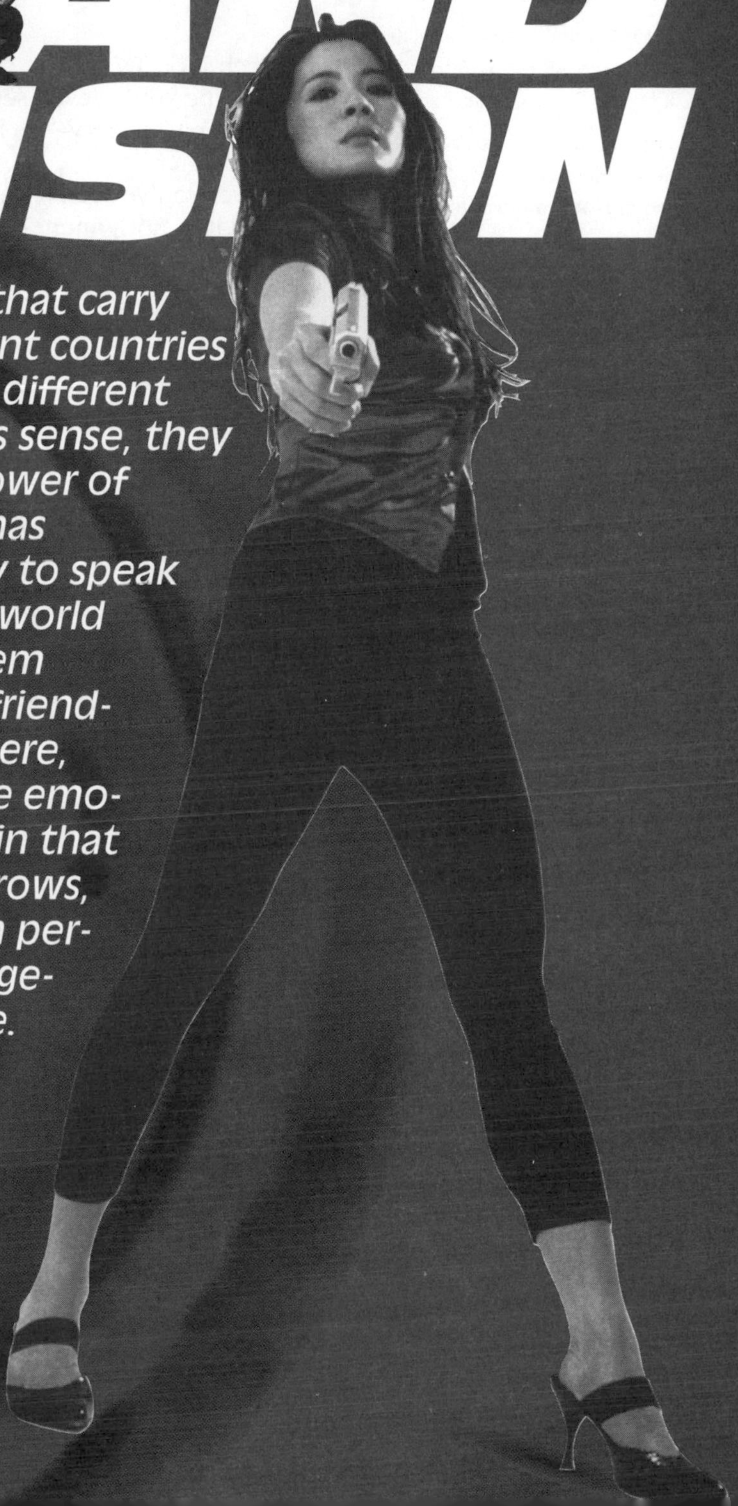

"Films are something that carry across to many different countries and are seen by many different kinds of people. In this sense, they have a tremendous power of communication. This has enabled me personally to speak to people all over the world and to understand them better and form new friendships. People everywhere, seeing a film, share the emotions of the character in that film—the joys, the sorrows, the dramas. Those film personages have no strangeness for their audience. Somebody like John Wayne is a personality the Japanese feel very close to. To the Japanese, he is a household word, not a stranger."

—Akira Kurosawa

Anime Attacks!

You've seen it on TV. You've seen it in music videos. Maybe you've even seen it in all its full chrome-and-pastel glory—on a big screen, in a darkened theater.

Wherever you've seen it (and whether you've recognized it or not), anime—Japanese animation—has attracted a huge and thriving audience in America, leading kids, teens, and many, many adults to recognize for the first time that cartoons aren't just kids' stuff after all.

Which, in Disney's America, is a fairly understandable mistake: Once you begin worrying about serious issues like puberty, the antic trials of animated rabbits become largely irrelevant. Not so in

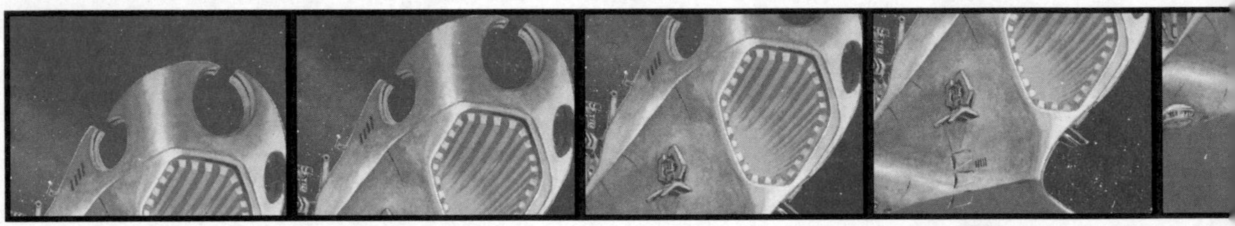

Star Blazers

Japan, where approximately 55 percent of all domestic box office revenue is generated by animated films. According to Masahiro Haraguchi, contributing editor of *Animage* (one of Japan's leading anime magazines), the turn towards animation was a cost-saving device in an industry that couldn't keep up with Hollywood's big-budget special effects. "[Japanese producers] increasingly turned to animation, where anything is possible," he says.

As a result, in Japan, animation isn't perceived as a genre, but rather a mass medium, a way of telling stories. There are anime for people of all ages and backgrounds, with themes ranging from the comic, to the melodramatic, to the horrific. Even those for younger audiences tend to have plots confronting sophisticated themes, like love, death, and coming of age; for example, the stars of the popular girls' superhero series *Sailor Moon* died en masse—and quite brutally—at the end of their first series. Anime created for more mature audiences, meanwhile, range from harsh but gripping portrayals of reality, as in the wrenching wartime drama *Grave of the Fireflies,* to subversive and often disturbing fantasies, such as in *Urotsukidoji: Legend of the Overfiend,* a prime example of the uniquely Japanese genre of horror porn.

Anime first arrived in America in 1961, in the form of two early features, *Alakazam the Great* (a loosely adapted version of the Chinese legend of the Monkey King, **👁32**) and *Panda and the Magic Serpent*. Unfortunately, neither film was successful, and Disney's domination of the U.S. animated-feature universe continued unchallenged. But if the big screen was Walt's unquestioned domain, mere anarchy ruled on the small screen, where the networks were engaged in a battle royal for kiddie viewers. The stage was set for anime's first real beachhead in the West—with the 1963 debut on American television of Osamu Tezuka's lovable robot crimebuster, *Astro Boy*. Though his Japanese origins were occluded by the show's producers, Astro's jet-propelled success led to a feeding frenzy among American TV execs for similar series, and the following years saw the debut of *8th Man* (about a crime-fighting robot detective), *Gigantor* (about a crime-fighting giant robot controlled by a young boy), and Tezuka's followup to *Astro Boy*, the jungle adventure *Kimba the White Lion*. In 1967, *Speed Racer* zoomed onto syndicated television, in the process becoming one of the most popular—and enduring—cartoons of all time.

Then, in the late '70s and early '80s, two television series arrived that captivated the animation appetites of a generation American fans. The first was 1979's *Space Cruiser Yamato*, known in the

ANIME THROUGH THE AGES

1914: Japan's first animated motion picture debuts.

1918: The first Japanese animated film screens in the West: Kitayama Seitaro's Momotaro.

1962: Japan's first animated series, Manga Calendar, debuts, running for two years on TV.

1963: Tetsuwan Atom debuts in Japan, then becomes the first anime to screen on American TV, as the legendary Astro Boy.

1966: Several other Japanese animated series come to U.S. TV, including Gigantor and Kimba.

1967: Speed Racer go, go, goes on the air in the U.S.

1972: In Japan, Go Nagai's Mazinger Z [👁**70**] debuts, and the giant robot is born; it comes to the U.S. in 1985 as TranZor Z.

1979: The stalwart crew of Space Cruiser Yamato debuts on U.S. TV, renamed Star Blazers.

1981: Anime slapstick comedy finds its first superstar in Lum, Rumiko Takahashi's alien princess in a tiger-striped bikini.

1985: Carl Macek's hybridized space epic Robotech debuts in the U.S.

1989: Having inspired a generation of anime fans with Robotech, Macek releases Katsuhiro Otomo's science-fiction epic Akira to American art-house theaters through his new company Streamline Pictures. It becomes the first blockbuster U.S. anime hit, selling over 100,000 copies on video, and thousands of movie tickets.

1989: Osamu Tezuka, the "God

Dragonball

U.S. as *Star Blazers*; the second was *Robotech*, a cobbled-together reenvisioning of three Japanese space-warfare series that enthralled schoolkids five days a week throughout 1985. Both were distinctive in that they had complex storylines, believable (if futuristic) situations, and realistic characters in changing, organic relationships.

"My brother and I used to race home every day from school to watch *Star Blazers*," says Trish Ledoux, editor of *Animerica* and the co-author of *The Complete Anime Guide*. "I still consider it one of my favorite shows ever." Mike Tatsugawa, cofounder of the nation's biggest anime fan convention, Anime Expo, remembers a similar obsession with *Robotech*. "*Robotech* was always the talk of the classroom," he remembers. "It didn't have a kiddie storyline, it covered relationships, and it had violence; it was like an animated soap opera. I remember *Robotech* was on at 4:30, and *The Smurfs* were on at 3:30. The dichotomy was really frightening." Unlike their predecessors, *Star Blazers* and *Robotech* made relatively little attempt to hide their Japanese origins. Most viewers recognized that the two series were different—and better—than the pale plastic fodder produced by most American cartoon companies. And many viewers wanted more: unadulterated, uncut, and straight from the Japanese source.

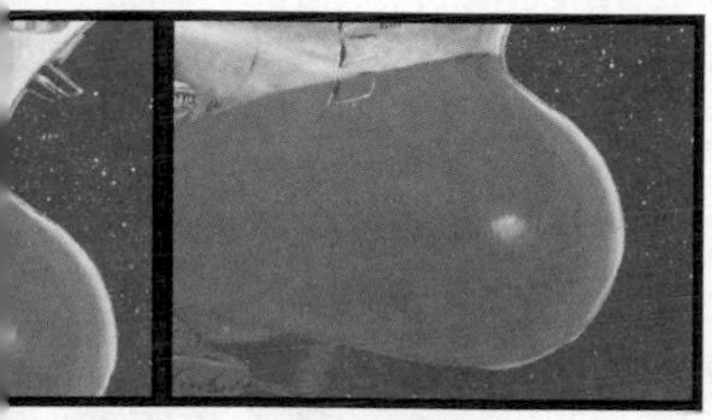

Luckily, in 1975, a technical innovation had arrived that made direct infusions of anime possible for the very first time: this was, of course, the VCR. Giant robot enthusiasts, *Robotech* junkies, and *Star Blazer* boosters slowly crafted a vast pirate underground, a jury-rigged network of computer bulletin boards and bootleg video exchanges that made subtitled versions of Japanese animation available—for free—to all who flocked to the anime banner. But if nature abhors a vacuum, then capitalism abhors an unexploited business opportunity, and it was just a matter of time before entrepreneurs arrived to feed the hunger of the American anime audience.

Since then, anime has grown from being a cult pleasure to a surging mini-industry—with annual revenues of some $60 million in the U.S. There are now well in excess of 200 anime titles available, in English, for sale or rent at a video store near you. And anime has even made it back to nationally syndicated television, with international mega-hits *Dragonball* and *Sailor Moon* airing in early-morning and afterschool slots across the nation. All of which has led some long-time fans to mourn the passage of a time when copyrights were winked at and tapes were traded by mail between addicts across the nation.

Other fans are more pragmatic, and philosophical: "In 1985, an import tape of *Macross: the Movie* cost you $150," says Tatsugawa. "Now, you can get the English-language version of *Macross II* for $20. People who had fuzzy, fourth-generation tapes of *Yamato* used to be considered big shots, but the stuff being released commercially is crystal clear. If you're a fan, there's no question what you're going to choose."

And for fans of anime today, the choices are as limitless as the imagination. —J.Y.

Gigantor

of Manga" and the father of Astro Boy, dies in Japan [46].

1991: The first U.S. anime fan convention, AnimeCon, is held.

1994: Hayao Miyazaki's children's classic My Neighbor Totoro is released in the U.S., selling 500,000 copies and providing the first real Japanese challenge to Disney. In 1996, Disney buys the U.S. rights to all of Miyazaki's works.

1994: Pioneer becomes the first Japanese anime company to enter the U.S. market, releasing

their enormously popular OAV series Tenchi Muyo almost simultaneously in America and Japan.

1994: Over 40 Japanese cartoonists sign a letter complaining to Disney that the megahit The Lion King draws uncredited inspiration from Tezuka's Jungeru Taitei (Kimba in the U.S.) [46]; Disney denies any connection.

1995: Two of Japan's biggest television hits, Sailor Moon and Dragonball, arrive on U.S. TV.

1995: Michael "The King of Pop" Jackson uses images from Akira in his video for "Scream."

1996: Manga Entertainment coproduces Ghost in the Shell, the most expensive Japanese anime feature ever (with a budget of nearly $10 million). The film is a moderate commercial success, but critics rightly hail it as a brilliant achievement.

SPEAKING ANIME:
A Glossary

ANIME: Japanese animation; preferred over "Japanimation" or "Japanese cartoons."

BISHOUJO; BISHONEN: "Beautiful girl" or "beautiful boy"; the former is a common prefix for stories of the "magical girl" genre (see **MAGICAL GIRL**), while the latter refers to the pretty, fey lads who populate girls' comics (see **SHOUJO**).

CELS: The clear polyvinyl sheets which are shot to produce animation; often collected by fans, who pay hundreds of dollars for original cels featuring their favorite characters.

COSPLAY: Short for "costume play," i.e., dressing up as your favorite character; a common sight at fan conventions.

FANSUB: Bootleg subtitles of anime shows, produced by fans with computer editing equipment; the primary means by which anime first spread throughout the U.S.

HENTAI; H; ECCHI (the Japanese pronunciation of H)**:** Perverted; used to describe someone with an unhealthy or unusual degree of lust, or to denote a pornographic work (like Urotsukidoji).

IDOLSINGER: A young teenybopper pop singer, better known for being cute than talented [👁265]. Often provide vocals and soundtracks for anime.

MECHA: Any anime device, robot, or vehicle [👁70]. Short for "mechanical."

MAGICAL GIRL: A genre of anime series featuring super-powered young girls as [continued on 59]

Anime 101: The Classics, and How to Watch Them

Wanna impress the gang with your theoretical and practical knowledge of anime? Watch the following classic works, covering the range from slapstick comedy to erotic horror. Then engage your friends with a discourse on recurring themes in anime (whose cultural and anthropological roots you'll have to research for yourself). Here's a bluffer's guide to some common anime themes:

1. BODY HORROR—A theme common to anime horror stories: the body out of control. Protagonists or victims find themselves transforming in grotesque, organic fashion, with appendages or organs swelling into monstrous form.

2. FEAR OF TECHNOLOGY/THE BOMB/THE FUTURE—Progress run amok, either in the form of cybernetic creatures that turn against their masters, or future dystopiae in which society is controlled by technology. Often combined with fear of ecological apocalypse or nuclear armageddon.

***Katsuhiro Otomo's cyberpunk classic* Akira**

3. INNOCENCE REGAINED—The theme of eternally chaste love, in which pursuer and pursued perform a tango of ambivalence, missed opportunities, and miscommunication.

4. INNOCENCE LOST—The theme of sexual adventurism, in which a protagonist engages in an endless series of sexual conquests, or in which the young or naive are subjected to depraved lusts.

5. GENDER TWISTS—Reversals of traditional gender roles, either through the depiction of strong, aggressive women, and weak, passive men; through open depiction of homosexuality; or through actual physical gender transformations.

Company Abbreviations

A18—Anime 18; **ADV**—A.D. Vision; **ANI**—AnimEigo; **BES**—Best Home Video; **FOX**—Fox Home Video; **MAN**—Manga Video; **PIO**—Pioneer; **STR**—Streamline; **USM**—U.S. Manga Corps; **VIZ**—Viz Video

Akira (**1., 2., 4.**)—For most modern anime fans, this is where it all began: a searing tale of the terrible potential that lies in the human mind. Biker boy Tetsuo is kidnapped and subjected to experiments designed to unleash his latent psychic ability. They succeed—but in the process, he becomes a monster. He storms through NeoTokyo on a collision course with the first recipient of these wild talents, the being known as Akira. And only his friend Kaneda can stop him. **(1988; STR)**

Battle Angel (**1., 2., 4., 5.**)—Above the earth hangs Zeram, the city in the sky, where humanity's artists, scientists, and intellects dwell. The surface below crawls with mutants and half-machine monsters, who live only to kill and cannibalize the organs of others. Ido, an exile from Zeram, uses

Dragonball

Without a doubt, the epic martial arts comedy-adventure *Dragonball* is one of the most popular cartoons in the history of the world. Even after nearly 500 televised episodes, dozens of videos and theatrical features, and millions of comic pages, it continues to thrill audiences, not just in its native Japan, but throughout the world. "*Dragonball* was so huge in Spain that, during the Barcelona Olympics, there were more *Dragonball* items being sold on the streets than Olympic mascot items," says Gen Fukunaga, whose company Funimation has brought *Dragonball* to American TV. Creator Akira Toriyama's effervescent combination of musclebound action, quirky characters, and slightly bawdy humor tickles the funnybone while delivering an adrenaline kick. Kids love it. Teens love it. Merchandisers, who've sold billions of dollars worth of *Dragonball* toys, lunchboxes, clothing, and more, thank God in heaven for it. And though the comic series has finally been brought to a kind of conclusion, the phenomenon shows no sign of stopping. Keep those lunchboxes coming.

The Story

Goku, a young, orphaned boy, has spent his childhood living on his own in the wild woods, practicing martial arts, and guarding his most prized possession—a strange golden ball given to him by his grandfather. What Goku doesn't know is that the ball is one of the seven mystical Dragonballs, which, if gathered together, can be used to call Shen Long, the Dragon God, who will grant the summoner's greatest single wish. Into Goku's placid existence comes Bulma, a cute teenage girl obsessed with finding the seven balls, as well as a host of odd friends—and enemies—with their own wishful agendas. Goku and Bulma travel together in search of the Dragonballs when Goku's own ball is stolen; they soon run into Yamcha, a wandering bandit, and his companion Puuaru, as well as a strange shape-changing pig named Oolong. The whole gang travels to the island of the Kamesennin, or Turtle Master, and Goku begins to train his martial arts in earnest. Over the course of a decade of training and questing, Goku meets many friends, competitors—and enemies. He gets married, has children, and dies (several times), eventually staying dead and passing the spotlight onto his son Gohan, who becomes *Dragonball*'s new hero. He travels to distant planets, saves the world more times than he could count, and defeats galaxy-smashing villains—Vejita the Saiyajin, Freeza, the androids of Dr. Gero, the super-android Cell, and the mystical monstrosity Buu. Throughout it all, Goku remains basically the same innocent, wide-eyed boy he was when the series began. And maybe that's why *Dragonball* has remained so popular. Goku is Peter Pan with a terrific flying kick—the boy every boy wishes he were, and wishes he could stay forever. —J.Y.

KAMESENNIN—An ancient martial artist (his name means "Turtle Master") who wears Hawaiian shirts, flip-flops, sunglasses, and a turtle shell. He has a mind even dirtier than Oolong's, but he's incredibly wise and skilled; he becomes Goku's teacher, showing him the secret of the Kamehame-ha energy blast and giving him the magical Kintoun Cloud, which can only be ridden by the pure of heart.

YAMCHA—A teenaged male bandit who has a swift, ferocious wolf-style martial arts technique, but completely falls to pieces around women. He's looking for the Dragonballs too—to wish for a girlfriend. He has a sidekick, PUUARU, a shape-changing flying cat. Also joining the gang at the same time as Yamcha and Puuaru is OOLONG, a shape-changing pig with a dirty mind.

BULMA—The perky daughter of a brilliant inventor who always has a plan—and something up her sleeve. When Goku's Dragonball is stolen by evildoers, she convinces him to join her quest.

SON GOKU—Loosely based on the Monkey King of Chinese legend, Goku begins the series as a naive, but powerful young orphan. Over the course of the series, he grows into a naive, super-powerful young man.

protagonists—or as the romantic partner of the hapless male lead.

OAV: Original Animation Video; a "straight to video" anime series.

OTAKU: Originally a term referring to "your house," this became a slang term in Japan for a generation of computer-literate but socially inept teens who spend all of their time gathering useless information about trivial obsessions—pop singers, military technology, or, commonly, anime and manga. The term "otaku" has since been rehabilitated by the teens themselves—particularly in the U.S., where American fans use the term with pride. The anime studio Gainax (known as the "otaku company") even created Otaku no Video ("Tales of the Otaku Generation"), an OAV spoofing the lifestyles of the young and geeky.

SEIYUU: The Japanese term for voice actors, who have the status of celebrities in Japan (and, when they make it over to the U.S. for fan conventions, in America as well. Many are also IDOLSINGERS.

SHOUJO: literally, "for girls"; shoujo manga and anime tends to be dreamily romantic, featuring ridiculously slender characters with big, starry eyes. It's impossible to tell boys and girls apart in shoujo works, which may be one reason why homosexuality is such a rampant theme in these stories.

SUPER-DEFORMED; SD: A comically miniaturized rendering of an animated character, with enlarged head, shrunken body, and cutesy, childlike features.

his mechanical skills to resurrect a lovely young cyborg named Gally, only to find that she is much more—and much deadlier—than her shape reveals. And when Gally fights for those she loves, no one had better get in her way. **(1993; ADV)**

Bubblegum Crisis **(2., 5.)**—In the bleak, cyberpunk future of 2042 A.D., MegaTokyo is controlled by the evil Genom Corporation—manufacturers of android servants and soldiers known as "boomers." When a wave of boomer-related destruction begins, a sexy all-girl vigilante force known as the Knight Sabers swings into action, using armored power-suits created by the dead inventor of the boomers themselves. **(1987; ANI)**

Ghost in the Shell **(1., 2., 5.)**—A lovely cyborg agent hunts a mysterious terrorist known only as the Puppet Master through virtual and actual reality. But slowly it dawns upon her that the Puppet Master is neither human nor even an enemy—and she's driven to question not just her own humanity, but the nature of existence itself. The animation is awe-inspiring. **(1995; MAN)**

Ghost in the Shell

Giant Robo **(2.)**—Daisaku is a young boy with a very good friend—the all-powerful robot Giant Robo. He and his cyber-pal work as part of a secret organization, fighting the terrorist gang Big Fire. A loose remake of the live-action *Johnny Sokko and his Flying Robot, Robo* is a throwback to the old days—when boys were boys, and robots were really, really big. **(1992; MAN)**

Kimagure Orange Road **(3., 5.)**—Young Kyosuke is forced to choose between two lovely girls—the dark-haired, mysterious Madoka and the cute, blonde, but incredibly shrill Hikaru. The twist: neither of them knows that he comes from a family of psychically gifted ESPers. **(1989; ANI)**

Maison Ikkoku **(3., 5.)**—Yusaku Godai, a tormented student who's failed his college entrance exams multiple times, must study hard to prevail—despite distractions like annoying neighbors and Kyoko, his boarding house's lovely manager. Unfortunately, he's got competition for Kyoko's favors... A sweet romantic comedy, from the wacky imagination of Rumiko Takahashi. **(1990; VIZ)**

My Neighbor Totoro—What if the forest were home to a fuzzy bearlike spirit? What if the spirit decided it wanted to be your friend? In this children's classic by master Hayao Miyazaki, it is, and he does. Totoro, the magical beast who comforts young sisters Mei and Satsuki while their mother is in the hospital, rivals any of Disney's creations for sheer lovableness. A must-see for anyone who's young, or young at heart. **(1993; FOX)**

Giant Robo

Oh My Goddess! **(3., 5.)**—Hapless college student Keiichi, attempting to order takeout food, accidentally calls Dial-a-Prayer instead. The result: "Helping Goddess" Belldandy descends from Heaven to fulfill his wish, which turns out to be for a "beautiful girl like Belldandy" to love him. Naturally, the wish is granted—and that's just the

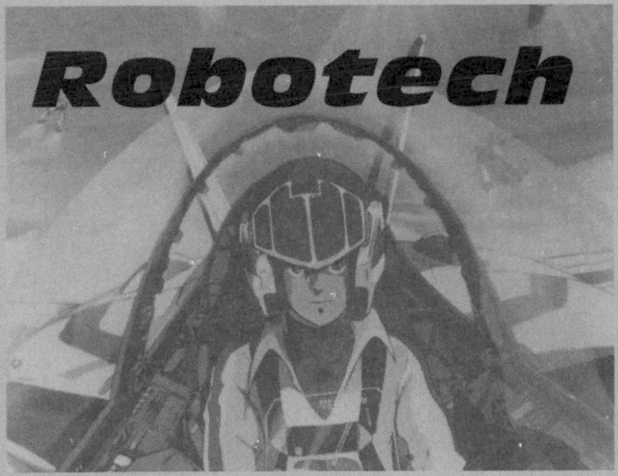

Robotech

A spacefaring spectacle that obsessed a generation of young fans, *Robotech* today remains one of the five best remembered science fiction TV shows of all time. Part of its uniqueness lay in its sheer scope: It spanned galaxies and generations, with a cast of characters in the dozens; it featured gigantic warships, mysterious aliens, and ultracool robot technology; and, like its TV predecessor *Star Blazers*, it featured characters driven by love, death, jealousy, and revenge—enlivened with a sophistication never before seen in American cartoons. Few of those who thrilled to *Robotech*'s outsized plot and vivid characterizations realized that it had been woven together from three unrelated anime series:1982's *Super Dimension Fortress Macross*, 1983's *Genesis Climber Mospeada*, and 1984's *Super Dimension Cavalry Southern Cross*. Their only common ground was that each featured aliens, robots, and intrepid human soldiers, a fact exploited by cartoon producer Carl Macek in amalgamating the three for American television.

There was method behind Macek's madness. Though rights to the series *Macross* had been acquired by U.S. cartoon company Harmony Gold, the show—with just 36 episodes—was too short for broadcast. Given the task of preparing something that could air across an entire television season of 13 weeks (a minimum of 65 episodes), Macek had Harmony Gold purchase the rights to *Southern Cross* and *Mospeada*, then imagined a fanciful new storyline covering three generations—"Macross," "The Robotech Masters,"and "The Invid War"—dubbing and editing the shows together to fit his epic vision. The finished three-arc saga was 85 episodes—more than long enough for their purposes. In October 1985, the cut-and-paste miracle aired for the first time anywhere, and a generation of space cadets fell in love.

The Story

The year is 1999, and Earth is at war. Only one thing could end a near-decade of ceaseless global struggle: The realization that humanity is not alone. The crash-landing of a mammoth spacecraft, dubbed the "Super-Dimensional Fortress," causes widespread destruction; it also forces mankind to act in concert for the first time in its history, working together to unravel the SDF's secrets. The technology around which the fortress is designed is known as Robotech, and behind its unbelievable power is an organic substance known as Protoculture, derived from an alien plant known as the Flower of Life.

Just as human scientists are mastering Robotechnology, however, the Zentraedi—servants of Robotech's true masters—arrive to reclaim their lost battleship. The SDF must launch before it's ready, emerging from a wild subspace jump beyond the orbit of Pluto. On board are young but determined career soldier Lisa Hayes; accidental stowaways Lynn Minmei and Rick Hunter; and thousands of military and civilian personnel, who together realize that to get back home they must fight their way through vastly superior forces. This marks the beginning of one of the most ambitious spacefaring adventure ever to be put to animation: Following the *Robotech* story's first arc are the tales of two additional generations, the descendants of Earth's original space warriors, set against new and more deadly alien enemies... loving, losing, fighting, and dying in an intricate and brilliantly conceived world never imagined by the series' original creators. —J.Y.

LISA HAYES (Misa Hayase)—Stern and forbidding, Hayes is the businesslike first officer of the SDF-1. At first she and the rambunctious Hunter are at odds; eventually, they fall in love.

MAXIMILLIAN STERLING (Maximilian Jiinas)—The SDF-1's top pilot, after he defeats his Zentraedi counterpart Miriya, they fall in love and marry. Their daughter Dana is the key character of Robotech's second arc ("The Robotech Masters").

ROY FOKKER (Roy Focker)—The veteran leader of the "Skull Squadron" serves as Hunter's mentor—until he dies in an epic dogfight with enemy ace Miriya.

CAPTAIN HENRY GLOVAL (Captain Henry Grobal)—The stolid commanding officer of the SDF-1.

NOT SHOWN: MIRIYA (Miria Fariina)—Beautiful and deadly, the Zentraedi pilot Miriya cuts a murderous swath through the Earth defense forces...until she runs into Max Sterling, the ace of the SDF-1.

RICK HUNTER (Hikaru Ichijo in Japan)—Trapped on the SDF-1 while saving Lynn Minmei, Hunter quickly becomes one of its top aces and greatest heroes.

LYNN MINMEI (Lynn Minmay)—An accidental stowaway on the SDF-1, the pretty but vain singer initially bonds with Hunter, but Minmei's self-obsession leads to their breakup. Ironically, her voice proves to be the ultimate weapon against the Zentraedi.

Oh My Goddess!

Tenchi Muyo!

Patlabor

beginning. Because Belldandy has two lovely sisters named Urd and Skuld, and when she doesn't come back...*they* come looking for *her*. **(1994; ANI)**

Patlabor **(2., 5.)**—Noa Izumi is a tomboy whose greatest passion is robots—the bigger, the better. When the opportunity comes for her to join the Patrol Labor unit—a police team that fights android crime using the robots called "labors"—it's a dream come true. **(1989; MAN)**

Ranma 1/2 **(1., 3., 5.)**—Martial artist Ranma Saotome has returned from a trip to China with an unusual problem: whenever he's splashed by cold water, he turns into a cute, red-headed girl. It takes hot water to revert him to his "normal" self. Add a father who turns into a panda, a rival who turns into a pig, and would-be love interests for both boy *and* girl forms, and you get another sexy, hilarious classic from Rumiko Takahashi. **(1994; VIZ)**

Tenchi Muyo **(3.)**—High school student Tenchi accidentally releases Ryoko, a sexy "demon," only to discover that she's an imprisoned galactic criminal. Meanwhile, lovely alien princess Aeka, her cute-as-a-button younger sister Sasami, and airheaded space-cop Mihoshi arrive in hot pursuit. Wild slapstick, clever design, and memorable characters make this a standout. **(1992; PIO)**

Urusei Yatsura **(3., 5.)**—Hapless loser Ataru Moroboshi is randomly chosen as Earth's representative in a deadly game of tag; his opponent is a beautiful alien named Lum. If he catches her, the Earth is saved; if he doesn't, all is lost. He wins—but in the process, accidentally asks her to marry him. She then proceeds to turn his life into an electrically charged nightmare. Another comic classic, courtesy of Rumiko Takahashi. **(1982; ANI)**

Urotsukidoji: Legend of the Overfiend **(1., 4.)**—Repulsive, yet—in its way—a classic, and the instigator of an entire genre of erotic horror. Urotsukidoji recounts the search for a messiah who, legend has it, will unite the worlds of humanity, the Man-Beasts, and demonkind into a single enlightened kingdom. Unfortunately, it becomes apparent that this paradise is instead an infinite hell, as demons run loose on Earth, raping and killing with abandon. Works like this have given anime an unsavory reputation—and, unfortunately, after you've seen an animated demon tentacle invading the orifices of a young schoolgirl, you may be inclined to agree. **(1989; A18)**

Wings of Honneamise **(2.)**—Stirring and gloriously epic, *Wings* recounts the story of the conquest of space in a world similar to our own, with images and music lauded as some of the greatest ever created for animation. **(1987; MAN)** —J.Y.

Ranma 1/2

Urotsukidoji: Legend of the Overfiend

Wings of Honneamise

Sailor Moon

She's perky, she's clumsy, and she's...not all that bright. Still, to millions of young Japanese girls, the "pretty soldier for justice" Sailor Moon is a hero among heroes. They've made her series *Bishoujo Senshi Sailor Moon* into one of the most popular shows in cartoon history. Little wonder, then, that someone would eventually introduce this quirky series in America. In September 1995, top animation company DIC did just that, debuting *Sailor Moon* on U.S. TV. Unfortunately, disappointing ratings caused its cancellation. No such end is in sight in Japan, where fans have kept ratings (and merchandise purchases) at appropriately lunar levels: it's been estimated that *Sailor Moon* generates close to $3.4 billion per year in gross revenue for its Japanese creators and licensees. This is one moon that isn't due for an eclipse anytime soon.

SAILOR MOON—About as unlikely a hero as you're likely to find, Serena (Usagi Tsukino in Japan) is lazy, bubble-headed, and something of a crybaby.

SAILOR VENUS—Mina (Minako Aino) is fun-loving, athletic, and affectionate, and perhaps the friendliest of the five original Scouts. Despite her seeming normalcy, Mina has actually been fighting crime longer than the others, under the dashing alter ego of "Sailor V."

SAILOR MARS—Strong-willed and hot-tempered, Raye (Rei Hino) grew up living with her grandfather, a Shinto priest. She's training as his apprentice, and has already learned some mystical tricks, such as reading the future through the temple's sacred flame, or sensing the presence of evil.

SAILOR JUPITER—Tall, strong, and aggressive, Lita (Makoto Kino) seems to be the most tomboyish of the Scouts, except for her love of domestic things, like cooking and cleaning.

NOT SHOWN: DARIEN (Mamoru Chiba)—This handsome classmate of the Scouts begins the series as Serena's tormentor, and eventually reveals himself to be the love of her life. In secret, he's the top-hatted hero, TUXEDO MASK.

SAILOR MERCURY—In contrast to her friend Serena, whiz kid Amy (Ami Mizuno) is a cool-headed, brilliant student who loves school more than anything.

RINI (Chibi-Usa)—This pink-haired cutie drops out of the sky one day (onto Serena's head, in fact) and instantly insinuates herself into the lives of Serena and the Scouts. Despite initially thinking of her as a brat, Serena becomes quite attached to the Rini—later revealed to be her and Darien's daughter, sent back from the far future.

The Story

A thousand years ago, the Earth's moon was the capital of a glorious kingdom, whose reign of peace and harmony over the galaxy was called the Silver Millennium. Its benevolent ruler was the beautiful Queen Serenity, who possessed two great magical artifacts: The Silver Crystal and the Crescent Moon Wand. Little did Serenity and her subject know that, in the shadows, the evil Queen Beryl was plotting to overthrow the Silver Millennium, using the terrifying power of the Negaforce. Beryl and her minions attacked, slaying the Queen's most trusted and capable warriors. After even the Queen's daughter gave her life fighting the army of the Negaverse, Serenity took aside her two most trusted advisors, magical cats named Luna and Artemis, and gave them the crystal and the wand. She told them that the Moon Kingdom would soon be destroyed, but that the future promised hope—if the power of the two artifacts could be used for good. Then, using her magic, she sent the spirits of her daughter and her bravest female warriors into the future, where they all took on secret new incarnations. Last of all, she transported the two cats, with instructions to find and teach Serena and the Sailors the skills they would need to build a new Silver Millennium.

In the 20th century, a junior high student named Serena saves a small black cat from a group of small boys. That evening, she's woken by the very same cat—who shocks her by speaking in human tongue. The cat Luna tells her that she's not just a simple schoolgirl, but a disguised warrior, and gives her a brooch which enables her to transform, with a shout of "Moon Prism Power!", into Sailor Moon. Serena soon meets four other girls who join her fight to defend Earth from Negaverse demons, sent to Earth to steal human souls; together, the Sailor Scouts foil plan after plan, often with the help of a mysterious young man in evening wear: Tuxedo Mask.

Numerous other complications develop over the course of the show's first season, which concludes with the *death* of all five Sailor Scouts; luckily, the Scouts recover in time for new adventures with new allies and a fresh set of foes. So far, there have been five seasons of *Sailor Moon* in Japan—and no end is in sight. —J.Y.

Speed Racer

KEY CAST

SPEED (Go Mifune in Japan)—At just 18 years of age, Speed is a precocious competitor in the fast-paced world of international auto racing. While winning races, Speed has busted up the plots of arch-villains like Tongue Blaggard time and again.

TRIXIE (Michi Shimura)—At 17, Trixie is no less accomplished than her boyfriend Speed, and just as fearless—saving the day more than once when it looked like Speed was headed for that Big Pit Stop in the Sky.

REX/RACER X (Kenichi "The Masked Racer" Mifune)—Probably the coolest member of the regular cast, this mysterious driver is a rival of Speed's in many of the top races of the world. He's never seen without his X-marked mask, and for a good reason: Underneath that mask is the face of Speed's older brother Rex. Racer X is also an undercover agent of Interpol, code numbered Agent 9.

SPRIDLE (Kuryo Mifune)—A hyperkinetic tot whose best friend is a chimp, Spridle is Speed's younger brother, and a holy terror—constantly stowing away in the trunk of the Mach 5 with his pet monkey Chim Chim.

THE MACH 5—The world's most sophisticated driving machine, it can leap over chasms, blaze across any terrain, has rotary buzzsaws that can cut through obstacles), and even drive underwater. Not available in stores.

Who's the fastest guy on wheels? If you don't know the answer, you don't know Speed Racer. Owner of the slickest vehicle ever to set four tires on the tarmac, the Mach 5, when Speed drove onto American TV in 1967, he became the boy-hero of millions of kids across the nation. Boys wished they were Speed (though the really cool ones idolized his enigmatic rival, Racer X); girls wanted to be Trixie; and annoying little brothers everywhere hid in car trunks and demanded pet monkeys, just like Spridle.

The Story

When genius mechanic Pops Racer first unveiled his plans for a super-car to his employers, they scoffed in his face, leading him to quit and start his own business. He quickly built a name for himself as a top-notch car designer, and his small company, Pops Motors, became quite successful. But making normal cars was nothing to Pops: He wanted to create the fastest, most technically advanced car in the world, which he dubbed the Mach 5. It took him years to design his dream, during which time he raised his children—eldest son Rex, middle son Speed, and baby Spridle—to love cars and racing as much as he did. Upon coming of age, Rex Racer began driving professionally, but wrecked a prototype car Pops had spent years on in his first race, prompting Pops to ban him from driving competitively ever again. While Pops, upon cooling down, soon thought better of his hasty demand, it was too late: Rex had left, vowing not to return until he'd become a champion on his own.

While Pops and Mom Racer were devastated, no one was hurt more than Speed, who idolized his older brother. He decided to become a race driver as well, to follow in Rex's footsteps, and soon became one of the best on the pro circuit. It was Speed who was given the Mach 5 when it was finished, and he continues to drive it in competitions throughout the world, proving both his skills and the marvelous abilities of the Mach 5—which could travel over virtually any terrain, had secret built-in weapons, and was built for awesome acceleration, the car of choice for any "demon on wheels." Joining Speed in his adventures: the entire Racer family, plus his pretty girlfriend Trixie, who never forgets to tell Speed to "be careful!" before he sets out on another dangerous mission. And who's that masked racer, coming up on the inside track? Racer X—Speed's mysterious shadow, his greatest rival, and unknown to everyone, his lost brother Rex. —J.Y.

The Speed Racer Theme Song

Here he comes, here comes Speed Racer
He's a demon on wheels
He's a demon and he's gonna be chasing after someone

He's gaining on you so you better look alive
He's busy revving up the powerful Mach 5
And when the odds are against him and there's
dangerous work to do
You bet your life Speed Racer will see it through

Go Speed Racer
Go Speed Racer
Go Speed Racer go

He's up and flying as he guns the car around the track
He's jamming down the pedal like he's never coming back
Adventure's waiting just ahead

Go Speed Racer
Go Speed Racer
Go Speed Racer go!

Star Blazers

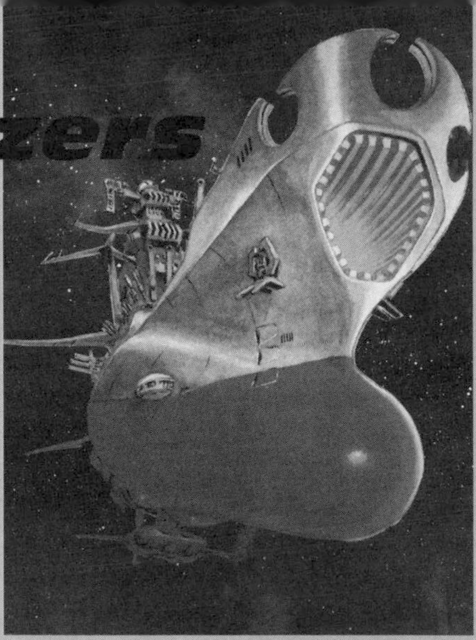

In 1981, millions of kids across America pedaled their bikes faster, in order to get home in time for the next episode of the galaxy-faring adventures of the spaceship *Argo*. Led by the dashing Derek Wildstar, the *Argo*'s crew fought adrenaline-charged star battles; braved unknown horrors in the depths of interstellar space; and raced against time to the mysterious planet of Iscandar, where the secret to humanity's salvation lay. But it wasn't simply the science-fiction excitement that drew fans to *Star Blazers*: It was also the show's melodramatic web of passion, unrequited love, rivalry, and petty jealousy, which gave the series a complexity and sophistication unparalleled by any other cartoon show on the air. Few fans realized that it was an English-language dub of a Japanese TV series entitled *Uchu Senkan Yamato* (*Space Cruiser Yamato*), directed by popular comic artist Leiji Matsumoto; few cared. All they knew was that there was no better reason to get home from school, five days a week, as fast as possible.

The Story

The year is 2199. From a world far beyond the reaches of our solar system, the Gamilon warrior race has attacked humanity without provocation, besieging the Earth with a deadly barrage of world-destroying bombs. To survive, mankind is forced to descend into the depths, huddling in underground cities against the threat of a planet ravaged by radiation. All of Earth's combined space defenses are soon overcome by the superior Gamilon forces, who demand immediate and total surrender; when the Earth Defense Command refuses to give up, the prospect of the extinction of all life on Earth becomes extremely likely. The bombs continue to fall, and the radiation sinks deeper into the Earth's crust, toward humanity's surviving remnants.

Then, the Defense Command is alerted to the crashdown of a courier vessel on the surface of Mars, bearing a message from Starsha, ruler of the planet Iscandar. She offers hope for Earth and its inhabitants in the form of a mechanism which can eliminate the Gamilon barrage's radioactive threat.

But Queen Starsha is 148,000 light years removed from Earth—and in the 21st century, mankind has yet to travel beyond the solar system. Scientists alike conceive of a bold, perhaps foolhardy plan to send the *Argo*, an experimental light-speed vessel, to Iscandar. Just one year remains until the Gamilon radiation reaches the underground cities. Can the Star Force of the *Argo* make it to Iscandar and back before Earth's time is up? —J.Y.

The Original Star Blazers Theme Song

We're off to outer space
We're leaving Mother Earth
To save the human race
Our Star Blazers

Searching for a distant star
Heading off to Iscandar
Leaving all we love behind
Who knows what danger we'll find?

We must be strong and brave
Our home we've got to save
If we don't in just one year
Mother Earth will disappear

Fighting with the Gamilons
We won't stop until we've won
Then we'll return and when we arrive
The Earth will survive
With our Star Blazers

KEY CAST

DEREK WILDSTAR (Susumu Kodai, in Japan)—The young deputy captain of the Argo, the brash Wildstar takes command of the ship when its captain falls ill, and gradually learns to temper his emotions and lead his crew. Over the course of the series, his attraction to Radar Operator Nova becomes mutual, and blossoms slowly into a relationship—demonstrating an emotional evolution never before seen in American cartoons.

NOVA (Yuki Mori)—As one of just a handful of women on the original Star Force, Nova acts almost as the crew's jill-of-all-trades—operating the Argo's radar, aiding the ship's doctor, and heading the Star Force Survey team. She's as brave as she's resourceful; it's her display of love for Wildstar that ultimately convinces Gamilon leader Desslok to abandon his goal of destroying the Earth and its people.

MARK VENTURE (Daisuke Shima)—A boon companion to Wildstar since their days as cadets, the Argo's Chief Navigator is an important balancing force for his impetuous friend and leader.

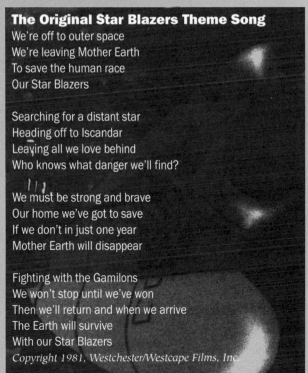

L-R: Derek Wildstar, Nova, Queen Starsha, Mark Venture

Astro Boy

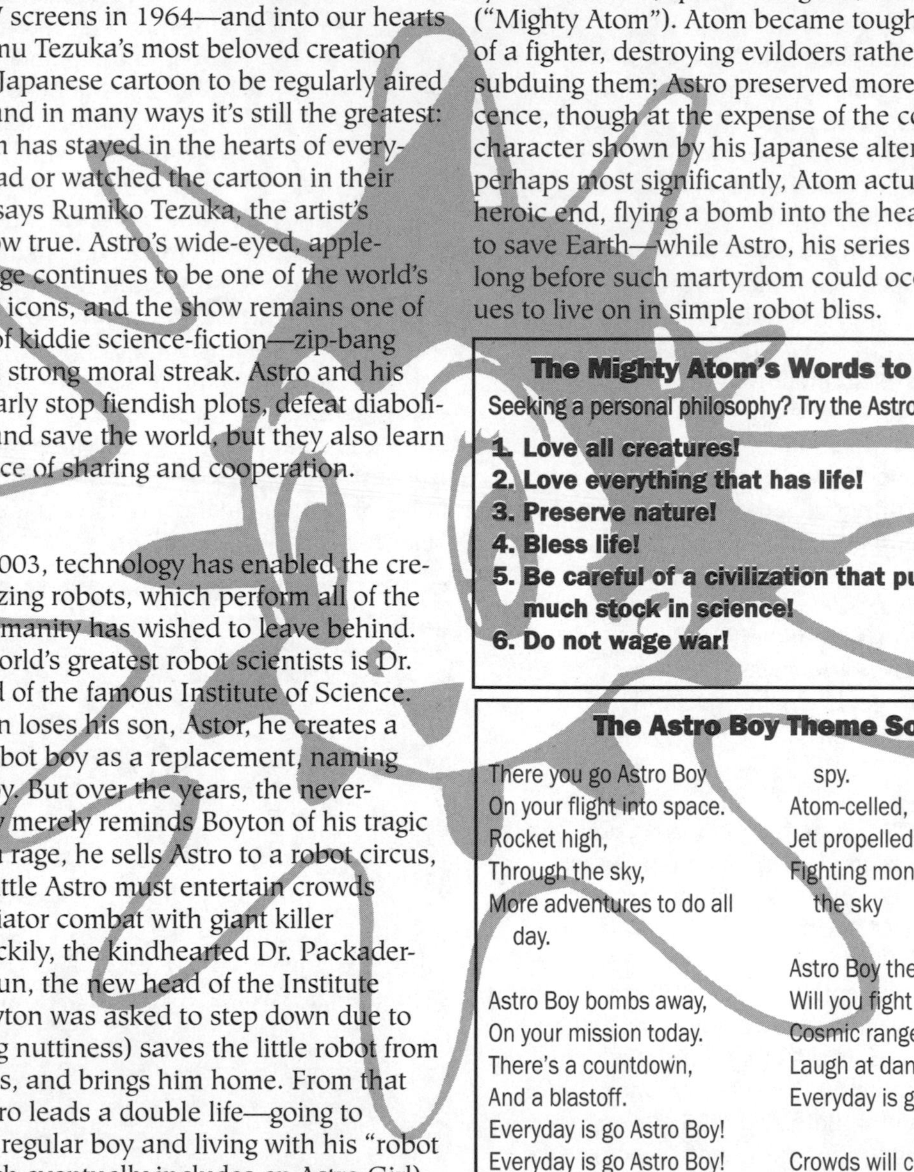

Innocent, honest, and insufferably cute, the little robot boy with the tricorner hairdo burst onto American TV screens in 1964—and into our hearts forever. Osamu Tezuka's most beloved creation was the first Japanese cartoon to be regularly aired in the U.S., and in many ways it's still the greatest: "I think Atom has stayed in the hearts of everybody who read or watched the cartoon in their childhood," says Rumiko Tezuka, the artist's daughter. How true. Astro's wide-eyed, apple-cheeked visage continues to be one of the world's most revered icons, and the show remains one of the classics of kiddie science-fiction—zip-bang action with a strong moral streak. Astro and his friends regularly stop fiendish plots, defeat diabolical villains, and save the world, but they also learn the importance of sharing and cooperation.

THE STORY

In the year 2003, technology has enabled the creation of amazing robots, which perform all of the tasks that humanity has wished to leave behind. One of the world's greatest robot scientists is Dr. Boyton, head of the famous Institute of Science. When Boyton loses his son, Astor, he creates a new super-robot boy as a replacement, naming him Astro Boy. But over the years, the never-changing boy merely reminds Boyton of his tragic loss, and in a rage, he sells Astro to a robot circus, where poor little Astro must entertain crowds through gladiator combat with giant killer androids. Luckily, the kindhearted Dr. Packadermus J. Elephun, the new head of the Institute (after Dr. Boyton was asked to step down due to his increasing nuttiness) saves the little robot from his dire straits, and brings him home. From that point on, Astro leads a double life—going to school like a regular boy and living with his "robot family" (which eventually includes an Astro Girl), and meanwhile, saving mankind from the machinations of evil robots, like Atlas and Satan.

Interestingly, because of the restrictive nature of American children's television guidelines, over time, Astro Boy diverged in both character and storyline from the Japanese original, *Tetsuwan Atom* ("Mighty Atom"). Atom became tougher and more of a fighter, destroying evildoers rather than just subduing them; Astro preserved more of his innocence, though at the expense of the complexity of character shown by his Japanese alter ego. And, perhaps most significantly, Atom actually met his heroic end, flying a bomb into the heart of the sun to save Earth—while Astro, his series cancelled long before such martyrdom could occur—continues to live on in simple robot bliss.

The Mighty Atom's Words to Live By

Seeking a personal philosophy? Try the Astro Credo:

1. **Love all creatures!**
2. **Love everything that has life!**
3. **Preserve nature!**
4. **Bless life!**
5. **Be careful of a civilization that puts too much stock in science!**
6. **Do not wage war!**

The Astro Boy Theme Song

There you go Astro Boy
On your flight into space.
Rocket high,
Through the sky,
More adventures to do all day.

Astro Boy bombs away,
On your mission today.
There's a countdown,
And a blastoff.
Everyday is go Astro Boy!
Everyday is go Astro Boy!

As-tro Boy as you fly,
Strange new worlds you will spy.
Atom-celled,
Jet propelled,
Fighting monsters high in the sky

Astro Boy there you go,
Will you fight friend or foe,
Cosmic ranger,
Laugh at danger,
Everyday is go Astro Boy!

Crowds will cheer you,
You're a hero,
As you go, go, GO ASTRO BOY!

KEY CAST

ASTRO BOY (Tetsuwan Atom in Japan)—Innocent, trusting, yet tremendously brave, Astro is a Pinocchio of tomorrow—always ready to help his friends, or save the world. He's enormously strong, has the ability to fly, and can sense if people are good or evil. Perhaps to show the positive side of nuclear energy (Godzilla and his ilk being the dark side), Astro is powered by atomic fission. He's the creation of mad, but brilliant scientist Dr. Boyton.

DR. BOYTON (Professor Temma)—Dr. Boyton is the director of the Institute of Science, whose resources he uses to craft Astro after his boy Astor is killed in a tragic car accident. However, after building him, he comes to realize that no mechanical boy can take the place of his own son; insane with grief, he sells his creation to the nefarious owner of the Robot Circus.

DR. PACKADERMUS J. ELEFUN (Dr. Ochanomizu)—The new head of the Institute of Science, Dr. Elefun saves Astro from the circus and becomes his foster father, teaching the little robot how to act like a human. As a result, Astro Boy commits himself to forever use his powers to help and support mankind, although he always wonders what it would be like to be real live boy himself.

THE CREATOR

Before making the leap to the small screen, Astro Boy started out, like many cartoon legends, in the funny pages; unlike others, he didn't begin as a star, but rather as a minor character in a comic entitled *Atom Taishi* ("Ambassador Atom"), penned in 1951 by Osamu Tezuka **[👁46]**. However, the android kid quickly outstripped the rest of *Taishi*'s cast in popularity, and in 1952, was given his own comic: *Tetsuwan Atom*. The series lasted for 17 years. In 1963, Atom was turned into a black and white cartoon—Japan's first ever animated television show. It was a phenomenal success, leading NBC to purchase the rights to produce an U.S. version. The development of the English-language version was turned over to veteran animation producer Fred Ladd, and in September 1963, Astro Boy was born—as a robot boy living in 21st Century New York.

Of course, even as Astro was taking shape in America, Atom continued to air in Japan. At first, the release of *Astro Boy* in the U.S. proved to be a positive thing for *Tetsuwan Atom*, since NBC gave Tezuka the money and freedom to make the animation quality of the series equivalent to American standards; however, the honeymoon would soon come to an end. Despite its popularity in the States, NBC chose to cease buying new episodes from Tezuka's production company after two seasons, or 104 shows. In part this was because parents' groups in the U.S. were beginning to complain about the rough-and-tumble nature of children's cartoons. As *Tetsuwan Atom* developed, his enemies had grown in their fiendishness, and Atom's smash-'em-up antics had grown more outrageous in response, delighting his Japanese fans. Meanwhile, it became increasingly difficult to assemble American episodes that complied with censorship guidelines. NBC told Ladd to tell Tezuka to cut out the violence, and Ladd shuttled between the U.S. and Japan attempting to mediate between the two partners, to no avail; by 1964, NBC ended its *Astro Boy* run. But that wouldn't spell the end of NBC's relationship with Tezuka's production company. Far from it: NBC's next project with Tezuka was a full-color cartoon series set amidst the beauty of the African savannah, with cuddly animals and none of the robot battles that had increasingly begun to define *Astro Boy*. This was *Jungeru Taitei* ("Jungle Emperor"), which would become *Kimba, the White Lion* in America.

Despite the popularity of *Jungeru Taitei* and Tezuka's later works, the artist continued to prize Tetsuwan Atomu as his most cherished creation. He attempted to revive the series in a color format in 1980, but this new cloyingly cute version failed to win an audience either in Japan or in the U.S.

While neither version of *Astro Boy* is currently shown on U.S. television, videotapes of the original 104-episode series are available from:

The Right Stuf Incorporated
P.O. Box 71309, Des Moines, IA 50325
(800) 338-6827

—J.Y.

ASTRO'S POWERS

His complex computer brain gives him the ability to speak in over 60 different languages, making him truly a hero for the world; he can also sense whether someone has good or evil intentions.

His wide and innocent eyes can work as searchlights, and he has machine guns built into his hips—a last ditch Astro-attack when the going gets too rough for his atomic fists.

With a nuclear fission generator beating in his cute little chest, Astro Boy is an efficient and incredibly powerful little package (though one wonders about issues like radioactivity levels and waste disposal).

His arms can exert a 100,000 horsepower push, or deliver that force as a punch strong enough to smash steel. Moreover, if he pushes his two ear-buttons, his strength can briefly increase over a thousandfold.

He has atomic jet engines in his feet that can send him flying at speeds up to Mach 5. They also work as rockets in outer space.

CLASSICS OF THE BLADE

TALES OF THE TAIRA CLAN (1955, dir. Kenji Mizoguchi)—The age-old story of honorable warriors versus their corrupt feudal lords. In the end, justice triumphs over loyalty: the samurai turn against their masters.

THE SEVEN SAMURAI (1957, dir. Akira Kurowasa)—Helpless villagers under attack by gangs of bandits hire—who else?—seven samurai to protect their village.

THE TWO MUSASHIS (Futari no Musashi, 1960, dir. Kunio Watanabe)—Two master swordsmen who both claim to be named Musashi have it out with each other for honor, revenge, and bragging rights as the best blade in the East.

THE MISSING LEAF (Kagero-zamurai, 1961, dir. Kazuo Ikehiro)—In exchange for payment of his gambling debts, a no-good playboy samurai is recruited to find a thief who has stolen proof of a valuable inheritance.

YOJIMBO (1961, Akira Kurowasa)—The story of a loner samurai for hire who annihilates both sides of two warring clans—not without humor.

SANJIRO (1962, Akira Kurowasa)—A sequel to Yojimbo, featuring the same loner samurai. This time, he helps young, clumsy samurai fight the corrupt superiors of their clan.

CHUSHINGURA (1962, Hiroshi Inagaki)—The famous story of 47 ronin (masterless samurai) who take revenge for their lord, who was forced to commit hara-kiri for another man's crime.

Chambara!: Samurai Cinema

Until the mid-'60s, nearly half of the films produced by Japan's then-prolific cinema industry were of the genre known as *jidaigeki*—stories set in Japan's feudal era, between the 12th and the middle of the 19th century, before Japan's forced Westernization. Though some of these films were satires and standard dramas, the vast majority were violent action melodramas, featuring the adventures of brave, sword-slashing samurai. Known as *chambara*, short for "*chanchan barabara*" (the sound-effect for the clashing of blades), these films were more than just bloodthirsty entertainment; they were cinematic set-pieces that defined Japan's standards for honor and masculinity, while reflecting in the glint of a swift-drawn blade the soul of a nation come of age.

Pre–World War II samurai films tended toward moodiness and dialogue, with contemplative protagonists who reasoned rather than slashed their way out of conflicts. In the 1950s, chambara became darker and more swashbuckling. Postwar samurai protagonists were loners, physically and mentally scarred, fighting the injustices of the feudal system. These men drew their swords as they introduced themselves; a split-second later, the high-pitched sounds of blade hitting blade would cut through the air, and one man would be left standing amidst a field of dead bodies.

Given the parallels between the genres, it should come as no surprise that some of the classics of chanbara have been adapted into American horse-opera form. The influences of samurai cinema can be seen in such films as Sam Peckinpah's *The Wild Bunch,* for which he borrowed the final massacre scene from Kurosawa's classic *Seven Samurai,* as well as in *The Magnificent Seven,* a direct copy of Kurosawa's work. And, of course, echoes of Kurosawa's *Yojimbo* ripple through Clint Eastwood's spaghetti-Western classics. Which goes to show that some things—like betrayal, vengeance, and justifiable homicide—mean the same thing in every language. —F.T. & J.Y.

LEGENDARY HEROES OF THE SWORD

Grim of visage and swift of blade, the following are some of the most popular samurai heroes to have cut a bloody swath across television and the silver screen, as well as in the pages of best-selling comics (*Lone Wolf and Cub*, featuring the adventures of Itto Ogami, was one of the first English-translated manga):

ITTO OGAMI, THE LONE WOLF—Once a rising young samurai of the Iemitsu Shogunate, Itto Ogami is framed by members of the rival Yagyu clan, his wife murdered by ninja, and his rank stripped from him in disgrace. Alone with his young son, he leaves the decision as to their joint fate up to the infant child: Placing a ball on one side of the boy and a sword on the other, he tells him that should he choose the ball, they will take the honorable route of ritual suicide; should he choose the sword, they will "travel the road to Hell" and gain vengeance at the expense of honor. The boy touches the blade, and Ogami becomes the Lone Wolf on a mission of revenge, pushing his cub along with him in a booby-trapped baby carriage...

SAOTOME MONDONOSUKE—Known as the "Bored Samurai," Mondonosuke is a swordsman who leaves his rich castle to right wrongs not out of a sense of justice, but to break the tedium of the noble life.

TANGE SAZAN—At the hands of a jealous rival swordsman, Sazan has his right arm cut off and right eye put out; by the exacting code of bushido, the samurai way, this should have ended his career with the blade, since to fight with the "improper" hand is unthinkable. Instead of retiring (or committing suicide), Sazan rejects bushido and becomes a ronin, fighting against oppression with a backwards blade and an eye for justice.

ZATOICHI, THE BLIND SWORDSMAN—Perhaps the greatest of all Japanese screen swordsmen, Zato Ichi is not a samurai but a sightless wandering masseur who hides his blade in a cane; seeking not to right wrongs but simply to be left alone, he nevertheless runs into those who seek his destruction at every turn, and must kill in self-defense. The beloved Zato Ichi was featured in 26 films and a hit television series, played by Shintaro Katsu, who subsequently became a megastar (his brother Tomisaburo Wakayama played Itto Ogami in the *Lone Wolf and Cub* films, which were made by Katsu's production company). Unfortunately, in 1990, Katsu fell from grace, arrested for attempting to bring cocaine and marijuana into Hawaii. He died some years later, but the blind hero he brought to life lives on in the hearts of millions of fans.

Sonny Chiba

If you're a fan of gut-wrenching, hell-bent, hands-on destruction, there's only one Asian screen hero who'll deliver it—raw, bloody, and steaming on a silver platter—and it's *not* Bruce Lee. True fans of knuckle-on-bone violence know that Sonny Chiba, the actor behind the rampaging *Streetfighter* movies, is the true master of disaster. (A typical Chiba maneuver: emasculating a rapist with his bare hands.) One avid admirer is Asian cine-groupie Quentin Tarantino. "I look forward to the day when I can put Sonny Chiba in a film of mine, but it's very important to me, so it has to be right," says Tarantino.

Chiba was born Sadao Maeda on January 23, 1939, in Fukuoka, Japan. The eldest of an army test pilot's five children, he and his family were moved to a military base in Chiba Prefecture during World War II; it was from this childhood home that Maeda later took his stage name. His days of action began not with karate, but gymnastics. As a teen, he enrolled in the Physical Education Department of Nihon University, with the goal of reaching the 1964 Olympics in Tokyo. It was at this time that Chiba studied under World Karate Grandmaster Mas Oyama, as a complement to his gymnastics education. To help pay for his training, Chiba took a part-time job as a construction worker; unfortunately, at this job Chiba suffered a hip injury that eliminated him from Olympic contention. Desolated, Chiba took the advice of friends and entered a competition sponsored by Japan's most prominent production company, Toei: the 1960 "New Face Contest." To his surprise, he won, and was given a contract by Toei TV.

After lead roles on several popular TV series, including the superhero actioner *Spectrum Mask, JNR Inspector #36,* and the secret-agent action series *Key Hunter*—Toei's most successful TV show ever—Chiba was ready for a new challenge. The the release and international success of *Enter the Dragon* provided him with the inspiration he was looking for. He would make his own martial arts film—with a twist: the violence of hand-to-hand battle would be shown in its grim entirety, no holds barred. The 1975 release of *The Streetfighter* introduced to the world the unstoppable killing machine Terry Tsurugi, while stirring up a whirlwind of controversy. Its over-the-top brutality went far beyond anything yet shown on American screens. For instance, in the climactic final fight, the camera shows Tsurugi smashing his opponent's skull open with his bare hands—first in slow-motion, then as an X-ray effect replay, showing the *internal* destruction. Is it any wonder that *Streetfighter* became the first movie in the U.S. given an X rating for violence?

As a result, *Streetfighter*'s sequels—*The Return of the Streetfighter* (1976) and *The Streetfighter's Last Revenge* (1977)—were never shown uncut in U.S. theaters. New Line Cinema has since re-released the films on videocassette, unedited and unrated. (Also part of the box set: 1978's *Sister Streetfighter,* featuring Chiba's dynamic protege, Sue Shiomi.)

After the Streetfighter films, Chiba continued to make movies—though none had the international impact of the Tsurugi epics. Even today, Chiba is still revered as the grand old man of Japanese action. And, should Tarantino have his way...he'll be back. —J.Y.

Overlooked Facts:

CALL HIM MR. CHIBA—Some actors get by on their looks and stuntmen: Chiba is the real deal. He studied under the renowned karate master Baitatsu "Mas" Oyama for five years, and won a series of intimidating martial arts degrees: a 2nd dan black belt in judo, a 4th dan black belt in ninjutsu, a 1st dan black belt in kendo, and a 1st dan black belt in shoriji kempo. Which makes Chiba one guy not to mess with.

THE CHIBA LEGEND, PART ONE—The posters created by New Line Cinema upon the original release of The Streetfighter proclaimed the arrival of a new martial arts superhero: "6-foot-6 of half-breed fury." The tagline was written by Robert Shaye, the founder and head of New Line; it was only after a decade that Shaye actually met Chiba, to find out that he was neither a "half-breed," nor was he anywhere near six feet tall. His true height: five feet six inches.

THE CHIBA LEGEND, PART TWO—New Line's elaborations on the truth didn't rest with the poster: his official press bio said that he was the " son of an unknown father and a dancer" who "grew up to be leader of a street gang called the Kamikaze Lords, learned kung fu on the streets, and after a motorcycle accident became a serious student of karate." After Streetfighter became a monster success, the company added that Chiba "became a Shinto monk living in the foothills of Mount Fuji."

Gamera

Created by Daiei Studios as a deft attempt to counterprogram rival Toho's *Godzilla* films **[👁71]**, this curiously popular series also featured a giant, radioactive reptile, but was otherwise vastly inferior. Its special effects were rudimentary at best, featuring patently fake monster models, with wires and control rods visible in every frame; moreover, the enormous nuclear turtle had a predilection for befriending small children, whose dorky antics and high-pitched dubbed voices made the *Gamera* films a study in how to irritate. All have been dubbed into English, and should be available at your local video store. —J.Y.

GAMERA (Daikaiju Gamera) (1965)—Also known as Gamera the Invincible, this was the last Japanese monster movie shot in black and white. Unlike its sequels, it was theatrically released in the U.S., but was not well received. The plot: Fire-breathing turtle Gamera is awakened by a nuclear explosion, goes on a rampage, and is subdued with the help of a small child.

GAMERA VS. BARUGON (Gamera Tai Barugon) (1966)—Also known as War of the Monsters, this has the distinction of being the only Gamera film that doesn't star a small, annoying child. Treasure hunters discover a gem-like object on a deserted island, and bring it back to Japan. Sadly for the monster-ravaged Asian nation, the object is actually the pupal form of a monstrous creature. Enter everyone's favorite turtle.

GAMERA VS. GAOS (Gamera Tai Gyaos) (1967)—Also known as Return of the Giant Monsters, this was the most successful of the Gamera series in its original Japanese release. Gaos is a giant rubber bat, released from the bowels of the earth by a volcanic eruption. Gamera arrives to deal with the winged rodent, but is overwhelmed. Scientists plot to lure Gaos to its doom with a blood substitute, placed atop a rotating hotel restaurant, but the plan goes awry, and Gaos escapes to bedevil Gamera—and Japan—another day.

GAMERA VS. THE OUTER-SPACE VIRUS (1968)—Also known as Destroy All Planets, this blatant attempt to feed off the popularity of the Godzilla film Destroy All Monsters featured invaders from space, not one but two annoying children, and a giant squid creature. Aliens land in Japan, only to be met with the nation's pet giant turtle; unfortunately, the aliens quickly manage to turn the tables by placing a mind-control device on Gamera's neck. Gamera goes berzerk—until a pair of kids destroy the alien device.

GAMERA VS. GUIRON (Gamera Tai Guiron) (1969)—Also known as Attack of the Monsters, this film features the return of Gaos the bat-critter, two (different) annoying children, and more space beings. This time, the action takes place not on our Earth, but on an Earth-like planet on the other side of the solar system, where two Japanese boys, stowing away on an alien spaceship, have landed. There they meet two alien women who offer them a life of royal leisure (but secretly want to consume them, like the irritating little piglets that they are). Distressingly for the movie-watching audience, the boys are saved by their pal Gamera, before becoming alien hors d'oeuvres.

GAMERA VS. JIGER (Gamera Tai Jiger) (1970)—Also known as Gamera vs. Monster X, this was the only film in the series to feature a female monster—

Jiger, a dinosaur-like beast that is released from subterranean bondage by the moronic actions of Japanese scientists. The triceratops-like Jiger escapes from its underground pen and promptly rumbles with Gamera, who loses. Jiger then wreaks havoc, as expected, in Japan, only to have Gamera show up again for a grudge rematch. Gamera eventually wins, but not before a complication—he's "impregnated" with Jiger's parasitic spawn.

GAMERA VS. ZIGRA (Gamera Tai Zigra) (1971)—Just months after the release of this final film in the original Gamera series, Daiei went bankrupt. The plot: Aliens again harass the Earth. Gamera stomps them, but releases Zigra, a sharklike monster. There's some underwater fisticuffs, then a fight on land, during which Gamera actually plays his theme song on Zigra's body with a boulder!

GAMERA—GUARDIAN OF THE UNIVERSE (Gamera-Daikaiju Uchu Kessen) (1995)—After seven years of bankruptcy, Daiei re-emerged as a cinema player and began making small, higher-quality films—until 1995, when they decided to return to their franchise series with a new effort. More of a serious monster flick than its predecessors, this Gamera has better effects and a somewhat ballsier giant turtle, battling yet another version of Gaos, the monster bat.

GAMERA 2—GAMERA VS. LEGION (Gamera-Region Shurai) (1996)—After the nostalgia-driven success of 1995's Gamera flick, Daiei decided to pop for a sequel. A meteor hits the Earth, bearing a swarm of giant insects and plants. The silicon-based insects eat glass and seek to destroy sources of electrical energy, which puts high-tech Japan on the crunch 'n' munch menu; luckily, Gamera saves the day, though not before getting severely injured by exploding flowers and revived by the prayers of a group of children.

Giant Robots

Majestic machines the size of battleships, powered by nuclear energy, armed with heat-seeking missiles and enormous flaming swords! Every adolescent boy should have a giant robot pal. In the world of Japanese pop culture, it seems as if they do. From the live-action adventures of *Johnny Sokko and his Flying Robot* to its contemporary animated remakc *Giant Robo,* enormous mechanical fighting machinesare an indelible part of Japanese comics and cinema. Here's a brief history. —J.Y. & E.N.

Giant Robots Launch (1958-1972)

As the Japanese economy rebounded from the Second World War, its robots grew proportionately in size and prowess: Mitsuteru Yokoyama's mechanical crimefighter **Tetsujin 28** ("Iron Man 28") was large enough to be called **Gigantor** when he hit U.S. airwaves in 1965. Besides showing that size matters, *Gigantor* also introduced another important concept in the giant robot genre: the human pilot. The fear that unchecked technology might transcend humanity's ability to command it is common in Japanese pop culture, and the fact that many of these titanic mechanicals are powered by nuclear energy only enhances their potential for terror; they're literally walking, flying bombs, waiting to explode. In giant robot cartoons from *Gigantor* onward, this danger is counteracted by making the robot subject to the orders of a human controller—usually a young boy or girl. There's a built-in moral to these stories: if such a techno-titan can be controlled by a mere child, why should adults fear the march of progress?

Robot Invasion (1972-1975)

The next leap for giant robot evolution came at the hands of the acknowledged king of giant robots, manga artist Go Nagai. In introducing **Mazinger Z** in 1972, he simultaneously breathed new life into the giant robot genre and invented a new and lucrative market segment for the toy industry. Mazinger Z was a true original: He was the first giant robot actually "piloted" by his controller— dashing hero Koji Kabuto activated and directed Mazinger from a command ship that docked in his enormous metal skull, in effect serving as Mazinger's brain. Mazinger's design, half retro-samurai, half techno-dynamo, was another novelty. Both innovations contributed to his enormous popularity, and Nagai immediately churned out a number of sequels, including *Great Mazinger* (1974) and *UFO Robo Grandizer* (1975). The giant robot army had arrived.

Transformers! (1975-1981)

As hordes of giant robots burst onto the scene, it became harder and harder to distinguish one sword-wielding, missile-firing monster machine from another. It took **Getta Robo** (1974) and **Brave Raideen** (1975) to set the next standard for giant robot technology: Mix-and-match parts. Getta Robo, another Go Nagai invention, was the first robot who could be reassembled into different android forms; Brave Raideen did Getta Robo one better, in that it could transform not just into other humanoid shapes, but into something entirely differnet—a jet fighter called the Godbird. Soon the ability to transform, separate, or conglomerate was a must-have giant robot feature. Leading the West into the Transformer Era was a robot called **Go-Lion**, known in the United States as **Voltron, Defender of the Universe.**

The Modern Era (1982-present)

Since the arrival of transforming robots, the giant robot genre has continued to evolve. Robots have gotten considerably bigger—the **Gunbuster** robot of *Gunbuster! Aim for the Top* is a mind-boggling 795 feet tall—and more exotic—the **EVA** of *Neon Genesis Evangelion* has in its arsenal of weaponry something known as an "Absolute Terror Field," an all-powerful defense necessary because the foes it must fight are the bastard children of God! Regardless of size, shape, and armament, however, one thing hasn't changed: giant robots are still a boy's (or girl's) best friend.

TETSUJIN 28/GIGANTOR (40 FEET TALL)

Invented by Dr. Kaneda ("Dr. Franken" in the U.S.) to fight against the Allies in World War II, after the war Tetsujin 28 was converted to the more peaceful (if no less violent) pursuit of criminals. He's controlled by Dr. Kaneda's young son Shotaro ("Jimmy Sparks").

VOLTRON (80 FEET)

The legendary Voltron is a composite robot able to separate into five mechanical lions, each with its own powers. Explorers from Earth's Galactic Alliance discover the robot on Arus, a distant planet devastated by the evil King Zarkon. Coming upon the last remaining survivor of the Arusian royal family, the lovely Princess Allura, the explorers volunteer to pilot Voltron themselves, to defeat Zarkon before he's able to turn his attention towards Earth. And so, Voltron's Blazing Sword rises again to defend the innocent.

MAZINGER Z (50 FEET)

A brilliant scientist named Professor Kabuto ("Dr. Wells" in the U.S.) discovers a new substance known as Super Alloy Z. His arch-rival Dr. Hell ("Dr. Demon") wants the alloy in order to create an army of super robots, but Kabuto refuses; the evil Hell kills him and his family, except for his grandsons Koji ("Tommy") and Shiro ("Toad"). With his dying breath, Kabuto tells the two boys to stop Dr. Hell at all costs, using the robot avenger he created: Mazinger Z.

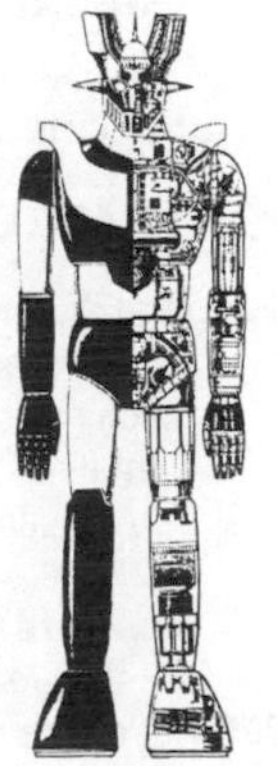

Godzilla

When Toho Studio's Gojira debuted on the big screen in 1954, he was like no other monster in cinema. The cranky former dinosaur stomped cars, smashed skyscrapers, spat radioactive flames, and destroyed buildings, all the while sending viewers the message: It's not nice to fool with Mother Nature. Two years later, the movie—with absurd English-dubbed dialogue and spliced-in footage of Raymond Burr—and the monster were unleashed upon the United States as Godzilla, King of the Monsters.

Like the atomic bomb, whose terrors the Toho Titan has been said to symbolize, *Godzilla* was created by a team of experts. Producer Tomoyuki Tanaka was a veteran of films by Horoshi Inagaki and Akira Kurosawa. Director Ishiro Honda collaborated with Kurosawa before and after Godzilla. After making his name as a special effects wizard on the *Godzilla* films, Eiji Tsuburaya left Toho to go solo, applying his monster-suit and miniature-set design techniques to TV, in the phenomenally successful *Ultraman* shows [👁**114**]. Together with screenwriter Takeo Murata, these artists wove a fantastic and layered story that incorporated such themes as nuclear fear (Godzilla was awakened and mutated into his killer form by nuclear bomb testing); the power of nature (Godzilla is a personified elemental force); and political discontent (Godzilla crushes the Japanese Diet onscreen). The combination of latent symbolism and overt violence was cathartic: Though the film was the most expensive Japanese movie ever made at the time—it cost approximately $900,000 to produce (about $65 million in today's dollars)—it was an instant hit in Japan; meanwhile, *Godzilla*'s subtext of post-atomic paranoia struck a nerve is Cold War America, too.

The success of the original led Toho to produce a parade of new post-atomic predators, many of whom, like Mothra and Rodan, became stars in their own right; and, as additional Godzilla adventures were filmed, the monster lizard's popularity eventually led to his conversion into a hero—defending Japan from an endless chain of rubber horrors. It seemed as if Japanese audiences would never tire of their radioactive reptilian hero—but, by the dawn of the third decade of the King of Monsters' reign, the crowds were beginning to thin. Toho brought back the original, savage Godzilla for their *Godzilla 1984*, giving the lizard a new lease on life. However, after stomping on for another decade, Toho pulled the plug on their prehistoric star in 1995's *Godzilla vs. Destroyer*—killing him off, apparently for good.

Is it the end for the Lizard King? Not likely. Death hasn't stopped him before, and his millions of Japanese and American fans are already clamoring for more. Three million Godzilla toys and collectibles were sold in 1995 alone, and blockbuster filmmakers Roland Emmerich and Dean Devlin (*Stargate* and *Independence Day*) have committed to make a big-screen American remake for the Sony-owned Hollywood studio TriStar Pictures. All of which attests to the fact that Godzilla is the King of Monsters—now and forever. —J.Y.

PORTRAIT OF THE LIZARD AS A YOUNG REPTILE: A GODZILLA TIMELINE

1954 Toho Studios releases the first *kaiju eiga*, or "mysterious beast movie"—**Gojira**, a bleak allegory in which nuclear testing mutates and awakens a giant dinosaur, who begins a terrifying rampage through Japan. It's a smash hit in Japan and in the U.S., where it's released as **Godzilla, King of the Monsters** (1956). The first, and in many minds, still the greatest Godzilla film.

1955 Hot on the heels of the original, Toho rushes out **Gojira no Gyakushu** ("Godzilla's Counterattack"). Apparently, the death of the first Godzilla didn't eliminate the species. Indeed, this sequel features not one but two boffo giant lizards: Godzilla II, who looks essentially like a slightly goofier version of the original, and Angurus, a dinosaur with a single horn on his muzzle. Once again, blame them pesky atom bombs, which wake the beasts from their Pacific slumber. They battle, and Godzilla kicks Angurus's horny butt, then levels Osaka. He's finally stopped by the heroic efforts of a single airman, who sends an avalanche of snow from Mount Fuji cascading down on him, encasing him in ice. The movie is released in the U.S. as **Gigantis, the Fire Monster** (1959), since Warner Brothers, the American distributor, is too cheap to pay for the rights to the Godzilla name; audiences are confused, but the film still proves popular.

1956 Toho, desperate for another *Godzilla*-sized success, releases **Rodan**, which features a giant pterodactyl, hatched by an atomic blast and incubated by warm radioactive water. While *Rodan* doesn't float the box office boat the way *Godzilla* did, he does give Toho their first new monster of what would prove to be many.

1958 Toho makes another attempt at duplicating Godzilla, this time with **Varan the Unbelievable**, who looks like Godzilla on all fours. Varan is hated by all, and the movie sinks with a faint whimper.

1962 One more try for the home team: Toho runs a giant insect named **Mothra** up the flagpole, and gets a hearty salute from the fans. Mothra is the first Toho monster with good intentions; she only goes berserk when her larva is stolen by greedy humans. The film is memorable for featuring a pair of miniature girls named the Ailenas, who chant Mothra's name in unison and generally act cute.

1962 Even with the success of *Mothra*, Toho realizes that its meal ticket is the original atomic lizard, and decides to make another sequel—this one created deliberately with an American release in mind: **King Kong vs. Godzilla**. Despite a plot riddled with loopholes, a script notable for its inanity, and incredibly shabby special effects (rather than using stop-motion miniatures, King Kong is performed Toho-style by a man in a horrible ape suit). As bad as it is, the film is released in the U.S. in 1963. The Japanese version features a victory by the King of the Monsters; the U.S. release puts the super-sized simian on top. The first Godzilla film in color.

1964 Toho releases **Atragon,** named not for a monster but for a Japanese nuclear submarine, coveted by the evil underwater Mu Empire. The Mu people send yet another rubber creature out to try to steal it: Manda, the giant sea serpent. The film flops.

1964 The mix 'n' match period of Toho's monster canon begins, with the King of the Monsters facing off against big bug Mothra in **Mothra vs. Godzilla**, released in the U.S. as **Godzilla vs. the Thing** (1964). When Godzilla bursts from the depths once more to assault Japan, the only recourse for the hapless Japanese is to call in Mothra, the other rubber giant on the backlot. The army uses one of the moth-monster's eggs as a lure to draw the two titans together, and in the ensuing struggle, Godzilla incinerates Mothra with his atomic breath. Then the egg hatches...releasing two caterpillars, who together force the lizard back into the ocean. The Ailenas make their second appearance here.

1964 Godzilla's busy year continues, as he joins an all-star monster cast in **Sandaikaiju Chikyu Saidai no Kessen** ("Three Giant Strange Creatures' Greatest Decisive Battle on Earth")—otherwise known in the U.S. as **Ghidrah the Three Headed Monster** (1965). This show is notable for two reasons: First, it does *Godzilla vs. The Thing* one better by upping the creature count to four. Second, it begins the transformation of Godzilla from the menace we know and love into a benevolent buddy of humanity. When a meteor lands and hatches Ghidrah, a three-headed space dragon with laser breath, mankind seems doomed, until Godzilla makes one of his perennial jaunts from the ocean to butt heads with Rodan—the pterodactyl star of the earlier Toho flick. Scientists realize that they could be Earth's salvation, but they're too busy beating each other up to pay attention. Finally, the Ailenas convince Mothra to intercede; he chats with his reptilian peers and gets them to join forces against the unwelcome alien, sort of like a monster INS. They win; Ghidrah flies off into space. (How does he fly in airless space? Who knows?)

1965 Ghidrah is so popular that, a year later, he's drafted for service again, in **Kaiju Daisenso** ("Strange Creature Giant War"), known in the U.S. as **Invasion of the Astro Monster**, or **Godzilla vs. Monster Zero** (1969). Astronauts land on mysterious Planet X only to find that it is being menaced by King Ghidrah; Japan agrees to "lend" Rodan and Godzilla to the Xians for their defense. Instead, the X'ers reveal a plot to control all three monsters and conquer the Earth. They almost succeed, too.

1966 The first Godzilla film not to be helmed by originator Ishiro Honda (Jun Fukuda takes over the directorial reins), **Nankai no Daiketto** ("South Seas' Giant Duel") features the radioactive reptile saving the world from a giant crab named Ebirah. A mess, with one of the dopiest monsters of all time. This is also the first Godzilla film sold directly to U.S. TV, without a theatrical run. It's shown in America as **Godzilla vs. the Sea Monster** (1966).

1967 The series, which has already softened considerably, takes a cloying turn with **Gojira no Musuko** ("Godzilla's Son"). It's not specified whether the appalling little beast named Minya is actually Godzilla's spawn or just a freakish mutant adopted by the kindly Lizard King. However, Godzilla's attachment to the pop-eyed squawker suggests a blood tie, bringing up a second question: Is Godzilla male or female? And who's the mother—or father? One of the most stomach-turning displays of monster mush you'll ever see. Americans were subjected to it as **Son of Godzilla**.

1968 Toho brings back Inoshiro Honda, who promptly tries to juice things up with a sort of Ultimate Fighting Challenge for latex titans, **Kaiju Soshingeki** ("Strange Creature All Attack"). It features not just popular kids on the block Godzilla, Rodan, Mothra, and Ghidrah, but also the hateful mistakes of Toho's monster past—Minya, Manda, Spiega, Angurus, Varan, Gorgosaurus (from *King Kong Escapes*), and a giant lizard named Baragon, who'd debuted in the ill-considered *Frankenstein Conquers the World* (1965). The alien Kilaaks take control of all the world's monsters, setting them loose on major cities (Godzilla does New York!). When a moon-based transmitter is smashed, the monsters snap out of it and attack their erstwhile masters. This film might have been cool, except for Toho's stingy decision to force Honda to use stock footage for most of the city-smashing scenes, as well as an incredibly bad script. The film is released in the U.S. as **Destroy All Monsters**.

1969 The nadir of Godzilla, **Oru Kaiju Daishingeki** ("All Strange Creatures Giant Attack"), released in America as **Godzilla's Revenge** (1971), is a sort of childhood allegory in which a young boy learns how to defend himself against bullies by daydreaming about Minya and Godzilla. The extra kaiju here are Angurus and Gorgosaurus, plus a new, tailless reptile named Gabera.

1971 A new director, Yoshimitsu Banno, brings a twist on the Godzilla premise: Instead of warning about the dangers of atomic energy, the film **Gojira tai Hedora** ("Godzilla vs. Hedorah") offers a parable about...pollution. This is one K-Razy acid trip of a film, with go-go dancers, weird snap cuts, and a bizarre, English-language song entitled "Save the Earth." Hedorah is a slime beast who lives on pollution; Godzilla defeats him, but not the Underlying

***Kong gets atom breath right where it hurts, in* King Kong vs. Godzilla**

Problem of Uncontrolled Environmental Damage. The big lizard is, by this point, unrecognizable from the original city-smasher. This film is seen in the U.S. as **Godzilla vs. the Smog Monster** (1972).

1972 Another attempt to draw in a kiddie audience, **Chikyu Kogeki Meirei Gojira tai Gaigan** ("Earth Destruction Directive Godzilla vs. Gigan") features Godzilla and Angurus teaming up against Ghidrah and a new, birdlike creature from the "Hunter Nebula" named Gigan. The pair of interstellar foes have been drawn to the U.S. by aliens who have taken over...an amusement park! Americans saw it as **Godzilla vs. Gigan** (1978).

1973 Gigan's back, and he's under the control of undersea fiends known as Seatopians, who send him and their god—a giant mutant cockroach named Megalon—to attack surface dwellers, in **Gojira tai Megaro** ("**Godzilla vs. Megalon**"). With the help of the robot Jet Jaguar, Godzilla saves the day.

1974 Getting back some steam, the series offers up not one, but two Godzillas in this new Fukuda-directed entry, as the once-friendly lizard seemingly returns to his bad old city-stomping ways. He defeats his old foe Angurus, then is confronted by...another Godzilla! They tussle, and the first Godzilla is revealed to be an alien robot, named MechaGodzilla. Our reptilian hero defeats the droid with the help of the weird-looking King Seeser, a kind of giant lion dog. It's released in the U.S. as **Godzilla vs. the Cosmic Monster** (1975).

1975 Inoshiro Honda comes back, and so does MechaGodzilla, for what was intended to be the last Godzilla film: **Mechagodzilla no Gyakushu** ("Counterattack of MechaGodzilla"). Aliens (again!) from the Third Planet of the Black Hole rebuild the robot destroyer, and send him and a creature called Titanosaurus to attack Godzilla. Our hero handily defeats them and strolls off into the sunset. Originally released to TV as **Terror of MechaGodzilla** in 1978, it has a brief run the following year in theaters as *Terror of Godzilla*—a version for kiddie consumption with most of the violence edited out. Honda never directed another Godzilla film; this film proves a sad epilogue for the filmmaker's proud career.

1984 Emulating the Hollywood revival of *King Kong* in 1976, a *Godzilla* remake project kicks around Toho for years, finally hitting the screens as **Godzilla 1984** (**Godzilla 1985** in the U.S.). This film returns the series to its roots, with Godzilla as a destroyer rather than an ally of mankind; it is a huge success in Japan, and a moderate one in the U.S., where it is re-edited and released with footage of American actors (including Raymond Burr, featured in the U.S. version of the original *Godzilla*).

1989 Godzilla is on a rampage and only a giant, acid-squirting rose bush can stop him in **Gojira tai Biorante**, which is better than it sounds. As **Godzilla vs. Biollante**, it is distributed on video but has no theatrical release in the U.S.

1991 A very strange, but cool new entry in the series involves the plot of time travellers to destroy Japan (which, by the 23rd century, is the dominant world power) by removing the dinosaur that would become Godzilla from the atomic-test island where he'd receive his power-up dose of radiation. The time-hoppers plant three cute creatures known as the Dorats on the island instead, and the bomb tests fuse them together into the mutant menace King Ghidrah. Japan quickly surmises that only Godzilla can defeat the monster, and subjects the poor dinosaur to a modern nuclear blast, whereupon he stomps on Ghidrah and goes on a killing rage of his own. One of the time travellers, having a change of heart, saves Japan by constructing a cyborg from Ghidrah's remains. The film is notable for a new Godzilla suit (with bigger muscles and a nastier look) as well as a palpable anti-U.S. streak—Americans are portrayed in the film as weak, spiteful, and chicken. Americans see it (on video only) as **Godzilla vs. King Ghidrah**.

1992 More of a remake of *Mothra* than of *Godzilla vs. The Thing*, 1992's **Gojira tai Mosura** ("Godzilla vs. Mothra") features an epic battle between "good" and "evil" moth-beasts (Mothra and her caterpillar sibling Battra), with Godzilla more or less a sideshow attraction.

1993 **Gojira tai Mekagojira** ("Godzilla vs. MechaGodzilla") brings back some old favorites—the flying monster Rodan, and, of course, the robosaur known as MechaGodzilla, this time controlled by the "United Nations Godzilla Counter Measure Center," whose mission is to kill the Big G once and for all. It also makes the mistake of reviving Godzilla's son, here given a new origin and called Godzillasaurus, or sometimes "Baby."

1994 In **Gojira tai Supesu Gojira** ("Godzilla vs. SpaceGodzilla")'s feat of pseudoscientific legerdemain, Godzilla's radioactive cells are swept into a black hole, producing a Bizarro progeny, SpaceGodzilla, who looks like Godzilla except with scary mutant icebergs sticking out of his shoulders. The Ailenas and Mothra warn humanity of this new foe, and once again, it's Godzilla to the rescue. By this time, audiences are beginning to tire of the endless variations of this theme, and Toho decides it's time to play its biggest trump card yet...

1995 It had to happen sometime: **Gojira tai Desutoroia** ("Godzilla vs. Destroyer"), the last of the Toho Godzilla films, features the death of the great lizard—for real, this time. An army of praying mantis–like things have emerged from Tokyo Bay and are wreaking havoc. Meanwhile, scientists noticing certain changes in Godzilla's body chemistry, conclude that he's about to experience a meltdown that could cause the end of the world. When the giant mother of the mantis-monsters, known only as Destroyer, threatens Godzilla's son, the scene is a set for a showdown. Godzilla saves Japan—moments before blowing apart from the forces raging within him. But in the final moments, it is revealed that, even though Godzilla is gone, his son survives. The legacy continues. Akira Ifukube, the greatest soundtrack composer of the Godzilla series, came out of retirement to create the score to this final episode; it proves to be a blockbuster—but not as big as the one to come...

1996 ...as Hollywood's TriStar Pictures announces that it has finally gotten its own Godzilla project off the back shelf, recruiting mega-movie specialists Roland Emmerich and Dean Devlin to do the honors of bringing the G-thang to life in big-budget America. Using computer effects rather rubber suits, the new Godzilla promises to be like nothing fans have seen before. Long live the King!

Robot vs. mutant in a battle to the finish! Team Godzilla takes on Mecha-G and pals

Hong Kong Cinema

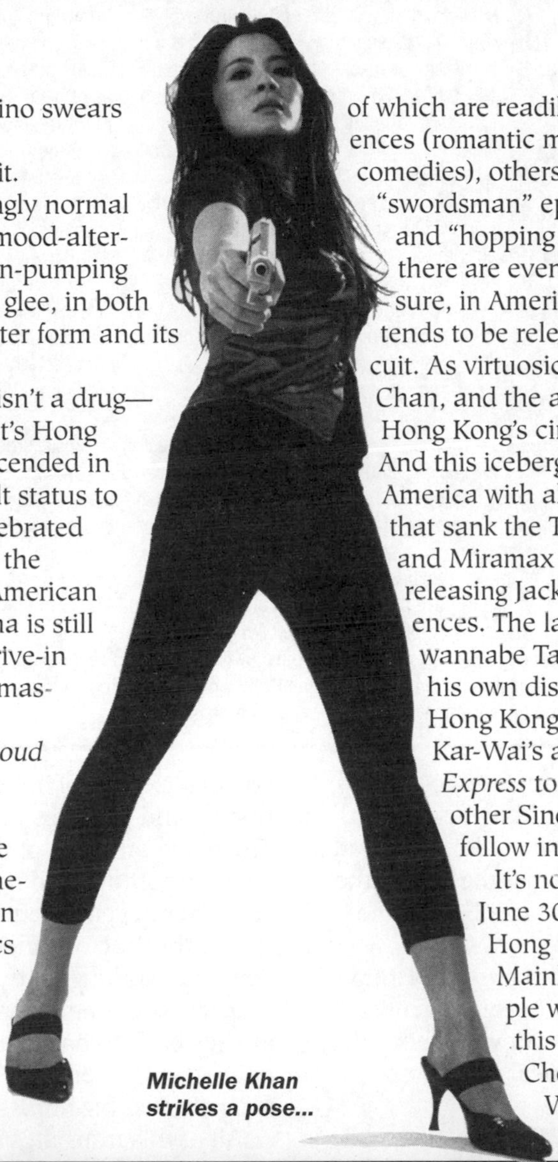

Michelle Khan strikes a pose...

Pulp auteur Quentin Tarantino swears by it.

Hollywood is hungry for it.

And thousands of seemingly normal individuals, addicted to its mood-altering, mind-bending, adrenalin-pumping rush, consume it with eager glee, in both its legitimate, over-the-counter form and its illegal black-market variety.

The product in question isn't a drug—though it might as well be. It's Hong Kong cinema, which has ascended in recent years from furtive cult status to become one of the most celebrated and imitated film canons in the world. Of course, to many American watchers, Hong Kong cinema is still synonymous with cheesy drive-in chopsocky ("You killed my master! Now, you die!" *<primal screech of rage, followed by loud slapping noises>*). And even most of the enlightened are aware only of its least subtle expressions, such as the kinematic ballistic-ballets of John Woo and the hilarious antics of kung-fu clown-prince Jackie Chan.

The truth is, of course, that Hong Kong cinema spans a huge and diverse spectrum of genres, some of which are readily familiar to Western audiences (romantic melodramas and slapstick comedies), others totally alien (period "swordsman" epics, "gambling king" films, and "hopping vampire" flicks). And yes, there are even art films—though, to be sure, in America, anything with subtitles tends to be relegated to the cappucino circuit. As virtuosic as they might be, Woo, Chan, and the action clan are just the tip of Hong Kong's cinematic iceberg.

And this iceberg is careening toward America with all the mighty force of the floe that sank the Titanic. New Line Cinema and Miramax have had huge successes releasing Jackie Chan films to U.S. audiences. The latter, which has given Woo-wannabe Tarantino a blank check and his own distributing label, has also sent Hong Kong New Wave prodigy Wong Kar-Wai's artsy actioner *Chungking Express* to Stateside screens—with other Sino-cinema selections likely to follow in short order.

It's not just the films, either. As June 30, 1997—the fateful date of Hong Kong's return to the Chinese Mainland—approaches, the people who made them are heading this way as well. Screen icon Chow Yun-Fat and mentor John Woo are already ensconced in Hollywood; Tarantino-muse

The Magnificent Butcher

The Chinese Boxer

An early swordsman epic

THE CANON: A Baker's Dozen Must-See Hong Kong Films

AN AUTUMN'S TALE (1987)—A gorgeous romantic-comedy classic—Hong Kong's When Harry Met Sally. Chow Yun-Fat plays a rough-and-tumble merchant marine who must play host to his Hong Kong cousin, the dreamy Cherie Chung Chor-Hok. The film, set in New York's Chinatown, was so popular that visiting tourists would regularly flock to the site of Chow's apartment to pose for photographs. (Well, the site where it was supposed to be, anyway—the building doesn't exist in real life.)

A BETTER TOMORROW I (1986), II (1987), III (1989)—This film series broke John Woo into the top ranks of action auteurs, touched off a fusillade of noisy imitators, and turned Chow Yun-Fat into the King of Hong Kong. Tomorrow I takes brotherhood and betrayal to its epic limits, as two siblings choose different paths in life—Ho (Ti Lung) becomes a Triad, and Kit (Leslie Cheung) becomes a cop. When Kit's discovers his brother's misdeeds, he goes on the hunt, repulsed that his idol is a criminal and a murderer. Chow plays Ho's partner-in-crime Mark, who, in a sequence so iconic that it approaches cliche, takes explosive revenge against the bosses who betrayed Ho and himself. The film's climax, which sees Ho and Kit reuniting as a self-sacrificing Chow absorbs a virtual tsunami of lead, seared the image of the Honorable Gangster into the minds of Hong Kong audiences forever. The sequel, made reluctantly by Woo under pressure from his studio, features Chow as the twin of slain antihero Mark, and is generally regarded as a mediocre effort. The third, however, takes a surprising twist; a prequel to the original made by the ever-stylish Tsui Hark, it brings in Anita Mui to play the dangerous damsel who taught Mark all he needed to know about love and war—not necessarily in that order.

C'EST LA VIE, MON CHERIE (1993)—A down-in-the-mouth jazz musician (Lau Ching-Wan) is dragged out of his sullen existence by a lovely young girl named Wing, who shows him the meaning of life. The Love Story–ish plot won't let them be happy together, of course: perky teen angels can't live long in our mundane world, and Anita Yuen as Wing is no exception.

A CHINESE GHOST STORY I (1987), II (1990), III (1991)—The Chinese Ghost Story movies are probably the best known of Hong Kong's supernatural thrillers, and certainly—due in large part to producer Tsui Hark's taste for lavish detail—the most stylish. In the trilogy, mortals and ghosts fall in love and suffer the consequences. Leslie Cheung is a humble scholar in the first two, Jackie Cheung a bumbling swordsman in the latter two, and Joey Wang steals the show as the ghostly enchantress in all three.

CHUNGKING EXPRESS (1994)—Not one film but two, joined at the hip, Wong Kar-Wai's refresh-

TSUI HARK: EPIC PROPORTIONS

Tsui was born in Vietnam and raised in Hong Kong; an unexceptional student, he applied to schools in the U.S. after it became clear that he wasn't going to have much of an academic future in the supercompetitive Hong Kong system. The only school to accept him was the University of Texas, which luckily had a film studies program. Against his parents' wishes, Tsui followed his dreams, and learned the tools of his eventual trade.

After graduating in 1975, Tsui made a documentary about New York Chinatown garment workers, then returned to Hong kong, where he found work as a television director, making a miniseries, *The Gold Dagger Romance* (1978), which was roundly acclaimed as a seminal work. Soon afterwards, Tsui was given the opportunity to do his first feature film: *The Butterfly Murders* (1979), a stylish fantasy-swordsman flick which brought him international acclaim as part of an emerging "Hong Kong New Wave." Tsui may not have been a great student, but he was a quick study: recognizing that pure art and the Hong Kong film industry were barely on speaking terms, Tsui quickly veered toward the commercial mainstream. His 1983 smash *Zu: Warriors of the Mystic Mountain* combined imported Western special effects and a very Chinese plot of outlandish martial arts fantasy and mysticism; it also established Tsui as a director uniquely capable of blockbuster cinema. 1986's *Peking Opera Blues*, a jaunty caper comedy, featured a trio of star ingenues—singer Sally Yeh, then-screen queen Cherie Chung, and cool beauty Brigitte Lin. It also drew some of Tsui's greatest international acclaim.

But Tsui's biggest successes aren't always those which he's credited as directing; it's as a producer, working his magic through another's hands and eyes, that he's made Hong Kong cinematic history. He produced John Woo's *A Better Tomorrow* and *The Killer*, as well as frequent collaborator Ching Siu-tung's *Chinese Ghost Story* and *Swordsman* trilogies—making stars out of Chow Yun-Fat and the lovely Joey Wang Jo-Yin, and jump-starting the career of screen legend Brigitte Lin through his curious casting of her as a hermaphroditic supervillain in the latter.

The biggest of Tsui's cinematic triumphs may be the epic historical action-drama *Once Upon a Time in China*, which since its beginnings in 1991 has stretched across five feature films and an ongoing television series, in the process transforming Jet Li Linjie into an international superstar and reviving the cult of folk hero Wong Fei Hung.

Whether working as director, producer, writer, editor, storyboarder, special effects technician, soundtrack supervisor, or, more likely, a little of each, Tsui has made himself synonymous with Hong Kong cinema. Which might, perhaps, make one wonder what would have happened had he followed his parents wishes—and become a physician.

Ringo Lam is on his way, as are directors Ronny Yu and Tsui Hark. With Hong Kong in a precarious state and the film market there both saturated and shrinking, it's no wonder that the lure of the Gold Mountain's silver screens has become so much greater.

So study the following basic course in Hong Kong cinema closely, and pay special attention to the names and faces. Because, any day now, they could be coming—to a bijou near you.

HOW THE INDUSTRY WORKS

Don't make the mistake of thinking that Hong Kong's movie industry is a Far East photocopy of Tinseltown. Compared with Hollywood—or even American independent cinema—the Hong Kong movie industry's production budgets are rock-bottom, and the orientation of most of its filmmakers relentlessly commercial. Films are generally considered commodities, not works of art, and the way that they're produced, packaged, and marketed reflect this orientation. If a film is successful, you can expect the release of dozens of sequels, ripoffs, and parodies in the months that follow. The name and face of the featured talent is often more important than irrelevancies like storyline, character development, or visual coherency. As a result, "hot" actors and actresses are in constant demand, working on two or three projects simultaneously, shooting different scenes from different movies back to back, and collapsing with exhaustion—just long enough to recover before signing on for their next big film.

All of this translates into the wild irreverence, pinball plotting, and stylized production values that many people associate with run-of-the-mill Hong Kong cinema. But this isn't to say that all Hong Kong films are the same—despite what many Western enthusiasts might suggest. There are films which have brilliantly superseded the chains of genre, demonstrating that on this most mercantile of islands, art is not dead. And there are even a number of directors—Stanley Kwan, Ann Hui, and Wong Kar Wai—who have developed international status as cinematic auteurs. Still, these are exceptions; the standard rules of the Hong Kong movie game demand that players be rough, random, and ready for anything

A standard Hong Kong production might proceed as follows:

I. A storyline, often a retread of a recent Hollywood or Hong Kong hit, is conceived of by a producer or director, who fleshes it out—with or without the help of a screenwriter.
Even if a screenwriter is hired, he or she usually does no more than craft a scene-by-scene outline. Many films are shot without a completed script, with dialogue invented on the spot or ad-libbed by the actors.

II. The production company, if it hasn't already chosen a star from its roster of contracted talent, shops around for a headliner: an actor whose mere presence in the film will be enough to book the film into theater chains.
Getting a top, bankable star (say, Chow Yun-Fat, Stephen Chow, or, if you're Golden Harvest, Jackie Chan) guarantees that a movie will at least break even for the studio, since its presales to distributors in Hong Kong and key markets like Taiwan and Southeast Asia will cover the cost of making the film itself. Actresses generally don't have the box office clout of actors—but the casting of an ingenue-of-the-moment opposite your leading man adds to the probability that the film will hit "breakthrough" b.o. After the headliners are cast, the supporting roles are filled from the pool of regular character players, usually based on established types: the fat slob, the sex-starved woman, the senile old man, and so on.

III. The studio hits up distributors for presales.
This can make or break a film: if the stars attached to a film aren't of sufficient luminosity, Asian distributors may turn up their noses, presales will be low, and the number of theaters carrying the film domestically and abroad will be small—small enough to guarantee that it won't earn out its budget. There isn't such a thing as a "platform" release in Hong Kong: A film is launched into a set number of theaters and runs as long as it's making enough money to warrant keeping it there. Even if a film scores a surprise hit, it can't expand its outlets, so getting a film into as many marquees as possible is critical. Unfortunately, because of the drop in quality in Hong Kong productions, distributors have been cutting back presale offers, sometimes to as little as one-fifth of their '80s peaks.

IV. The shoot begins, with or without a script.
There's relatively little post-production in Hong Kong—stunts are shot "live" with wires and harnesses and trampolines, not faked with blue-screen or computer effects; monsters and supernatural beasts are costumed actors or puppets, not animation. Since the headline talent is usually booked solid for months beyond the project (a hot actress like Anita Yuen can appear in as many as 10 movies a year; crooner/actor Andy Lau **[👁256]**, one of the four "Heavenly Kings," has appeared in more than 70 films in the past decade), the shoot can't—and won't—last more than about a month. Besides, every day spent shooting is another bite into a budget that can be as low as a few million HK dollars ($250,000 U.S.).

V. Postproduction. Such as it is.
The film is edited and the soundtrack is polished—

A Better Tomorrow

A Chinese Ghost STory

The witch is possessed. Kill her!
The Bride with White Hair

ing Express is less sober and more commercial than his earlier Days of Being Wild. Both of Express's stories are quirky tales of young policemen in love; the first stars Takeshi Kaneshiro as a the moony-eyed cop and Brigitte Lin as a mysterious and formidable femme fatale, and the second features Tony Leung

Chiu-Wai as the amorous flatfoot and perky-punky singer Faye Wong as a young girl who worms her way into his life.

DRUNKEN MASTER I (1978) and II (1994)—Contemporary chop-socky fans know the historical hero Wong Fei Hung via Jet Li's sober, prouder performances in the Once Upon a Time in China series. In the classic Drunken Master, Jackie Chan gives the master a zany spin—playing him as a lazy buffoon who's trained in the Drunken Style by a foul-mouthed, sadistic derelict. The movie made Chan a star—so when Chan announced plans to make a sequel to his early hit, people were revved up for a masterpiece. They got it: DM II is Chan at his best, with masterful turns by Ti Lung as Chan's pop, Anita Mui as his stepmom, and director Lau as yet another kung-fu hobo. It's since become one of Chan's biggest hits ever.

FROM BEIJING WITH LOVE (1994)—Stephen Chow parodies Bond, and nobody does it better. Even if you don't like his shtick,

you'll love this nail-on-the-head takedown of everyone's favorite secret agent cliche. Anita Yuen, as his perky (and possibly traitorous) sidekick puts in a typically winning role—but the fun here comes from Chow's deadpan performance.

HE'S A WOMAN, SHE'S A MAN (1994)—What do you get when

you combine a starstruck fan, a neurotic songstress, and her temperamental producer-cum-boyfriend? The funniest comedy of cross-dressing and crossed communications ever to emerge from Hong Kong. Anita Yuen plays Lee, a groupie desperate to meet pop-queen Rose (Carina Lau). When Rose's mentor/lover Kim (Leslie Cheung) holds an open call for new singing talent, Lee seizes the opportunity, hoping to get close to her idol. The problem is, Kim's search is for a male vocalist, so Lee dons guywear and goes undercover. And when Lee is picked from the crowd, she thanks her lucky stars—until she finds herself falling in love with Kim, and Rose falls in love with her...The rest is gender-bending farce in the grand tradition of Tootsie and Victor/Victoria.

THE KILLER (1989)—Chow Yun-Fat is a retiring assassin who decides to take on one last job—to save the eyesight of an innocent bystander played by singer Sally Yeh, blinded in Chow's

Police Story

Swordsman II

The Chinatown Kid

or *created*, if the film was shot without synch sound. Sometimes the headline talent is too busy to do their own dubbing, in which case a voice actor is hired to plug in the star's lines. A real hatchet-job production might even include scenes for which dialogue wasn't completed in time for shooting; in this case, the director might simply tell the actors to count to 20 in front of the cameras, and wait to dub in appropriate words in post. Music, a major part of the film's atmosphere, is added: if you have a singer/actor as your headliner, it's a must to put in a music video–like "interlude," where the lead and his leading lady go through a series of touching moments as the singer's voice floats across the soundtrack. Sometimes the final cut isn't ready until the very last minute—hours or minutes before its domestic premiere.

VI. The midnight premiere.

If the film is an "event," say, a big studio's Lunar New Year film (Lunar New Year being the big moviegoing holiday, equivalent to Memorial Day here in the U.S.) or the latest release by a top-tier star, it'll open with a special midnight premiere. This media-heavy shindig can turn into a mob scene if a film is a smash. Or a disaster.

VII. The run.

The film will play in theaters domestically for three weeks on average, during which it must make a return on the studio's profits—especially if it hasn't had big Asian presales. Most don't earn out. The plethora of crappy cut-out films that were created in the late '80s and early '90s led to a collapse of the domestic industry, as audiences stayed away in droves: In 1989, 44.8 million movie tickets were sold, which made Hong Kong residents amongst the most frequent moviegoers in the world. In 1994, just 29.1 million tickets were sold. Big-name stars had big disasters. Comedian Stephen Chow, the number-one b.o. draw in Hong Kong, starred in *The Mad Monk*, which scored HK$20 million (U.S. $2.5 million)—a drop of more than half from the HK$49 million (U.S. $6 million) of his *Justice My Foot*, then the biggest Hong Kong hit ever.

After (and sometimes during) its runs in Hong Kong and Asia, a film will go on to play in Chinatowns in the West. It will also have video and laserdisc releases; unfortunately, because of endemic piracy (video-store owners regularly buy a single copy of a film and dupe it as often as they like), these won't turn a bomb into a bloom.

FROM THE ABOVE EXAMPLE, A FEW BASIC GUIDELINES TO HONG KONG FILMMAKING CAN BE EXTRAPOLATED:

I. Expect low budgets. Really low budgets.

A top-of-the-line production in Hong Kong will run a studio about HK$30 million (U.S. $4 million)—just one-tenth of the production budget of a comparable Hollywood film. This means that Western luxuries like multiple takes, high-end special effects, and second-unit cameras are rare or nonexistent. Until very recently, even synch sound—which no American movie would do without—was uncommon. Not that completing a movie takes long: Shooting schedules are measured in days and weeks. (One charity film, shot in the late '80s and featuring nearly every major star in Hong Kong, was completed, from concept to postproduction, in just three days!)

II. Distributors rule.

Even more than in the U.S., distributors have

clout. Jackie Chan's career was almost stalled at birth when, after an early flop, Asian distributors demanded that his production company stop using him: he was too ugly to be a marquee idol, they said. (Luckily for us, his company didn't listen.) Hong Kong has 70 percent of Asia's film market share, making it a powerhouse in the region—but, by the same token, the industry must play to the tastes of a very broad market, and thus often take the word of regional distributors as gospel.

III. Names are everything.

Since presales are so important, packaging a film with the right stars is critical. The big three—Stephen Chow, Jackie Chan, and Chow Yun-Fat—have been reliable sources of presale revenue (though the latter two have gone to Hollywood). The four "Heavenly Kings"—Andy Lau, Jackie Cheung, Aaron Kwok, and Leon Lai [👁254]—are also strong headliners, particularly the first two. Leslie Cheung also continues to be popular, and the two Tony Leungs—"Big" Tony Leung Kar Fai and "Little" Tony Leung Chiu Wai—are strong favorites throughout Asia. Hong Kong's only "bankable" female star is the now-retired Brigitte Lin, although action demigoddess Michelle Yeoh and star-for-all-seasons Maggie Cheung come close.

Sometimes, however, combinations can be stronger than the sum of their parts. Lau Ching Wan and Anita Yuen costarred in the smash hit *C'est La Vie, Mon Cherie*; they've been paired up in a half-dozen more movies since, in hopes that lightning would continue to strike. Young actors Nicky Wu and Charlie Young, whose chemistry drove Tsui Hark's *The Lovers* to box office heights, have also been paired up several times since. And of course, if all else fails, putting as many big names as possible into an ensemble can't hurt.

The result of this worship of box-office name-power has been that the Hong Kong industry has, like Hollywood, moved slowly away from the studio system, with low-paid contract actors under the thumb of big studios, toward a star-based sys-

JOHN WOO: THE MASTER OF DISASTER

Woo's career in Hong Kong spans most of the island's modern cinematic history. Originally hired in 1969 by tiny Cathay Studios as a script supervisor at the age of 23, within a few years he'd jumped over to the studio that dominated Hong Kong cinema throughout the '70s: Shaw Brothers. In 1971, Woo became assistant to Chang Cheh, the company's greatest director, and learned both the master's technique and the themes that serve as the bedrock for his later work: the ineffable fraternal bond that exists between men (even if one is trying to kill the other), and the need to return to chivalric ideals. Two years later, Woo got his first opportunity to direct on his own—an independently made, low-budget martial arts film, *The Young Dragons*. Despite its lightweight content, the film drew the notice of Golden Harvest—the home of Bruce Lee, and the heir to Shaw Brothers' cinematic crown. Harvest signed him to a directing contract, first putting him to work at low-budget martial arts films, and then giving him his big break, as the director of a series of slapstick farces starring the Hui Brothers, then the biggest comedy stars in Hong Kong. His 1977 film with Ricky Hui, *Money Crazy*, became one of the year's standout box office smashes; for the next decade, Woo made 10 more films for Harvest, of which eight were comedies.

As successful as he seemed to be as a farceur, Woo's vision lay elsewhere; his dream project was an epic, on the scale of Coppola's *Godfather* movies, that would tell the tale of brotherhood and betrayal in the bloody criminal underworld. Since Woo's career had recently run aground on a handful of critical and box-office flops, Golden Harvest understandably saw the film as a commercial risk. Coming to his rescue was a filmmaker whom Woo had gotten his first break: Tsui Hark, who was riding high on successes like *Zu: Warriors of the Mystic Mountain*. Hark offered to produce the film, which was enough to appease the studio. *A Better Tomorrow*, starring a popular but untested TV actor named Chow Yun-Fat, became the highest-grossing Hong Kong film to date upon its release in 1986. Woo's new career was launched: pulse-pounding, incredibly sophisticated action epics, focusing on the relationships between men and the men who want to kill them. By the early '90s, his international star had risen to the point where a chance at Hollywood's gold ring was inevitable. *Hard Target*, featuring Jean Claude Van Damme, was a solid hit in 1993—though the experience left a sour taste in Woo's mouth. Woo's 1995 loose-nuke followup, *Broken Arrow*, consolidated the resurrection of once-and-future-star John Travolta's career, while reaching the top five in the year's box-office charts.

Now, not only has Woo become a household name in America, with the clout to pick his projects, but he's also opened the door for a new wave of Hong Kong arrivistes to follow in his wake.

penultimate firefight. Gonzo Danny Lee plays the obsessed cop who develops a love-hate relationship with his target; the film's incredible action sequences and way, way over-the-top finale have made it required watching for any contemporary crime-film buff.

ONCE UPON A TIME IN CHINA I-V (1991-95)—A brilliant and gorgeous deconstruction of the life of folk hero Wong Fei Hung, the first three Once Upon a Time pics feature Jet Li as an acrobatic, proud, but romantically innocent incarnation of the great master, and Rosamund Kwan as his Western-educated love interest Aunt Yee; after a salary dispute with filmmaker Hark, Li left the series, to be replaced by the somewhat less charismatic Chiu Man Chiuk.

PEKING OPERA BLUES (1986)—Good things come in threes—in this case, we mean Cherie Chung, Sally Yeh, and Brigitte Lin, who headline this caper-comedy set in China's pre-Revolution 1930s. Chung plays a vixenish gold-digger, Yeh the child of an opera master longing to join the stage's male stars, and Lin the boyish daughter of one of the period's warlords. The three find their fates intertwined, when Lin's secret conspiracy to overthrow her father's iron-fisted rule brings the strangers together in the worst of circumstances. The resulting confusion combines wild action, mistaken identity, and yes, Peking Opera, in a heady, hilarious mix.

POLICE STORY I-III (1989-96)—A cop in trouble is a temporary

thing, at least if that cop is Jackie Chan's intrepid Chan Kui—who uses his fists, kicks, and a heavy dose of improv to pull himself out of hissing hot water throughout the Police Story films. Especially good: the third, subtitled Supercop, in which he's paired up with the fabulous Michelle Khan to bust an international arms smuggler.

SWORDSMAN I-III (1990-92)— The first Swordsman features singer Sam Hui as Ling, a warrior trapped between clans fighting for possession of a mystic scroll. The second replaces Hui with kung fu star Jet Li, and vaults the story to a period after the scroll has been stolen—by Invincible Asia, a devious martial arts master who seeks nothing less than the usurpation of the Imperial throne. Asia has used the secret of the scroll to gain immeasurable power, at a price—self-castration. As played by the statuesque Brigitte Lin, Asia is at turns icy and coquettish; the action is balletic and baroque. Swordsman III: The East Is Red brings back Lin as Asia hundreds of years after her supposed death, in a time when dozens of false Asias have popped up around China. One of the most powerful happens to be Asia's former concubine, played by Ghost Story's Joey Wang. The finale is a spectacle of love, death, and flying femmes.

tem. Salaries for actors have crept upward—and, in a market where budgets of HK$10 million are common, hiring one or two stars at HK$2 million a piece leaves little for actual production values.

IV. If it works—copy it.

"One hit, and you have three or four sequels and a hundred imitations," says distributor, film critic, and director Shu Kei. A smash success like *Once Upon a Time in China* might produce as many as four sequels, which brings up the question of how many times "once" can take place. This cloning goes far beyond the quesion of "legit" sequels; the commercial desperation of the industry has led to slavish mimicry among competing studios. Every hit spawns an entire generation of copies—John Woo's *A Better Tomorrow*, for instance, led to the creation of an entire sub-industry of gangster movies, while the success of Tsui Hark's *Swordsman* movies produced an early-'90s renaissance of the period costume epic. And companies are not above copying themselves, either. Win's Films had a big hit with the Chow Yun-Fat starrer *God of Gamblers*. When he refused to star in the sequel, they hired up-and-coming comic star Stephen Chow to play a clownish would-be apprentice to the *God of Gamblers* in the film that made Stephen a superstar—*All for the Winners*.

Winners surpassed *A Better Tomorrow* (and *God of Gamblers*, for that matter) as the top-grossing Hong Kong film of all time. The "gambling film" was launched as a thriving genre. Stephen Chow headlined in *God of Gamblers II* and *God of Gamblers III: Back to Shanghai*, both of which were commercial successes. (In *Gamblers II*, Stephen Chow's character even meets up with Chow Yun-Fat's—via the use of a handy clip from the first film.) Then, in 1995, Chow Yun-Fat agreed to make an "official" sequel...but, since the name *God of Gamblers II* was already taken, the film was titled *Return of the God of Gamblers 2*, confusing audiences; after all, there'd never been a *Return of the God of Gamblers 1*.

Meanwhile, other studios had jumped on the bandwagon—with *Queen of Gamblers* and the trickily named *All of the Winners*.... —J.Y.

WONG KAR WAI: ODD MAN IN

Wong was a graphic design student at Hong Kong Polytechnic, before following a path taken by many of Hong Kong's brightest entertainment names: He enrolled in a course at the Shaw Brothers' TVB, and upon graduation received a job as a production assistant. He also began to indulge his desire to write, and went on to pen a number of scripts for top directors. Then, in 1989, he got the opportunity to helm his first picture—the rebel-without-a-cause gangster pic *As Tears Go By*, featuring singer Andy Lau and rising ingenue Maggie Cheung. The film was popular—but it also established him as a director capable of bringing out uniquely rich performances. In an industry where actors are routinely treated as commodities, Wong was a revelation, and when he cast his followup, *Days of Being Wild*, every young actor in Hong Kong lined up for parts. The film, a steamy, dreamy collage of teen lives beset by ennui and unfulfilled desire, proved to be a turning point on two levels: It demonstrated to international audiences that Wong was a director worth watching, and it demonstrated to local studios that Wong was a director whose return on investment was going to be awards—not box office.

Wong's followup, *Ashes of Time*, was a budgetary and scheduling boondoggle (at $5 million and three years, it broke Hong Kong records for cost to completion); however, released shortly after the quickie-pic *Chungking Express*, it also consolidated Wong's global reputation. The inevitable embrace by Hong Kong fetishist Quentin Tarantino followed soon thereafter, as did offers to turn his lens to the West. And, though Wong has made it clear that he's not interested at joining the Hollywood exodus, it remains to be seen whether his quirky urban surrealism will play in Hong Kong post-1997. If not, Q.T. could soon face some canny competition.

The Stars of Hong Kong

JACKIE CHAN SING LUNG

Born on April 7, 1954, as the only child of a cook and a maid, Chan's family was so poor that his parents considered selling him to the British doctor who delivered him. (The price? $26.) When he was just seven years old, Chan's parents placed him at the China Drama Academy, run by Beijing Opera master Jim Yuen. The academy, home of the Seven Little Fortunes Beijing Opera Troupe, was a collection of cast-off children bound by long-term contracts to learn from—and perform for—a master who was given the power to beat them, starve them, and discipline them "even to death."

The head apprentice at the academy was a stocky boy named Yuen Chu, who, along with a younger lad named Yuen Biao (all of the Little Fortunes took their master's surname) became fast friends with the mischievous new kid. Their friendship continued into their later careers, and Chu, who changed his name to Samo Hung, Biao, and Chan are still referred to as the "Three Brothers."

At the school, the students trained exhaustively in the weapons skills and acrobatic stunts that are the hallmark of Beijing Opera. But the Opera was on the wane in Hong Kong, and, without audiences to watch or new students to train, the school shut down in the early '70s. Without too many options, Chan and his peers went on to become stuntmen at the pioneering Shaw Brothers film studio. He then acted in a number of rather terrible chopsocky films in the mid '70s, but in 1975 was finally "discovered" after starring in a film called *Hand of Death,* directed by a young John Woo.

The discoverer was Lo Wei, the star producer-director who'd also found the first kung fu superstar, Bruce Lee. But Lo's attempts to groom Chan into a new Bruce were disasters (although Lo did give Chan his English name, Jackie; before that, Chan had called himself "Paul"). Chan soon realized that Lo was ruining his career, and managed to struggle out from under Lo's thumb long enough to make two films for seasoned martial arts whiz Yuen Woo Ping. The first was *Snake in Eagle's Shadow,* which became an unexpected hit—mostly because it was the first "comedy fu" flick, making best use of Chan's considerable slapstick talents. The second of Chan's Yuen films was *Drunken Master*—a box-office record-breaker, and one of the great classic kung fu films of all time.

After *Master,* Chan's place in the pantheon was assured. First, however, he had to settle with a seething Lo, who refused to let Chan escape his grip the way Bruce Lee had. Eventually, Raymond Chow of Golden Harvest stepped in and resolved matters, and Chan began making his own films, with unprecedented artistic control. His trademark became his commitment to doing all of his own incredibly dangerous stunts, and very nearly killing himself, again and again. (This means that the best part of any Jackie flick is often the end-credits, under which he screens clips of his "N.G.'s", or "no goods"—scenes of Jackie crashing into the asphalt, catching on fire, or being rushed to the hospital after a failed stunt.)

After the U.S. success of *Rumble in the Bronx, Supercop,* and *First Strike,* the biggest star in Asia has now set his sights on America. Can Chan (whose reputation as a control freak precedes him) actually work with Hollywood-sized egos? Time will only tell.

EYE, EYE SIR—Like many other Hong Kong stars, Jackie Chan, at the urging of early mentor Lo Wei, had "opening" surgery to make his eyes larger. He also had his teeth fixed. Didn't do anything about the nose, though.

LOVE WILL TEAR THEM APART—Big secret: Jackie Chan is married (to Taiwanese actress Lin Feng-chiao) and has a son named Jackson. Well, okay, it's not really a secret—but neither Jackie nor the media openly acknowledges his married status, ever since a female fan of his in Japan threw herself in front of a moving automobile after hearing a rumor of his non-single status. Another Japanese fan-girl once showed up in his offices unannounced and, declaring her hopeless eternal love for him, took poison. She was forced to vomit and fortunately survived. Suffice it to say, Jackie is very, very big in Japan.

REAPING THE HARVEST—Up until his move to the West, Jackie Chan worked for Golden Harvest, and only Golden Harvest. Why? Some sources say that Jackie's loyalty is in part a debt of blood. Director Lo Wei, who "discovered" him, was allegedly a high-level officer in the Sun Yi On Triad. When Jackie broke away, Lo threatened to have Chan chopped into hamburger if he ever returned to Hong Kong. As a result, Chan stayed in Taiwan for two years, until Golden Harvest's Raymond Chow "bought his life" from Lo and Sun Yi On for U.S. $1.5 million.

DEAD SOLID PERFECT—In 1992, Maggie Cheung's slender figure was chosen in a poll of Asian women as the "most ideal" of all female celebrities. Asian men would probably agree: she measures out as 168 cm tall, 50 kg, and 83-58-87 cm.

"La Cheung" in Irma Vep

A LANGUAGE OF HIS OWN—The bizarre patter which made Stephen Chow famous has become a kind of cult slang among youth in Hong Kong. Called mou lei tau, which means, more or less, "without a shred of meaning," the slang involves the use of Chow's patented obscure puns and left-handed non sequiturs. Mo lei tau kids take pride in behaving and speaking as if nothing has meaning. Some academics have associated the popularity of mo lei tau (and Chow himself) with the "deadline" of 1997, after which the future is, to say the least, uncertain.

MAGGIE CHEUNG MAN-YUK

Born in Hong Kong, Cheung spent the better part of her childhood in England, emigrating there with her diplomat parents at the age of eight. She didn't return to Hong Kong until after finishing her secondary education, in 1982—and then only on a visit, having been reluctantly lured by the promise that during the trip she would get to meet one of her TV soap-star idols. While walking in the street with her mother, however, she was "discovered" by a producer of television commercials. She decided to stay on the island, and began working as a model. "Modeling for a year helped because people knew my face, even if they didn't know my name," she says. "Then my model agency suggested I try for Miss Hong Kong; I was runner-up, and suddenly I became famous overnight." Schlock-hit director Wong Jing cast her one week after the pageant in a comedy called *Prince Charming*, where she played a supporting role to then-screen-queen Cherie Cheung (no relation). Then, since the Miss Hong Kong runner-up contract included a television contract, Cheung worked in TV for two years as a soap and serial ingenue, which she calls a "nightmare." Luckily, around that time her film career began to explode.

Since then, Cheung has made over 70 films that span the entire range of Hong Kong cinema—action films, light comedies, romantic melodramas, period pieces, and art films, winning numerous awards along the way, including the Best Actress award at the Berlin International Film Festival for her role in the biodrama *Centre Stage*. Having matured as an actress, Cheung seems well poised to make her mark beyond Hong Kong; Cheung is among a very select few Hong Kong actors who speaks perfect English and has a global reputation. Rumor has it that she's already getting the lay of the land, having acquired an agent in Hollywood.

STEPHEN CHOW SING CHI

Chow was born in poverty, and graduated from high school to work first as a street peddler and then as an office boy, before joining TVB's television-actor training program in the early '80s. Unfortunately, TVB's brass soon decided that Chow was not up to snuff and canned him. A friend of his, actor Jamie Chik, pleaded with TVB to give him another chance—which they did...hosting a *Romper Room*–like children's show called *4:30 Space Shuttle*. A producer chanced upon the show one afternoon, and noticed the incredibly bored Chow's sarcastic attitude towards the show's kiddie audience: In the show's quiz segment, Chow asked the names of the ancient Three Kingdoms, and received from one wretched child the response "Hong Kong, China, and Taiwan." Chow embraced the boy and said, "You are very smart! Someday, you'll be a great man!" The producer split his sides laughing and decided that Chow had the potential to be a star.

Chow's early films were martial arts and dramatic vehicles, which didn't play to his strength: still, Chow's deadpan comic mugging drew notice, and Win's Films finally cast him in the comedy *All for the Winners*—the film that made him Hong Kong's box-office king. He's since starred in six of Hong Kong's 10 all-time top-grossing movies, and makes more than $1.7 million U.S. for each of his star turns; despite the inconsistent quality (and box office) of his recent films, he's still one of Hong Kong's top draws.

CHOW YUN-FAT

Chow was born in 1956 on Lamma Island, a tiny isle off Hong Kong, in poverty, the son of an oil worker and a cleaning lady. His nickname at the time was *Gao Tsai,* or "Little Dog." When he was 10, his family moved to Kowloon, where he had his first formal schooling. However, at age 17, he dropped out of high school to work to support his family—his several jobs included postman, bellboy, office clerk, and camera salesman. Finally, one day he saw a newspaper ad for a "free training program" for television actors, which he answered. "Free training" at the Shaw Brothers' TVB meant being a bit actor in their series—without pay. After the program was over, Chow was signed to a three-year contract, at the pitiful rate of $500 a month. In 1976, he hit it big with audiences as a soap-hunk on a show called *Hotel,* and was able to renegotiate his contract—extended for 10 more years—in his favor. In the '80s, he headlined a gangster series set in the late '20s called *Shanghai Bund,* where his suave crime-boss portrayal presaged his later success as Hong Kong's most famous cinematic antihero. Then, in 1986, he hooked up with mentor, imagemaker, and favorite director John Woo for *A Better Tomorrow.* The rest is history, as Chow developed an enormous following throughout Asia, and then around the world—leading to his decision to leap the Pacific into the waiting embrace of Hollywood. Never has a newcomer to Hollywood had so much advance hype; while still working on his English (which even now can be graded at best as "passable") he was already dubbed with the title of "The Coolest Actor in the World" by the *Los Angeles Times.*

***Chow Yun Fat rocks hard in* Hard-Boiled**

MICHELLE KHAN (MICHELLE YEOH)

Khan, born in Ipoh, Malaysia, was a ballet dancer, model, and beauty queen whose first screen break was a TV commercial she did with Jackie Chan. After appearing in a window-dressing role in *Owl vs. Bumbo,* produced by Samo Hung, she was tapped by Hung to star in a visionary new project—a movie that would pair two women as butt-kicking, bullet-blasting heroes. Khan was quickly trained in the basics of movie fighting, and cast in *Yes Madam*. When that film took off, she realized she'd found her forte, and made two more action films, *Royal Warriors* and *Magnificent Warriors*. Then, after stunt incidents aggravated the back injury that had ended her career as a dancer, she retired to marry retail magnate Dickson Poon.

Their divorce in 1991 freed up Khan to make her triumphant return to the screen, paired with her early TV-ad costar Jackie Chan in *Supercop*. Khan is now the top action heroine in Hong Kong, earning U.S. $400,000 a movie. Still, with her chronic back trouble likely to eventually curtail her daredevil-stunt career, will Khan be able to switch gears into more sedate roles? Her first attempt at a non-action film, *Easy Money* (1988), was a flop. But a switch to a more special-effects oriented arena—say, Hollywood—will give her a new lease on risking her life. She's doted on by top Western

PAS Á DEUX FU— Like Shaw Brothers mainstay Cheng Pei Pei [👁94], the hard-kicking, high-flying star of another era, Michelle Khan began her career with no martial arts training, though she learned quickly, translating her skills as a Western-trained ballet dancer into the agile moves of an action heroine. Her debut in Corey Yuen Kwai's Yes Madam (1985), which paired her with American action queen Cynthia Rothrock, soared at the box office—and so did her martial arts career.

THE (FRENCH) WORLD LOVES A LOVER—In 1991, a poll of women by a French magazine named Tony Leung Kar-Fai the "Asian man whom French women would most like to have sex with."

DOWN AND OUT IN HONG KONG AND MACAO—During his mid-'80s dry period, Tony Leung Kar-Fai was forced to go to the streets, selling fake Gucci purses from a pushcart to supplement his meager earnings as a TV actor on the government-owned station RHTV.

JET CRASHES—Following the success of Once Upon a Time in China and its first sequel, he fired his manager (the son of chopsocky director/triad boss Lo Wei), then hired film producer Jim Choi Chi Ming to negotiate richer terms. Just months later, Choi was gunned down by hired assassins, sending Li scurrying back to Beijing, where he found himself detained by the Mainland government. Police suggested that Choi's death was due to his alleged drug trafficking; others suggest that the killing was an unsubtle "warning" to the fickle actor by the Sun Yi On triad.

VOX NOT-SO-POP—Anita Yuen's voice, now considered one of her uniquely appealing features, was originally considered a major liability. Producers thought it was "unfeminine," and even went so far as to overdub her lines with the voice of a more traditionally girlish-sounding actress.

filmmakers like Oliver Stone, speaks perfect English, and is that rare commodity, a serious female action hero. And when interviewed on *Prime Time Live* for a special profile of costar Jackie Chan, she seemed cooler than Jackie, no easy task. All of which should stand her in good stead as she makes her Hollywood debut alongside 007 as the latest "Bond Girl." Now that Chanmania has taken root in America, watch for Khanmania to follow suit.

TONY LEUNG CHIU-WAI

Born in 1962, Leung was a home appliances salesman before he joined TVB's training program in 1982. There, he became host of the same kiddie show that produced megastar Stephen Chow, and then came to prominence playing Jin Yong's

famous character Wei Xiaobao in the TVB period-drama *Duke of Mount Deer* **[👁41]** (Curiously enough, Stephen Chow played this role himself in two hit comedies, *Royal Tramp I* and *II*.)

After winning considerable recognition and popularity playing Hong Kong "everyman" roles, Leung garnered the respect of critics with his performance as a dazed, lovelorn cop in Wong Kar-Wai's *Chungking Express*. He's since cut back his work in "commercial" movies, saying that if he were to make 20 movies a year just to rake in the cash, he "wouldn't be an artist but a factory worker." Recently, he also won international acclaim for his role as a poetry-quoting pimp in the art-theater Vietnamese film *Cyclo*. He speaks good English, and there have been rumors of his imminent arrival in America. Still, since he's neither a hunk-type idol nor an action icon (though he did play an agonized undercover cop in John Woo's *Hard-Boiled*), it's difficult to say what kind of place Hollywood has for him.

TONY LEUNG KAR FAI

After graduating from a Hong Kong arts college, the young Leung sank his savings into the startup of a graphic design magazine, which folded after just one issue. Luckily, in 1981, Hong Kong filmmaker Li Hanxiang spotted him on the street and decided to give him a chance to make it in showbiz, as the lead in a two-part historical saga, *Burning of the Imperial Palace* and *Reign Behind the Curtain*. The films, shot on the mainland, were critically lauded when they were released in 1982, and the novice star was awarded Best Actor at the Hong Kong Film Awards for his performances.

Then misfortune struck again: just as he began to receive accolades, Leung was virtually exiled from the Hong Kong industry after complaints from Taiwan's strongly anticommunist distributors. He worked in small roles on TV, sold counterfeit goods on the street, and struggled to get auditions. "In those days, people often labelled actors who worked in China as communists," Leung says. "Works shot there were not distributed in Taiwan and some parts of Southeast Asia, which are big markets. I was not a leftist, but still no producer approached me."

In 1990, he got his second big break, signing a

Michelle Khan gets a leg up

contract with Cinema City. Unfortunately, his films—despite being well received by critics—were box-office poison. It took a third, and final, knock by opportunity to open the gates of fame: *The Lover,* which Leung got almost by accident. "One day, I happened to be where [director Annaud] was staying, and dropped by to see him," says Leung. As *The Lover* sent his international star soaring, Leung starred in the satirical local hit *'92 The Legendary La Rose Noire,* a wacky musical parody of '60s-era Hong Kong caper flicks—playing a preening, somewhat effeminate cop. *La Rose* made over HK$20 million. A Tsui Hark remake of the classic swordplay epic *Dragon Inn,* costarring Brigitte Lin and Maggie Cheung, followed soon after, and Leung was finally catapulted to his rightful place in the Hong Kong pantheon.

JET LI LINJIE

Li began studying at the prestigious Beijing Wushu Academy at the age of eight, where he trained in the stylized forms of kung fu that are the only officially recognized martial arts in the People's Republic of China **[👁182]**. He was immediately recognized as a superior talent, and won the national championships in *wu shu* performance five times as a child and teen. He also studied less rigid forms of kung fu under the Shaolin monks, and, by the time he was a young man, had become a spokesperson for wu shu and the Shaolin Temple, travelling the globe to pump the glories of Chinese martial arts. He was even a member of the first wu shu team to tour the West, performing at Nixon's White House.

In 1980, he was discovered by filmmaker Fu Qi, and made his breathtaking debut in *Shaolin Temple*—China's top-grossing film ever at the time. Unfortunately, Li's followups did not prove as successful, and for four years, his movie career foundered. Then, in 1987, Li was given a two-year exit visa from the Chinese government to go on an educational mission—"to spread the glory of wu shu" in the U.S. Li pulled a fast one and somehow managed to secure an Ecuadorean passport and U.S. residency, then relocated to Hong Kong, where he signed on with Golden Harvest and made his first *Once Upon a Time in China* film in 1991, with Tsui Hark at the helm. The film was an enormous success; Li made an appealingly naive, yet appropriately potent Wong Fei Hung, and Li was signed on for two more sequels. With his star seemingly on the rise, Li decided to renegotiate his fee with Hark, who hotly refused. Li went on to make another, mediocre Wong Fei Hung movie, *Last*

Hero in China, with ultracommercial schlock director Wong Jing, then turned away from his Wong Fei Hung meal ticket and toward more contemporary fare. (Not that he's given up the period stuff—he enlivened another semi-mythical hero, mama's boy martial artist *Fong Sai Yuk,* in a hit film and its sequel.)

BRIGITTE LIN CHING-HSIA

Lin was born in Taiwan, the daughter of a military physician, and a striking beauty even as a teen. Her adolescence was filled with propositions from agents and producers offering to make her a star. "The first one chased me down the street," she says. "I ran away from him because it scared me—a stranger approaching you like that." After rejecting a series of offers, Lin finally agreed to listen to one scout's proposal. His pitch, involving rather more casual nudity than Lin was interested in, almost led her to bolt again—but then the agent, sensing her dismay, offered to introduce her to well-known director Sung Tsun-Shou, who cast her immediately in *Outside the Window* (1973), a tragic love story about the illicit love between a teacher and his young student. The film was a gigantic hit throughout Asia...except in Lin's native Taiwan, where it was never screened due to a legal battle that erupted shortly after the film was completed. Lin's second film (which did get released in Taiwan) made her an icon in her own country, with media exposure and hype that was all a bit too much for a girl still in her teens; even worse was the seemingly endless amount of work that came her way, which Lin found impossible to refuse. For 10 years,

Lin worked almost without rest, starring in as many as a dozen films a year, often simultaneously, learning, as she put it, "to sleep standing up, leaning against a wall."

In 1979, the pace finally took its toll. Lin had a notoriously bad romantic encounter, and then, hounded by gossip columns and exhausted both physically and mentally, she left Taiwan for the United States, spending the next year and a half in California. When she was ready to return to work, she chose Hong Kong as her new base of operations, and resolved to make films that took her away from the romantic-heroine roles she'd been boxed into.

In 1985, she starred opposite Jackie Chan in his first *Police Story* flick, as a slightly ditzy witness under Chan's protection—which led to her taking her first action lumps. Lin's next big role was in Tsui Hark's groundbreaking *Peking Opera Blues* (1986), an all-girl romp that featured Lin, Sally Yeh Qian-Wen (later of John Woo's *The Killer*), and Cherie Cheung Chor-Hok, then the most popular actress in Hong Kong. Lin's character, the daughter of a 1920s warlord who sports dapper men's garb and incites a revolution against her own father, was a startling transformation for the actress. Her fans were surprised, but not so much that they stayed away. And that was just the beginning: in 1992, Lin made the film that shocked her fans out of their seats for good—*Swordsman II*, featuring Lin as the martial arts master Invincible Asia. Directed by Ching Siu Tung and produced by the inevitable Tsui Hark. The story's twist: Asia, a biological male, has sacrificed his manhood for the sake of a dark mystic power—and is thus transformed into a woman in appearance. As Asia, Lin carries on dalliances with both the male lead (played by Jet Li) and a female concubine, and performs feats of martial arts wonder, involving sewing needles and other "feminine" implements. The film was a gigantic hit, and Lin repeated the role of Asia in a third *Swordsman* in 1993 subtitled *The East Is Red*. From then on, Lin's past as a sweetheart of the soaps was banished from memory—and her position as a screen icon was set forever.

Lin, the biggest female star in Hong Kong, is currently retired. She's had a baby, and is happily married to a wealthy husband. After having had two big careers—and managing to preserve her unearthly beauty well into a period when many actresses have moved on to more matronly roles—it seems incredibly unlikely that Lin will be satisfied with the domestic life for long. Even money says Lin will come out of retirement...for the right script. And the right script might be in the U.S. Lin, who speaks English, has spent a fair amount of time on this side of the Atlantic; she also has enough of a cult following that her swan-song role, in Wong Kar-Wai's *Chungking Express* (released stateside by Miramax) could well lead to Hollywood opportunities.

ANITA YUEN WING-YEE

Yuen was born in 1971 as the middle of three children (she has an older brother and a younger sister). After a gawky adolescence, she blossomed into a lovely teen—beautiful enough to be selected as a candidate for the 1991 Miss Hong Kong Contest shortly after graduating from Ching Yee Lui Ji high school.

Her surprising victory in the pageant launched her into showbiz—but, unlike many beauty contest winners, she was able to move from early "window dressing" roles into parts where she was given an opportunity to actually act. She won Best Newcomer at the Hong Kong Film Awards for a small supporting role in the gangster-film parody *Days of Being Dumb*, and was then hand-picked by filmmaker Derek Yee for the part of Wing, the optimist with a terminal disease in his tragicomedy *C'est La Vie, Mon Cherie*. Yee's warm-hearted weepie was a surprise smash hit, and Yuen, just 22, was awarded Best Actress for her moving and uninhibited performance.

Yuen's stock as a serious actress skyrocketed—but it was her role in a more traditionally commercial film, Peter Chan's *He's a Woman, She's a Man*, that made her Hong Kong's most sought-after female lead. In the latter film, she plays Lee, a young groupie who disguises herself as a boy to get closer to her favorite pop-star couple, and ends up becoming part of a hilarious love triangle, rife with crossed genders and intentions. Yuen subsequently made Hong Kong film history by winning an unprecedented second Best Actress in a row for her portrayal.

Since then, the former beauty queen has been working around the clock; after just a few short years as an actress, Yuen has managed to perform in a huge and uneven set of productions, ranging in quality from the execrable to the delightful. Some say that Yuen's high-volume output is diminishing her performances and burning audiences out; others suggest that making as many movies as she can in the years she has available to her is a necessity—since the span of an ingenue's career in Hong Kong is shorter than Yuen's perky 'do, and younger, newer stars are already cutting into her franchise. —J.Y.

Getting It in America: Where to Find Hong Kong Movies

The smash success of Jackie Chan's *Rumble in the Bronx* (1996) was the harbinger of a new era for Hong Kong films in America. After all, the resounding failure of Chan's previous efforts to win Stateside hearts and minds—1980's *The Big Brawl* and 1986's *The Protector* were both critical and commercial flops—had seemingly all but doomed Hong Kong cinema to the backwaters of cult oddity. To Drive-In America, Hong Kong was a cheesy, campy in-joke: the source for martial arts films with rock-bottom special effects and endearingly amateurish English dubbing.

Still, never underestimate the power of cult odditics. As the '80s advanced, in rec rooms and on college campuses across the nation, a generation of young Americans raised on Bruce Lee were discovering Hong Kong cinema with a vengeance. They wrote garish, obsessive fanzines. They exchanged tapes and info on computer bulletin boards and later, the Internet. And they hosted furtive, gleeful screenings of videos liberated from Chinatown video stores, reveling in Hong Kong's wacky comedies, opulent costume dramas—and especially, the balletic action flicks of masters like Ringo Lam and John Woo. When Woo's *The Killer* was released to art-house crowds in 1989, a hip, tuned-in audience was there to receive it. The dam had broken; the rush to embrace Hong Kong as the next cinematic hothouse had begun. But insiders know that Hong Kong film has been available here in the U.S. all along: You just needed to know where to look.

GETTING IT ON VIDEO

I. The Fan Underground

On the Internet and through bulletin boards, many fans of Hong Kong cinema request and offer movies for trade or sale. Beware, however: check to make sure you aren't receiving a dubbed copy of an original. This is, of course, illegal—and will ensure that your viewing experience is marred further by scratchy sound, flickering subtitles, and distressingly poor video quality.

Even if you don't actually purchase used stuff over the Net, you may find that cyberspace is the best place to get information on what to watch: the phenomenal **Hong Kong Movie Database** (*http://egret0.stanford.edu/hk/hkquery.html*) contains a nearly comprehensive list of film reviews, hyperlinked by director and performers. If you find one movie you like, a click into the Database will let you find other films featuring the same actors, actresses, or auteurs.

II. Mail Order Mayhem

The easiest way for Hong Kong dilettantes to get their cinefix is probably by mail. Mail-order houses, which often tout a variety of "cult" films in addition to works of Hong Kong cinema, can be a particularly good source for older or more obscure works. By the same token, mail-order houses can be disconcertingly narrow-minded in their selection, stocking, for instance, only ballistic-action and Category III films; if you're looking for more thoughtful or highbrow wares, look elsewhere. The other thing to be wary about is the possibility of getting ripped off. Many video mail-order houses are fronts for one-man pirate operations, with no guarantees on tape quality, copyright legality, or even ability to ship product. If a mail-order house doesn't advertise that its titles are legit, then they probably aren't—and any price below $20 is almost certainly going to get you a bootleg.

DUB PANIC

Most people with even a vague awareness of the fact that a continent known as Asia exists know that Hong Kong is—or was, up until June 1, 1997—a British colony. While this has had both positive and deleterious effects on the island and its people, for American fans of Hong Kong film, the impact of British rule is a big linguistic win: Since the early '80s, nearly every movie made in Hong Kong has been subtitled in English, to allow for their consumption by Hong Kong's expat Brit population.

Unfortunately, no one said the subtitles had to be easy to read. They're often printed in flickering, spidery type, and, since video transfers in Hong Kong tend not to be adjusted for different screen proportions, the first and last words of long sentences can be cut off by the edges of the television screen. Even if you're lucky enough to catch a film in a theater or in a letterboxed version, you may be dismayed by the semantic gymnastics displayed in a typical Hong Kong subtitle: Only in Hong Kong will you see brave heroes praised for their "mandom." Still, these English subtitles mean that Hong Kong cinema is the only Asian film product that is already (sort of) video-ready for American viewers, a fact that contributed to its rise as an underground sensation.

A NOTE ABOUT RATINGS

Hong Kong films, like American ones, are given ratings to pre-

vent the unwary exposure of small children to the extremes of sex and violence. The ratings, usually found on the cover of the film in a small black triangle, are as follows:

CATEGORY I—Equivalent to an American G—the province of innocuous kiddie-stuff.

CATEGORY II—Ranges from PG through a moderate R. These can have profanity (though it's probably untranslatable anyway), quite a bit of violence, and "suggestive themes," but no actual nudity or explicit sex. The vast majority (perhaps 70 per cent) of Hong Kong films available in the U.S. are Category II.

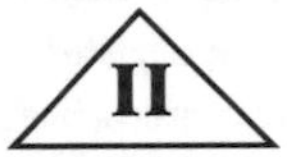

CATEGORY III—Hard R to X. Category III films are a mixed bag of grotesquely gory horror and explicit pornography. "Quality" films occasionally fall into this category (for instance, The Untold Story, a stomach-turning Cat-III murder reconstruction, won several Hong Kong Golden Statue awards); most III flicks, however, are pure exploitation, and are certainly not for children. Or many adults, for that matter.

III. Chinatown

If you're in a major metropolitan center, the first and best place to head for Hong Kong goodies is your local Chinatown, where you can rent and sometimes buy just about every film you're likely to ever want. However, if you're not a fluent speaker and reader of Chinese, you may face a serious linguo-cultural barrier, not to mention some extremely stony expressions; Chinatown video stores rely on pencil-and-paper level technology, and if you don't know the Chinese name of a video, clerks will have no way of helping you, and little incentive to try. Luckily, most stores have binders filled with the covers of videos they carry. These will usually give a committed browser access by the point-and-gesticulate method.

The standard operating procedure for video membership is straightforward: Pay $100 in cash up front for anywhere from 50 to 100 rentals, receive a membership card, and pick out what you like. Usually, stores will let you take out up to seven videos for approximately one week at a time. Note that the English-subtitle law affects theatrically released works only, so television shows (generally distributed via TVB Video) carry no translation.

One warning: many small video stores are not above buying a single copy of a movie and duplicating it multiple times for their rental customers. This is just as illegal as if you bought a pirated copy by mail, but attempts at copyright enforcement have so far proven nearly impossible. If you rent a tape with a photocopied label, stuck on with yellowing glue, with picture quality verging on pointillism, you know that your store is flouting the law. Rent at your own risk. The only legal distributors of Hong Kong films on video in the United States are Tai Seng Video and a number of small, licensed Tai Seng representatives (most notably UE Enterprises)—so if a film is clean and Tai Seng labeled, you're probably safe.

IV. Your Local Video Hell

After years of sleepy ignorance, Blockbuster and other national video chains are finally beginning to stock contemporary Hong Kong product. Some of the older martial arts films (early Golden Harvest and Shaw Brothers works) have long been widely available; on the highend, Voyager's Criterion Collection has released John Woo's *The Killer* and *Hard-Boiled* in spiffy subbed-dubbed laserdisc versions with amazingly comprehensive liner notes. Meanwhile, the initiation of a bidding war on the works of Jackie Chan and Jet Li by indie giants Miramax and New Line Cinema will likely result in their eventual appearance in strip-mall venues. The catch: Virtually everything you find in chainstores is going to be dubbed into English. One saving grace for purists: Tai Seng, waking up to America's infatuation with Hong Kong cinema, has begun a push to get its subtitled goods on mainstream shelves as well.

HONG KONG ON FILM

I. Festival Fare

If you're in a college town or major metro, you're likely to see at least one blaring ad for a Hong Kong film fest every year, which may be your best chance to catch unadulterated works on the big screen. Rim Films, based in Los Angeles, is the primary distributor of films for these festivals, which draw sell-out crowds in Manhattan and Los Angeles every year.

II. The Downtown Double-Feature

What Chinatown residents know (and purist Hong Kong fans have learned) is that everything you can see "uptown" at artsy film festival venues has long since come and gone "downtown" at neighborhood Chinatown theaters. There isn't a better bargain around: Chinatown theaters offer two films for a ticket price of around $6, and the ambiance, while a far cry from the cappucino-scented environs of the art circuit, is authentic. If you don't mind uncomfortable seating and a distinct lack of popcorn, nachos, and surly ushers, try catching a downtown double-dip—you'll notice a healthy number of *gwailos* **[👁336]** in the seats around you, since people are beginning to catch on.

III. Your Local Cineplex

Expect a barrage of Hong Kong fare at your nearby cinema, as, over the next few years, Miramax and New Line release the films they've hoarded from masters like Jackie Chan and Jet Li. Lights! Camera! Action! —J.Y.

Movies Masala:
Bollywood and Indian Cinema

What's the film capital of the world? Some might point to the dream factory of Hollywood; others to the rip-roaring action machine of Hong Kong; still others to the austere stylists of Japan or the sophisticated auteurs of France.

Those who really know film will know that every single one of the above cinema centers pales in comparison to the prodigiously prolific film industry of Bombay, India dubbed "Bollywood" by its devoted fans and detractors alike. Bollywood's annual output is almost three times that of Hollywood; more than 800 works are churned out every year, producing revenues of more than $1 billion. Audiences pile into some 13,000 venues across India to watch them, and, unlike in most other film-watching countries, their numbers only continue to grow.

How does Bollywood do it? The answer's simple. First of all, Bollywood's films are cheap—most films are made for the equivalent of less than $2 million. Quality is not an integral concern, so long a film is completed and so long as one or more bankable stars can be attached to it. And somehow they do get completed, they get released, and they get seen—in spite of a barely functioning distribution system, unpredictable independent producers, even stars that sometimes end up in jail. If they're truly successful, they'll gross maybe $3 million—quite respectable, considering that the average Indian movie ticket costs a mere 65 cents.

The second staple of Bollywood success is hewing to a long-established formula, with little or no experimentation on the well-worn themes. The true Bollywood creation, which usually runs three hours long (luckily, there's usually an intermission, so you can excuse yourself to the john), contains everything, including half a dozen musical numbers, a "wet sari" scene (the closest you'll get to sex), romance, politics, family relations, and (of course) some gratuitous violence. Fans say, once you've seen one, you've seen them all. Which doesn't stop them from seeing them again and again—to the tune of hundreds of movies a year.

Even if the movie's a flop, investors and studios still have a very strong chance of making back their money. The musical portion of the film (absolutely critical to every Bollywood creation) is recorded on cassettes and sold nationwide. (The most famous singer of film songs, Lata Mangeshkar, is in the *Guinness Book of Records* for being the most-recorded individual in history.) Called *filmi,* Bollywood hits are constantly played on radio stations, until people on the streets are whistling and humming the tunes, and, of course, buying the albums. So soundtracks serve as Bollywood's insurance policy—something that's becoming increasingly true in Hollywood as well.

Meanwhile, Bollywood is supposedly going high tech. After watching dubbed versions of flashy Western blockbusters like *Jurassic Park* and *Speed* mesmerize audiences, Bollywood's Spielberg wannabes are setting up their own special-effects studios, with the help of Silicon Graphics, the California-based company whose equipment generates most of the eye-popping computer effects seen in Hollywood's recent summer sensations.

Indeed, the latest buzz is that, as capital and equipment floods into the industry, Bollywood may become the next hot center for advanced animation. India has long been known as a software-producing giant, an asset in a time when even Mickey Mouse is given motion via workstation. Until then, however, the lilting tones of filmi and the beckoning arms of the Bollywood hit continue to draw them in and get them dancing in the aisles.

While film snobs might not exactly understand its allure, Bollywood has already extended far beyond its borders; its films are a staple commodity for Indian communities throughout North America and Great Britain, where "Bollyhouses" have sprung up by the dozens.

And, while many of their patrons are die-hard fans, curious clientele of all ethnicities are beginning to smell their way to the samosas, found right next to the popcorn. —T.H. & J.Y.

A BOLLYWOOD CONSTELLATION

Note: Following the careers of Bollywood stars requires dedication; each works as many as 10 films at once.

Actresses

MADHURI DIXIT—Currently the unquestioned queen of Hindi film; her film Hum Aapke Hain Kaun is perhaps the century's biggest Indian cinema hit.

MANISHA KOIRALA—The second-biggest starlet in Bollywood. She's not above taking risks, either: Her hit film Bombay was banned in parts of india, as well as in many Muslim countries.

KARISHMA KAPOOR—The daughter of Randhir Kapoor and Babita, '60s and '70s heartthrobs, she is known for her dancing, and is often mentioned as Bollywood's number-three star, despite her relatively recent entry.

SRIDEVI—She earned the nickname "Miss Thunder Thighs" for her astounding, swivel-hipped dancing in scanty clothing.

POOJA BHATT—The daughter of well-known director Mahesh Bhatt, Pooja boasts a pleasant innocence and an alluring appearance. A rising star.

REKHA—The daughter of actress Gemini Ganeshan, she was the number-one leading lady in Bollywood in the '80s. She allegedly engaged in a scandalous love affair with frequent costar Amitabh Bachchan—despite his very married status.

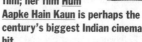

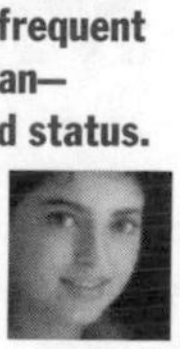

JUHI CHAWLA—Ubiquitous at the turn of the '80s; for a

while, she reportedly was able to bring success to a movie simply by appearing in it.

HEMA MALINI—This classic actress ruled Hindi film for over a decade, and initiated the first big B-wood scandal when she had an affair with (and then married) her frequent costar Dharmendra, despite knowing that he was already otherwise married. She remains one of Bollywood's most beloved icons.

Actors

AMITABH BACHCHAN—Often called "Mr. Bollywood," for over two decades Bachchan has ruled Hindi film. When he was accidentally injured during a film shoot, virtually the entire Indian population went into an anxious frenzy of prayer for his recovery. Though semi-retired today, he's still, for many, synonymous with the Indian film industry, and the very definition of a star.

SALMAN KHAN—Khan's debut, Maine Pyar Kiya, became one of Bollywood's top grossers of all time, in part because of Khan's good looks and fresh attitude.

ASHKAY KUMAR—Compared by some to John Travolta, Kumar is a phenomenal dancer, with dashingly handsome looks.

AAMIR KHAN—Khan's charm and charisma, not to mention his acting and dancing abilities, have made him one of Bollywood's most endearing leading men.

SHAHRUKH KHAN—One of three unrelated Khans in the Bollywood top echelon, Shahrukh is known for his portrayal of antiheroes, which he does with palpable passion and a broad emotional range.

Satyajit Ray: The Master of Indian Cinema

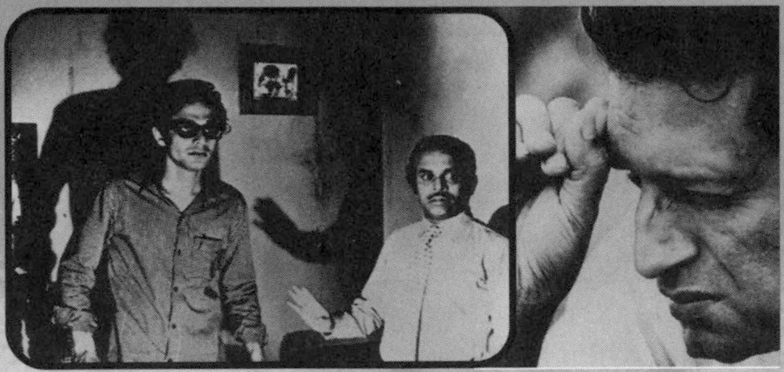

Born on May 2, 1921, into a high-caste Calcutta, India family, Ray died on April 23, 1992, at Belle Vue Hospital in Calcutta, leaving behind a legacy as India's premier filmmaker—and, indeed, as one of greatest filmmakers in the world.

The Ray family was artistic aristocracy, tracing back 15 generations of cultural contribution to Bengali society. Ray's grandfather, Upendra Kishore Ray, wrote children's books and founded the first Bengali children's magazine, *Sandesh*; Ray's father, Sukamar, was a photographer, writer, and painter, and his mother specialized in handicrafts. Upon the death of Ray's father when Ray was just three, he was raised in the home of a maternal uncle, an aficionado of both Eastern and Western music. Ray grew up on imported Hollywood films, loving the repartee and glamour of Fred Astaire and Ginger Rogers, but at first he gave little thought to pursuing a filmmaking career. After graduating with honors from the University of Calcutta, then studying painting for three years, Ray joined the Calcutta office of a British advertising agency in 1943. While on a business trip to London in 1950, Ray saw Vittoria de Sica's just-opened film, *The Bicycle Thief,* made primarily with non-professional actors and crew. Then and there, Ray decided he would make his first film, without the help of professionals; on the voyage back to India, he wrote the screen adaptation that would become his landmark first work. Upon returning to India, Ray met Jean Renoir, who at the time was filming *The River.* Ray helped Renoir scout locations while Renoir provided artistic and moral support to the filmmaker-in-the-making.

Ray's first film, *Pather Panchali* ("Song of the Open Road"), was based on a novel by Bhibuti Bashan Bannerjee that Ray had illustrated. It began in 1952 as a weekend project with a $3000 budget and an unpaid, unprofessional crew (except for one assistant and an 80-year-old actress, who required a daily pipe of opium). To keep the project going, Ray sold all his possessions and pawned his wife's jewelry. Eighteen months later, the film seemed doomed, until visiting American director John Huston saw a rough cut of the film, praising it so highly and publicly that the West Bengali government provided $35,000 for its completion sight unseen. (When it was finally finished in 1955, government officials were bewildered; they thought they had financed a travelogue.) *Pather Panchali,* which introduced young Apu and his childhood in rural Bengal, won a Grand Prix at the 1956 Cannes International Film Festival, eventually garnering more than 15 international awards. Today, the work is considered one of the finest films ever made.

After this spectacular debut, Ray continued the story of Apu in two more films, which became the legendary "Apu Trilogy." In spite of their status, for decades, watchable prints of the triptych were almost impossible to find—until recently, when a multi-million dollar restoration campaign finally resurrected Ray's brilliance for the big screen.

In 1968, Ray, clearly a filmmaker with an international reputation, made a trip to Hollywood during which time he approached numerous studios about a script, *The Alien,* about an extraterrestrial who lands in a small village and befriends a young Indian boy. Although the script was widely circulated, the film was never made.

Or was it? Imagine the surprise, 14 years later, when Ray saw the mega blockbuster *E.T.... The Alien* transported to California. Spielberg, of course, vehemently denies any connection, and even Ray, after voicing initial disgust with Hollywood, eventually claimed he was tired of the comparison. In any case, Ray ultimately received a kind of justice, when he was awarded an Oscar for Lifetime Achievement on March 16, 1992—three weeks before his death. —T.H.

The Chrysanthemum Camera:
Great Japanese Directors

It might be said that no Asian country has contributed more to world cinema than Japan, whose greatest talents have shaped the art in ways admired and envied by in the west. From the epic spectacle of Kurosawa to the pointillist intimacy of Ozu; the earthiness of Imamura, the romantic idealism of Mizoguchi, and the quirky flamboyance of Oshima—the visions of the great filmmakers of Japan have mesmerized audiences not only in their home country, but around the globe. —J.Y.

AKIRA KUROSAWA

Kurosawa was born in 1910, in Tokyo, the son of a gym teacher and former soldier whose family was of samurai stock. He was not the most pleasant child: by his own description, awkward and spoiled. Indeed, his nascent talents might

***Kurosawa's* Ran**

have never developed had he not been taken under the wing of a schoolteacher who encouraged him to pursue his interest in art, as well as introduced him to *kendo*— Japanese swordplay **[👁183]**. Kurosawa's childhood interest in the clash of blades was a harbinger of his future as the man who raised the samurai movie to high art. His cinematic career began in 1936, when he joined PCL Studios (later part of cinema giant Toho) as an assistant director, after several years of attempting to survive as an artist. In 1943, Kurosawa made his sure-handed directing debut with *Sanshiro Sugata*. It was in 1946, however, that Kurosawa met the man who would serve as his muse for nearly two decades: Toshiro Mifune **[👁107]**. With *Rashomon* (1951), which won an Academy Award—the first ever awarded to a Japanese film. Kurosawa and Mifune vaulted into the international spotlight; *Seven Samurai* (1954), *Yojimbo* (1961), and *Sanjuro* (1962), all starring Mifune, sealed Kurosawa's reputation. Their collaboration would last through 16 films, many of which are cited as among the greatest in cinema history. But Kurosawa's perfectionism and temperament finally proved to be too much for Mifune, as well as for Toho, leading to his firing from the studio. After his dismissal, he continued to produce works of brilliance, but his artistic vision clearly began drifting away from his audience. In 1968, Kurosawa left Japan to take his first and last taste of Hollywood, co-helming the epic World War II film *Tora! Tora! Tora!* for Fox, before being relieved of his duties by exasperated studio execs. He then returned to Japan to make his first color film, *Dodes'kaden* (1970), which proved to be such an enormous commercial failure that, a year later, Kurosawa attempted suicide. Despite having fallen out of favor in Japan, Kurosawa continued to be embraced by international audiences, and for each of his projects since he has relied on Western financing, filming *Dersu Uzala* with Soviet money in 1975, and enlisting Francis Ford Coppola and Steven Spielberg as producers for *Kagemusha* (1980) and *Dreams* (1990) respectively. Even his most celebrated recent work, his *King Lear* interpretation *Ran* (1985), was a coproduction between Toho and Serge Silberman Productions. All of which might indeed be proof of the adage that a prophet is not without honor except in his own country.

KENJI MIZOGUCHI

Mizoguchi was born in Tokyo in 1898, and showed as a young child a talent for art; as an teen, he studied painting, and then worked for several years as an advertising designer in Kobe. At the age of 21, a restless Mizoguchi returned to the city of his birth, where he became an actor and then a director for the Nikkatsu Motion Picture Company. Though his early work tended towards sentimentality, he made a stark breakthrough in 1936 with two films that portrayed female characters with unprecedented realism—*Osaka Elegy*, about a young phone operator taken advantage of by her manipulative supervisor, and *Sisters of the Gion,* which follows the divergent paths of two geisha, one a "modern" girl who climbs the social ladder, man by man, the other a "traditional" girl, hidebound by custom and social expectation. His subsequent output marked him as one of Japan's greatest visual stylists, and its greatest creator of female characters—strong, independent, suffering, tragic, but always rich, and always resonant. By the time he died of leukemia at the age of 58, his influence had extended well beyond Japan's borders, making him an inspiration to such Western filmmaking greats as Godard and Rivette.

NAGISA OSHIMA

Oshima was born in Kyoto in 1932, and was brought up by his mother, having lost his father at the tender age of six. He would later give his fatherless upbringing credit for his extraordinary character, and even added that he occasionally wished he'd been an orphan, since lack of parental protection would have made him an even *more* un-average individual. He attended Kyoto University, where he was active with the leftist movement, and joined Shochiku as an assistant editor upon graduating in 1954—less because of a calling than because he was unable to find a job elsewhere, in part due to his student activism. He soon was given the opportunity to direct, but ran afoul of his superiors politically and creatively, and left to form his own production company, Sozosha. His first independent film was entitled *The Catch* (1961), based on a short story by Kenzaburo Oe [👁**45**], about a black pilot captured and killed by Japanese villagers during the war. It was both commercially and critically successful, and as a result Oshima was able to easily find funding for additional projects. The work for which Oshima is best known—and perhaps infamous—is 1976's *In the Realm of the Senses,* a lush, sexually explicit portrayal of an obsessive relationship, notable for its shock ending and for the fact that the sex scenes performed for the film were real. Though it was shown widely in France and elsewhere in the West, it was blocked from release in Japan,

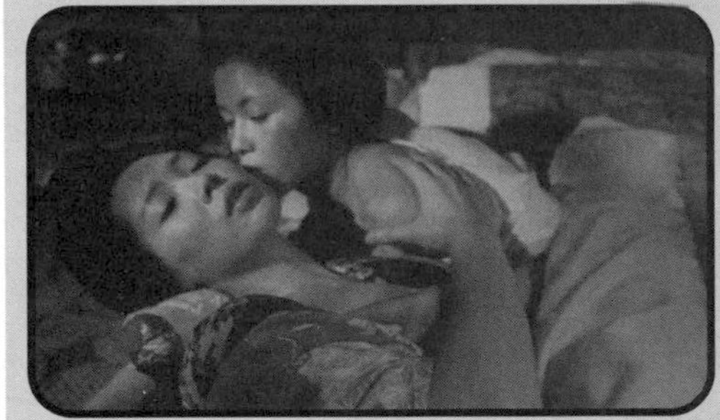

Oshima's **Empire of the Senses**

and Oshima was tried on charges of obscenity. Once again, Oshima would emerge victorious: His name was cleared, Senses received global acclaim, and its followup, *Empire of Passion,* won him the coveted best director prize at the 1978 festival at Cannes.

YASUHIRO OZU

Born in 1903, Ozu was a quiet boy, possessed of a wry sense of humor. He attended an all-male high school, but was expelled before graduation for sending a love letter to a fellow student (it's unclear whether the letter was serious, or a prank). He was hired in his early 20s by Shochiku, one of the four great studios of the time, and was quickly put to work as assistant to the director Tadamoto Okube. Ozu was offered opportunities to direct several times during his apprenticeship, before finally agreeing that he was ready to take the helm; similarly, although "talkies" became available in Japan in 1931, Ozu refused to indulge in the new technology for years, finding it an annoying distraction. With the onset of World War II, Ozu was called into military service, and spent time in a British P.O.W. camp, before returning home as one of the last Japanese prisoners to be repatriated. Upon his return, Ozu turned his attention to a genre with which he later became synonymous: the "home drama"—sentimental explorations of family relationships, often among the lower middle class. Ironically, the view of family that Ozu framed so poetically was entirely alien to him; his father had died in the mid '30s, and Ozu himself, a lifelong bachelor, lived alone with his mother for nearly his entire life. Still, no one was more observant when it came to family affairs. During Ozu's 36 year, 54-film career, he received widespread acclaim for such films as *Late Spring* (1949), in which a father, concerned about his daughter's future, tricks her into marrying, and *Tokyo Story* (1953), about an old couple's disappointing visit to the home of their children. Three decades after his death in 1963 of cancer, Ozu—who never felt that his work would find a broad audience—would be surprised to see himself enshrined as a filmmaker for the centuries. But most who've seen his work agree: far from being limited, Ozu is that rare artist able to transcend time, space, and the boundaries of culture.

SHOHEI IMAMURA

Perhaps more than any other Japanese director, Imamura has dedicated himself to depicting the regional culture of Japan—its rural fringes and isolated margins. He was born in 1926 in Tokyo, and grew up hearing stories of the countryside from a schoolteacher who declared his city-bred charges to be soft and pampered. Imamura's interest was piqued; after graduating from Waseda University, Imamura decided to pursue a career in film, hoping for the opportunity to explore the world outside of the urban confines

Imamura's **Black Rain**

in which he was raised. He found a job with Shochiku as Yasujiro Ozu's assistant, working on such films as *Tokyo Story*. Eventually, however, growing disgusted with what he saw as Ozu's excessive refinement and aesthetic remove, he left to work under Yuzo Kawashima—another cinematic pioneer, whose tastes and interests were more in line with his own. After writing the script for the enormously successful film *Bakamatsu Taiyoden* (1958), Imamura was given the opportunity to direct on his own, making an award-winning debut with *Endless Desire* (1958). He went on to create a rough and roiling world of peasants and rogues and outcasts—reserving a privileged place in his work for women, whom he saw as the "conscience" of Japan. Unlike the romantic heroines of Kenji Mizoguchi, however, Imamura's women are earthy, vigorous, and "true to life," as he has declared: The determined, ambitious protagonist of *The Insect Woman* (1964), or the lower-class housewife who triumphs over abusive men through sheer endurance in *Intentions of Murder* (1964). In the '70s, Imamura turned to television documentaries, indulging his early bent toward investigative anthropology. Returning to the feature screen in the early '80s, he received his greatest honor in a lifetime of accolades for *The Ballad of Narayama* (1983)—the Cannes Palme d'Or, which has been given to just one other Japanese director in history: Akira Kurosawa. Now in his seventies, Imamura has not made a film since his wrenching *Black Rain,* about a family of atom bomb survivors, or *hibakusha* [👁**320**], but continues to teach at the Tokyo Film Technical School, an institution he founded and still heads.

Takeshi Kitano

Most Americans have never heard of him, but the man called "Beat" Takeshi Kitano has been named the most admired man in Japan by readers of *Spy! Magazine* four years in a row. In a 1994 poll of the Japanese electorate, he was voted the man they most wanted to see as prime minister. And, in 1995, a rumor even circulated that Beat was, in fact, going to run in the Tokyo gubernatorial elections. (The rumor proved false, but it wasn't as absurd as it seems: The winning candidate, Yukio Aoshima, was another well-known comedian.)

Why should he bother with politics? Kitano is probably content ruling his vast entertainment empire: He writes, directs, edits, and stars in his own films; writes books (40 novels and essay collections to date) and newspaper columns; and at one point graced the tube in eight different prime-time slots each week. There's never been a star in Japan as big as Beat, and the Beat keeps getting bigger.

Takeshi Kitano was born January 18, 1947, in downtown Tokyo, the youngest of four children of Kikujiro and Saki Kitano. Though the Kitanos were working-class, they strived to give their children the best: When Takeshi was at the tender (and impressionable) age of nine, his family was the first on their street to purchase a television. It was through constant exposure to TV that Kitano developed his deadpan humor, as well as his passion for entertaining; though he attended college for three years, the wayward young Kitano dropped out before graduation, hoping to break into showbiz.

After working as a janitor and a coffeehouse waiter, Kitano got his big chance when he took a job as elevator boy in a strip joint. He and a friend, Kiyoshi Kaneko, put together a comedy routine, calling themselves the Two Beats; they convinced the manager to let them perform as the scantily clad femmes cavorted, and—oddly enough—patrons ate it up. In 1970, a talent scout caught the act and booked the team on a live variety show, where they had the studio audience rolling in the aisles. They continued to perform at local comedy venues, before being discovered by a producer for NHK, Japan's largest TV network, in 1974. The pair captured top honors at NHK's comic showcase, and were signed on to do a regular series, which proved to be a phenomenal hit.

But Kitano had eclipsed his buddy Kaneko; Japan soon forgot that there were two Beats, and the one and only Beat began his meteoric rise. He soon became well-nigh ubiquitous on television, while branching out as an author, pundit, and screenwriter.

In 1983, he made his international big-screen debut, playing a supporting role as a sadistic Japanese army officer in Nagisa Oshima's *Merry Christmas, Mr. Lawrence* (it costarred countryman Ryuichi Sakamoto [👁**278**] and British rocker David Bowie). The experience was somewhat frustrating for Kitano, used to running his own show; consequently, in 1989, he made his own bid for auteur glory, when the director of a policier he was cast in—the vividly titled *Violent Cop*—stepped down. Kitano rewrote the script to give it a bleakly nihilistic undertone, and, as the tough-as-nails Detective Azuma, did his best *Dirty Harry* tribute—beating confessions out of delinquent teenagers, and driving over thugs with a car.

Violent Cop achieved moderate popularity in Japan, but found its real audience abroad, where it became a cult hit in Europe. Kitano's equally raw followup *Boiling Point* broadened his appeal in the West. But it was *Sonatine* (1993), a quirky film about a disillusioned gangster who's been around the block one too many times, that framed Kitano as a director to take seriously: screened out of competition at the Cannes International Film Festival, it was acclaimed as a work of subdued brilliance, garnering accolades from, among others, Asian-cult-film-patron extraordinaire Quentin Tarantino, who has optioned *Sonatine* for release through his distribution deal with Miramax. It shouldn't be long before America, like Japan, gets in synch with the Beat. —K.L.

Overlooked Facts:

REPORT THIS!—When a freelance gossip reporter harassed a woman rumored to be Kitano's mistress, Kitano rounded up the 12 costars of his comedy show, the Takeshi Gundan, to beat a modicum of respect into the pathetic muckraker. Despite the flagrant nature of Kitano's offense, he served just a six-month abbreviated sentence, while a countersuit assigned the reporter a 10,000 yen fine. Far from being shocked at Kitano's behavior, his fans staged a boycott of all gossip magazines, sending their circulations plunging. The message was clear: Mess with Beat, get beaten.

BEAT DOWN—On August 2, 1994, a scooter accident left Beat "lying in a pool of blood from his brain on a street in Shinjuku, downtown Tokyo." The incident left half of his face paralyzed, thus keeping him off the airwaves for nearly a year. Fortunately for Beat-o-philes, he staged a full recovery, no worse (or less popular) for the wear.

AIIIEEEE! A Pantheon of Kung Fu's Classic Greats

KWAN TAK HING—The original Wong Fei Hung [👁100], Kwan was Hong Kong cinema's first real star, playing the master in a series of 99 successful films.

ALEXANDER FU SHENG—The Jimmy Dean of kung fu cinema, Fu was Jackie Chan's [👁80] predecessor as a comic martial artist, as well as a "serious" kung fu hero in films like Heroes Two and Disciples of Shaolin. Unfortunately, Fu's promising career was cut short by his tragic death in a car accident

JIMMY WANG YU—Wang, a former swimming champion, attained enormous popularity in his early The One-Armed Swordsman. This set him up for typecasting as a mono-limbed hero throughout his long career, in such films as Return of the One-Armed Swordsman, The One-Armed Boxer, and so on.

CHEN KUAN TAI—Originally a fireman who'd studied martial arts from the age of eight (mastering, among others, the Monkey style), Chen began with Shaw Brothers in the final film of the 99-piece Wong Fei Hung saga, entitled Bravely Crushing the Fire Formation. He became a Shaw contract player, and evolved into one of the studio's major stars.

GORDON LAU KAR FAI—The adopted brother of directing great Lau Kar Leung was one of the most popular Shaw contractees, toplining movies such as 36th Chamber of Shaolin, which transformed his bald-head-

Nine Deadly Venoms: Martial Arts Classics

Yes, Virginia, kung fu *did* exist before Bruce Lee. The following films are must-see cinema for anyone seeking to become literate in the genre of high-kicking flicks:

Vengeance (Chang Cheh, 1970)—This film marks the beginning of the juggernaut reign of Shaw Brothers, the studio that launched Hong Kong's modern cinema industry. Directed by Cheh, who would become Shaw's hallmark filmmaker, and starring David Chiang and Ti Lung, who would become the studio's most resilient stars, *Vengeance* is a grimly intense martial arts manifesto with Ti Lung as a Beijing Opera player forced into deadly serious combat.

The One-Armed Boxer

The One-Armed Boxer (Jimmy Wang Yu, 1970)—Written, directed, and starring Wang Yu, *Boxer*'s story contains all of the genre's now-classic elements: an insulted martial arts school, masochistic training, and bloody vengeance. However, in this film, after the hero loses his arm, the new technique ("the iron fist") requires killing the nerves in his *remaining* arm, and the final confrontation involves a tournament with Tibetan lamas, tae kwon do masters, a karate expert, twin Thai boxers, and an Indian yogi. Could you ask for anything more?

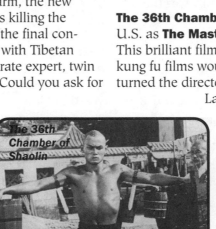

King Boxer (released in the U.S. as **Five Fingers of Death**; Cheng Chang-Ho, 1972)—While Bruce Lee's *The Big Boss* was the chop heard 'round the world for kung fu films on an international scale, it was *King Boxer* that turned the martial arts flick into a phenomenon here in the States. *Boxer* features Indonesian-born Lo Lieh as Chao Chih-Hao, a wandering martial artist with lightning-fast hands. Incorporating references to classic American Westerns—including 1953's *Shane*—*King Boxer* showed to American audiences that honor, guts, and quick-draw speed are a universal language.

The Five Venoms or **The Five Deadly Venoms** (Chang Cheh, 1978)—The ultimate "warrior team" film, this oddball work has a 15th-century martial arts master teaching five of his students the most murderous of martial arts stances (known as "the venoms"—Snake, Centipede, Lizard, Toad, and Scorpion) only to see them descend into evil behavior. The dying master tells his sixth student (who has learned a smidgen of each form) to halt their rampage—by any means necessary. After the smash susccess of this film, the five martial artists playing the Venoms went on to star in a dozen more movies together, in similar roles.

The 36th Chamber of Shaolin (released in the U.S. as **The Master Killer**; Lau Kar Leung, 1978)—This brilliant film set the mold which all other kung fu films would have to either fit or break. It turned the director's bald-headed adoptive brother, Lau Kar Fai, into an international superstar, playing a wimpy young scholar who transforms himself through 35 stages of intense and intricate Shaolin training into the temple's top fighter. Bearing a heart full of vengeance against the Ching Dynasty, whose troops have demolished his family and townspeople, Lau asks his masters for the right to build a 36th

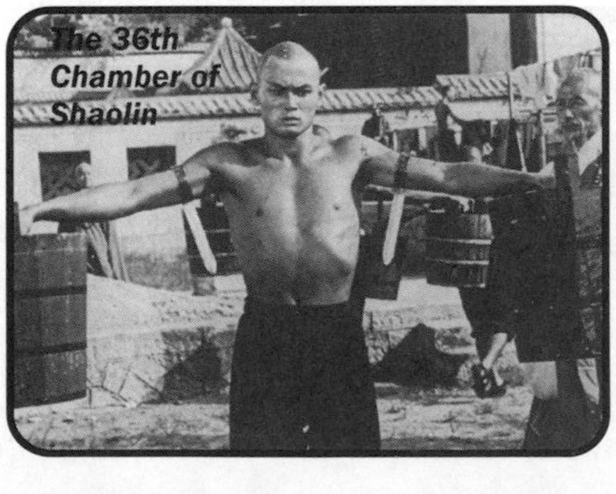
The 36th Chamber of Shaolin

school of Shaolin. After creating a new fighting weapon, the three-sectioned staff, he passes the temple's test of one-on-one combat and is given the rank of master. He travels to his home to enact bloody vengeance against the Manchus, then returns to the temple to open the secret 36th Chamber. Note that *Chamber*'s story is based loosely on the life of folk hero San Te, a Shaolin monk whose nobility, virtue, and fighting prowess has been much detailed in novels and on film. Like other "legendary heroes," whether or not he actually existed is debatable **[👁100]**.

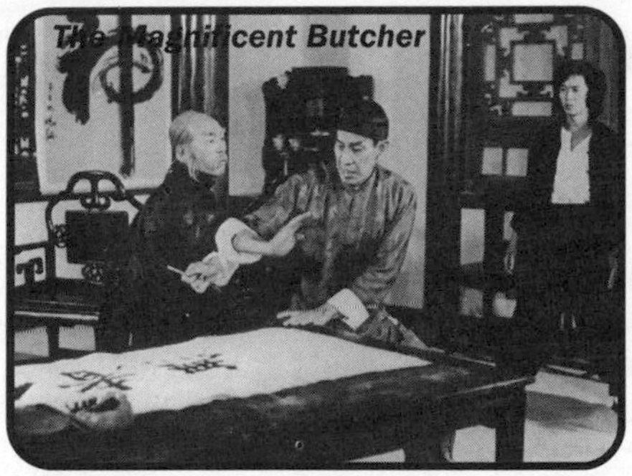
The Magnificent Butcher

The Magnificent Butcher (Yuen Woo Ping, 1979)—Perhaps the finest fighting moment for overweight hero Samo Hung, in this semi-comic postscript to the Wong Fei Hung legend, Hung plays Lam Sai Wing, one of the great master's best students. *Butcher* not only showcases the talents of the "Fat Dragon," it also features the return of Kwan Tak Hing to the screen as Wong—the role which he originated and made famous.

Legendary Weapons of China

Dirty Ho (Lau Kar Leung, 1979)—Lau Kar Fai, the most evocative of Shaw Brothers' stable of martial arts maestros, plays Imperial heir Wang Chin-Chin, a young, rather sheltered royal who befriends a garrulous thief and kung fu renegade named Ho Chih, played by *One-Armed Boxer*'s Jimmy Wang Yu. Blending comedy and spine-tingling action, Ho takes a Shakespearean plotline and makes it effortlessly Eastern and endlessly engaging. The tagline for the film's promotional posters is one of the most memorable in chopsocky history: "You haven't lived until you've fought Dirty Ho...and then you're dead!"

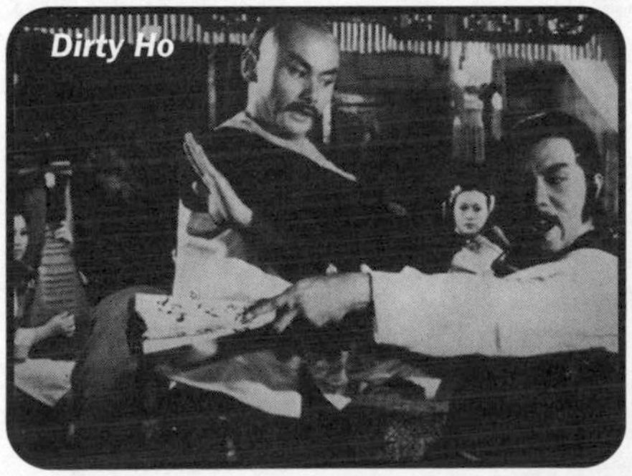
Dirty Ho

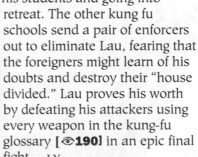

Shaolin Temple (Chang Hsin Yen, 1981)—Shot on location over three years in China using a cast of genuine martial artists, *Shaolin Temple* was the People's Republic of China's first kung fu movie. The epic revenge story features breathtaking photography and kung fu choreography, plus charismatic Jet Li in his debut role, as a young man who undergoes Shaolin training in order to kill the Sui soldiers who murdered his father. The epic on-screen results inspired so many students to leave school in search of training at the legendary temple that the Chinese government had to make an official announcement persuading them to do otherwise. Its massive success triggered a "Shaolin craze" during the '80s, and launched the career of then-18-year-old martial artist Li into the stratosphere.

Legendary Weapons of China (Lau Kar Leung, 1982)—A purist's kung fu masterpiece, *Legendary Weapons* is set in the fertile Boxer Rebellion period of China's history, when thousands of "boxer" sects were experimenting with mystic means to defeat the white foreign devils and their coward's weapon, the gun. The director himself plays an old monk who refuses to go along with the boxer madness, dispersing his students and going into retreat. The other kung fu schools send a pair of enforcers out to eliminate Lau, fearing that the foreigners might learn of his doubts and destroy their "house divided." Lau proves his worth by defeating his attackers using every weapon in the kung-fu glossary **[👁190]** in an epic final fight. —J.Y.

ed monk's cut into a signature look.

CHENG PEI PEI—Dancer turned actress Cheng rose to glory in Come Drink With Me, and then starred opposite Jimmy Wang Yu in Golden Swallow (also known as The Girl with the Thunderbolt Kick); the first major female kung fu star.

ANGELA MAO YING—The queen of kung fu cinema, Taiwan-born Mao began as a ballet dancer and Beijing Opera player and moved into films when that medium collapsed in popularity; she was contracted to Golden Harvest and made a huge number of films for that studio, including a role as Bruce Lee's sister in Enter the Dragon.

LILY LI—One of Shaw Brothers' top female stars, and perhaps their most durable, starring in dozens of films (including the great Executioners from Shaolin); she was eclipsed only by Golden Harvest's Angela Mao and Shaw's own Hung Wei-Yin.

KARINA HUNG WEI-YIN—Hung was leading a rather disreputable life as a dancer and (allegedly) a streetwalker before she was discovered by Lau Kar Leung; she became his favorite actress, and (after Angela Mao) one of the top female kung fu draws, in movies such as My Young Auntie.

DAVID CHIANG TAI-WEI—With Ti Lung (who would later star in John Woo's A Better Tomorrow [👁78]), Chiang was half of Shaw Brothers' deadliest duo, starring in dozens of movies, including the SB debut kung fu flick Vengeance.

Bruce Lee

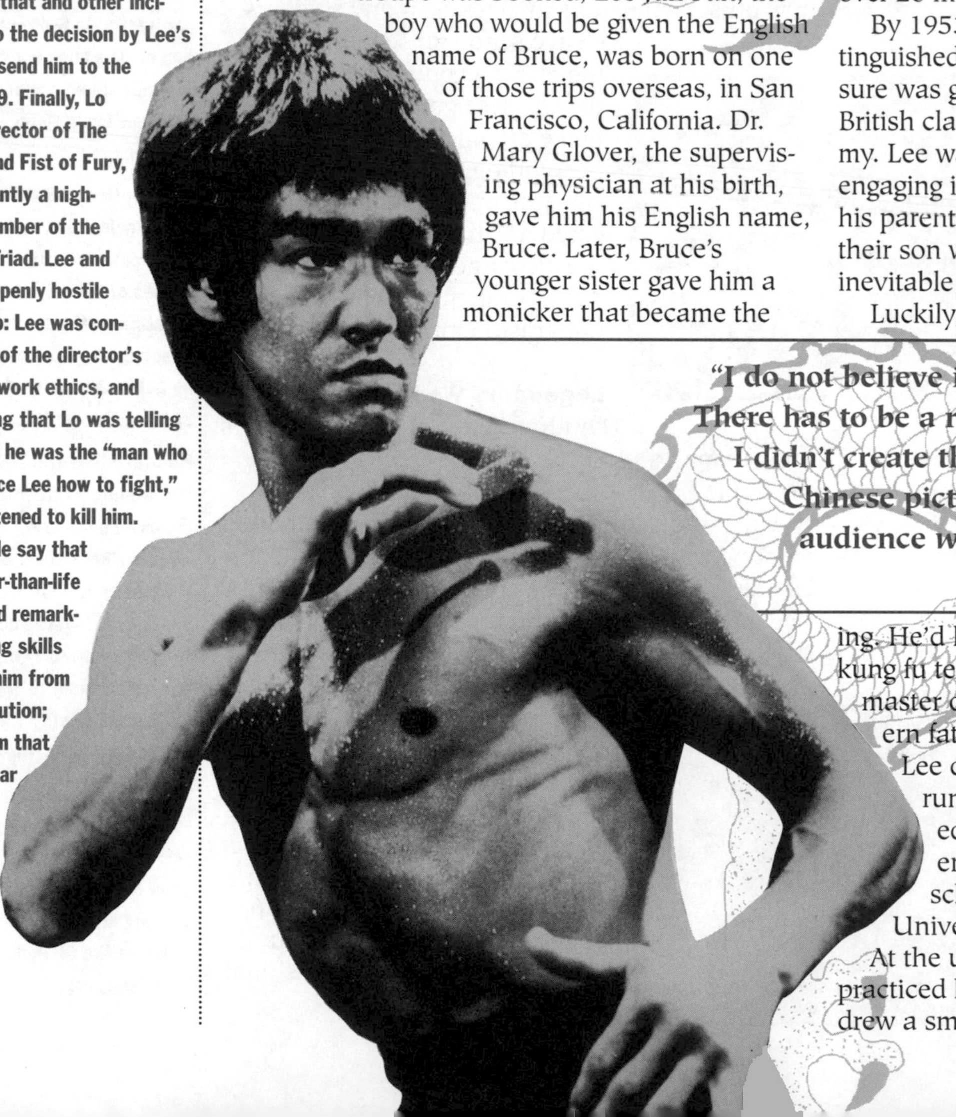

Overlooked Facts:

AN INCH IS ENOUGH—In the world of martial arts competition, Lee was widely famous for the "One-Inch Punch"—his ability to strike with such force from just one inch away that his opponent would fly backwards several feet.

TALES OF THE TRIADS—Lee apparently had his first run-in with triads in 1954, when he was still a juvenile delinquent in Hong Kong. While the confrontation was minor, that and other incidents led to the decision by Lee's parents to send him to the U.S. in 1959. Finally, Lo Wei, the director of The Big Boss and Fist of Fury, was apparently a high-ranking member of the Sun Yi On Triad. Lee and Lo had an openly hostile relationship: Lee was contemptuous of the director's ability and work ethics, and upon hearing that Lo was telling people that he was the "man who taught Bruce Lee how to fight," even threatened to kill him. Some people say that Lee's larger-than-life persona and remarkable fighting skills protected him from triad retribution; others claim that his death, far

Lee was born in November 27, 1940, the son of Lee Hoi Chuen, a well known comic actor and a member of the ensemble cast of the 99-episode Wong Fei Hung series that launched modern Hong Kong filmmaking. His mother, Grace, was a Shanghainese transplant to Hong Kong who had been raised a Catholic, and was the daughter of a German father and a Chinese mother. The Lees frequently traveled abroad from their home in Hong Kong, going wherever Hoi Chuen's opera troupe was booked; Lee Jun Fan, the boy who would be given the English name of Bruce, was born on one of those trips overseas, in San Francisco, California. Dr. Mary Glover, the supervising physician at his birth, gave him his English name, Bruce. Later, Bruce's younger sister gave him a monicker that became the name by which he conquered Asia, and then the world—Siu Long, or "Little Dragon."

Though Bruce was a sickly baby, he grew into a boisterous and mischievous toddler, and was nicknamed by his family "Mo Si Tun," or "never sits still." His self-assurance and spunk drew the notice of Hoi Chuen's filmmaking coworkers, and the young Bruce was soon cast in a series of films (he would eventually appear in over 20 movies as a child actor).

By 1953, when Lee was 14 years old, he'd distinguished himself as a boy whose primary pleasure was getting into fights—particularly with his British classmates at the prestigious LaSalle academy. Lee was eventually expelled from LaSalle after engaging in fisticuffs one too many times. In 1959, his parents sent him to California, hoping that their son would avoid what seemed like an inevitable descent into thuggery.

Luckily, Lee's fighting wasn't just street brawling. He'd learned the basics of Northern Shaolin kung fu techniques from an uncle, and became a master of Wing Chun under Yip Man, the modern father of that technique.

> **"I do not believe in blood for the sake of blood. There has to be a reason! Why do I start fighting? I didn't create this monster—all this blood in the Chinese pictures. Hopefully, I can show the audience *why* these things are happening."**
>
> **—Bruce Lee**

Lee didn't stay in San Francisco long; after running into some sort of trouble, he headed for the state of Washington, where he enrolled at the Edison High Technical school, and then was accepted into the University of Washington.

At the university, Lee studied philosophy and practiced kung fu in public; at one exhibition, he drew a small group of admiring street toughs, who

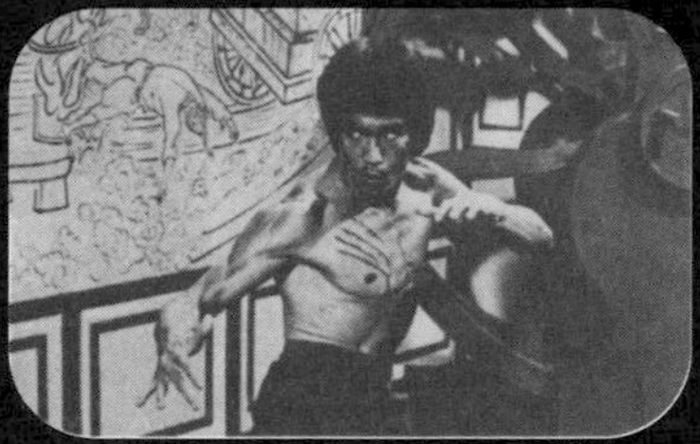

became his first students. He also met a 17-year-old girl named Linda Emery, who studied under him, then said yes when he asked her out on a date—a picnic outing at Seattle's Space Needle. At this time, Lee wrote his first book, entitled *Chinese Gung-Fu: The Philosophical Art of Self-Defense.*

Lee and Emery got married in 1964, moved to Oakland, and, at Emery's suggestion, opened up the first of Lee's kung fu academies. This blatant flouting of the unspoken rule—that the gwailo, or foreign devils, must never learn the secrets of kung fu, led to a challenge match from an opponent representing the traditional kung fu schools, which Lee won. During this fight, however, Lee realized that the traditional skills he had trained in were too formal for real-life combat; he resolved to create a new way of kung fu, based on Wing Chun **[👁188]**, that placed a precedent on speed, flexibility, and practicality.

To publicize his school, Lee began giving kung fu exhibitions at martial arts competitions. At one of them, Ed Parker's Invitationals in Long Beach, California, he was filmed by Jay Sebring, a Hollywood hairstylist who worked with the producer of TV's *Batman* superhero series, William Dozier. An impressed Sebring showed the film to Dozier, who auditioned Lee for a part in a pilot entitled *Number One Son*—an action-oriented spinoff of the *Charlie Chan* stories **[👁34]**. While that series never came to fruition, Dozier was convinced enough by Lee's abilities that he paid Bruce an $1800 retainer to not accept any other Hollywood offers, until Dozier's new project, *The Green Hornet,* would begin.

Lee, the new father of a son named Brandon, accepted the money, the deal, and the part. A year later, in 1966, Bruce debuted as Kato, crimefighter Britt Reid's driver and sidekick. While the show was not a success, Lee's outstanding action performances created an enormous fan audience for Bruce himself, and, upon *Hornet*'s cancellation at the end of that year, he sent out feelers about new projects that would put Lee—and kung fu—at the center of the spotlight.

Lee met with producer Fred Weintraub, and developed with him the idea of a show about a wandering Chinese loner in the old West, a man with a mysterious past who uses ancient wisdom—and kung fu—to protect the weak and punish evil. Unfortunately, TV executives doubted that a Chinese man could draw an audience base, and cast white actor David Carradine **[👁99]** in *Kung Fu,* in the role Lee had created for himself.

While the wound from this overt racism festered in Lee's soul, he decided to bide his time, doing cameos in television shows and movies, and continued to train students—including actors Steve McQueen and James Coburn, basketball player Kareem Abdul-Jabbar, and screenwriter Stirling Sillipant. He also began to develop the underlying concepts behind what he called "Jun Fan Kung Fu," or "Jeet Kune Do"—the "Way of Intercepting Fist" **[👁184]**. Jeet kune do emphasized fluidity in motion, and eliminated the traditional blocks and ripostes in favor of moves that simultaneously served as defense and attack.

But Bruce Lee—always yearning for greater heights of success—couldn't be satisfied with teaching classes and taking bit parts for long. Unfortunately, while his more influential showbiz students tried creating opportunities for their *sifu* ("teacher"), each of them ended as *Kung Fu* had—with Lee frustrated at Hollywood's inability to accept him as the star he knew he could become.

Only one road seemed open for the former child star: a return to his other home, Hong Kong. While *The Green Hornet* had drawn middling audiences in its U.S. run, in Hong Kong—where it was retitled *The Kato Show*—it had become amazingly popular. Lee hoped to use that lingering fame to

from being a tragic accident, was actually a triad assassination. The truth died with Lee.

Quirks:

BRUCE LEE...GIRLY-MAN?—Sickly as an infant, Lee—his parents' firstborn son—had his ear pierced and was dressed as a girl in order to fool evil spirits, under the assumption that said spirits wouldn't bother to harm a girl.

DANCING KING—Lee's remarkable agility was first demonstrated on the dancefloor, where he spent evenings and weekends at the Champagne nightclub in Hong Kong's glammy Tsimshatsui district, strutting the night away with dancing partner Pearl Cho. (Indeed, his moves were so graceful that he was crowned "Cha-Cha King of Hong Kong" at the young age of 18.) Lee's footwork would prove to be a useful commodity: Lee gave dancing lessons to his uncle, Siu Hon Sang, in exchange for instruction in kung fu techniques, and on his voyage to San Francisco in 1959, he taught shipmates the Cha Cha to earn pocket money.

FILMS OF THE DRAGON

THE BIG BOSS (Lo Wei, 1971, released in U.S. as Fists of Fury)—Lee plays a young man forced to leave his home because of constant brawling. After promising his parents that he will not fight, he travels to Bangkok and takes a job in an ice factory, which turns out to be a front for a drug operation; after Lee discovers its secret, the owners first seek to appease him, then kill him, but succeed only in slaying his friends. It's then that Lee throws off his vows and becomes the martial arts machine we know and love. NOTABLE MOMENT: Lee throws an evil minion through a wall, leaving a hole in the exact shape of a flailing man.

FIST OF FURY (Lo Wei, 1972, released in U.S. as The Chinese Connection)—Lee is a martial arts student whose teacher is killed by members of a rival Japanese school. Lee dons a series of disguises, smashes the murderous dojo, and then dies in a hail of Japanese bullets. NOTABLE MOMENT: Lee comes across a sign that states "No Dogs or Chinese Allowed." He smashes it with a single kick.

ENTER THE DRAGON (Robert Clouse, 1973)—Lee plays a government assassin who performs his mission with lethal efficiency, and simultaneously busts a drug ring and avenges his Shaolin ancestors. NOTABLE MOMENT: Trapped in a hall of mirrors, Lee smashes his reflections and finds the passage to the villain's inner sanctum.

launch his screen career overseas; contacting the dominant studio of the era, Shaw Brothers, he was offered the standard Shaw studio contract, which paid a pittance and demanded virtual indentured servitude. Lee laughed in Shaw's face, and took an offer more worth his time and self-opinion—a lucrative contract from Golden Harvest's Raymond Chow. Chow assigned Harvest's top director, Lo Wei, to their new property, and in October 1971 started shooting in Bangkok on the film that proved the Dragon's star power: *The Big Boss*. The film, a revenge thriller pitting Lee against evil druglords, cost just HK$100,000 (U.S. $14,000) to make—and grossed HK$3.2 million (U.S. $457,000) upon its Hong Kong release. An ecstatic Chow quickly put Lee and Lo into production on a second film, with double the earlier picture's budget. That film, *Fist of Fury*, was so phenomenally successful throughout Asia that its run was cut short in some countries to prevent the collapse of their native film industries. In Singapore, demand from eager viewers drove the price to see *Fist* from the standard $2 to over $45 a ticket. *Fist* earned HK$4.3 million (U.S. $633,000) domestically, making it the highest-grossing Hong Kong film ever; the cumulative gross from *Fist* and *Boss*, after their international release, was over HK$20 million (U.S. $2.86 million)—blockbuster numbers.

By this time, the tension between Lee and his director had mounted to a point where Lee refused to work under Lo; rejecting Lo and Chow's latest project, *Stern Faced Tiger*, he demanded instead to pursue a story of his own creation—written, produced, directed, and starring himself. Released under the banner of his own Concord Productions, his 1972 film *Way of the Dragon* was the story of a young, proud martial artist who struggles to find his way in a foreign land, defeats countless enemies (including a Lee student named Chuck Norris), and emerges victorious—to walk into the sunset alone. The only film that Lee wholly controlled, it was perhaps his most personal film. It was also his greatest domestic success, grossing HK$5.3 million, and setting the stage for his triumphant return to the land that had rejected him.

Fred Weintraub, the producer with whom Lee had developed *Kung Fu*, contacted Lee on the set of *Game of Death*, his followup to *Way*. He offered Lee the lead in a film entitled *Blood and Steel*, a cartoonish thriller set on an island ruled by a cruel druglord named Mr. Han. Lee would play an agent sent to infiltrate the villain's annual martial arts tourney, uncover the island's macabre secrets, and slay Han himself.

Lee accepted the role, on the condition that the film be made in collaboration with his company Concord. He stopped production on *Death* and flew to Los Angeles, where he tinkered with the script, written by Michael Allin, and renamed it *Enter the Dragon*.

Upon its release in 1973, *Dragon* set off Brucemania throughout America and around the world—eventually grossing over U.S. $150 million in multiple releases. Lee's dismantling of Han's minions with fist and nunchuck, his smashing of the druglord's room of mirrors, and his final condemnation of Han with the lethal line, "You have shamed my family and the Shaolin Temple," are all eternal moments in cinematic history. Meanwhile, the grim tournament that anchors *Dragon*'s storyline became a staple paradigm for martial arts movies—and martial arts video games—for time immemorial.

Dragon made Bruce Lee the most famous Asian star in the world. Lee's untimely death soon after—in strange circumstances, of unexplained causes, and at the tender age of 32—sealed his legend forever. —J.Y.

Fall of the Dragon

Lee was a man who inspired both great loyalty and hatred. When Lee was making *Enter the Dragon,* he decided to show off his skills in a sparring match with his much older counterpart, Shek Kin, who played the evil Mr. Han. At over 70 years of age, Shek was nowhere near Lee's match—and after admitting that Lee was superior, he issued a glowering warning to the young warrior: "Be careful, nephew! There are many hidden tigers in Hong Kong."

Some claim that the Dragon was the victim of Hong Kong's "hidden tigers"; others say he died at the hands of his own inner demons. Whatever the cause, when Lee was buried in Seattle's Lakeview Cemetary in 1973—wearing the Chinese fighting outfit he wore in Enter the Dragon—the rumors lived on. Was he slain by gangsters? By kung fu masters, using a secret delayed-reaction death touch? By evil spirits? By drugs, or overtraining? Is he, in fact, dead at all, or is he—like Elvis—merely biding his time for a return when the Dragon is needed once more? Judge for yourself: The following is a timeline of Bruce Lee's final hours, on the fateful day of July 20, 1973. —J.Y.

2 p.m.: Lee meets with Raymond Chow to discuss finishing Game of Death. Lee, at this point in his life, is far from his peak of physical prowess—he has lost weight, is engaging in obsessive training, and spending much of his free time carousing, drinking as many as 20 sakes per night. (Indeed, on May 10, Lee had actually gone into convulsions and lost consciousness while editing Enter the Dragon. Doctors diagnosed cerebral edema—swelling of the brain—and prescribed medication, but pronounced him fit for duty.)

4 p.m.: The two leave Lee's home together, driving to the apartment of Lee's mistress, Betty Ting Pei—a Taiwanese actress cast in a lead role in the film. The three sit and discuss the script.

7 p.m.: Chow departs from Ting Pei's home to attend a dinner meeting, and the couple is left to their own devices. They are expected to join him at the meeting later.

7:15 p.m.: Lee complains to Ting Pei that he has a headache. She brings him a tablet of a prescription painkiller, Equagesic, and a soft drink, which he consumes.

7:30 p.m.: Lee decides to take a nap. He lies down and falls asleep, missing Chow's telephone call. Chow asks Ting Pei why she and Lee haven't left yet for the dinner, and she attempts to wake Lee—unsuccessfully.

7:40 p.m.: Ting Pei anxiously tells Chow that she can't get Lee to wake up.

8 p.m.: Chow arrives at Ting Pei's apartment and also tries to wake Lee without success. They call a doctor.

8:15 p.m.: The doctor spends 10 minutes trying to revive Lee, then calls an ambulance. Before it arrives at Queen Elizabeth Hospital, Lee is dead. He is pronounced D.O.A. by doctors at the hospital, and his body is turned over to coroners.

There are no injuries on Lee's body or skull, but his brain has swollen from 1400 to 1575 grams in size; the only unusual substances found in Lee's body are the Equagesic and traces of cannabis, neither in a quantity large enough to cause harm. The hospital's clinical pathologist, Dr. R.R. Lycette, suggests that Lee died as a result of an allergic reaction to the Equagesic, which contains aspirin and a number of herbal ingredients. R.D. Teare, a professor of forensic medicine at the University of London, confirms Lycette's hypothesis; as a result, Lee's death is ultimately ruled a case of "misadventure."

Over 20,000 people attend Lee's memorial service in Hong Kong, many of whom are weeping uncontrollably. His body is flown out to Seattle, where he is interred in Lakeview Cemetary beneath a simple stone, decorated with an open book, an engraved yin-yang symbol, and the words "Your Inspiration Is Our Guide To Our Personal Liberation."

Lee's tragic and inexplicable death is a shock to all who know and love him, but is not, perhaps, a surprise to the dead man himself. "If I should die tomorrow," he was given to saying, "I will have no regrets. I did what I wanted to do. You can't expect more from life."

WAY OF THE DRAGON (Bruce Lee, 1972, released in U.S. as Return of the Dragon)—Lee plays Tang Lung, a young martial artist who moves to Rome to help relatives out with their Chinese restaurant. When gangsters attempt to extort money from his family, Lee teaches them a lesson. After defeating increasingly deadly thugs, Lee faces Chuck Norris in a climactic battle at the Roman Colisseum. Guess who wins? **NOTABLE MOMENT:** Lee grabs a handful of Norris's chest hair, looks at it, and blows it contemptuously off his palm.

GAME OF DEATH (Lee/Clouse, 1973/1978)—Lee only completed three fight scenes for Death, one with Daniel Inosanto, one with B-baller Kareem Abdul-Jabbar, and one with Chi Hon Joi. The original plot has Lee climbing a tower, defeating new and deadlier enemies on each floor. When Lee died before completing the film, Raymond Chow hired Enter the Dragon's director to finish it, in the process transforming its storyline. The ludicrous result purports to be a bio-drama about Lee himself, attempting to evade the designs of an evil theatrical agent-slash-crimelord. **NOTABLE MOMENT:** A Lee "double" (played by Kim Tai Chung [👁99) looks into a mirror as the camera moves in over his shoulder. To preserve the illusion that Chung is actually Lee, a photograph of Lee has been pasted on the mirror, where the stand-in's face should be.

Clones of the Dragon

True icons never die; like Elvis, they live on in the form of inferior—and sometimes absurd—imitations. Bruce Lee was no exception to the rule. After his untimely death, unscrupulous producers went into a frenzy attempting to invent a replacement; the result was a buffoonish lineup of Dragon wannabes, passed off to a naive public as the real deal resurrected. —J.Y.

David Carradine

David Carradine—After swiping the lead role of Kwai Caine in *Kung Fu,* the TV series Bruce helped to develop (and hoped to star in), Carradine realized he'd struck gold. He's since then made a career out of playing a pale version of the Dragon, releasing workout videos, books, and yes, a sequel to the original *Kung Fu* called *The Legend Continues.* Kwai Caine wasn't the only role Carradine stole from Bruce. A Stirling Silliphant film titled *The Silent Flute*, originally starring Bruce and James Coburn, was finally made in 1987—starring Carradine. According to Carradine, a staunch believer in his own hype, it only stands to reason. After all, he says, "when Bruce died, his spirit went into me. I'm possessed."

Dragon Lee

Dragon Lee—Another Korean martial artist, with a dim resemblance to Bruce; one of the most prolific Lee-clones.

Bruce Le (Huang Kin Lung)—The star of *Bruce the King of Kung Fu* was a credible fighter but didn't look like Lee facially or physically; moreover, he acted about as well as a wooden training dummy. He, too, eventually dumped his phony name and attempted to launch a career under his own name, and ended up doing stuntwork on Golden Harvest's later *Teenage Mutant Ninja Turtle films*.

Bruce Li (Ho Tsung Tao)—A Taiwanese actor who bore a moderate resemblance to Lee, Ho was a decent actor who, after making such exploitation titles as *Bruce Lee Superdragon* and *Fist of Fury 2*, dumped the "Bruce Li" moniker and tried to go it on his own. Since you've never heard of him, you can guess how successful that idea was.

Bruce Liang (Dorian Tan Tao Liang)—A stylist known best for his kicks, Tan actually starred in a number of decent films, including John Woo's debut, *Hand of Death*. Like other wanna-Lees, however, getting sucked into the Bruce-clone game marred what would otherwise have been a fine if undistinguished career. (Note: he didn't look anything like Lee either.)

Bruce Li

Tang Lung (Kim Tai Chung)—This clone wasn't even Chinese! Kim, a Korean martial artist, was brought in to double for Lee after his untimely demise, finishing off Lee's incomplete last film, *Game of Death,* as well as the equally terrible jigsaw-puzzle sequel, *Game of Death 2.*

Bolo Yeung—The broad-shouldered, thuggish Yeung (he was a former Mr. Hong Kong) has made a name for himself playing nemeses to some of the top names in American martial-arts action. He played a Bruce-oid in the terrible *Bruce's Fingers* and other films, but notably also played the traitorous opponent who breaks Bruce's back in the biopic *Dragon: The Bruce Lee Story.* Yeung has stated that his goal is to someday make a sequel to *Enter the Dragon*, starring himself in the role made famous by Lee.

Bolo Yeung

Live, On Screen:
The Legendary Heroes of Kung Fu!

On screen, they perform dazzling stunts of martial prowess; their foes quake at the very sound of their names. These are Hong Kong's traditional heroes, whose deeds have transcended history to become legend. But were they men—or myth? —J.Y.

Name	Cinematic Portrayal	Historical Reality
Wong Fei Hung	On film, Wong Fei Hung is portrayed as an incomparable fighter and a man of great pride and honor, whose two secret weapons are "Drunken Style" fighting and the "No-Shadow Kick," an impressive, flying multiple-kick. He's a champion at combat Lion Dancing, and is in love with his young Aunt Yee. As played by Jet Li: *Once Upon a Time in China 1-5, Last Hero in China*; as played by Jackie Chan: *Drunken Master 1* and *2*; as a very young boy, encountering an earlier "legendary hero" played by Donnie Yen: *Iron Monkey*; as an older, wiser man, as played by early star Kwan Tak-Hing: *The Skyhawk*, *The Magnificent Butcher*, *Dreadnaught,* 99 serial films.	Born in Guangdong in 1847, Wong was the son of a another famous martial artist, Wong Kei Ying–one of the ten "Tigers of Guangdong." Wong honed his Hung Gar skills at the feet of his father's teacher, then founded an academy that was unsurpassed in martial arts competitions,. He was also an herbalist who tended to the ill and a fighter who defended the weak. However, the character of Aunt Yee (Wong's love interest) is fictional, and there's no record of Wong having been a master of the "Eight Drunken Gods" style of kung fu. And as for the No-Shadow Kick, it's shown on-screen as in reality, it's a kind of feint-kick which uses the arms to divert attention from a solid leg blow–wires not included, or necessary.
Fong Sai Yuk	In contrast to the stately Wong Fei Hung, Fong–China's most formidable mama's boy–is portrayed as a young, arrogant hero with a brash sense of his own abilities and a gleeful lust for street brawling. The novelty of Fong is that he learned his considerable martial skills (as well as his feisty temperament) from his mother–with the result that Fong's cinematic adventures are a uniquely humorous exploration of the bond between a mom and her son. As portrayed by Jet Li: *The Legend of Fong Sai Yuk 1 & 2*. As portrayed by Alexander Fu Sheng and Jimmy Wang Yu: numerous Shaw Brothers' films. Portrayed by Leslie Cheung:in a popular television series..	Another of Guangdong's fighting legends, Fong's training at his mother's knee made him a kung fu adept at a very young age–so good, in fact, that he was challenged to a deathmatch by a master at age 14. He won. His exploits as a freedom fighter against the Manchu and as a freelance defender of the oppressed made him famous, but it was his quick-trigger temper and readiness to fight that sealed his fate in the storybooks. Like the duellists of the American West, he made his name and lost his life while he was still a very young man–dying in action in his early twenties.
Wing Chun	As portrayed in the eponymous film, Wing Chun is the daughter of a tofu seller, who has been trained by a mysterious mountain recluse in the acrobatic techniques of a new form of kung fu. Given to dressing in man's clothing and acting very much the tomboy, Wing Chun eventually discovers the "true secret" of the technique that would bear her name after giving in to her "soft," feminine side. As portrayed by Michelle Khan: *Wing Chun*	The intricate training techniques of the Shaolin Temple were far too slow and obvious for the training of a revolutionary army under the watchful Manchu eye, and so five great kung fu masters met to design a new form, focusing on efficiency and ease of learning. The Ching learned of their conspiracy, torched the temple, and sent the masters fleeing. One of them, a nun named Ng Mui, escaped to the White Crane temple on Tai Leung mountain, where she met and trained the woman who would become Wing Chun. **[👁188]**

Kung Fu Theatre

Who says white men can't chop? With a guttural screech and a thump of a hairy chest, the following six masters proved that you don't have to be a son of the Shaolin Temple to register your hands and feet as deadly weapons. —H.L.

	Steven Seagal	Jean-Claude Van Damme	Chuck Norris	Don "The Dragon" Wilson	Marc Dacascos	Brandon Lee
Style	Bits of Aikido, plus guns when things start looking bad	Karate	Karate (though he was also a student of Bruce Lee)	Kickboxing	Kung fu; capoeira, at least in the movies (*Only the Strong*)	Dad's Jeet Kune Do, similar to Wing Chun kung fu
Disposition	Provokes violence in a freakishly calm manner; bullies opponents.	Romantic: the self-proclaimed "Muscles from Brussels" wants to prove that he's a master of the martial arts—and amoré!	The archetypal reluctant but capable American; shows less restraint in third world countries.	Strangely hates killing for one so good at it. However, once angered, his characters become relentless killing machines.	He's got more soul then Zen. Marc's little secret—happiness and dancing, not meditation, are a hit with the kids.	Somewhat morose, in keeping, perhaps, with his ultimate fate.
Acting ability	His characters are basically Seagal, but wearing different clothing. Unfortunately, Seagal is only adequate at playing himself.	Because he is not yet hooked on phonics, most appropriate role would be the world's deadliest mime. Van Damme would teach his sad mime lesson of existentialism—the hard way!	Starred in comedy with furry canine sidekick (*Top Dog*); make your own conclusions.	Acting skills negligible, which is not a problem, since none of Don's 25 *Bloodfist* movies were, in fact, penned by Shakespeare.	Similar to Van Damme, only with rhythm and good English.	Deep, action-as-art-film line readings—emoted with the deadpan brilliance of master thespian Keanu Reeves.
Best known for...	Putting opponents in wrist and arm locks; humiliating remarks before and after each attack.	Leg splits that emphasize the near-perfect spherical shape of his buttocks.	None. He might consider joining the World Wrestling Federation, where all wrestlers are awarded a signature maneuver of their very own.	A furrowing of his hawk-wing eyebrows—not unlike Bruce Lee, whose title Don also shamelessly borrows.	Handstand kicks to opponents' heads with his bare feet.	Being Bruce Lee's son, and dying young and tragically in a horrible accident during the shooting of *The Crow.*
Qi level (Potency of "Inner strength," on a scale from 1 to 10)	**4.** Mysteriously wrinkle-and-stain-proof black outfits might be evidence of high qi, but points must be deducted for his ponytail and ballooning physique.	**4.** With ludicrous movie promo lines such as, "So Van Damme good!" he drops down a couple of qi points.	**3.** "The Best Way to Defend is not to Offend..." or so his Right Guard deodorant commercial went. Chuck has given himself away. People with a lot of qi don't smell.	**2.** Having made *Bloodfist One, Two, Three, Four, Five, Six,* and possibly *Seven,* this lack of imagination almost certainly is an indication of low qi.	**1.** So far, the cumulative box-office of his films could be exceeded by a festival of driving instructional films. This seems to be evidence of subpar qi.	**4.** His qi is mostly inherited, and he died young without ever getting the chance to use it. Still, he deserves a higher qi rating than Chuck Norris.

Mainland Chinese Cinema

There's a saying about prophets going without honor in their own country, and another about cutting off one's nose to spite one's face. Where Mainland China's film industry is concerned, both sayings are appropriate. It's an oft-mentioned irony that the Mainland's greatest films are screened and revered everywhere but in their nation of origin, and that the filmmakers of China's Fifth Generation have been crassly repressed for the very acts of penetrating creativity which make their work brilliant.

***Chen Kaige's* Yellow Earth**

Then again, would the subtle, politically charged art of directors like Zhang Yimou, Chen Kaige, and Tian Zhuangzhuang have been possible in a more open (and commercially anarchic) environment like Hong Kong? Probably not.

GENERATION FIVE

The story of contemporary Mainland cinema begins with the rehabilitation of Deng Xiaoping, who had been purged during the Cultural Revolution. In 1977, Deng became part of a ruling tribunal, and initiated a wave of social, political, and cultural reforms—one of which was the reopening of the Beijing Film Academy, shuttered in 1966 as a decadent influence. Among the members of the first new class to enroll—the Class of '82—were a former Red Guard, the bourgeois son of a former studio head, and a textile factory janitor: Chen Kaige, Tian Zhuangzhuang, and Zhang Yimou.

"I'm not sure who the first four generations were, but Chinese like everything to have a number," says Zhang. "Actually, I don't think all of us in the 'Fifth Generation' have that much in common. Our styles are very different. We like different subjects....The only similarity I see is that we're all innately rebellious."

Rebellious or not, upon finishing their academy training, the '82 grads were sent to a backwater locale, the Guangxi Film Studio, where they were assigned to be assistants. Unfortunately, the Cultural Revolution had essentially demolished the ranks of experienced directors, which meant that there was no one around for the apprentices to assist. They petitioned to form their own directing collective, and became known as the "Youth Team." In 1983, the Youth Team's Zhang Junzhao directed *One and Eight,* with Zhang Yimou manning the camera, and followed it a year later with Chen Kaige's phenomenal *Yellow Earth*—also filmed by Zhang.

It was *Yellow Earth* that gave the West notice of the Fifth Generation's arrival. Debuting at the Hong Kong Film Festival in 1985, it put the team of Chen and Zhang at the forefront of world cinema. When Zhang took the director's chair in 1988 with *Red Sorghum*, winning the Golden Bear at the Berlin International Film Festival, he established the Fifth Gen as a commercial success as well: the first pairing of Zhang and his muse/lover Gong Li was a tremendous success both in Asia and abroad, in one fell swoop creating China's first star director and first star *star.* But in the belly of the Beijing beast, a thunder was beginning to rumble.

CRACKDOWN

Even as *Sorghum* was establishing Zhang's global stature, China was undergoing a radical shift to the right, as Deng suppressed outspoken academics and "rabblerousers," purged reform-minded leaders, and restricted political freedoms. In 1989, Zhang released his masterpiece, *Ju Dou,* to unprecedented international critical and commer-

THE BOYS OF THE BANNED China's Record of Cinematic Crackdown

The following are some of the films by Fifth Generation filmmakers that China has banned or "withdrawn" due to their political incorrectness.

Chen Kaige

YELLOW EARTH (1984)—Set in 1939 in China's rural north, Earth is a visually stunning portrayal of a girl's resistance to the tradition of arranged marriage. While the film seems to toe the Marxist line, it was criticized for allegedly exposing China's backwardness. BANNED, THEN RELEASED.

LIFE ON A STRING (1991)—A blind musician in the last years

of his life reveals a stunning secret to his (also blind) apprentice: Within his instrument is the formula to a medicine that can restore lost sight—but the instrument will only open if the young man remains devoted to his master until the sanxian breaks its thousandth string. The New York Times, among others, suggested that the film's patriarch was a coded depiction of Mao Zedong, though Chen vigorously denied any political references. EFFECTIVELY BANNED.

FAREWELL MY CONCUBINE (1994)—Adapted from Hong Kong author Lilian Lee's potboiler, Farewell's epic scope covers more than half a century as it tracks the evolving relationship between two male Beijing Opera stars from childhood, through adult stardom, and then separation and betrayal. Concubine's frank depiction of homosexuality (officially "nonexistent" in China), as well as its portrayal of the grotesque abuses of the

Cultural Revolution made the film a particularly hot potato. BANNED, THEN (DUE TO WORLD OPINION) RELEASED...AFTER BEING CENSORED.

Zhang Yimou

JU DOU (1989)—An elaboration upon the themes Zhang raised in Red Sorghum, Ju Dou features Gong Li once again as a young woman married against her will, to an abusive and impotent dye-shop owner. Ju Dou falls for her husband's nephew, gives birth to her lover's baby, and then plots to end her husband's life—only to sow the seeds of a terrible and ironic fate. Zhang's combination of coded gibes and allegorical referents—the crippled tyrant in his swaths of flowing red—were more than enough to cause officials to choke the film, upon seeing it. BANNED INSTANTLY ON RELEASE; GIVEN APPROVAL FOR SCREENING—TWO YEARS LATER.

cial success. But its subtle antigovernment subtext—in one scene, the titular heroine smashes a small vase, a "*xiao ping*," against a wall—soon led official censors to declare it anathema, banning its domestic release and later attempting to rescind its nomination for a Best Foreign Film Academy Award.

Zhang Yimou's Ju Dou

Then, on June 4 came an act of repression that transfixed the world: the massacre at Tiananmen Square. The rolling of tanks through the Gate of Heavenly Peace was a horrific, overt expression of the rolling back of China's short-lived progressive era. The guideline of *zhu xuan ying pian*—that filmmaking should cater to ideology—became the rule of the land once more.

"'In the process of making a film," notes Tian Zhuangzhuang, who was at one point banned from making films in China, "you write a script and submit it to the Film Bureau, and the Film Bureau submits it to the Radio, TV, and Film Bureau at a higher government level. If they agree with the script, then you can go ahead with shooting the film. If they don't like the script they will make suggestions, and they want you to rewrite. If you don't rewrite, then you don't make the film."

MAINLAND MOVIEMAKING TODAY

The question that may come to mind is, why would China's film studios allow mavericks like the Fifth Generation to make films at all? Wouldn't it be easier to simply return the industry to its earlier propagandist roots? The answer is simple: Even under socialism, money talks. Virtually every big-name Mainland film is a foreign coproduction, with a budget largely or wholly underwritten by Hong Kong, Taiwan, or other investors. (In 1993, 56 of the 151 films made on the mainland were joint-produced with Hong Kong or Taiwan companies, and 81 were produced "privately"—usually with some sort of foreign investment. Just 14 were made solely within China's studio system.)

In these ventures, the Chinese Ministry of Radio, Film, and Television provides nothing more than facilities, locations, and, of course, a cast and crew. Movies have thus become an important source of hard currency for China's economy—and, though it means that ownership of such films is in the hands of foreigners, this can actually be politically expedient, if the film contains problematic content.

Of course, China doesn't make the coproduction process easy. All films must have their scripts preapproved by censors at the studio and the Ministry level; as of February 1994, the Ministry mandated that films shot in China must also go through postproduction in China, which gives the Ministry yet another measure of control over the process, and gives producers headaches—since Chinese editing and film development technology can be decades behind that available in Hong Kong, Taiwan, or abroad.

What keeps foreign producers coming back is the extremely low cost of shooting on the Mainland. A lush feature like *Raise the Red Lantern* might cost in excess of $30 million if lensed in the U.S.; due to low labor costs and other savings, the same film can be made in China for one-tenth the budget. And, due to the international prominence of filmmakers of the Fifth Generation, coproducers can usually recoup their costs with sales in the U.S. and Europe alone, garnering substantial profits in Asia.

The great audience frontier, of course, is the Mainland itself, with its billions of potential filmgoers. Unfortunately, the same inefficiencies that balk film production turn film distribution there into a nightmare. While ticket prices have risen substantially—from about 12 cents to between 60 cents and $3—little money from domestic box office sales ends up in the hands of producers. "[*Farewell My Concubine*] made almost $30 million at the box office in China, but we only got back about $116,000," says producer Hsu Feng. "Making money from distribution in China is impossible under the current system."

MAIN MEN (AND WOMAN): THE MAINLAND'S TOP DRAWS

The following four individuals—three directors and one actress—have been the public face of Fifth Generation Chinese film to the West.

Zhang Yimou

Zhang was born in 1950, in the northern city of Xian. In a time when parentage was all-important, Zhang had the misfortune to be the child of an officer in the Nationalist Army and a medical doctor, making him and his family politically suspect. Of his siblings, one brother was forced to flee to Taiwan (where the KMT had taken power) and another was accused of espionage. In 1966, when Zhang was just entering his prime teen years, the Cultural Revolution thundered through China, crushing those whose class background was inappropriate or problematic. Zhang was taken out of school and sent into a "work reform" program, where he spent more than a decade in menial labor, first on a farm and then at a textile mill. Still, Zhang was unbowed by his hard luck. After purchasing a camera (selling blood to pay for it), Zhang began snapping pictures, publishing his work in the province's *Shaanxi Daily,* and gaining a small amount of fame as a photographer. Eleven years after Zhang's removal from school, Deng Xiaoping returned to power and began a program of reform. Zhang saw the reopening of the Beijing Film Academy as his opportunity to escape his heretofore lousy life; after passing the entrance exam and convincing the administration to admit him despite his advanced years, Zhang became a member of the Beijing Academy's first post-Revolution class—the class of 1982, which would produce China's greatest modern filmmakers, the "Fifth Generation."

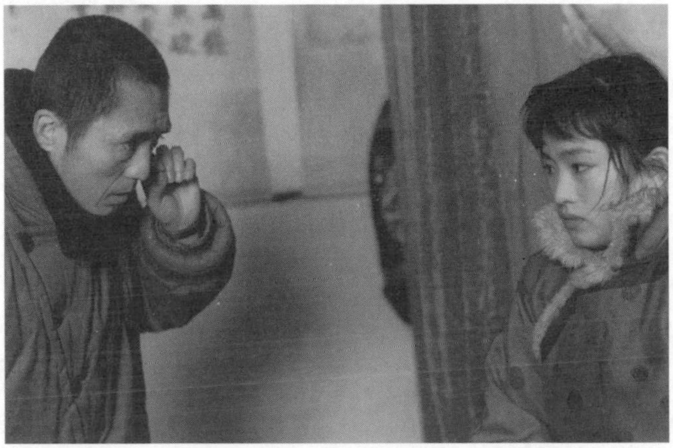

***Zhang Yimou directs Gong Li in* Raise the Red Lantern**

Because of his photographic experience, Zhang was put into the cinematography program rather than the directorial track he preferred. Upon graduation, Zhang and three other 1982 grads were sent to Guangxi's small film studio, where they convinced the studio head to let them work on their own project—the drama *One and Eight.*

The second project of the so-called "Youth Team," *Yellow Earth,* catapulted its director Chen Kaige and its cinematographer—Zhang—into the international spotlight. After shooting two more well-received films for other directors (Chen's *The Big Parade* and Wu Tianming's *Old Well*), Zhang finally got permission to direct his own film—*Red Sorghum,* the film that made his star go supernova. Of perhaps equal import: In casting *Sorghum*'s female lead, Zhang put aside the list of established actresses and instead went straight to Beijing's Central Drama Academy, where he discovered a fresh-faced, remarkable young actress named Gong Li. Li and Zhang became an inseparable pair in the movies and in life, despite the initial refusal of Zhang's wife Xiao Hua to grant him a divorce. Zhang's international recognition and acclaim expanded with each film that he did, as did his problems with the Chinese government. Each time he stepped over the line, however, he managed to accrue enough foreign support to prevent a too-rash reaction by the Chinese government. In short, despite frequent official sanctions, Zhang seemed untouchable, the golden boy of Chinese cinema. Then, in 1995, his relationship with his golden girl abruptly ended, as Gong Li took up with a Singaporean businessman (whom she later married). Since then, the two have talked about collaborating again, but their days as the First Couple of Chinese cinema are clearly over.

Gong Li

Li was born in Shenyang in 1966, the daughter of

RAISE THE RED LANTERN (1991)—Set in the same time-frame as <u>Ju Dou, Lantern</u> fea-

tures Li as yet another unwilling wife—this time to a patriarch who has three other concubines. The four wives are called for in turn by the sign of the red lantern, raised at the house of the one who has most recently struck his fancy; the slow, poisonous rivalry that has existed between the three older women explodes upon the arrival of the young, beautiful Li. Once again, tragedy ensues. Reviewers suggested that, once again, an allegory was being raised for communism and its establishment of strict hierarchy; however, the official reason for government enmity with the film was a scene in which Li is given a foot massage—whether due to implicit eroticism or other reason is unclear. BANNED UPON COMPLETION; APPROVED FOR RELEASE YEARS LATER.

TO LIVE (1994)—An epic, decades-spanning work that

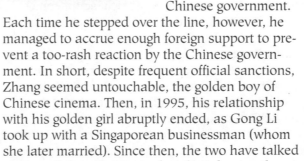

examines the effects of history on the individual. A wealthy city-

dweller succumbs to his gambling addiction, then rides the rollercoaster of modern China through the Great Leap Forward, the Cultural Revolution, and more. To Live's raw portrayal of China's corruption and incompetency, almost a direct indictment of communism, was not withstandable. BANNED; ZHANG FORBIDDEN TO WORK ON FOREIGN COPRODUCTIONS FOR FIVE YEARS, THOUGH THE SANCTION IS LATER WITHDRAWN.

Tian Zhuangzhuang

ON THE HUNTING GROUND (1983)—Tian's first feature film, an exploration of life amongst the horseclans of the Mongol grasslands, opens with nearly a quarter hour of animal killings, and centers on an ethnic minority that China would rather forget about entirely, Hunting Ground was officially offensive in both form and content. ONLY TWO PRINTS ARE EVER STRUCK OFF OF TIAN'S MASTER, MAKING IT EFFECTIVELY IMPOSSIBLE TO DISTRIBUTE.

THE HORSE THIEF (1987)—Breathtaking cinematography enlivens this 1920s reverie of a young, Tibetan tribal family; the

father, Norbu, is a model Buddhist, husband, father, and citizen by day—and a horse thief by night. When Norbu's deeds are exposed, he and his family are exiled from the tribe, endur-

academics; both of her parents were economics professors at a local university. Since she was much younger than her siblings—she was born when her parents were advanced in years—she was often left to her own devices. Li forsook her parents' hopes that she would follow in their footsteps to enroll in the nation's oldest drama academy. There, in just her second year as a student, she met Zhang Yimou, and began her most significant creative—and intimate—relationship.

"I happened not to be on hand when he arrived," she says. "I was working in a TV drama, and I almost missed my chance to audition; I went to it not really caring whether or not I got the part." Of course she did, and that film, *Red Sorghum,* became an international success, while Li's intense yet restrained performance made her a darling to critics and audiences alike. *Ju Dou* and *Raise the Red Lantern,* the first two Chinese films to ever be nominated for Academy Awards, consolidated her appeal. By the time that she and Zhang ended their personal relationship (though, perhaps, not their creative one), she had become Asia's biggest star—winning a Best Actress award from the New York Film Critics Circle award for her performance in *Farewell My Concubine,* directed by Zhang's colleague and rival Chen Kaige, and going on to star in Chen's eagerly awaited followup, *Temptress Moon.* Meanwhile, Li is learning English, and has already been offered roles—notably the part of Robert De Niro's girlfriend in the Michael Mann film *Heat.* She declined upon finding out that she'd have to accept the role without reading the screenplay first. However, when the right script comes along, Li will surely test the climate in Tinseltown.

Chen Kaige

Chen's father, Chen Huaikai, was one of China's most respected directors of his generation; as a result, Kaige was brought up in the nation's capital, Beijing, an educated and privileged young man. But 1966 heralded the arrival of the Cultural Revolution; everything, especially the notion of class privilege, was about to turn upside down.

"My school class was full of the kids of high-ranking officials and they put on their fathers' army uniforms and became Red Guards overnight," remembers Chen. "I was pretty jealous." Chen, then just 16 years old, was swept up in the tide. He joined the Guards, and enlisted in Mao's war against traditional art and culture. Then came a pivotal moment for the young idealist: "One day there was a 'struggle session,' and I was asked by the Red Guards to denounce my father, who had been identified as a former member of the Kuomintang. I not only criticised my father; I denounced him as a spy....The saddest thing is that I knew I was telling lies. I remember my father's eyes—he just stared at me in great confusion." The "spy" and his son were both sent into rural exile for "reeducation" among the peasants. Kaige spent the next three years in the mountainous southern province of Yunnan, slashing bamboo with a machete and living in a dirt-floored hut. The only way for Chen to escape was a route that, if anything, proved even more onerous: Joining the People's Army, where for four years he worked as a road engineer for the North Vietnamese.

In 1975, Chen returned to Beijing, where he worked in a film developing plant until the reopening of the Beijing Film Academy—where, like Tian Zhuangzhuang and Zhang Yimou, he became a member of the Class of '82. Chen was the first of the Fifth Generation to break out of the pack, with the 1984 feature *Yellow Earth.*

While each of his three subsequent films enlarged his international reputation, his former cinematographer Zhang's successes soon eclipsed him. Perhaps in response to the West's embrace of Zhang, Chen reevaluated both his style and choice of subjects. Formerly best known for small, relatively intimate films, he picked as his next project a soapy historical page-turner by Hong Kong novelist Lilian Lee: *Farewell My Concubine.* The result-

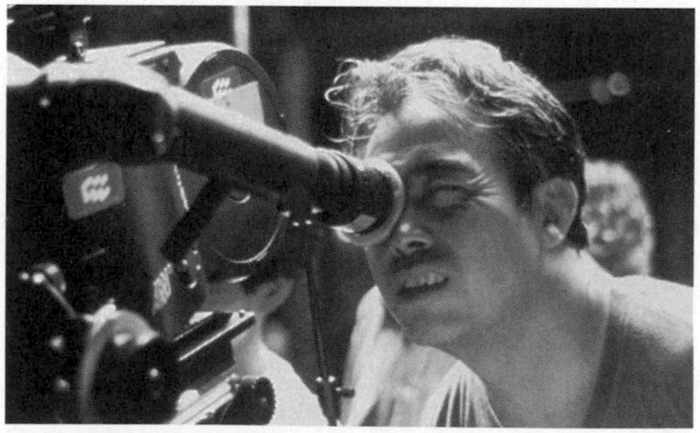

ing film, which even featured Zhang's leading lady Gong Li, was a sprawling epic of unrequited love, betrayal, and despair played out against four decades of Chinese history. Concubine shared the top prize at Cannes with Jane Campion's *The Piano,* and established Chen as a filmmaker capable of making movies that are successful at the box office as well as critically acclaimed. "My early films were personal, direct, and primitive," says Chen. "The films I do now involve the consideration of the audience and commercialism."

Tian Zhuangzhuang

Tian was born in 1952 with a considerable legacy of filmmaking in his genes. His father was a former actor who had risen to become the first head of the Beijing Film Studio, while his mother was a star actress who later took the reigns at China's Children's Film Studio. When he was just 14, the Cultural Revolution dawned, and he was sent, like many other privileged young men, into the countryside to expiate the sins of their class. After working several years in the northeast part of Manchuria, Tian joined the People's Liberation Army and took up still photography. Returning to Beijing after the Revolution was declared to be at an end, he became a cinematographer's assistant at the Beijing Agricultural Film Studio, learning the craft while working on industrial films.

Then, like contemporaries Zhang and Chen, Tian enrolled in the Beijing Film Academy's class of 1982. Unlike the other two top Fifth Gen talents, Tian was assigned not to a film studio but to television work, where he made children's films and documentaries, leading to his first fictional feature work: the brutal ethnographic exploration of Mongol tribal life, *On the Hunting Ground*. He followed that work with another film examining the lives of minorities under Chinese rule—a film that simultaneously incensed authorities and awoke the attention of the film world: *The Horse Thief,* which was filmed on location in a Tibetan village. Pilloried for bluntly depicting the Chinese persecution of Tibetans and for uncritically showing Tibetan life, it took eight months of crushing examination by censors before authorities allowed *Thief's* release. It was soon abruptly withdrawn, with officials citing a concern that the film might prove offensive to Tibet. Tian was deeply in disfavor, and, in order to continue making films, he was forced to make several "contract" movies: an absurd attempt at "commercial filmmaking," *Rock Kids,* and a historical drama, *The Imperial Eunuch*.

In 1993, Tian was finally given approval to make a film he believed in—*The Blue Kite,* coproduced by Hong Kong's Longwick Film Production company. Unlike his earlier ethnographic work, *Kite* was set in the mainstream of China itself, but brought the same raw, uncompromising sensibilities to bear, with the result that the ravages of the Cultural Revolution were presented without the allegorical camouflage used by his contemporaries. The reaction of authorities was swift and harsh. Upon seeing his raw footage, they accused him of departing from his approved script, and suspended production before editing could be completed. While Tian vigorously denies smuggling the footage out of China, in one or another manner, a Dutch production company, Fortissimo Films, managed to get a hold of the raw material, and edited it according to his instructions. The film played to enthusiastic audiences in its premiere at Cannes, and then was featured as a main selection of the Tokyo International Film Festival. At its scheduled screening, the entire Chinese delegation promptly stood and walked out of the theater in protest. Soon thereafter, Tian was banned from filmmaking and blackballed from the use of Chinese production facilities. The sentence was withdrawn under pressure, and Tian has returned to work as a producer—though undoubtedly his rebellious streak remains. —J.Y.

ing hardship until Norbu begs forgiveness. The film again focuses on an ethnic group China would rather pay as little attention to as possible—the Tibetans, who have long lived under the Chinese thumb. RELEASED, THEN WITHDRAWN

THE BLUE KITE (1993)—The story of a family caught up in the turmoil of China in the "50s and '60s, beginning with the wedding preparations of a young

librarian and his schoolteacher fiancee in 1953, and following their trials as they and their son are crushed under the Great Leap Forward and later, the Cultural Revolution. As postproduction began, the Chinese Film Bureau suspended the production "indefinitely," after an anonymous charge was made that the film's content was "problematic." Finally, after the film had sat gathering dust for almost a year, the shooting reels were mysteriously acquired by a Dutch film company, which finished the film by following Tian's detailed inntructions. BANNED; TIAN BANNED FROM FILMMAKING (SANCTION LATER WITHDRAWN)

Toshiro Mifune

Overlooked Facts:

THE SHOGUN MUST GO ON— Though he's played hundreds of roles, the one that reached the broadest audience is probably his pitch-perfect portrayal of Lord Toranaga in the TV miniseries Shogun, adapted from the novel by James Clavell. The reason why he was so ideal for the role? Clavell wrote the character with Mifune in mind to play it, should it ever be brought to the screen.

WHY SEVEN WASN'T HEAVEN— Mifune remembers the shoot for Seven Samurai (remade in America as the classic western The Magnificent Seven; 👁67) as one of the worst he ever endured. Due to Kurosawa's painstaking pace, the production dragged out over an entire year, and the climactic final conflict, which was supposed to have taken place during the summer, was actually shot at the height of Japan's winter. To complete the battle scene, Mifune spent over a month struggling in the mud, drenched with water that was supposed to represent a torrential storm—all in sub-freezing weather. After production wrapped, Mifune had to be hospitalized for a week.

LIFE IN THE OLD DOG YET— Mifune and his wife Mika have two adult sons; however, in 1982—at the ripe age of 62—Mifune had his third child, a daughter, named for her mother. "I can't help it," he says. "When I was young, I played old men's roles. But now I'm an old boy!"

One of the greatest Japanese actors ever to live, Toshiro Mifune was born on April 1, 1920, in Tsingtao, in Japanese-occupied China. He grew up there, and during World War II, enlisted in the Japanese Air Force and served as an aerial photographer. After his military term, he thought it only natural to look for a job in the motion picture industry as a cameraman, and, in 1946, applied for a position at Toho Studios. Due to an odd administrative quirk, he was directed to the wrong interview session, and arrived at the room only to be asked to "pretend to laugh." A confused Mifune grew angry at the strange request, since he'd expected to be asked about matters more related to photography. When he refused, the irritated interviewers asked him to "act drunk." This simply sent Mifune over the edge, and he flew into a rage, shouting curses and threats. The committee, which was just as frustrated as Mifune, told him to leave—but fortunately for cineastes everywhere, an actress named Hideka Takamine informed young but promising director Akira Kurosawa of the raw passion of the amateur who had stumbled into the open auditions. Kurosawa came in and watched Mifune rant, immediately deciding that he was an untrained talent of enormous proportions.

Mifune starred in a number of uninspiring films by other directors before finally joining his patron in *Drunken Angel,* playing a gangster with tuberculosis. The film put the duo on the Japanese cinema map, but it was their followup, the classic *Rashomon,* that thrust them into the international spotlight. In *Rashomon,* Mifune plays a bandit accused of rape and murder. He based the character on a lion he'd seen in a jungle film; the performance helped to win the film top prize at the prestigious Venice International Film Festival, as well as a 1954 Oscar for best foreign film—the first ever awarded to a Japanese film. That same year, he played Kikuchiyo, a farmer's son turned warrior, in *Seven Samurai*. Among the other roles Mifune made famous were that of the ronin Sanjuro in *Yojimbo* (1961), for which he won the Venice International Film Festival's best actor award; the role of Taketoki Washizu in *Throne of Blood* (1957), Kurosawa's adaptation of *Macbeth*; and the ruthless warlord in *The Hidden Fortress* (1958).

His collaboration with the director ended in 1964, almost two decades after it began, with another dynamic performance as a 19th century country doctor in *Red Beard*; Mifune won yet another Venice best actor award for that portrayal. The reason Mifune gives for their parting of ways is that Kurosawa was fired from Toho after *Red Beard*, while Mifune remained under contract. Both parties claim that no bad blood exists between them, though Mifune says that it is unlikely at this point that they will ever work together again: he simply doesn't have the time to spare one of Kurosawa's painstaking pieces. However, as Mifune went on to become a real estate mogul and the owner of a production company of his own, the star and his patron maintained contact. "Kurosawa edited the first film I produced," says Mifune. "Later on, when he was in trouble and came to me for money, I gave him 5 million yen, which at the time was a lot of money."

In recent years, Mifune's production company has survived by churning out samurai shows for TV, while Mifune the actor starred in Steven Spielburg's horrendous comedy *1941 (TKTK)* and NBC's *Shogun* (1980). In 1995, however, Mifune accepted a role as a *benshi,* a travelling narrator of silent movies, in the U.S. indie film *Picture Bride.* Director Kayo Hatta wrote a letter to Mifune to invite him to do a cameo; when he accepted, says Hatta, "we were terrified!" Not so frightened that she and Mifune didn't conjure an inside joke for careful watchers: the benshi takes time to amuse two young boys, whose names are Toshiro and Akira. —A.M.G. & J.Y.

Mighty Morphin Power Rangers

They're mighty! They morph! They come in perky designer colors! Combining fight footage from the hit Japanese superhero series *Zyuranger* (1992-93) with scenes shot in the U.S. featuring a multi-culti cast of teenaged actors, the hybrid action series *Mighty Morphin Power Rangers* overcame parental resistance and critical disdain to become a collosal kiddie hit—and a merchandising phenomenon. Through 1997, the Power Rangers reigned supreme in ratings among the target two-through-11 age group. For two straight Christmas seasons, toys of the Rangers and their robotic steeds the Dinozords caused battles worthy of the show itself among parents eager to procure them for their children. And, in the surest evidence of their popularity yet, the show has spawned a horde of imitators: *Superhuman Samurai Syber Squad* (based on Japan's *Gridman*), and two of Saban's own, *VR Troopers* (based on two Japanese shows, *Spielvan* and *Metalder*), and *Masked Rider* (based on *Kamen Rider Black RX*). None, however, has been able to rival the original for the attention and merchandise dollars of young consumers.

Power Rangers Zeo

"What the Power Rangers comes down to is a perfect expression of good versus evil—saving the weak and prevailing over the bad guys," says a spokeswoman for Bandai. "We think the reason American children like it so much is that it's really the first action program aimed specifically at them. Until now, there's mainly been animated cartoons and programs."

Whether *Power Rangers* was the first action show aimed at kids in the U.S. is debatable. As novel as they may seem in the U.S., however, these high-kicking costumed heroes have a long and illustrious history in Japan. *Zyuranger,* the foundation for the original Power Rangers, is the 16th show from Toei TV to feature color-coded costumed crusaders, going back over two decades to *Go Ranger* (literally, "Five Ranger"), which debuted in 1975. Indeed, Toei's superhero team shows have been so popular for so long that they've now become a genre—referred to as the sentai (or "task force") show. Sentai shows obey a remarkably consistent formula that determines everything from the makeup of the team to the kinds of evildoers they battle—but despite the cliche nature of the format, they remain overwhelmingly popular in Japan. Several new sentai series have debuted since the passing of *Zyuranger,* two of which (*Dai Ranger* and *Oh Ranger*) have been incorporated into recent seasons of *Power Rangers,* and there seems to be no end in sight.

"We never dreamed it would come to this," says Susumu Yoshikawa, a division chief at Toei Television supervising the *Ranger* series. "Still, as long as the Rangers are popular, we'll do it forever."

The Power Rangers Story

Ten thousand years ago, the evil enchantress Rita Repulsa was thwarted by the cosmic being Zordon. On August 28, 1993—the date of the first airing of *Mighty Morphin Power Rangers*—Rita is accidentally released from her confinement. With her henchmen Goldar, Finster, Baboo, and Squatt, as well as an endless series of rubbery monsters, Rita seems poised on the brink of universal conquest, beginning with the planet Earth—until Zordon directs his android Alpha 5 to recruit five teens to fight the vile sorceress. The teens—Jason, an expert in martial arts; Zack, a dancer and rapper; Billy, a science whiz; Kimberly, an athlete and acrobat; and Trini, a strong-willed student of kung-fu—are given magical coins containing special powers. With their weapons and robot steeds, the Dinozords, the Power Rangers are well equipped to defend their home of Angel Grove, California, as well as the rest of humanity. And that's just what they've done, weathering cast changes, catastrophe, and the biggest crisis of all—fading ratings. —J.Y.

SENTAI IN A NUTSHELL

The secret of sentai's enormous popularity is not its originality, but rather its consistency: when fans tune in to a new set of Rangers, they know exactly what they're getting, whether the prefix is Dai or Oh or Kaku. Curiously, the basic formula of sentai originated not with 1975's Go Ranger, the first show in the genre, but three years earlier with a cartoon called Science Ninja Team Gatchaman (1972), known in North America as Battle of the Planets (1978) or G-Force (1986). The Gatchamen were a secret task force whose mission was to use advanced weapons and flying kicks to save the world from alien invasion. Like in the later live-action shows, the team dressed in color-coded, skin-tight uniforms, commanded powerful vehicles, and fought a different space monster every episode. They also had stock character roles that would become sentai archetypes:

KEN ("Mark" in Battle of the Planets)—the straight-shooting leader of the force

JOE ("Jason")—the hot-headed second in command

JUN ("Princess")—the girl

JINPEI ("Keyop")—the youngster

RYU ("Hooter")—the big guy

The creators of Go Ranger learned Gatchaman's lessons well; from then on, sentai would follow this blueprint nearly to the letter. After all, if it ain't broke, why morph it?

NINJA ATTACK!
A Timeline in Black

1967—Ninjas leap stealthily into the Western pop consciousness in the James Bond vehicle You Only Live Twice. Sean Connery, as Bond, may be the first white man to be shown learning the secret arts of ninjutsu on-screen; he isn't the last.

1974—Sam Peckinpah's The Killer Elite (starring American tough guys Robert Duvall and James Caan) has the dubious honor of being the first Western movie featuring ninjas that completely confuses Chinese and Japanese cultures; it isn't the last.

1981—The success of Chuck Norris's The Octagon triggers a flood of cine-ninjas, though Lord knows why. In the film, Norris learns the ancient and secret arts of ninjutsu from his adoptive father, and must battle his evil adoptive brother, who has embraced the dark side. Along the way, Norris is forced to kill and kill again. This proves to be a successful box office formula.

1981—Enter the Ninja arrives, a $2 million crapfest that launched the career of Japanese martial arts expert Sho Kosugi, while earning 10 times its budget for Cannon Films, its producer.

1983—Kosugi and Cannon return with Revenge of the Ninja, in which Kosugi plays the surviving scion of a ninja clan massacred in Japan. He subsequently (and sensibly) moves to California with his mother and son, then gets snarled in some sort of drug scheme. In order to avenge his family and disentangle him-

Enter the Ninja

***Sho Kosugi in* Enter the Ninja**

During the Shang Dynasty in China (1700-1100 B.C.), the shadowy Lin Kuei clan perfected a series of secret techniques for survival, self-defense, and murder. Their methods made them hotly sought after as killers and spies for hire; they also made them too dangerous to be allowed to survive, and the clan was eventually hunted down by the very warlords who'd utilized their services.

Hundreds of years later, the techniques of the Lin Kuei emerged in Japan, adopted by the warriors later known as the ninja, or "stealers-in." Hated and feared by the ruling samurai, the low-born ninja initially waged a guerrilla war of subversion and ambush against the nobility. Eventually, however, ninja would be secretly retained by noble clans as surveillance operatives, scouts, and—occasionally—assassins.

It's this facet of the ninja that popular culture has embraced, with everything from video games to cinema portraying ninjas as star-slinging murderers (a depiction that modern-day ninjutsu initiates find ignorant at best and offensive at worst).

The secret world of the ninja was first introduced to Western moviegoers in the James Bond film *You Only Live Twice* (1967), in which Sean Connery's 007 has the opportunity to train with a group of ninjas, who subsequently lend their sword-swinging and sharpshooting prowess to the film's finale. Ninja subsequently proliferated in B-grade cinema like maggots in a year-old pork chop—propelling black-bodysuit-wearing "actors" like Sho Kosugi and Michael Dudikoff into instant stardom.

That stardom would prove momentary; after the peak of the heinous monstrosities known as the Teenage Mutant Ninja Turtles in the early '90s, ninjas fell in popularity, dropping quickly out of the spotlight—perhaps forever. Then again, who knows? It's when a ninja *can't* be seen that he or she should most be feared... —J.Y.

SPEAK SOFTLY AND WEAR A BLACK MASK: Screen Ninja Sho Kosugi

Born in Tokyo in 1949, Sho Kosugi was Japan's national karate champion by the time he was 18. Even so, he hardly dreamed of an international film career, hoping only to go to college to practice the slightly less deadly and more practical arts of business. After failing Japan's higher education examinations, he travelled to America at the age of 19 to visit universities in California. Unfortunately, while in Los Angeles, he got on the wrong bus—and instead of arriving at his intended destination, L.A.'s "Little Tokyo" area, he ended up in Watts, an unhealthy place for a young, non-English-speaking Japanese tourist to wander. "Three people came up to me because I had a big suitcase, a camera around my back, and $500 in cash in my pocket," says Kosugi. "One guy grabbed me, and two guys started talking to me. I didn't know what the hell they were talking about." Finally, the altercation transcended the language barrier, as one of the would-be muggers pulled a knife. "Bam! I kicked him." The muggers scattered.

> **"There is a difference between the Hollywood image of ninja and my own. For example, for us Japanese, a ninja is not someone who walks a down a city street in broad daylight."**
>
> **—Sho Kosugi**

Kosugi not only survived his first American experience, he made a significant discovery: the West was unfamiliar with, and intimidated by, the martial arts. He proceeded to attend Pasadena City College, and then California State University, earning degrees in economics; meanwhile, he opened two dojos in L.A., teaching karate to all comers. In 1981, after serving as a stunt extra or bit player in dozens of marginal martial arts movies, Kosugi was invited by producer Menahem Golan to play a small role in Cannon Films' latest small-budget extravaganza, *Enter the Ninja*. Golan was so impressed that he had Kosugi's part expanded, then cast him as the star of the film's sequel, *Revenge of the Ninja,* which outearned the original hit. Unfortunately, Golan's idea for a sequel—combining ideas from *The Exorcist* with the earlier ninja hits—was sufficiently absurd that Kosugi decided to walk away from the production. "I said, 'It doesn't work,'" says Kosugi. "[Golan] was believing in ninja mystery, plus trying to include breakdancing and psychic concepts." *Ninja III: The Domination* was made in 1984, without Kosugi, and proved to be a modest hit, though not on the scale of the first two films.

Kosugi continued to star in small but profitable ninja films like *Pray for Death* and *Rage of Honor* until the genre waned in popularity, around the same time that ninjutsu became identified with sewer-dwelling turtles. Kosugi has no regrets. "It happened like this," he says. "A car called 'the ninja boom' passed in front of me as I was driving down the road, so I took it for a ride." And he's philosophical towards those who accuse him of abetting the onscreen misrepresentation of Asian tradition and culture. "There is a difference between the Hollywood image of ninja and my own," he admits. "For example, for us Japanese, a ninja is not someone who walks a down a city street in broad daylight. There were many scenes in which I was asked to do the unthinkable. We held many discussions on whether or not scenes that would strike Japanese as odd should be tolerated in the name of entertainment. In many cases, I was forced to give in. After all, these were Hollywood movies. In those days, I had no authority to correct the things I found wrong. I was just happy to be offered a role and was unwilling to do anything that might spoil it." And Kosugi has managed to avoid getting run over by the "ninja boom" car he rode to success; he demanded a healthy percentage of the grosses of his later releases, saved his money, and began producing his own films. And nearly 30 years after he showed a few thugs the meaning of the Japanese foot, he continues to live in L.A. with his wife and three children, including two sons, Kane and Shane. —J.Y.

self from the frame-job he's been subjected to, he must kill and kill again. Another hairpin-budget flick, it grosses $32 million.

1984—The third of Cannon's original trilogy (though certainly not their last ninja film), <u>Ninja III: The Domination</u> manages to displace Kosugi with a young woman who is possessed by the ninja's ghost, causing unintentionally wacky havoc. It still manages to gross $7.6 million.

1985—Otherwise known as <u>White Guys Wear Black</u>, the unimaginably awful <u>American Ninja</u> hits screens like a giant turd, with Michael Dudikoff in the lead lending support to the theory that a key part of ninja training is "How to Act Really Badly."

1986—Kosugi is back in his franchise role, donning the dark duds for <u>Pray for Death</u>. In it, nearly 90 people are killed (and killed again) by Kosugi, leading to <u>Pray</u>'s receipt of an X rating due to violence. It's recut to an R, which does little for its cohesion of plot, which is something about stolen jewelry, gangsters, and police corruption.

1984—Lee Van Cleef, that staple of the spaghetti Western, goes noir in NBC's short-lived TV series <u>The Master</u>, playing a white guy who has learned the ancient and secret arts of ninjutsu. He's now running from an arch-rival (Sho Kosugi, naturally) and searching for his daughter, dragging along his protege Timothy Van Patten. Since it's on TV, they can't kill and kill again, but they do kick a lot of ass.

Stereotypes

As the old saying went, in a perfect world, one would have an American house, a Japanese gardener, and a Chinese cook. Throw in a suicidal geisha wife, a horde of die-on-command soldiers, a simpering houseboy, a fey Oriental sleuth, and a high-kicking cabaret of gold-hearted Hong Kong prostitutes, and you've hit the Asian stereotype trifecta.

Cooked up by an exclusively white male film industry, the Hollywood representation of Asians in film has historically caricatured when it has sought to depict, damaged when it has aimed to entertain, and outraged when it has endeavored to inform. Here are some examples: —K.L.

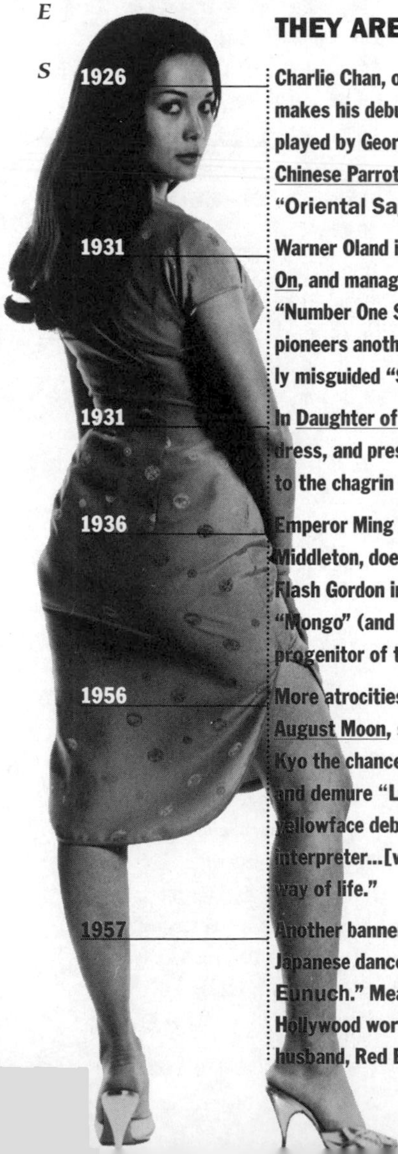

THEY ARE CURIOUS, YELLOW

1926 Charlie Chan, of the rotund build and fortune-cookie mouth, makes his debut in a serial called House Without A Key, he's played by George Kuwa, and he returns in a bigger role in The Chinese Parrot, this time played by Kamiyama Sojin. The "Oriental Sage" has arrived [👁34].

1931 Warner Oland in hideous yellowface stars in Charlie Chan Carries On, and manages to make Chan a household name. Chan's "Number One Son"—played by Asian American actor Keye Luke—pioneers another stereotype: the loyal and assimilated, but utterly misguided "Second Banana."

1931 In Daughter of the Dragon, Anna May Wong dons diva headgear, dress, and press-on nails to give birth to the "Dragon Lady," to the chagrin of Asian American actresses thereafter.

1936 Emperor Ming (surname Merciless), played by Charles Middleton, does battle with buff, coiffed, and tights-clad hero Flash Gordon in the 25th century. Despite being an alien from "Mongo" (and thus not Asian at all! Really!), Ming becomes progenitor of the "Diabolical Tyrant."

1956 More atrocities than you can shake a stick at! Teahouse of the August Moon, set in post–World War II Okinawa, gives Michiko Kyo the chance to offer the Hollywood debut of the soft-spoken and demure "Lotus Blossom." Meanwhile, Marlon Brando in yellowface debuts the "Sneaky Backstabber," as a "wily interpreter...[who] helps America troops succumb to the Oriental way of life."

1957 Another banner year: Ricardo Montalban plays a mincing Japanese dancer in Sayonara—the very picture of the "Sexless Eunuch." Meanwhile, "Madame Butterfly" [👁118] gets a Hollywood workout as Miyoshi Umeki committs hara kiri with her husband, Red Buttons.

1957 In the television series Bachelor Father, "Houseboy" Peter Tong (Sammee Tong) performs traditionally female domestic functions in the Bentley Gregg household, to comic effect.

1960 A Hong Kong prostitute (Nancy Kwan) frolicks with an American artist expatriate in The World of Suzie Wong and unleashes the myth of the secret innate sexual prowess of the "Asian Harlot."

1961 Breakfast At Tiffany's casts Mickey Rooney [👁118] as the "Goofy Guy from Japan"—complete with squint-goggles and buck teeth.

1966 Masked man Bruce Lee costars on The Green Hornet series in all his whirlwind-kicking splendor as the Asian Sidekick...

1972 ...and David Carradine [👁99] plays the Shaolin half-breed monk who walks the Earth in Kung Fu, the TV series, dispensing the wisdom of Inscrutable Ancients while proving either that Asians can still be played by white people or that white people are actually Asian...

1973 ...but Enter The Dragon soon grosses over $100 million, propelling Lee [👁95] to superstardom, and creating the (occasionally helpful) myth of the innate fighting prowess of all young, poorly barbered Asian men—the "Martial Arts Killing Machines."

1985 Year of the Dragon, director Michael Cimino's "inside" look at the dens of iniquity of New York City's Chinatown, reaffirms a slew of old stereotypes, while launching a few new ones onto the silver screen, including the "Asian Broadcast Babe" (which, granted, originally surfaced on TV news; 👁319) and the "Brutal Chinese Gangster."

1984 Director John Hughes seals the fate of adolescent Asian males for generations to come with his casting of Gedde Watanabe as "Wassa happening hah-stuff?" Long Duk Dong in Sixteen Candles—the first, but far from the last "Super Nerd"

1986 Watanabe pioneers another screen stereotype with his turn as the "Japanese Corporate Drone" in Gung Ho.

1993 Philip Kaufman's Rising Sun puts a spin on the Drone stereotype by making it more vicious than a stray Velociraptor. L.A. is shown as a hotbed of horny Japanese businessmen hell-bent on world domination, not to mention collecting harems full of blond bimbos. Put the welcome mat out for the "Japanese Corporate Predator."

1994 Falling Down and Menace II Society offer back to back renditions of the latest stereotype to jump out of the pack: the "Rude Korean Storekeeper"—the most current, but probably not the last, bit of image vandalism to come from the belly of Hollywood and news headlines. Watch this space.

Taiwanese Cinema

Ang Lee's **The Wedding Banquet**

By some standards, the heyday of Taiwanese film was several decades ago, during the '60s and '70s, when a powerhouse industry churned out some 200 films per year—mostly light comedies, melodramatic soapers, and silly action films. By others, however, Taiwan is at its peak right now—with emigre filmmaker Ang Lee scoring big as an American transplant, while young mavericks like Edward Yang and Tsai Ming-liang generate heat among critics around the world. In 1995, the Taiwan film industry could boast just 27 productions—but from that total, received invitations to 52 international film festivals, including three from Cannes.

Part of the reason for Taiwan's turn from quantity to quality was the rise of Hong Kong as film powerhouse; with the explosion in popularity of the martial arts film, Hong Kong soon grew to dominate film export in Asia. Taiwanese studios were hit hard, and soon concluded that the slogan "if you can't fight 'em, join 'em" best applied to the situation, whereupon they began investing their funds in Hong Kong coproductions—letting the domestic industry falter.

Rather than watch Taiwanese film fade entirely away, the Central Motion Picture Corporation—a Nationalist Party–run state studio, created as a propaganda instrument in 1954—threw its hat into the ring. It began by producing anthology films, featuring collected short works by emerging directors who would later be labeled the Taiwanese New Wave. One of these films, *In Our Time*, featured Edward Yang; another, *The Sandwich Man*, launched Taiwanese master Hou Hsiao-hsien. Despite the often controversial nature of these works, CMPC was committed to breathing life into the industry, and (despite some censorship) did not crack down on directors in the manner of the Kuomintang's Mainland counterparts. Even Hou's 1989 *A City of Sadness*, which examined the KMT's brutal slaughter of native Taiwanese on February 2, 1947, was allowed broad release, and later won the Golden Lion at the Venice International Film Festival.

In the '90s, a generation of young directors have followed in the footsteps of Yang and Hou. With the support of the government, which has set aside a pool of funds to subsidize the work of filmmakers and which rewards selection by international film festivals with additional funds, these filmmakers are recreating the Taiwanese cinema in the tradition of the American independents. "[In Taiwan,] the burden is on the film-maker," says Lien. "We don't have a film industry here: Film is more like a manual product. Filmmakers have to use all their energy to finish a film, looking for money, looking for support." Without the Mainland's pressures of state information control or Hong Kong's pressures of pure commercial viability, Taiwanese filmmakers are free to explore difficult, sometimes painful issues—most notably the question of Taiwanese identity. Taiwan has been a political football since its original colonization, having been variously occupied by the Dutch (1624-1674), the Manchus, the Japanese (1886-1945), and most recently, Chiang Kai Shek and his Nationalists in the late '40s; filmmakers have been at the forefront of the exploration of Taiwan's muddled history and its equally uncertain future. So, while Hou Hsiao-hsien has examined the officially denied outrages

TAIWAN'S YOUNG TURKS

EDWARD YANG—Yang's international acclaim is rivaled only by his fellow New Waver, Taiwanese elder statesman Hou Hsiao-hsien; at 48 years old, his sensibility bridges that of Hou's (classic and contemplative) and those of his younger peers (jagged, aggressive, flashy). Educated in the U.S., where he studied film at the University of Florida and UCLA, he's fully bilingual—and ready to break out of the Taiwan market: He's currently making his first film Stateside—an indie project about a Chinese American policeman convicted of excessive use of force. His most noticeable films include A

Brighter Summer Day (1991), A Confucian Confusion (1994) and Mahjong (1995)

TSAI MING-LIANG—The Malaysian-born Tsai's feature debut, Rebels of the Neon God, won awards at festivals in in Taiwan, Tokyo, and Berlin. His 1995 film Vive L'Amour won the Golden Lion at Venice (in hot competition with Edward Yang's

Mahjong). Tsai's heavy Truffaut influence no doubt contributed to his popularity in France—he was signed by a French television channel to make a film "representative of Asia," in celebration of the coming millennium.

STAN LAI—Lai grew up in the U.S. and received his dramatic arts Ph.D. from the University of California at Berkeley; he began as a playwright, establishing his mark on the stage with The Peach Blossom Land, an innovative work that explores the continuing questions of Taiwanese identity by intercutting a modern romantic melodrama and a traditional comic farce. When approached to turn Peach Blossom into a film in 1992, he experienced creative differences with the director and decided to do the adaptation himself. The film (which starred Brigitte Lin; 74) took second prize in the Tokyo International Film Festival's Young Cinema Competition. His followup, Red Lotus Society, which explores the anchorless status of Taiwanese youth through the metaphor of the ancient mystical art of "vaulting" (flying through the air without wires or propulsion), played at festivals around the world, including New York and Vancouver.

of the Nationalists in *City of Sadness*, and Wang Tung has depicted the Japanese occupation in *Hill of No Return*, young guns like Tsai Ming-liang, Ho Ping, and Hsu Hsiao-ming are holding the modern, materialistic Taiwan up to the light, with its anomic youth and neon gauderie hiding a very Confucian confusion.

"[Taiwanese directors] wanted to explore their own history," says Peggy Chiao, founder of the Taiwanese Film Centre. "To do this, they chose to formulate a film language which was very Chinese, very Taiwanese. Their films are very original, and I think that's why they appeal to critics and festival programmers. The films are different from art films from other countries, and very different from other Chinese films."

HOU HSIAO-HSIEN: Taiwan's Movie Master

Considered by many world critics as the most expansively talented filmmaker of any of the Chinas, Hou, born in Guangdong in 1948, fled to Taiwan with his family a year after his birth—escaping, as many did then, the juggernaut of the Communist Revolution. When he was 12, his father passed away; five years later, his mother died of throat cancer, just as Hou was graduating from high school. Now orphaned, Hou entered into Taiwan's compulsory military service, and then, in 1969, enrolled in the National Taiwan Arts Academy, studying film. In 1973, a year after graduation, he got his first job in film—working as a scriptwriter, assistant director, and production assistant for senior directors in Taiwan's well-established cinema industry. But the industry was on the wane, buffeted by competition from Hong Kong, and by the time Hou got his first chance to direct—1980's *Cute Girls*—Taiwanese cinema was a mere shadow of its original powerhouse self.

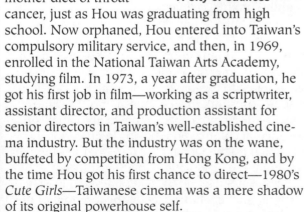

A City of Sadness

Luckily for Hou, the government, which rightly saw film as an important tool for the establishment of an international reputation, wasn't going to take the flagging output of its studios lying down. Through the Kuomintang Party-owned studio CMPC, the government began subsidizing young directors whose work was receiving international attention. Hou's gentle, commercially popular *Green, Green Grass of Home* (1982)—popular in part because it starred a Cantopop singing idol—had already earmarked him as a major talent. His segment in the CMPC anthology film *The Sandwich Man* served to entrench his status as the greatest of Taiwan's New Wave filmmakers.

The *Boys From Fenquei* (1983), an ironic critique of modernization and big-city affectation, was the first of Hou's films to be invited to a major world venue—the 1984 Hawaii International Film Festival. *Boys* also won the top award at the Festival of Three Continents at Nantes, France.

Still, it was the autobiographical *A Time to Live and a Time to Die* that was Hou's first true global triumph. Charting the passage to maturity of a young man through Taiwan's restless '50s and '60s and a series of family tragedies, it is an emotional but restrained work that was instantly hailed as a masterpiece. Hou has had more success on the festival circuit than in theaters. Still, he managed an unexpected domestic success with *A City of Sadness*—the first Taiwanese film to examine the massacre of natives by the Nationalists, upon their arrival on and subjugation of Taiwan. *City* was awarded the Golden Lion for Best Picture at the 1989 Venice International Film Festival.

Hou's sophisticated eye and frank but considered way of confronting hard topics has made him much emulated by his juniors, but never matched; though his work has rarely screened in the West, he has managed to impact his contemporaries in Taiwan, Hong Kong, and even on the Mainland—and continues to explore the identity of Taiwan as no other director has, and few have tried. —J.Y.

Ultraman

Ultraman defeats the Giant Space Beast of the Week

After a decade of making giant rubber monsters for Toho (including such classics as Godzilla, Rodan, and Mothra), it's no wonder that, in 1966, special effects master Eiji Tsuburaya decided to create a new type of hero for Japanese television. That's when he unveiled Ultraman, a 40-meter tall, silver and red, bug-eyed alien whose mission was—ahem—to stop giant rubber monsters from destroying Japan.

The Ultraman phenomenon actually began in 1965, with Tsuburaya's black and white series *Ultra Q*. In *Ultra Q*'s 28 episodes, an author (Kenji Sahara, of Toho's *Rodan*) and a photojournalist (Hiroko Sakurai, who would star in *Ultraman*) travelled around the world, examining strange occurrences and exposing the monsters that caused them. (Curiously enough, just as every unexplained supernatural event in *Scooby-Doo* could be pawned off on a disgruntled caretaker, each of *Ultra Q*'s weird happenings were the result of some mutant latex critter. Go figure.)

While Q was extremely popular, Tsuburaya was ready to go one step further in his followup series. Tsuburaya took the monsters from Q and made them gigantic. Then he replaced the investigators with an organized "Science Patrol." Finally, he added the superhero who would become one of Japan's most enduring icons: Ultraman.

Since the original *Ultraman* series, Tsuburaya Productions has produced eight sequels—some serious, some silly, some animated, some live action, and even one, *Ultraman Powered,* which was filmed in America. Dozens of members of the Ultra family have been introduced, not to mention a legion of goofy-grotesque arch-enemies. And meanwhile, Ultraman's popularity keeps growing. Like Superman in the U.S., Ultraman's image, his cross-armed "Specium Beam" attack pose, and even his theme song are national institutions in Japan. Other masked heroes have followed him; none have superseded him—and even today, his visage is a staple on Japanese products ranging from candy to bathroom supplies. —M.W. & J.Y.

The Ultra Story

Two hundred and sixty thousand years in the past, the World of Light in Nebula M78 is threatened with destruction, due to the untimely explosion of its sun. A scientist known only as the Ultra-Elder saves his people by replacing the dead sun with an artificial star called the Plasma Spark. The Spark surpasses its inventor's intentions: it not only gives warmth and light to his desperate people, but it also grants them powers far surpassing those of ordinary mortals. For a great many centuries following the invention of the Spark, the Ultras live in peace and harmony. Thousands of years later, however, the Emperans—jealous aliens from a nearby planet—decide to attack the glorious World of Light, sending invading hordes of mind-controlled monsters against the unsuspecting Ultras. Despite their advanced powers, the Ultra-folk seem doomed—until a leader called the Ultra-Father unites his people to defeat the menacing creatures. Though he is wounded in the battle, he is nursed back to health by a warrioress known as Ultra-Mother, and together they organize a team to patrol the spaceways against the Emperans and other bloodthirsty races. Led by their parents, the children of Ultra-Father and Ultra-Mother become the greatest warriors of the Intergalactic Security Force—saving the cosmos time and again. —J.Y.

THE ULTRAS: A Family Affair

While Ultraman gets most of the publicity, the fact is, over the course of the three-decade-long Ultra reign, nearly two dozen Ultra brothers and sisters have been introduced to an enthusiastic viewing public. Each has had a similar space-gladiator appearance and powers—the ability to grow to over 200 feet in size, the ability to use funky martial arts, and the ability to generate a deadly blast of "Specium" energy. Most also share one major weakness: a limited energy supply, which leads to their falling into a state of near-collapse after just three minutes of combat (apparently, despite their advanced technology, the Ultras never developed Energizer batteries). Worry not—our Ultra heroes never fail to perform a last-ditch, energy-draining Specium Beam assault, defeating their slavering rubber opponents and saving the cosmos, time and again.

The Reel War: Vietnam on Film

> **"If they're running, they're VC gooks. If they aren't running, they're dead gooks. What's the difference?"**
>
> —Helicopter gunman in Stanley Kubrick's *Full Metal Jacket*

Some American G.I.'s unlucky enough to have been sent to Vietnam quickly developed a sharp paranoia—a gripping fear that the enemy was everywhere and nowhere at the same time. After a few screenings in a row, any Asian forced to trudge through the savage jungles of the Vietnam War movie might easily develop the same pathology.

Beginning with John Wayne's *The Green Berets* (1968), Hollywood has mostly presented a view of the Vietnamese as a people less human than simian in nature, though, based on these portrayals, the comparison might well serve as an insult to the monkeys. Viet Cong guerrillas (pardon the pun) lurk everywhere in the densely foliaged jungles; they swing out of trees and greenery with simian gusto, shrieking like howler monkeys, AK-47s cocked and ready to fire. They are without conscience, mercy, or honor; they value no life, least of all their own, in their mindless thirst for blood. Michael Smith, a communications instructor at Ball State University who has researched war-film images of U.S. enemies from the silents to the present, notes that even the Germans were shown saluting "our boys" after being shot down in a good dogfight; the Vietnamese, on the other hand, only shoot them in the back. When the Vietnamese aren't being drawn as a savage horde, they are presented instead as characters invoking inveterate stereotypes—pimps and prostitutes, brutal wardens, and the like.

Meanwhile, battle-scarred vets "returning from hell" (at least they got to leave it) are given the benefit of human complexity, of tragic moment, either as heroes or as victims, and occasionally both. Granted, latter-day explorations of the war attempt to even out the balance of brutality, but by placing the acts of American soldiers in the context of a vast and abstract struggle—good versus evil, sanity versus insanity—the Vietnamese are once again stripped of their humanity. The true tragedy of atrocities like the massacre at My Lai, these films seem to suggest, is that they tarnished the innocence of young American men—good, red-blooded boys, who found themselves confronted with unknown inner demons while in a terrifying land far from home. And the Vietnamese? Living or dead, they're props in America's own internal morality play.

Where fair representation is concerned, the enemy, it seems, is everywhere. Everywhere in Hollywood, that is.
—K. L.

Film/ Year	Director/ Stars	Synopsis	Southeast Asia Is:	The War Is:	The Vietnamese Are:
The Green Berets (1968)	dirs. John Wayne, Ray Kellogg; John Wayne, Jim Hutton	Typical John Wayne fare: Special Forces defend a fire base and neutralize a Viet Cong general. Notable for its legendary scene in which the sun sets in the east.	...another jungle that America must conquer.	...another excuse to quell communism; a chance to wave small flags and sing off-key.	...affable and harmless when young; deadly—yet easily mowed down by superior American weaponry—after puberty.
The Deer Hunter (1978)	dir. Michael Cimino; Robert DeNiro, Christopher Walken, Meryl Streep, John Cazale, John Savage	Three small-town steelworkers are sent off to Vietnam and return—jaded, confused, and stripped of what made them men.	...like a sweaty S&M bordello where young men lose their moral virginity.	...the end of innocence.	...trigger-happy sadists with a bloodcurdling penchant for Russian Roulette.

Film/ Year	Director/ Stars	Synopsis	Southeast Asia Is:	The War Is:	The Vietnamese Are:
Apocalypse Now (1979)	dir. Francis Ford Coppola; Martin Sheen, Marlon Brando, Robert Duvall, Frederic Forrest, Dennis Hopper	An army captain (Martin Sheen) treks to Cambodia in search of a Special Forces colonel (Brando).	...the Heart of Darkness.	...a harrowing, meaningless journey into the blackest part of the human soul.	...dead; surreal and cerebral manifestations of American guilt.
The Killing Fields (1984)	dir. Roland Joffe; Sam Waterton, Haing S. Ngor, John Malkovich	A *New York Times* reporter solicits the help of a Cambodian translator, only to escape the country without him; leaving his Asian pal waist deep in shit.	..where Pulitzers are won; a breeding ground for sanguine revolutionaries.	...a time to cry.	...screwed (Cambodian translator); ruthless killers (Khmer Rouge).
Missing In Action (1984)	dir. Joseph Zito Chuck Norris, M. Emmet Walsh, David Tress, James Hong	Norris plays a bearded American vet with an M16 slung around his mud-soaked body, going back into the jungles of Vietnam to rescue MIAs amidst feckless political maneuverings.	...a hotbed of sadistic corruption and missing POWs.	...unforgettable, that's what it is...	...Filipino, not Vietnamese.
Rambo: First Blood Part II (1985)	dir. George P. Cosmatos; Sylvester Stallone, Richard Crenna, Julia Nickson	Betrayed by the CIA, beleaguered vet Sly returns to Vietnam, aided by a pretty local woman, to rescue MIAs Chuck Norris missed; instead he's captured and tortured by both the Soviets and the Vietnamese. Yahoo!	...where the protagonist's warmest years were spent.	...the reason why the U.S. government is not to be trusted.	...dusted at the rate of one per minute.
Platoon (1986)	dir. Oliver Stone;Tom Berenger, Willem Dafoe, Charlie Sheen, Forest Whitaker, Johnny Depp	A rookie joins a platoon of cynical veterans as they meander through the deadly jungles of South Asia.	...a mythical battle between the good and evil in Man.	...a hell-hole where batty soldiers turn on each other.	...hurt real bad; victims of the barbarous acts of American GIs.
Full Metal Jacket (1987)	dir. Stanley Kubrick; Matthew Modine, Adam Baldwin, Vincent D'Onofrio	A two-act movie about the mental aftermath of the war. The first half follows trainees, whipped into shape by a merciless drill instructor. The second offers field action as told by a soldier/reporter graduate of that training.	...reduced to rubble, literally and figuratively.	...dehumanizing, in keeping with Kubrick's time-honored theme.	...horny, broke, and entrepreneurial (if pimping is considered a legitimate business).
Good Morning, Vietnam (1988)	dir. Barry Levinson; Robin Williams, Forest Whitaker	A thigh-slappingly hilarious radio jock entertains the troops as they're getting shredded by shrapnel in the field, but is distracted by a hot Vietnamese babe. Later he learns an important lesson about humanity, and still gets the babe.	...a great audience, thank you, thank you.	...grim enough to provide a nicely stark backdrop to Robin Williams's goofy antics.	...available, so long as you impress their fellow villagers by teaching them baseball.
Casualties of War (1989)	dir. Brian De Palma; Michael J. Fox, Sean Penn, Thuy Thu Le, John Leguizamo	A young soldier struggles with morality and loyalty in the face of American aggression gone buck wild.	...getting tired of being filmed.	...a 113 minute metaphor for the loss of innocence.	..."portable R&R to break up the boredom and to keep up morale."
Heaven and Earth (1993)	dir. Oliver Stone; Hiep Thi Le, Tommy Lee Jones, Joan Chen, Haing S. Ngor, Debbie Reynolds	The true, if dramatized, story of a Vietnamese village girl who survives getting beaten and raped by the Vietnamese, only to start a life with an ex-Marine who unfortunately goes postal by movie's end.	...like a big wet, weepy woman at the mercy of a shining white knight.	...a national (cinematic?) tragedy.	...martyred; peace-loving and poetic.
Operation Dumbo Drop (1993)	dir. Simon Wincer; Danny Glover, Ray Liotta	Based on a true story where a platoon of soldiers transported a four-ton elephant to a remote village.	...pachyderm-deficient.	... a great time to be amused by animal mayhem.	...hostile and anti-American when young, spiritual after puberty; big fans of elephants.

The Reel War: World War II on Film

The soldiers did the fighting in the Pacific theater, but where movie memories were concerned, Hollywood dictated how the war would be portrayed for generations to follow. The conclusion: The foreign forces of evil as personified by the Germans and, even more glaringly, the Japanese, would be easier to hate if the enemy were always represented in one of two ways: enigmatic and faceless, or crudely caricatured. Over 2,500 films were made between the years of 1939 and 1945, as Hollywood contributed its propaganda skills to the war effort. Leading the pack—with a release date just shy of the two-month memorial of Pearl Harbor—*A Yank on the Burma Road* (1942) depicted the adventures of a tough truck driver in the Far East, who abandons his trade after he uncovers the plans for a sneak Japanese attack. Later that year, *Wake Island* hit the theaters, and immediately was a box-office smash, despite its less than heartening plot: a battalion of Marines is overwhelmed by swarming Japanese soldiers.

The portrayal of Japanese as an unseen but omnipresent horde would evolve in later films into that of a treacherously pathological race given to irrational, compulsive behavior—not because they were under orders, like the noble and beleaguered Germans, but because senseless killing was a part of the deranged Japanese nature.

Neither portrayal, of course, was flattering—but they scored boffo b.o. —K.L.

FILM/DATE	DIRECTOR/STARS	PLOT	ASIANS ARE:
Wake Island (1942)	dir. John Farrow; Brian Donlevy, MacDonald Carey, William Bendix, Robert Preston	A small Marine garrison is haplessly left to its own devices against Japanese invaders on a remote island. No white man survives.	...a mindless horde; a useful propaganda tool.
China (1943)	dir. John Farrow; Alan Ladd, Loretta Young, William Bendix, Iris Wong, Victor Sen Yung, Richard Loo	An oil salesman is swayed to join a Chinese guerrilla force after the Japanese butcher his sidekick's son.	...(Chinese are:) freedom fighters and closet Americans; (Japanese are:) ruthless killers and closet sadists.
Destination Tokyo (1943)	dirs. Delmer Daves, Blake Edwards; Cary Grant, John Garfield, Alan Hale, John Forsythe, Dane Clark	A U.S. submarine is sent on a secret bombing mission in Tokyo harbor.	...backstabbing losers; faceless minions.
Bataan (1943)	dir. Tay Garnett; Robert Taylor, George Murphy, Thomas Mitchell, Desi Arnaz, Lloyd Nolan	Thirteen soldiers hold a bridge and are slaughtered by Japanese forces one by one.	...expert snipers; dishonorable chumps prone to breaking all rules of war decorum.
Back To Bataan (1945)	dir. Edward Dmytryk; John Wayne, Anthony Quinn, Beulah Bondi, Richard Loo	When Bataan is taken over by the Japanese, Wayne organizes a guerrilla resistance.	...sometimes Mexican or otherwise ethnically confused (Anthony Quinn plays a Filipino guerrilla, for instance); but Charmin-squeezable when young.
The Sands of Iwo Jima (1949)	dir. Alan Dwan; John Wayne	Tough marine sergeant leads his patrol in the takeover of Mount Surirachi where they pose for the famous picture, hoisting the flag.	..."those lemon-colored characters"—the Duke
From Here to Eternity (1953)	dir. Fred Zinnemann; Burt Lancaster, Montgomery Clift, Frank Sinatra, Deborah Kerr, Donna Reed	A tale of relationships between three soldiers that leads up to Roosevelt's "day that will live in infamy."	...sneaky attackers, though ironically, not all that central to the story
The Bridge on the River Kwai (1957)	dir. David Lean; William Holden, Alec Guinness, Jack Hawkins, Sessue Hayakawa	British POWs are forced to build a bridge for the Japanese in Burma while fellow Brits conspire to blow it up.	...ruthless, slave-driving, and brutal, so what else is new?
Tora! Tora! Tora! (1970)	dirs. various; Martin Balsam, Joseph Cotten, James Whitmore, Jason Robards	A re-creation of the events leading up to and during the attack on Pearl Harbor, from both perspectives.	...not as evil as we were led to believe, but rather pawns of military machination.

Yellowface

In his book, *Our Films, Their Films,* director Satyajit Ray [👁89] recalls a meeting with a Hollywood film studio executive in August 1958. The Hollywood host claimed to have a "wonderful plan" which Ray explains was not, after all, so wonderful: "He was going to produce a film about a great Indian....He said this with an earnestness that I found disconcerting. I remembered Ramon Navarro as Karim, the son of a Brahmin who wore the sacred thread and a silk turban; and I remembered Banerji, the westernised Hindi in *The Rains Came,* performing cabalistic rituals to appease the Rain God. 'Which great Indian?' I asked. 'The Lord Buddha,' he said. 'Light must come from the East, you know.' I said: 'That's fine, but who're you going to cast in the lead?' 'Guess who,' said the Executive. I made a quick mental survey of all the Oriental faces available to Hollywood, and could not think of one that filled the bill. I said I could not guess. The eyes of my host now gleamed with what I took to be a sneak preview of the light to come. 'Why,' he said, 'Robert Taylor, of course!'" At the time, Ray was the Indian film director only recently made famous by his rave-reviewed 1956 film *Pather Panchali,* a movie in which Asians play Asians. A novel concept? For the time, apparently so.

The films below demonstrate that "yellowfacing"—where whites portray Asians—was not only prevalent, but went unquestioned for decades in England and America. Some of these films were highly acclaimed creations; a few even won Academy Awards. Still, as New York Times film critic Andre Sennwald remarked in 1932 about the first speaking version of *Madame Butterfly,* nearly all yellowfacing "smacks less of the Orient than of the studio mills." But that's Hollywood for you—half dream machine, half nightmare. —K.L.

Film/Year	Director/Stars	Synopsis	Sample Reviews
Madame Butterfly (1915)	dir. Sidney Olcott; Mary Pickford, Marshall Neilan	The ultimate Asian-woman-as-sacrifice story with the virtuous geisha Cho Cho San (Pickford) committing suicide over the loss of her American soldier.	"By adopting 'yellow face' for her role, Pickford frees herself from...Victorian prohibitions against sexual display while maintaining a sense of innocence." —Gina Marchetti
Broken Blossoms (1919)	dir. D.W. Griffith; Lillian Gish, Richard Barthelmess, Donald Crisp	based on the short story, "The Chink and the Child," by Thomas Burke. A battered child (Gish), lives in London's squalid Limehouse district with her abusive father (Crisp). Chen Huan (Barthelmess), a Chinese poet and philosopher, helps her escape her gloomy life, butshe is eventually killed by her father. Chen kills the father, then himself.	"a genuine attempt to bring real tragedy onto the screen as opposed to machine-made drama" —*The London Times* "Richard Barthelmess is Lillian Gish's able partner...and makes his reputation here" —LizAnne Bawden
Charlie Chan Carries On (1931, followed by more than 40 other *Charlie Chan* films, as well as a television series)	dir. various; Warner Oland, among others	After three previous non-blockbuster Chan flicks with Asians in the lead, Fox hit it big when Oland made his yellowfaced Chinese detective in *Charlie Chan Carries On*, a role he reprised in over 15 films. In 1938, Sidney Toler took over the role, then Roland Winters in 1947, J. Carroll Nash in a 1950s TV series, Ross Martin in 1971, and even Peter Ustinov—in 1980!	"In 1931...began the fully-fledged *Chan* movies, which entertained a generation....They were never noted for production values, but many retain interest for their scripts, their puzzles, and their casts of budding stars, as well as the central character"—Leslie Halliwell "Ustinov is badly miscast, gives one of the worst performances of his career"—Leonard Maltin
The Bitter Tea of General Yen (1932)	dir. Frank Capra; Barbara Stanwyck, Nils Asther, Toshio Mori, Walter Connolly	A missionary in Shanghai (Stanwyck) is captured by a Chinese warlord (Asther), grotesquely outfitted in the style associated with Hollywood's fantasies of evil Mandarins. Lo and behold, she falls in love with her captor—but, of course, there is no consummation; in expected Hollywood style, the emasculated Asian man is ruined and commits suicide. Bitter tea indeed.	"It is doubtful whether this picture can make the grade without support...photographic advantages cannot overcome the queer story"—*Variety*

Film/Year	Director/Stars	Synopsis	Sample Reviews
The Son-Daughter (1932)	dir. Clarence Brown; Helen Hayes, Ramon Navarro, Lewis Stone	Hayes and Novarro play two star-crossed Chinese lovers whose happiness is shattered when Hayes' family pressures her into an arranged marriage. Warner Oland portrays Fen Sha, the vulgar husband whom Hayes eventually strangles with his own pigtail.	"Naturally handicapped...because the faces which have been embellished with seemingly shaved skulls, pigtails and slanted eyes belong to such familiar actors as Lewis Stone, Warner Oland, Ralph Morgan and H.B. Warner"—*New York Times*
Mysterious Mr. Wong (1935, followed by five sequels with Lugosi;he was replaced by Keye Luke in the sixth)	dir. William Nigh; Bela Lugosi, Wallace Ford	A Chinatown Mandarin (Lugosi) will stop at nothing to collect the 12 coins of Confucius. He turns his hatchet men loose, and although they retrieve the coins for Mr. Wong, the men themselves are soon out of circulation.	"Passably exciting"—*Variety* "The bloody biography of a power-mad Chinese...very juvenile"—*New York Times*
The Good Earth (1937, based on the Pulitzer-winning Pearl Buck novel; 👁**33**)	dir. Sidney Franklin; Paul Muni, Luise Rainer	A Chinese peasant grows rich but loses his beloved wife. Anna May Wong wanted the lead, which went instead to Rainer (who won an Oscar!). The director instead asked Wong to play a concubine; she refused in disgust.	"Prestigious boredom, and it goes on for a very long time"—*The New Yorker*
Dragon Seed (1944, also based on a novel by Pearl Buck)	dir. Jack Conway; Harold S. Bucquet, Katharine Hepburn, Walter Huston, Aline MacMahon	The impact of Japanese invasion on a small Chinese community; MacMahon, whose hair appears to be spray painted black, was nominated for an Oscar for her portrayal of a Chinese peasant.	"badly cast actors mouth propaganda lines in a mechanical script which provokes more...unintentional laughter than sympathy"—Leslie Halliwell "a kind of slant-eyed *North Star*...awkward and pretentious, it nevertheless has moments of moral grandeur"—*Time*
Love is a Many-Splendored Thing (1955, based on a semi-autobiographical novel by Han Suyin)	dir. Henry King; Jennifer Jones, William Holden	A Eurasian doctor (Jones) falls in love with a war correspondent (Holden). The good doctor describes her love for him as a conflict between her Eastern and Western halves; West wins out, though she's left in misery when her lover is killed on assignment.	"Self-admittedly sentimental soaper with a tragic ending; the theme tune kept it popular for years" —Leslie Halliwell
Teahouse of the August Moon (1956)	dir. Daniel Mann; Marlon Brando, Glenn Ford, Eddie Albert	In post-World War II Okinawa, Brando plays a Japanese interpreter who helps introduce American troops to an embarrassingly stereotypical version of so-called Japanese life. Hard to watch Brando again yelling "Stella!!!" or complaining "I could have been a contenduh" after this one.	"Adequate, well-acted screen version of a Broadway comedy which succeeded largely because of its theatricality. A few good jokes remain"—Leslie Halliwell
China Gate (1957)	dir. Samuel Fuller; Gene Barry, Angie Dickinson, Nat King Cole	*Pocohontas* in Vietnam. Lucky Legs (Dickinson), a French-Chinese barkeep, helps a unit of French legionnaires. In the unit is her husband, who deserted her upon discovering her Asian background. By film's end, she's just another sacrificial Asian woman.	"Slick but undistinguished"—Leslie Halliwell
Breakfast at Tiffany's (1961; 👁**112**)	dir. Blake Edwards; Audrey Hepburn, George Peppard, Mickey Rooney	A social and emotional whirlygirl, Holly Golightly, finds herself in love with her handsome writer neighbor. Sounds innocent enough, but their intolerant, bucktoothed, landlord is Mr. Yunioshi, (Rooney), whose yellowfacing accoutrements include taped-back eyes.	 "Mickey Rooney's bucktoothed, myopic Japanese is broadly exotic"—*New York Times*
My Geisha (1962)	dir. Jack Cardiff; Shirley Maclaine, Yves Montand, Robert Cummings, Edward G. Robinson	An American actress (Maclaine) secretly follows her husband to Japan, where he is working on a remake of *Madame Butterfly*. She dons a geisha costume and supposedly fools her director husband into not only casting her as the lead, but even into falling in love with her make-believe alter ego. Yeah, right.	"Careful to relegate any discussion of race or miscegenation to a minor role. Any discomfort created by the treatment of interracial sexuality is, at its most basic level, alleviated by the fact that the viewer knows from the outset that both Paul and Bob are attracted to a Caucasian woman"—Gina Marchetti

FOOD AND DRINK

"Has the American diet changed with the increased exposure and availability of Asian foods and ingredients? Of course—to the extent that Americans are becoming more adventurous. Practically every household in the country has a bottle of soy sauce. You can go out to a restaurant and get grilled salmon with black bean sauce, or ginger, or mustard sauce—served with baked potato and a salad. And a recent study showed that one-third of American restaurants serve at least one stir-fried dish. When most chain or hotel restaurants have some kind of 'Asian' thing—whether it's 'Mandarin chicken salad,' a stir-fried dish, or kung pao chicken—it's a very good indication of how American palates have become acclimated to Asian cooking."

—*Chef Martin Yan, cookbook author and host of the cooking show* Yan Can Cook

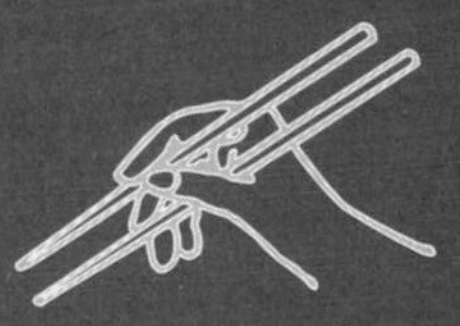

West Drinks East:
Asian Cocktails

Was the Singapore Sling really invented in Singapore? Did Japanese pilots down a Kamikaze before their suicidal bombing missions? Is the Mai Tai named after a tiny Asian village? The problem with finding the answers to these questions, as cocktail historian William Grimes explains, is that "barroom etymology—a pseudodiscipline that bears the same relation to real etymology that barroom conversation does to the philosophy of Hegel—rests on the wobbly premise that each and every cocktail was invented on a specific occasion by a particular bartender, who looked upon his new drink, cried 'Eureka!' and endowed it with a fanciful name." Or, as bartender extraordinaire Gary Regan puts it more succinctly, "Cocktail history is full of legends rather than history." That said, the bleary pasts of "Asian" cocktails can be broken down into a few main categories:

THE COLONIAL ERA

"The origin of most of the 'Asian' drinks we know today comes from the colonial era. And there are quite a lot of famous ones," says John Poister, author of the best-selling *New American Bartender's Guide.*

• The **gin and tonic** (gin, tonic water, lime wedge)—"The British were wild for gin," says Poister. In the 19th century, the British company Schweppes imported an Indian tonic water made with quinine, which was taken as a preventive for malaria. "In actual fact, there wasn't enough quinine in a bottle of Schweppes tonic water to have any medicinal value," says Poister. "But it tasted good." According to Poister, the gin and tonic originated in India, circa 1870. "It was an instant hit." It then moved to London, when officials of the British Raj brought it home, and then poured its way into the hearts of the world.

• The **Gimlet** (gin, lime juice, lime peel)—Another gin drink that, according to Poister, most likely originated in India in the early 19th century. It was made with Rose's Lime Juice, which was created as a substitute for fresh limes and sold throughout the British colonies.

• **gin and bitters** (gin, Angostura bitters)—A classic cocktail, also invented in the middle of the 19th century, and called gin *pait* in India. "Gin and bitters or gin *pait* was invented as a means of keeping fit," says Poister. "They thought bitters were very good for your stomach; in those days, in the Far East, they had a lot of problems with the drinking water."

• The word "**punch**" is reputedly derived from the Hindi word *panch*, or "five"—possibly through the compound word *panchamrit*, "a mixture of five ingredients." Why? Because most traditional punch recipes follow the "Rule of Five": "One sour, two sweet, three strong, four weak," with the fifth element being spices and flavorings. Like most colonial era drinks, punch was probably a British expatriate idea. Some classic punches created in India in the18th and 19th century include the East India, the Bombay Punch, and the Bengal Lancer's Punch.

THE HOTEL ERA

Many cocktails originated in hotel bars, the crossroads of the drinking world. Bartenders and other staff at these hotels were usually natives who had the burden of accommodating the strange tastes of Western foreigners. Bartenders in Asia, says Poister, "were catering to the tastes of Europeans, but adding their own creative touch. That continues today."

• The **Singapore Sling** is perhaps the most famous Asian drink of this era. It was invented in 1915 by legendary Singaporean bartender Ngiam Tong Boon at the Raffles Hotel. The hotel, named after Sir Stamford Raffles, had been established in 1886 by four Armenian brothers, and had soon become a magnet for world travelers. W. Somerset Maugham, after his visits in the 1920s, wrote that the hotel "stands for all the fables of the exotic East"; as a reward for this bit of PR, a hotel suite was named after him. Considered by some the "pina colada of the Orient," this notorious pink drink was intended to be a ladies' cocktail, which doesn't prevent modern-day hotel visitors of every gender from slinging the $9 cocktails down at a rate of 2,000 per day. The Sling is considered a classic cocktail, though many variations exist.

• **Tiger's Milk** (gold rum, cognac, half-and-half, sugar syrup, grated nutmeg or cinnamon) originated in the capital of China in the early 1920s. It was first served at the Hotel Des Wagon-lits, which was owned by a consortium that operated trains (like the infamous Orient Express) and hotels all over Asia.

• **The Mount Fuji** (gin, lemon juice, heavy cream, pineapple juice, egg white, cherry brandy, maraschino cherry) was the offical house drink of the Imperial Hotel in Tokyo, which opened its doors in 1922. The drink was once popular in the U.S., and could be again. "People travel to India and China and Japan, have these drinks, and bring them back," says Poister. "Next thing you know, they're making them here."

THE PSEUDO-POLYNESIAN ERA

The fruit-bedecked Singapore Sling spawned many Polynesian-styled varietal coolers, invented on the American mainland in the '40s and '50s. These

would-be tropical cocktails, notes Grimes, "reflect a strange, synthetic exoticism." The most prolific producer of these cocktails was Trader Vic's, the island-themed restaurant chain created by Vic Bergeron. Bergeron's original restaurant, Hinky Dink's—founded in Oakland in 1934—was reportedly more like a deer-hunting lodge. After visiting Don the Beachcomber, an L.A. restaurant with an island theme, in 1937, Bergeron was prompted to turn Hinky Dink's into a Polynesian fantasy. In 1939, his chef Chan Wong added Chinese wood-fired ovens. The popularity of the original led Bergeron to open a second Trader Vic's in Honolulu. Seattle, San Francisco, New York, and other major cities followed; at its peak, the chain boasted a total of 19 restaurants.

"Perhaps returning American servicemen found themselves growing nostalgic for the South Pacific," shrugs Grimes. "Or perhaps the musical *South Pacific* **[👁252]** stirred a national longing to drink out of coconuts. But the concept and the execution were bogus, and Bergeron himself made no secret of it. Diners feasted on a thoroughly Americanized version of a less-than-compelling cuisine—and loved it. The drinks were about as authentic as the dishes." (Not that this shouldn't have been obvious from names like Dr. Funk of Tahiti, Rangoon Ruby, and so forth.)

"The fact that nobody in Polynesia had ever seen one of these elegant, showcase libations is unimportant," says Poister. "The ingredients—fruits, spices, and flavorings from faraway places combined with rare rums—the toppings, like aromatic liqueurs, and the decorations—hibiscus, orchids, and gardenias—proclaimed to adoring patrons: 'This is what you drink in a tropical paradise.' I don't think anybody really cares when they're drinking them."

Famous Trader Vic cocktails include the Fog Cutter, the Scorpion, the Shark's Tooth, and Tonga Punch. Of course, Trader Vic is most celebrated for his faux Polynesian classic, the Mai Tai. But before he died in 1984, Bergeron admitted that—along with his restaurant's faux Pacifica decor—the rum drink was "inspired" by Don the Beachcomber.

Bergeron claims he first mixed the Mai Tai in 1944. The name comes from the fact that, when he served it to two visiting friends from Tahiti, they exclaimed, "*Mai tai—roe ae*!" According to Bergeron, this translates to: "Out of this world—the best!" Of course, his story should probably be taken, like a tequila shooter, with a pinch of salt. —D.G.

Asian/American Cocktails

Sometimes inspired by "Asian" ingredients (ginger liqueur or orgeat, an almond syrup), but mostly the result of random invention, American cocktail makers have named drinks after everything Asian from places (China, Kowloon, Shanghai, Yokohama Mama) to plants (Orange Blossom, Cherry Blossom)to animals (Panda) and even religious icons (Buddha Punch). The mythical dragon is another common leitmotif (Golden Dragon, Green Dragon, Rocky Green Dragon), as are musicals (Mikado, South Pacific). Names have ranged from the war-related (Pacific Pacifier, Burma Bridge Buster) to the cute (the saketini, a sake martini) to the inexplicable (John Poister's Geisha Cup, of which he says, "I can't remember why I named it that.")

No one is really certain when or where the Kamikaze (triple sec, vodka, lime juice) was invented, although it was surely an American invention. Poister quips, "The Japanese would be embarrassed to have invented this drink." Gary Regan believes the drink was invented on New York's Upper East Side. Around the time of its invention, a friend of his walked into a bar. After watching the bartender make the drink, the friend noticed that the ingredients were similar to a gimlet's. He asked about the difference between the two drinks. The bartender responded: "Well, you don't want to commit suicide after a gimlet."

Sweets from the East: Asian Candy

What makes Asian candy so uniquely satisfying? Part of it is packaging: the vibrant colors, unfamiliar cartoon animals, and bizarre slogans decorating the boxes and wrappers of these imported sweets offer fantasies of otherworldly delights. There's buttery-sweet White Rabbit candy, delivered from the moon by the bunny who resides there (according to Chinese tradition) [👁237]. There's caramelly Milky, the only treat recommended by round-faced 'toon gal "Peko-chan." And there's also the inexplicable confection known as "haw flakes," made—naturally—out of "haw," and beloved throughout China and Southeast Asia.

Consider yourself lucky that you can even find the stuff (and more and more you can, at local delis and in ethnic centers everywhere); the history of the candy industry in Asia is a bitter tale indeed, featuring cutthroat competition, ripped-off recipes, and trade warfare. The mid-1980s in Japan, for example, saw extortionists threatening to poison Valentine's Day sweets; the kidnapping for ransom of the president of confection giant Glico; and a threat by U.S. business interests to impose trade sanctions against the Japanese maker of what they perceived to be a cheesy clone of M&Ms. Fortunately, the extortionists were paid, the head of Glico escaped unhurt, and the M&M/Mars company cooled off. Now Americans can truly enjoy some of the sweetest treats Japan—and the rest of Asia—has to offer.

Here are a myriad of sugary choices from Asia available somewhere near you. A warning: They're all high on sentimental and curiosity value, but not, unfortunately, nutritional. —D.G., T.H., J.Y.

Name/photo	Country/Company	Fun Wrapper Slogan
Botan Rice Candy	Japan (JFC International)	"Each candy has an edible inner wrapper that melts in your mouth"
Fresh Mint, Cool Mint, Green Gum, Black Black	Japan (Lotte, a Korean company)	"Enjoy the delight only possible from Lotte."
Ginseng gum	Japan (Lotte)	None, but the ginseng root on package looks like a person sitting down.
Ginseng gum	Korea (Haitai)	"Keep foil wrapper to put gum in after use."
Haw flakes	Korea (Haitai)	"Store in a cool dry place away from direct sunlight."
Pastilles	Philippines (Goldilocks Bakery)	None (they're wrapped in a plain white-paper wrapping).
Polvoron	Philippines (Goldilocks)	"Polvoron" in a nice flowery script.
Preserved fruit	Macau (Tai Sun)	None. Fruit is fruit.
Queen cup jelly	Japan (Eishindo)	None, unless you count "Product of Japan."
Soft Milky	Japan (Fujiya)	"Any time with Peko."
White Rabbit (classic)	China (White Rabbit)	"Creamy candies."

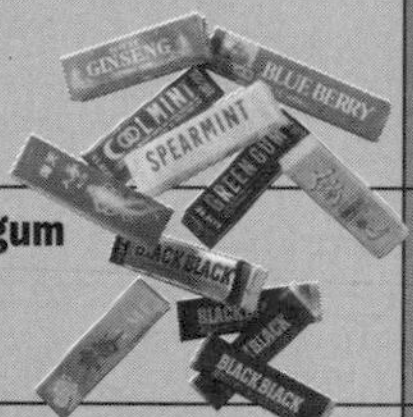

Description (including scary ingredients)	How It Looks and Tastes
Gummy rice candy made of millet jelly, sweet rice, and lots of sugar	This mildly sweet, amber-colored chewable has the taste and texture of the insides of a plain ol' jellybean, but its popularity in Asia (and in the U.S., among kids in the know) is phenomenal. Why? Well, the green-and-red box, which has been decorated with the same chrysanthemum, cat, and sumo baby for decades, is cute. And like Cracker Jacks, Botan includes a toy surprise in each box, though nowadays we're talking "cheap paper sticker" rather than "nifty collectible surprise." Despite the advice on the box flap, people still insist on trying to peel off the rice paper. Connoisseurs know that the best way to eat the candy is to let the rice paper melt slowly in one's mouth before biting.
Whatever gum's made of, it's got to be worth a lot less than what it costs. Such steep profit margins have made Lotte's Korean owner, Shin Kyuk-Ho, one of the 50 richest people in the world.	Lotte has flavors with bite. According to their wrappers, Green Gum, Cool Mint, and Fresh Mint all have "a light and mild sweetness coupled with lasting flavor and comfortable chewiness." They taste like Wrigley's Spearmint, Peppermint, and Ginseng (if Wrigley's made a ginseng gum), but with an extra minty kick. BlackBlack's "triple combination hi-tech" action makes it "a tasty breath freshening gum for beautiful white teeth." It tastes vaguely like licorice. And it's not black, it's charcoal grey.
"Ginseng extract/powder" and chewing gum	Austere green–and-white package, with each piece individually wrapped in copper foil. Unlike Lotte Fresh Mint, which tastes like mild ginseng, Lotte Ginseng smells like dry dirt and tastes like minty dirt.
Ginseng and chewing gum, as well as "softeners" and menthol	Lacquer-red package with a ginseng root on the front (looks like a headless person, but ginseng root always looks human); each piece wrapped in gold foil. Tastes like mentholated dirt. Perhaps we must conclude that ginseng in general tastes like dirt.
Round, Necco wafer–like coins of pressed, preserved, dried fruit; contains "new coccine C.I. 16255" and, of course, "haw"	Cool green, yellow, and magenta wrapping. For would-be Catholics, these sweet, tart, purplish-pink wafers are good for playing "Holy Communion." There are about 20 wafers in each individually wrapped cylinder.
Dry candy made of sugar, milk, and egg	Even though one kind of pastille resembles a white conte crayon and another looks like nothing more than a moist lump of sugar, both are very accessible to the novice taster. It's like eating a vanilla cupcake with milk all in one little bite. The packaging on this homemade-style candy is strictly no-frills; their idea of ornamentation is cutting fringes into the plain white paper wrapping.
Same as above, but different; sometimes contains *pinipig*, which is toasted young rice	Unwrap the jewel-toned cellophane carefully or these bite-size circular or oval cakes will crumble into fine dust before they make it to your mouth; once there, they melt sweetly on the tongue; eaten especially around Christmas and special occasions.
Mashed preserved fruit made into a pasty lump and wrapped for individual consumption; contains "The Five Spices"	Once you unwrap the cheerful layers of rice paper and plastic, you are met with a piece of preserved, dried fruit that looks like doo-doo; these are an acquired taste—the sweet, pungent fruit pastes leave a sour aftertaste.
Little plastic cups of sweetened agar jelly in neon colors. Agar, or "agar-agar," is made from seaweed.	Tastes like warm Jell-O. After peeling off the foil top, you should suck the whole chunk of agar out at once. Comes in lemon, lime, orange, and strawberry flavors, but alas, they all taste the same.
Chewy milk candy; there is no "hard" Milky	Milky is the color of butter. It tastes sweet and...milky! The red-and-white package features Peko-chan, a wholesome-looking pig-tailed girl, tongue dangling at the thought of eating Milky.
White, bite-sized tubes of sugar-freak, cavity-creep hell. Kids love it, but you'll find it stuck to furniture and drapes afterward.	The blue, white, and orange wrappers have a sort of Art Deco feel to them; the chewy candies are like ersatz caramel, with a milky aftertaste; and yes, you're supposed to eat the inner rice-paper wrapping. Brings one back to the days of snuggling on Mom's lap.

STICKING IT OUT: A Primer

1 If the chopsticks are wooden disposables, gently pull them apart with both hands. Many people like to rub the chopsticks against each other to brush off stray splinters. This is perfectly acceptable, but rubbing them a few times should suffice; otherwise, you might start a fire.

2 Grasp both chopsticks together, points facing down, letting the bottom chopstick rest in the crook of your hand. Keep the bottom chopstick stationary by positioning it firmly between the inner joint of the thumb and the first joint of the curled ring finger. Diagrams printed on paper disposable chopstick sleeves advise you to grasp one chopstick and place it into position before adding the second, but if you do it this way, you may as well announce to the world that you're a chopstick virgin.

3 Secure the upper chopstick by holding it between the thumb pad and first two fingers. The pincering motion is controlled for the most part by the movement of the first two fingers. Chopstick wrappers commonly instruct you to hold the upper stick "as you hold a pencil," but when writing with a pencil, the thumb is a primary mover, along with the index and middle fingers. With a pair of chopsticks, this is impractical. Let your middle finger help move the upper stick. If you don't, you'll end up crossing your chopsticks, which can result in the awkward flip-flopping of food morsels, turning them into dangerous projectiles.

Chopsticks

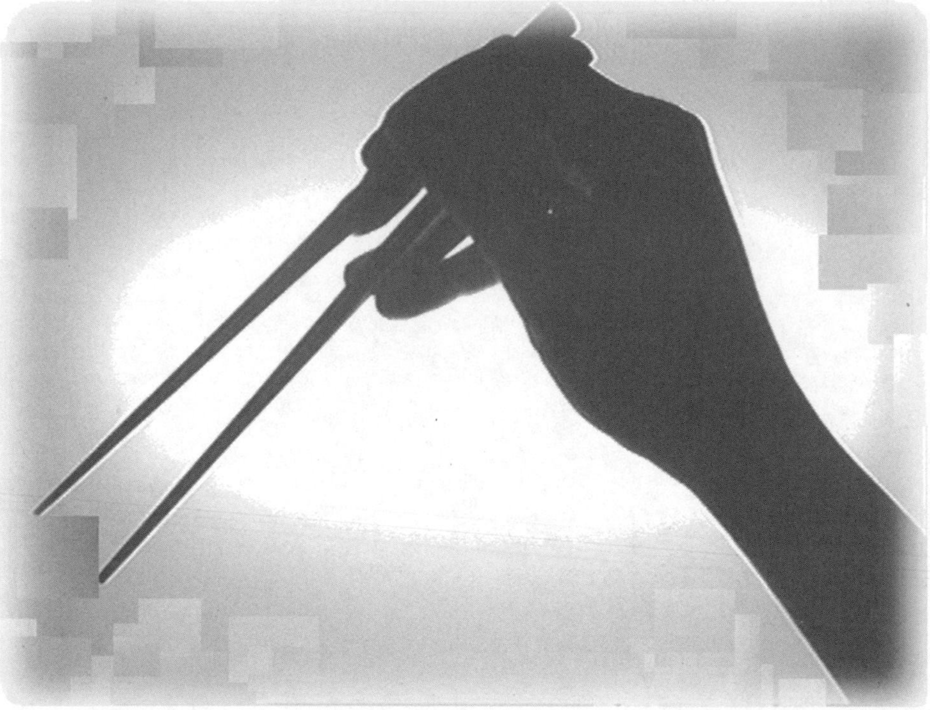

Regardless of how difficult you may find chopsticks to use, these thin, eight-to-10-inch-long eating utensils are used by more than a quarter of the world's population. Known as *kuai zi* ("fast fellows") chopsticks were used in China as early as 400 B.C., and exported to other East Asian countries by 500 A.D. The Japanese made them slightly shorter and more pointed at the ends and called them *hashi* ("bridge"), because chopsticks form a bridge between bowl and mouth; the Korean variety (*jhuk kha rak*) are usually made of stainless steel. Ancient Asian royalty commonly used chopsticks made from silver, since it was believed silver blackened upon contact with poison. (This is not strictly true. Silver does not change color in the presence of toxins such as cyanide or arsenic, but it may turn black from exposure to the hydrogen sulfide released by rotten eggs, onions, or garlic.)

These days, chopsticks for eating are made from plastic, as well as any light but strong wood, including bamboo, cedar, sandalwood, teak, and pine. Chopsticks used for cooking are often made from unlacquered bamboo, because it can withstand high temperatures and doesn't conduct heat.

Unfortunately, wooden chopsticks are a potential breeding ground for bacteria. The modern answer to this threat, disposable chopsticks, currently poses a severe ecological problem: the Southeast Asian rainforests from which disposable-chopstick timber is harvested are shrinking from excess demand—Japan alone consumes as many as 20 billion disposable chopsticks (*waribashi*) a year. Japanese households customarily reserve a pair of personal chopsticks for each member of the family; recent conservation efforts include the toting of hashi around in carrying cases, to avoid wasting waribashi.

Although chopstick evolution basically halted in 500 A.D., that hasn't stopped the odd innovator from trying to build a better hashi. Recent chopstick inventions issued patents by the U.S. Patent Office include plastic chopsticks with corrugated tips to provide better grippability of slippery foods; telescoping chopsticks for environmentally minded chopstick users on-the-go; a combination fork and chopsticks for those who want the best of East and West; and "tweezer" chopsticks connected by a spring-loaded device "to give the correct feel for the use of chopsticks" without the agony of actually having to master them.

1

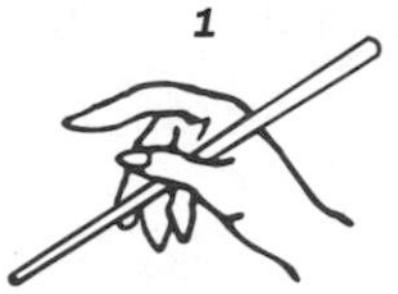

Chopstick Hints and Etiquette

• Square chopsticks are easier to use than round ones; unfinished ones are easier than lacquered ones.

• Don't grasp them too tightly or your hand will cramp. Snapping them in two is considered poor etiquette.

2

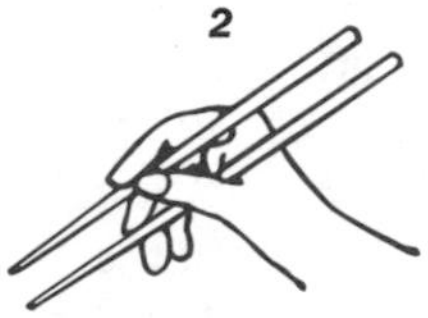

• If serving spoons are not provided for shared dishes, you may serve yourself by turning your chopsticks around and placing food on your plate with the bottom ends of your chopsticks instead of the tips. Turn them back around before you begin eating. Note, however, that when dining in familiar company (friends or family), it is considered a breach of etiquette to serve yourself this way, since it shows an unseemly lack of desire for intimacy.

3

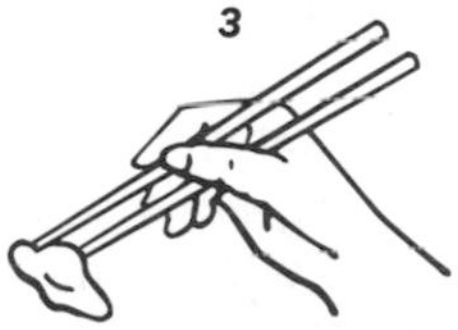

• Don't place your chopsticks across your plate or directly on the table when they're at rest. Lean the tips against the side of the plate, letting the bottoms rest on the table. Japanese restaurants often provide chopstick rests, called *hashigaki* or *hashioki,* which are made of wood, glass, or ceramic, and can add a decorative touch to the dinner table.

• Never stick your chopsticks upright in your rice bowl. This is based on the fact that upright sticks look like the incense sticks used to honor the dead.

• Never take food from someone else's chopsticks. In Japanese funerary custom, bone fragments from the dead are picked from a pyre and family members pass them to one another using ceremonial chopsticks. Afterwards, the chopsticks are thrust into the ashes, points down.

• Never reach across a neighbor's chopsticks. "Chopstick fencing" will, at best, cause a mess and, at worst, result in the loss of an eye.

• Never lick or bite your sticks, since this is considered barbaric. So is fishing around for the best pieces in a serving dish.

• Japanese food, such as pickles or dumplings, may be speared with a chopstick, but it is bad form to stab pieces of Chinese food, which is generally served cut up into bite-size pieces.

• In the case of soups, eat solid pieces with chopsticks, then sip or spoon the liquid from the bowl.

• According to Miss Manners, the definitive rule about using chopsticks as hair ornaments is: "Do not put chopsticks in your hair. Especially after lunch." The hair sticks you see sticking out of hairdos in woodblock prints of Japanese women are actually called *kanzashi* or *kogai.*

• If you really want to impress the waiters in a Chinese restaurant, eat rice from a bowl the way the Chinese do: Raise the rice bowl with one hand and perch the edge of the bowl on your lower lip. Hold the chopsticks together with the other hand, and shovel the rice into your mouth, being careful not to spill grains on the floor. In Chinese custom, rice symbolizes life's blessings, so it is important to suck them in with gusto rather than pick away at them. —D.G., J.Y.

How *Not* to Eat with Chopsticks

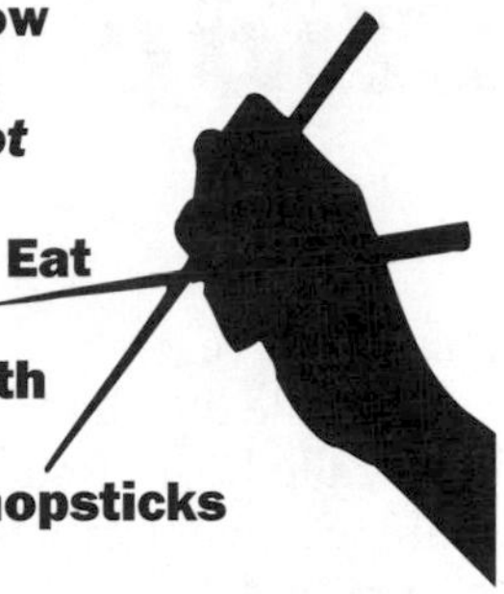

1 THE "POKE 'N' CHOKE": Take chopsticks firmly in one hand and puncture food morsels, skewer-style. Although this is perfectly acceptable for young children, this method is unsightly for adults.

2 THE "SCISSOR GRIP": Grip chopsticks in one hand, crossed into an awkward "X" shape. Use misunderstood principles of leverage to pinch food and bring some of it toward mouth. Allow remainder to fall on lap.

3 THE "BALANCING ACT": Hold chopsticks closely together. With the fingers of your opposite hand, slide a chunk of food onto the tips of the chopsticks. Raise chopsticks, with food teetering precariously, in general direction of mouth. Drop food. Repeat.

4 THE "SWEET SURRENDER": Use chopsticks to signal waiter. Ask for fork.

Chopstick superstitions

• How you hold your chopsticks can say a lot about you. If you clutch them close to the tips, you are short-tempered. The further back you hold them, the more gracious your personality. However: The closer your fingers are to the tips, the closer you live to your eventual mate. If you grasp them from high up, you will marry a foreigner.

• A more modern superstition is that if you can break waribashi cleanly, so that the bottom ends are even in size and shape, then the rest of your day will be lucky. Another tale says that if the chopsticks are broken apart unevenly, then it means that the affections in your current relationship are shared unevenly. However, disposable chopsticks are not interchangeable with wishbones.

Chop Suey

This meat, vegetable, and noodle dish has been called "Chinese soul food"; contrary to popular belief, however, chop suey first appeared in *America*, circa 1850, and was in fact unknown in China until after World War II. As a result, variations such as "chop suey sundae," "farmer's chop suey" (raw vegetables mixed with sour cream), and "American chop suey" (ground beef, noodles, and tomato sauce) aren't necessarily less authentic than the standard Chinese takeout version, which contains some combination of beef, noodles, bean sprouts, mushrooms, carrots, celery, onions, tomatoes, soy sauce, sherry, sugar, and corn starch, stir-fried and served over rice.

So where *did* chop suey come from? A number of competing origin myths exist:

1. A display at Idaho City's Boise Basin Museum claims that a Chinese man who had been invited to the White House for dinner was displeased with the food, so he cooked his own dish and called it "chop suey."

2. Another story explains that Chinese ambassador Li Hung-Chang couldn't stomach the rich foods served at foreign banquets, so—during a visit to New York—he and an aide concocted the bland dish as a substitute. J.N. Kane's *Famous First Facts* pinpoints the date of this diplomatic debut as August 29, 1896.

3. Another, similar story places the date of chop suey's invention earlier, in the 1850s, when a different visiting Chinese dignitary had dinner with President Grover Cleveland at the Waldorf-Astoria—declining the sumptuous hotel food in favor of the stir-fry created by his personal chef.

4. Yet another simply claims that chop suey was invented by an *Irish* waiter working in a Chinese restaurant in San Francisco.

5. A more reasonable (and detailed) origin story also takes place in San Francisco—where, during the Gold Rush of 1849, more than 300,000 Chinese travelled in search of fortune. It was only a matter of time before immigrant entrepreneurs set up "chow-chows," the precursor to the Chinese restaurant. Popular with both Asians and non-Asians, chow-chows served all you could eat for $1. One night, a group of hungry miners burst into a popular chow-chow, which had closed early after running out of food. The miners demanded to be fed anyway; the desperate but ingenious cook tossed together some leftover meat and vegetables, which he would otherwise have thrown out. The miners gobbled up the impromptu dish and proclaimed it delicious. They asked the cook what the dish was called, so they could order it again. *"Shap sui,"* said the cook, which the miners understood to be "chop suey." *Shap sui*, in Cantonese, means "mixed pieces" or "odds and ends." In other words, the first chop suey was literally table scraps.

6. The *real* story—or at least the most "official" one—is as follows. In 1988, a mock Court of Historical Review and Appeals determined that chop suey *was* first concocted in San Francisco during the Gold Rush. Annie Soo, secretary of the San Francisco–based Chinese Historical Society of America, testified that the chef who invented chop suey under duress was her husband's grandfather's boss. According to Soo, whose testimony is based on years of family legend, one of the miners went so far as to threaten the cook with a gun. As in the story above, he hastily threw together some vegetable scraps and discarded meat entrails, which the miners gobbled up like ambrosia. When they asked the cook what the dish was called, he told them, *"Chop sui,"* which in Cantonese literally means "garbage bits." Other witnesses testified in the 1988 ruling that many of the Chinese who worked in mining towns were forced by circumstance to subsist on chop suey–like dishes thrown together from "whatever crawled or moved." And the reason why chop suey is served over white rice instead of fried rice, says Soo, is "because the white rice cleanses the palate in between bites of the many tastes of chop suey." —D.G.

"Chop Suey: Real Chinese Cuisine."
—Neon sign spotted in New York City, c. 1933

"Genuine American Chop Suey."
—Another sign, in post–World War II Shanghai

Curry

When you think of Indian restaurants, you think of curry. When you think of Thai restaurants, you think of curry. When you think of Chinese, Japanese, or Vietnamese restaurants, you probably *don't* think of curry, but it's there anyway. Curry is one of Asia's most traveled foods, popping up in different guises throughout South, Southeast, and East Asia—not to mention Europe and the world. Considering that the spice trade was a primary reason for European colonialism throughout Asia, it could be said that the British came to India for curry, and subjugated the population as an afterthought.

Certainly, however, the origin of what is commonly known in the West as "curry" lies in India, where it has been eaten with gusto (not to mention rice) for five millennia. But what the West considers "curry" is a result of vaguely remembered curry powder recipes (for the most part, haphazardly converging around turmeric and chilies, with saffron for coloring) brought home by British, Dutch, and Portuguese traders and conquerors; versions of this poor substitute were available by 1860 in both Europe and America. This led to curry's gradual degeneration from hundreds of combinations of spices and cooking styles into the uniform, boring, dirty-yellow dust you buy in supermarkets today. Sadly enough, most people, who think of curry as a single spice rather than a blend of many, don't know that any other kinds of curry exists. Even the name "curry" is a Western invention, most likely the British corruption of a Tamil (Southern Indian) word, *kari*, meaning "spice," or possibly *karahi*, meaning the wok-like pot that Indians use for cooking.

The truth is, curry is best thought of as a style of cooking than a spice or a dish. Just about anything can be "curried." What makes a dish a curry is the combination of meats and/or vegetables prepared with a richly spiced sauce or gravy—which implies that many, if not most of the diverse dishes in the traditional Indian repertoire can be called curries.

Thanks to the peripatetic efforts of spice traders, curry traveled from India to other Asian ports. It's an integral part of most Southeast Asian cuisines. In China, curry dishes have existed for at least a thousand years; in Japan, for only about a century, due primarily to the efforts of the British, who brought curry with them when Japan was opened for foreign trade during the late Meiji era, 1868 to 1912. These days, especially in U.S. restaurants, the most popular curry dishes feature beef, lamb, and chicken, though you'll also see fish and seafood, pork, and sometimes goat. On the other hand, if you overhear someone mentioning "currying a horse," he's more likely to be discussing grooming than gourmandizing. Still, you never know. Check the kitchen for hoofprints.

SO WHY IS CURRY SPICY?

Like many other warm-climate cultures, Indians developed a cuisine that ranges from moderately spicy to suicidally hot in flavor. Scientists assure that on a sweltering day, spicy food actually makes you feel cooler, triggering sweat glands to release refreshing perspiration into your armpits and clothing. While this may seem counterintuitive, it does seem to account for the predominance of spicy foods in Southern and equatorial cuisines. —J.Y., T.H.

Curry in a Hurry

A quick curry tour of the world

garam masala (literally, a "warm mix")—Cinnamon, nutmeg, cloves, cardamom, cumin, and saffron. A classic of Northern origin; the Moghul style also features ground nuts, dried fruits, and creamy yogurt. Medium-hot.

Vindaloo—Fresh red chilies, dry mustard, coriander, and fenugreek. Spices and herbs are ground in vinegar to make a paste that results in a sweet-sour taste. From the Goa region of South India; the spiciest of Indian sauces.

Madras—Dried chilies, coriander, cumin, mustard seeds, peppercorns, curry leaves, ginger, and turmeric. Southern Indian. Fragrant, fairly spicy.

Thai green curry—Fresh green chilies, basil, dark herbs; coconut milk. Very spicy; for cast-iron stomachs only.

Thai red curry—Fresh and dried red chilies; coconut milk. Provides lingering heat.

Thai yellow curry—Red chilies, turmeric; coconut milk. Mild.

Thai orange curry—Red chilies, vinegar, shrimp paste; coconut milk. Used for seafood and soup; a sour curry.

Massaman—Dried red chilies, potatoes, cinnamon, cloves, cardamom, mace, and nutmeg; white potatoes; coconut milk. Mildest of the Thai curries.

Dim Summing Up

In the good old days, after satisfied customers finished their dim sum repasts and pushed themselves gently away from their dish-laden tables, a waiter would come and count the empty plates remaining to tally the fiscal damage; unfortunately, sneaky diners began sticking plates on other tables, under chairs, or in their pockets in order to stiff their bills. Nowadays, after each point-and-click order you make, cart-pushers will mark your bill with a little stamp to denote a dish consumed. Dim sum comes in three price categories, small, medium, and large, with more exotic or bulkier items demanding higher rent. To pay your bill, just signal a waiter (not a busboy); he or she will run the tally and write it down in plain numerals. A solid dim sum should run you between $8 and $15 a person, and you'll be stuffed. Now comes the big question: How much should you tip? We advise being generous, since the waitering trade is not a particularly jolly one; but if you need a rule of thumb, ten percent is the minimum (if you haven't bothered your waiter at all), and make it 15 percent if you've demanded any kind of table service whatsoever. Especially if you've asked for forks.

Dim Sum

The Chinese answer to meals on wheels, dim sum isn't just a brunch—it's an adventure. A dim sum repast consists of appetizer-size portions of food, picked from rolling carts as they pass from table to table. The selection is enormous, ranging from dumplings to roast meats to sweet buns, to more challenging delicacies like duck feet; purportedly, more than a thousand varieties of dim sum dishes exist, although a typical dim sum restaurant serves just 50 to 100.

Dim sum has its origins more than 2,000 years ago in southern China, where, according to Jack Tang, dim sum chef at New York's HSF Dim Sum Restaurant, wives would prepare the appetizing morsels for their husbands as a small token of their love. Thus the name: in Cantonese, *dim* means "a little bit," and *sum* means "heart," making dim sum "a little bit of heart."

When inviting a platonic friend to eat dim sum, however, you might say "Let's go *yum cha,*" which literally means going to drink tea. But don't expect quiet brunchtime conversation; the atmosphere is loud, rowdy, and family-style. Get there early to avoid waiting and to get the freshest food (no later than 11 a.m.). Go in a crowd, to improve the dish selection and avoid sharing a table, a common experience for pairs and trios. Six or eight people is best, since dim sum dishes tend to come in units of three or four items per plate.

Most dim sum dishes are eaten with chopsticks, although buns, tarts, and egg rolls can be eaten with your hands. Feel free to place a small amount of hot sauce or mustard on your plate for dipping purposes (you can also ask for soy sauce or chili oil, though purists will frown at you). If you must have rice, order fried rice rather than white. And the *only* proper beverage to drink with your meal is tea: most large dim sumptuaries will have at least two varieties—regular black tea and sweet jasmine tea. Above all, relax—to do a proper yum cha, you'll need at least two hours.

Dining Dim Sum

Rule number one: Be ready to point. Sometimes servers will pause at each table and show off each dish as they pass. Other times, they'll steamroll on by, shouting the name of the item (in Chinese, of course). In this case, advises HSF manager Eddie Yee, you should just stop them and point at your selection. "The hardest part of dim sum," says Yee, "is finding out what you want." Figure on ordering about two to five dishes per person in your party, depending on your crowd's appetite. Typical dishes like *har gow, shiu mai,* and other dumplings range in cost from $1.50 to $2.50 per order. More elaborate dishes like lotus leaf-wrapped sticky rice or cold jellyfish are higher priced—$3.50 and up. For the meek of appetite, the two most popular (and nonthreatening) dim sum dishes are har gow (shrimp dumplings) and shiu mai (open-topped pork and cabbage dumplings). But don't be afraid to pick things you don't recognize. Part of the experience is the excitement of discovery; if you stick to meaty, fatty old standards—dumplings, spare ribs, and the like—your dim sum experience will be heavy and nutritionally appalling. Many dim sum dishes are steamed and made of healthy ingredients like shrimp, Chinese cabbage, and tofu. Most Westerners like the deep-fried dishes, such as fried wonton, observes Chef Tang. It's your loss.
—D.G., T.H., J.Y.

KID STUFF

cha won ton
(fried wonton made of pork or beef).

Don't bother.

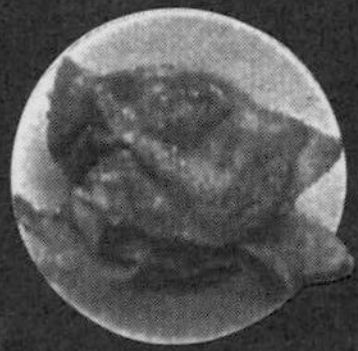

ja hyee keem
(fried crab claw).

Neither Chinese in origin nor dietician-approved.

churn gyoon
(spring roll).

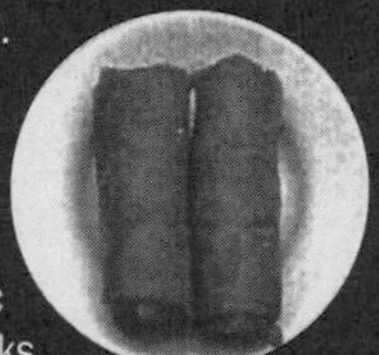

Ordering these inauthentic grease sticks will provoke contempt from the waitstaff.

daan tut
(egg custard tart).

Mmmm...

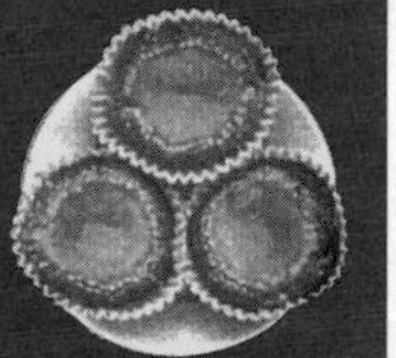

FOR THE NOVICE

shiu mai
(open-topped meat dumpling made of pork or pork and beef).

No dim sum experience is complete without it.

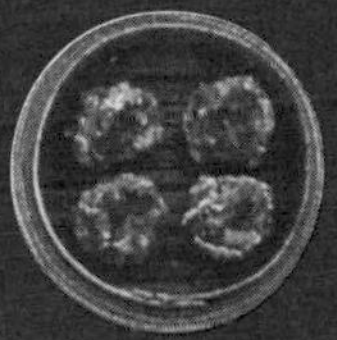

har gow
(shrimp dumpling).

Absolutely essential.

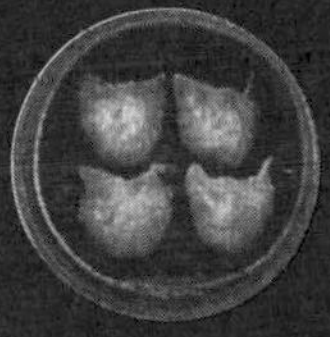

ji ma eun
(sesame balls filled with lotus or bean paste).

Heavy and unappealing for some, but a taste treat for the kids.

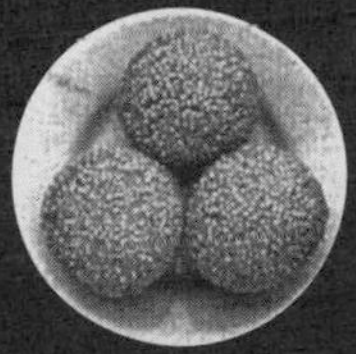

ngor my guy
(sticky rice wrapped in lotus leaf).

Don't eat the leaf.

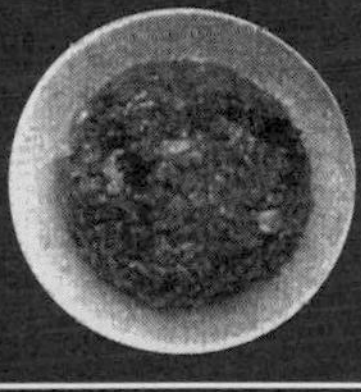

INTERMEDIATE

law bak go
(white turnip cake).

Dip it in the oyster sauce. Don't miss it.

yuu daan
(fish balls).

Better consumed in a soup noodle bowl.

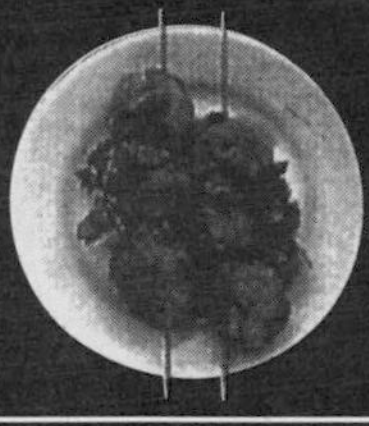

tofu fa
(tofu in honey).

A great authentic dessert.

hung yun
(almond tofu).

Not tofu, but an almond gelatin. Light and refreshing.

EXPERT ONLY

fung jao
(chicken feet).

Order it just so you can tell your friends.

ap gurk
(duck feet).

A double-dare order.

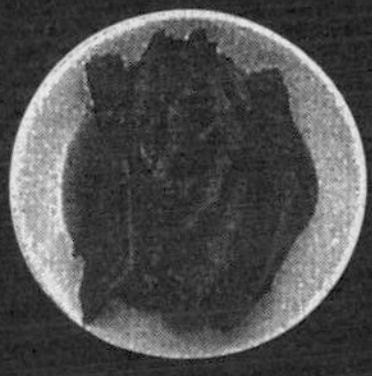

ngaw jhap
(beef tripe).

Tastier than you'd think.

hoi gi pei
(cold jellyfish).

Rare and worth getting if you see it.

GWO TIEH: fried pork dumpling

CHURN GYOON: deep-fried pork, shrimp, and vegetable spring roll

CHA SIU PAO: roast pork bun, toasty-brown baked, or fluffy-white steamed

CHING JING PIE GWOT: spare ribs, steamed in black bean and pepper sauce, a must-order for meat-eaters

HAW FUN: steamed canelloni-style rice noodle containing beef, roast pork, shrimp, or other fillings

SONG CHAO NGOR MAI FON: steamed, glutinous rice containing pork, mushrooms, bamboo shoots, and other tasty surprises

TOFU PEI: steamed, wrapped bean curd sheet containing pork or pork and beef

YUU DAAN: steamed, white balls of minced and pounded fish

TOFU FA: light, cool tofu curds in a sweet, syrupy honey sauce.

HUNG YUN: almond tofu, a white almond-flavored gelatin usually served with a spoonful of fruit cocktail in syrup.

NOTE: Cantonese has no standard romanization system, and intonations are difficult to transliterate; pronunciations are provided as a guideline only.

Dumplings

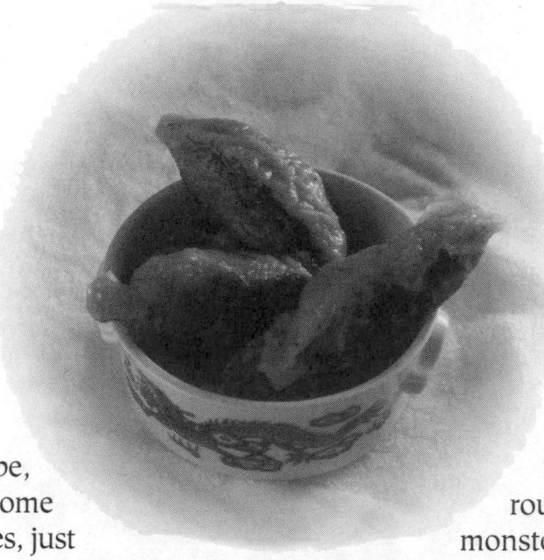

History has it that Marco Polo returned triumphantly from China to his native Italy bearing a bounteous array of new foodstuffs—including noodles, which became that starchy Italian staple, pasta. Did he tote dumplings—a.k.a., "Asian ravioli"—with him as well? Probably not; unlike noodles, over the months-long sea voyage from Asia to Europe, meat and vegetable-filled dough would become very unpleasant trade goods indeed. Besides, just about every culture has its own version of the dumpling, though the Chinese have transformed the humble dish into something like an art.

The Chinese have made dumplings for over a thousand years old; *won ton* in soup—the oldest known dumpling variant—can be traced back to the Tang period (618-907 A.D.). According to legend, the filling of the first dumpling was the ground flesh of a fearsome beast slain on New Year's Eve by a wandering traveler in the northeastern mountains of China. Thereafter, in celebration, the villagers that the stranger saved (as well as the rest of northeastern China) prepared dumplings on New Year's and holidays.

These days, dumplings are eaten all year round, requiring neither an excuse nor ground monster flesh for preparation. Uncooked, they keep well frozen, and can be purchased in large quantities in plastic bags at most Asian supermarkets, and steamed, boiled, or fried at your leisure. They're also a staple part of a dim sum meal. As can be seen below, every country has its own variation on the theme—but if it's doughy on the outside and stuffed with stuff, it's a dumpling. —D.Y.

Country	Name	Description	How is it prepared?
China	**Won ton**	Small, succulent, meat-filled; smaller than dumplings, with a thinner, more translucent wrapper made from wheat flour and egg dough.	In a clear, chicken-stock soup; also, in America, anyway, deep-fried served with duck sauce (which is not actually made out of duck, but rather plums, apricots, and sugar).
China	**Guo tie** (literally, "pot sticker"), Chinese or Peking ravioli, fried style.	Browned on one side to a slight crisp, tender elsewhere. Usually has a minced pork and vegetable filling. Sometimes available vegetarian.	They stick to the pot when they're being pan-fried, and thus the name. Legend has it that a cook's slip-up in China's Imperial Palace kitchen led to their creation; the inattentive cook, who was making boiled dumplings, allowed the water to boil dry. Usually served with a soy sauce and vinegar dipping sauce.
China	**Steamed dumplings**	Similar to pot stickers, but with a thicker, chewier, more bread-like wrapper.	Steamed; served with a soy sauce and vinegar dipping sauce.
China	**Xiao long bao**	A tasty, juicy pork-and–Chinese cabbage dumpling originating in Shanghai, where entire restaurants are devoted to them. And they're always crowded.	Steamed on a bed of Chinese cabbage in round bamboo baskets; must be eaten while hot, with a ginger, vinegar, and soy sauce dip or just alone. Good ones are so juicy that you have to eat them with chopsticks *and* a spoon.
Japan	**Gyoza**	A delicate Japanese version of the pot sticker, made with a slightly thinner wrapper; usually served as an appetizer; the meat filling is usually pork, sometimes beef.	Pan-fried, served with soy-based dipping sauce.
Korea	**Mandoo**	Korean version of the dumpling, with a ground beef, tofu, and vegetable filling.	Cooked in soup, usually with rice cake slices, cellophane noodles, and meat slices (mandoo guk); steamed or pan-fried, served with a sesame, soy-based dipping sauce; sometimes deep-fried, served with same dipping sauce.

Fortune Cookies

These sweet, crispy, bow-shaped sugar cookies have now become a part of Chinese restaurant tradition, arriving as dessert (usually on top of your check)—despite the fact that 1. the Chinese have no tradition of dessert, and 2. fortune cookies are very much an American invention.

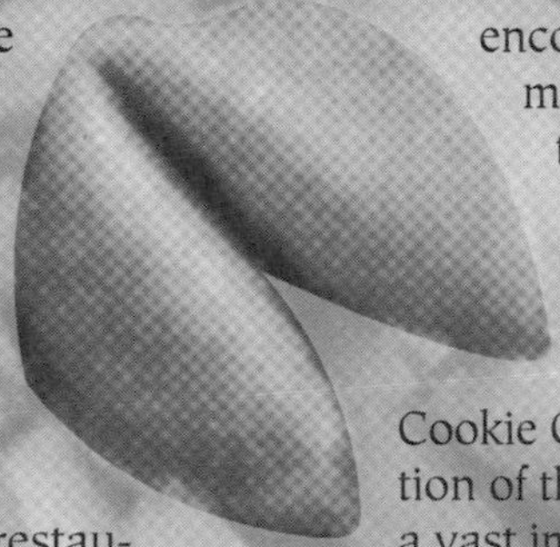

Several competing legends exist concerning the origin of the fortune cookie. One suggests that it was actually introduced in the Japanese Tea Garden in San Francisco's Golden Gate Park and was subsequently taken up by a Chinese entrepreneur who pirated the idea for his restaurants. Those who claim a Japanese American heritage for the fortune cookie contend that it descended from the flat, round, rice cracker called *sembei*. The Chinese, however, believe that the fortune cookie is a modern Chinese American take on moon cakes, which were allegedly used in the 14th century as an aid in the repulsion of the Mongols. Chinese soldiers disguised as monks communicated military strategies by stuffing notes into the sweet buns; the idea of note-stuffed pastry survived, although the regime that invented them did not.

A more plausible story traces the origin of the fortune cookie to the early 20th century—specifically, to the Los Angeles of 1918, where David Jung, founder of the Hong Kong Noodle Co., invented the dessert as a snack and encouraging word for the unemployed men who hung around outside on the street. (Some say he invented the fortune cookie merely as a gimmick to jump start his noodle business.) Edward Louie, founder of the Lotus Fortune Cookie Company, followed with the invention of the fortune cookie-folding machine, a vast improvement over the previous method done with chopsticks.

Whatever its origin and however they make them, the fortune cookie has been so popular in the United States that it has since been exported to its alleged ancestral home: China and Hong Kong (the fortunes remain written in English). But the largest market for fortune cookies is still by far the United States, where they have been made in every imaginable flavor, including cheese nacho and chocolate, and have had everything from personalized messages to wedding invitations to resumes to condoms put inside them. —D.G., T.H.

> "The Chinese believe that the fortune cookie is a modern Chinese American take on moon cakes, which were allegedly used in the 14th century as an aid in the repulsion of the Mongols. Chinese soldiers disguised as monks communicated military strategies by stuffing notes into the sweet buns; the idea of note-stuffed pastry survived, although the regime that invented them did not."

The Fortune Top 10

According to Sunny Kwan, author of the seminal fortune-cookie history Wisdom, the following are the most popular of the 1000-plus stock messages used by cookie-makers. Incidentally, none of them are attributable to Confucius. (And don't forget to add "...in bed.")

1. You will have great success.
2. You will soon be promoted.
3. You will step on the soil of many countries.
4. Your destiny is to be famous.
5. Your love life will be happy and harmonious.
6. Your present plans are going to succeed.
7. Good news will come to you from far away.
8. Now is the time to try something new.
9. Be confident and you will succeed.
10. You will be rich and respected.

Garden Varieties: Asian Fruits and Vegetables

Of the world's 20,000 to 80,000 edible food crops, the average American is exposed to only about 150. It's hard enough to get some people to eat their vegetables, and this narrow selection doesn't help. Luckily, the horizons of the American consumer have been broadening, in part due to the efforts of produce specialists like Frieda's, Inc., which has perfected the art of cross-ethnic merchandising. "We sell Asian food to non-Asians," boasts Karen Caplan, president of the company her mother founded in 1962. Frieda's "discovered" the kiwifruit, which found supermarket stardom only after its name was changed from the Chinese gooseberry. Frieda's was also the first produce company to sell domestically grown shiitake mushrooms, which at first they marketed as "black forest" mushrooms—because the Japanese word looked a little too much like the word for where mushrooms might grow.

The recent influx of immigrants from Southeast Asia and Latin America, a greater openness to ethnic cuisines, and a higher degree of health consciousness have made Americans ripe for a shift in the consumer paradigm. "Twenty years ago, people didn't even want to know varietal names," says Caplan. "Now they want to know everything." Still, there's no such thing as an overnight success in the produce world. It took decades for the kiwi to become a household name, and it may take decades more before the more exotic fruits and vegetables in Asia's larder become as ubiquitous in America's produce aisles as bananas and oranges.

—D.G.

lychee

plantains

persimmons

FRUITS

- **Citrus fruits** have been cultivated in their native Southeast Asia and in India for thousands of years, and were not introduced to Europe until the 12th century. Now, of course, citrus fruits grow all over the world.
- Despite its name, the **mandarin orange** or **tangerine** is not a true orange. Japan grows about a third of the world's tangerine supply, exporting a variety called the Satsuma mandarin. Originally indigenous to China, the mandarin was introduced to Europe through the Moroccan seaport of Tangiers, and was first called the Tangiers orange—thus the name tangerine. Hybrids of this fruit include the tangelo and the temple orange.
- The **pummelo,** the largest of the citrus fruits, is native to India and Malaysia. Also called the shaddock or Chinese grapefruit, the pummelo has a drier, meatier pulp than the grapefruit, and was introduced to Florida by the Spaniards in the 17th century. When served at a Chinese New Year banquet table, the pummelo is a sign of fertility. Don't confuse the pummelo with the pomelo, which is the archaic progenitor of the grapefruit, and no longer exists as a species.
- The **durian** is a smelly, heavy, green, spiny, tropical fruit, native to Southeast Asia. The pulp of the durian is soft and can be eaten raw, or cooked like a vegetable. Its taste, which has been described as "onions and ice cream," is one that must be acquired—that is, if you can get past the durian's legendary stench to take a taste. In Singapore, where durian is a delicacy, it is illegal to consume it in public or to carry it onto public transportation.
- The **mango** is a Southeast Asian native, and has been cultivated for more than 6,000 years in India, where legends say that the Buddha was presented with a mango grove as a place of repose. The fruit is also known as the "Apple of the Tropics," since it is regularly consumed by more than one-fifth of the world's population. Now grown in Florida, where it arrived in 1833.
- The **lychee** originated almost 2,000 years ago in China. In 1059, it became the subject of the first published work on fruit, written by Chinese scholar Cai Xiang. Lychee trees, which can take up to 15 years to mature, now grow in subtropical regions of Florida and Mexico. Be forewarned: eating too many lychees can cause a sore throat.
- The **kiwi fruit** is also known as the Chinese gooseberry. Native to south central China, the kiwi was first taken beyond the Great Wall by an Englishman, who sent its seed to be cultivated in the Royal Botanical Gardens. The fruit was introduced to New Zealand in 1906, and then exported to the U.S., where its unmarketable, original name was changed to kiwi, after New Zealand's national bird, whose feathers resemble the fruit's fuzzy, brown skin. A little-known fact: Never use kiwis in making Jell-O. An enzyme in the fruit prevents gelatin from setting.
- **Bananas** originated in Malaysia about 4,000 years ago and first spread in the Pacific region from India to the Philippines and New Guinea. Two thousand years later, bananas can be found throughout the equatorial band. After the discovery of America, Europeans introduced banana plants from Africa to Haiti and the Dominican Republic.
- The **plaintain** is otherwise known as the plantano, the macho, the plantano macho, and the cooking banana. Believed to be a Southeast Asian native, plaintains grow only in tropical climates, such as Central America, Columbia, Ecuador, Puerto Rico, and Hawaii. Plaintain leaves have been found in Peruvian tombs dated prior to the landing of Columbus in South America. Technically a fruit, plaintains are treated as vegetables and used like potatoes, but they can be baked or sautéed with brown sugar and cinnamon as a dessert.
- The **Asian pear** has the look of an apple, but the taste and texture of a pear. The fruit, which dates back to 1100 B.C., is the oldest known cultivated pear. Asian

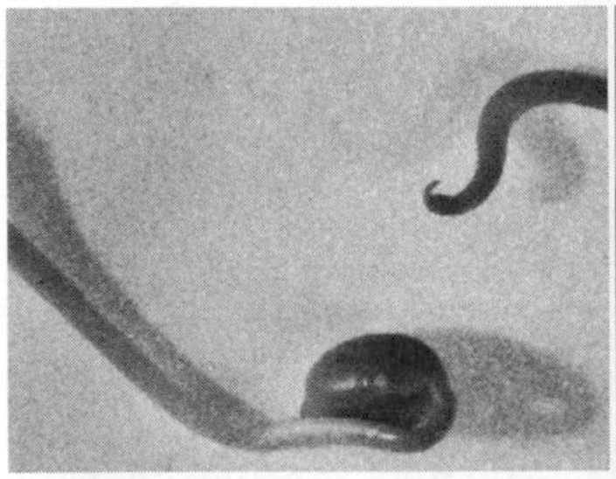

bean sprout

kiwi fruit

shiitake mushroom

asian pear

pear seeds were introduced to California by Chinese miners during the Gold Rush era, and were first planted along the waterways of the Sierra Nevada. More than 25 varieties of Asian pears are grown in California and Washington, and more than 100 in Japan. Also known as *nashi* (Japanese for pear), water pear, apple pear, sand pear, salad pear, Chinese pear, Oriental pear, and Asian apple.

• **Persimmons** originally come from China and Japan. Commodore Perry brought these reddish-orange, apple-like fruits to the U.S. from Japan in the 19th century. *Fuyu* persimmons (also *haru, kaki,* Japanese tomato, persapple, possum apple, or Olympic fruit) are of the non-astringent variety, and can be eaten fresh. The *hachiya* persimmon, which is better known in the U.S., is an astringent variety and, as such, must be processed or very ripe before eating.

• The exact origin of the **starfruit** (*Averrhoa carambola*) is unknown, but it is believed to be native to the Malayan region, and was brought to the Hawaiian Islands by Chinese sandalwood traders more than 75 years ago. References to starfruit appear in ancient Sanskrit writings, suggesting that the fruit was around in India before the time of European colonization.

Vegetables

• **Bean sprouts** are the germinated seeds of grains and legumes. The practice of sprouting seeds dates back thousands of years in Asia, and originally caught on in the U.S. with alfalfa sprouts. The most popular sprout used in Chinese cooking, however, is the mung bean. Bean sprouts are popular with vegetarians and can be eaten raw or cooked.

• **Bok choy** goes by many names, including Chinese chard, *tai sai,* and *lei choy*. Bok choy is believed to have crossed with the Chinese turnip in ancient times, producing the michell and napa cabbages. It has dark green leaves, and a milder flavor than cabbage.

• **Daikon**, or lo bok in Chinese, is also called Chinese, Japanese, or Oriental radish. Raw or cooked, daikon can be used like the radish; pickled daikon, which is often bright yellow, is a common side dish in Asian cuisine. Daikon looks like a long (up to 12 inches), very thick, white, misshapen carrot. "*Daikon ashi*" (literally "daikon legs") is a Japanese insult for a woman with short legs. In ancient Japan, it was believed that if you ate a daikon radish sprout during the summer festivals, you would stay healthy for the whole year.

• **Snow peas** are also called sno peas, China peas, or edible pea pods. Originally from Central Asia, other ancient cultures, such as the Greeks and Romans, quickly assimilated them into their cuisines. Sixteenth-century European aristocrats considered them a delicacy, eaten raw and immature. New World explorers brought snow peas to America in the 18th century, where they've since become a regular part of the American diet.

• The **shiitake mushroom** is known as "Elixir of Life" in Asian countries, but here it goes by the more mundane black forest, golden oak, or Chinese black mushroom. Shiitake used to be harvested from moist forests, particularly in Japan, where they've been grown from the trunks of rotting oak trees since the 17th century. Now they are cultivated on artificial logs or sawdust trays in sterile laboratories. In the U.S., shiitake farms are located in California, New York, Pennsylvania, Virginia, and Minnesota. The shiitake mushroom should never be eaten raw.

• **Enoki mushrooms** are also called *enokitake, enokidake,* enok mushrooms, golden mushrooms, or velvet stems. Enokis grow in the wild in North American forests, but their cultivation in a rice bran and sawdust medium originated in Asia about two decades ago. This sunless cultivation method produces the domesticated enoki's creamy-white color, which is quite different from the wild variety. Enoki mushrooms can be eaten raw and used like bean sprouts in salads and sandwiches. When cooked, they need just a few moments of heat before they are deliciously tender.

• **Wood ear mushrooms** are also called cloud ear, tree ear, silver ear, or Judas ear. They don't really look like your ears at all, unless you have some mangy disease. Usually sold in dried form and reconstituted in warm water before using, the rather bland-tasting mushroom is used mainly for its gelatinous crunch, which adds texture to a wide variety of dishes. The Japanese word for them is *kikurage*; Korean is *mook yee.* In Asia, wood ear mushrooms are believed to prevent heart disease.

• The **leek** has been around since prehistoric times, spreading westward from Asia to the Mediterranean and Europe, where they grow in the wild. The leek is the national plant of Wales. American leeks, which resemble an "overgrown green onion," are larger than European ones.

• The **taro root** also goes by the names dasheen, tannia, eddo, and the Polynesian potato. Native to Southeast Asia, taro root was brought to China and Japan, where the dasheen strain developed and was taken to the West Indies in the 16th century. Boiled taro is used for Hawaiian poi and African fufu; dried taro is used as a basis for flour. A fresh taro is about the size of a turnip, with brown, ringed skin, white flesh, and a taste like potatoes and water chestnuts. Taro must not be eaten raw, since it has an acrid, skin-irritating juice. Wear gloves when peeling taro root, and then bake, boil, or steam it as a potato substitute. Taro chips are a good alternative to potato chips.

• **Water chestnuts** are widely cultivated in China, but they're also grown in Georgia, Florida, Alabama, and California. Raw water chestnuts are tart, but when cooked, the taste is more like nutty sweet corn. Good water chestnuts are rock hard with some mud residue, which keeps them from drying out. Scrub and peel them before cooking or tossing them in a salad raw.

Fusion Cuisine

While the term "fusion cuisine" is a holdover from the '80s, the concept it defines began over 500 years ago. After all, were it not for foods crossing borders, Italians would never have perfected tomato sauce—nor would they have had pasta to pour it on; the Irish would never have had a potato famine, since they would never have had potatoes; the Swiss would be without their chocolate; and even Chinese Szechwan dishes would lack that definitive chili kick. According to Hugh Carpenter, considered the foremost aficionado of fusion cuisine in America and the author of *Fusion Food Cookbook*, "Historically, 'fusion cuisine' is an integration of ingredients and/or techniques of one or more cultures into a single dish. It does not necessarily mean a combination of foods from East and West."

However, the contemporary definition of fusion food does involve hemispheric bonding. It began in the restaurants of the West Coast, where a huge Asian population, and thus Asian ingredients, were readily available. Chefs started experimenting with Asian seasonings, got the attention of the media, and the fusion phenomenon exploded.

Peking Duck Pizza

More specifically, believes Carpenter, nouvelle fusion cuisine began in the town of Hanford, outside of Fresno, California. It was there that, shortly after World War II, Richard Wing—a one-time aide to General George Marshall—and his brother Paul founded Imperial Dynasty, the first East/West fusion restaurant in the U.S. "That's decades before Wolfgang Puck even learned to *cook*," notes Carpenter.

So famous was the restaurant's fare that, legend has it, representatives of the first U.S. delegation from the People's Republic of China got off the plane and immediately asked where Hanford was and how they could get there. "It may be just a story," says Carpenter, "but it's pretty amazing just the same."

While sources vary about the "founder" of fusion cuisine—going so far to even name names—Carpenter insists that no single inventor exists. "How can one person be given credit for a global phenomenon?" he says. "Besides, this type of cooking without boundaries has been going on since man has been eating."

Today, by most definitions, nouvelle fusion—also called multicultural, cross-cultural, and even "blendo" cuisine—has spawned such tasteful offspring as sashimi-wasabi pizza (a thin crust topped with raw tuna and a wasabi sauce); Tex-Mex fajitas made with Chinese ingredients such as duck, hoisin sauce, and red bean paste; hibachi salmon; grilled chicken satay over a frissee salad; and tempura onion rings.

"Food today is changing at an astonishing rate," says Carpenter. "Just speaking about the U.S., all the different food trends that we've been going through—Cajun, Nouvelle French, Southwestern—these are all branches of the fusion cuisine tree."

With the enormous rise in immigration from around the world, new groups are bringing with them different cooking styles and ingredients that eventually end up in your local supermarket. "Think about what was available 15 years ago in U.S. groceries and what's available now," says Carpenter. "Not just in major metropolitan cities like San Francisco or New York, but tiny little places like Hendersonville, North Carolina, where I can get fresh shiitake mushrooms, exotic fruits, and every other ingredient for Asian cooking."

Fusion cuisine has undeniably reached the heart of America—the right way, through its stomach. Even McDonald's has jumped into the culinary melting pot: would you like a side of "Oriental" Chicken Salad with that Big Mac? —T.H.

Kung Pao Pizza

Asian Snack Attack

The Snack Food Association ("Don't call it *junk* food!") informally defines a snack food as "anything you eat that's not considered a meal." Now while junk—excuse me, snack food may be a universal concept, every culture has its own unique idea of what a good between-meal munchie means. Most Asian snack foods feature juxtaposed tastes (such as sweet and sour), and less salt than American snacks, but more spices and MSG. And while Cheetos are being marketed to China, numerous snack foods from Asia are finding their niche here.

Some of them have been around for centuries; perhaps the oldest Asian snack food clogging up American arteries today is pork rinds. According to Evans Food Products, the largest producer of pork rinds in the world, the skins of pigs were reportedly first fried as a hi-calorie nibble in China during the Ming Dynasty.

Now, of course, they're available the world over, wherever disgustingly greasy, cholesterol and nitrate–laden snacks are sold. —D.G., T.H.

JUNK CLASSICS

Here are some Asian snack foods that you should try, if you're not hopelessly addicted to them already:

DRIED AND FRIED FRUITS AND VEGGIES:

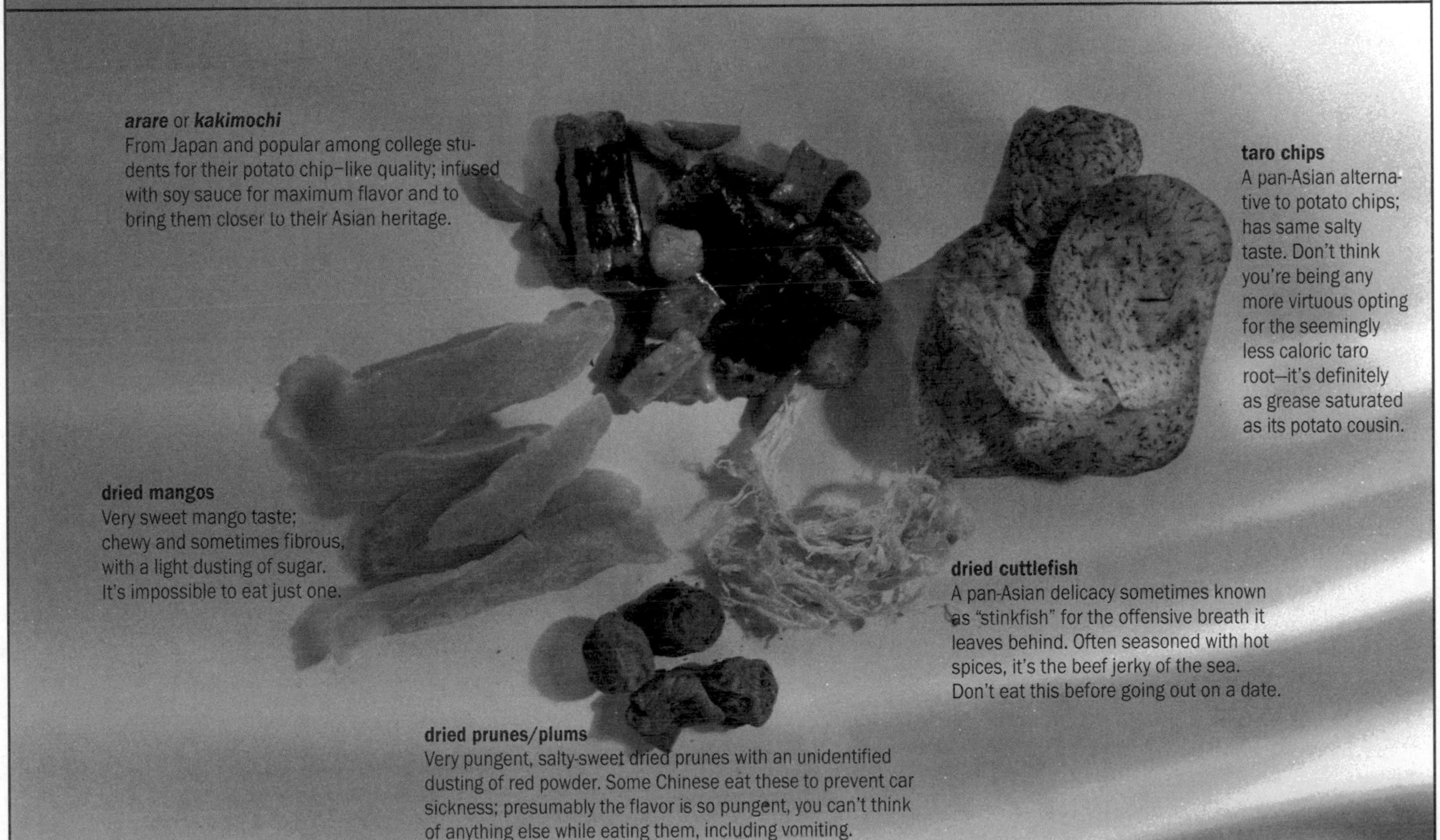

arare **or** ***kakimochi***
From Japan and popular among college students for their potato chip–like quality; infused with soy sauce for maximum flavor and to bring them closer to their Asian heritage.
taro chips
A pan-Asian alternative to potato chips; has same salty taste. Don't think you're being any more virtuous opting for the seemingly less caloric taro root—it's definitely as grease saturated as its potato cousin.
dried mangos
Very sweet mango taste; chewy and sometimes fibrous, with a light dusting of sugar. It's impossible to eat just one.
dried cuttlefish
A pan-Asian delicacy sometimes known as "stinkfish" for the offensive breath it leaves behind. Often seasoned with hot spices, it's the beef jerky of the sea. Don't eat this before going out on a date.
dried prunes/plums
Very pungent, salty-sweet dried prunes with an unidentified dusting of red powder. Some Chinese eat these to prevent car sickness; presumably the flavor is so pungent, you can't think of anything else while eating them, including vomiting.

CRACKERS AND COOKIES

First made in 17th century Japan, **sembei** ("rice cracker") come in all shapes and sizes, from palm-sized circles and squares to small seed-shapes flavored with red pepper.

Sesame candy from China: Very sweet, like peanut brittle, except with teensy-weensy sesame seeds; it also comes in black sesame variety that has a weird burnt taste to it.

Pan-Asian **prawn crackers** look like french fries and taste like shrimp chips; light, crispy, with diagonal stripe pattern.

Roasted green peas. A Japanese "happy present from the earth," or so says the slogan. You'd think this is a great junk food way to eat your vegetables, but what's "Tartrazine" and "brilliant blue FCF" doing in a happy present from the earth?

THE POCKY CONNECTION

Every Asian country seems to have its version of these plain, unsalted pretzel sticks dipped in chocolate. But Pocky is really the standard. How did they think of this unique treat? Someone must have put his pretzel stick in someone else's chocolate.

Pocky—The original Japanese "Super Snack." Other flavors include bitter chocolate, strawberry, almond crush, and "marble Pocky." The lucky few will come across the rare box of Giant Pocky.

Lucky is also from Japan. These sticks are slightly thicker than Pocky; also, the edges are rounded. The curious slogan proclaims simply: "I'm Lucky. It's good."

OK-OK is Taiwanese. The reason why the serving size is only four pieces is that these sticks are twice as thick as Pocky sticks. Kind of like a Twix without the caramel.

Pepero—Pocky's slighter shorter Korean cousin; the chocolate doesn't really taste like chocolate.

Menus Made Easy
CHINESE

China covers a lot of territory, and the food of each region has its own characteristics—varying according to neighbors, climate, and tradition.

In the north, cold, harsh weather is more conducive to growing wheat than rice. As a result, there are a lot of bread and noodle dishes. Some popular northern dishes include Peking Duck and Mongolian barbecue.

The west has the hottest food. Many dishes utilize red chili peppers in pastes, oils, or just by itself; these are relative newcomers to Chinese cuisine, since they were brought to Asia by the Portuguese and are not native to China. Fortunately, rice grows well in the "land of abundance," to offset the spiciness. Bamboo, black mushrooms, and duck are all good bets in western, or Szechwan, style cuisine.

Eastern provinces are known for their seafood and waterfowl. In Shanghai, gourmands enjoy shrimp, shellfish, and carp, as well as geese and duck. The food can be heavier and oilier than in other varieties of Chinese food, but the drunken chicken and shellfish remain quite popular.

It's commonly accepted that the southern school of cooking is China's best. (Certainly southerners will say so.) Southern, or Cantonese, food is traditionally fresh, light, and simple. Other provinces have their own versions, but Cantonese dim sum, noodles, and vegetables are generally accepted as the finest.

Other than the "standard" regional styles of cooking, some special styles—such as Hakka, which is the food of an indigenous and discrete tribe within China, and Taiwanese, from the Republic of China—also exist. These, however, are usually found at specialty restaurants, rather than on your standard menu. Regardless of what style of Chinese food is being served, there are general guidelines to follow when ordering dishes. Most pertain to balance. For example, a sweet dish should be countered by a salty dish and a spicy dish should be countered by a bland one. Likewise, a meal should include a variety of cooking methods (steamed, stir-fried, baked, and so on), textures (crunchy, chewy, soft, hard, stringy, and whatnot), and colors. Rice always serves as the equalizer between these extremes. This isn't just for reasons of taste; the principle of bodily humors is very important in Chinese medicine. An excess of foods with "heat" in them, like oily foods, for instance, can precipitate bad skin and other symptoms.

For a traditional family meal, all one needs to do is choose a meat dish, a fish dish, a vegetable, and soup. Then decide on whether you want rice, noodles, or bread with your meal, though even if you're having the latter two, you'll probably also want rice. For informal occasions, everything is served at once—except, perhaps, for a cold appetizer. —M.W., T.H.

SURVIVAL OF THE FITTEST

Liking Chinese food is not simply a matter of taste—it's an important survival technique, for several reasons:

1 CHINESE FOOD IS AVAILABLE AT ANY HOUR. **Why settle for greasy donuts in the morning when you can get greasy dim sum instead? Likewise, long after Italian trattorias and Mexican restaurants have closed for the night, Chinese barbecues are just warming up.**

2 CHINESE FOOD IS INEXPENSIVE. **Unlike in French bistros and steak houses, how much you spend on Chinese food doesn't relate to its quality. Some of the best noodle joints are also the cheapest. Family style dining and unlimited tea make it even more affordable.**

3 CHINESE FOOD IS HEALTHY. **If you order properly, you can eat well without being bogged down in calories or fat. A basic Chinese meal is sparing in meat and heavy on vegetables and grains.**

4 CHINESE FOOD TASTES GOOD. **From hot and sour soup to cold cuts to Buddha's delight to spare ribs, there's something for everyone. Those who don't like Chinese cuisine simply haven't tried the right variety.**

A FEAST FOR ALL REASONS

For birth and death and on every occasion in between, Chinese people love to throw banquets. After all, it's a great way to show off. If possible, have a grandmother or other expert handle the awesome responsibility of choosing the menu. (Assuming you have a Chinese grandmother.) However, if you're bold enough to take charge, it's a good idea to start with cold cuts, a soup, and dry or crisp dishes; these are well-suited for drinking and toasting. Then follow up with main courses, like whole fish, duck, or chicken. More toasting will occur during these courses. Finish off with simple dishes that go with rice. (During banquets, instead of getting white rice with the meal, you serve fried rice at the very end.) As the meal winds down, you'll make many more toasts, while other people will be toasting you. You may have to go from table to table, toasting each in turn; if it's a wedding banquet, and you're the bride or groom, this is required The number of dishes should run from 10 to 15, depending on event and budget. End with fruit—fortune cookies are for tourists. By meal's end, you will have spent a bundle. You will have no idea who attended your fiesta; they'll all be gone, taking leftovers and centerpieces with them. And you will be very, very, drunk. Still, the Chinese have survived banquets for millennia, so can you. Enjoy.

STARTERS

The standard Chinese meal does not include appetizers and salads, although for banquets (*see sidebar*), two smaller courses—one cold, followed by hot—are served at the beginning. What constitutes an appetizer section on most U.S. menus are actually popular dim sum **[👁129]** items, such as spring rolls and pot stickers. By the way, that small plate of duck sauce, hot mustard, and fried noodles found on restaurant tables is not at all a Chinese custom, but was devised to please Western customers. Chinese people never touch them, and sometimes ask for the offending substances to be taken away.

Spring rolls/egg rolls - *What's the difference? It's subtle, at best. It's usually in the wrapper: spring roll wrappers are made of wheat flour and water; egg roll wrappers are made of wheat flour, water, and beaten egg. Spring rolls are sometimes smaller than egg rolls. The name spring rolls is derived from the fact that they are traditionally served on the first day of the Lunar New Year, which happens to be in early spring.* **[👁160]**

Guo tie **("pot stickers," or fried dumplings)** - *Crescent-shaped dumplings, usually filled with a mixture of pork, cabbage, scallions, ginger, and other spices. Served with a dipping sauce of soy sauce, vinegar, and sometimes sesame seeds and scallions. Also available in some restaurants vegetarian-style, with the pork replaced by tofu.* **[👁131]**

Scallion pancakes - *Crisp-on-the-edges, chewy-on-the-insides pancakes filled with chopped scallions. The best ones are multi-layered, almost like filo dough. Served with a vinegar-ginger-soy dipping sauce.*

Jellyfish salad - *Cold slices of cooked jellyfish and sometimes raw cucumbers, tossed in a light vinegary sauce. Rather chewy, like shredded latex, and an acquired taste.*

Szechwan sesame chicken - *Cold boneless chicken, sliced and tossed with a spicy dressing of sesame seed paste, Szechwan peppercorns, sesame oil, hot chili oil and various spices. Can also be served with noodles and other meats.*

SOUPS

Won ton soup - *This dumpling-laden clear soup is actually more of a lunch entree. Vegetables such as bok choy, bamboo shoots, and/or Chinese mustard greens, as well as meat slices, are often added to make it a one-dish meal.*

Hot and sour soup - *A thick, spicy Szechwan-style soup, usually made with pork, wood ear mushroom, bamboo shoots, bean curd, and seasoned with pepper, vinegar, sesame oil, and hot oil. Most restaurants make this in large vats beforehand, but some will definitely make a vegetarian version to order.*

Cabbage and shredded pork soup - *Strong chicken-stock soup of Szechwan origin, seasoned with sautéed shredded pork and crunchy, vinegary Szechwan-style preserved vegetables.*

Sizzling rice soup - *Clear soup (usually chicken-stock) with assorted seafood (or chicken), chopped shiitake mushrooms, bamboo shoots, scallions, topped with sizzling fried rice (which is made by taking the crust of rice left at the bottom of the rice cooker, drying the pieces, then deep-frying to create a puffy, crunchy rice puff; the puffs are taken directly from the oil and dropped into the hot soup, which makes the signature sizzling sound).*

Bird's nest soup - *Rich soup which includes the dried saliva of a special species of swallows that keeps nests together. Believe it or not, the saliva glue is an outrageously expensive delicacy, long prized for its health benefits. Usually served at banquets and the most special of dinners.*

ENTREES

Peking duck - *Roasted duck with thick, crispy, caramelized skin and juicy meat, usually requiring advance ordering. Pieces are sliced off the duck by a waiter before your eyes, and the skeleton taken back into the kitchen (where, if you're getting the traditional*

Peking duck complete meal, it is turned into a rich soup). The meat and skin are eaten with a dab of hoisin sauce and a scallion shoot, sandwiched between halves of a steamed bun or—more commonly—wrapped with a Mandarin pancake, the flat crepe made of wheat flour and water.

***Kung pao* chicken** - *The original, developed by a governor of Yunnan and Guizhou with the rank of Kung Pao (literally "Guardian of the Royal Heir's Palace"), featured maize corn, but peanuts are used everywhere else in China, and in U.S. restaurants. Diced chicken with a garlicky, sometimes fiery sauce. Shrimp and other meats may be substituted for chicken.*

Moo goo gai pan - *Stir-fried chicken slices with fresh mushrooms. The dish varies from chef to chef, and is one of the oldest Americanized Cantonese dishes; emphasis should be placed on fresh ingredients.*

Lemon chicken - *Chunks of lightly breaded chicken in a citrus sauce; a Canton specialty which emphasizes the aromatic tang from the lemon rind. The chicken should be braised so that the flavor permeates the chicken thoroughly. A common take-out staple, usually transformed into a deep-fried, syrup-coated mess.*

Drunken chicken - *Cold, alcohol-base marinated chicken pieces—hence its name. An East China specialty, made originally with yellow wine. In the U.S., the wine is often substituted with rum.*

Steamed fish with ginger and scallion - *Cantonese believe steaming is the best way to prepare fish as it beings out the natural flavor, without using oil or other unhealthy additives. The entire fish, usually a white-meat fish such as rock cod, snapper, or sole, is steamed, and served with a ginger and scallion sauce. Other variations include a ginger and vinegar sauce or a white sauce with chopped ham.*

Hunan crispy fish - *Whole deep-fried fish, topped with garlicky sweet-and-sour sauce.*

***Mu shu* pork** - *Mu shu dishes offer a stir-fried mixture of meat, eggs, and vegetables which are wrapped in a Mandarin pancake with a dab of hoisin sauce, burrito style. Adaptable to any meat, though pork is traditional, and also available vegetarian-style.*

Peking pork chops - *Marinated in rice wine and soy sauce, then deep-fried. Mixed with thick, savory brown sauce.*

Twice-cooked pork - *Szechwan-style pork slices and scallions, mixed in a hot bean sauce (or hoisin sauce). The term "twice-cooked" means that the meat is first simmered in water, then sliced and braised in the sauce; also called "double-cooked."*

Shredded chili beef - *Slices of beef and carrots, deep-fried, and glazed with a spicy, tangy sauce. Deliberately dry, chewy, and fiery. Szechwan specialty.*

Mongolian beef - *A Northern Chinese creation of marinated beef slices, stir-fired with chilies, scallions, soy sauce, and sesame oil; served over crispy glass noodles.*

Chinese broccoli with oyster sauce - *The perfect accompaniment to any meal. The Chinese broccoli (a slender, flavorful version of its Western cousin) should be crisp and crunchy, not drowning in thick sauce.*

Eggplant with garlic sauce - *Szechwan-style slices of Asian eggplant (smaller and softer than the Western aubergine), quick stir-fried in garlic sauce. The eggplant should not be too soft and hold its slightly chewy texture. Warning: if done improperly, this dish is oil-soaked, heavy, and a must to avoid.*

***Ma po* tofu** - *A rich stew-like dish of braised bean curd cubes, mixed with ground pork, water chestnuts, wood ear mushrooms, garlic, chili paste, and scallions. Can be made vegetarian style, but the original is one of the classic homestyle dishes.*

Buddha's delight - *An adaptation of the Louhan Cai, the vegetarian dish for the 500 disciples (louhans) sworn to protect the Buddhist way. Has a myriad of textures in a single plate, with various vegetables, bean curd, noodles, and herbs and spices. If you're a strict vegetarian, be sure to ask about the stock; sometimes restaurants use chicken-based stock.*

NOODLES

Noodle dishes are lunch, snack, or late-night items. That they appear on dinner menus in U.S. restaurants is basically a nod toward pleasing the Western palate [👁157].

Chow mein - *Crispy pan-fried noodles, topped with vegetables and your choice of meat. Another dish that was Americanized early in Chinese cuisine's coming to the States.*

Chow fun - *Stir-fried fresh rice noodles, with or without a sauce; usually tossed with meat, onions, and peppers.*

Singapore-style *chow mai fun* - *Stir-fried vermicelli rice noodles, with barbecued pork, chicken, shrimp, vegetables, all topped by a spicy curry-based sauce. Sometimes available vegetarian-style, with fried bean curd used to substitute for the meat.*

Lo mein - *Egg noodles, usually pan-fried, and mixed with soy sauce, oyster sauce, scallions, bean sprouts and a choice of meat.*

RICE

Steamed rice is the accompaniment of choice at dinner. Fried rice, with its many ingredients, is thought to interfere with the textures and flavors of the rest of the meal [👁159].

DESSERT

Chinese, like many other Asians, mainly eat fresh fruit for dessert, except maybe at a giant banquet. Catering to Western palates, many restaurants offer ice cream, sometimes battered and deep-fried in a hideous concoction.

BEVERAGES

Clear, light soup is considered the beverage of choice at a traditional Chinese meal. The other important beverage, of course, is tea, which is usually served at the end of a meal. However, in most U.S. restaurants, a teapot will arrive minutes after you have been seated; this is again to please Western tastes.

Tea - *Served in three basic varieties: green, black (also called red tea by the Chinese), and Oolong* [👁167].

Beer - *Tsingtao, a pilsner with a light bouquet, is the best-known Chinese beer.*

Menus Made Easy
INDIAN

At most Indian restaurants in the U.S., the menu is primarily North Indian, with a smattering of South Indian dishes. What's the difference? After all, Indian food is Indian food, isn't it? Not exactly. North and South Indian cuisines are as different as French and Mexican. Even within the divergent cuisines of the North and South, significant differences within regions also exist. In general, however, North Indian food is known for its elaborate, often spicy, meat dishes, while South Indian food is spartan and almost entirely vegetarian. Southern food is steamed, compared to Northern, which is cooked in oil (or clarified butter, known as *ghee*)—lots of it. Southern cuisine, on the other hand, emphasizes rice, lentils, pancakes, vegetables, seafood, and coconut. Southern food is healthier.

In U.S. Indian restaurants, one of the best ways to fully enjoy a complete Indian meal is to order a *thaali.* Thaali literally refers to the circular steel tray which is used to hold the elements of the complete meal, which includes a bowl of plain rice or *pullao* (rice pilaf), placed in the tray's center, surrounded by numerous smaller bowls (called *katoris*) filled with various typical Indian dishes. Thaalis can either feature vegetarian or non-vegetarian katoris. While at most restaurants you'll be provided with utensils, traditionally, Indian food is best enjoyed when eaten with your hands. If you want to try this, first warn your tablemates; should any object, wait until you're eating alone or with more adventurous diners. If they agree, wash your hands.

When eating, use only one hand. Try not to dirty your fingers beyond the second knuckle, and do not use the dirty fingers for any other activity except eating. Transfer food from communal serving dishes to your individual plate before your hands get dirty. When eating rice, gather rice and any other food in one hand, mold into a small roll, and raise it to your mouth. Use the thumb to push the food into your mouth. Don't flick your fingers to get rid of food; don't suck them, regardless of how much sauce might be dripping from them. The idea is to minimalize the exchange of saliva between parties at the table, while sharing trays of often sloppy food.

One last word of advice: never order your food spicy, for if you do, it will be very spicy—the kind which opens your tonsils and makes your scalp sweat. The best option is to order it mild. Odds are that it will suit your palate quite well. —O.P. M.

SOUPS

Soups were created by Indian chefs during the British occupation to accommodate western palates, and therefore are not traditional to the Indian dining experience. However, that shouldn't stop you from enjoying them.

Mulligatawny Soup - *Traditional meat-stock soup with chicken, lentils, tomatoes, and spices. Recipes can differ extensively from restaurant to restaurant, family to family.*

Shorba - *Chicken or mixed vegetable soup with mild herbs and spices.*

Alu tikki - *Mashed, deep-fried potatoes with fresh herbs and spices. This should always be topped with tamarind sauce and yogurt.*

Alu chaat - *Lightly fried potatoes marinated in spicy and tangy sauces, including coriander and tamarind chutneys.*

APPETIZERS

When going for a complete dinner, it's actually not a very good idea to order appetizers; dishes like shammi kebabs or alu chaat are complete meals in themselves. By the time you push away your chair, much of the food is likely to be destined for the trash.

Shammi kebab - *Deep fried lamb and lentil patty with coriander and tamarind sauce. They tend to be on the heavier side and should be consumed in moderation before ordering a complete meal.*

Dosa - *South India's most popular dish. A large, thin southern Indian rice and lentil pancake, eaten with Sambar, a watery, spicy, tangy lentil curry. Dosa is usually served with coconut chutney and a spicy mix, popularly known as "gunpowder." Gunpowder is rightly named; you'll break into a sweat after a mere taste of it. Available in many forms,* dosa is best when eaten by hand. Masala dosa is a regular dosa wrapped around a potato, onion, and nut filling. A "paper" dosa is a larger, thinner, crispier version of a simple dosa.

Papadam - *A crisp lentil wafer, flavored in various ways—with peppercorns, garlic, or cumin seeds. Served as a snack with tea, or with main meals. Note that papadam are eaten like chips and are not meant to be used to scoop up food, as are the soft breads.*

Samosa - *Deep-fried, curry-flavored triangles. These originated in Persia as a meal-in-a-pocket. Here, it's served as a snack food or appetizer, and available with meat or all-veggie fillings.*

TANDOORI

Tandoori cuisine comes from the word *tandoor,* which is a simple clay oven about three feet deep and two feet wide. Tandoori dishes, which are mostly meat, are cooked over red-hot charcoals on long, steel skewers. Tandoori bread is made by baking it on the hot side of the oven. Tandoors are said to have come to India from Persia (modern Iran) and are believed to have been brought to India by the Mughals (or Mongols), who took Tandoori dishes to new heights, and then renamed them Mughlai cuisine. Similar to barbecuing, the meat cooked in this earthen pot is moist and tender and obtains some of the earthy aroma of the pot. The meat is cooked very slowly, and tends to be well-done—if cooked badly, tough and stringy. Tandoori dishes in India are served with raw onion relish and fresh lime. Some restaurants—particularly those in New Delhi's famous restaurant row, Pandara Road—also serve onions pickled in vinegar. These are a delicacy in their own right, but you won't see them here. When dining on tandoori dishes, insist on raw onion relish and mint sauce.

Tandoori chicken - *The healthiest Indian dish you can order: Chicken marinated in yogurt and freshly-ground herbs and spices. Broiled in the tandoor, it's devoid of fat and non-oily. Best enjoyed when accompanied by either lassi or a beer.*

Malai kebab - *Chicken marinated in ginger, garlic, and herbs and roasted in the tandoor.*

Chicken tikka - *Boneless chicken marinated in yogurt and broiled in the tandoor. An average order brings you four pieces.*

Seekh kebab - *Minced lamb seasoned with onions and herbs, and broiled in the tandoor with a light coating of oil or butter. Your average order gets you two kebabs. Heavy, and should be consumed in moderation.*

CHICKEN DISHES

Chicken curry - *Chicken cooked in a gravy full of herbs, spices, onions, tomatoes, and parsley. Best served mildly spicy.* **[👁128]**

Chicken makhni - *Tandoori chicken cooked in butter and tomato gravy; a cholesterol-bomb best left alone.*

Chicken tikka masala - *Diced chicken in a tomato-and-cream gravy, oven-baked. This dish can prove to be very heavy; a single order is usually good for three people.*

Chicken jalfrez - *Boneless chicken cooked with green peppers and tomato gravy; extremely spicy for those not used to spicy foods. A dish for the adventurous.*

LAMB DISHES

Rogan josh - *A traditional North Indian entree. Cubes of lamb cooked in a light gravy, heavy on the oil, extremely fattening.*

Keema mutter - *Ground lamb cooked with peas and herbs. Despite being a red-meat dish, can be healthy if the restaurant uses oil or butter in moderation.*

Lamb pasanda - *Boneless pieces of lamb cooked in cream sauce and mildly spiced; great dish to have with Indian breads.*

VEGETARIAN DISHES

Malai kofta - *Fresh vegetables and homemade cheese balls cooked in mildly spiced gravy.*

Mattar paneer - *Homemade cheese cooked with green peas and a light gravy made of tomatoes and fresh herbs.*

Navratan korma - *Mixed vegetables cooked with nuts, mild spices, herbs, and cream.*

Dal makhni - *Lentils prepared with butter, cream, spices and a dash of yogurt. No Indian meal is complete without this dish.*

DALS

Especially in South India, *dal* is served with nearly every meal. In the U.S., it is harder to find, although not impossible. Dal is the Hindi word for legumes; it also refers to the seasoned, prepared legumes that are cooked in water, most commonly the *chana dal* (yellow split peas) or the *masoor dal* (orange lentils), although there are a vast variety of beans, peas, and lentils that can used to make dal. It is usually prepared mildly spiced, to counteract the spiciness of other meat and vegetable dishes. At many restaurants, you'll get dal, plus an onion relish and boiled cabbage, free with your meal.

BREADS

Most restaurants can be judged by their breads, which should be fresh and fluffy, and not microwave-reheated. Note that there are no definitive recipes for these breads, and they can differ vastly from one establishment to the next. One way to test the authenticity of an Indian restaurant is to check their nan. If, instead of nan, they serve pita bread, you're better off going to McDonald's.

Nan - *Slightly leavened white flour bread. Baked in tandoor oven without fat or oil. Not the same as pita.*

***Roti* (or *chapati*)** - *Whole wheat flat, unleavened bread cooked in the tandoor oven (for roti) or on a griddle (for chapati).*

Paratha - *Many-layered unleavened whole wheat bread, cooked with butter on a griddle. Extremely heavy.*

Alu paratha - *Paratha bread stuffed with potatoes spiced with onions, peppers, cilantro, and sometimes more.*

Poori - *Deep-fried whole wheat bread puffs; surprisingly light.*

RICE DISHES

In India, as in most Asian cultures, rice is a very important part of any meal. Rice is more a staple in South India, since Northerners tend to rely more on breads, but there are a number of unbeatable North Indian rice dishes. Indians prefer basmati rice, which has longer grains, more aroma, and more taste than any other variety. According to a popular saying in Northern India, good rice is worth its weight in gold, and the older the rice, the better it is. In the U.S., while most Indian restaurants will serve you rice, breads are only served upon request. However, the easiest way to recognize basmati is by its long grain and its color, which is white to pale yellow. Grown in the foothills of the Himalayas, basmati rice is sweet and nutty in flavor. [👁159]

Chicken biryani - *Tender pieces of chicken cooked with saffron rice.*

Peas pullao - *Basmati rice cooked with mild spices and fresh green peas. Pullao, or pilaf, is a dry rice dish and much more subtle in taste than biryani. A good pullao has many ingredients like nuts, dried fruits, and spices. Saffron, of course, is a must in any Indian rice dish.*

CONDIMENTS

Raita - *Cool whipped yogurt with cucumbers, potatoes, and fresh mint leaves. Takes the edge off spicy foods.*

Chutney - *An Indian relish which serves as an accompaniment for almost all Indian meals. Chutney can be either fresh or cooked. One of the most popular chutneys is made from mangoes and prepared ahead of time, sometimes months before actual consumption. Fresh chutneys are made daily from vegetables, fruits, herbs, and spices.*

Pickles - *Indian pickles range from salty to fiery, from hot to sweet. The most popular are lemon and mango pickles. Indian pickles are marinated in oil and spices and, like kimchi, help digestion. Really!*

DESSERTS

Rasmalai - *Homemade cheese sweetened with condensed milk, and flavored with rosewater*

Kulfi - *Indian ice cream with pistachio nuts.*

Gulab jamun - *Cheese balls dipped in honey syrup.*

Kheer - *Rice pudding flavored with rose water and nuts.*

BEVERAGES

Many Westerners have debated what kind of wine best complements Indian food. Since much Indian food served in restaurants tends to be spicy (in varying degrees), chilled white wine is recommended to soothe inflamed taste buds. Still, the best liquid accompaniment for Indian food is lassi, a yogurt drink, which is healthy, low on calories, and tends to enliven your taste buds. The cooling effect of lassi is also a big plus, especially when ordering extra spicy food.

Lassi - *Cold yogurt drink; available plain, salty, sweet, or with mango.*

Chai - *The most common Indian teas are Darjeeling and Assam. True chai is prepared Indian-style, that is, by steeping tea leaves directly into a combination of hot water and milk; it's often sweetened before it arrives at your table.* [👁166]

Masala chai - *Chai flavored with spices.*

Madras coffee - *Freshly brewed coffee with milk. This South Indian–styled coffee is made by brewing the coffee, then adding sweetened boiling milk to create a froth at the top, almost like a cappuccino. In the south, the coffee is one-third milk, while in the north, coffee is perceived in the same way as it is in the West: black with a dash of milk.*

Menus Made Easy
JAPANESE

Contrary to popular belief, the Japanese diet does not consist solely of raw fish. Neither do most Japanese restaurants make you take your shoes off and eat your meal kneeling on a tatami mat. In fact, only the more expensive restaurants provide that traditional dining experience, and for the privilege of a tatami room you'll probably have to make a reservation. Japanese cuisine is intensely varied—from quick-snack specialties like ramen and curry rice, to elaborately presented and prepared dishes with an extra helping of pomp and circumstance. —E.N., T.H., D.G.

APPETIZERS (ZENSAI)

Edamame - *Boiled soybeans; literally, "beans on a branch," because traditionally, the branch of a soybean tree was cut off and the whole thing boiled. The boiled beans were then salted and served, either cold or warm. To eat these, bite down gently on the bean pod and wiggle out the bean with your teeth, letting slip them directly into your mouth. The pod should be politely discarded in the provided bowl, not consumed or tossed on the floor.*

Hijiki - *Black seaweed cooked with dashi (fish stock), soy sauce, and mirin (rice wine). Salty-sweet, with a prickly-soft texture. Believed by Japanese to promote hair growth.*

Oshinko - *An assortment of pickled vegetables, including cucumber, Asian eggplant, and daikon, or white radish. (The latter is traditionally a bright lemon yellow in color; do not be alarmed.)*

Sunomono - *Seafood and vegetables, especially sliced cucumber, pickled in sweet vinegar.*

Agedofu - *Cubes of tofu, deep fried to a golden color, served with a savory salty/sweet dipping sauce.*

Yakko-tofu - *Cold tofu cubes, with grated ginger, bonito (dried fish flakes), scallions, and soy.*

Gyoza - *Delicate pan-fried meat dumplings, served with a vinegar and soy dipping sauce.* **[👁131]**

Negimaki - *Thinly sliced grilled beef strips rolled with scallions and served with a savory salty/sweet dipping sauce.*

SOUPS

To eat soup, use chopsticks to pick out any solid pieces, then sip the liquid as you would from a cup, using both hands to grasp the bowl, or use the white soup spoon, if provided.

Suimono - *Clear soup with tofu, fish, chicken or egg, and decorative vegetables. Properly consumed at the start of a meal.*

Misoshiro - *Soybean paste soup, usually with tofu, scallion and seaweed. Misoshiro, along with white rice, is eaten at almost every meal. Miso soup is traditionally consumed after the meal, but before dessert. However, in a bow to Western custom, most Japanese restaurants serve it prior to the entree. Miso—fermented soybean paste—is one of the basic flavorings of Japanese cuisine. Made of soybeans, salt, and koji (a fermenting agent made of rice, wheat, or soybeans), it's a great source of protein, especially the amino acids lysine and threonine. Although most U.S. restaurants don't offer a selection, hundreds of varieties of miso exist, differing in color, texture, aroma, and taste, depending on the ingredients used, how they are combined, and where the miso was made. The two main categories are sweet miso (also known as mellow miso and white miso), which is usually light in color (beige or yellow), high in carbohydrates, and fermented for just two to eight weeks, and red miso (also called brown rice miso or barley miso), which is darker in color, saltier in taste, and fermented for a much longer time—anywhere from one summer to up to three years.*

During the 7th century, Korean Buddhist monks first brought miso from China to Japan, where fermentation techniques were unknown; the use of miso throughout Japan became widespread during the Muromachi period (1333-1568). In spite of its Chinese origins, most Westerners associate the soybean paste with Japan.

But miso has long since burst free of its ethnic origins, and is now available to non-Asian consumers in many mainstream restaurants. Its most common incarnation is miso soup, made of water, soup stock (dashi), kelp (kombu) and bonito flakes (katsuoboshi); additional ingredients may include a wide variety of vegetables, tofu, shellfish, and seaweeds. So popular is this light soup that it's now available in dry instant packets in supermarkets. Miso is also becoming an important seasoning in salad dressings, dipping sauces, and marinades; don't be surprised if you find broiled salmon with miso sauce over julienned seasonal vegetables, or a three-color salad with carrot miso dressing on the menus of your trendier eateries.

Miso's culinary versatility may be just part of its attraction. Recent studies suggest that the daily use of miso may lower cholesterol, alkalinize the blood, neutralize the effects of some carcinogens, and ward off the effects of smoking and pollution. In 1990, conclusive reports linking miso's ability to protect against radiation were confirmed by

POP SUSHI

What goes inside the rolls or on top of the rice? Just about anything. In approximate order of popularity, sushi mavens' favorite fish are:

1. **MAGURO (tuna)**
2. **TORO (the marbled belly of tuna)**
3. **UNI (sea urchin)**
4. **CHUU-TORO (the marbled mid-underside of the tuna)**
5. **EBI (shrimp) and amaebi (sweet shrimp)**
6. **TAI (sea bream)**
7. **IKA (squid)**
8. **AKAGAI (ark shell)**
9. **HAMACHI (baby yellowtail)**
10. **BUTI (adult yellowtail)**

Professor Akihiro Ito at Hiroshima University's Atomic Radioactivity Medical Lab. As a treatment for stress, high cholesterol, pollution and radiation, this ancient ingredient may well be a staple food for modern times. The secret to good miso soup: Add the miso gradually only after the rest of the ingredients have fully cooked in the broth. To preserve flavor, do not bring the soup to a boil after the miso is added.

SUSHI and SASHIMI

There's a reason why sushi is so popular, and it isn't the rice: though sushi comes in many forms with many ingredients—various seafoods, raw and pickled vegetables, and cooked egg among them—the essence of sushi is fish. Raw fish. For culinary neophytes, the act of eating fish raw is almost unimaginable. They have a point. It is, after all, soft, slippery on the tongue, and a bit too close to being alive for comfort. But it's also delicious and healthy (if prepared properly), and full of subtleties in flavor that cooking destroys. The Japanese have eaten sushi for thousands of years, and although there's the occasional report of people sickened or worse from less-than-fresh fish, well, the nation as a whole seems to be doing just fine.

Sushi's ancestral precursors are in ancient China, in a common seaside method of preserving fresh fish. There, the catch of each day was packed in rice and salt, and then left to ferment up to a year. Once fermentation occurred, the rice was disposed of and the "pickled" fish consumed. This technique arrived in Japan sometime during the Yayoi period (300 B.C.-300 A.D.). Through the centuries, the process evolved. Layers of fish fillets were laid onto a layer of unsalted rice and then weighted down with a heavy stone. As the rice fermented, it produced a sharp, sweet taste approximating that of modern-day vinegared rice. People stopped throwing the rice away, and ate the two layers together.

Then, in what was then called Edo in the early 19th century (some reports even peg it down to an actual date, 1824), this pickling process was replaced with a technique of serving fresh raw fish on top of newly cooked rice doused in rice vinegar. Sushi was born; it only remained for Edo to be renamed Tokyo before Japan entered its modern era.

During this period, sushi was sold as a snack food by street vendors—the original Japanese fast food. Stalls gave way to restaurants and bars, and quickly sushi moved from the quotidian to gourmet.

Having come into its own in modern times, sushi now proliferates in many forms. In addition to *nigirizushi,* a small pad of lightly vinegared rice topped with a slice of raw fish, there is *norimaki,* sushi wrapped with seaweed into cylinders and then sliced into round cross-sectional pieces. (A modern variant of norimaki, *temakizushi* or hand roll, involves seaweed rolled around the rice and fish on a bias, making an ice-cream-cone shape. There is also *chirashizushi,* in which raw fish is laid over a bed of vinegared rice, usually served in a laquered bowl or box.

Sushi first entered the American vocabulary in the 1970s, when Japanese cuisine was first gaining widespread recognition. A decade later, when diners were searching en masse for simpler, healthier grazing alternatives, sushi bars developed into a culinary phenomenon. Before the decade was over, sushi had reached the pinnacle of American pop culture—it had become an icon, a symbol for a kind of reckless, materialistic self-indulgence. In our current, simpler era, sushi has gone back to humbler roots. People eat it not because it's exotic or pricey, but because it tastes good, and it's good for you. The common thread of sushi is the freshness of its ingredients. Seafood must be as close to fresh-caught as possible, even if this means seeing the ingredient alive and pulsating just moments before consumption (and there are restaurants that offer "live" sushi). Unpleasant? Perhaps. But at least with sushi, you know exactly what you're getting.

Other, somewhat less popular sushi are *tako* (octopus), *ikura* (salmon roe), *anago* (conger eel), and *awabe* (abalone). But why stop with fish? Among the most daring of Japan's sushi-eaters, sushi topped with raw chicken or raw horse meat has developed its own small following. And for the ultimate raw thrill, there's always fugu—the blowfish whose ovaries and liver contain a potentially deadly poison (*see FUGU below*).

For those inclined to stay away from raw flesh, there are less challenging choices: *kappa* (cucumber), *kampyo* (pickled gourd), *tamago* (thick, sweet omelet), *oshinkomaki* (pickled daikon radish), and *futomaki* (literally, "fat roll," filled with strips of egg, a dried gourd called *kampyo*, sweet pink fish powder, and vegetables). Sushi-lovers take note: That all-time favorite, the California roll—a *makizushi* of avocado, crab, cucumber, mayonnaise—is an American creation. Southern Californian, if you want to get specific. And yes, it's gone back to Japan and become a sushi staple there as well. —T.

TEMPURA

Tempura (say tem'puhruh, not tempoo'rah) is a myriad of meats and vegetables, coated with a thin flour-based batter and deep-fried. In America, the shrimp and vegetables come out crispy like fish and chips, but in Japan it's usually softer and a bit moist. It's served with a light dipping sauce, called tempura sauce or *tentsuyu,* made out of sweet rice vinegar, soy sauce, seaweed, and bonito flakes.

Though tempura was first introduced to the Japanese by the Portuguese in the latter half of the 16th century, like sushi, sukiyaki, and teriyaki, tempura is a dish that Westerners exclusively identify with Japan. And—after teriyaki—tempura

is probably the Japanese entree that Westerners have most embraced. Tempura can consist of any of a variety of delicately battered and deep-fried seafood and vegetables, usually served hot. Commonly used foods for tempura range from prawns, shrimp, squids, scallops, eels, and different types of fish, to shiitake mushrooms, green peppers, burdock, and eggplant. Though prepared by frying, tempura shouldn't be confused with french fries and onion rings. Like most Japanese foods, it's actually light, relatively grease-free, crisp, and succulent. This lightness is due to its specialized method of cooking. After the ingredients are washed and dried, they are dipped into a thin batter of egg and flour mixed with water. The thinness of the batter is important, since it absorbs little oil during cooking. After dipping, the battered pieces are placed into a carefully temperature-regulated (usually 340 to 360 degrees F) combination of sesame and vegetable oils. At just the proper instant, when the tempura turns a diaphanous golden color, it is taken out and served. —T.

NOODLES [👁157]

Ramen *- Japanese name for Chinese wheat noodles. Although ramen is quickly becoming synonymous with*

WRITING SUSHI: A FINE KETTLE OF FISH

With the dish's many-layered history, it's not surprising that the characters for the actual Japanese word sushi has at least three incarnations:

鮨

1 The left half of the character by itself is <u>sakana</u>, which means fish; the right half by itself is <u>umai</u>, which means delicious. Both parts together make up the compound word "sushi."

鮓

2 Again, the left half is <u>sakana</u>; the right half by itself is <u>nagara</u>, which means "during," "while," "notwithstanding," or "suddenly."

寿 司

3 The first character is <u>kotobuki</u>, an auspicious word which means "longevity" or "congratulations." The second character is <u>tsukasadoru</u>, a commanding word which means rule, administer, conduct. While the individual characters don't seem to have anything to do with sushi, this version is the most common way of "spelling" the word. If you read Japanese, however, you're likely to eventually run into all three.

TEMPURA'S EASY! (You Don't Even Need a Wok)

1 Heat vegetable oil in a deep frying pan filled about 3/4 full to 350 degrees.

2 Prepare an egg-water mixture of one part beaten egg to three parts water.

3 Combine equal parts of the egg-water mixture and flour, but don't overmix it. Good tempura batter is thin and still contains small lumps of flour.

4 Dip whatever you're frying (shrimp, carrots, broccoli florets) into the batter, and then drop it gently into the oil. Remove it when the oil around the tempura stops bubbling, or when the batter has bloomed into a pale golden cocoon.

instant noodles, the homemade variety hardly resembles its packaged neighbor; fresh, silky noodles in a robust soup base. (See also RAMEN.)

Udon - *Thick, wheat noodles, served with a soup base, usually topped with fish cakes, vegetables, or tempura.*

Soba - *Buckwheat noodles, traditionally served cold with dried seaweed and scallions, and a vinegar-soy dipping sauce. When served in a hot soup base, referred to as kakesoba.*

Yakisoba - *Pan-fried noodles with sliced meat and vegetables. Most often accompanied by okonomiyaki (see below).*

Somen - *Rice noodles, available in an array of colors, usually served in a cold soup base topped with chilled julienne vegetables, egg, and sometimes seafood.*

RICE DISHES (*GOHAN*)

Donburi - *Any kind of Japanese entree meal placed in a bowl over hot white rice. The most popular is oyakodon, literally "parent and child" donburi, because it is a mixture of cooked chicken and egg. Other types of donburi include fresh water eel (unaju), salt water eel and egg (anagotojidon), beef and egg (tanindon), tempura and egg (tentojidon), and breaded fried chicken or pork and egg (katsudon). The proliferation of Yoshinoya chain restaurants is an example of how donburi has gotten popular here in America. Or just step into a Jack-in-the-Box fast food joint, where the Teriyaki Chicken Bowl is a hot seller.*

Kare (Curry) rice - *Although curry originated in India, the Japanese have their own distinct version, which is milder and thicker. Usually bright yellow in color and served over hot rice, sometimes with sliced pork or chicken katsu strips laid over it.* **[👁128]**

Tonkatsu - *Breaded pork cutlet, deep fried, served with a thick sweetened soy sauce. Chicken cutlet also available, although this is a Western concession.*

ONE-POT DISHES (*NABEMONO*)

Both *sukiyaki* and *shabushabu* are Japanese dishes classified as *nabemono,* food cooked at the table in a single pot or pan, usually during the winter. Both are products of modern Japan which arose in the Meiji era, 1868 to 1912, when the country was opened to foreigners and their influences. Traditional prohibitions against the eating of beef were lifted in Japan's sweeping efforts to modernize; the result is stewed-cuisine history.

Shabushabu, the lighter of the two dishes, consists of thin slices of marbled beef and vegetables cooked by dipping them with chopsticks into a pot of simmering kelp broth. (The name comes from the sound made when one swishes meat in the soup.) After a few seconds of swishing, the morsels of meat are dipped in a sesame- or citron-flavored sauce and eaten, usually with rice. Other ingredients in the mix include tofu, Chinese cabbage, chrysanthemum leaves, scallions and mush-

rooms—all of which are simmered in the stock to add flavor to the meat. The uniqueness of shabushabu cooking is that the extra fat and harshness of the beef is drawn off by the boiling broth, leaving a relatively light meaty treat.

Sukiyaki, perhaps the better known of the two nabemono outside of Japan, is similar to shabushabu, but uses as its cooking medium a stock of soy sauce, sweet sake, and sugar. Unlike its swishing cousin, sukiyaki has a distinctly sweetish taste—which has made it among the most popular of Japanese dishes. The most common ingredients in sukiyaki are marbled beef slices, scallions, and thin, gelatinous noodles made of buckwheat. Vegetable ingredients include onions, grilled tofu, mushrooms, and chrysanthemum leaves—all of which bring to the tender beef a freshness not usually associated with red meat. Just before consumption, the cooked meat is dipped into a bowl of beaten raw egg, which makes the meat even more succulent.

The Japanese culinary imagination associates the experience of shabushabu and sukiyaki with conviviality. Both types of nabemono are seen as a kind of communal food, attended with a classical image of a family dining over a steaming pot of beef and vegetables on a cold winter evening. Americans have no similar tradition (save, perhaps, for the communal bucket of fried chicken or roasting marshmallows over a campfire)—but with the spread of nabemono restaurants, they're learning.

GRILLED FOOD (*YAKIMONO*)

If you see a dish with *yaki* in the name, rest assured it isn't raw. "Yaki" refers to grilled or broiled foods.

Teriyaki - *A method of cooking, referring to meats marinated and grilled or broiled with a thickened sweet soy sauce. Meats commonly used are beef, chicken, and fish (usually salmon).*

Teppanyaki - *Refers to a cooking method adapted by the Benihana chain into a comedy routine. Rather than a table, customers sit around a large grill on which meat, seafood and vegetables are prepared before your eyes. A specialty restaurant fare.*

Okonomiyaki - *Literally, "grilling what you like." An eggy, cabbage-and-flour pancake with your choice of meats and/or vegetables inside, topped with a thick sweetish-salty sauce and bonito flakes. Usually accompanied by a heaping plate of yakisoba. Another specialty restaurant fare.*

Yakitori - *Literally "grilled chicken." Yakitori is also used as the generic name for skewered, marinated meat cooked over hot coals, much like a barbecue. Certain Japanese restaurants, called izakaya, specialize in selections from a yaki bar; items range from chicken, beef, fish, and vegetables, even rice balls, but it's easy to get gingko beans, smelt, beef tongue, liver, chicken giblets, chicken skin, and quail eggs if you really want them.*

SPECIAL DISHES

Kobe beef - *Actually, Kobe beef doesn't really come from Kobe at all. Where in that massive metropolis would you put a cow anyway? Raised in the samurai club meds of the Japanese cattle world (in Sanda, a rural area outside of Kobe, and also in the north of Japan), these super-fat-marbled, cholesterol-packed brutes are known to afficionados, correctly, as wagyu. Virtually from birth, they're gorged on a diet of beer, soy products, and grain, with the goal of decreasing their lean body mass to the lowest possible percentage without making them literally drown in their own flab, or break a bone from holding up over 1,800 pounds of flesh. (American cows buckle at 1,200 pounds).*

Wagyu black cattle are raised through a secret process that includes staying still for most of their three-year-short lives in small pens, in a relaxed environment, with music and daily hand-massages by owners to keep their flesh soft and tender. The steaks from these cows, with their tiny, liberally distributed droplets of fat (shimofuri in Japanese, literally "frost-fallen" because the white fat droplets crystallize like frost formations) are known to melt on your tongue, especially when served raw, as they sometimes are, in Japanese restaurants.

This oh-so-delicate pampering for the slaughter might be seen as a kind of penance on the part of the breeders. From the 6th century, when Buddhism entered Japan, it was forbidden to kill cows for food. Even in Japanese bullfights, it was the bull that ran away first or fell to its knees that lost the fight; no blood was shed. But in the mid 19th century, a hairy barbarian named Townshend Harris, who was the first American Consul in Japan, shocked his neighbors in the port town of Shimoda by rudely killing one of his heifers and eating its flesh; a monument to the poor animal still stands today.

Still, what's done is done. Since then, the Japanese beef industry has boomed, particularly since the brief rice shortages following World War II. And at $75 for an eight-ounce steak, a Kobe beef meal will leave you light in the wallet and empty in the stomach—but the experience, most say, is well worth the cost. —M.S.

Fugu - *The ultimate double-dare dish, fugu is the deadly Japanese globefish that has nearly done in both Homer Simpson and James Bond, as well as approximately 100 real-life Japanese each year. Why would anyone eat a sea creature which, if misprepared, can cause paralysis and death within minutes? Part of it is the death-defying excitement of it all; part of it is the mildly hallucinogenic, tingling sensation that trace amounts of toxin causes in consumers; but at least some of it must be due to the taste—chewy, rich, and delicate. In Japan, the Emperor and Empress are prohibited any enjoyment of the fish, presumably to spare them the annual fate of 100 of their subjects; in the U.S., professional chefs must first apply to the government, and then take a series of oral and written exams before they are licensed to serve fugu to the public. The Japanese insist that the danger of eating fugu lends to its pleasure. In fact, of the 30 varieties of fugu (ranging from the popular mafugu to the highly prized torafugu), the more poisonous the fish, the more prized it is to eat. For a serving of fugu sashimi, the going rate in New York will run a sophisticated diner some $250 to $400. Just what does one get out of the experience, if not death? The Japanese have long believed in its powers as an aphrodisiac. Fugu has also inspired artists, poets, and musicians. Ingesting just a touch of the poison was deemed to be good for the heart, blood circulation, and muscular relaxation. If still unharmed afterward, one is believed to be stronger physically, morally, and emotionally for it.* —J.R.

BEVERAGES

Your beverage choice is simple: *ocha*, or green tea, goes well with everything **[👁166]**. You might also try sake, though it is best consumed before or after the actual meal **[👁161]**.

Menus Made Easy KOREAN

How to Eat *Kalbi* or Bulgogi

1 Take the raw, sliced meat and place it on the grill. It's ready when you think it's ready—usually within a minute or so, less if you like it rare.

2 Place a grilled piece of meat in a leaf of green or red lettuce held in your free hand.

3 Smear on a dab of samjahng (a spicy mixture of hot red-pepper paste, soybean paste, and sesame oil). If you like, add a mouthful of rice or a sprig of scallion.

4 Fold the leaf over the filling and consume in one or two bites. If it takes more than that, you're overstuffing. This is bad form and probably messy.

5 Alternate with bites of white rice and kimchi. Repeat.

Eating Korean food is a postmodern dining experience. Sitting down at a typical Korean spread, the diner is simultaneously faced with a colorful variety of side dishes, stews, and entrees, with no obvious starting point for a meal. The uninitiated are liable to think the waitperson mistakenly unloaded the orders for several strangers at your table, as a half dozen small plates of seasoned vegetables are often delivered, all without the asking. But a Korean meal need not begin with a taste of disorientation. With a little foreknowledge, anyone can enjoy this healthful and delicious cuisine, from the popular Korean barbecued meats to the more traditional, spicier fare. —N.K.

SIDE DISHES (*PANCH'AN*)

Although they don't appear on the menu (or the bill), these small dishes are usually set on the table shortly after your order has been placed. The various kinds of *panch'an* can be eaten directly from their respective plates throughout the meal. Depending on the generosity of the restaurant, they may prove substantial enough to take the place of appetizers. Note that more side dishes accompany a large meal, like barbecued meats, than less expensive orders, like noodles. A standard panch'an selection:

Kimchi - *Pickled vegetables, such as cabbage, radish, or cucumber. The standard accompaniment to any Korean dish, kimchi ranges from mild to red-hot and, believe it or not, is an aid to digestion. (See KIMCHI box below)*

Namul - *Seasoned vegetables or roots, flavored with spices and sesame oil. Separate plates bearing blanched spinach, bean sprouts, sesame leaves, and mountain roots are popular offerings.*

Mook - *A translucent acorn gelatin, either white or brown, garnished with scallions and soy sauce.*

Grilled fish - *Fancier restaurants serve a mild fish, slightly salted and grilled whole, called gongchi.*

TRADITIONAL APPETIZERS

Bindaeduk - *Lightly fried pancakes made from ground mung beans, prepared with vegetables and sometimes a little meat. Before eating, dip into the mixture of soy sauce and rice vinegar that comes with the dish.*

Mandoo - *Steamed or fried dumplings, filled with beef.*

Japchae - *Cellophane noodles sauteed with julienned vegetables and strips of beef.*

THE MAIN COURSE

If you're eating barbecue, you don't ordinarily need any other entrees, though a large party might mix barbecue orders with rice or noodle dishes. Korean stews are virtually meals in themselves, and if you go to a restaurant that specializes in *gomtang*, or slow-cooked beef broth, you shouldn't mix it with a heavy grilled-meat dish—gomtang has a delicacy and heartiness that should be enjoyed separately.

Korean barbecue - *Kalbi, marinated beef short ribs, and bulgogi, thinly sliced marinated beef, are the most popular entrees for nonvegetarian newcomers to Korean*

cuisine. These grilled meats are distinguished by a savory marinade of soy sauce, sesame oil, scallions and spices. A similar dish prepared with chicken or pork uses the same flavoring.

In fancier restaurants, the meat is cooked on a metal grill set over a deep pot of glowing coals that fits into a hole in the table's center. Otherwise, a portable stove is brought to the table and lighted. Diners usually grill their own pieces, using chopsticks to turn the meat over; a waitperson may lend a hand.

Along with the meat, fresh green vegetables are brought out to make the meal complete. These are used to wrap the grilled meats for easier consumption by hand, and aren't meant to be eaten separately. (see sidebar)

RICE DISHES

Bibimbap - *This spicy rice-based mixture starts with a large bowl of fresh julienned vegetables and seasoned meat, topped with an egg fried sunny-side-up. The diner adds a bowl of steamed white rice and a dollop of hot-pepper paste before thoroughly mixing the whole caboodle with a spoon. Vegetarians can request this dish without meat and egg.*

Tolsot bibimbap - *The rice, meat, and veggie combination served in a heated stone bowl. Mix the ingredients quickly as they sizzle. When almost finished, be sure to scrape and savor the crunchy rice that crusts on the bottom of the bowl.*

Yookhwe dihimbap - *The mixed-rice dish served with thinly sliced raw beef.*

Hwedupbap - *A more recent adaptation of bibimbap, crossed with Japanese sashimi. Raw fish, chopped lettuce, and other vegetables are served over rice, ready to be mixed by the diner with a vinegary hot-pepper sauce.*

NOODLES

Nengmyun - *Cold buckwheat noodles, served in a clear broth and sometimes cooled with ice cubes. Topped with beef, pickled radish and thinly sliced pears, this dish may be eaten as is, or seasoned to taste with optional condiments. Try vinegar, hot mustard and hot-pepper paste, if you want to sample the authentic concoction.*

Bibim nengmyun - *Very spicy, cold buckwheat noodles without broth. In addition to the beef, radish, and pears, these noodles are to be mixed with a spoonful or two (or more, if you can handle it) of hot-pepper paste.*

Onmyun - *Literally "warm noodles." These white noodles, made from wheat flour, come in a mild soup with beef, egg, and sauteed vegetables.*

Kal-gooksu - *Prepared properly, these noodles are hand-rolled and knife-cut before being placed in a beef broth with sliced vegetables.*

STEWS

These salty stews, which go well with plain white rice, are classic Korean fare and are usually eaten communally.

Denjang-jigae - *Thick, miso-based stew with cubes of tofu, potato, and zucchini.*

Kimchi-jigae - *Kimchi and tofu simmered in a pork broth.*

Soondubu-jigae - *Soft tofu and egg with whole clams (shells included) in a spicy soup base.*

Haemul-jigae - *Spicy fish stew with miso and vegetables.*

HOTPOT (*JUNG-GOL*)

Thinly sliced beef and vegetables cooked in a simmering broth by diners at the table. Similar to, and probably descended from, Mongolian hot pot and Japanese sukiyaki. **[👁147]**

SOUPS

Numerous in variety, soups hold a place in most Korean meals, whether as a starter, on the side, or as the main event. Although usually served piping hot, soup is not only served in the winter. In fact, according to Korean folk wisdom, a good way to beat the heat during the sweltering summers is to eat soups and other hot foods. The resulting perspiration has a cooling effect, and the surrounding air seems relatively less steamy.

Duk mandoo gook - *Sliced rice cakes and dumplings in beef broth.*

Gomtang - *A simple slow-simmered broth made from beef bones and rich in flavor. To eat, spoon in a bowl of white rice, a little coarse salt, and chopped scallions. This soup tastes best when eaten with radish or cabbage kimchi. Also look for ggort gomtang (beef oxtail soup), solongtang (beef broth with cellophane noodles), and kalbitang (beef soup).*

Yook gejang - *Hot and spicy vegetable soup with beef shreds.*

Miyuk gook - *Seaweed soup in a clear light broth, eaten alongside rice dishes or as an appetizer.*

Samgyetang - *A summertime soup consisting of a whole chicken stuffed with glutinous rice and a ginseng root, all cooked in a rich broth.*

HOW TO EAT KIMCHI

1 **When eating "family-style" at a table, pick out one piece at a time rather than spooning a pile onto your plate. Be careful to avoid touching with your chopsticks other pieces of kimchi that you are not taking. If you're eating "buffet style," serve yourself as much as you think you can eat.**

2 **If pieces of cabbage kimchi are too big to consume in one bite, put a slice on a small plate. Then tear it into manageable pieces using the tips of your chopsticks, holding a chopstick in each hand.**

3 **Koreans often wrap a mouthful of rice with a leafy piece of kimchi. Spread the leaf on top of your rice, then pinch a bite-size morsel with your chopsticks and pop the whole bundle into your mouth.**

4 **When eating kimchi, be sure to have some steamed white rice nearby. The two taste great together, and the rice acts as a good buffer to kimchi's spicy heat.**

DESSERTS

At the end of a meal, many Korean restaurants serve a complimentary plate of fresh sliced fruit, sometimes accompanied by cold dessert drinks.

Soojeung kwa - *Spiced persimmon drink flavored with ginger and cinnamon, and garnished with pine nuts.*

Shik he - *Sugary sweet punch prepared with rice water and cooked rice grains.*

BEVERAGES

Bori-cha - *Roasted barley tea, with its nutty flavor, is poured at the table instead of water.*

OB beer - *Korea's favorite brew.*

Soju - *Korean vodka, sometimes served in a pot with sliced cucumbers, which soften its alcoholic edge. Warning: this distilled liquor has a stallion-like kick, and too many little bottles of soju, combined with a spicy, hearty Korean meal, will likely provide you with the opportunity to experience that meal all over again.. Plus, in the morning your head will feel like a much-used anvil.*

Kimchi

Perhaps the most famous of Korean foods, kimchi—spicy preserved vegetables—has gained global notoriety for its incendiary flavor and pungent aroma. Even those who've never seen or tasted kimchi seem to have been forewarned: This is hot stuff. Don't be discouraged. There are over 200 varieties of kimchi—including cabbage, radish, and eggplant—and only some of them leave charred spots on your tongue.

Kimchi has long been a staple of the Korean diet, dating back about 2,000 years. Present on the tables of royalty and peasants alike, the beloved pickle provided a dependable food source during long, harsh Korean winters. The hot chili, pickling salt, fresh ginger, garlic, and other spices used in its creation act as natural preservatives, making kimchi eminently storable. And, thanks to enzymes produced during the fermentation process, kimchi is also an aid to digestion.

Although kimchi has become synonymous with a hot flavor and frightening red color, chilies were not introduced into Korean cuisine until the late 16th century. The chili, which originated botanically in Mexico and Guatemala, came to Korea via Portuguese Catholic priests who accompanied Japanese troops during the seven-year Korean-Japanese War that began in 1592. Chilies, in powder and paste form, as well as fresh off the stem, are used in making most kinds of kimchi, but kimchi can also be made with a simple garlic brine—although you may not want to make it yourself. The time-consuming process involves washing, soaking, and salting dozens of cabbages or radishes before mixing in a potent combination of spices, and letting the vegetables ferment in glass jars. Depending on the desired ripeness, the jars of kimchi must then be transferred to a cool place to keep. Some Korean American households dedicate entire basement refrigerators to kimchi storage.

Meanwhile, kimchi has come into its own as a tourist draw. In 1993, the Korea National Tourism Corporation surveyed 2,700 foreign tourists and found kimchi ranked second only to leather goods among the items bought in Korea, more popular than liquor or ginseng. (Travelers can drop by the Myongga Kimchi Museum, which opened in 1986 at the Korea World Trade Center in Seoul.) In Korea, the U.S. and elsewhere, kimchi has also started appearing in fusion dishes: Atop pizza and stirred into pasta sauces, kimchi distinctive flavor adds a salty-sour, spicy bite.

Menus Made Easy
THAI

Four basic flavors dominate authentic Thai cuisine: salt, from such ingredients as dried anchovies and shrimp, fish sauce, shrimp paste; sour, from lime juice and vinegar; spicy, from peppercorns and chilies; and sweet, from sugar and natural fruits. A meal, usually enjoyed family-style (rather than in separate assigned entrees), should include a large bowl of steaming hot white rice, complemented by a number of dishes with a range of various tastes and different textures.

While it shows marked influences from China, as evidenced by many stir-fried and noodle dishes, India, as shown by many curries, and Portugal, from where chilies were first imported, Thai food reflects a definitive and unique style all its own. Typical Thai ingredients include lemongrass **[👁162]**, *galanga* (related to ginger, with a peppery paste), kaffir limes (both the dark, bumpy-skinned citrus fruit and its leaves are used), coconut milk (used instead of dairy cream), tamarind (a type of fruit which contains a sour-sweet pulp), and basil.

How the Thai eat is another example of their independent spirit. During the 19th century, King Chulalongkorn decreed that all Thais should give up eating with chopsticks, and instead begin using forks and spoons, which they did...for rice dishes and entrees. However, they refused to give up the ubiquitous utensil when eating noodle dishes—so when in the presence of *pad Thai*, break open the chopsticks.

To look like a real Thai aficionado, be prepared with some basic vocabulary, and you'll be able to order just about any typical dish without looking at a menu. Choose a main ingredient and add the Thai phrase that describes the cooking method: for example, chicken *kaprow* is chicken sauteed wth basil and chili. Other terms to know: *pad* (sauteed), *pad king* (with ginger), *nam man hoi* (sauteed with oyster sauce), *kratiem* (with garlic), *prik* or *prik Thai* (with chilies). —J.R., T.H.

SAUCES AND CONDIMENTS

Nam pla - *Fish sauce, the basis for most Thai sauces. Thin, transparent brown sauce made from salted, fermented fish or shrimp.*

Nam prik - *Spicy dipping sauce containing red chilies, scallions, garlic, lime juice, and fish sauce; on the table at every meal. Recipes for this dish vary wildly.*

Nam prik pao - *Roasted, hot sauce. Commonly accompanies plain rice, cooked vegetables, and salads.*

APPETIZERS

Appetizers are usually not served as a separate course in Thailand, although they are listed on most menus in the U.S.

Satay or sate - *Marinated meat (usually chicken or beef) grilled on skewers and served with spicy peanut sauce and a small cucumber salad on the side. Satays are street vendor fare throughout Asia.*

Kanom pan nar moo - *Ground shrimp and pork, scallions, coriander, garlic, and fish sauce spread onto toast and then deep-fried. Served with a cool dip.*

Tofu tod - *Small cubes of deep-fried bean curd; outside is hard and the insides easy to hollow out. A small spooned-out area is filled with ground pork and shrimp, fish sauce, minced roasted peanuts, and various hot peppers. The stuffing overflows the opening, so it sits on top in a small mound, usually garnished with chopped scallions, coriander, and cilantro.*

SALADS

Yam (also spelled *yum*) refers to a group of hot-and-sour salads, comprised of cooked meat, fish, or shellfish, mixed with a spicy, fish sauce and lime juice–based dressing. Other garnishes include crushed peanuts, fried onion or garlic, powdered dried shrimp, and herbs and spices.

Yam nuer - *Cooked beef slices with garlic cucumber tomato, chilies, onion, and lime juice, served over lettuce.*

Yam pla muok - *Spicy squid salad with pickled garlic, chilies, lemongrass, lime juice, and fresh mint, served over lettuce.*

Laab - *Pan-fried ground meat (pork, beef, or chicken), with ground chilies, onion, mint, lime juice; served at room temperature with lettuce, cucumber, and tomato.*

SOUPS

Soups accompany almost every Thai meal. Variations range from a thick, one-meal dish filled with noodles and some kind of meat, to lighter, clear consommes. In restaurants, soups are usually served in a fire pot which has a central funnel of burning coals, which helps to keep the soup the same constant temperature, whether you're having a first helping or the final serving.

Tom yum - *The different variations of tom yum, characterized by a fresh and hot-flavored broth, are the most popular soups in U.S.*

Thai restaurants. Tom yum goong, made with shrimp, and tom yum gai, made with chicken, are the best known.

Kao tom goong - *A porridge-like soup, often eaten at breakfast or as a late night snack. Less flavorful than other dishes, but meant to be seasoned by each individual with such assorted condiments as scallions, cucumber, lime, green chilies, and/or preserved fish.*

NOODLES

Noodle dishes are usually served with an assortment of condiments, including *nam pla, nam prik,* ground peanuts, lime juice, and crushed dried chilies. At some restaurants, these condiments are not served automatically to non-Thai customers, but if you ask for them, they will come.

Pad Thai - *Its main ingredient is the sen lek noodle, a dried, thin and flat rice noodle remoistened after soaking and combining with sesame oil, lemon juice, fish sauce, ground shrimp or pork, bean sprouts, egg and scallions. Chopped radish and peanuts add texture, while cilantro and garlic add spunk. A lunchtime favorite.*

Mee krob - *Sweet, crisp, fried noodles topped with a caramelized ground meat sauce and pickled garlic. Served at room temperature. Should not be overwhelmingly sweet.*

Lard na - *Fried egg noodles with Chinese broccoli. Comes with choice of chicken or various seafood.*

Pad kee mow - *Flat rice noodles with basil, chilies, garlic, and a choice of meat*

CURRIES

Thai curries feature coconut milk, fresh herbs, chilies, shallots, and sometimes garlic. The herbs and spices are ground together to create a paste. The following four types are the most popular. **[👁128]**

Massamun - *The mildest of the three; the name may derive from a mispronunciation of the word "Muslim." Made with red chilies, potatoes, and spices. Subtly sweet.*

Red curry - *Spicier than Massamun, but not as hot as green curry.*

Green curry - *A bit of a misnomer, as it is actually pale yellow in color. Made with green chilies and potentially very spicy.*

Penang curry - *Very spicy, thick, and dark in color. Made with ground peanuts.*

ENTREES

"During the 19th century, King Chulalongkorn decreed that all Thais should give up eating with chopsticks, and instead begin using forks and spoons, which they did... for rice dishes and entrees. However, they refused to give up the ubiquitous utensil when eating noodle dishes—so when in the presence of *pad Thai*, break open the chopsticks."

With most Thai entrees, the type of meat used is interchangeable. The sauce or cooking method is basically the same, whether for chicken, beef, pork, fish, or shellfish. Listed below are a number of the most popular Thai cooking methods.

Pad kaprow - *Sauteed, sliced meat with fresh basil and chilies. Usually quite spicy.*

Kaeng kew wan - *Meat in green curry sauce with kaffir lime leaves, coconut milk, basil, and eggplant.*

Yang - *Meat marinated in herbs and spices, especially garlic, chilies, lime juice, then grilled.*

Pad king - *Sliced meat sauteed with ginger, Chinese mushrooms, scallions, and chilies.*

Pad pak nam man hoi - *Sauteed meat with mixed vegetables and oyster sauce.*

Kratiem prik Thai - *Pan-fried in garlic sauce, with chilies, cilantro, and tomato. A favorite Thai version features frog legs, very popular in Thailand, where they are often served to mark special occasions. In U.S. restaurants, Kob kratiem (frog legs, Kratiem style) are more often than not deep-fried, although in Thailand, they tend to be pan-fried.*

Pla lad prik - *Whole red snapper stir-fired with roasted curry paste, red curry, and tamarind.*

RICE

Thailand is referred to as "the rice bowl of Asia," as it is one of the top rice-growing nations in the world. The preferred grain is jasmine rice, a long-grained rice with a subtle nutty flavor. White steamed rice is served at most meals. **[👁159]**

DESSERT

Dessert is reserved for special occasions. Like other Asian countries, rather than a sweet concoction, most Thai tend to finish a meal with fresh fruit.

Sang ka ya - *Pumpkin custard made with coconut milk.*

Khao niew mamuang - *Sweet, sticky rice flavored with coconut cream and served with mango slices.*

BEVERAGES

Thai iced tea and iced coffee - *Made with brewed tea or coffee, sweetened milk, and ice. Can also be flavored with cinnamon, star anise, vanilla, or other sweet spices. Very refreshing, but possibly better as a dessert rather than to drink with your meal.*

Singha Beer - *A popular pale Thai lager.*

Menus Made Easy
VIETNAMESE

Ironically, Vietnamese food is sometimes referred to as the "nouvelle cuisine of Asian cookery," although it is thousands of years old. That's because, after thousands of years of occupation by various military forces, it's become one of the clearest examples of the fusion of East and West culinary styles. You're just as likely to find crusty bread at the table as rice, understandable since China dominated Vietnam for a thousand years and France for hundreds. In spite of these at-the-time-unwelcome influences, the Vietnamese have managed to preserve their own distinct, unique cuisine—one which is growing rapidly in popularity here in the U.S. (which dominated Vietnam for a few decades too, if you recall).

The major difference between Vietnamese and Chinese cuisines has to do with seasonings. While soy sauce is the primary flavoring in Chinese cooking, it's rarely seen in Vietnamese recipes. Instead, the basis of Vietnamese dishes is *nuoc mam,* which literally translates as "fish sauce"—a clear amber liquid produced from layers of fresh fish, preferably anchovies, and salt, fermented in large barrels. Nuoc mam is used as a basic flavoring during the cooking process; it is also the base for the most popular of Vietnamese sauces, *nuoc cham,* a combination of nuoc mam, garlic, chili peppers, fresh lime, and sugar, which accompanies almost all dishes and takes the place of salt at the Vietnamese table. Other noticeable traits of Vietnamese cuisine include the regular use of shallots, which are not usually seen in Chinese cooking; scallions are also plentiful in Vietnamese dishes. Other characteristic spices include coriander and lemon grass. Moreover, lamb or mutton are never eaten in Vietnam. Preferred meat dishes are most often made of pork; chicken is also prevalent. Although much appreciated, beef dishes tend to be rare, due to its high cost in Vietnam (though you'll certainly find them at U.S. restaurants).

Today, you can find Vietnamese restaurants in most major metropolitan areas, often near or within Chinatowns. Don't fear that you might have trouble ordering, since most restaurants have extensive English translations and descriptions on their menus—though occasionally you may come across a word that is unfamiliar even in English. —J.R., T.H.

SAUCES AND CONDIMENTS

Nuoc mam - *Salty fish sauce; the basic flavoring of Vietnamese cuisine. Can be added to soups or other dishes, to taste.*

Nuoc cham - *Salty-sour fish sauce, made of nuoc mam, garlic, chili peppers, fresh lime, and sugar, and sometimes vinegar to make it more sour. Served at almost all meals, just as Westerners serve salt and pepper.*

Hoisin peanut sauce - *A dipping sauce, especially for appetizers like summer rolls (see below), made of hoisin sauce, vinegar, sugar, garlic, and a sprinkling of chopped peanuts.* **[👁164]**

APPETIZERS

Cha gio - *Fried spring roll, made with meat and veggies, rolled in egg-based wrapper. Served warm, with dipping sauces as above. A must.*

Goi cuon - *Summer roll with shrimp and pork, served cold, wrapped in rice paper; can be dipped in nuoc cham or hoisin peanut sauce.*

Banh tap - *Grilled pork on shrimp-flavored chips. The meat is served warm and the chips cool, served separately.*

Ga xe phay - *Chicken salad, made of cold, dry chicken with shredded cabbage, onions, and sometimes other vegetable, served with nuoc cham, which is poured on top like salad dressing.*

Banh mi chien tom - *Shrimp toast, made of whole shrimp or spiced ground shrimp coated in batter, placed on top of French bread and deep-fried; served warm, to be dipped in nuoc cham.*

Cha lua - *Boiled pate, a pate roll made of pork or chicken, wrapped and steamed in a banana leaf; sliced pieces, dipped in nuoc mam, can be served as an appetizer, or on French bread as a sandwich.*

SOUPS

Pho - *Long-simmered beef broth with linguine-size rice noodles; comes in many variations with various meats and/or vegetables. Virtually the national dish of Vietnam.*

Mieng ga - *Chicken vermicelli soup; pretty much self-explanatory—chicken broth with vermicelli threads.*

Canh chua tom - *Spicy sour shrimp soup. This soup has no noodles, but scallions, tomatoes, bean sprouts, and celery may be included. Can also be made with fish instead of shrimp.*

ENTREES

Banh vot thit nuong *(Barbecued meat-wrapped in rice paper): In traditional Vietnamese households, this is never eaten as* an entire meal, but it has been adapted as an entree in U.S. Vietnamese restaurants to suit American tastes. You usually get three plates, one with the cold rice wrappers, which have been blanched, another with vermicelli noodles topped with grilled, marinated beef, pork, or chicken, and a third with vegetables including fresh leaf lettuce, mint leaves, cilantro, bean sprouts, cucumbers, and a pickled mixture of cabbage, carrots, and onions, each in separate piles. Usually, you wrap the rolls yourself. Carefully take a wrapper in your palm, cover it with a lettuce leaf to protect it against moisture from the veggies, then use chopsticks to add small amounts of noodles and meat, and whatever veggies you like, roll like a fajita, and eat, dipping in nuoc cham if desired.

Bo kho - *Beef stew, made of beef cubes and carrots stir-fried and seasoned with a five-spice powder (star anise, cinnamon, cloves, fennel, and Szechuan peppercorns) and lemon grass; eaten with French bread, steamed rice, or rice noodles.*

Ca-ri ga - *Chicken curry stew, a coconut-milk flavored stew of chicken and potatoes, stir-fried and curry-seasoned; eaten with French bread or steamed rice.* **[👁128]**

Thit kho tieu - *Caramel pork with black pepper—browned meat in caramelized sugar sauce, simmered in its own juices and eaten with rice. Can also be made with fish.*

Cha chien - *Whole fish pan-fried with ginger, scallions, garlic, eaten with rice and nuoc mam.*

Cha thit - *Ground pork and shredded crabmeat mixed with cellophane noodles, a beaten egg, and shredded black mushrooms, then steamed together.*

Com tay cam - *Hot pot chicken rice pilaf: chicken, mushrooms, onion, cashews, and rice cooked slowly in a clay pot with coconut milk and chicken stock.*

Bang xeo - *Resembles a large omelette; made of a rice flour batter mixed with scallions. The batter is first cooked in large wok and swirled around (crepe-batter style), then shrimp, mushrooms, bean sprouts, mung beans, and grilled pork are added. The concoction is folded in half like an omelette and served with nuoc mam.*

"Ironically, Vietnamese food is sometimes referred to as the 'nouvelle cuisine of Asian cookery,' although it is thousands of years old. That's because, after thousands of years of occupation by various military forces, it's become one of the clearest examples of East and West culinary fusion."

NOODLE DISHES

"While soy sauce is the primary flavoring in Chinese cooking, it's rarely seen in Vietnamese recipes. Instead, the basis of Vietnamese dishes is *nuoc mam,* **which translates as "fish sauce"—a clear amber liquid produced from fresh fish, preferably anchovies, and salt, fermented in large barrels. "**

Bun cha gio - *Spring rolls cut in pieces, laid on a bed of rice noodles, and served with fresh vegetables, including lettuce, cucumbers, bean sprouts, and mint. Eaten with nuoc cham.*

Thit nuong banh hoi - *Grilled pork meatballs over a bed of rice noodles, served with fresh vegetables.*

Bun thit bo nuong or **Bun thit ga nuong** - *Lemon grass beef or chicken over rice noodles: The meat is grilled with lemon grass and laid on a bed of rice noodles; also served with shredded lettuce and cucumbers.*

BEVERAGES

Cafe pin sua da or *Ca phe da* is iced coffee, served black, if you can take it, or with sweetened condensed milk. You can also get it hot; coffee is served with drip-through metal filters placed over a mug, with an extra side Thermos of hot water should you wish to have a second cup. The hot water slowly filtrates through the coffee in the top, into the mug, where it blends with the condensed milk (and ice, if it's iced) at the mug's bottom. Very rich, and very strong.

Soda chanhh muoi - *"Pickled lemonade": The lemons are cured in salt water and allowed to ferment until the lemons become pickled. The salted lemons are squeezed into a glass of seltzer water or club soda, with sugar added to taste. Served over ice; a very odd, acquired taste.*

Soda si mui - *"Salty plum soda": Salted, dried plums are placed in a glass of iced soda water, sugar is added, and the resulting drink is served over ice. Another acquired taste.*

Sua dau nanh - *A sweetened, watery soybean drink, very slightly gritty in texture (from the soybeans), with vague resemblance in taste to sweetened condensed milk.*

Sam bo luong - *Made of longan* **[👁133]**, *lotus seed, and syrup, served over ice.*

Che ba mau dau xanh va dau do - *Rainbow ice—a drink made of green and red beans, mixed with tapioca (which looks like gelatin), coconut milk, and ice water.*

MSG Attacks and Cures

Some people go through life without ever knowing about monosodium glutamate. Others spend much of their lives trying to get away from it. For those in the latter category, the food additive is allegedly responsible for headaches, dizziness, blurred vision, tingling faces, tight chests, and other symptoms of "Chinese Restaurant Syndrome." Who knew that a simple seaweed extract would cause such controversy?

It all began in 1908, when Japanese scientist Kikunae Ikeda developed MSG as an isolate of *kombu* ("sea tangle," a form of kelp), which has been used as a flavor-enhancing ingredient in Japanese cuisine for thousands of years. The following year, Ikeda became a partner in the first company to market MSG as a seasoning: Ajinomoto, literally "the essence of taste." Ajinomoto has since become synonymous with MSG throughout Asia, and remains the world's largest producer. In 1993, the multibillion-dollar company opened its first American MSG-manufacturing plant in the heartlands of Iowa.

MSG is sold in liquid and granulated form in grocery stores, and is widely used as a food additive. It's not fully understood how it works to enhance the taste of food. Western science believes that it stimulates the taste buds, while having no distinct taste of its own. Eastern cultures believe MSG has a fifth taste—beyond salty, sweet, sour, or bitter—called *umami,* from the Japanese word for "deliciousness."

Although the industry's Glutamate Association reports that MSG is perfectly safe, and some researchers have labeled stories of reactions to the flavor enhancer as "superstition," many individuals have cited adverse effects—including skin rashes, breathing problems, and irregular heartbeat. More extreme findings have suggested links to Alzheimer's and Lou Gehrig's disease; Dr. George Schwartz, a toxicologist and the author of *In Bad Taste: the MSG Syndrome,* claims to have recorded incidents of brain damage, heart attacks, and even deaths linked to MSG. "It's the DDT of the '90s," he warns. Schwartz theorizes that MSG's toxic effect is derived from its rapid absorption as an artificially isolated "free glutamate." Naturally occurring glutamates, found in meat and anything with protein, are linked to other amino acids by peptides, which are broken down slowly in the digestive process. Laboratory tests have shown MSG to act as an "excitatory neurotransmitter," which can cause damage to nerve cells in the brain. Regardless, the U.S. Food and Drug Administration still lists MSG as "generally recognized as safe," although it must be listed on the ingredient label of any food to which it is added. —MW., D.G.

CURES FOR THE MSG ATTACK

Since there is no clear understanding of the syndrome and no generalized anti-MSG medication, the best you can do is treat the symptoms. Dr. Schwartz suggests the following remedies:

Symptom	Treatment
heartburn	Alka-Seltzer or Tagamet
stomach upset	Pepto-Bismol
bloating, bags under eyes	a sauna or steam bath
headache	aspirin, acetominophen, ibuprofen
migraines	analgesics, plus isolation in a dark room
asthma	inhalers, over-the-counter asthma preparations
rapid heart rate	vigorous exercise (sweating to get MSG out of system)

(There are also certain ubiquitous folk remedies for the syndrome, including drinking lemon juice with a vitamin C tablet, taking magnesium tablets, and smearing Tiger Balm on the forehead.)

MSG, BY ANY OTHER NAME. CAN STILL MAKE YOU SICK

THE FOLLOWING COMMON INGREDIENTS CONTAIN MSG:

- hydrolyzed vegetable protein
- hydrolyzed animal protein
- autolyzed yeast extract
- vegetable protein
- textured soy protein
- sodium caseinate
- calcium caseinate

THESE MAY HAVE MSG IN SMALL TO SIGNIFICANT AMOUNTS, DEPENDING ON FORMULATIONS OR MANUFACTURING CONDITIONS:

- broth
- boullion
- stock
- seasonings
- natural flavorings
- tomato paste
- texturized protein
- whey protein
- dried yeasts, Torula yeast, yeast nutrients

Noodles

Noodles, or *mein,* supposedly originated in northern China during the Han dynasty (206 B.C. to 220 B.C.), around the time when the Chinese learned techniques for large-scale flour grinding. The popularity of this staple food soon spread to all of East Asia, especially Japan (a country thought to consume the most noodles in the world), Korea, Thailand, and Vietnam. People still speculate whether, in 1295, Marco Polo really did bring back to Italy the dish that would become the grandfather of pasta; most people give him the benefit of the doubt.

As a specialty food, noodles are often eaten by Chinese on birthdays and New Year's, because the shape of noodles—long and thin—symbolizes longevity. That's why it's taboo to break noodles before cooking them. The following is a selection of some of the most common noodle variants found throughout Asia:

Cellophane or **vermicelli noodles**, are thin, translucent noodles made from mung bean starch. Especially popular in Southeast Asia, these "bean threads" are usually cooked in soups or deep-fried. The Japanese version, made from sweet potato starch, is called *haruame,* or "spring rain." The dish is usually served cold and can be topped with shredded cucumber, radish, chicken strips, or shrimp. Korean vermicelli is also made from sweet potato starch, and often used in soups. It can also be flavored with sesame oil, soy sauce, sugar, onion, garlic and topped with sliced meats and vegetables to make the staple dish *japchae* [👁149]. Both the Korean and Japanese versions are slightly thicker than East and Southeast Asian vermicelli.

If the superstition tying noodle-length to lifespan is true, eating **haw fun** could be your doom; they're wide, white, flat, slippery rice noodles, usually pan-fried as chow ("fried") fun, but also boiled in stock as noodle soup. In Thailand, a slightly thinner version of fun is known as *gwaytio,* and used in such entrees as *lard na* [👁152].

Mein is simply the Chinese word for noodle, but chow mein—pan-fried egg noodle—is probably the noodle dish most commonly connected with Chinese take-out cuisine. These wiry, wavy, yellowish noodles are seared brown and crispy on the outside (if done right). The same egg noodles, boiled, drained, and stir-fried, make a dish called lo mein; unfortunately, at some restaurants lo mein is called chow mein, so if you want crispy noodles, ask for crispy noodles [👁140].

The making of **La mein**, or Chinese "pulled noodles," is a most exhilarating culinary spectacle to behold. A noodle chef in action repeatedly stretches a piece of wheat flour dough until a network of thin noodle strands materialize. The resulting noodle is thicker than regular egg noodles; in most restaurants, however, you can probably count on getting machine-made rather than hand-pulled la mein. After being boiled and drained, it doesn't get deep-fried, but instead is stir-fried with meats and vegetables.

Rice sticks are thin, translucent noodles made from rice flour, usually cooked in soups or stir-fried with meats and vegetables. They're popular in Southeast Asia, especially in Vietnam, where they bulk up treats like spring rolls, as well as in Southern China and Taiwan. In dried form, they're wiry and resemble dry vermicelli, only whiter. Rice sticks from the Philippines are called *pancit luglug*.

Soba, popular in northern Japan, is a thin, brownish noodle made from buckwheat flour. If made with green tea (which is mostly a coloring agent, not a flavor enhancer), it has a green, translucent color. Soba is traditionally served cold and bare of garnish in a wooden box, with a soy-based dipping sauce on the side. Soba has been shown to have numerous health benefits, including lowering of cholesterol and prevention of heart disease. [👁147]

Juzo Itami's **Tampopo**

Somen, a fine, vermicelli-like wheat noodle, is a southern Japanese noodle that's always served cold. It can come in an array of colors besides the standard white: pink (which comes from perilla oil), bright yellow (from egg yolk), and green (from tea powder). In Kyoto, you can still experience one particularly pastoral way of serving it, called *nagashi somen*: Cooked somen is slid straight out from the kitchen, down a bamboo chute, and into the waters of an icy, mountain stream. Diners lounge around the water, taking in nature, and occasionally dipping their chopsticks into the stream to grab fleeting strands of somen, which are dipped into a chilled broth.

Udon, a fat, white noodle made from wheat, is the staple of southern Japan. It's usually cooked in soups, though revisionist restaurants have taken to stir-frying it. Since udon is extremely soft, stir-frying can produce a distasteful glop. Stick with tradition—you'll feel better. [👁147]

Ramen is the speed-lunch of Japanese salarymen, who slurp it down feverishly in tiny cafes before bolting back to work. An entire movie by director Juzo Itami, *Tampopo* (1986), had as its plot the quest for the perfect bowl. There's even a museum in Yokohama dedicated to this popular noodle treat. The Japanese love ramen, and well they should—properly prepared, it's a tasty, nutritious meal in a bowl. What most Americans don't realize (most Japanese probably don't either) is that ramen is not a Japanese dish. They originated as la mein (*see above*), a traditional Chinese pulled-wheat noodle, but were adapted by a population motivated by convenience. And how much more convenient can you get? Boiled ramen, usually in a miso or soy-based stock, is garnished with slices of roast pork, bean sprouts, bamboo shoots, fish cakes or other tidbits, then served in a bowl. Preparation time is usually minutes, and consumption time takes not much longer. The answer, of course, is instant ramen—convenience in a crisp plastic package, synonymous with desperate living throughout Japan and America. Originally intended as a snack for children, instant ramen was created in 1957, and is now consumed at a rate of 4.5 billion packets a year. Unfortunately, to get that familiar brick-like form, wheat noodles must be flash-fried in oil, then dried—breaking down what little fiber and vitamins the noodles contain, and replacing it with fat. Usually, to further preserve it, BHT and other chemicals are added. To top it off, instant noodles contain a package of broth powder which is mixed into the noodles as they're boiling: the powder is a bouquet of preserved spices, salt, nitrates, and MSG. Regardless, instant ramen is a reliable empty calorie, with the benefit that it makes *real* meals taste great, once you can afford to make them. So stock up. It's the survival food of the '90s. —D.Y.

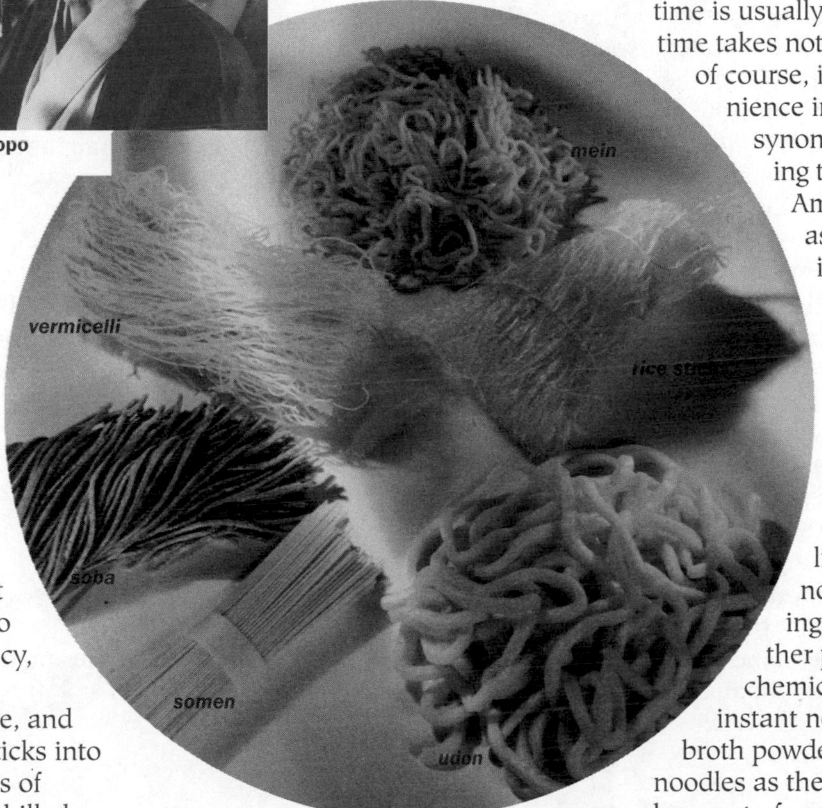

Rice: The Sticky Staff of Life

If food were a language, rice would be the lingua franca of Asian cuisines. The primary food staple for two-thirds of the world's population, rice fills bowls and bellies throughout Asia.

Rice cultivation was probably indigenous to India, spreading to Indochina and Southeast Asia as early as 7,000 years ago, and then up through other Asian countries. Today, an estimated 40,000 varieties of rice are cultivated internationally, with mainland China, India, Thailand, Burma, and Vietnam among the world's largest producers. While 90 percent of the world's rice is grown in Asian monsoon territory, only a small fraction of this is exported. Domestic consumption accounts for much of the rice harvests in many countries, and thus the well-being of their populations is tied closely with the production and availability of rice. For instance: Compare the worldwide per capita consumption of around 145 pounds of rice per year, to that of the average Burmese—408 pounds per year. Other Asian countries follow close behind: Vietnam's population accounts for 367 pounds per year, and Japan's, 167.

Not surprisingly, this huge market has whetted the appetite of American agribusiness. Unlike Asian producers, half of the annual yield of the U.S. rice industry is targeted for export. For years, Asian governments, particularly Japan and South Korea, resisted American trade pressures in their determination to keep cheap foreign rice off their soil. They argued that self-sufficiency in their staple food was necessary to national security, and that their increasingly urban economies had a responsibility to protect the livelihood of rural folk. During the early 1990s, controversy boiled over in both Japan and Korea, when their respective leaders lifted bans on foreign rice—the former to alleviate a shortage due to bad weather, the latter to comply with international trade agreements.

Domestic consumption in the U.S. is no slouch either. According to the U.S. Department of Agriculture, rice is currently the nation's fastest-growing food commodity. Annual American consumption now averages about 25 pounds per capita, roughly twice that of the early 1980s. Some attribute this trend to the influx of Asian and Latino immigrants, and to the increasing mainstream interest in ethnic cuisines and health foods.

Meanwhile, one perennial use of the grain is on the decline: the tossing of rice at newlyweds. The practice, which symbolizes fertility and abundance, is believed to have been adopted in the West from the example of early Asian American immigrants. But in recent years, couples have opted for birdseed or rose petals over the rigid rice grains, to avoid the post-nuptial risk of wedding guests slipping on the sidewalk, not to mention the hazard that rice poses to feathered friends: overconsumption of raw rice, which expands upon contact with liquids, can cause severe gastrointestinal distress and even death in birds. —N.K.

GOING WITH THE GRAIN

A shorthand guide to rice:

INDICA (also long-grain rice)—The standard in the West and postcolonial nations; the finest long-grain reputedly comes from Iran, although its export is no longer allowed. More granular and textured than short-grain rice, and, some say, more flavorful, though you'd be hard-pressed to tell the difference by taste alone.

JAPONICA (also short-grain rice)—The standard in East Asian cooking. More sticky and softer than long-grain rice. All East Asian dishes (Chinese, Japanese, or Korean) are perfect complements to this rice, which, though bland on its own, holds flavors well and absorbs sauces readily.

BASMATI—Native to India and Pakistan, this variety of Indica is aromatic and distinctive, strong enough to stand up to the punch of curries and other spicy foods; a U.S.-native hybrid called "Texmati" is similar in taste, and widely available.

GLUTINOUS (also sticky rice)—Used for special dishes in China and Japan, upon cooking, this starchy rice becomes extremely sticky, clumping in clusters.

JASMINE—A variety of Indica from Thailand, this looks much like any other long-grain, but cooks up moister and stickier. More delicate than basmati, with a flowery "nose."

BROWN—Only in the U.S. is this considered a delicacy. This is standard rice that hasn't gone through the polishing and bleaching that produces white rice.

Roll With It: Wrappers Delight

The original Chinese egg roll—that ubiquitous cylindrical-shaped finger food filled with all the ingredients for a balanced meal—has made a beeline path into the American palate. It's quick; it's got vegetables, protein, and carbohydrates; best of all, it's cheap (often thrown in free with your take-out special). Today, Americanized versions of the roll can be found everywhere, from hors d'oeuvre platters at the Ritz-Carlton to your grocer's freezer.

So what's the difference between the egg roll and spring roll, anyway? Basically, very little. Both refer to the same thing, although the egg roll's wrapper counts a beaten egg among its list of ingredients and a spring roll usually includes shrimp and more vegetables. Both are deep-fried; sometimes, the spring roll is smaller **[👁138]**.

But these are just the tip of the iceberg. Every culture has its variant on wrapped food, from Mexican burritos and fajitas, to French cràpes, to Greek pita pockets, and with the explosion in ethnic cuisines, American consumers are being rocked by a growing number of rolls. Some arrive already prepared, while others require a little hand-made creativity. Either way, the result is a bundle of culinary delight. —J.R., T.H.

Name	Country	Wrapper	Ingredients	Sauces	How to (where applicable)
chuen juan (Spring roll/egg roll)	Shanghai, China	Thin squares of flour-and-water dough. Spring-roll wrappings tend to be flaky and delicate, egg roll heavier and textured	Beef, pork, or chicken, shrimp, Chinese cabbage, mushrooms, bamboo shoots, scallions, Chinese parsley, eggs; Westernized versions often include carrots.	A dipping sauce of oil, dry sherry, sugar, and light soy sauce; salt, white pepper.	Just enjoy! Note that the Americanized takeout version tends to feature a preponderance of cabbage and a very thick wrapping, which absorbs oil.
Mu shu	Northern Chinese	A supple flour and water crepe	Traditionally pork, cabbage, tree ear mushrooms, lily buds, bits of scrambled egg.	Plum or hoisin sauce.	Hold the flour crepe flat in one palm, fill with combined ingredients, drizzle sauce, add scallions, then fold.
Cha gio (spring roll)	Vietnamese	Dried rice paper	Ground or shredded meat, cellophane noodles, onions or scallions, garlic, and spices. Deep-fried and served hot.	Nuoc cham, a blend of fish sauce, chilies, lime juice, vinegar, and sesame oil, chopped peanuts.	Served with lettuce leaves, cilantro, milk, and pickled cucumber and carrots. Spread lettuce leaf, place the spring roll and other ingredients onto the lettuce, roll into cylinder, dip into the nuoc cham.
Goi cuon (summer roll, soft or fresh spring roll)	Vietnamese	Thin, moist sheets of rice paper	Shrimp, pork, lettuce, mint, garlic, rice vermicelli, . Served at room temperature.	Nuoc cham, peanut or hoisin dipping sauce	Open wide!
Lumpia	Filipino	Thin sheet of noodle dough	Shrimp or pork, julienne hearts of palm, garlic, and spices.	Cooked vinegar, soy sauce, crushed garlic, black pepper, tomato.	Enjoy as is!
Lumpiang sariwa	Filipino	Paper-thin, soft, white crepe; held together by a layer of waxed paper	Lettuce, julienne carrots, string beans, minced pork, and shrimp; not fried.	Topped with sweet-and-sour sauce.	Eat with your hands by tearing off strips of the sheet of waxed paper as you go.
Hae koon	Thai	Dried bean curd sheets	Ground pork, fish sauce, shrimp, garlic, ginger; deep fried	Vinegar and soy sauce.	Dig in!

Sake

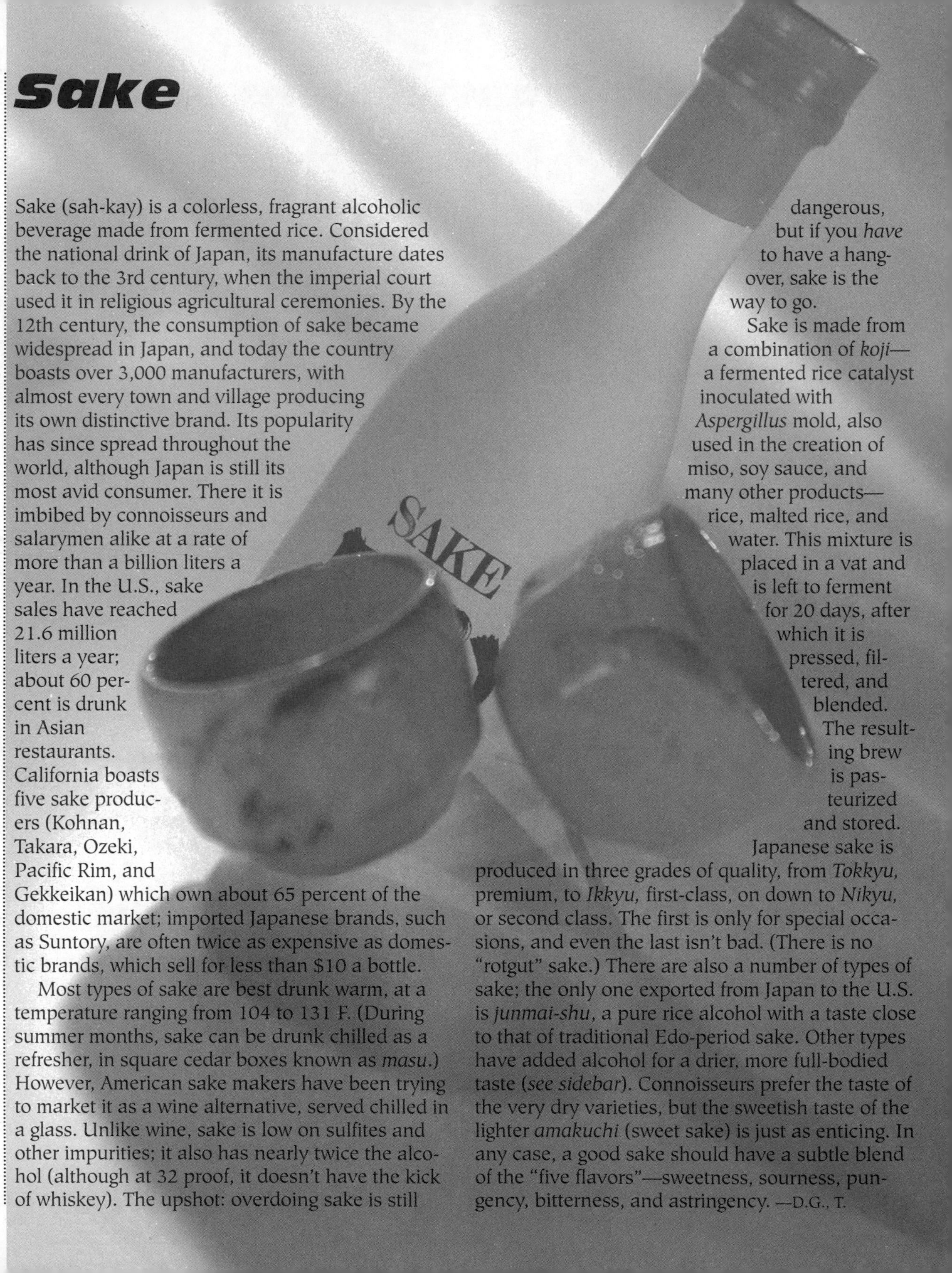

Sake (sah-kay) is a colorless, fragrant alcoholic beverage made from fermented rice. Considered the national drink of Japan, its manufacture dates back to the 3rd century, when the imperial court used it in religious agricultural ceremonies. By the 12th century, the consumption of sake became widespread in Japan, and today the country boasts over 3,000 manufacturers, with almost every town and village producing its own distinctive brand. Its popularity has since spread throughout the world, although Japan is still its most avid consumer. There it is imbibed by connoisseurs and salarymen alike at a rate of more than a billion liters a year. In the U.S., sake sales have reached 21.6 million liters a year; about 60 percent is drunk in Asian restaurants. California boasts five sake producers (Kohnan, Takara, Ozeki, Pacific Rim, and Gekkeikan) which own about 65 percent of the domestic market; imported Japanese brands, such as Suntory, are often twice as expensive as domestic brands, which sell for less than $10 a bottle.

Most types of sake are best drunk warm, at a temperature ranging from 104 to 131 F. (During summer months, sake can be drunk chilled as a refresher, in square cedar boxes known as *masu*.) However, American sake makers have been trying to market it as a wine alternative, served chilled in a glass. Unlike wine, sake is low on sulfites and other impurities; it also has nearly twice the alcohol (although at 32 proof, it doesn't have the kick of whiskey). The upshot: overdoing sake is still dangerous, but if you *have* to have a hangover, sake is the way to go.

Sake is made from a combination of *koji*—a fermented rice catalyst inoculated with *Aspergillus* mold, also used in the creation of miso, soy sauce, and many other products—rice, malted rice, and water. This mixture is placed in a vat and is left to ferment for 20 days, after which it is pressed, filtered, and blended. The resulting brew is pasteurized and stored.

Japanese sake is produced in three grades of quality, from *Tokkyu*, premium, to *Ikkyu*, first-class, on down to *Nikyu*, or second class. The first is only for special occasions, and even the last isn't bad. (There is no "rotgut" sake.) There are also a number of types of sake; the only one exported from Japan to the U.S. is *junmai-shu*, a pure rice alcohol with a taste close to that of traditional Edo-period sake. Other types have added alcohol for a drier, more full-bodied taste (*see sidebar*). Connoisseurs prefer the taste of the very dry varieties, but the sweetish taste of the lighter *amakuchi* (sweet sake) is just as enticing. In any case, a good sake should have a subtle blend of the "five flavors"—sweetness, sourness, pungency, bitterness, and astringency. —D.G., T.

THE FIVE MOST COMMON TYPES OF SAKE

1 **JUNMAI-SHU:** pure rice sake with no additions.

2 **HONJOU-ZUKURI:** 3/4 rice sake and 1/4 added alcohol, milder in taste than Junmai-shu.

3 **GINJOU-ZUKURI:** a variation of both of the above, considered to be the ultimate sake, brewed only in small quantities.

4 **GENSHU:** slightly more alcohol than normal (20 percent added alcohol), has a full-bodied taste, often drunk chilled.

5 **TARU-ZAKE:** sake aged in wood, which gives it a somewhat raw, muscular flavor.

SAKE RULES

Through its ritual use in marriage ceremonies to funerals, sake retains a sacerdotal character. Filling one's own sake cup while dining with company is considered rude. And one should always lift one's cup while being served by another. Finally, you should never refuse an offer of more sake if your host is still drinking, although as a final option you can turn over your cup (called sakazuki), or simply slump over unconscious.

A Pan-Asian Pantry of Spices and Sauces and Everything Nice

Had it not been for the Western obsession with Asian spices, America would never have been discovered: Christopher Columbus, searching for a better, faster route to get to the tangy, aromatic, much-valued spices available only in the Far East, made a wrong turn and ended up in the Caribbean.

Asians ingredients like cinnamon, ginger, and coriander have long been an integral part of the Western diet. Today, the East continues to be a cornucopia for the spice pantries of the world, infusing global cuisine with new and unique concoctions of roots, flowers, seeds, and bulbs of an endless variety of plants.

SPICES

Basil (Sweet basil)—Native to India and Persia, the leaves add an appetizing aroma to sauces, gravies, and stews.

Cardamom—The dried fruit of a large-leafed perennial plant, which is native to India. One of the oldest spices in the world, and the third most expensive after saffron and vanilla. Has aroma initially reminiscent of camphor, with a sharply bitter, strong, lingering taste. Used throughout Chinese and South Asian cooking, especially to season meat dishes.

Cassia (Chinese cinnamon)—Another ancient spice, recorded as a Chinese herb as early as 2700 B.C., although it is believed to be a native to Assam and northern Burma. Can be used interchangeably with cinnamon, although cassia is thicker and coarser, and its taste less delicate. Slightly sweet with a bitter edge.

Cinnamon—Discovered (for culinary use) growing in Sri Lanka by a Westerner in the 13th century; used in China since ancient times for medicinal purposes. It adds an aromatic, sweetish flavor to myriad foods, including meats, vegetables, sauces, and drinks.

Cloves: Originated from the Moluccas Islands (also known as the Spice Islands) in eastern Indonesia; mentioned in Chinese literature in the 3rd century B.C., and in Indian writings by the start of 1st century A.D. Used especially for meats and in stews and soups. Has a sweetish, lingering taste, with a complex "nose."

Coriander (Chinese parsley, Mexican parsley, cilantro)—One of the most common herbs in Chinese cuisine. Graceful, tender leaves have unique spicy flavor. Coriander is the seed, and used as a spice; cilantro is the plant and used as a garnish.

Cumin—Native to Western Asia. Only the seeds are used—dried and ground. Not to be confused with caraway, though in French, caraway was often called cumin des pres. Has a nutty, aromatic taste. A member of the parsley family.

Five-spice powder—Of Chinese origin, made of a powdered blend of fennel, Szechwan peppercorns (see below), star anise (see below), cinnamon (see above), and cloves (see above).

Galangal—A member of the ginger family. There are two main types: "lesser," native to southern China, and "greater," native to Indonesia. Lesser galangal has a more pungent aroma with a hint of eucalyptus, and a taste reminiscent of ginger and cardamom; greater galangal is more of a mix of ginger and pepper, with a hint of sour lemon.

Ginger—Cultivated in tropical Asia for more than 3,000 years. Widely used throughout Asia, especially in China and India. First spice to make it out of Asia into wide usage in the West. It has a warm aroma with woody undertones; the flavor is hot and slightly biting. In most Asian counties, fresh ginger is used as a cooking ingredient, often with fresh garlic, but it's available in any number of ways: ground, dried, crystallized, candied, pickled, and so on.

Lemongrass—Used predominantly in Southeast Asia, where it is believed to have originated. Most popular in cuisines of Thailand, Vietnam, and Indonesia. Available by the stalk: up to two feet in length, pale yellow-green, and fibrous. Adds a citrine flavor to soups and stir-fried dishes.

Marjoram—Native to western Asia and the Mediterranean; cousin to the more familiar oregano. Used especially with vegetables and to flavor lamb dishes.

Nutmeg and mace—Original to the Moluccas Islands. Nutmeg is the nut, while mace is the lacy growth (the "aril") which envelops the nut and becomes visible when the fruit is stripped away.

Pepper—Native to the monsoon forests of the Malabar coast of southwest India, pepper was so highly valued at one time that it was traded ounce per ounce for gold; for centuries, pepper was used as a currency substitute throughout the East and West. Black pepper is the dried unripe fruit of the vine *piper nigrum*; white and green peppercorns are berries picked at different stages of maturity from the same vine. Pink peppercorns are from a wholly different plant, and aren't used in Asian cooking (the peppercorns are mildly toxic).

Saffron—Native to Asia Minor. The most expensive spice in the world, costing 10 times as much as vanilla and 50 times as much as cardamom. Utilized in the cuisines of all ancient civilizations, though it was hardly a common spice; its use was first recorded in China in the 7th century. Has a highly aromatic taste. A small amount will flavor large dish and add a bright gold color.

Star anise—Native to southern China and Vietnam. The fruit of a small evergreen tree of the magnolia family; its shape is that of an irregular, eight-pointed star. Has a pungent licorice-like taste. Old recipes reveal that star anise travelled from China to the West in the 17th century, where it was used in fruit syrups and jams. Has been recently rediscovered in the West, especially to add flavor to fish stews.

Szechwan peppercorns (fagara, wild pepper, anise pepper, Chinese pepper, flower pepper): Not related to familiar black and white pepper, it's actually the reddish-brown dried berries of a Chinese prickly ash tree. It has a distinctive aroma, but it isn't "spicy" hot. Used in marinades, seasonings, and coatings.

Tamarind (Indian date)—Particularly good with fish and poultry dishes, with a slightly sweet aroma and a sour, fruity flavor, it was first cultivated in India, then introduced to Europe by returning Crusaders.

Turmeric—Native to India. A member of the ginger family of rhizomes, or "underground stems." A fragrant spice with warm, spicy taste, it adds an orange color to foods, and to curry powder. Fresh turmeric root is also used in Southeast Asian cooking.

Zedoary—A highly aromatic plant related to turmeric. Native to India and Indonesia. Its taste has slight resemblance to rosemary, with a musky aroma; the flavor is pungent and resembles ginger but is not bitter.

SAUCES AND CONDIMENTS

Black vinegar—Made from the fermentation of a mixture of rice, wheat, millet, or sorghum; used predominantly in Chinese cooking. Less tart, smokier, sweeter, more flavorful, and darker in color than common white vinegar.

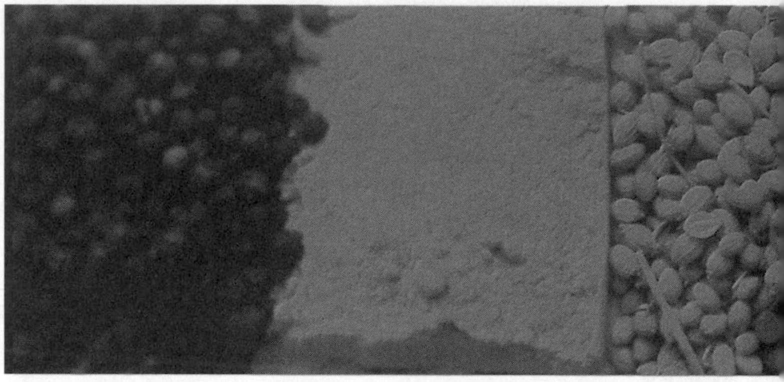

Brown bean sauce (also soybean paste or *min see jeung*)—Of Chinese origin. A brown, salty, thick paste made of ground fermented soybeans, flour, and salt. Often used in recipes which include bean cake and minced ground pork.

***Char siu* sauce** (barbecue sauce)—A Chinese sauce with a thick, jam-like texture, made from fermented soy beans, vinegar, tomato paste, chili, garlic, sugar, and other spices. Adds a sweet and spicy taste to grilled and roasted meats and poultry.

Chili oil—Of Chinese origin, although the chili pepper itself didn't arrive in China until the 13th century, via the Portuguese. Made by steeping whole dried chilies and dried red pepper flakes in hot oil. Used to add extra spiciness to food.

Chili sauce or paste—Primarily made of minced chili peppers, vinegar and garlic, it's used in Chinese cuisine (particularly Szechuan and Hunan), as well as Vietnamese and other Southeast Asian countries, where you'll usually find a bottle of chili sauce on your table for use as a condiment. The ingredients may vary, but it's always spicy.

Chinese mustard—Typically a mix of dry mustard and water, found in many restaurants and in Chinese take-out bags; not used in cooking, and rarely (in authentic Chinese cuisine) as a condiment. Probably a Western-introduced concept.

Curry powder or paste—Includes an almost limitless number of different sauces that range across borders and palates. Original to India, but adapted and completely changed by other Asian countries. Major types include yellow curry (containing a blend of various dried spices), red curry (containing a greater portion of dried red chilies), and green curry (containing a greater portion of dried green chilies). **[128]**

Duck sauce—Oddly enough, it's not made of duck, nor is it used to season or sauce duck. This Chinese sweet dipping sauce, usually pale orange in color, is made of plums, apricots, and sugar, and common to Chinese restaurants in the U.S., where it's used as a condiment for fried wontons and egg or spring rolls. Like hot mustard, evidence points to it being a Western concept.

Fish sauce (*Ngoc mam, nam pla*)—A strong-smelling liquid made by packing small fish with salt in a barrel and leaving to ferment. Of Southeast Asian origin, but also used in Filipino cuisine; both cultures use it as a condiment as well. The highest quality sauce is from the first draining of the barrel, producing an amber-colored, clear liquid with a good aroma, especially if made only with anchovies.

Hoisin sauce—Of Chinese origin. A reddish-brown, sweet and pungent sauce made of fermented soybeans, spices, vinegar, and chili. Excellent as a marinade for roast pork or spare ribs.

Mirin—A Japanese sweet rice wine traditionally made by a complex distillation and double-fermentation process, used as a cooking wine to give "body" and aroma to foods.

Oyster sauce (*Ho yow*)—Of Chinese origin, made from the essence of oysters. Contrary to what you'd believe, it doesn't have a strong fishy taste; it's used in beef and vegetable dishes, and some soups.

Plum sauce—A sweet, spicy Chinese sauce made of plums, sugar, ginger, chili, and garlic. It has a dark, opaque color. Served with *mu shu* dishes.

Red-hot sauce—A Malaysian creation; a biting ginger and chili sauce.

Rice malt—A natural sweetener usually made of malted barley, rice, and water. Used for sweetening sauces.

Rice vinegar—Used throughout East Asia for cooking and pickling vegetables, particularly Japan. Not as sharp or pungent as regular white vinegar.

Sambal—A category of Indonesian spicy hot pepper relishes, served in small dishes as an accompaniment or condiment; food cooked sambal-style is usually bright red, extremely saucy, and very hot.

Sesame oil—A highly refined, fragrant oil, made of pressed, roasted sesame seed. Not used for cooking, but as a seasoning in soups and some stir-fried dishes. Sesame seeds are believed to be native to Africa, but records show that the seeds and oil were used in China more than 2,000 year ago.

Shrimp paste—Originally Chinese, but used throughout Southeast Asian cuisines. Made of ground shrimp fermented in brine; extremely salty, and should be used sparingly in cooking or as a condiment.

Soy sauce—Ubiquitous, versatile, and indispensable to all East and Southeast Asian cooking, soy sauce is a brown, liquid seasoning made from fermented soybeans, wheat, and salt. Introduced to Europeans in the 17th century by Dutch traders who visited Japan, it can now be found in mainstream restaurants and most households across the U.S. Most historical reports agree that soy sauce, *jiang you* in Mandarin, originated in China more than a millennium ago, although Korean soy sauce is believed to be at least as old. The Japanese version, *shoyu,* dating back to the 1500s, is the best known soy sauce in the West, and differs both in taste and process from its Chinese ancestor, tending to be fuller in flavor and less salty. Two kinds of modern Japanese soy sauces exist: shoyu, which is what most Westerners recognize as soy sauce, and *tamari,* a sauce made by the same process and ingredients as shoyu but without wheat. It has a much more intense flavor and more staying power during cooking. Chinese soy sauce comes in various intensities. "Dark" soy sauce has a viscous texture and contains molasses. It is sweet, rich, and mahogany-colored, and is used only for cooking (as opposed to in dipping sauces, since uncooked it easily overpowers any other flavor). "Light" or thin soy sauce, on the other hand, used both as a condiment and in cooking, is saltier, paler in color, and has a watery consistency compared to regular Chinese soy sauce. This is not to be confused with "lite" soy sauce—a reduced sodium version, inspired by Western tastes, that has about 40 per cent less sodium than regular soy sauce. Traditionally, soy sauce is made by incubating steamed soybeans and roasted wheat or barley with the fermented rice-and–*Aspergillus* mold mash called *koji* by the Japanese. This mixture is fermented with salt for 18 months in wooden casks. After pressing, the soybean oil is squeezed out, leaving behind soy sauce. More realistically, however, about half of the soy sauce sold in the U.S. tends to be made in a one-day process, without fermentation; the other half is made using chemically processed soy meal in an accelerated fermentation process, with sodium benzoate as a preservative. The results are often disastrous; if you plan on cooking any kind of East or Southeast Asian cuisine, buy your soy sauce in an Asian market or Chinatown. Or look for Kikkoman, the largest soy sauce producer in the world and the only authentic version that you're likely to find in America.

Sweet bean sauce—Made from crushed yellow beans combined with sugar. Chinese in origin, but found throughout most Asian cultures.

Wasabi—From the mountain hollyhock, which grows only in Japan along the marshy edges of mountain springs. It's known as Japanese horseradish, although not a member of the Western horseradish family. The edible root, with brown-green skin and pale green flesh, is grated finely and made into a paste or powder. Used as accompaniment to many Japanese dishes; in addition to sushi and sashimi, it's also served to flavor the dipping sauce of soba. Available in small tins of powder (to be mixed with tepid water and left for 10 minutes to develop its flavor) or pre-prepared in tubes. —T.H.

"ORIENTAL" FLAVOR

It's puzzling. Sauces, crackers, and salad dressings are only a few of the mass-marketed foods that come in "Oriental" flavors. But what is Oriental flavor? Unlike "sour cream and onion," "mint chocolate chip," or even "atomic fireball," "Oriental" doesn't seem to describe a specific taste.

Oriental flavor varies from food product to food product, but typical ingredients include soy sauce, garlic, sesame, and—of course!—MSG. In many products, the flavor seems to be secondary to the packaging: boxes or bags decorated with chopsticks, bamboo, snow peas, or "Asian"-style art or calligraphy.

What does this all mean? Nothing in particular. Like the ingredients, the images are chosen to convey a general idea and not a specific (or authentic) country, culture, or dish. —M.W.

"Oriental" = inscrutability

Knott's Berry Farm, which prides itself on old-fashioned country-style food, released Oriental Chicken Salad Dressing in 1994. A spokesperson was unable to say exactly what made it Oriental: "It was just a name they picked out."

"Oriental" = stir-fry

Lipton, the soup and tea giant, introduced "Oriental Style" Golden Sauté rice mix during the spring of 1995. According to a company representative, the Oriental quality comes from the preparation method that the mix is used with: "It's any kind of stir-fry. I don't know if it's Chinese, Japanese, or Korean."

"Oriental" = health, flavor—adventure!

In the summer of 1995, the ubiquitous Campbell's Soup Company unleashed Swanson Oriental Broth, "the perfect marriage between healthier cooking trends and consumer interest in more flavorful, adventuresome cooking." The fat-free blend of "the classic taste of soy, sauteed onion and sauteed garlic" can be used as an oil or butter substitute. A spokesperson noted that, by using the broth, "people who can't cook Oriental-style can be Oriental chefs." And isn't that a dream we've all had at one time or another?

Are such products authentic or insulting? Perhaps it ultimately depends on the consumer. However, purchasing "Oriental" foods in a non-Asian supermarket is ultimately like ordering Mexican food at a coffee shop: it's convenient and it may be tasty, but one can't really complain if it's slop.

Tasty treats from the oriental pantry!

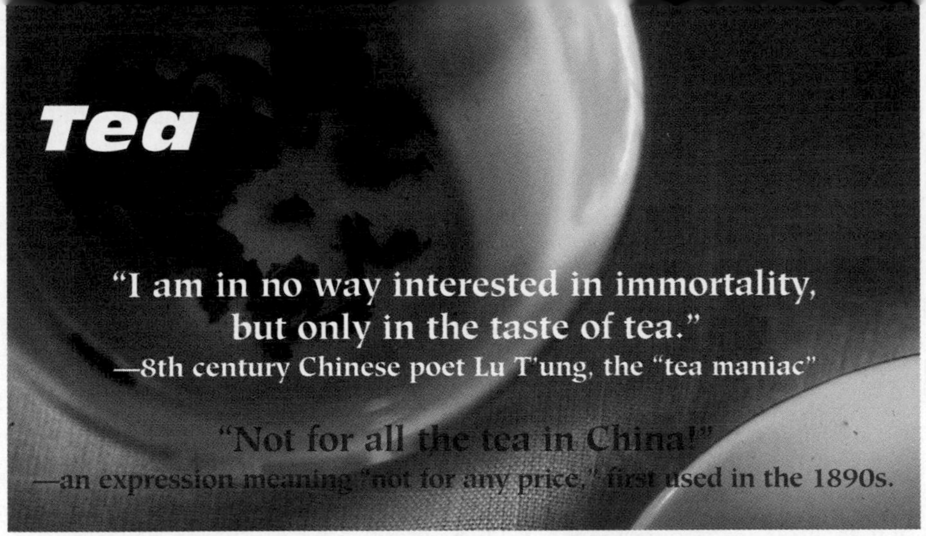

Tea

"I am in no way interested in immortality, but only in the taste of tea."
—8th century Chinese poet Lu T'ung, the "tea maniac"

"Not for all the tea in China!"
—an expression meaning "not for any price," first used in the 1890s.

Call it the universal beverage. Although tea originated in Asia—the wild tea plant was first found in the Yunnan province of China, and later in the Assam region of India—it's enjoyed around the globe. In fact, next to water, tea is the most consumed liquid in the world. And although China is tea's original source, the Chinese aren't even among its top five per capita consumers: the Irish wear the global tea-drinking crown, drinking more than three cups per capita every day of the year, followed closely by the U.K., Turkey, Qatar, and Iraq. (Although, to be fair, China's tea consumption rates are difficult to measure. Like the Japanese—and unlike Westerners, who prefer to make a fresh cup with each serving—Chinese use the same tea leaves all day, simply adding hot boiled water to the pot.) In the U.S., which is just ahead of China in tea consumption, tea salons are proliferating, much as coffee bars have. "Tea is to the '90s what coffee was to the '80s, and wine was to the '70s," says tea importer John Harney, of Harney & Sons, Ltd. Particularly favored among the "tea set" is Indian *chai*, served milky, spicy, and sweet.

TEA, THE UNIVERSAL LANGUAGE

The Mandarin word for tea is *cha,* as it is in Japanese, Korean, and Hindu. In Tibetan, it's *ja*; in Arabic, *shai*; in Turkish, *chay*; and in Russian, *chai*. So why is tea "tea" in English? In the Fukienese dialect, the word for tea is pronounced *tay*, which is how the Dutch learned it when they met Chinese tea traders from the Fukien province, who sailed into the port of Java. Since all European countries (except Portugal and Russia) first bought tea from the Dutch, they use words based on the pronunciation learned from the Fukienese traders.

LEGENDS OF THE CHA

- One day in 2737 B.C., Shen Nung, China's "Divine Cultivator" and mythical father of agriculture and herbal medicine **[👁248]**, was boiling water outdoors. Wild tea leaves fell into the water. Naturally, he drank it.
- Shen Nong was also what might be called a recreational herb-user, ingesting various kinds of plants to discover their effects. It is said that he used tea as an antidote to his accidental poisonings.
- A Japanese legend credits the creation of tea to Bodhidharma, Daruma, the

12TH CENTURY B.C.	**First reported use of tea, in the 347 A.D. Treatise on the Kingdom of Huayang.**
3RD CENTURY B.C.	**The Chinese begin drying and processing tea leaves. Surgeon Hua Tuo, father of anesthesia, remarks that tea makes one feel more alert and awake.**
420-479 A.D.	**Sung Dynasty; tea is well-established as a medicinal digestive aid and stimulant.**
589-620 A.D.	**Sui Dynasty; tea becomes China's unofficial national beverage; tea bricks are used as currency in trade.**
620-907 A.D.	**Tang Dynasty, the Golden Age of Tea. In 725, the tea plant gets its own character so it no longer has to share the one for "sow-thistle"; Poet Lu Yu writes the tea classic Chaking in 780 A.D., inspiring Lu T'ung, the "tea maniac," to devote his life to tea and its preparation; the first recorded tea tax is imposed by the government. Buddhist monks take tea seeds home to Japan.**
960-1279 A.D.	**Song Dynasty; tea-drinking becomes an art; tea rooms and houses crop up everywhere.**
1368-1644 A.D.	**Ming Dynasty; two other types of tea besides green—black and Oolong—emerge. In Japan, Sen Rikyu elevates the tea ceremony to a way of life. Tea becomes a key trade good with Europe.**
1600s-1830 A.D.	**In India, the British cultivate tea stolen from China. In 1820, tea plants are found growing near the Burmese border. In 1830 the forests of Assam and Darjeeling are cleared and planted, producing the world's best black teas. On the other side of the world, in 1773, some people are having a tea party.**

E

A

E

A

The Way of Tea

The great master Sen Rikyu, codified the Japanese tea ceremony (chanoyu, literally "tea's hot water") in the 16th century. A typical ceremony, which can take four hours, might go like this:

1 Proceed with decorum to the tea room.

2 Pretend to read the scroll hanging in the shallow alcove. If you can't read the calligraphy, look at the picture illustrating it. Check out the single flower in the vase below it.

3 Kneel and bow from the waist as you poetically express your thoughts about the scroll, the flower, or, for variety, the kettle boiling over the charcoal fire.

4 Eat the moist, gelatinous confection provided by the hostess. Then eat the dry one. Be patient as the hostess rinses the tea bowls and wipes them three times using a cloth napkin.

6 Watch the hostess make the tea, scooping a bit of matcha into a bowl, adding three and a half mouthfuls of water (she doesn't use her mouth), and stirring it with a bamboo whisk.

7 Accept the bowl and say "I gratefully accept the tea you have prepared."

8 Drink the tea, then wipe the bowl dry with a paper towel. Turn it upside down and look at the craftsman's mark. (This is considered polite, not nosy.)

9 Bow. Leave quietly. Be at peace.

Indian monk who sold the Chinese on Buddhism circa 520 A.D, and who, according to Shaolin legend, invented martial arts [👁6; 188]. To demonstrate the benefits of meditation, he stared at a wall in a cave outside Nanjing for nine years. He only fell asleep once, but to prevent his eyelids from drooping again, he cut them off. Where they fell, a tea plant grew, from whose leaves come a drink that fends off sleep.

TEA TYPES

There are only three types of tea, classified according to how they are processed:

black tea - fermented, then heated and dried to produce a reddish-brown cup of tea; favored in Western cultures; China exports almost all of its black tea; black teas are distinguished by a series of letters:

*O.P. = **Orange Pekoe**; the Pekoe comes from pak ho, literally an expression for a newborn's fine hair, which refers to tea buds harvested early; Orange has nothing to do with the fruit; it's an arbitrary term, refering to the house of Nassau's princes of Orange, first slapped on by Dutch merchants to give their tea an air of nobility*

*F.O.P. = **Flowery Orange Pekoe**; "flowery" refers to the tips of the tea buds, plucked even earlier in the season than O.P.; the more "flowery" and "tippy" the tea grade, the better, hence:*

*G.F.O.P. = **Golden Flowery Orange Pekoe***

*F.T.G.F.O.P. = **Finest Tippy Golden Flowery Orange Pekoe**; comprised mostly of tea bud tips; produces a light but aromatic brew*

*B.O.P. = **Broken Orange Pekoe**; the finest broken tea, not inferior to whole-leaf teas, but makes a stronger brew*

*F.B.O.P. = **Flowery Broken Orange Pekoe***

green tea - unfermented, producing a bitter greenish tea; favored in Asian cultures; green teas are whole-leaf teas, except for *matcha*, Japanese powdered green tea; green tea should always be drunk without milk or sugar.

Oolong - (literally, "black dragon") partially fermented to produce tea that is milder than black or green. The two main types are China Oolong, which is common in China and rarely exported, and Formosa Oolong, which undergoes more fermentation, is closer to black tea, and appeals more to Western cultures. Formosa is another name for Taiwan, which produces the latter type of Oolong for export.

Descriptive Tea Terms

***Assam** - a strong tea from Assam in Northern India; the base for Irish Breakfast Tea*

***Congou** - any black tea from China*

***Darjeeling** - a northern Indian province that produces fragrant black tea; an afternoon tea that is considered the rarest and most precious of black teas*

***Earl Grey** - a Chinese and Indian blend of black tea scented with bergamot oil; a packet of this tea was given to the second Earl Grey, the British prime minister in the early 1800s, as a token of appreciation for saving a Chinese official's life*

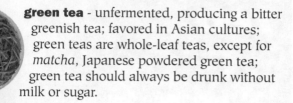

***gunpowder** - young green tea, the leaves of which are rolled into a ball, and thus the name; widely used to produce mint teas*

***hojicha** - a roasted green tea, producing a brown brew*

***Keemun** or **keemum** - a fine grade of black tea produced in the Anhui province of China; a frequent base for scented blends*

***Lapsang souchong** - a smoky Fujian black tea produced by withering the leaves over pine fires*

***matcha** - a powdered green tea used in the tea ceremony* —D.G.

Tofu: Four Reasons Why It Could Be the Best Bland White Cube You Ever Ate

Tofu, or bean curd, has been a staple of Asian cooking for centuries. Called "meat without bones" by the Chinese, tofu—or *toufu* (DOE-foo) in Mandarin—was first produced in China about 2,200 years ago. The light, springy, delightfully cool comestible is made by adding a coagulant to soy milk, which separates its curds and whey; no legend exists explaining why the original tofu maker was coagulating soy milk in the first place. The separated curds are then pressed into soft blocks—and voila.

Four thousand years after tofu's invention, tofu was sold commercially in the U.S. for the first time in the early 1900s. Some of America's largest tofu shops opened during World War II in the internment camps where thousands of Japanese Americans were incarcerated. In fact, the word "tofu" is Japanese; bean curd is known as *dowfu* or *daufu* in Cantonese, *tahu* in Indonesian, *dubu* in Korean, *tokwa* in Tagalog, *tao-hu* in Thai, and *dau hu* or *dau phu* in Vietnamese.

Today America has more than 200 tofu manufacturers, who collectively produce 65 million pounds a year. They'd better gear up the curd compressors: in light of a 1995 *New England Journal of Medicine* report indicating that soy protein can drastically lower cholesterol levels, even more Americans are expected to make tofu a regular part of their diets. But if preventing strokes and heart attacks isn't enough, here are six more reasons:

1. It's really good for you.
Move over, cottage cheese—tofu's a dieter's real best friend. Tofu is unique among natural high-protein foods in that it is low in calories and saturated fats, and entirely free of cholestrol (as mentioned above, it even reduces the cholesterol you already have). Next to soybean sprouts, tofu has the lowest ratio of calories to protein found in any plant food.

Trust us: If you start eating more tofu and less meat as a protein source, your body will thank you. One cup of firm tofu provides eight ounces of soy protein; protein from tofu is complete, which means it contains all eight essential amino acids, and helps your body build muscle and repair tissue. Tofu also provides a good supply of iron, phosphorus, potassium, sodium, essential B vitamins, choline, and vitamin E. And, as a side effect of the solidifiers used in its making, tofu has 23 per cent more calcium by weight than standard dairy milk.

2. It's so versatile, it's scary.
This is the Zelig of foods. Plain tofu absorbs flavors readily; sauteed in sauces or stirred into soups, tofu cooperates agreeably with a large array of dishes. Smooth and soft-textured, it can be grilled, boiled, steamed, marinated, deep-fried, baked, mashed, or pureed. Innocuous as the mild-mannered curd might appear, tofu's versatility landed it a starring, albeit disguised, role in the 1973 sci-fi thriller *Soylent Green,* In the movie, set in the year 2022, the world is dependent on Soylent Green, a foodstuff with a thousand faces. In the end the hero discovers the hard-to-swallow truth: *Soylent Green is people*!

Not to worry. Most tofu comes from soybeans, although researchers have found that tofu can also be made from peanuts, okra seeds, and other mundane protein-rich legumes.

3. With so many varieties, there's a tofu for everyone. Even you.
The two most popular types of tofu are firm (or "Chinese-style") and soft (or "Japanese-style"). Though dairy-free, tofu is often called the "cheese of Asia," and its preparation actually does resemble cheese-making. In addition to these standard tofu types, there are known to be seven types of Japanese and almost two dozen kinds of Chinese tofu variants, including salt-dried tofu, silken tofu, a very soft custard-like variety, sweet bean curd sticks, and pressed tofu sheets.

4. No tummy trouble.
Unlike other high-protein foods, namely meat and dairy products, tofu is easy to digest. With a digestion rate of 95 percent (it's not clear how nutritionists calculate this), tofu is an excellent food choice for babies, the elderly, and folks with digestive problems. So dig in, and be well! —N.K.

WOK THIS WAY
How to Stir-Fry

PREPARATION

All peeling, slicing, dicing, and marinating should be finished before you begin, and all sauces or spices laid out where you can quickly grab them. The reason Chinese takeout is so speedy is that there, stir-frying has been raised to a science. One wok and one utensil, plus tubs of fresh, sliced ingredients and seasonings means fast, wok 'n' roll action. Remember not to overcrowd your wok, since this will make stirring a pain and guarantee soppy, over- or half-cooked results.

1 Heat your wok for a minute or so over high heat. (Wait until you can literally feel it radiating into your palm.)

2 Add a small amount of vegetable or peanut oil; two tablespoons will do. Lift it by the side handle using a kitchen glove and circulate the oil evenly around the sides of the wok. Wait 15 seconds, but not so long that the oil starts smoking.

3 Throw in your "taste" ingredients, like ginger, garlic, chilies, or scallions.

4 Still holding the handle, take your bowls of cut "bulk" ingredients and pour them into the wok. Meats usually go first, then chunky veggies (like sliced carrots), then leafy ones. If you have fresh mushrooms, place them in last. When pouring, don't just plunk the stuff into the center of the wok, since this is sure to precipitate a painful

Woks and Stir-Frying

Stir-frying without a wok is like draining spaghetti without a colander. It's possible, but potentially unpleasant. The risks are also greater: ruining your fresh-cut vegetables, spattering your stove and clothing, and causing a minor grease fire are, if anything, more of a hazard than just watching noodles slide down the drain. Moral: If you're going to stir-fry, a wok you should buy.

Luckily, you probably already have, even if you don't regularly prepare Chinese-style cuisine. While the wok is thousands of years old, today most cooks have found it to be an efficient and reliable cooking utensil for stir-frying, deep-frying, steaming, boiling, poaching and stewing alike. The wok is even good for making popcorn. (Although for the latter, a lid is essential.)

The modern wok, a round-bottomed pan with sloping sides, ranges in diameter from nine to 30 inches; the most common size is usually 12 to 14 inches. It is generally made of carbon steel, which allows heat to spread rapidly. Since the round bottom retains a constant, concentrated high temperature, food can be cooked rapidly and efficiently, which means that nutrients, colors, textures, and flavors will not fade with prolonged exposure to heat. The graduated heat along the sides means that various ingredients can be cooked at the same time; with proper use, both tender meat and crispy vegetables are practically guaranteed—with a minimum of after-meal scrubbing.

A wok works best when used with its traditional utensils. The Chinese spatula (*wok chann*), with its shovel-shaped blade perfect for the wok's sloping sides, and the scooper (*wok hauk*), a large Chinese version of the slotted spoon, are two such indispensable tools. Also helpful are the Chinese ladle (wider and shallower than its Western counterpart), extra-long wooden chopsticks, and a lid—especially for steaming. Or popping corn.

Wok cooking is best suited for gas stoves, but electric ranges can also be used. Just remember that the wok will take longer to reach the desired temperature with electric heat, and the food may take longer to cook.

These days, the number of competing manufacturers and styles makes shopping for woks a dizzying experience. In addition to traditional carbon steel, woks can also be made of stainless steel, anodized aluminum, and other compounds. Electric woks are an alternative favored by many spatter-shy amateur chefs, but don't expect to get

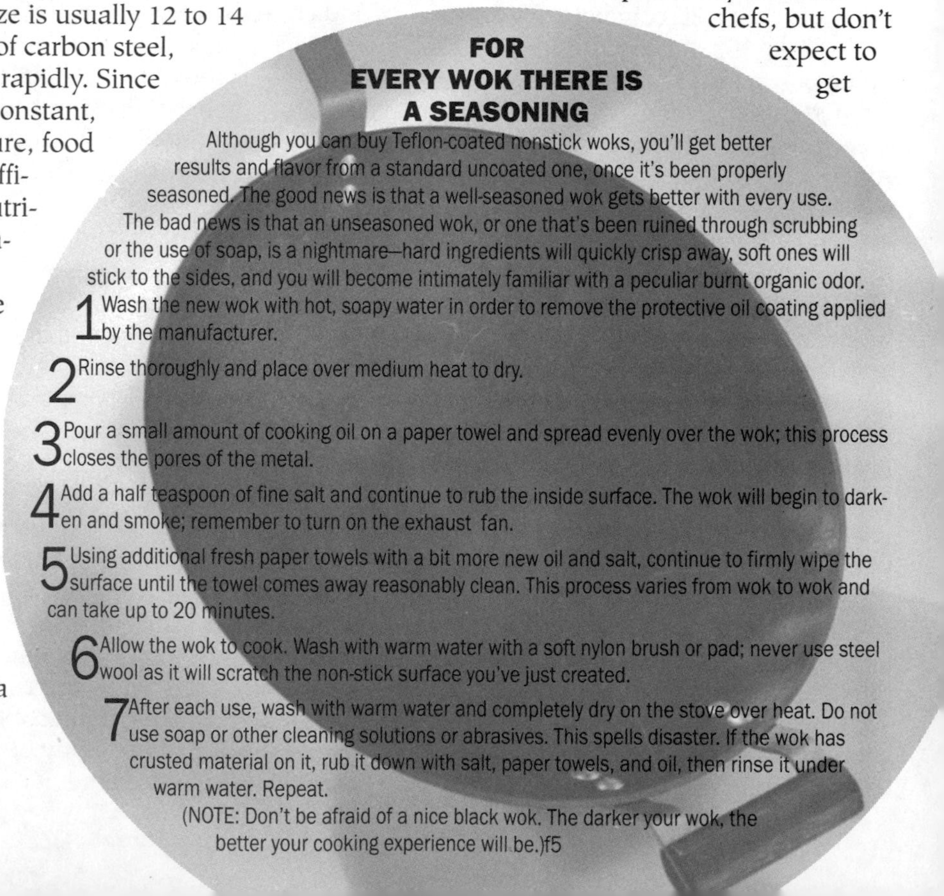

FOR EVERY WOK THERE IS A SEASONING

Although you can buy Teflon-coated nonstick woks, you'll get better results and flavor from a standard uncoated one, once it's been properly seasoned. The good news is that a well-seasoned wok gets better with every use. The bad news is that an unseasoned wok, or one that's been ruined through scrubbing or the use of soap, is a nightmare—hard ingredients will quickly crisp away, soft ones will stick to the sides, and you will become intimately familiar with a peculiar burnt organic odor.

1 Wash the new wok with hot, soapy water in order to remove the protective oil coating applied by the manufacturer.

2 Rinse thoroughly and place over medium heat to dry.

3 Pour a small amount of cooking oil on a paper towel and spread evenly over the wok; this process closes the pores of the metal.

4 Add a half teaspoon of fine salt and continue to rub the inside surface. The wok will begin to darken and smoke; remember to turn on the exhaust fan.

5 Using additional fresh paper towels with a bit more new oil and salt, continue to firmly wipe the surface until the towel comes away reasonably clean. This process varies from wok to wok and can take up to 20 minutes.

6 Allow the wok to cook. Wash with warm water with a soft nylon brush or pad; never use steel wool as it will scratch the non-stick surface you've just created.

7 After each use, wash with warm water and completely dry on the stove over heat. Do not use soap or other cleaning solutions or abrasives. This spells disaster. If the wok has crusted material on it, rub it down with salt, paper towels, and oil, then rinse it under warm water. Repeat.

(NOTE: Don't be afraid of a nice black wok. The darker your wok, the better your cooking experience will be.)f5

restaurant results. Some brand names you'll find at the mall are Joyce Chen's Products, Farberware, Taylor and Ng, and the Meyer Corporation. All of these make solid products—but if you want to save on price and up your authenticity, go to your local Chinatown, where brand-free woks, imported directly from Asia, will be widely available. Look for one with stoutly attached handles (riveted ones are huskier; if it has a wooden grip, all the better), a smooth finish with no obvious bumps, dents, or imperfections, and an even curve.

STIR-FRY BASICS

Quick, efficient, and so simple that any culinary idiot can learn it, when done properly, stir-frying is also a lo-cal delight—tasty and healthy. Anything can be stir-fried, so long as its sliced into small, uniform pieces (no larger than an inch or so in diameter). Don't overdo the protein: even for a "meat" dish like kung pao chicken, about 3/4 of a pound of poultry for two to three people is enough, with the rest being bamboo shoots, peanuts, and other veggie products. For your own original 'fries, consider keeping a 1:3 ratio between meat and vegetables, by volume.

STANDARD STIR-FRY INGREDIENTS

Meat—Chicken (boneless, skinless breasts); pork (fresh loin or roasted char siu); beef (flank steak); shrimp or prawns; other shellfish (always "in shell," and usually as a separate entree rather than as part of a stir-fry mix)
Vegetable—Chinese broccoli; bean sprouts; baby corn; snow peas; bok choy; bamboo shoots; Chinese eggplant; long beans; watercress; scallions and other onions [👁133]
Other—Tofu (soft, fermented, fried, or hard); bean threads; noodles (generally pre-cooked); mushrooms (wood ear, straw, shiitake)
Seasonings—Soy sauce; black bean sauce; soybean paste (brown bean sauce); dried chilies, chili oil, and chili sauce or paste; cornstarch or flour (for sauce thickening); fresh garlic (minced or sliced); ginger; MSG (optional, of course); oyster sauce (brown, salty, and yes, made of oysters); salt; black and white pepper; sesame oil (for flavor, not cooking); broth (chicken, pork, seafood, or beef) [👁163]
—T.H., J.Y.

fountain of hot oil. Pour it in gently off-center, then lift the handle to center it.

5 Once your ingredients are in—and they all should go in within minutes of one another—begin stirring with your spatula, flipping and tossing food vigorously, and making sure no food element spends too much time at the hot bottom of the wok. The best technique is the wok-handle-in-one-hand, spatula-in-the-other style—it lets you shake the wok to re-center ingredients, and prevents the disaster known as "Wok Flip," wherein your stir-fry stir-flops to the ground.

6 Add your liquid seasonings. If you desire a thick, gravy-like consistency to your sauce, add a mixture of cornstarch dissolved in cold water.

7 Add your powdery seasonings, like salt, pepper, or the dreaded MSG.

8 Eat immediately. Your meat should be flavorful, your vegetables crisp, and the whole thing should be very, very hot. Enjoy!

GAMES AND LEISURE

"Good video games all have a few essential elements in common. First, there must be an appropriate balance of challenge and reward: if players meet the challenge the game poses too easily, he will become bored and cast it aside; if it is too difficult, he will stop playing in frustration. `Second, good games must deliver substantial play value–they must offer hours and hours of entertainment. Finally, all good games allow the player to immerse himself in the character, the environment or the action. If you really feel you are the hero, chances are you're playing a great game.

If you ask me what Japan's most important cultural influence is on America, I would have to say it's a tie—between sushi and video games."

—Minoru Arakawa, President of Nintendo of America

Chess

Yoko Ono's* Play It By Trust, *a 1988 version of the original 1966 piece Chess Set.

Played by millions around the globe, chess is the world's favorite game of strategy. Throughout history, people have lived for it, won love with it, and (not a few times) killed for it; no game has aroused more passion, or inspired more obsession. And, while chess as we know it today—with its medieval knights and its Christian bishops—is intimately entwined with Western imagery, its origins are actually Asian.

Around 550 A.D., a game called *chaturanga* emerged into popularity in Northwest India. In chaturanga (Sanskrit for "four-membered"), two players faced off across an eight-by-eight board, with each player controlling a set of six game-pieces representing a military force. Unlike modern chess, which has no element of chance, chaturanga may have used six-sided dice, which players rolled to determine which of their six gamepieces they would be allowed to move on a given turn.

There's no historical evidence of the name of chaturanga's inventor; however, a popular chess myth says that it was created by the Brahmin Sissa, who devised the game as a way to teach his king that he could not win battles without soldiers, nor could his reign survive without the support of his subjects. It's not clear whether the object lesson was embraced, but the king was certainly overjoyed by the new toy, and offered Sissa any reward he wanted. Sissa replied that all he wanted was one grain of wheat for the first square on the board, two for the second, four for the third, eight for the fourth, and so on to the 64th square. The mathematically impaired monarch readily agreed, and ordered his servants to begin counting out the reward. After 20 or so squares, the enormousness of Sissa's request hit the rajah; 64 squares would have cost the king 18,445,744,073,709,551,515 grains of wheat—more than there are atoms in the universe.

The legend isn't clear on what happened next: One version says that the ruler was humbled and made Sissa his grand vizier. Another says that he swopped off the impudent Brahmin's head. Those who are knowledgeable about the ways of kings can decide for themselves which is more likely to be true.

In any case, from India, chaturanga was introduced into Persia (modern-day Iran) sometime during the reign of Khusraw I Nushirwan (531-578). The Arabs took it and renamed it *shatranj* after their invasion of Persia; the primary differences between *shatranj* and modern chess were that in place of the modern queen was a piece called the *firzan*, while in place of the bishop was the *fil*. Pawns could only move one square at a time, and could only be promoted to firzans. Because of the reduced power of the pieces in shatranj, it was often difficult to achieve what we call "checkmate" in modern chess, and victory was often given to the player who managed to capture all of the opponent's pieces other than her king, which, like in modern chess, could be moved only one square in any direction on a turn. (Castling was not introduced until the 13th century.)

From India, the game of chess began its migration all over the world. In East and Southeast Asia, it spawned multiple variations ranging from Japan's shogi and China's xiang qi to Burma's *sittuyin* and Tibet's *chandaraki*. Following Arab trade routes, the game eventually reached Europe in the 11th century.

Perhaps the most significant European change wrought on the ancient game was the phonetic transformation of the weak, masculine firzan into the feminine "virgin," which became the "Holy Virgin," and then the queen—rising to become the most potent piece on the board. Otherwise, however, the pieces and play of chess have remained remarkably constant throughout history and around the world—a challenge for the ages. —J.Y., J.C.

OTHER WORLDS, OTHER BOARDS: Chess Variations

SHOGI: The Japanese strategy game shogi is a close relative to Indian/Western chess, with the primary differences being a larger board (nine by nine), more pieces (20 per side), promotion of pieces to more powerful ranks when they've crossed over into "enemy" territory, and—most important—a rule that enables you to take captured enemy pieces and drop them back into play on your side. This means that taking enemy pieces becomes considerably more critical, and the kind of slow-rolling strategy available in chess is virtually impossible.

XIANG QI: Like shogi, xiang qi is a kissing cousin to the Euro-Indian game, and is in fact often called "Chinese Chess" in the West. One primary difference in xiang qi is its board: the two enemy sides are divided by a "river" which certain pieces cannot cross, and each side's king and counselors (there is no queen) are restricted to a "palace" with limited mobility. xiang qi also has some unusual pieces, including "cannons" that move by leaping unlimited squares in a straight line, so long as they pass over exactly one other piece in doing so. The object of the game isn't to "mate" the king, but to capture it; there's no namby-pamby declaring of "check," and a sloppy player might leave his king exposed only to see it captured and the game over while many pieces are still on the board.

Child's Play: Children's Games from Asia

Long before the Nintendo [👁199] ever existed, American kids were playing with toys that had their ultimate origins in Asia. Here are just a few popular examples:

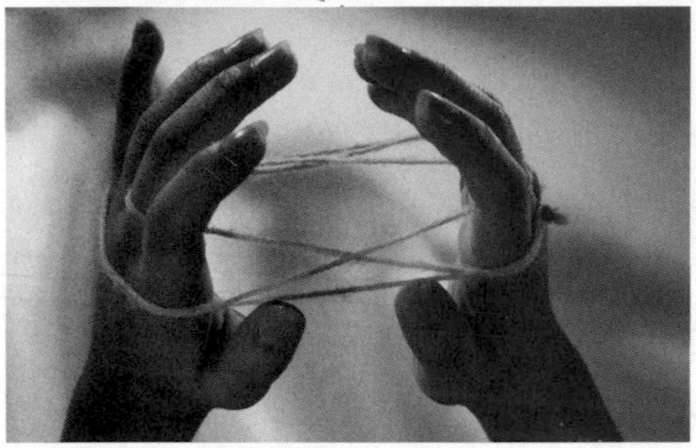

CAT'S-CRADLE

Cat's-Cradle (also known as "Cratch-Cradle" or "string figures") is a children's string game in which designs are created with a loop of string six feet in circumference woven between the player's fingers. In Japan, Cat's-Cradle is called *aya ito tori* (literally "woof pattern string-taking"). In Korea, it is a popular girls' game called *ssil-teu-ki* ("woof-taking"). In Southern China, where it is played by young girls and Cantonese laborers alike, Cat's-Cradle is *kang sok* ("well-rope"). The string game originated in southeast Asia, and from there traveled east and southward through Polynesia and into Australia. In the 17th century, Cat's Cradle journeyed westward into Europe along with the tea trade. In 1898, a special language of loops, strings, basic positions, and moves was developed for the first time by two anthropologists, Dr. A.C. Haddon and Dr. W.H.R. Rivers, enabling string figures to be officially recorded and passed on to others. —E.L.

CHINESE SKIPPING

Chinese skipping, or *tiao houpijang*, ("jump rubberband"), a children's jumping game involving an elastic rope joined at the end with a knot, is also known as Yoki, Elastics, and Jumpsies. Two players stand facing each other with feet spread apart inside the rope, which should be taut around their ankles. The third player hops between the ropes to a chant or rhyme while trying not to touch the rope. To make the game more challenging, advanced Chinese skippers twist or cross the rope in patterns while jumping. In the 1930s, a young Canadian girl, Margaret Burbidge, learned Chinese skipping while in Korea with her missionary parents. Upon returning to North America, she taught the game to her classmates. The spread of Chinese skipping during the Depression was facilitated by the cheap price of elastic, which made the game affordable when more expensive toys were verboten.
—E.L.

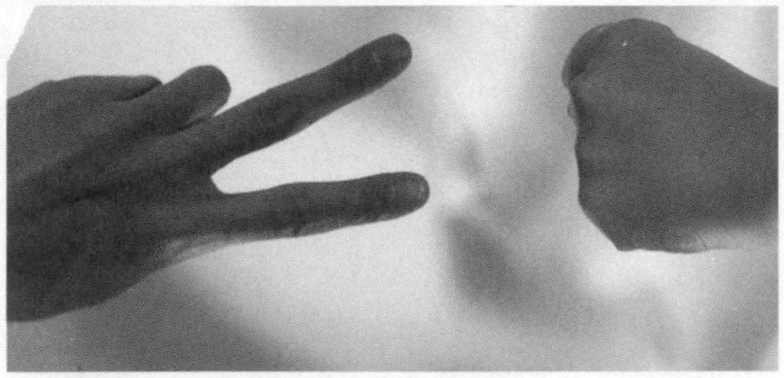

ROCK, SCISSORS, PAPER

This centuries-old traditional Japanese game—one of many *ken* (literally "fist") games played by children—is known in its native country as *Jan-Ken-Pon* or *Jan-Kem-Po*, in China as *Jiandao-Shitou-Bu*, and in Korea as *Kai-Bai-Bo*. Two opponents stand with one hand hidden behind their backs. After one person calls out "jan, ken, pon!" (or in America, at the count of three), both players bring their hand out in front, making one of three possible gestures–rock, paper, or scissors. The object of the game is to anticipate which gesture the opponent is going to make in order to make a gesture that will defeat it. Scissors (two fingers held in the "victory" sign) beats paper (an open hand) by cutting it, paper beats rock (a closed fist) by wrapping it, and rock beats scissors by dulling their edges. This can be played as a game in itself, but it is often used to determine who will be "it" for another, more entertaining game. —E.L.

YO-YO

The yo-yo is often considered a quintessential American toy, but, as with most things "American," the yo-yo is an immigrant. The yo-yo as we know it in America originated in the Philippines. Originally conceived as a weapon, in the 16th century Filipino jungle fighters used retrievable string-tied chunks of flint to stun enemies and prey. Over time, the weapon evolved into a toy (probably because kids liked to emulate their yo-yo-toting fathers), and Filipinos became adept at making them with materials such as mahogany and water buffalo horn. Americans can thank Filipino immigrant Pedro Flores for their yo-yo fun. In 1920, he brought to the U.S. his ability to whittle a toy that caught the attention of soon-to-be yo-yo-entrepreneur Donald F. Duncan. The rest is kiddie-toy history.
—L.P.

CHUTES AND LADDERS

Chutes and Ladders, the game popularized by toymaker Milton Bradley as the "exciting up and down game for little people," actually originated as a Hindu **[231]** religious game which sought to teach young children the consequences of good and evil behavior. According to Hindu sages, both good (*pap*) and evil (*punya*) are present in humanity's soul. In the game *moksha-patamu*, or "snakes and ladders," children are instructed that leading a moral life will get them more quickly into paradise. Acts of virtue are represented on the gameboard by ladders, along which the soul travels until it reaches an incarnation of ultimate perfection. Acts of vice are symbolized by the bodies of snakes, down whose slithery slopes the soul slides, leading to reincarnation in lower animal forms. As in life itself, a throw of the dice decides which path one's fortune will take.

Of course, all this stuff about spiritual perfection and reincarnation is more than American game manufacturers can comfortably swallow, and when Milton Bradley adapted the game in 1943, they gave it a less threatening name and a set of rules devoid of religious symbolism. According to company spokesperson Mark Morris, "I guess we figured it'd be a lot more fun for kids ages four to seven to make it chutes instead of snakes." —D.G.

PARCHEESI

According to Webster's, Parcheesi is the "trademark used for a board game adapted from *pachisi*." So what's pachisi? Well, that's in the dictionary too. Pachisi is "an ancient board game played with dice and counters on a cruciform board in which players attempt to be the first to reach the home square."

Pachisi originated in India more than 1400 years ago; in the 16th century, the Moghul Emperors played the game using slave girls wearing colorful saris **[312]**, instructing them to move around marble courtyards laid out to resemble the board. The remains of these life-size boards still exist at the Agra, Allahabad, and Fatehpur Sikri palaces of India. The literal meaning of pachisi is "25," the maximum throw possible in the original game, which used cowrie shells or coins to determine a player's move; modern Parcheesi replaces the shells with dice, and eliminates the slave girls entirely.

Nineteenth-century puzzle designer Sam Loyd (d. 1911) has been credited with inventing the American version. The story goes that a manufacturer had

approached Loyd wanting to dispose of a large surplus of cardboard squares; after a little bit of consideration, Loyd adapted Parcheesi from the Indian game, and presented it to the factory owner. Because the idea for Parcheesi came to him so easily, Loyd took just $10 for his efforts, refusing to accept a penny more. (The ancient Indians, of course, got nothing.) The boardgame, eventually acquired by Milton Bradley, is now considered a classic, with sets in the millions gathering dust in family rooms around the world. And, with begrudging consideration for history, its box cover still touts Parcheesi as "A Royal Game of India." —D.G.

POGS

Walk into your favorite convenience store, and next to the register you'll probably find colorful packages of round cardboard or plastic cut-outs, often depicting superheroes or cartoon characters. These are Pogs, collectible gaming pieces used to play a game called, naturally, Pog. Pog is a trademarked term, owned by the World Pog Federation; the generic term for the little cardboard disks, which now rival trading cards in popularity, is "milk cap"—although it's rare to find any that have ever capped a bottle of milk. Other manufacturers label their products Herocaps, Skycaps, Tonx, or Trovs.

The roots of Pog can be traced back to Japan's Kamakura period (1185-1333), when a game called *menko* was played using pieces made of wood, lead, or clay. Menko (literally, "little face") were often decorated with pictures of sumo wrestlers and samurai: later, cardboard menko depicted movie stars and manga **[46]** characters. Japanese immigrants brought the game to Hawaii, where children improvised menko games using milk bottle caps, calling the "slammer" piece a "*kini*" ("king" in Hawaiian). POG, as people in Hawaii are quick to tell you, stands for Passionfruit, Orange, and Guava, a fruit juice invented in 1970 by the Haleakala Dairy on the island of Maui. As a promotion for the new drink, the dairy issued decorated POG pieces for use in milk-cap games. While milk-cap games have always been popular among kids in Hawaii, the contemporary craze was unleashed in 1991, when Oahu teacher Blossom Galbiso reintroduced the game to her students using pieces donated by the dairy. Pogs spread like wildfire, first throughout the islands, and then to the mainland—D.G.

Kites

ON THE WINDS OF THE WORLD

• In Korea, kites are called yon and have been flown for at least 13 centuries. The first written reference to them likens them to a "ball of fire." Two basic models are the kaori yon (literally, "ray kite"), a square kite with three tails flying off one corner. There's also the pang pae yon (literally, "shield against bad luck"), a decorated rectangular shape with a hole cut out of the middle, making it an aerodynamically excellent fighter kite.

• In China, kites are called feng zheng (literally "wind zither"); these elaborately painted fantail swallow kites are a specialty of Beijing, as well as Tianjin and other parts of China. Professional kitemakers must go through three years of apprenticeship. The structure of Chinese kites tends to be more complicated than that of other countries; common kite design motifs are Chinese folk heroes, birds, fish, and insects.

• In Japan, which has more kite museums than any other country, kites are called tako (literally "wind cloth"), which is also the pronunciation for "octopus," a common kite shape in Japan. O-dako are huge kites, some as large as 40 by 50 feet and weighing almost a ton, which are launched at Chldren's Day festivals in May. (One American kite society tried to stage its own o-dako festival using kites made of bedsheets, with mixed results.)

Without kites, Ben Franklin would never have discovered that lightning was electricity, and Charlie Brown would have saved himself a lot of frustration. And without the ancient Chinese, kites would never have existed. Most scholars of the elegant wind-driven toy believe the kite was invented in China more than 2,000 years ago. According to Valerie Govig, editor of *Kite Lines* magazine there are many stories of origin, mostly on the order of "A Chinese farmer's hat blew away and the tether on it showed him that a hat shape could fly." The earliest Japanese reference to kites was in a 10th century dictionary of Chinese characters, in which a kite was defined as "a paper hawk which rides the wind and flies well."

Regardless of their origin, one fact remains a truism: When you put a kite in the air, you look up. In Asian countries, kites have had a religious significance, where they were once considered a sort of concrete prayer, a link between heaven and earth. Kites have also had military utility, serving as signals and message carriers. But by the end of the 17th century, kites were primarily used as a form of amusement. Now, kites are flown all over the world by children and adults alike. Kites come in all shapes and sizes, from tiny three-inch miniatures to huge ones as much as 50 feet long. And the two and three dimensional shapes can fly, dance, and perform stunts.

America's interest in kites was first piqued in 1876 by an exhibition of Chinese kites at the Philadelphia Centennial Exposition. The nonprofit American Kitefliers Association, based in Rockville, Maryland, was founded in 1964 and has grown to more than 5,000 members in 33 countries. Membership has its privileges, including kite-flying insurance coverage of up to $100,000, and "bragging rights" of belonging to the only national kite-fliers' organization. In 1966, museum curator Paul Garber founded the Smithsonian Kite Festival in Washington, DC, which has since become an annual spring event. Meanwhile, in 1977, Govig founded *Kite Lines,* a publication for kite fliers and enthusiasts of kite battles, which over the years has grown to an international circulation of 13,000.

FIGHTING KITES

Kite battles have taken place for centuries in most Asian countries, including Japan, Korea, and India. The object of a kite fight is to bring down your opponent's kite, or cut its control lines, sending it soaring out of control; individual combat uses small kites with lines coated with crushed glass, while team fighting (the most popular mode in the U.S.) uses larger kites known by the Japanese term *rokkaku,* a name derived from the kite's huge (up to eight feet long) hexagonal shape; each kite has multiple controllers, and a battle can be a truly epic sight, depending on the skills of the wielders and the arbitrary shifts of the wind.

According to *Kite Lines,* the Rokkaku Kite Capital of the World is the city of Sanjo, Japan, which in 1650 started to hold annual kite battles every June. Legend has it that Sanjo's ruler at that time, Lord Mizoguchi, solved a clash between two villages by suggesting they take their street battles to the sky, using kites instead of fists. In America, "Rokkaku Challenges" of varying skill levels have been a popular feature at many kite festivals since the mid-1980s. While most kite battlers are male, there is an all-female international team called the Mama-sans who compete in kite battles wearing traditional Japanese dress. —D.G.

Consumer Electronics

Time was when America was the undisputed technology leader of the free world; times have changed. In the latter half of the 20th century, from computers to telecommunications to video games, Japanese companies have lurched past their American rivals and revolutionized the electronic media by which we communicate with one another and entertain ourselves.

Most of today's Japanese giants emerged in the wake of World War II, along with a generation of aggressive Japanese industrialists struggling to rebuild and resuscitate war-torn Japan. Notably, the consumer electronics titan we know as Sony began as the young upstart company Tokyo Telecommunications Engineering Corporation. Founded in 1946, it would later rename itself—but not before unveiling to the world the phenomenally popular compact AM transistor radio in 1955, and then its FM cousin four years later. Sony was quick to utilize American innovations to miniaturize American products, and they've put American technologists on the run ever since.

The compact transistor was merely an omen for what was to follow. Miniaturization became an earmark of Japanese innovation. From televisions to computers to stereos, the Japanese have developed a reputation for taking Yankee electronic gadgetry, shrinking it, and selling it back to an eager American market. More recently, however, the adjective "Japanese" has also stood for "quality" and "value": Purchasing Japanese-made stereos, cassette players, CD players, TVs, and home video game systems have all come to mean getting more and better—in a smaller, niftier package. A new lifestyle that merged convenience and entertainment was practically created overnight.

Though the U.S. once output more than half of the world's manufactured goods, many things formerly associated with the phrase "made in America" have since been replaced by things made in Asia. With the purchase of Zenith in July 1995 by Korean company LG Electronics, formerly Goldstar, the last American television manufacturer exited stage East; practically all American pictures and sound now emanate from Asian-made machines. By way of consolation, America is still the world's number-one creator and exporter of entertainment—so even as we sit here watching TV on our Sony Trinitrons, it's very likely that, in Japan, glassy-eyed adolescents are slouched in front of a particularly hypnotic episode of *Baywatch*. —H.L.

AUDIO REVOLUTION

1979

Sony debuts the Walkman, generically known as the PORTABLE CASSETTE PLAYER. It's an instant success, and thousands of second-rate imitations surface in its wake. Still the only widely available recordable medium for audio, the cassette tape continues to enjoy life well into the 1990s.

1982

As record sales lag, Sony introduces the COMPACT DISC. Although CD technology —which uses a low-powered laser to read data off of a semireflective plastic disc—was codeveloped by Holland's Philips Electronics, it's Sony that manages to convince everyone that they need it. Suddenly, LPs become "vintage" novelties and CD sales skyrocket, due in part to such handsome features as digital-quality sound, nonlinear playback (allowing you to choose a track without having to cycle serially through the ones preceding it), random selection, and a longer usable life. The compact disc quickly becomes the standard for consumer audio recordings. To date, over 120 million CD players and 3 billion CDs have been sold in the United States alone.

1986

Like the CD, the DIGITAL AUDIO TAPE (DAT) is simultaneously developed by Philips and Sony, but is first introduced and aggressively marketed by the later. Effectively a souped-up cassette tape (only digital!), it goes beyond CDs by offering playback <u>and</u> recording, though it shares the analog cassette's lack of nonlinear playback. The threat of DAT causes a consternation among record companies, who fear a plague of digital-perfect pirating. They effectively kill DAT in its cradle; no longer a force in the the consumer market, the medium still has life behind the scenes for production purposes, and as a computer data-backup medium.

1992

Sony aggressively begins marketing the MINIDISC (MD), essentially a miniature CD that features playback (for normal people) and recording and playback (for the excessively wealthy). Like DAT, the MD phenomenon is over practically before it begins: MDs, though cute, hold less music than CDs, and offer only the benefit of being less prone to skipping than their larger cousins. Meanwhile, record companies utterly fail to offer MD variations of their wares, with the result that half a decade after its introduction, the MDs got one foot in the grave and the other foot on the edge.

VIDEO DREAMS

1941

The Radio Corporation of America (RCA) conducted the first experimental TELEVISION BROADCASTS in the early 1930s, but consumer use of TV begins when the FCC formally okays television broadcasts in 1941. The TV goes on to keep people riveted and couch cushions depressed for more than 50 years. Like for most consumer electronic products, Sony later proves to be the key innovator in TV, winning an Emmy in 1972 for its TRINITRON MONITOR and another in 1976 for its U-MATIC broadcast-quality videotape recording system, which quickly replaces 16mm film in television broadcasting. Sony continues to be a leading television set manufacturer.

1975

The "BETAMAX Debacle," now the stuff of marketing legend. Filled with hubris after the popularity of its industrial-

strength U-Matic video recorder, Sony decides to launch a consumer version, called the Betamax "VTR" (video tape recorder). Initially, in fact, it's a big hit too. But then Sony rival Matsushita (known in the West as "Panasonic") and Victor Company of Japan (JVC) abruptedly decide to challenge Sony's hegemony with their codeveloped competing format, VHS format. (VHS stands for "video home system," for those who have always wondered, but were afraid to ask.) In America, RCA jumps in and agrees to license and sell it. A free-for-all battle royale, ensues. You know what happens next. Why does VHS crush Betamax, despite being an inferior system? Number one: Sony refuses to license Betamax technology to its competitors, preferring to keep the potentially lucrative market to itself. Number two: Sony expresses no interest in providing consumers with prerecorded films. What do you get when you add one and two? In this case, zero. The VHS license, on the other hand, is made widely available, and many pre-taped movies are released for purchase, inventing a whole new industry. VHS systems multiply like bunnies; Betamax users endure mockery similar to eight-track tape player owners. Later, Sony swallows its pride and jumps into the VHS fray as well, having learned a valuable lesson.

1981

Japan's Pioneer Electronics introduces the first **LASERDISC** player (the year after video kills the radio star), and goes on to be one of the leading manufacturers of consumer laser disc equipment (especially karaoke systems, for which Pioneer's products have become the standard to beat). Basically an application of CD technology to video storage, laser discs have similar advantages: non-linear playback and crystal-clear digital pictures. "LaserDisc" begins as the intellectual property of Pioneer, but in 1989, Pioneer kindly releases the term into the public domain, formalizing the right for others to freely use it. Though popular among high-end video buffs, LDs have not had the penetration of CDs among consumers—in part because of their cost and their lack of availability at Blockbuster outlets.

1985

Sony debuts its **WATCHMAN**—just like regular TV, but smaller. The concept is novel, but brilliantly useless: Portable TV sounds great until you actually have one. Too distracting to use while walking, too dangerous while driving, too impractical while swimming, portable TV is only for the hardcore electronics freak—and deadbeats who can't afford a real TV.

1987

HIGH DEFINITION TELEVISION (HDTV) is proposed by Sony as a "next generation" television standard that will produce high-resolution, near-cinematic-quality images in a wide-screen format. In the West, Zenith picks up on Sony's lead, forming a consortium to develop a competing HDTV standard. By the early '90s, two separate and incompatible standards for HDTV exist: one created by Western companies, and one created by Sony and its cronies. The primary difference is that the Western one is digital (and not yet technically feasible), while the Japanese one is analog (and ready to go right now). Japan goes ahead and implements <u>its</u> standard, while the digital standard created by Zenith and its development partners becomes snarled in demands by broadcasters for additional television bandwidth to accommodate HDTV broadcasting. In Japan, Sony, Matsushita, and Hitachi are the first to sell HDTV receivers, though their high cost and restricted programming (programs must be specially recorded for HDTV to really flex its muscle) limits its sale to hotels, post offices, and the like. Meanwhile, the superior Western standard finally seems to be nearing launch, which will likely send the existing analog version into obsolescence.

1995

After a heated battle between warring consortiums—Sony/Philips on one side, Toshiba/Time Warner on the other—a collaborative standard for the **DIGITAL VERSATILE DISC (DVD)** is arrived at, and both computer and electronics companies target Christmas 1996 for the first launch of a consumer technology that's basically CD on steroids, packing the information of a 12-inch LD on a CD-sized disc. (Originally, DVD stands for Digital Video Disc, but computer companies demand a name change, since, as they note, the standard is to be used for data storage of all kinds, not just video.)

THE INTERACTIVE ENTERTAINMENT INDUSTRY COMES HOME

1976

The **GAME CARTRIDGE** is invented by Fairchild Camera and Intruments, whose Channel F becomes the first full-color home video system to use removable software cartridges. This flexible system allows game systems to play as many games as the players' parents can afford, and soon other companies adopt similar standards. They quickly beat the underwhelming Fairchild at their own game (pardon the pun). In particular, America's Atari Systems creates a game platform, the Atari 2600, that essentially conquers the world, becoming the starter kit for increasingly tech-wise generations to come. (Thinking about Atari is like remembering first love: Both of you were a bit klutzy and inexperienced, no one really knew where all the plugs should go, but it was highly addictive once you got started.)

Early 1980s

With the downfall of Atari, the oversaturated home video game market flatlines. But then Japan's Nintendo Entertainment [199] swoops in and does the unexpected—tantalizes American children with something they're no longer supposed to want. In doing so, Nintendo simultaneously jump-starts and dominates the **HOME GAMING** industry throughout the 1980s and early 1990s, until it makes a tactical mistake that nearly sends it to its doom—underestimating adult appeal for home gaming, as well as a crafty, nimble rival: Sega Games.

1985

In keeping with the electronics industry's fascination with shiny round discs, the computer industry adapts Sony/Philips's CD standard for data storage as the CD-ROM (ROM stands for "Read Only Memory"—around 600 megabytes of it.) Like its audio/video cousins, CD-ROM-stored data is retrieved via laser technology. Since then, CD-ROM players have gotten ever-faster: single (1X), double (2X), triple (3X), quadruple spin (4X), etc. Featuring the same basic inflexibility of CD technology, CD-ROMs cannot conventionally be used to record, and content must be provided. (CD-ROM "burners" are available, but for a high price.) Still, they fill the market demand for high-storage needs, though the arrival of the DVD will eventually push the CD into obsolescence.

Luck of the Draw: Asian Casino Games

It's a Saturday night and the neon-lit hall is packed wall to wall. Eager crowds of Chinese, Vietnamese, and Japanese throng around green felt tables, as dice are rolled, cards are turned, and chips raked in and replaced. Gamblers shout words of encouragement and disgust in a dozen dialects; the games they're playing feature ornate rules and eye-popping stakes of tens of thousand per hand. The only thing familiar about this exotic scene is the setting: not Macao, but Atlantic City, New Jersey, the newest home of the gambling fad that's swept the nation: Asian games.

These fresh challengers to casino mainstays like blackjack, roulette, and craps—with names like Pai Gow and Sic Bo revealing their non-European origins—were brought across the Pacific by turn of the century Chinese immigrants. Illegal "underground" games continue to thrive in Chinatowns across the country, generating millions for organized crime, while serving as a chronic burden for many Chinese and Southeast Asian communities. "We have cases where parents spend all of their [welfare] money on gambling, or sell their food stamps for a very low price," says Northern Californian social worker Tuan Tran. "It's a disease, and right now...there's nothing we can do."

Casinos and card clubs, on the other hand, have done plenty—adding these traditional Asian games to their gambling rosters in a heated attempt to exploit a vast new revenue opportunity. The results have been nothing short of spectacular: In California card clubs, where the Asian game craze first took legal root in the mid '80s, nearly two-thirds of all annual revenues are generated from Asian gamblers. "Nobody realized the potential of the Asian market," says George Hardie, general manager of the Bicycle Club, the oldest and largest card club in Los Angeles County. "It is now the lifeblood of our business."

Seeing California's successes, Nevada was not long in following suit, with Vegas and Reno institutions racing to offer more and more Asian-oriented amenities. Alongside its faux Roman temple, Caesars Palace installed an opulent Buddhist shrine, donated by a pair of Asian tycoons. Rival hotels began booking Asian comedians, singers, and other entertainers for holiday extravaganzas like "A Chinese Christmas." Even the notorious Chicken Ranch brothel had its menu of sexual delights translated into Japanese.

Still, in the City of Lights, the key attraction has always been the action. Hoping to milk the Pai Gow cash cow while adapting the complex game for Western audiences, casino operator Bill Zender invented the first of the "hybrid" Asian games—Pai Gow Poker—and introduced it on the floor of the Maxim in Las Vegas. The game was an instant gold mine. Along with Super Pan 9, a variant of baccarat (which, translated as *bai jia le*, or "100 happy families," has long been a favorite of Asian high rollers), Pai Gow Poker has spread to wherever games of chance are played.

THE RULES OF PAI GOW

Syd Helprin, the author of European and Asian Games, has called Pai Gow (literally "heavenly dominoes" or "make nine," depending on the dialect used in translation) "the most complicated [and] confusing game the non-Oriental is likely to encounter in any casino anywhere." With its unfamiliar equipment—three dice, a brass bowl, and a set of 32 domino-like tiles—and its completely counterintuitive hand-ranking system, first-time players are well advised to bone up on the rules before venturing anywhere near this fast-paced, high-stakes challenge.

The play itself is deceptively simple. Each gamer receives a deal of four tiles and must set them into two hands, a "front" and a "back." Gamers then take turns comparing their hands with the banker's two hands, "front" to "front" and "back" to "back." If the player's hands both outrank the banker's, she wins her bet. If the reverse is true, the banker wins. In the case of splits, the player "pushes," losing nothing. Exact ties, however, are won by the banker—accounting for the

AN ASIAN GAMING GLOSSARY

The following are slang terms often used (in both Chinese and English) by gamblers in the fast-paced world of Asian gaming.

BIG ROOM: The high-stakes tables, usually in a separate room from the rest of the club, where table minimums often start at $1000 or more. There are usually no maximums.

BLACK CAT: A professional jinx, who gets tipped by players to stay away from them—usually someone with a reputation as a loser (in life or in gambling) or someone who simply looks unkempt or unattractive.

BOMBER: A petty thief, who stalks card clubs hoping to sneak chips away from drunk, unwary, or non-Asian gamblers.

COVER ALL!: The shout that a high-roller makes to indicate that she's willing, as banker, to cover all Pai Gow bets placed, regardless of the amount. Everybody gets all the "action" they want.

JADE: A semiprecious stone worn by many Asian gamblers because they believe it brings good luck. Casino dealers are often prohibited from wearing jade because Asian gamers will refuse to play against a house that has jade on its side [295].

JUICE COLLECTOR—A high-interest "asset-based loanmaker." In essence, a walking pawnshop who takes valuables in exchange for a gambling stake, but demands "juice," or interest, on a daily basis until the stake is returned or the valuable is forfeited to the collector. Often

juice collectors demand extra "juice," above and beyond the set amount, if a gambler has won on the collector's stake.

KUM-KUM: To go partners on a bet. It's perfectly legal to jointly place a wager in California card clubs. Since the atmosphere in the scene is almost familial—despite the fact that players are all playing each other, rather than the house—going partners to raise the stakes necessary for a Big Room wager is common.

SHOESHINER: The opposite of a black cat—a professional good-luck charm, who flatters gamblers or gives them advice, or simply hangs around them in exchange for tips if they win. The problem is, shoeshiners whose fortune runs foul can easily turn into black cats.

TIP: Tipping is not only encourage among Asian gamblers, it's the rule. If you win, you tip the dealer. And the waiter who brought you your most recent drink. And anyone else who might have brought you luck, tipped the odds in your favor, or just happened to be standing around while you struck it rich. The old adage that what comes around, goes around has more meaning in this scene than anywhere: When you're up, you loan or give money to other gamblers. When you're down, they're supposed to do the same for you. Ultimately, of course, the biggest winner—as always!—is the house, who gets a cut regardless of whether you're up, down, or even. If you want to be certain of keeping above water, you should simply stay at home.

banker's 2.5 per cent edge against the players.

The two things that make Pai Gow drastically confusing for the uninitiated are the betting system and the way that hands are ranked. Because the tiles themselves have an origin in 13th century Chinese divination techniques [👁224], higher numbered hands don't necessarily beat lower numbered ones, and pair hands don't always beat unmatched hands. Real players, the ones who exchange hundreds of thousands per deal at "Big Rooms" in California card clubs, have the rankings memorized, and can often play by feel alone—fingering their tiles with Braille-like precision.

> **"Gamblers shout words of encouragement and disgust in a dozen dialects; the games they're playing feature ornate rules and eye-popping stakes of tens of thousand per hand."**

SIC BO (or DAI SIU)

A much simpler game than Pai Gow, Sic Bo is fairly common in Nevada and East Coast casinos. It has the thrill of craps without the betting complexity, and provides a fun, fast-paced way of losing all of your money in record time.

The rules are fairly basic. Players place their bets. A house dealer jostles three dice in a shaker, then removes the cover, announcing the numeric value of each die. Players win or lose, and continue if they have any money or interest left. Unlike craps, the only bets in Sic Bo are on dice combinations. A "large" bet is a 1:1 bet that the sum of the dice will be 11 or more. A "small" bet is one that the sum will be 10 or less. Players may also bet on sets like three of a kind, two of a kind, on the exact total value of the dice (from three to 18), and other combinations. But the even-money bets, like in roulette, are the most popular, and give the game its alternative name of "Dai Siu," or "Large-Small."

FAN TAN

Unlike the Pai Gow and Sic Bo, Fan Tan has still not made it into the legal gambling sphere of American casinos. Part of the reason is that its manner of play is completely unlike the card, dice, and machine games that casinos have accounted for in their security procedures, and thus more susceptible to irregularities. Basically, gameplay goes like this: The house dealer takes a silver cup and upends it over a pile of colored porcelain buttons. Some go under the cup; some go outside of the cup. The cup is moved to one side, and players place their bets on a layout that offers them a choice of the numbers one through four, plus multiple-number options like one and two, two and three, odd, even, and so on. The dealer lifts the cup and counts the buttons out with a stick in groups of four. The number of buttons remaining after all groups of four have been counted out—one, two, three, or four—is the winner. The game is popular in Macao and other Asian sites; the card game that shares Fan Tan's name is a Western invention, and bears no the counting game no relationship.

THE HYBRIDS

When Vegas operators decided to try to siphon off the Asian business of the Cali card clubs, they first had to reckon with two problems. The first was the alien equipment used by Pai Gow—the 32-piece set of tiles, each of which was small enough to palm, sleeve-drop, or otherwise mishandle by an adept cheat. The second was the game's user-unfriendly rules, which bore no resemblance to any Western game. Bill Zender, who ran Las Vegas's Maxim casino, came up with an innovative solution—one which used standard casino equipment and had rules that were easy for novices to learn and similar enough to the original for veterans to like. This was Pai Gow Poker. Its success led to the adoption of other "Asian"-esque games, such as Super Pan 9 and California Aces, though none of these has the direct bloodline of Pai Gow (and, in fact, are grouped with Pai Gow only because they are notably newer than games like poker, and blackjack). These are likely just the tip of the iceberg; as long as there's money to lose and gamblers to lose it, casinos will happily embrace multiculturalism in pursuit of the ultimate gilded mousetrap. —J.Y.

Go

It's considered a road to enlightenment, and it's the oldest of all known games; it's also been called one of most difficult to master. It's *go*, or as they call it in China, where it originated, *wei qi*, (literally, "surrounding pieces"). According to *The Go Player's Almanac*, the most credible theory about the inception of go maintains that the game evolved between 1300 and 900 B.C. from early methods of divination **[👁224]** in which Chinese kings and shamans used to cast black and white stones onto a board marked with geomantic symbols. By the time the Tang Dynasty (618-906 A.D.) rolled around, go was considered one of the "Four Accomplishments" of a Chinese gentleman-scholar, alongside calligraphy, brush painting **[👁4]**, and the ability to play a stringed instrument.

During the Sui and Tang dynasties (581-907), the game found its way to Japan, where it was first called *igo*, via Korea, where it's called *paduk*. In 1603, Japan set up a government Go Bureau, which was "devoted to the regulation and orderly development of go." As a result, Japan soon eclipsed China in technique and skill. Japan's fervor about go is encapsulated in the saying, "*Go uchi wa oya no shini me ni mo awanu*," ("a man playing go would not interrupt his game even to attend the deathbed of his parent"). Professional go players shaved their heads and dressed like Buddhist monks, in obedience to ancient tradition; soon, however, go reached the masses and pretty much everyone became obsessed with the game, as evidenced by this translated snippet of Edo-period verse: "'Just one game,' they said, and started to play. That was yesterday."

GO TO AMERICA!

The first go games were played on U.S. soil among Chinese and Japanese immigrants during the 19th century. In 1908, non–Asian Americans were exposed to the game through a book called *The Game of Go* by Arthur Smith. The modern American go movement took off after 1934, when reknowned German chess authority Edward Lasker, who had immigrated to the U.S. two decades earlier, wrote a widely read book on the game. The American Go Association was founded in January 1935, and began publishing *The American Go Journal* in 1949. Regional U.S. Go championships have been held since the 1960s, and national US Open Championships have been held since 1988. Victors compete in tournaments of the International Go Federation, established in 1983, as well as in corporate-sponsored ones. Globally, go is reportedly played by 30 million people. The best players are found where the game is most popular: in Korea, China, Taiwan, and Japan. The '90s has brought the Internet Go Server, where every year hundreds of thousands of go games are played, bringing the most ancient of games into the electronic era. —D.G.

The Basic Rules

The game is played on a square board with 19 horizontal and 19 vertical lines forming a grid of 361 "points." Two players take turns placing black or white "stones" on the points to demarcate their territory. Stones surrounded by opposing stones are removed. The object is to dominate the most territory by strategic formation of groups of stones which cannot be surrounded. Sounds easy, but there are a staggering number of possible play sequences: 10^{750}, to be exact (1 followed by 750 zeros). No wonder it takes a lifetime to master.

BLACK AND WHITE AND PLAYED ALL OVER

Othello, the board game that "takes minutes to learn, a lifetime to master," was invented by a Japanese barber named Goro Hasegawa in the early 1970s. Hasegawa, an impressively literate hairsmith, was inspired to named the game after the Shakespearean drama because of its black and white pieces, constantly in conflict. Though it is widely assumed that Hasegawa based the game on Go, in actuality, Othello is much more closely related to Reversi, a public-domain game that originated in England in the 19th century. In 1973, Hasegawa sold the rights to his game to the Japanese toy company Tsukuda, who released it the following year to great success. In 1975, Tsukada took the game to the U.S. for a licensing meeting with toy inventor James Becker; Becker immediately chose to become Othello's exclusive worldwide agent. In 1976, the year Othello was first released in America, over one million game sets were sold, making it the largest-selling licensed strategy game in the world. In the two decades that followed, about 30 million more games were sold. Two decades later, Othello continues on strong, with U.S. consumers purchasing about 500,000 sets annually. "There's something sort of magical about a game that lasts 20 years," says James Becker's son, Jonathan. Especially if it takes just seconds to learn. (And, uh, a lifetime to master.)

Mah Jong

Whether it's played by blue-haired suburban matriarchs or high-stakes gamblers in smoke-filled dens, the Chinese game of *mah jong* has a curious appeal. In the hands of the skilled, the slick tiles, decorated with baroque patterns, have lives of their own; they flip and mix with lightning speed, until finally a shout of victory ends their churn. Don't let *The Joy Luck Club* fool you: even among friends, mah jong is no friendly game—and among strangers risking cash, it can range from nerve-wracking to decidedly dangerous.

Modern mah jong developed in the Ningpo region of China in the 1870s, although elements of the game date back to the Han Dynasty (202 B.C. to 220 A.D.). A game similar to mah jong known as *mah chuek,* played with domino-like pieces, was popular during the Chung Dynasty (960 to 1279 A.D.). The game then evolved, reaching its current form during the Taiping Rebellion when Northerners, exiled by the rebels of the South, found themselves with plenty of spare time to devise systematic rules for the game. After it evolved into its present form near the turn of the century, it spread westward, eventually being brought over to America by a former Shanghai resident named Joseph Babcock. In the 1920s, it became popular among upper-class American sophisticates; a decade later, however, the fad faded, though the game survived among middle-class women, who turned it into a much more social game.

"Playing mah jong is about so much more than the game," says Ruth Unger, the 1995 president of the National Mah Jong League. "It's about camaraderie and bonding." Today, the National mah jong League, which establishes the rules for the American game each year, counts about 150,000 members across the country, plus an estimated 100,000 more who are not members but observe its rules.

THE JOY OF THE CHALLENGE, THE LUCK OF THE DRAW: The Basic Rules of Mah Jong

Although Chinese and American (also known as international) mah jong differ in details, the basic objective of each game

is the same—that is, to "go out" by completing a hand composed of four sets of three tiles each, plus a pair (known as the "eye"). A set is composed of either three, sometimes four, identical tiles, or three consecutive tiles of the same suit (in mah jong, there are three suits—circle, crack, and bamboo—each of which has tiles numbered 1 through 9). There are also special tiles, such as flowers and seasons, which enable the drawing player to score extra points and draw new tiles, and "wind" and "dragon" tiles that deliver bonuses if used as part of winning sets. Four players are required to play, each of whom are initially dealt 13 tiles from the horizontal rows of tiles set in a square shape at the center of the table. A throw of dice determines where among the four stacks the first set of tiles are dealt from; upon receiving their tiles, players exchange one per turn, either by choosing from the stacks of undealt tiles or picking up other players' discards, in obedience to certain guidelines.

When a player goes out, he or she declares "mah jong," the words apparently referring to the sound of the tiles clicking against one another (*mah* means "flax" or "hemp" in Chinese and refers to the sound of its leaves crackling in the wind, while *jong* means sparrow, a reference to the chattering of the bird). In Chinese mah jong, the winner receives the total of his or her points as winnings from each of the other three players, while in the American version points are assigned relatively to all players, based on what they had when the game ended.

This makes Chinese mah jong (which is played in Japan, as well as in Chinese-speaking regions of Southeast Asia like Hong Kong and Singapore) much more competitive than its U.S. counterpart, the emphasis being on going out with a strong hand and preventing other players from going out at all. Indeed, in China, the game is primarily played by men as a serious form of gambling, while here it is predominantly a woman's game and is much more social. The other major difference is that, in the American game, what hands you can go out with varies slightly every year in accordance with the decisions of the National Mah Jong League, obligating American players to buy a new rules guide from the League each year. –N.W.

MARTIAL ARTS

Martial artist Roger Yuan

The tattered ad stapled to the telephone post reads, "Fully certified Warrior and Assassin training in three months...or your money back!" Your pulse rises. You breathe deep, and think: *Like the half-breed Shaolin monk, Kwai Chan Caine in* Kung Fu, *I too will walk the earth in search of peace while snapping the necks of those foolish enough to cross my path, defend the sanctity of my fellow men, and deal a heavy hand (or foot) to those who threaten it. And, as an added bonus, snappy retorts of Confucian wisdom will come easier to me, once I wield the deadly arts!*

Unfortunately, you now have a problem. You must decide which martial arts discipline you will follow. And there are *so* many. Ever since the first shiploads of gold-seekers from China docked at the shores of *Gom San* (the "Gold Mountain," California to you and me) during the mid 19th century, martial arts have been a part of the American cultural landscape. At night, away from the prying eyes of Americans, Chinese compatriots secretly taught martial arts techniques to each other as a means of self defense in the harsh foreign land. These early *sifu* (martial arts masters), who stayed and instructed others after their day's work was finished, were weaving these uniquely Asian arts into America's rich cultural tapestry. However, it wasn't until the first decade of the 20th century, when a pioneer by the name of Takugoro Ito opened the first judo *dojo* (gym or school) in Seattle, Washington, that non-Asian Americans were initiated into the once clandestine circles of martial arts. Bruce Lee and other kung fu legends on the big screen and small made the business a household name in the late '70s. And since then, more than 10 million Americans have followed suit.

But what about you? As your delusions of grandeur subside, you must ask yourself: "Which is the most effective for my lifestyle?" Do you want to hurt someone, or defend yourself and your loved ones? Are you looking for a martial art replete with pithy philosophical ruminations, or just a quick and dirty means of self-protection?

Let following chart serve as your first step down the warrior path. However, before you embark on your barefoot journey through the California dustbowl, a note of advice is in order: any "master" who promises deadly skills in three months is probably lying. Mastery over *anything* requires years of training and practice.

So what are you waiting for? —K.L.

A Guide to the Martial Arts

Name and literal meaning	Description	Founder	What can you do with it?	Does it really work?	What will your teacher make you practice over and over?	What weapons do you get to use?	Intimidation factor (on a four fisted scale, with four fists striking terror in those merely unfortunate enough to bear witness)	Where have you seen it?
Aikido The "Way of Peace"	A "soft" art with an emphasis on the redirection of an attacker's energy	Morihei Ueshiba created it in 1942, influenced by Japanese fencing (*kenjutsu*), spearfighting (*yarijutsu*), and *jujutsu* (*see below*).	Restrain or disable people without maiming or killing; you can use it for defense without offense.	Only after years and years of training; no overnight wonder here.	Seizing control of attacker's balance by means of leverage and timing; throws, pins, and wrist and arm locks	A serene, clear, sound mind and a reasonably fit physique, as well as *tanto* (foam rubber or wood knives), *jo* (five-foot staff), and *bokken* (wooden sword)	**2;** It looks great but it's not very practical. Your ass will be whupped if your timing is off.	Steven Seagal movies. But these days, he usually uses guns.
Jujutsu (a.k.a. **jiu jitsu, jujitsu)** The "Art of Suppleness/ Gentleness/ Flexibility"	The no-holds-barred precursor to Judo: here, unconscious carcasses and groveling opponents (as opposed to points and neat little bows) are the goal.	In 1532, Takenouchi Hisamori established the term "jujutsu" as referring to the modern incarnation of Japanese martial art forms originating over 2,000 years ago and found in Japanese mythology; from Jujutsu sprang Aikido and Judo.	Get your opponent on the ground begging for mercy, screaming "Uncle." Or "Auntie."	Three words: Ultimate. Fighting. Challenge.	*Atemi*, kicks, throws, locks, strikes, knees, joint-locking, and holding; ground-fighting and close work	Some short weapons, but mostly hands and legs	**4;** Like judo, but better.	*Lethal Weapon* (Mel Gibson), *Bad Days* (Spencer Tracy)
Hapkido The "Spirit Way"	Hapkido is characterized by three things: passivity, circular movements, and the water principle (absolute penetration of an opponent's defenses).	Hapkido was first recognized as such in 1964 by Yong Shul Choi.	Lots of damage.	Did rushing water create the Grand Canyon?	A hybrid of Aikido's pacifist, flowing philosophy, Tae Kwon Do's kicks, Karate's power, and Judo's leverage	Fast legs	**4,** if you're fighting a bunch of *gi*-clad guys; **4+**, if you're a product of the '70s who remembers *Billy Jack* .	*Billy Jack* (actor Bong Soo Han made Hapkido famous by choreographing and stunt doubling for the title character), *Trial of Billy Jack*, *Billy Jack Goes to Washington*
Kendo The "Way of the Sword"	A sport discipline derived from ancient sword-fighting arts, except using bamboo equipment, because it's against the law to kill.	Based on *kenjutsu*, the 1,500-year-old art of samurai sword-fighting.	Compete; or partake in a mock grudge match.	It depends. The likelihood that you'll be suited up and ready to spar on the street is nil; however, being seen in your Kendo getup can be highly effective, since your opponent may never recover from uncontrol-	Stance, footwork, cuts, thrusts, feints, and parries	*Shinai* (four polished shafts of bamboo held together by a long sheath; kind of looks like a light saber, but much less deadly); *Bokken* (hardwood sword); *Katana* (real metal longsword only used for demonstrations)	**4** with gear, since you'll look like an Iron Maiden; **0** without gear, in which case you will be *killed*.	*The Hunted* (Chris Lambert)

Endurance /Stealth" [👁**109**]	learn to: survive certain death, throw stuff accurately, climb walls, prepare poisons explosives, and other practical jokes.	military operations.	detection				*will* hurt them, even if they never see it coming.	*American Ninja* series I, II, III, IV, etc., *The Master* (with Lee Van Cleef), *You Only Live Twice* (James Bond)
Kali, Escrima, Arnis (aka ***arnis de mano***, or "Harness of Hand")	**Kali:** a native Filipino system of hand and weapons **Escrima:** traditional Filipino fencing **Arnis:** Modern derivation of the ancient Kali fighting system. *Kali* was invented in the Philippines in the 9th century, before the Chinese arrived; *Escrima* and *Arnis* are soldiers' arts dating back to the 17th century, in response to Spanish invaders.	Originally derived from *tjakalele*, an Indonesian method of combat, modern *arnis* was innovated by Remy Presas.	Fight with a rolled-up newspaper or hard object of any length you can find	Sure, if you're cornered in a garbage alley rife with broken broomsticks, or if you're on the train with a rolled up newspaper; or if you're carrying a "postal"-style Rambo blade—even if you're a wheelchair-bound 80-year-old.	The independent use of hands and feet to do two different things at the same time; not blinking (blinking in combat can prove fatal).	*Kali* (knife system): *sinawali* (two sticks of 2.5 feet), *kali* (large bladed weapon), *kris* (wavy blade of different sizes); *Escrima*: *tabak* (pointed short wooden stick), *The New York Times* (or other newspaper); *Arnis*: *espada y daga* (sword and dagger), *muton* (two sticks), *baston* (single long stick), *bidio* (dagger)	**1**, if you whip newspaper out; **4**, if you whip blade out and speed through some basic forms *muoy muoy rapido*.	*Under Siege* (Steven Seagal knife-fights Arnis style), Mohammed Ali used Filipino footwork in boxing; Jeff Speakman (in *The Perfect Weapon*); *The Pacific Connection* (choreographer: Modern Arnis Grandmaster Remy Amardor Presas)
Muay Thai (Thai Kick-boxing	A martial art in which lithe young men with oiled and tanned bodies kick and elbow each other till one drops.	It was part of warrior training during the reign of King Naresuen the Great (1590-1605), but the record of its actual origins was destroyed in 1769.	You can bust a nut, ANYTIME!	Depends on how lithe and oiled you are.	Boxing, hard-kicking, and knee and elbow strikes, but not in the strict formal way of other martial arts	Shins of steel 	**3**, if you can do the traditional Thai dance before your bout and hum the Muay Thai anthem to let 'em know you're a badass.	Don "The Dragon" Wilson movies, Saskia Van Rijswijk movies
Jeet Kune Do The "Way of Blocking Fsts"	The "no-style" style of martial art used by Bruce Lee [👁**95**].	In 1967, Lee came up with the art form, which is more of a concept than a rigid system.	Whomp skilled veterans of martial arts and ruffians of all shapes and sizes.	One word: Bruce.	Conservation of movement, non-telegraphic movements (i.e. resisting the urge to flail legs or arms like windmills)	Loose limbs, footwork, the evil eye, gut-piercing shrieks	**4**, especially if you can hit Bruce's soprano catcall.	Bruce!, Bruce!, Bruce! (*Fists of Fury*, *The Chinese Connection*, *Return of the Dragon*, *Enter the Dragon*, *Game of Death*); also, *Fist of Legend* (Jet Li)
Wu Shu "Fighting Arts"	*Wu shu* is the official umbrella term for martial arts adopted by the People's Republic of China.	The Chinese government formalized it in the 1950s, based on ancient *kung fu* disciplines [👁**188**].	Impress people.	Most disciplines have been refined for competition, but knowing some *Wu Shu* moves may make you feel safer walking around alone at night.	Exercising the complete physical body	A healthy body; weapons including swords, broadswords, hooks, halberds, whips, double headed spears, three-sectional staffs, et cetera	**4**; just tell 'em you know *Wu Shu* to send 'em running.	*Shaolin Temple* (with a 17-year-old Jet Li), *The Master Killer*, *Iron & Silk*

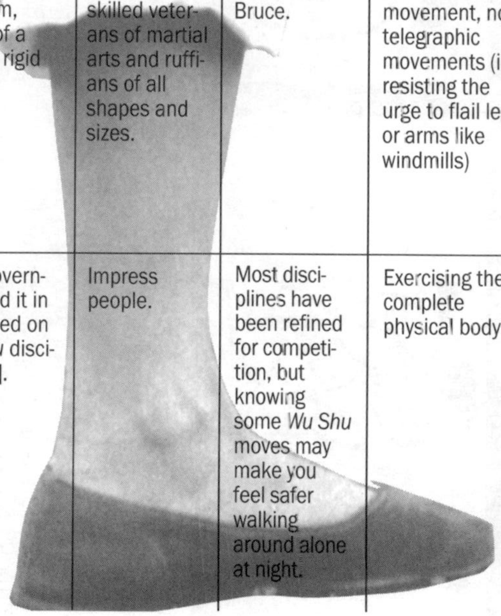

Actress/filmmaker Tiana

JUDO

Judo, literally translated as the "gentle way," is the sporting derivative of the deadlier, ancient martial art of *jujutsu* ("the art of suppleness/flexibility/gentleness"). Serving as a vivid example that *the bigger they are, the harder they fall*, *judo* is guided by two principles established by its founder, Dr. Jigoro Kano: maximum efficiency with minimum effort (*seiryoku zenyo*) and mutual benefit and welfare (*juta kyoei*). Armed with these ideas and a complete bare-handed system of grappling, choking, pinning, throwing—and, at black-belt levels of study, *atemi*, a system of effecting temporary but excruciating pain through attacking vital points—vertically challenged folks from all corners of the globe have finally been able to face down lifetimes of humiliation.

Its history goes back to 1882, when Kano, professor and president of Tokyo University, refined the combative, and potentially lethal, art of jujutsu to include a previously absent attention to moral and character development. Renaming *jujutsu* to *judo* further distinguished the new form from the older one, which had fallen into decay and modern disrepute. The suffix "*do*" (or "way") is different from "*jutsu*" (or "art"), representing Kano's intent that the new fighting form stress harmony of mechanics as well as a way of thinking and acting. His new "way" would perfect one's body and mind for the good and welfare of all mankind. One of Kano's students, Yoshiaki Yamashita, introduced judo to the U.S. in 1902, making Kano's "way" the first formally introduced martial art in America.

Still, Japanese *judokan* (judo practitioner), typically of smaller stature than their European and American counterparts, wreaked havoc on the international competition trail until the mid-20th century; with a dexterous élan afforded by a lower center of gravity, they were probably the most feared non-tall folks in the world. They continued undefeated until 1961, when 6-foot 6-inch Dutch terror Anton Geesink rocked the judo world by besting the bantam Japanese champion in the Third World Championships in Paris—proving that excessive height did not necessarily preclude judo prowess.

Today, over 200,000 members are registered in the International Judo Federation, the sport's governing body, in member countries including the U.S., France, and Russia. In Japan, judo is a sport within the national school system. Its popularity culminated in the inclusion of *judo* as a competitive sport in the 1964 Olympic games in Tokyo. Unfortunately, Kano's motive of better living through *judo* has been obscured under the hype of athletic competition. As a result, the "overall balance established by Kano has been lost," writes martial arts scholar Donn F. Draeger in the seminal *Comprehensive Asian Fighting Arts*. "Judo's [original] purpose was not to win a contest." –K.L.

KARATE

One of the most widely practiced—and most fragmented—of all martial arts in the world today, *karate* is a broad term for a system of Asian martial arts where practitioners deliver blows with their hands, feet, and use other body parts in defending and blocking. In contrast to the circular movements of Chinese kung fu, karate's blows, blocks, and parries are sharp and linear.

Karate's humble beginnings speak of the industriousness of human potential. Originally conceived on the island of Okinawa, a former colony of China located south of Japan, the development of this empty-handed form of combat was an urgent imperatives for a people besieged. When the Japanese occupied Okinawa in 1470, they issued a ban on all private ownership of weapons. This led to the practice of weaponless and unconventional-weapon combat techniques, rooted in Chinese martial arts. Then, in the early 17th century, Japan permanently conquered the island, and forbade the practice and development of martial arts. This prohibition drove practitioners underground (as most nettlesome government restrictions inevitably do). Gradually, traditional Chinese forms took on unique Okinawan characteristics. These styles were given the innocuously generic name *te* or "hand" by early practitioners, in an effort to maintain secrecy from the Japanese. Traditional Okinawan *te* incorporated weapons styles loosely adapted on agricultural implements, so as not to arouse suspicion; these deadly farm tools included the wooden flail *nunchaku* made famous by Bruce Lee, and the three-pronged metal *sai.*

Following the Meiji Restoration of 1868, the Okinawans were forced to undergo complete assimilation into Japanese culture, which included traditional Japanese martial arts training. In return, the skills of te were brought forcibly back to the mainland as well. By 1903, Okinawan te had been introduced into physical education programs in Japanese schools. Te was renamed *karate-jutsu* —the ideogram "*kara*" meant Chinese or China, "*te*," hand, and "*jutsu*," art—a name that stood as tribute to its multi-ethnic influences. A noted master and scholar of *karate-jutsu* named Gichin Funakoshi demonstrated the Okinawan fighting form at Tokyo University by invitation of the Japanese Ministry of Education, giving the art a national spotlight; by 1924, *karate-jutsu* dojos, or gyms, could be found at most universities, and students in Japan had outnumbered those in Okinawa.

Tai Chi

The Japanese shortened the term to simply karate, and exchanged the ideogram of "*kara*," which had once denoted "Chinese," for a same-sound prefix that meant "empty"—signaling a uniquely Japanese derivation of Okinawan traditions. Furthermore, they eliminated the practice of weapons from the new, sanitized "empty-hand" martial arts.

The Okinawans were understandably infuriated over this blatant disdain for Okinawan tradition, but were forced to accept the new ideogrammatical changes; meanwhile, however, masters who remained in Okinawa continued to develop new forms of the original art, both armed and weaponless.

Karate didn't make its way to America until 1946, when ex-G.I. Robert Trias opened the first karate dojo in Phoenix, Arizona. Stationed on the British Solomon Islands during World War II, he had studied with masters there and in Singapore, where he was trained in *kempo*, a Chinese form of self defense similar to karate. Two years later, he formed the U.S. Karate Association, the first and one of the largest karate associations in America.

Since then, systemized competition has been established, in which modern day *karateka* (practitioners of karate) fight to win points in sanctioned bouts. Today, approximately 4 million people in the U.S. study over 16 styles of karate from Okinawa and Japan. Who knew breaking boards could be so much fun?

–K.L.

TAE KWON DO

Ancient Korean warriors were not known for beating around the bush. Why waste the time, when you could be beating your opponents instead? *Tae kwon do*, the fighting form that they developed, is stripped clean of the euphemisms or self-righteous doctrines proclaimed by other martial arts disciplines, a fact made clear from its very name, which translates as "the way of kicking and punching."

Utilitarian though it might be, the martial art tae kwon do took almost 2000 years to develop; then, in 1909, the discipline was nearly lost forever, when Japan annexed and did its best to wholly assimilate Korea. It wasn't until 1946, a year

JHOON RHEE: The Father of American Tae Kwon Do

Jhoon Rhee, born January 7, 1932, says that there were three events that changed his life forever. First of all, when he was six, he got slapped by a five-year-old girl. Then, when he ran home crying, his mother slapped him again for getting slapped by someone a year younger than him, and even worse, a girl. But then he discovered tae kwon do, and everything changed—in time for his third primal event: When he was in the 11th grade, he accepted a challenge to fight the school bully after school. He was a brown belt then, with a bantam build of just five feet six inches and 120 pounds, and was facing the first real test of his newfound fighting abilities. "He swung at me first," Rhee writes in his memoirs, "and I gave him a black eye." Then Rhee kicked him in the throat, to which the bully replied, "You got me."

Jhoon Rhee with Bruce Lee

Rhee knew then that his years of tae kwon do training had worked. He also knew that the rest of the world needed to experience the miracle for themselves. In 1956, a still-wet-behind-the-ears Rhee opened the first American tae kwon do dojang (studio), in San Marcos, Texas, after teaching the art at the nearby college he attended. In 1962, the Grandmaster founded the Jhoon Rhee Institute of Tae Kwon Do, a chain of schools based in Washington, D.C. Since then, Rhee has taught congressmen, senators, and even the Secret Service. And if boxing champ Muhammed Ali, one of Rhee's early students, and Bruce Lee, whom Rhee taught kicking techniques, could learn a thing or two about fighting from the master, well, anyone could.

after Korea's liberation, that the nation's traditional martial arts were resuscitated. Hong Hi Choi, then a second lieutenant in the Korean Army, is credited with tae kwon do's revival. In 1946, he began instructing Korean soldiers in the skills of *taekyon*, an early precursor to modern tae kwon do. Three years later, Choi introduced the martial art to American troops on a trip to the United States.

Meanwhile, numerous *kwan*, or schools, opened in Korea, each preaching unique and disparate philosophies and styles. By 1954, there were nine major kwans teaching different variations of Korean fighting forms. On April 11, 1955, Choi—now General Choi—submitted the name "tae kwon do" during a formal convening of the masters as an umbrella term to encompass the nine kwans of Korean fighting arts. Although discord arose over what was so uniquely Korean about the martial arts that fell under the new name, most agreed that "tae kwon do" represented a native system of kicking, punching, jumping, blocking, dodging, and parrying, whose distinctive calling card was high-flying, acrobatic side kicks. Under Choi, this new form would grow, amalgamating time-honored Korean traditions of combat, sport, self-defense, and art.

But Choi's lock on the development of tae kwon do ruffled feathers. Dissension among the ranks of masters continued until 1961, when the Korean government decreed the formation of the Korean Tae kwon do Association, with Choi as its first president. The KTA's mission was to oversee the proliferation of tae kwon do throughout the world. And Choi, as its leader, saw to it that demonstration teams traveled far and wide to promote this legacy of the Korean art of war.

Today, according to the U.S. Tae kwon do Union, over 2.5 million practice the art in the U.S., and another 20 million worldwide, in 112 countries. Although tae kwon do—in its present incarnation—is less than 50 years old, dynamic and tireless spokespeople like Choi and, in the U.S., Grandmaster Jhoon Rhee (*see above*), assure its continued prominence in the global martial arts lexicon. –K.L.

TAI CH'I

You're walking through the neighborhood park and see people slowly stroking the air with their arms and legs. They turn slowly and embrace the sky. They raise one leg like a flamingo. Unless you've wandered into a mime rehearsal, chances are good you're witnessing the practice of something which rightly has earned the nickname "slow meditation." It is a form of Chinese martial arts called *tai ch'i chuan*, literally, "Ultimate Fist."

"While watching a fight between a snake and a bird, he noticed that each animal battled using a series of quick slashing assaults, coupled with slower and seemingly wavering moves."

Since its introduction into the U.S. in the 1930s by master Yang Cheng-Fu, this meditative form of martial arts has gathered fans ranging from dancers to doctors. Those who practice it do so for its advantages in five areas: the relaxation of the body and mind, as a nonaggressive form of self-defense, for better circulation of ch'i (or qi, internal energy; **[👁241]**), for progression down the spiritual path, and ultimately, for a great full-body workout.

Legend has it that the form was invented by Chang San-Fen, a Taoist priest living in the Kiang Hsi Province of China during the early 14th century. While watching a fight between a snake and a bird, he noticed that each animal battled using a series of quick slashing assaults, coupled with slower and seemingly wavering moves. Duly inspired, Chang (who sources say looked like an animal himself) created a new fighting style. Legends aside, however, *tai ch'i chuan* was systematized in the late 15th century by the Chen family, who practiced in the Honan province of Southern China. The Chen family had learned tai ch'i from Wang Tsung-yueh, allegedly Chang's best student, and for nearly 500 years tai ch'i was kept a restricted Chen family affair. One day in the early 19th century, a Chen houseguest, the young kung fu master Yang Lew-Shen, was let in on the secret by master Chen Chang-Hsin. From the Chen style evolved the Yang style, which ultimately spawned the school of Wu, developed by Wu Yu-Hsin toward the end of the 19th century.

Known primarily for its usage of lower-body stances, Chen's is the only one of the three schools to utilize quick, forceful blows within its routines. It would be difficult to mistake a rigorous Chen routine for pantomime. The branch of tai ch'i which most approaches formlessness is the Wu school. At its highest level, the practice of the Wu routine can appear to be nothing more than a series of normal ordinary actions, such as getting up from a chair and walking across the room.

These days, however, the Yang school is the most popular tai ch'i style, perhaps as a result of the family's own self-promotion. It was the Yangs who took the practice to Beijing and taught the royal court before the fall of the Ming dynasty. Yang sons also taught non-royalty, spreading tai ch'i around the world. This school of tai ch'i is often practiced for the cultivation of health. Its various motions involve up-down sweeps of the arms and simultaneous bends at the knees. Some say the motions approximate modern dance, but despite their aesthetic appeal, they were in fact created for self-defense and attack. If applied for these purposes, the tactics can kill or maim. Which is something that can't be said about ballet.—K.M.L.

Everyone's Kung Fu Fighting!

Some say that the history of kung fu is the history of China, and considering the confusion that surrounds the latter, it's probably understandable that no one knows for sure who invented kung fu. Then again, the term "kung fu" merely means "ability or skill"—and there are many abilities and skills that fall under its rubric.

The devoted seeker of the truth behind the legends might do well to begin from a modern point of reference: In 1953, the National Traditional Sports Meet convened to organize over 1,500 different styles of kung fu from four millenia of Chinese history into a single set of skills to be studied as wu shu (literally, "war arts")—the new official term for martial arts in the new official People's Republic of China. To uphold the Communist maxim of making every aspect of culture a way to serve the people, the new regime sublimated old-fashioned kung fu fighting under the guise of promoting health. By 1959, the State Physical Culture and Sports Commission had outlined five basic categories of wu shu forms: boxing, sword fighting, broadsword fighting, spear fighting, and stick fighting. It was decreed that these skills, adapted for performance and sport rather than battle, would be the only valid forms of kung fu in China.

Non-Chinese would have to wait until 1967 before being properly introduced to Chinese martial arts. "There was an unwritten rule that you just didn't teach Caucasians," says Dave Carter of *Inside Kung Fu*. Today, of course, the skills are practiced widely throughout the world, by people of diverse races and origins. One thing to remember: a kick in the head feels the same, regardless of the color of the foot delivering it.

KUNG FU AND YOU

As noted above, there are dozens of different styles encompassed under the umbrella designation "kung fu." The best known are described here, divided into two categories: *External,* which are penetrating and outwardly focused, and *internal,* which are flowing and inwardly focused. —K.L.

External Styles

Wing Chun is the most popular of all Chinese martial arts today, and often considered the deadliest **[👁100]**. The only martial art known to have been systematized by a woman, it also takes a shorter time to master—about three years—than almost any other fighting discipline. Its history can be traced back to the early 1700s at the Shaolin Temple, where the traditional methods of training required more than 18 years to master. When the threat of a Manchu attack loomed, Shaolin monks convened to devise a quick and dirty method to train their young disciples. Unfortunately, they weren't quick enough; the temple suffered an attack and burned down. A handful of disciples escaped, including a nun, Ng Mui, who had participated in the discussion. Legend has it that Ng Mui eventually completed the system and named it Wing Chun, or "Eternal Spring," after the name of the hall at the temple where the meetings convened. Ng Mui also renamed her first student, the folk heroine "Yim Wing Chun," after the style.

Wing Chun's efficacy lies in finding the most economical distance between two points. For instance, if your opponent initiates a hook punch at the same time you launch a direct straight punch to his face, he's going to be hurt first. Each line of attack of Wing Chun, consisting of straight and intercepting lines or deflecting arcs, also doubles as a defensive move.

Northern Shaolin, the "original" kung fu style, is a direct descendant from the orthodox temple styles. Its basic premise is that kicks are more effective

KUNG FU: THE LEGENDS CONTINUE

So where did kung fu really come from? Some of the most popular legends follow here:

- **Once upon a time in the 6th century A.D., Buddhist priest Bodhidharma ("Tao Mo" in Chinese) [👁6] made his way from India to Shaolin, China, to spread the good word. When he was turned away at the temple, he stalked off to a nearby cave and meditated for nine years. His unblinking gaze bored a hole through the wall; this was enough to convince the monks to admit him. Once in, he noticed that other monks had a tendency to snooze during meditation. Miffed at this lack of mental and physical discipline, he devised the legendary I-Chin Ching ("Muscle Change Classic"), blueprinting early kung fu as a training regimen. Tao Mo's system was later adapted into the Shaolin Ch'uan Fa ("Shaolin Way of the Fist").**
- **Another theory holds that—since Buddhists aren't supposed to fight—it must have been wayward rogues hiding out at the Temple who came up with the tough stuff. Later, monks reasoned that kung fu wasn't really fighting, merely "redirecting aggression" from attackers. As a result of this, berserk monks began redirecting aggression all over the place.**
- **The least widely known theory names two monks, Hwei-Kuang and Sung-Chou, as the founders of kung fu. However, no one believes this theory except the two monks. And they're dead.**

than punches since legs have longer reach than arms—hence its balletic movements, typified by spinning kicks and bold, overextended punches.

Choy-Li-Fut is one of the most powerful kung fu styles. Famous for its long-range fist techniques, the system was founded in 1836 by a man named Chan Heung who was trained by Shaolin temple monks. It combines the long arm and fancy footwork styles of Northern China with the low stance and brute strength characteristic of the south. Vital to the practice of this system is a loose, powerful waist, which practitioners use to whip their arms at foes. Considered one of several "revolutionary" kung fu styles, Choy-Li-Fut was developed secretly by rebels toiling beneath the 18th century Manchurian rule, and incorporated an arsenal of weapons including spears, tridents, lances, and varying lengths of chain whips to counter the well-armed Manchurian troops.

Hung Gar hails from the Southern Shaolin Temple in the Fukien province. *Once Upon a Time in China*'s real-life Wong Fei Hong **[👁100]** practiced this style, typified by low, strong stances and powerful hand techniques. It's especially useful for developing arm and leg strength, albeit in a less fancy way than Northern counterparts.

Nary a martial arts parody passes without some mention of the **Praying Mantis** style. One day, the great martial arts master Wong Lung, who wasn't so great that he didn't lose challenge after challenge against even the lowest levels of Shaolin monks, was wandering the woods dejectedly, when he noticed the predatory prowess of a mantis. Observing its don't-mess-with-me swagger and skills at deflecting attack, he captured the mantis and studied its natural forms. Lung then devised a system in which a practitioner, as martial arts writer Jane Hallander puts it, might "block a punch, grab with his blocking hand and pull his attacker off balance, then close into him while simultaneously striking with the opposite hand...Once you hit with the first, your opponent's guard is down, and you follow with three or four more strikes to totally disable him." He won't come back for more.

Monkey Style is the primate equivalent of Praying Mantis. Though playful in nature, and hilarious to watch, this simian-inspired kung fu, known for its squats, tumbles, and rolls, is deadly on the receiving end. Legend has it that martial arts master Kau Tze, in attempting to dodge the draft during the Ch'ing dynasty, accidentally killed his conscription officer. Unwilling to fight the entire Manchu army, he surrendered, and thus experienced a long holdover at a Beijing jail. There, he observed a pack of feisty monkeys employed to guard one of the prison doors. Feebly attempting to keep fit, Tze mimicked the leader of the pack for the next decade until his release. Voila! Monkey kung fu! This system is governed by several principles: 1. Be tricky and cunning; 2. Be poisonous; 3. Destroy all attacks; 4. Bluff like a master poker player on his last chip; 5. Be unpredictable and flaky, like a real monkey. And hey—have fun!

Chin Na is probably the least structured, most practical, and least famous of all the external styles. Developed over 370 years ago during the Ming dynasty, Chin Na has become an integral component of hand-to-hand combat training for the police and military forces of many Asian countries. But Chin Na is not an offensive form; rather, it's a system of seizing and disabling perpetrators. Its practitioners seek to locate and "address" the most vulnerable parts of the body as a means to subdue without unnecessary force.

Internal Styles

Hsing Yi (literally "form-will"), founded in the 17th century, is rooted in the belief that all fights should be ended as quickly as they are started. By incorporating the Taoist "five elements" **[👁241]** and 12 animal forms of movement (dragon, tiger, monkey, horse, iguana, cock, hawk, snake, eagle, bear, swallow, and ostrich), Hsing Yi allows thought and action to work in unison, creating a system of linear movements that can be performed at lightning speed; the body remains completely relaxed until the final devastating moment of action.

Pa Kua, founded sometime between the late 18th and 19th centuries, is another form based on Taoist principles, in this case, the I Ching **[👁224]**. Pa Kua moves are aligned along the eight-sided I-Ching trigram to form eight directions of attack and defense, in movements that are primarily flowing, soft, and circular. Its distinguishing feature is that it uses no closed-fist attacks, but rather only open palm attacks and deflects.

Martial Arts Weapons

Imagine the blind-as-a-bat evil abbott in *The Flying Guillotine* without his screeching, head-ripping, woven-rattan hatbox on a chain. Or the Dragon himself, taking down his staff-wielding foe-for-hire in *Game of Death* without his bone-cracking, air-whipping nunchakus. Or an inebriated Jackie, god forbid, without his—ahem—benches of pain. Martial arts may be most widely known as techniques of the fist and foot, but true masters of death never scoff at using a weapon if one's at hand. Here are some of the most popular:

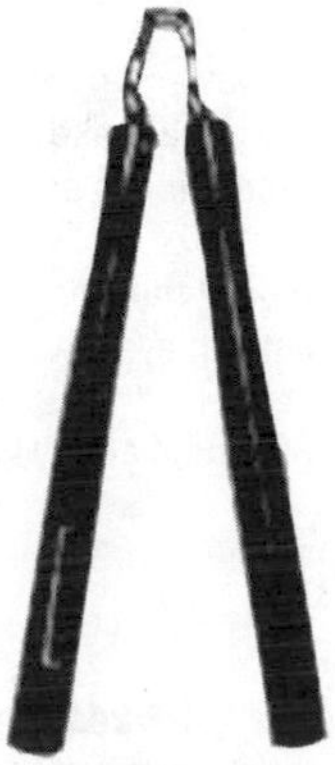

Nunchaku (none-cha-koo)—Originally a tool for flailing grain, its use was developed as a fighting style by Okinawan masters. One can disarm an opponent with a longer weapon by trapping it with the chain and twisting. To confuse and distract an opponent, one can swing them in zig-zag patterns around the body, striking suddenly from an unknown direction. However, to really inflict damage and watch grown men cry, one can *ensnare* with the nunchaku by catching the opponent's finger, hand, or wrist in a nutcracker grip. Hear them scream! Bruce did.

Staff—Indisputably the simplest of all martial arts weapons, the staff, in varying lengths and thickness, has been incorporated into nearly all weapons systems in Asia. In Japan, big sticks are called *bo*, and the study of *bo* is known as *Bojutsu*. In China, the generic Cantonese word for staff is *guan*. Attach metallic points on the ends, and a staff becomes a *cheung*. The Okinawans call their sticks *rokushakubo* and taper them at the ends to increase damage potential when the ends connect with their target. In India, staffs are *lathi*. The Thai love their staffs so much that they dance with them. Hooked on staff? All fightin' Asians are.

Shuriken (shoo-ree-ken)—Watch it; after a quick Sho Kosugi fix [👁109], kids using these'll put your eye out in a second. The razor-sharp stars are flung with a strong flick of the wrist, or released tangentially along the arc of a swinging arm at a foe's throat, eyes, temples, and limbs. They can be dabbed in lethal poison for added efficacy. Shuriken were among the ninja's favorite weapons—portable, concealable, and lethal.

Katana (kah-tah-nah)—First forged by

expert swordsmiths during the 8th century in Japan, this long sword was the samurai's principal weapon. Drawing a katana was serious business—it was not uncommon for a reputation and life to fall before a samurai's *katana* was resheathed. In obeyance of the art of Japanese sword-fighting—*kenjutsu*—only four points on the body were allowable targets for the *katana*: the top of the head, the wrist, the side, and the leg below the knee.

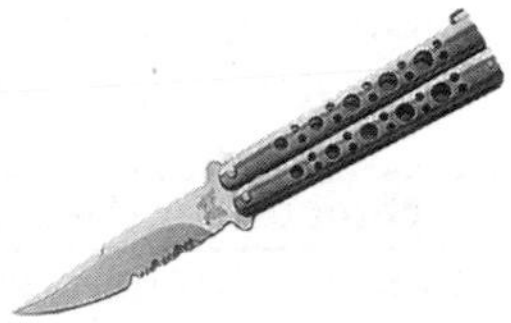

Balisong (ba-lee-song)—Otherwise known in America as the "butterfly knife," this fan-like, hinged Filipino blade has a locking system which allows the user to flip it open with one hand, freeing the other to wield another weapon. Smuggled into America by servicemen stationed in the Philippines after World War II, the balisong became a fighting implement of choice among teenaged Asian gangsters. These days, however, Uzis are much easier to come by.

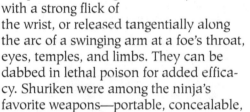

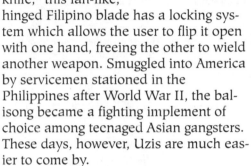

Tonfa or **Tui-Fa** (ton-fah) (twee-fuh)—One of five Okinawan weapons that began as farming implements, the *tonfa* was originally a handle used to manually turn millstones for grinding rice. By keeping the long end of *tonfa* parallel to the forearm, one can effortlessly punch and poke offenders. Look closely next time you're in a donut shop: Your friendly neighborhood policeman's billy club is essentially a *tonfa*.

HONORABLE MENTION

Wooden benches (wuh-dun ben-chez)—Eat, drink, schmooze with the waiter, and if he shall be so unlucky as to miscalculate the bill, grab the wooden bench you sit on and wield the deadly art of Choy-Li-Fut southern-style kung fu popularized by Jackie Chan in *Drunken Master*. He'll never forget his arithmetic again. —K.L.

Five Ways to Kill a Person with a Single Unarmed Blow

In the Old Days, when trekking across the Chinese badlands, travellers would often fall prey to treacherous rogues. Unless, of course, they were skilled in the Ancient Deadly Arts. We speak here of the dreaded Death Touches—the legendary attacks that could send foes to their doom with a single blow. The means by which masters achieved these powers have long been hidden. No longer. These secrets are revealed below, to be used against evil in the defense of good, and *only* as a last resort. —K.L.

Technique	Description	Secret training method!
The Red Sand Palm	This allows you to kill assailants simply by rubbing your palms together and aiming them at your foes. Victims of Red Sand Palm suffer immediate injury, followed by death within 15 days.	1. Fill a basin with fine, red sand. 2. Scoop up a handful of sand and rub it between your palms, crushing it into a powder. Continue until you get tired. 3. Repeat daily for years, until you can grind the sand to powder by simply rubbing your empty palms over the basin. 4. Repeat steps 1-3, using coarser sand. 5. Repeat using iron beads. 6. Repeat using 5-pound iron balls. If you can rub your palms over the basin and make an iron ball bounce out, you've mastered Red Sand Palm. Take care at performances, since your applause now has killing force.
One-Finger Kung	This skill allows you to point and shoot your enemies with the tips of your fingers. Legend recounts that high-level users were able to affect objects staggered behind others without damaging the one in front.	1. Suspend a heavy iron bell in the hallway of your house. 2. Poke it with your finger whenever you walk by. 3. Do this for several years, until you can point at the bell from two feet away and make it move. 4. Repeat as necessary until you can point at the bell from three feet away and make it ring. 5. Repeat steps 1-4, except with a lighted candle, increasing distance until you can snuff it from 20 feet away. 6. Repeat using a candle inside a paper lantern. 7. Repeat using a glass lantern. If you can put out the flame without breaking the glass, you have mastered One-Finger Kung. Watch where you point; it's all very fun until someone puts an eye out.
Dragon Claw Kung	"Birds flying across the sky will fall as if shot by arrows at a stretch of the gripping fingers. Wild horses can be managed as if bridled and the reins in one's hands." Rooted in Chin Na **[👁189]** techniques, Dragon Claw Kung makes your targets suffer as if talons were ripping their flesh. Masters were able to project their skills upon distant objects or people. Now you can, too.	1. Figure out which of your two hands is stronger. With this hand, lift a 30-pound empty jar for three months until it stops slipping from your grip. 2. Repeat, except fill the jar with water. 3. Repeat, except with sand. 4. Repeat, but use lead beads. 5. Pat yourself (carefully) on the back, 'cause your hand now possesses Yang **[👁241]** powers. 6. Now it's time to develop the Yin: Practice the same claw grip, but this time aim it at the sun and pretend that you're trying to grip it. You may not know it, but you're trying to undo your Yang in order to develop Yin. 7. After you find that you possess the same ability, only this time through the Yin, rather than the Yang, you've harnessed this power. Wipe the sweat from your brow, and relax, because now you've got Yin. Remember, although Dragon Claw can be deadly, it was most often used to restrain rather than kill. Modern users will find it helpful for popping bottlecaps, unscrewing sticky jars, and so on.
Jade Belt Kung	No, this isn't a fashion statement: Jade Belt Kung is actually a terribly effective bear hug in disguise. Wielders of this kung are able to crush anything by wrapping their arms around the object and squeezing.	1. Throw your arms around a tree trunk and clasp your hands together. 2. Squeeze for 3 minutes and relax for 1 minute. 3. Repeat Step 2 for half an hour a day, five days a week for a few years, until, with the slight shaking of your arms, a shower of leaves is released. 4. Uproot the tree and congratulate yourself. You've just advanced to the next level. 5. Repeat Steps 1 through 3 with a 500-pound boulder. 6. In two years, you'll be able to walk briskly with a boulder cradled in your arms. You've mastered Jade Belt Kung!
Ch'i Kung	George Lucas modeled "the Force" of his Star Wars saga after this art. Shockingly, of all the clandestine skills described here, *ch'i kung* (*qi gong* in Mandarin) s the only one practiced today, albeit in dwindling numbers. Masters and young practitioners who are trained in ch'i kung are able to withstand incredible feats of peril: Trucks roll over them without harm; large needles impaled through their cheeks draw no reaction and cause no pain; brick walls don't stand a chance against ch'i kung head butts, et cetera. Through ch'i kung, practitioners can inflict pain simply by controlling and redirecting their qi. The consequences are too scary to be taken lightly, and no directions are provided here, because—in the wrong hands—these methods are far too deadly.	

Motorcycles

Ever heard piston slap coming from the layshaft of a fuel-injected double-knocker? If so, you might need a feeler gauge to determine if the bore/stroke ratio is wrong for the master cylinder. No, this isn't a description of androids having sex; it's motorcycle tech-talk, and it's a language that two-wheeled motor enthusiasts in Japan and the U.S. speak quite fluently. Since 1980, four Japanese motorcycle companies have cornered nearly 75 percent of the U.S. market, and the majority of the global market. Honda is the most popular Japanese motorcycle brand in America, with 25 percent of the market, on par with Harley Davidson. Kawasaki and Yamaha aren't far behind the leader of the J-pack, with Suzuki bringing up the rear. For down and dirty mastery of the open highway, you still can't beat a classic hawg—but for a phenomenal combination of technical sophistication and raw power, check out these rides of the Rising Sun: —N.G.

HONDA

Slogan: *"Follow the leader— he's on a Honda."*

Soichiro Honda, a guy who liked to party, play music, and make whiskey in his spare time, sold his first company, a piston-ring factory, to Toyota in 1945. The next year, he founded Honda Technical Research Institute, running it out of his garage. In 1949, Takeo Fujisawa (owner of Japan Machine and Tool Research Institute) joined Honda, and together they opened a branch of the company in Tokyo in 1950. The rest is automotive—and motorcycle—history. Today, the **C90 P Cub** is the oldest motorcycle still in production, and the **Fireblade** has practically defined the category "sportbike" since its introduction in 1991.

KAWASAKI

Slogan: *"Let the good times roll."*

Shozo Kawasaki started out in the late 1800s as the owner of two shipyards in Tokyo and Kobe, which he then merged in 1896 to form the Kawasaki Shipyard Co. In 1939, the company changed its name to Kawasaki Heavy Industries, Ltd.; it began making motorcycles in 1949, after dabbling in steel, rail coaches and wagons, planes, and other metal things. Kawasaki's **ZX-11**, which was first released in 1980, is still one of the fastest and most powerful bikes on the market.

The **Ninja** series is currently synonymous with sport cycling.

YAMAHA

Slogan: *"The cruising spirit lives."*

Torakusu Yamaha started out in 1887 as a manufacturer of organs (the musical kind). The company he founded soon diversified, creating a motor vehicle division that, in 1955, spun off from its corporate parent, and exists today as its own entity, Yamaha Motor Company. Musical instruments are still the parent company's main thing (note Yamaha's three tuning forks logo, illustrating this concept), but they also make everything from semiconductors to stereo equipment. In 1993, its **GTS 1000** won more titles than any other bike in history.

SUZUKI

Slogan: *"The ride you've been waiting for."*

Company founder Michio Suzuki's first business was the Suzuki Loom company, which he launched in 1909 in Hammamatsu, Japan. Suzuki used to bicycle to his favorite fishing spot when not working; after a great deal of exhausting pedaling, he realized that motorbikes were sure to catch on. He made his first motorcycle engine in 1937, and started his motor vehicle company in 1952. You may remember Suzuki autos like the **Sidekick** and the ill-fated **Samurai** (think "sudden involuntary rollover"). Cyclically speaking, Suzuki introduced the three-cylinder two-stroke **750** and the **500 RGA** four-cylinder water-cooled racer to the industry.

Origami

Origami is a traditional Japanese craft by which three-dimensional objects are created by folding square pieces of colored paper. Believed to have originated in China more than a thousand years ago, the practice spread to Japan during the Heian period (794-1185 A.D.), where it developed as a part of Shinto ceremonies in which a special type of "shrine paper" was cut and folded to make *katashiro*, or symbolic representations of deities. At first, only the rich could do origami because paper [👁233]—then made by hand—was very expensive. After the Meiji Era (1868-1912), paper became more widely available, and schools adopted origami as an educational method, particularly in geometry, to teach about relationships between planes and solids. As origami became more popular, the complexity of the objects likewise increased. By the mid-1920s, patterns for more than 150 different types of origami figures had been formalized.

The person credited with introducing origami to the U.S. is Lillian V. Oppenheimer, who in the 1930s took it up to entertain her daughter, stricken with meningitis. In 1958, she began receiving television, radio, and newspaper publicity for her mastery of the craft. Oppenheimer wrote several books on the subject, founded the Origami Center of America, and taught eager students ranging from Boy Scouts to corporate executives. Now there are origami societies in just about every state, and virtually every schoolkid in the nation knows how to make paper balls, boats, and, of course, cranes—handy ways to recycle those dreaded D-minus compositions.

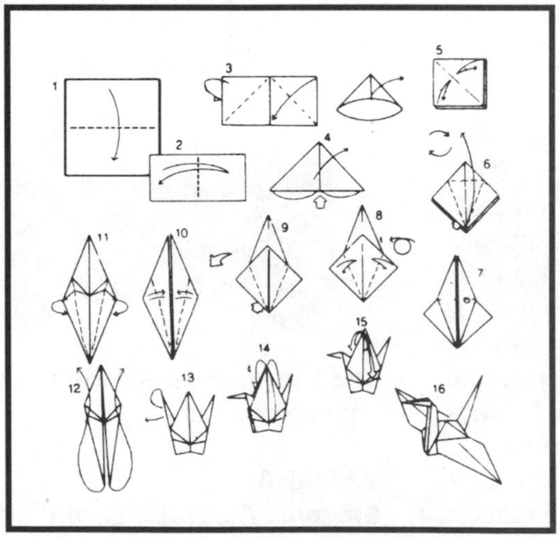

HOW TO FOLD A PAPER CRANE

The most popular origami figure both in Japan and the U.S. is the crane, a traditional symbol of fortune and longevity. A common saying in Japan promises that if you make "a thousand cranes" (*sembazaru*) and hang them together from the ceiling in a chain, you will have a long and fruitful life. Give it a try. What do you have to lose?

—D.G.

Origami Etiquette

In America, they're cute little ornaments, but in Japan, origami has long had ceremonial significance:

- **At weddings, bottles of sake are traditionally adorned with male and female origami butterflies, representing, of course, the happy bride and groom.**
- **When wearing a kimono, an origami billfold called a tato is carried within the folds of the garment.**
- **When giving gifts, it was once traditional for an origami ornament called a noshi to be attached to the present with a long, flat strip of abalone, the presence of which symbolizes a happy occasion. (There was once a Buddhist mandate against the consumption of flesh at times of misfortune.) These days, a strip of yellow paper is used instead of abalone, which makes for somewhat more pleasant (and certainly less pungent) gift-giving seasons.**

Pachinko

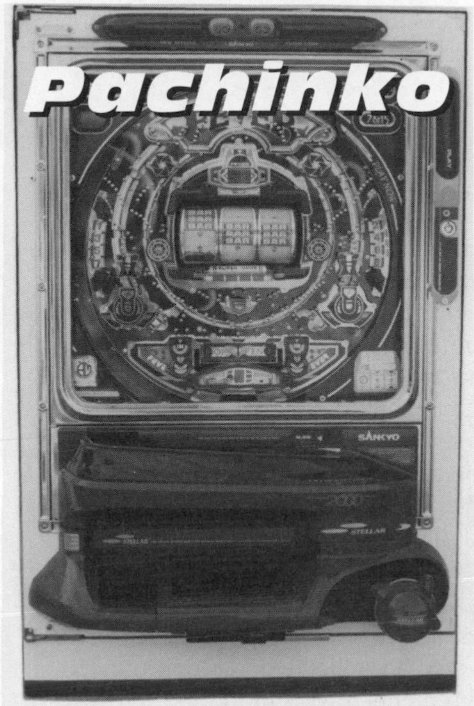

In the game of pachinko, which resembles a vertically oriented pinball machine, small silver balls are shot by players up into the top of a playing field, where they drain down a maze of pins, holes, bumpers, and trap doors. A just-right twist of the wrist at the game's single flipper can send the balls into higher-scoring pockets (though, to be sure, there's a significant amount of randomness involved). Instead of points, players are rewarded for high scores with more silver balls, which can be fed back into the machine, for hours of hypnotic fun. The game, named for the sound the balls make as they tumble down the board, was first played commercially in Nagoya in 1948; it originated as a children's game, reportedly adapted from American pinball.

By 1993, the Japanese pachinko industry was grossing more than $170 billion a year—four times more than the country spends on its military. Pachinko machines have made billionaires out of its manufacturers, in an industry whose size almost equals that of auto manufacturing. Today, more than 30 million Japanese—one fifth of the population—play the game at least once a week at one of the more than 16,000 pachinko parlors in Japan. The parlors are gaudy and flourescent-lit, filled with rows upon rows of machines, each of which buzz, ring, play music, and emit pre-recorded sounds, adding to the excitement; upscale parlor owners, in places like Tokyo's tony Ginza district, spend big bucks to cultivate a classy look, complete with coffee bars, art galleries, crystal chandeliers, and, of course, pretty hostesses.

AMERICA GETS ON THE BALL

When an American serviceman named Roy Giliotti first saw pachinko machines while on leave from service in Vietnam in 1973, he simply thought pachinko was an "awful nice looking game." He played the game at a parlor in Shinjuku and thought to himself, "if the Japanese love 'em. Americans'll love 'em, too." He bought 700 remaindered pachinko machines—the mechanical flip-handle kind—for just $7 each, and sent them home to Sacramento, where, on October 19, 1973, he opened a store called Pachinko Palace. A local newscaster happened to swing by with a television crew, and the next day Giliotti sold 40 of the machines for $29.95 each. By Christmas, they had almost sold out. Giliotti ordered more, but his Japan supplier couldn't deliver them fast enough. Undaunted, Roy sold them right on through the holiday, sending out coupons redeemable for machines upon delivery.

Giliotti's venture was so successful that, by December 1974, he'd opened 18 Pachinko Palace retail outlets all over the country, and was selling his machines wholesale to Sears and Montgomery Ward. Giliotti's business peaked when he sold 400,000 pachinko games in 1977, the same year in which he opened a pachinko parlor on the boardwalk in Atlantic City. (The parlor didn't succeed because "people kept taking the balls"—an unfortunate, but typically American problem.)

In 1980, Giliotti halted his import efforts when the industry shifted to computerized machines, which were out of his price range; a decade later, Giliotti retrieved his crown as the king of American pachinko, importing used computerized machines, reconditioning them, and selling them for $150 to $250 each. Giliotti says he has sold something in the realm of 1.25 million machines in his 20 years in business. Still, the game hasn't caught on here the way it has in Japan. "It's too complex for the simple American mind." theorizes Giliotti. —D.G.

PACHINKO PANIC: A National Obsession

Pachinko is highly addictive. Some pachinko players say the game is relaxing and induces a meditation-like state in which one can ponder life's quandaries. Others believe that pachinko parlors provide a sense of privacy in a society where space is at a premium: the player sits in a crowded pachinko parlor, surrounded yet isolated, a lone individual against a machine. Of course, another obvious draw is the gambling aspect of the game, which has perhaps been emphasized as pachinko machines have gone from mechanical to electronic, adding an element of luck to a previously skill-driven game. Gambling is illegal in Japan, but pachinko provides a way to circumvent the law. Players can legally trade in the balls they win for little prizes—everything from cigarette lighters and toothbrushes to marmalade and Chanel bags. They can choose to keep the merchandise or, as is more often the case, go around the corner to a discreet redemption window, where the prizes can be exchanged for cold hard cash. Where there's money to be won, there are people lining up to win it, and in Japan, there are professional pachinko players, called pachipuro, pachinko magazines, and even pachinko colleges which teach game strategy.

Asian Aphrodisiacs

You are what you eat—sensible nutritional advice, but also a modus operandi the ancient Chinese used in selecting amatory aids. In keeping with the belief that the sexual prowess of certain animals will be bestowed upon the person who consumes a potion concocted from the animal's sexual parts, the dried penises and testicles of animals like tiger, seal, deer, and beaver, have been (and are still) marketed as marital aids throughout Asia, as well as in Asian communities in the U.S. and Europe.

One unfortunate outgrowth of this unbridled lust for lust has been the threat of extinction of certain animals, all for the sake of their prized "heavenly root" (a soup bowl of which can cost up to $400), considered effective but costly treatments for a flagging human sexual drive—even if the tiger's own copulative experiences average only 15 seconds in length. (Female tigers have been unhappy for generations.) Not all aphrodisiacs need consist of the gonads of endangered species. Rhinos, who can go at it it for more than an hour, are prized for their priapic horns, which can go for as much as $18,000 per kilogram on the black market. Conservation groups have directed their efforts at changing the beliefs that fuel the demand. They often cite the studies of experts, who maintain that the effects, if any, of such aphrodisiacs, are merely psychological. (However, since the brain controls the libido, the imagination can be a most powerful aphrodisiac. To stem the tide of extinction, perhaps it might be better to inform would-be consumers that rhino horns are in fact just matted clumps of hair.) Other aphrodisiacs, from China and elsewhere, are made of plants or naturally recycling animal products.

Although in 1989, the FDA declared that over-the-counter preparations professing themselves to have aphrodisiac powers could not be recognized as safe and effective, many products containing the following ingredients have still found their way to America's Asian herbal pharmacies and health food stores. You're likely to find them in health products labeled "rejuvenators" or "energizers." —D.G.

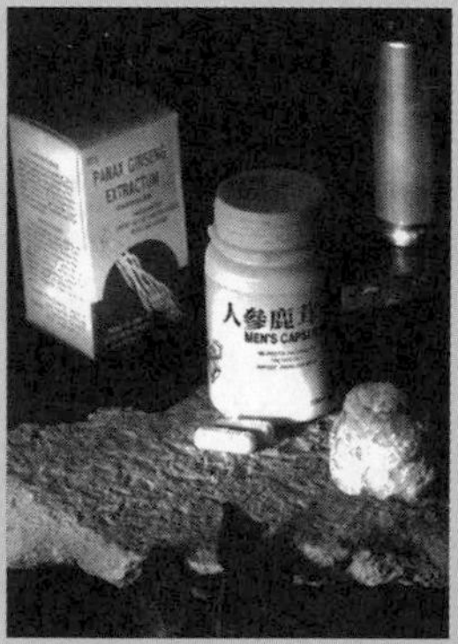

Ashwaganda • the "ginseng of India," Ashwaganda is used as a longevity herb and is known to boost the immune system, eliminate stress, and increase long-term memory.

Bird's Nest Soup • a spicy Chinese soup made from the nests of the rare vulture sea swallow. The sea swallow is found in Malaysian Borneo caves and the most prized nests are collected when they are light in color, consisting of little more than spit secreted by the birds. The darker nests usually contain feathers and are of lesser value. Harvesters collect the nests and clean, dry, and package them for export mainly to China and Hong Kong, where one can fetch up to $2000.

Eucommia • a member of the rubber tree family, Eucommia is all the rage in Japan not only for its sexual tonic effects but also many health and energy related benefits. Thought to be more powerful than ginseng.

Garlic • to the Ainu of Japan, this sacred herb was like ambrosia to the Greeks. The libidinous Ammites of China credit their lasciviousnous to high doses of garlic. Scientists have discovered that the chemical ingredient responsible for garlic's odiferous bouquet is the same as one of the constituents of the "female love juices."

Green oats (*Avena sativa*) • a fairly recent addition to the list of known aphrodisiacs, was discovered by a boy in China who accidentally fed the stuff to carp in his father's pond, which soon doubled in population. Controlled studies were done, including one by the Institute for the Advanced Study of Human Sexuality in San Francisco. Sure enough, they found that an extract of green oats loosens testosterone like cold water loosens gum from hair. A commercial product is available in the U.S. and consists of vitamin C, nettles, and green oats extract. Apparently effective for both men and women, it's not just for breakfast anymore.

Geoducks • the long-necked shellfish called the geoduck are equally valued in China and elsewhere in Asia for their priapic propensities. (Though, granted, anyone with a penis shaped like a geoduck should probably seek medical help.)

Ginseng • the grand herb of Asia [👁248]. Slip a little ginseng root in with tea and it's supposed to make your victim horny as a racehorse. Too much ginseng and you'll be experiencing nervousness, agitation, insomnia, heart palpitations; the perfect symptoms of love. But ginseng is now classified by the FDA as a dietary supplement, instead of the unapproved drug it used to be.

Royal Jelly • a by-product of bees once thought to be Cleopatra's cherished secret to her beauty. Today, it is regarded as valuable energy and longevity food in Asia, as well as a potent sexual tonic.

Schizandra Berries • the prized possession among Chinese empresses for their ability to preserve youth, maintain healthy and robust facial skin, and for their value as a sexual tonic. Known in China to increase the juice flow in female genitalia as well as to make the clitoris more excitable. Men have also found it a means to enhance sexual vitality. They are boiled alone and drunk as a tea, or used in tincture form.

Velvet deer antlers • Elk and deer antlers fall off in the spring and grow back at the end of the summer. When the new antlers are "in velvet" (pre-calcified and up to three feet long) they're cut off (humanely, using a local anesthetic) and processed for use in Asian sex potions. More than 750 ranchers in the United States raise elk, according to the North American Elk Breeders Association, and about $5 million worth of antlers are sold each year, about 65 percent to Asian countries and Asian medicine practitioners in the U.S., and the rest to North American makers of deer antler preparations.

Sumo

tsuki -thrust

oshi -push

yori-grapple

Envision yourself in a sumo match. You are now facing a 400-pound man who's psyching himself up to head-butt you, just before he grabs your crotch to throw you out of a dirt ring. The head-butt gives you a concussion; your crash-landing on the arena floor brings you ringing back to reality. This is sumo, the national sport of Japan, and an activity few Americans experience except as a spectator.

The exact origin of the 2,000-year-old sport is unclear. Legend has it that sumo was practiced as early as 23 BC. The earliest written record appears in the *Kojiki* ("Record of Ancient Matters") of 712 A.D., which depicts two gods in a sumo match to determine control over the island of Japan. In 720 A.D., the *Nihonshoki* ("Chronicles of Japan") mentions a sumo match between two commoners before the Emperor. Sumo matches of that era were staged to insure good harvests, though they had the practical side effect of causing massive contusions and other injuries.

During the peaceful Edo period (1600-1868), however, sumo rules were refined from no-holds-barred combat into today's somewhat (but not much) more gentle entertainment. The *Nihon Sumo Kyokai* (Japan Sumo Association) was formed in 1925, and began keeping official records such as win-loss statistics. However, it's not just *who* wins that matters—it's *how.*

THE RULES OF SUMO

A sumo match is simple: The first person who touches the ground or gets thrown out of the *dohyo* (a 15-foot diameter hard clay circle) loses. There are no groin kicks, hair pulling, biting, punching or eye gouging; however, grabbing an opponent's *mawashi* (belt), slapping, and tripping are allowed. Most of a sumo match centers upon a wrestler trying to get a firm two-handed grip on his opponent's mawashi in order to execute a move. There are over 200 methods that a wrestler can employ to beat his opponent; the Sumo Kyokai lists 70 official "winning techniques," of which 48 are considered classic moves. Prefixes describing these moves include *tsuki* ("thrust"), *oshi* ("push"), and *yori* ("grapple"); a thrust-out, for example, is called *tsuki-dashi.*

THE RITUAL

Just as important as the actual combat are the quasi-religious pre-match rituals, in which the

A TYPICAL DAY AT THE HEYA

4-5 a.m.: The youngest and lowest-ranked rikishi (wrestlers) wake up, ready the dohyo, and begin their exercises.

6: 30-7 a.m.: The Makushita wake up and enter the ring.

8 a.m.: The Juryo wake up and enter the ring, and the Makunouchi follow shortly after.

8 to 11 a.m.: the rikishi perform exercises (shiko, teppo, and matawari) [see next page]; fight in moshiai (practice bouts), in which younger wrestlers learn from senior wrestlers and practice with their peers; engage in butsukari-geiko (collision training), in which juniors charge at seniors to attempt to drive them across the dohyo; more matawari; a final round of shiko.

11 a.m.: Bath time—seniors first, followed by the junior ranks.

NOONTIME: Brunch, the first and largest meal of the day—heaps of chanko nabe (see below), rice, and beer; seniors eat first and juniors get leftovers

AFTERNOON: Juniors perform housekeeping chores.

EVENING: Evenings are free, but rikishi, especially junior ones, are expected in bed early—after all, the next day begins at 4 a.m.

SUMO ISOMETRICS

These are the three traditional sumo exercises, which condition balance, agility, and flexibility, not to mention a pair of powerful thighs.

SHIKO: Stand with your feet wide apart, take a deep breath, and tip your body to the left while raising your right leg sideways as high as possible. Stamp your right leg down hard while exhaling with a hiss. Repeat with left foot. Beginners should repeat this exercise at least 500 times a day.

MATAWARI: Sit in the dirt with your legs spread as close as possible to 180 degrees. Lean your torso forward until the entire front of your upper body is pressed against the ground. If you need assistance, get a senior wrestler to stand on your back. Warning: this exercise may cause intense pain.

TEPPO: Slam your open hands, left, right, left, etc. against this wooden punching bag.

wrestlers clap their hands to rouse the gods, toss salt in the dohyo to purify the ground, and stamp their feet to ward off evil. The opening ritual can last as long as four minutes; the actual sumo match might last just a few seconds. If a match goes longer and the wrestlers become tired, the *gyoji* (referee) can stop the bout for *mizu-iri* (water break). The two phrases one will hear a gyoji yelling are "*hakkeyoi!*" ("keep fighting") and "*nokkotta*" ("still in the ring"). Sportsmanship and decorum are the primary qualities by which the ringside *shimpan* (judges) make their decisions.

THE COMPETITIONS

Basho (tournaments), which last 15 days each, are held six times a year in January (Tokyo), March (Osaka), May (Tokyo), July (Nagoya), September (Tokyo), and November (Fukuoka), with numerous exhibitions and promotional events in between. The winner of a tournament gets the Emperor's Cup (which, like the Stanley Cup, must be returned for the next tournament).

SO YOU WANT TO BE A SUMO WRESTLER

Here's a rundown of what you have to do if you want to join the big boys in the glorious clay ring:

1. Meet the physical requirements. The minimum weight requirement for a sumo wrestler is 180 lbs. Unlike boxing or Greco-Roman wrestling, however, sumo has no weight classes, and it's entirely possible to have a rikishi like Mainoumi, who stands 5'8" and weighs about 210 pounds, go up against a grand champion like Hawaiian-born Akebono, who stands 6'8" and weighs in at around 500 pounds. Contrary to popular opinion, the heaviest wrestlers don't always win. The average top-ranked sumo wrestler weighs about 326 pounds and is about six feet tall. The minimum height requirement is 5'8"; wrestlers who came up short used to stretch themselves, club their heads till they were swollen, or have silicone head implants (removable after passing the one-time height test). The latter was banned, after a 5'3" wrestler named Koji implanted 5" of matter in order to make the height requirement. As for the eggplant shape of the typical rikishi, it's not a sign of beer-swilling sloth: large bellies allow them to maintain the lowest possible center of gravity. Oh—you also have to be male. There is not now, and likely will never be, such a thing as a female sumo wrestler.

This may or may not surprise you.

2. Move to Japan and find a training school that'll accept you. If you aren't in your mid-teens, you probably won't have much of a chance (this isn't a profession for middle-aged crisis victims). The training for sumo is incredibly difficult, and the only place where training is done is in Japan. A sumo school is called a *heya* (stable, literally "room"), and joining one means committing yourself to years of grueling work and humble groveling before more senior wrestlers. Unless you're married, you have to live in the heya throughout your career. Wrestlers of lower rank sleep in a communal room, while professionals earn the right to small private rooms.

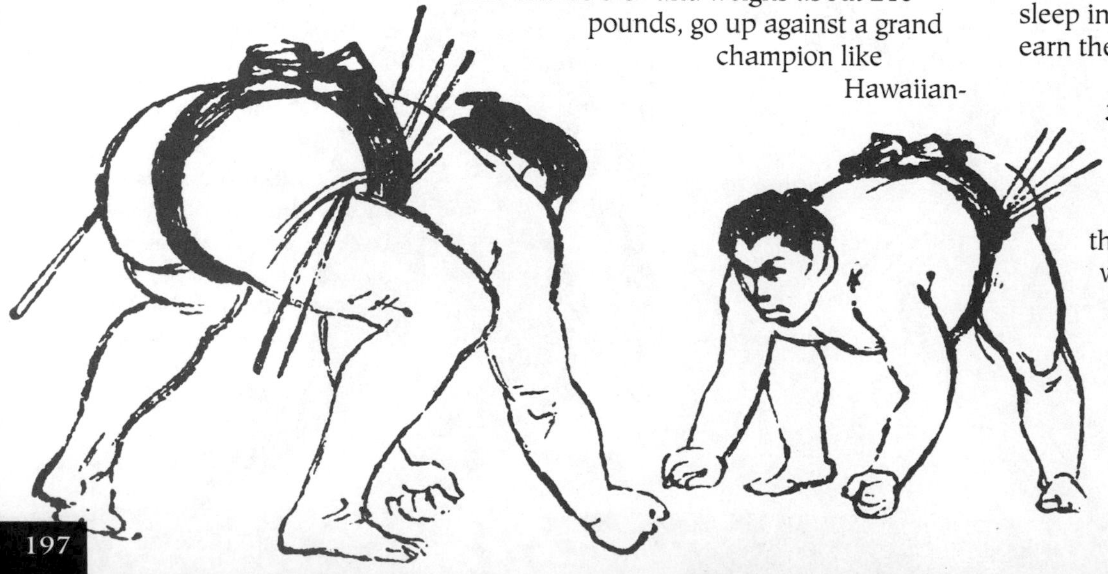

3. Get used to the wardrobe. The thong-like attire of the wrestler is known as the *mawashi*; it's no less revealing than a G-string, and if you're a sumo wrestler, there's a lot to reveal. During tournaments, wrestlers also wear a string apron called a *sagari,* which often falls off during the match. Professionals may also wear an elaborately embroidered apron during opening ceremonies. If your hair is long enough, you can wear it oiled and combed into the *oichomage* ("gingko-leaf") topknot. Only *sekitori* (top-ranking wrestlers) have the right to wear their hair in the oichomage style during tournaments.

3. Start at the bottom, work your way up. At the very bottom echelon of the sumo wrestler pyramid are the *Maezumo* (literally, "before Sumo"), followed by the bottom levels of *Jonokuchi* ("first step"), *Jonidan* ("second step"), and *Sandanme* ("third step"). With one good tournament, a wrestler can rise to gain access to the level of *Makushita* ("outside the curtain"). Getting out of that division, however, takes skill and perseverance. Many wrestlers get stuck at this level their whole careers, before deciding to give up. To get promoted at any level, one needs to have a winning record in a tournament. Wrestlers in these levels have only seven bouts per tournament.

The next two levels are a bit more difficult to break into, as it should be for divisions in which one earns money, the title of sekitori, and the privilege to wear their hair oichomage-style.

4. Go professional. The first sekitori level is *Juryo* (literally "10-*ryo* men," originating from the Tokugawa period when a good wrestler earned 10 ryo for a tournament). This is the level where a wrestler turns professional. You get your own attendant (a peon from one of the lower classes) and you receive a salary, around $7,000 a month.

5. Get really good, and rake it in. The creme de la sumo are the *Makunouchi* ("within the curtain"), the elites of the sport. They make anywhere from about $9,000 to $20,000 a month, plus bonuses, gifts, and fringe benefits like fame akin to pop stardom. Within this division in order of skill are the *Maegashira* ("senior wrestlers"), the *Komusubi* ("almost champions"), the *Sekiwake* ("junior champions"), the *Ozeki* ("champions"), and the very top level, *Yokozuna* ("grand champion"). The top divisions usually have between one and four members. There are no limits to the numbers of Yokozuna, and at times there have been none. The Sumo Kyokai decides who is able to gain access to the Yokozuna level, although the standard is winning two consecutive tournament championships.

6. Think about retirement. Most rishiki retire in their early thirties. Sumo wrestlers get no breaks or vacations, and in the event of sickness or injury, a wrestler's ranking can decline rapidly; rather than ending their careers at the bottom, many wrestlers cut it short while at the top. A retiring wrestler's hair is cut in a hair-cutting ceremony called *dampatsushiki*. Dressed in a formal kimono, the retiring wrestler sits in the dohyo, while friends, fans and relatives step into the ring to take a ceremonial snip at his hair with gold-plated scissors.

7. Now what? The Sumo Kyokai employs retired rikishi as security guards and announcers. Top wrestlers often form their own heya. If nothing else, you can always open a chanko nabe restaurant.

SUMO AMERICANA

Over the years (and over the protests of Japanese sumo purists) Americans have become a strong force in Japan's national sport. Hawaii's Daigoro Takamiyama (née Jesse Kuhaulua) was the first to win the Emperor's Cup in 1972. Since then, there have been several American Yokozunas, including Akebono ("Dawn," neé Chad Rowan). Today, Takamiyama heads the Azumaseki heya where Akebono trains. Perhaps the best known American rikishi, however, is Hawaii-born Konishiki ("Little Brocade," neé Salevaa Atisanoe), who at over 600 pounds is one of the world's heaviest athletes, and one of the top reasons for the sport's growing global popularity. —E.N.

WHAT DO SUMO WRESTLERS EAT?

The answer? Chanko nabe, a high-calorie vegetable and meat stew, along with bowl upon bowl of rice and quarts of beer.

The Recipe

- 1 medium chicken
- 2 onions
- 4 carrots
- 3 green onions
- 1 daikon radish
- 10 shiitake mushrooms
- 1 cabbage
- 2 deep fried tofu chunks
- 1 potato
- 1 block fresh tofu
- 1/2 cup soy sauce
- 1/2 cup sweet cooking sake or 1/2 cup sake with a tablespoon of sugar
- 1/2 teaspoon salt
- 1 or 2 packs udon noodles

DIRECTIONS

1. Slice carrots and onions and add to chicken bones in big pot. Cover with water, put on medium heat; cook for three hours.
2. Chop potato, daikon, boil separately.
3. Add remaining vegetables to pot; add potato and daikon. Then add soy sauce, sake, and salt. Simmer until vegetables are done.
4. Add noodles; cook until noodles are done.

Serves one really big sumo wrestler.

The Electronic Bestiary: An Evolutionary Scale of Video Game Characters

In times of hoary antiquity, there were raster graphics—images made of tiny line segments—from which Space Invaders and Pong were born, and they were good. And then there were vector graphics, unbroken lines, which begat Asteroids, Star Castle, and Tempest, and the arcades rang with cheers and the ka-chunk of quarters.

Then, in 1972, the home console revolution arrived, when Magnavox brought us Odyssey, with plastic overlays that could be taped over the television screen. The Atari 2600 ruled the home video market gloriously from 1976 to 1982, facing intermittent competition from Coleco Vision and Mattel Intellivision, but all were destroyed in the Great Video Game Burnout of 1983.

In Japan, Cassette Vision, Game Personal Computer M5, Pyuta, and MSX fell before the might of Nintendo. In America, Nintendo, utilizing bizarre foreign tactics that befuddled American businessmen (so it has been said), rose from the ashes of Atari to seize 80 percent of the home gaming market. The 8-bit NES possessed 2,000 bytes of RAM to Atari's 256 bytes and the graphic resolution was good enough to create cute

NINTENDO ERA

(1981-1989)

Pong
(Pongo monopaddleus)

Atari, not a Japanese company as many think, emerges from the primordial silicon ooze of Sunnyvale, California, ca. 1972, with **Pong**—and the coin-op video game on a converted television screen and its complete instructions read: "INSERT COIN. AVOID MISSING BALL FOR HIGH SCORE." So what made a '70s Californian company name themselves after a term from the Japanese board game go (*atari* meaning "prepare to be attacked") and model their logo after Mount Fuji? Must have been those zen vibes coming across the ocean, man.

Space Invaders
(*Quarterdevourius erectus*)

The video game evolves from Pong's invertebrate characteristics to the legs, claws, unblinking insectoid eyes, predatory attitude, and mass breeding of **Space Invaders.** Developed by the Japanese company Taito, they descend upon Yankee shores (that is, arcades and bars) in 1978 and become the first in a venerable line of "slide-and-shoot" games (Galaga, Galaxian, and Centipede were to follow in this grand tradition), while generating the first video game-induced mass hysteria in recorded history, not to mention a perfect metaphor for the cheaper, smaller, and less gas-guzzling Japanese products then swooping in, Space Invaders–style, on the U.S. marketplace.

Pac-Man
(*Pakupaku taberus*)

Based on a Japanese folk character with an insatiable appetite (*paku-paku taberu* meaning "to eat voraciously" in Japanese), **Pac-Man,** developed by the Japanese game manufacturer Namco, emerges with a streamlined, but colorful, early 1980s look—it's a yellow ball with a mouth. Early skeptics, put off by the maze-game format (no shooting, blowing up stuff) and the simple controls (just one joystick), are turned around by the game's highly addictive complexities, while it becomes one of the first video games with cross-over appeal to the female population. "Pac-Man Fever" ensues, with Ms. Pac Man, Pac Man, Jr., a top 40 radio song, and a plethora of toy spin-offs, while the Namco engineer who came up with the game was awarded a whopping $3,500 for his efforts. He quits the video game industry.

Donkey Kong
(*Enterus mario*)

In a desperation move, an apprentice artist with no video game design experience is assigned to create a game for the Kyoto-based company's failing American branch. Shigeru Miyamoto, the future one-man Lennon-McCartney of video games (the Mario Bros. series, Legend of Zelda and sequels), comes up with **Donkey Kong,** the first "platform" game (where a character moves up a screen, usually hopping over obstacles). "Kong" refers to the game's ape villain (as in "King") and "Donkey" is from Miyamoto's Japanese-English dictionary's crappy definition for "goofy." Despite being occasionally mispronounced as "Honkey Dong," the game is a smash hit.

and lovable characters, such as Mario, to capture children's hearts. But that, too, was just the beginning.

In the arcades, as the Golden Age of Defender and Centipede passed, Street Fighter II emerged. It became an age of martial arts combat games and ultra-realistic violence, and America's own Mortal Kombat mastered the art of graphic slaughter.

In 1989, Sega introduced the 16-bit home system, Genesis. The *Sengoku Jidai*, the Period of Warring States, had begun. Taking half of Nintendo's market share, Sega battled Nintendo for the bloated consumer soul of America. And then Sony entered the fray with a machine that blasted both rivals out of the water...until, like Godzilla, Nintendo rose from the depths again, with its awesome Nintendo 64 supersystem. Today, the video game world is in a time of crisis, as it looks forward to the next generation of technological evolution. Will the heroes of the new video age be CD-ROM, VR, or RISC? Will the future resemble Myst or Doom, or another creature altogether? Time will tell. –A.L.

PERIOD OF WARRING CORPORATIONS

(1989-PRESENT)

Super Mario Bros.

(*Nintendo monopolius*)

In 1983, the NES (Nintendo Entertainment System) revitalizes the home video machine market on the strength of Miyamoto's **Super Mario Bros**. The game's unfolding passageways are, he's said, based on the sliding *shoji* screens, maze-like corridors, and hidden rooms of Miyamoto's Sonebe (a town in the Kyoto countryside) childhood. "Mario," who debuted in Donkey Kong, was named after Nintendo's American branch's landlord, Mario Segali. In a 1990 survey, it is revealed that Mario is recognized by more American children than Mickey Mouse.

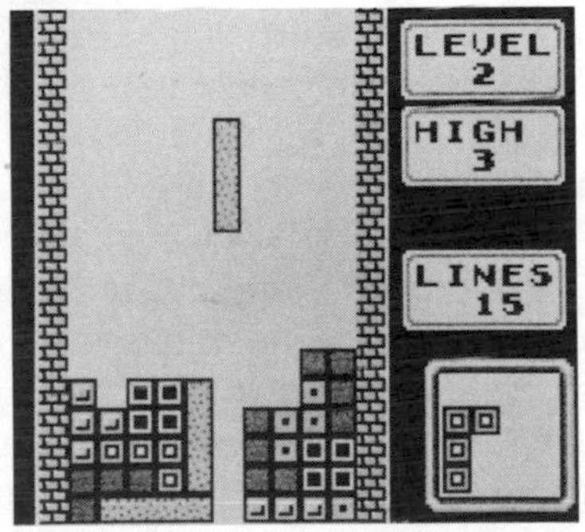

Tetris

(*Rectanguli addictyx*)

Tetris, the last and most lasting artifact of Cold War technology, evolves from the theoretical wanderings of Soviet mathematician Alexey Pajitnov, who, grasping some fundamental relationship between the human brain and geometric shapes, creates the most addictive video game ever. Meanwhile, Nintendo provides the perfect vehicle for Tetris via its innovative Game Boy, an ultra-portable game player designed by the R&D division headed by stalwart engineer Gunpei Yokoi, who had designed an early mini-game player the size of a pocket calculator, Game & Watch, that was also phenomenally popular for a while.

After a legal wrangle with several international companies, Nintendo wrests away home video rights and spreads the Tetris virus worldwide.

Sonic the Hedgehog

(*Marketsharus usurpex*)

Like his post-national parent company—Sega (SErvice GAmes), an American company turned Japanese turned transpacific ("NEC meets MTV," says *Business Week*)—**Sonic** is a postmodern and carnivorous beast, taking a bite out of Mario's dominance via hipness and blitzkrieg marketing.

Though the gameplay is similar to the platform format dominated by Mario, compared to the poky plumber, Sonic is fast-paced and furious. And impatient; he taps his foot when you don't do anything. Kidz luv him.

Streetfighter II

(*Manoymano combatus*)

East vs. West, or anybody vs. everybody else, courtesy of one-on-one kung-fu and the Japanese game maker Capcom, SFII offers warriors (woman and otherwise) from China, Japan, India, Thailand, Brazil, the U.S.S.R., the U.S., and Spain. The game's complex fighting maneuvers and special moves tap into adolescent testosterone reserves worldwide.

Learning maneuvers, by poring over "secret" books and practice, becomes a kind of martial art in and of itself. Its popularity unleashes a glut of similar games, including an American response, *Mortal Kombat*, which offers a pseudo-Orientalist storyline and sublimely gory *coup de grace* moves. Fighting games continue to be the driving force behind game-platform popularity, and the last few years have seen them become faster, more complex, more realistic (or surreal), and even 3-D—with entries like Sega's Virtua Fighter and Sony's home-gaming Battle Arena Toshinden serving as the literal cutting edge.

Nintendo vs. Sega: The Coke & Pepsi of Video Games

For years, Nintendo was It. When Sega introduced its 16-bit Genesis system in 1989, Nintendo not only possessed a virtual stranglehold on the American home video game market, but was set upon taking over the toy industry at large. The older company, which had long dominated the Japanese market, had achieved American superiority through a combination of well-supported research and development that ran contrary to marketing trends, a lean management structure that answered directly to the parent company headed by president and patriarch Hiroshi Yamauchi, and a ruthless, no-prisoners style of doing business that some called "Japanese" and some called "illegal."

In video game lore, Nintendo was the "old school" while Sega was the "new school," philosophies exemplified by the geography of their headquarters, Nintendo's in the ancient Heian capital of Kyoto, Sega's in cosmopolitan Tokyo. Nintendo worked methodically, bucking trends, and following the instincts of Yamauchi, who had the final word on everything. Many of Nintendo's biggest breakthroughs came about when they deliberately steered against American conventional wisdom; in 1981 Nintendo released the eccentric arcade game *Donkey Kong*, designed by a visual artist with no game design experience, and in 1983, they unveiled the NES (Nintendo Entertainment System) in a market that had just witnessed the burnout of Atari and was supposedly sick of video games. Much of this confidence came from the fact that Nintendo's Famicom, the Japanese equivalent of the NES, dominated the Japanese market and from Yamauchi's sense that what could work in Japan could also work in the US.

When 16-bit technology came along, Nintendo withheld their 16-bit machine, apparently because it felt that its older machine was doing so well, and waited. "We didn't really regard Sega as a competitor," Yamauchi said in 1991. "We felt above them," Howard Lincoln, chairman of Nintendo of America, admitted later. "There was some arrogance." The mistake is now legendary. Sega, from its American subsidiary headquarters in Redwood City, California, stormed the American market with a brilliant, blitzkrieg marketing campaign for its 16-bit machine that, more than anything, branded Nintendo as a children's toy and elevated the sleek, black-cased Genesis to the Next Level of cool. Where Nintendo had cute Mario, Sega had bristly, savvy Sonic the Hedgehog.

Sega, like Pepsi, was hailed as the new generation. While Nintendo was bogged down by its centralized management structure, Sega of America's CEO Thomas Kalinske worked with relative autonomy from Tokyo headquarters and president Hayao Nakayama. While Nintendo kept development in-house and worked cautiously with outside developers, Sega brought a fast-paced, wheel-and-deal, "American" style of business that allowed it to keep up with the latest technology.

But the game wasn't over. When Sega reached a peak 64 percent market share in America's 16-bit market in 1994, after years of Nintendo dominance, Nintendo struck back. The first move was Yamauchi's demotion of Nintendo of America's longtime chairman, Minoru Arakawa, also Yamauchi's son-in-law, for not being aggressive enough. Under Howard Lincoln, NOA won back market share in a highly publicized struggle. With a good deal of moral posturing, Nintendo brought Sega's admittedly sleazy game *Night Trap* before congressional hearings and blasted a Sega commercial showing an apparently mentally handicapped man playing a Nintendo game. Sega was forced to pull both.

In the summer of 1995, both companies were again thrown into a period of crucial transition as the *next* "Next Generation" of game machines was introduced—high-powered "64-bit" platforms. Sega released Saturn, a CD-ROM system showcasing its hit fighting game Virtua Fighter. Consumer electronics giant Sony entered the fray with its unexpectedly popular CD-ROM Playstation. Finally, a year later, Nintendo made its move—releasing the Ultra 64, a machine so powerful that it was a smash hit, even with just a handful of games to its name. Who'll win out? The future will tell—and the future is closer than you think. –A.L.

Yoga

With Spandex-clad urbanites crowding into yoga classes at pricey health clubs throughout the West, it's easy to forget that yoga is a 3,000-year-old philosophy with roots in India. Modern-day enthusiasts do yoga in the hopes of attaining slim, flexible loins; Patanjali, the guru [228] who first consolidated the Yoga *sutras* ("scriptures"), had something a bit less sexy in mind: His goal was to integrate mind and body in order to achieve a higher truth. It wasn't until 1893 that Swami Vivekananda introduced yoga to the United States, at a religious convention in Chicago. It didn't catch on with the turn-of-the-century populace, but since then, yoga has enjoyed two popular Western "rebirths": once in the 1960s among hippie types who favored its meditative aspects; another, in the late 1980s and 1990s, as a result of Western society's resurgent interest in physical health, not to mention New Age therapies. While critics bemoan the distortion of yoga into a physical exercise taught in the same venues (and with the same degree of seriousness) as aerobics and step classes, others say that even casual participation, with limited meditation and philosophical teaching, can improve one's well-being. It's difficult to estimate just how many Americans practice yoga, but the estimates run in the millions.

According to the *Encyclopedic Dictionary of Yoga*, yoga is not simply Sanskrit for "union." It's a means to achieve "centering"—the center being the transcendental Being, whether one calls that God or a "Higher Self." Centering is by no means an easy task. According to Patanjali, yoga is an eight-step process, only one of which involves twisting one's limbs this way and that. The following is an introductory guide to getting to the center, based on Patanjali's teachings.

THE EIGHTFOLD PATH TO YOGA

Before doing anything, recognize that there are many schools of yoga, each of which involve different disciplines. These include hatha yoga, a popular Western form that emphasizes physical postures; raja yoga, which stresses mental discipline; tantra yoga, which involves manipulating sexual drive; and mantra yoga, which focuses on meditation. All of these are divergent paths to the same goal, and rest on the same original principles. Choose your school carefully, and learn the specific requirements of each. Meanwhile, follow the following precepts:

1. Never lie, steal or be greedy. Never harm or wish harm on anyone.
2. Keep your body clean and your spirit pure. Be content. Give yourself to God/the Supreme Being/your Higher Self.
3. Meditate in special positions that involve both your mind and body. (This is where your neighborhood Health and Racquet Club's notion of yoga comes in.)
4. Turn your attention inward.
5. Remove all distractions.
6. Focus on an object (a spiritual one, not the TV). This can be a concept, nothingness, or a mantra, repeated again and again.
7. Meditate on it.
8. At this point, if you've done the previous steps correctly, you will have achieved *samahdi*—a oneness with your object of meditation, as well as union with *brahman* ("salvation"). Consider yourself centered—temporarily, of course; yoga isn't a project, but a process, that must be continued throughout one's earthly existence.

If you have completed the above program, but don't know whether you've achieved samahdi or not, you probably haven't. Don't fret. Yoga requires practice. Take it slow. No doubt, that's how famous yoga enthusiasts like wrestler Chris Campbell, Kareem Abdul Jabar, and the Beatles got started. "Even beginners who practice yoga once a day, earnestly, will feel a difference in a week," says Alice Christensen, founder of the American Yoga Association. Yes, you'll stretch your limbs. But you'll also expand your mind. —J.C.

top: camel pose, bottom: tiger posture

IDEAS AND PHILOSOPHY

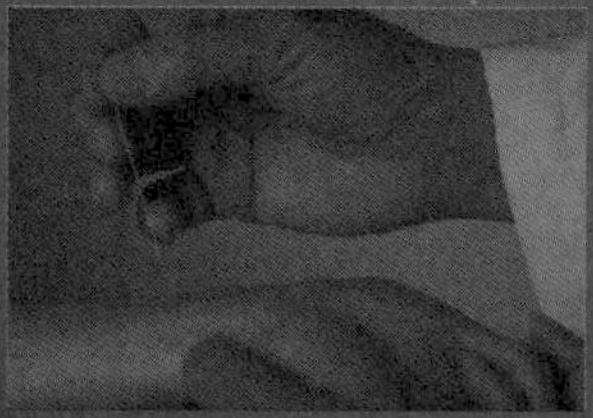

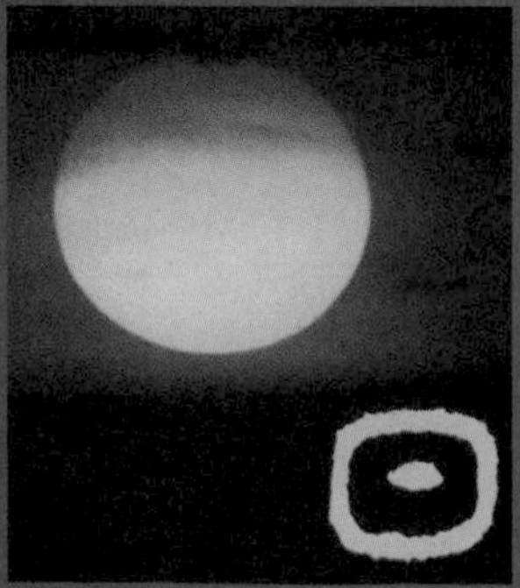

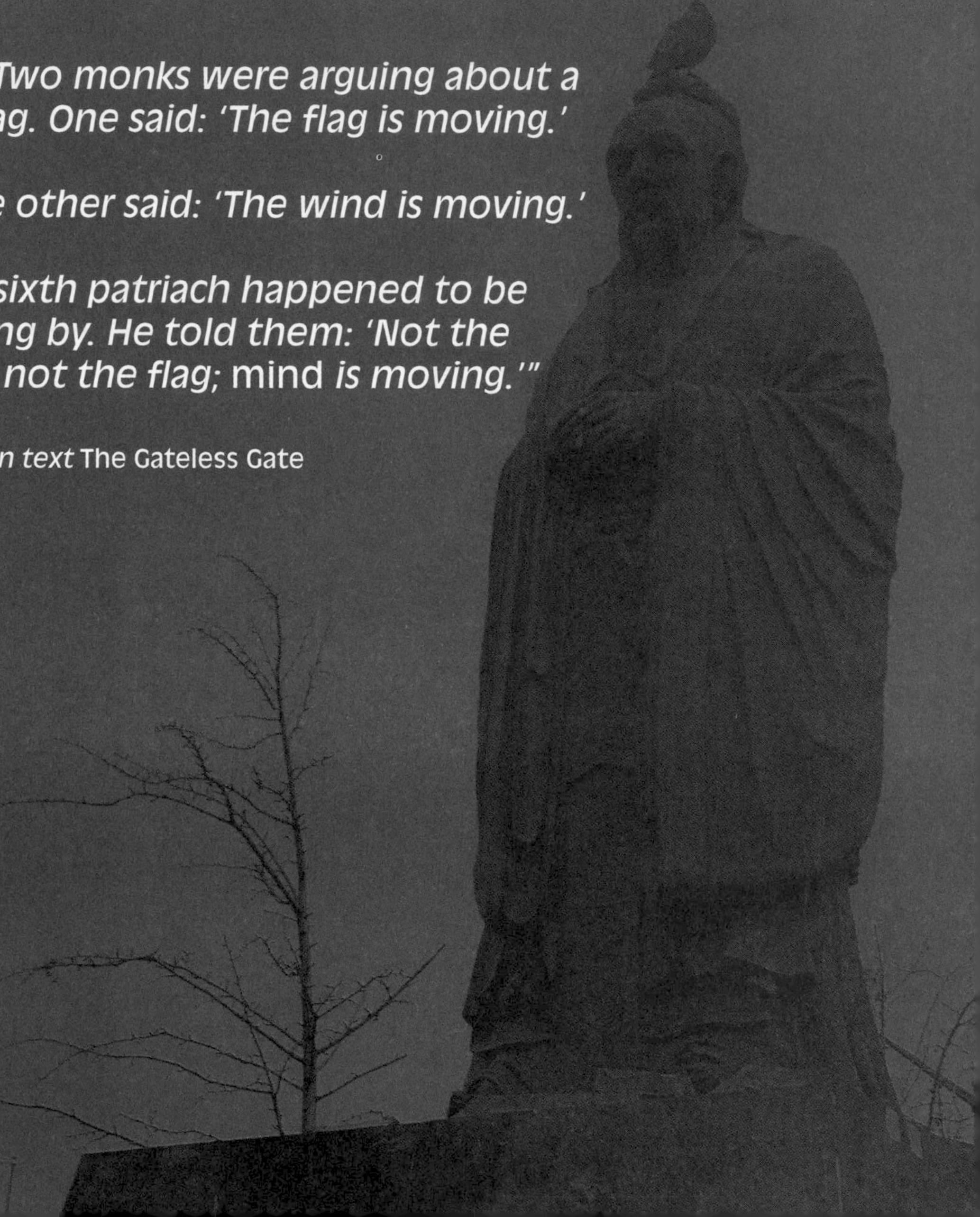

"Two monks were arguing about a flag. One said: 'The flag is moving.'

The other said: 'The wind is moving.'

The sixth patriach happened to be passing by. He told them: 'Not the wind, not the flag; mind is moving.'"

—From zen text The Gateless Gate

Abacus

It's compact. It's powerful. And it can calculate digits into the trillions at lightning speed. We're not talking about the latest high-tech digital assistant, but rather one of the simplest and most elegant mathematical tools ever invented, the *xuanban*, known in the West by the name of abacus. While the word "abacus" is from the Greek word *abax*, meaning "calculating table," the abacus itself was invented in China sometime during the Western Zhou dynasty (11th to 8th century B.C.). It was then introduced to Japan in the 16th century, where it was slightly modified and called the *soroban*, and then brought by the Arabs to the West during the Middle Ages.

Sadly, except for about 60 million die-hard accountants, bookkeepers, and clerks, this ancient calculation instrument has fallen out of general use in its country of origin. In Japan, however, the flicking of the beads is still routinely taught to children at the age of six, and abacus use is also widely taught in Singapore, South Korea, and in the "little Chinas" of Hong Kong and Taiwan.

Not so in the U.S., where the abacus has always been viewed as something of a children's toy. In 1965, however, a Japanese soroban expert named Koji Suzuki moved to the U.S., and ultimately taught the abacus to students at more than 300 public schools. Suzuki returned to Tokyo, but a sprinkling of American teachers picked up on the benefits of abacus training, and a number of other educational groups—including the U.S. International Abacus and Mental Mathematics Development Association, which offers community instruction in the skill in Southern California—became staunch advocates of its use. In 1993, a *New York Times* editorial even suggested that studies reporting better math skills among Japanese and Taiwanese were a result of the fact that Asian students are abacus-trained. Indeed, in 1995, Malaysian education officials mandated abacus training for nine-year-olds after finding that ethnic Chinese in Malaysia, who are regularly taught the abacus at home, consistently did better at math than their native Malaysian counterparts.

The main benefit of using the abacus is that it develops a balance between the two hemispheres of the brain, which researchers have found to be an ideal state for learning and memory retention. Japanese experts have found that abacus users process mathematical concepts on the right side of the brain, which is responsible for decision-making and creativity, rather than the left, where language, math, and logical problems are normally processed. Teachers of young abacus students in Asia say that learning the "mental abacus" (calculating by picturing the abacus in the head instead of moving beads with the fingers) simply "calms children," which automatically makes them more receptive to learning. Critics, on the other hand, maintain that the abacus admirably performs basic arithmetic functions, but it doesn't train users in underlying mathematical concepts.

Still, an expert abacus user can add and subtract up to 600 numerals per minute, which is about six times faster than a calculator. Why? In using a calculator, one has to punch more buttons. For example, to represent 1,000,000, one has to press seven buttons; with an abacus, one simply moves a single bead. For multiplication, division, and deriving square and cube roots, calculators are still substantially faster. (But then again, it's amazing that the abacus can be used to calculate square roots at all.) —D.G.

USING THE ABACUS—FOR FUN AND PROFIT

Learning the abacus is often likened to learning to type or play the piano. At first, one must think carefully where to put your fingers; with practice, however, the process becomes second nature. All abacuses have 23 or 27 columns of beads, but the Chinese xuanban and the Japanese soroban differ in that the former has two rows of beads above the crossbar and five below, while the latter has one row of beads above the crossbar and four below. The principle behind both forms of abacus is the same, and quite simple. Each bead above the crossbar represents five units of that digit, while each beat below the bar represents one unit. Depending on what column the bead is in, the unit in question can range from ones to trillions. Any bead pushed up against the crossbar is counted into the total, while any bead pushed away from the bar is subtracted or ignored; thus, a xuanban with three bottom beads pushed up against the crossbar in the "ones" place and one top bead pushed down against the crossbar in the "tens" place (with all other beads in all other columns resting away from the crossbar) displays a total of eight. It's just that simple.

The Ancient Asian Arts of Management

In the early '80s, the seeming triumph of Corporate Japan on the field of market warfare led to a desperate search by Western CEOs for a means to learn Asian management techniques—before it was too late. In the course of adopting innovations like quality circles and just-in-time inventory **[👁325]**, they also stumbled upon the writings of Chinese and Japanese military philosophers, which were advanced by winking Asian corporate chieftains as the "ancient oriental secrets" of success in business. While Sun Tzu and Musashi probably do offer useful insights for the would-be general of industry, the absurd popularity of their texts as management handbooks led to the publishing of more dubious (and less authentic) works, such as *Zen and the Art of Trading (Secrets of a Samurai Trader)* and *The Management Techniques of Attila the Hun*. Warning to wannabe corporate conquistadores: While a hostile takeover may or may not be approved by the Securities Exchange Commission, sacking, looting, and raping your competition is sure to be frowned upon by regulators. —D.C., J.Y.

A SAMPLING OF ASIAN MANAGEMENT GUIDES

THE ART OF WAR

An inspiration to leaders ranging from Napoleon to Mao Zedong, *The Art of War* has made the move from the battlefield to the boardroom more smoothly than any other work; it's now considered required reading for executives and politicians.

AUTHOR: A contemporary of Confucius, Buddha, and Alexander the Great, Sun Tzu wrote *The Art of War* over 2,000 years ago, during China's Warring States period. Little is known about him, except that he was born in the state of Qi (now Shandong Province). Around 500 B.C., he presented his *Principles and Tactics of Warfare* to King Helu of Wu, who asked him to demonstrate his ideas using an impromptu brigade of concubines. Dividing the women into two troops, Sun Tzu ordered them to perform a simple drill, at which the women broke into laughter. Sun Tzu took the blame, since he had not explained himself clearly. After making sure that the women understood his directions, he gave the order again. Again, the women giggled. This second insubordination was clearly the fault of the troops; so, to set an example, Sun Tzu had the troop leaders beheaded. This time, when he gave the order, the troops obeyed. The king was rather miffed, since the two beheaded women had been his favorites. Nevertheless, Sun Tzu had made an important point about the need for organization and discipline, and the king subsequently employed him as his general.

WHAT IT SAYS: Sun Tzu's tract offers surprisingly modern advice on leadership, strategic planning, business alliances, outsourcing, and the importance of market research. Best of all, it's only 13 brief dialogues long—perfect for the busy modern executive.

THE BOOK OF FIVE RINGS

Unlike Sun Tzu, who was best known for tactics involving large numbers of combatants, Miyamoto Musashi's *The Book of Five Rings* begins at the basic level of competition: one on one. The book sold hundreds of thousands of copies in its first printing, and continues to be snapped up today by eager scholars of the samurai-business tradition.

AUTHOR: The legendary samurai Musashi was Japan's greatest master of the blade. His exploits have been documented in theater and on film **[👁67]**, but his greatest contribution to contemporary society may be the book he wrote in 1645, after retiring from the martial world. In it, he distills the strategies he learned from killing more than 60 foes in single combat—apt training for success in the modern business world.

WHAT IT SAYS: *The Book of Five Rings* is divided into five sections, each themed after an element of the cosmos as defined in Japanese tradition: Earth, Water, Fire, Wind, and Void. In the Earth section, Musashi lays the groundworks for his teachings, placing them in context within Buddhist spiritual tradition. In the Water section, he discusses strategy, emphasizing knowledge of opponent's weaknesses and removal of "perceptual distortions"; the Fire section discusses combat, emphasizing flexibility and the willingness to risk total loss for victory; the Wind section contrasts Musashi's strategies with other schools of combat; and the Void section discusses the concept of nothingness, while imparting the lesson that training should be a process continued throughout one's life.

THICK FACE, BLACK HEART

Unlike the books above, Thick Face is not an ancient text translated from the work of a long-dead warrior, but rather a book written by business consultant Ching-Ning Chu as an adaptation of a text, *Thick Black Theory,* by 20th-century Chinese author Lee Zhongwu. Lee was a disgruntled politician living in tumultuous times; in 1911, Sun Yat-Sen led the successful overthrow of the Qing dynasty, creating the Chinese Republic. His theories were similarly Machiavellian, advocating deceit and lack of mercy as fundamental business practices. Rewritten and expanded by Chu in 1992, the book became a surprise bestseller in both the West, where it was subtitled "The Secret to Asian Success," and in Asia, where it was retitled "American Thick Black Theory"—an ironic example of the theory at work.

AUTHOR: Born of Manchurian parents who fled China to Taiwan during the Communist Revolution in 1949, the only two books she took with her in the escape were Sun Tzu's *The Art of War* and *Thick Black Theory,* Lee's obscure work of political strategy. At the age of 22, Chu left Taiwan with her husband, an American G.I., and began a new life in the United States—first working in real estate, and then eventually as a consultant to multinational companies around the world, including Eastman Kodak and Ritz-Carlton Hotels.

WHAT IT SAYS: The book reveals a hundred "warrior principles" for success, drawing upon the fundamental notions that one must be "thick" of face—that is to say, one must create a shield protecting inner thoughts or emotions from being seen or touched by the outside world—and "black" of heart, which says that one must be utterly ruthless and ready to take any action necessary for victory (frighteningly, Chu's examples of successful practitioners of these principles include, among others, Adolf Hitler). Business "virtues" touted by Chu include inconsistency, anger, procrastination, negativity, hatred, lying, and greed.

An Asian Calendar of Holidays and Festivals

If Christmas, Easter, and Thanksgiving aren't enough to satisfy your holiday jones, consider the following set of apt partying excuses, drawn from the traditions and cultures of Asia. After all, Asian countries have long benefited from the adoption of the Western holidays, with Christmas and New Year's showing up on Chinese and Japanese calendars right next to the Lunar New Year and O-Bon. So get on the cross-cultural bandwagon, and reap a bountiful harvest in vacation days. Of course, doing so is easier said than done: Many of the following holidays are based on lunar calendars (as opposed to the Western standard Gregorian solar calendar), and there's no easy way of converting between the two types of timekeeping—nor do all lunar calendars necessarily agree with one another. Still, if you bone up, you could be partying down—365 days a year. —D.G., J.Y.

Month	Date	Holiday	Origin and meaning	How is it celebrated in the original country?
January	the first three days, and sometimes the entire first week	**Shogatsu** (celebrated in Japan)	*Shogatsu* simply means January, but this New Year's celebration is one of Japan's most important holidays. Businesses close for one or two weeks, and distant family members gather for a big meal on. December 31, New Year's Eve, or **Omisoka**.	In preparation for Shogatsu, houses are cleaned, tatami mats are replaced, shoji screens are repapered, and boughs of pine are set up at doorways and entrances. On Omisoka, a huge, festive meal is prepared for the extended family, with sake and rice cakes; at midnight, all fall quiet to listen for the ritual 108 strikes of the temple bell (once to remove each of the 108 worldly desires, according to Buddhist tradition), while eating *toshikoshi*, or "year-crossing," soba noodles. They then dress in their best traditional finery **[👁299]** and together visit the Shinto shrine, where they receive fortunes telling them what to expect in the year to come.
January or February	the first full moon of the first month of the lunar calendar, which can be anytime between January 21 and February 21	**Lunar New Year** (celebrated in China and throughout Southeast Asia. In Vietnam, Lunar New Year is called **Tet**, as students of recent military history may remember.)	The beginning of the year under the lunar calendar (see above for explanations on how the lunar and solar calendars differ), this is a traditional time of renewal and celebration in which gods and ancestors are appeased, evil spirits driven away, and rites to ensure good fortune in the year to come are performed.	In **China**, in the days prior to the new year in China, families honor ancestors, clean house, make holiday food, and send millions of greeting cards. The lucky color red is put up throughout the home in the form of lanterns and *duilian* (strips of paper featuring inked wishes for health, long life, and prosperity). On Lunar New Year's Eve, families feast together, appease the Kitchen God with sweet offerings (so that his report on the family to the Jade Emperor in Heaven will be similarly sweet), and, at midnight, celebrate the coming of the new year with fireworks, lion dances, and other ceremonies. The doors of the house are closed tightly before the family goes to sleep, and opened again by the head of the household at dawn in a rite called "Opening the Gate of Good Fortune." On New Year's Day, families visit each other to exchange gifts, and kids get *li xi* (*lay see* in Cantonese)—red envelopes containing "lucky" money. In **Vietnam**, Tet celebrations take place over the course of three days, beginning two days before New Year's Day. As Tet approaches, flower stands are set up everywhere to meet the demand for peach blossoms, which stand for good fortune and abundance. On the day before Tet, *Ta Nien* or "The New Year of the Dead" is held, and families visit and clean the tombs of their ancestors, offering food and incense. Throughout all three days of the festival, firecrackers are exploded to ward off evil spirits.

Month	Date	Holiday	Origin and meaning	How is it celebrated in the original country?
February	3	**Setsubun**; celebrated in Japan	This was the first day of the New Year in Japan's ancient calendar; it's also the official first day of spring in Japan. Like other New Year's ceremonies, Setsubun is a day of cleaning, preparation, and purification. 	While the festivities of Shogatsu are more elaborate and widespread, the old Japanese New Year's Day of Setsubun has a separate and distinctive ritual of its own, known as *mame-maki* (literally, "bean-scattering"). On the evening of Setsubun, roasted soybeans are tossed into the nooks and corners of homes, buildings, and temples in order to drive out evil spirits; while the beans are being cast in all directions, the throwers shout *Oni wa soto, fuku wa uchi!* ("Devils out, good luck in!"). The beans also make a tasty snack; there are those who believe that they can achieve good health through the rest of the year by eating as many beans on Setsubun as their age in years.
February or March	a date two weeks before the second full moon in the lunar calendar	**Holi**; celebrated in Northern India 	A spring festival celebrating the vernal equinox, and promoting fertility in the half-grown harvest.	The festival of Holi takes its name from the term for half-ripened corn, *holika,* which is also the name of a legendary winter demon that consumed children; Holi commemorates both the well-being of the crops and the destruction of the demon.
March or April	dependent on the actual blossoming of the cherry trees	**Sakura Matsuri** (the "**Cherry Blossom Festival**"); celebrated in Japan 	The Japanese festival is a celebration of springtime and contemplation; the American festival commemorates the planting on March 27, 1912, of Japanese cherry trees at the Tidal Basin in Washington, D.C. The trees, actually the second such gift from Tokyo (the original 1909 gift of 3,000 trees was diseased and had to be destroyed), were paid for by chemist Jokichi Takamine, who had heard of then–First Lady Helen Taft's fondness for cherry trees.	*Sakura matsuri* take place across Japan during the flowering of the cherry blossoms, and generally feature parades and historical reenactments in traditional dress, as well as lots of *hanami*, or flower-viewing, which has been a traditional spring pasttime in Japan since the 8th century. TV and radio stations broadcast optimal times for cherry blossom viewing, just like ski reports, and thousands of people make excursions to orchards and groves, where they sit beneath the blossoms, drink sake, quote poetry, and contemplate life's *mujyo* ("transiency"). In the U.S., the Cherry Blossom Festival has been celebrated in Washington, D.C., annually since 1935 (except during World War II). At the Washington festival, paper lanterns are lit and a National Cherry Blossom Festival Queen is crowned; other celebratory festivities include a parade, a race, and a black-tie gala. Other cities with cherry blossom trees also celebrate springtime Cherry Blossom festivals, most featuring traditional Japanese arts and crafts.
March or April	Good Friday, between March 20 and April 23	**Penitencia**; celebrated in Pampanga, north of Manila, and a few other provinces of the Philippines	In 1962, the local residents of Pampanga province decided to highlight their annual Good Friday plays (*cenaculo*) by staging a real-life crucifixion; the Penitencia tradition of flagellation has been practiced since the era of Spanish colonialization.	On Penitencia, a dozen or so intensely devout Filipino Catholics have themselves crucified, complete with nails and crown of thorns, for several minutes (the record is 20) in atonement for sins or in the hope of a miracle; meanwhile, several hundred more "flagellants" walk the streets beating their backs bloody with wooden sticks and broken glass tied to ropes. The Catholic Church frowns on the practice, but tolerates the now-famous spectacle. Health risks have been minimized; the crucifixion nails are sterilized, and medical authorities say that the flagellation only produces gradual, blister-like third degree burns that heal without scarring in a matter of days. In 1994, the first non-Filipino, a Belgian woman named Godelieve Rombaut, had herself nailed to a cross in Pampanga. The event has become an international spectacle in recent years, with tens of thousands of American, European, Japanese, and local tourists thronging to witness the event.

Month	Date	Holiday	Origin and meaning	How is it celebrated in the original country?
April	4	**Ching Ming Festival**; celebrated in China	One of the most prominent festivals of the dead (it has an autumnal counterpart in the Hungry Ghost festival), this is a time for the living to remember their deceased ancestors.	As in other days in which the dead are honored, tombs are swept and cleaned, offerings of food are placed out for hungry spirits, and paper cash is burned to provide ancestral ghosts with floating-around money.
April or May	the first full moon in late April or early May	**Buddha Purnima**; celebrated in India, China, and wherever Buddhism has spread	The birthday of Buddha Siddhartha Gautama, as well as the day of his enlightenment, and of his passage into Nirvana, collectively called the Triple Blessing.	The day before this celebration is a day of fasting, prayer, and contemplation, as well as offerings of food, money, and incense; but upon the dawning of the next day, grand parades, dramatic reenactments of events from the life of the Buddha, and other spectacles are held, with much burning of incense and scattering of flowers. As the evening draws, lanterns are lit and every lamp in every building is turned on, as a symbol of Buddha's enlightenment and illumination of mankind. And—lest one forget—the sacred Bodhi Tree, under which Buddha sat as he meditated and achieved enlightenment, is ceremoniously watered.
 **May or June**	the 6th day of the 4th month of the lunar calendar	**Tuen Ng** (the "**Dragon Boat Festival**"); celebrated in China and Hong Kong	The Dragon Boat Festival has been held since 400 B.C., in honor of the ancient poet and minister Qu Yuan who, protesting government corruption, drowned himself in the Mi Lo River of Hong Kong. Local fishermen raced their boats out to try to save him, but—alas!—they were too late. Thus, each year commemorative Dragon Boat races are held.	Every year in June, teams from around the globe compete in the world championship Hong Kong Dragon Boat Race. Each team has 18 crewmembers, a tillerman, and a drummer (to keep the team rowing in rhythm), all crammed into a 39-foot teakwood shell, complete with dragon's head and tail painted red, yellow, and green. The 500-meter race takes about three minutes to finish—but since hundreds of teams enter and race in heats, it's an all-day event. In North America, Dragon Boat Festivals, first held in 1990, take place in July or August, when U.S. teams consisting of high-spirited yuppies compete in events in New York, California, and parts of Canada. In addition to the racing, festivals usually include a dragon dance, a ritual boat blessing by a Buddhist priest, and traditional Chinese food and crafts.
 **July or August**	three days in mid-July or mid-August	**Bon Festival** (also known as **O-bon, Urabon**); celebrated in Japan, and (somewhat less extravagantly) in China as **Yu lan p'en**.	First observed in Japan in 657 A.D., Bon is a Buddhist festival honoring the spirits of ancestors. Souls of the dead are believed to visit their descendents during this holiday, arriving on the 13th of the month and departing by the 16th. The Buddhist festival of Bon had its roots in the Chinese festival of the Hungry Ghosts, a Taoist-folk tradition.	One of Japan's major holidays, Bon is a three-day extravaganza that begins with the cleaning of gravesites, tombs, and ancestral tablets, the setting up of straw horses and oxen (to serve as vehicles for the spirits). On the evening of the first day, spirits are welcomed with a bonfire, then led home, following their families, who carry lanterns to show them the way. Upon arriving home, everyone shares a meal, prepared in advance, in the presence of their dead relatives. For the next few days, the spirits wander through their old homes and neighborhoods, while at night, celebrants gather in circles to perform Bon *odori* (Bon dances), usually dressed in traditional *yukata*. On the last day, spirits are sent off once more with a bonfire, and a ceremony is performed for those poor ghosts who have no friends or family: Paper lanterns in small boats are set adrift on streams, to guide lonely spirits back to the underworld.
July or August	celebrated on the seventh day of the seventh month of the lunar calendar	**Tanabata,** or the **Oxherd and Weaver Maiden Festival**; celebrated in Japan and China	 A tragic-romantic festival, celebrating an ancient legend of star-crossed love.	On this one day in the year, the Oxherd and Weaver Maiden—eternally separated for their forbidden love—are given permission by the gods to cross the Heavenly River of the Milky Way and meet together. Their reunion is celebrated with feasting, recounting of the legend, and the decorating of houses with fresh-cut bamboo and colorful strips of paper. More recently, young lovers (and would-be lovers) have celebrated by writing wishes of desire on paper strips and placing them on *tanabata* bushes, hoping that the Two Stars will make their romantic dreams come true.

Month	Date	Holiday	Origin and meaning	How do they celebrate in the original country?
August or September	the 15th night of the eighth month of the lunar calendar	**Jugoya** (also known as **Tsukimi**), the "**Moon Viewing Festival**"; celebrated in Japan, based on the Chinese **Mid-Autumn Festival**	During this nighttime festival, the moon is entreated to bring a bountiful harvest and to keep away storms. 	In **Japan**, public "moon-viewing" parties are held outdoors on patios, in gardens, or in open fields, often featuring picnic snacks, poetry, and music. Rice dumplings and rice cakes are eaten, and offerings of grass (symbolizing rice seedlings) are set out. The climax of the festival is usually a tremendous tug-of-war game, featuring teams composed of all of the able-bodied people in a village or neighborhood. (And it doesn't matter who wins—except to the participants.) In **China**, the celebration is similar, if less elaborate—there are nighttime moon-viewing parties where tea is drunk and mooncakes are consumed; many people purchase paper lanterns and gather in public parks, while others stay at home with family, to view the lunar face in quiet contemplation.
October or November	the last five nights of Kartikka, the last month of the Hindu calendar	**Diwali** (also known as **Deepawali** or **Lakshmi Puja**); originated in Northern India, now celebrated throughout India	Celebrated for over four millenia, this festival (named after the Sanskrit word meaning "garland of lights") commemorates the return to the throne of Lord Rama and his wife Sita, after a 14-year exile, during which Lord Rama triumphed over the evil Ravana. The king's subjects celebrated his return by lighting his path with candles and firecrackers.	Virtually a national holiday in India, even non-Hindus participate in the five-day festival, in which just about all of India is lit up with candles and clay oil lamps placed in windows, on streets and sidewalks, in trees, and floated down streams and rivers in coconut shells or little boats. Firecrackers are set off at dawn, families make desserts and visit other families, friends, and neighbors. Like in China's Lunar New Year, children "bow down" to adults and obtain their blessings (though not cash).
December	Celebrated on the first day of the first month of the Tamil calendar, which occurs on the winter solstice (the shortest day of the year).	**Pongal**; celebrated in Southern India	The Tamil New Year, and a seasonal festival celebrating the turning of the sun back towards the north (since with the passage of the winter solstice, the days will begin once more to grow long).	Pongal not only marks the turning of winter, but also the end of the monsoon season and the beginning of the harvest. In the days preceding Pongal, there's a frenzy of cleaning and burning of rubbish, while decorative patterns or *rangolis* are drawn on freshly cleaned floors. On the day itself, presents are exchanged, visits to friends and family are made, and then a renewal and harvest ceremony takes place: The married women in a household bathe themselves fully clothed, then emerge to boil rice in milk, which, when cooked (*pongal* literally means "boiled") is consumed by the family. Upon visiting a neighbor or friend, the ritual question "Has the rice boiled?" is asked, with the proper response being "It has boiled."

Values: The East-West Divide

People are people, regardless of color, creed, or nationality, right? Apparently not. Since virtually the dawn of recorded time, differences in everything from political systems to divorce rates to test scores have been noted between the nations grouped together as "the West" and those similarly grouped as "the East."

The culprit, more often than not? "Cultural values."

There are, of course, enormous fallacies in the cultural-value hypothesis. The first and most significant is that West and East are terms that are so loose that, in effect, they have no definition—"West" and "East" exist wholly in the mind of the observer. The second is that, even when the West is delineated as the "industrialized nations of Europe and North America" and the East is defined as being the "industrialized and developing nations of Asia," each of these groups contains enough variation in culture and religion that ascribing general values to either is impossible. At this point, those who still cling desperately to the idea that East and West have monolithic and contrastable values usually shrug and say that "Asian values" are those derived from and influenced by the social and ethical teachings of the Chinese philosopher Confucius, and "Western values" are those derived from and influenced by capitalism, democracy, and Christianity.

Are these two value sets that different? On the face of it, yes; after all, the central tenet in Confucianism would seem to be a respect for formal hierarchy and the good of the group, while the central tenet in capitalism and democracy would seem to be a shattering of social boundaries and rugged individualism. Look again and more deeply, however, and this shallow image reflects something altogether different: Although Confucianism does establish the importance of behaving appropriately to one's social position, it isn't as rigid a system as some might wish it to sound. Indeed, later philosophers explained that political rulers (and the social hierarchy in general) depended on the wisdom and benevolence of those on top, and that those on the bottom not only had the right but the responsibility to revolt against the established order, should government be unwise or cruel. The support of the people, these thinkers stated, was equivalent to the "Mandate of Heaven."

Meanwhile, the idea that Western values are representative of freewheeling individualism is simply wrong. Not only is the bedrock of Christianity—at least in its Catholic form—as rigid a hierarchy as any found in Asian countries, but, in any democracy, the individual good is regularly suppressed in favor of the will of the majority. In short, so-called Eastern values bear a notable resemblance to Western ones when examined under a microscope, and, of course, vice versa. There are unquestionably differences between Asian nations and Western ones—just as there are within each of these groups. And the dynamics of history are such that it's often easier to explain political disagreements as being founded on unalterable and fundamental differences, rather than as the twisting results of circumstance.

But circumstances do twist. After all, just a few centuries ago, Far Eastern nations—now seen as forming an unstoppable economic juggernaut—were being ridiculed as being incapable of engaging in contemporary commerce; and just a few decades ago, filial, family-loving Asians were seen as setting such a low value on human life that they readily sacrifice their own children for vague goals of propaganda. —H.S., J.Y.

FAMILY MATTERS, EAST VERSUS WEST

The illustrations below depict two stereotypical families, one representing "Asian values" and the other "Western values," strictly for comparative purposes.

The Lee Family

Guided by traditional Confucian belief in the family as the basic unit in society and of filial piety, the Lee family stresses loyalty and reverence to one's parents as the most important element in family relationships. The needs of individuals, particularly those of the younger generation, are subordinated to those of the whole. While there are household rules (and strict punishments if those rules are broken), by and large parents take an active interest in their children's daily schedules, and permission to go out or do other activities is always granted only after a period of negotiation. Children are obedient and study hard, supervised by their parents, often for extra hours after basic schoolwork is done. Older children are expected to guide younger children, who are expected to respect and defer to their elders. In addition to parents and children, grandparents, uncles, aunts, and cousins are seen as being significant parts of the family unit, with frequent gatherings of the entire extended Lee clan. Grandparents live with their children and grandchildren, expecting respect and care in return for the effort they spent raising their own children. Meanwhile, regardless of how old children are, they are never considered to be peers—once a parent, always a parent, and so forth. The key goals of the Lee family, as expressed by the family's patriarch, are economic security, household stability, and superior achievement on the part of the children, who after all represent the future.

The Leigh Family

While the Leighs are a family unit, more often than not, individual agendas outweigh the needs of the family. Upon reaching their teen years, the Leigh children are mostly unsupervised, though they're expected to obey household guidelines; it's not uncommon for people to pop in and out of the house during and between mealtimes, with the family gathering together on weekends, if then. The need for privacy and personal goals are stressed by both children and parents, and demands for "space" are not uncommon. So long as children aren't "getting into trouble," parents play a passive role in setting their children's schedules. Relationships are guided less by obligation than by "understanding." It's expected that if children have problems—even in touchy matters like sex—they should be willing to discuss them with their parents. In their teens, children enter a "rebellious" period, in which they often question or reject parental demands; parents must accept this as a "phase" in their path to maturity. Upon coming of age, children are expected to separate from their parents, and it isn't guaranteed that a parent will live with his or her children after achieving senior status. Gatherings of the extended family are also rare, occurring at most once a year. The key goals of the Leigh family, as expressed by both parents together, are economic security, household stability, and superior achievement on the part of the children—that is to say, exactly the same as the Lee family's. Or, to put it another way, "all roads lead to home."

Ayurveda

Ayurveda (from the Sanskrit, meaning "the knowledge of life") is one of the four Vedic sciences—along with self-knowledge, yoga [202], and Vedic astrology—described more than 5,000 years ago in the *Vedas,* a set of ancient Hindu texts [231] composed by a group of holy men known as the *Rishi.* Like Traditional Chinese Medicine [243], it is noninvasive, nontoxic, prevention-oriented, and emphasizes bodily "balance" rather than treatment of specific ills or diseases.

Ayurveda holds that there is a collective consciousness among all living things that naturally causes the body to seek harmony. Physical disease is caused by an imbalance in the body's three *doshas,* or regulatory systems. These doshas are re-balanced through the use of herbs, diet, and posture exercises derived from yoga, including meditation and breathing techniques. Ayurvedic practitioners assess patients by taking extensive questionnaires, studying a patient's tongue to measure general health, and measuring a patient's pulse at points along the wrist thought to indicate aspects of the body's physical and psychological constitution. Once a patients constitutional make-up is determined, any imbalances in that makeup can be corrected a physical therapy regimen known as *panchakarma*—which includes hot-oil massage, heat treatments, and cleansing of the intestinal tract—to rid the body of toxins.

In India, 80 percent of the population uses Ayurvedic techniques, and the system, with more than 250 million practioners and entire hospitals devoted to it, operates in parallel with modern allopathic medicine. Extensive clinical research on Ayurveda has been conducted at more than 40 research institutes in India over the last 70 years. In the West, by contrast, Ayurveda has the fewest certified practitioners of any of the alternative medicine systems, including TCM, homeopathy, and osteopathy; American Ayurvedic practice also tends to overlook the system's spiritual roots, emphasizing the finding of remedies for modern ailments (like "stress") instead. The good news for Ayurveda believers: In 1992, the National Institutes of Health established an Office of Alternative Medicine to research folk and traditional therapies, including Ayurveda. Since then, Ayruveda-related studies have been funded studying its role in the promotion of general health, as well as the treatment of Parkinson's disease, heroin addiction, and obsessive-compulsive disorder, among other ailments.

AYURVEDA IN AMERICA

The first major beachhead of Ayurvedic practice in America came through the teachings of the Maharishi Mahesh Yogi, also responsible for Transcendental Meditation [228]. In 1980, devotees of the Maharishi developed "Maharishi Ayur-Ved," an Ayurvedic approach which incorporates TM and seeks to return the practice of Ayurveda to its spiritual roots.

However, it wasn't the Maharishi but one of his proteges, Deepak Chopra, M.D. [228], who brought Ayurveda into the American mainstream consciousness. Chopra, an endocrinologist and former chief of staff of New England Memorial Hospital in Stoneham, Massachusetts, left the hospital to run the Maharishi Ayur-Ved Health Center in Massachusetts from 1987 to 1994. After deciding that his credibility might be impeded by the group's cultish reputation, Chopra distanced himself from the Maharishi, and has since written multiple bestsellers that have made him Ayurveda's best-known proponent.

HOW IT WORKS

The aim of Ayurveda is to maintain a lifestyle of health in balanced alignment with the individual's unique *prakriti,* or dosha pattern. Illness is a result of dosha imbalances in one's prakriti, and can be caused by stress, eating certain foods, lack of rest, environmental toxins, repressed emotions, etc. An imbalanced prakriti is called *vikriti,* or literally, "deviating from nature." In a state of vikriti, one's *agni* ("fire," or metabolic engine) is weakened and

KEY PRINCIPLES OF AYURVEDA

PRANA: the primal energy of life; analogous to the Chinese concept of qi [245].

DOSHA: bodily humor (can be either vata, pitta, or kapha)

PRAKRITI: the pattern of doshas manifested in an individual. Seven general patterns are possible: vata, pitta, kapha (if one dosha is clearly dominant in a person); vata-pitta, pitta-kapha, vata-kapha (combinations of two doshas); and vata-pitta-kapha (the most complex)

AGNI: the "fire" that governs one's metabolism

AMA: bodily toxins

THE THREE MALAS: sweat, urine, and feces, through which ama are eliminated

RASAYANA: a regimen, either herbal or behavioral, used on a regular basis to prevent or treat bodily imbalance

THE THREE DOSHA

VATA: Dispersive energy; the movement of cells and fluids throughout the body; organ and muscle activity; motor and sensory functions; flow of thoughts in the mind.

CORRESPONDING CHARACTERISTICS: Light, active, alert, restless; energetic, but may tend to waste it.

SUSCEPTIBLE TO: Intestinal gas, lower back pain, sciatica, arthritis, paralysis, neuralgia, diseases of the nervous system

PITTA: transformative energy; digestion, body temperature, and other metabolic functions.

CORRESPONDING CHARACTERISTICS: Fiery, angry, irritable, aggressive, competitive; activity often involves taking something and changing it into something else; would make a good CEO or lawyer.

SUSCEPTIBLE TO: gall bladder, liver, and bile disorders; hyperacidity, peptic ulcer, gastritis, inflammatory diseases, skin problems

KAPHA: accumulative energy; wound-healing, weight or muscle gain, physical strength and resiliency.

CORRESPONDING CHARACTERISTICS: heavy, slow-moving, solid, strong, stable, tranquil; doesn't move around much; would make a good middle manager or opera singer.

SUSCEPTIBLE TO: tonsillitis, bronchitis, sinusitis, lung congestion.

As one might expect, combination prakriti result in mixed characteristics.

ama ("bodily toxins") build up, causing the symptoms of disease.

Diagnosis, rather than focusing on curing specific symptoms, entails determining the patient's prakriti and vikriti. Practioners ask patients questions about their body, metabolism, habits, sleep patterns, self-image, interests, preferences, emotional state, and psychological characteristics. As in traditional Chinese medicine, Ayurvedic practitioners also make a detailed analysis of the patient's pulse. There are three basic pulses on each wrist, and myriad descriptions of possible soundings for each; skilled Ayurvedic physicians can diagnose disease from pulse readings as accurately as Western doctors can from a battery of lab tests. In addition, practitioners will examine the skin, tongue, lips, nails, and eyes, and administer basic lab tests for the blood, urine, or stool.

> **"The aim of Ayurveda is to maintain a lifestyle of health in balanced alignment with the individual's unique *prakriti*."**

AYURVEDIC THERAPY

Upon determining a patient's vakriti, a practitioner may prescribe any or all of the following therapeutic regimen:

Dietary therapy is based on the six tastes—sweet, sour, salty, pungent, bitter, astringent. Very specific diets of foods can be prescribed for balancing the body's doshas.

Herbal rasayanas—These may include fruit, herb, or mineral preperations in the form of teas, pastes, jellies, pills, powders, or liquid tinctures. An herbal regimen may contain 10 or 20 separate items taken in combination on a regular basis.

Behavioral rasayanas—These may include yoga, breathing exercises (*pranayama*), and meditation.

Abhyanga—Ayurvedic massage, entailing the stimulation of 107 *marma* points (similar to the pressure points used in acupuncture and acupressure). Abhyanga with sesame or medicinal oils helps stimulate the flow of prana and help move ama through the body for elimination.

Panchakarma—an intensive detoxification process that takes place over a few days or weeks. Done once or twice a year, panchakarma may involve abhyanga with herbal oils, *basti* (steam treatments and herbal enemas), *nasya* (nasal administration of herbs), oleation (ingestion of large amounts of clarified butter) followed by a hot bath and *virechana* (castor oil purgation), and *shirodhara* (having a steady stream of medicated oil poured on the forehead) to induce relaxation.

WHO TO SEE, WHAT IT COSTS

Ayurvedic physicians in India undergo five and a half years of study, a program that yields a Bachelor of Ayurvedic Medicine and Surgery; Indian practitioners may also obtain a conventional M.D. degree with a specialty in Ayurveda. In the U.S., however, there is currently no national certification standard for Ayurvedic practitioners. Many practitioners are licensed as conventional allopathic providers, with additional training in Ayurveda. Others may be unlicensed in primary health care, but experienced as Ayurvedic health consultants. Ayurvedic treatment is no less difficult to master than Western forms of therapy; among the aspects of Ayurveda that require considerable training and experience are pulse diagnosis and herbal pharmocology, both of which may require a practitioner to examine at least a thousand patients before he can be judged as skilled. If you would like visit an Ayurvedic practitioner, it's often best to seek one who has also gained a degree in Western medicine, or one that's affiliated with a credible health organization. Either way, expect to pay from $85 up to $350 for a first diagnostic exam, and $50 to $150 for treatment visits thereafter; an annual panchakarma treatment will cost approximately $200. —D.G. , J.Y.

Borrowed Words

For those who think that the primary Asian contribution to the English language is the Chinese takeout menu, think again: Words originating from Asian languages have been tripping off English-speaking tongues for centuries. As the British Empire expanded, so, too, did the English language; words rooted in Hindi, Sanskrit, Chinese, and other Asian languages bubbled their way into the English vernacular. In the latter part of the 20th century, American military escapades in Asia led to fresh linguistic assimilations, some of them unfortunate [336] and some of them serendipitous.

amok, amuck—This word originates from the Malay *amoq*, meaning "furious attack," thus explaining the phrase "to run amok."
avatar—From the Sanskrit word *avatara*, referring to the incarnated, human forms of the supreme god Vishnu, such as Rama the King and Krishna the Lover. Recently, it has been incorporated into Netspeak, becoming the term for an "on-screen representative" in a chat room or other online interactive milieu.
bangle—This term for a shiny, cheap bracelet, often worn in a myriad of embarassingly loud colors, isn't because it dangles or jangles, but because of the Hindi name for a colored glass bracelet, *bangri*.
brainwashing—Now associated with cults and spy movies, brainwashing first originated as military term during the Korean War. Unlike most other adopted terms, this English-language coinage is from a literal translation of the Chinese phrase for coercive indoctrination—*hsi nao*, "to wash the brain."
bungalow—This word, as well as the small cottage it describes, is Bengali in origin, and is derived from the word *bangla*, which doubles as the word for the Bengali nation.
crimson—Fledgling poets invoking this elegant adjective to describe rose blossoms or a lovelorn heart might be dismayed to learn that it comes from an ancient Indian word meaning "made by worms." Derived from the Sanskrit *krmi* ("worm") and *ja* ("produced"), the term described the red pigments made from the Kermes insect. Through commerce in finely dyed fabrics, early Spanish traders encountered the term and adopted it as *cremesin*, which emerged in English as crimson.

> **"For those who think that the primary Asian contribution to the English language is the Chinese takeout menu, think again: Asian words have been tripping off English-speaking tongues for centuries."**

gung-ho—Another Chinese term assimilated into English through the military, "gung-ho" is a shorthand phrase for *zhong guo gung yie hou tsou shi*—the Chinese Industrial Cooperatives Society. How did this come to represent feverish enthusiasm? In 1942, Lieutenant Colonel Evans Carlson of the U.S. Marine Corps was stationed in China to head the Second Raider Battalion. Carlson admired the fervent spirit and commitment of the Chinese Communists, and tried to instill a similar sense of unity and purpose in his men. Carlson defined "gung ho" to mean "work together," telling his battalion it was the motto of the Chinese cooperatives. While *gung* may be translated as "work" and *ho* as "together," a combination of the two characters doesn't mean "work together"—it's simply a guillotined version of a lengthy name.
guru—Originally the Sikh term for Nanak the founder and the other nine original leaders of Sikhism, it has come to mean a teacher or expert in any field (c.f., "computer guru"), particularly spiritual.
kamikaze—Literally meaning "divine wind," this term originally referred to a freak gust that blew a Mongolian invasion fleet away from the shores of Japan in 1281; later it was applied to the young Japanese suicide pilots who, flying rickety, explosive-laden planes, dived into Allied ships in an attempt to destroy them.
ketchup (or **catsup**)—the name of this most American of condiments actually originates from the Malay word *koetsiap*, which literally means "seafood sauce."
mandarin—An unusual example of a "boomerang" word that came from one part of Asia into the West, and was then applied to a phenomenon from another part, the term refers to the elite and educated official class of Imperial China, from whom mainland China's government-standard dialect gets its name. The word itself is not Chinese in origin, but an Anglicized synthesis of related terms from Spanish, Portuguese, and Dutch, dating back to 1589. "Mandarin" has also been used to describe any elitist, educated group, in reference to China's scholar class. The word's origin? It's derived from the Sanskrit term *mantrin* ("advisor"), which is adapted from another Sanskrit word, *manas*, meaning "mind."

paddy field—Rice paddies—the water-drenched fields in which rice is grown—are indelibly associated with Chinese, Japanese, and Southeast Asians. The English term "paddy" derives from the Malay *padi,* denoting rice in the straw.

pariah—Derived from Tamil, the word originally did not directly denote an "outcast"; it literally translated as "drummer." However, drumming at festivals and funerals was a hereditary duty of members of a low caste in southern India, and thus the English association of "pariah" with unclean or lowly individuals.

pidgin—A pidgin language is defined as a mixture of two or more languages developed as a means of communication between people who don't share a common tongue. The first pidgin was spoken between Chinese and British traders to perform commerce in the treaty ports; interestingly, the term "pidgin" comes not from a Chinese word, but rather from a British transliteration of the way traders heard Chinese pronouncing "business." Many commonly used American catchphrases are drawn from British-Chinese pidgin English, including "long time no see" and "no can do."

pundit—This word originates from the Hindi *pandit,* meaning "learned man," which itself had its roots in the Sanskrit *pandita,* meaning "learned" or "skilled." The first recorded English usage was in the 17th century, referring specifically to a learned man of India who was not only an expert in Sanskrit, but was also well versed in Hindi philosophy. In the 19th century, pundit became generally used in the sense of "a learned expert or teacher"; modern usage leans toward a media-centric definition, referring to an authority who makes authoritative statements in a public or journalistic forum.

serendipity—A favorite word among golden-age crooners of schmaltzy love songs, serendipity—meaning the ability to make unintended and fortuitous discoveries—came into the English language less by accident than by design. In 1754, the politician and intellectual Horace Walpole coined the word from the title of the Persian fairy tale "The Three Princes of Serendip," whose protagonists repeatedly make discoveries that are, well, serendipitous. Serendip, the old English name for what later became Ceylon and is now Sri Lanka, can be traced to the original Sanskrit name for the island, *Sinhaladvipa,* which itself came from the Sanskrit *sinhala,* "resplendent land."

shampoo—"[A Mahratta wife] first champoes her husband, and fans him to repose; she than champoes the horse."
—James Forbes, *Oriental Memoirs,* 1813
Your basic daily shower activity comes from the Hindi *capo,* a form of the verb *capna,* meaning "to press or massage." Each day, the typical Indian wife gave her husband a nice, relaxing head massage; no word as to how the horse felt about it.

thug—Today's version of a thug would hardly be mistaken for a religious practitioner, but the first thugs (or "thuggees") were worshippers of Kali, the Hindu goddess of destruction. They considered assassination a holy act and a religious duty carried out for the deity; thugees would follow wealthy travellers, and try by deception to gain their trust. Eventually, they would strangle the unlucky victim with a noose or handkerchief, before robbing and sacrificing the body. The term originally derives from the Hindi *thag,* meaning "a cheat or swindler"; it, in turn, comes from the Sanskrit *sthag,* meaning "to cover or conceal." When the word began to appear in British writing about India in the early 19th century, it tapped a macabre vein in the English-speaking public imagination, and was quickly extended to imply secular gangsters and cutthroats.

tycoon—Derived from the Cantonese words *ta* ("great") and *kiun* ("lord," "prince"), the Japanese adopted the word *taikun* to describe their shogun Iyesada, during treaty negotiations with Commodore Matthew Perry in the 1850s. (Since shogun literally means "general," the Japanese hesitated to use the term for fear that the Westerners would dismiss Iyesada as a mere military leader.) Perry then brought the word back to the U.S., where it gained currency as an affectionate nickname for Abraham Lincoln. It was extended to describe any important businessman or politician, but now refers more specifically to those who amass extravagant fortunes through business.

yen—The origin of this word isn't what you'd expect: Rather than coming from the Japanese term for its currency, yen actually comes from a Chinese term used to describe an opium addict's desperate hunger for the drug. During the 18th and 19th centuries, opium addiction in China rose steadily, eventually reaching staggering levels, under the pressures of Western traders, who encouraged widespread consumption of the drug. When Chinese first immigrated to the U.S. in the mid 19th century, they brought with them the phrase *in yan,* meaning "craving for opium. The word made its way into colloquial English as "yen-yen," which was shortened to yen, and generalized to refer to any (not necessarily pharmaceutical) longing or yearning. —N.K., D.G., H.S.

Buddhism

Buddhist relief in Aurangabad, India

About an eighth of the world's population is Buddhist, including the vast majority of Southeast Asians, many Chinese and Indians, and large numbers of Japanese. Buddhism has even made substantial strides in the West, becoming the most prominent of "alternative" religions to the Judeo-Christian mainline. In America, the number of practicing Buddhists has been estimated at up to five million people, including both immigrants who brought their faith with them and native-born Americans who have chosen to embrace Buddhist beliefs. In fact, like other Asian religions, Buddhist doctrine contains no exclusionary principle, and many who identify themselves as practicing Buddhists also subscribe to other faiths. Part of the reason, of course, is that, like Hinduism, Buddhism contains an enormous range of ideologies, each of which emphasizes different elements within the larger teachings of the faith.

THE BASIC TEACHINGS

The fundamental revelations received by the Buddha Gautama, which serve as the columns upon which the broadly divergent edifice of Buddhist thought rests, are known as the Four Noble Truths (*see sidebar*). These truths essentially link existence to suffering, and suffering to material and bodily desire. All of life is doomed to experience and re-experience the pain of existence, with release coming only from the following of the Eightfold Path. Achieving release from existence results in the state known as *nirvana,* a condition which cannot be adequately explained or described, except as "purified consciousness" and infinite bliss. (Note that, unlike its ancestor Hinduism, Buddhism does not believe in the concept of the eternal and individual soul. All things are impermanent, and subject to the wheel of change; there is no individual essence, but rather a bundle of *khandhas,* or senses and states, which must be dissipated in the pursuit of nirvana.)

THERAVADA VS. MAHAYANA

The original Buddhist school, Theravada Buddhism, focused on the personal inner quest, emphasizing asceticism, reflection, and study. However, this focus demanded self-involvement and separation from society, which were rejected by one sect known as the Mahasanghikas as being a form of egocentrism, and thus a barrier to enlightenment.

The new school of Buddhism they helped create was called Mahayana, or "Greater Vehicle." Besides being less weighted down by strictures than Theravada, it added the belief that some enlightened ones, upon attaining salvation, refused it so as to help others find liberation. These benevolent beings were known as *bodhisattvas,* and devotion to bodhisattvas became a second focus for Mahayana Buddhists, displacing the more austere emphasis on self-training and discipline. Mahayana Buddhism was egalitarian, since it suggested that (through the bodhisattvas) salvation was possible for anyone; it was also social, in that the temple became a place of group devotion rather than isolation and meditation.

A BRIEF HISTORY OF BUDDHISM

586 B.C.—Gautama Siddhartha, a prince of the Sakya people, is born. At his birth, it is predicted that he will someday rule the world. According to legend, his mother conceived him after experiencing a dream in which a white elephant magically entered into her womb. After the experience, she no longer had any desire for sex (which is probably understandable). Siddhartha is reared in luxury and, as an adult, marries and has children. However, after seeing four troubling sights while out walking one day—a very old man, an ill person, a corpse, and a holy mendicant—he leaves his home and family to wander the world seeking greater truth.

551 B.C.—After years of travel and study, Siddhartha arrives at a place known as Bodh-Gaya, where, sitting beneath a sacred Bodhi Tree, he has an insight into the grand pattern of the cosmos. Understanding the causes of suffering as well as the means by which to liberate humanity from it, he returns to the companions he had found on his journey and delivers to them his first lesson, known as the Sermon of the Turning of the Wheel. They become his first disciples, and he is given the title of Buddha, or "Englightened One."

506 B.C.—At the age of 80, the Buddha's material existence ends. Enlightened and thus beyond death and reincarnation, yet still maintaining a special form of existence, he is referred to by his disciples as Tathagata, or the "Thus-Gone One."

350 B.C.—A schism emerges among the Sangha (monks and nuns), as one sect known as the Mahasanghikas begins preaching a need for a more open and socially conscious orientation in Buddhism; they break away from the Theravadin, or followers of

the elder teachings. This results in the liberal school of Buddhism known as Mahayana.

268 B.C.—King Asoka comes to power in India, and converts from Hinduism to Buddhism; he then uses his rule to spread Buddhism into Central Asia, and from there into China, where it is interpreted as being a garbled form of Taoism.

4TH and 5TH CENTURY A.D.—Buddhism becomes the dominant faith in China, hitting its peak of popularity in the 7th century. In 520 A.D., the legendary Bodhidharma strolls into town bearing the secrets of another flavor of Buddhism: Meditative, or Ch'an, Buddhism, which, upon its introduction to to Korea, becomes dominant there.

6TH CENTURY A.D.—The Buddhist monk Naropa sees 12 disgusting (but mildly arousing) visions, leading him to break away from the Buddhist mainline to found Tantric Buddhism. This sect incorporates activities prohibited or discouraged in other forms of Buddhist practice, such as sex and the consumption of meat. Meanwhile, Buddhism is brought from Korea to Japan.

8TH CENTURY—Tantric Buddhism is brought to China and Tibet; this event is preserved in the Chinese legend of the Monkey King [👁32]. In Japan, the monk Saicho founds Tendai Buddhism, which incorporates Tantric beliefs as well as worship of traditional folk gods, and the monk Kukai founds Shingon, an esoteric form of Buddhism.

12TH and 13TH CENTURY—The monk Eisai brings Ch'an Buddhism to Japan, and establishes it as Zen, despite resistance from the dominant Tendai establishment. Later, the monk Nichiren proclaims a new, fiercely evangelistic school of his own. Through his sheer persistence, Nichiren Buddhism eventually gains a strong foothold in Japan.

THE JOY OF SECTS

Tantric Buddhism—Often associated with sex, this mystical offshoot of mainline Buddhism emerged in Northern India and Tibet, around 300 to 700 A.D. Concerned with discovering new means of transforming consciousness, usually with the help of a teacher or guru, Tantric Buddhism assimilated regional fertility beliefs, as well as elements of the Hindu pantheon (the original Hindu texts were written in the form of a dialogue between the Hindu god Shiva and the goddess Shakti, symbols of the masculine and feminine divine). Although in Tantric Buddhism, sex is a means (one of many) by which to achieve higher consciousness, in the West this orientation is reversed: many New Age practitioners see Tantric Buddhism as the key to transcendental sexual pleasure.

Tibetan Buddhism—An esoteric form of Tantric Buddhism in which meditation and the visualization of patterns known as mandalas are seen as the path to attaining unity with one's chosen Buddha-figure (the Buddha within, as it were). In an extension of the concept of the bodhisattva, Tibetan spiritual leaders are believed to remain on the wheel of rebirth in order that they might continue to instruct their flock. The leader of Tibetan Buddhism, the Dalai Lama (otherwise known as the living incarnation of Akalovitesara, the Bodhisattva of Compassion), is currently in his 14th material incarnation since the beginning of his spiritual line in 1391. Each reincarnated lama is identified as such by signs and portents left by his prior incarnation, so upon the death of a lama, a concerted search is held for his newest form. The young Llamo Dhondrub was discovered to be the latest Dalai Lama when, at the tender age of two years old, he recognized the Buddhist disciples, called them by name, and correctly identified items (including prayer beads and a walking stick) owned by his predecessor. At the age of four, he was whisked away to Lhasa, where he was raised and nurtured by monks in the sprawling Potala Palace. Upon turning 18, he was slated to commence spiritual and temporal rule of the country; that day never came, as neighboring China invaded the country in 1950, beginning a reign of cultural eradication that continues to this day. The Dalai Lama was forced into exile in India, from which he has fought tirelessly and nonviolently over the past half century against the ruthless domination of Tibet by the Chinese government. His pacifist message garnered him the 1989 Nobel Peace Prize, and has attracted multitudes of followers in the West as well as East, including celebrities such as Richard Gere, Uma Thurman (her father, Robert Thurman, is the president and founder of Tibet House), Courtney Love, Oliver Stone, Laurie Anderson, and Adam Yauch of the Beastie Boys (who raps about Buddha on "Bodhisattva Vow").

The Dalai Lama

Pure Land: A Mahayana sect based on Pure Land Sutra, which says that the spiritual nature of the world has been in decline since the time of the Buddha's material incarnation. Through prayer and devotion, followers cultivate a sincere intent to be reborn after death in a paradise known as the Pure Land of Amitabha (Amida in Japan), the "Buddha of Infinite Radiance." Its semi-apocalyptic elements and its incorporation of a heavenly afterlife make Pure Land unique among Buddhist sects; along with Zen, this is the dominant form of Buddhism in Japan.

Zen Buddhism—A Japanese school of Buddhism derived from Chinese Ch'an Buddhism, this sect emphasizes the achievement of satori (or "realization in experience") through meditation and (in Rinzai Zen) the contemplation of teaching riddles known as *koans*. Though Zen is distinctly a Buddhist sect, in the West it has been somewhat unbundled from its Buddhist roots; many New Age practitioners (like Chicago Bulls coach and "Zen

Christian" Phil Jackson) often embrace Zen's consciousness-awakening aspects while dispensing with other Buddhist doctrine, or fusing it with Western interpretations. Thus, Zen in America has become an all-purpose aid to motorcycle maintenance, business management, and basketball.

Nichiren Shoshu: Followers of Nichiren believe you can chant for "things": new car, fame, and fortune, and so forth; devotees hold rosary-type strings of beads with 108 beads, symbolizing 108 human desires, while chanting "*Nam Myo Ho Ren Keh Kyo*." This sect, founded in Japan by Nicheren Daishonin, has an estimated 8 to 10 million adherents around the world, with 140,000 in America alone, including celebrities such as Tina Turner, Roseanne and Patrick Swayze.

BUDDHISM IN THE U.S.A.

Americans have long been fascinated with Eastern religions. Henry David Thoreau, for instance, was the first to translate the Lotus Sutra into English. In 1950, D.T. Suzuki, a Buddhist scholar, set off a Zen trend with late afternoon classes at Columbia University that became popular with the cocktail crowd. At about the same time, Beat Poets such as Allen Ginsburg, Jack Kerouac, and Gary Snyder turned on to Buddhism, thereby hastening its spread. However, the hard-drinking, unchaste Beats weren't exactly model Eightfold-Pathers. Rick Fields, author of *When the Swans Came to the Lake: A Narrative History of Buddhism in America*, surmises that "psychedelics had more to do with this than most would like to admit." And Kerouac, in his poem "How to Meditate," likened the practice to "ecstasy like a shot of heroin or morphine."

MEDITATION, THE BUDDHIST WAY

Regardless of the flavor of Buddhist doctrine one follows, the practice of meditation is one of the golden keys to enlightenment. Even for non-Buddhists, meditation has been used as a means of stress reduction. Here's a sampling of Buddhist meditation techniques you might consider to help achieve that peaceful easy feeling:

Insight meditation (also "mindfulness" or *Vipassana*)—a free-form kind of meditation in which you let your thoughts run through your mind without analzing them. The technique was popularized by Buddhists like the Vietnamese monk Thich Nhat Hanh, who draws crowds in the thousands when he speaks publicly in the U.S.

Dzogchen meditation—a Tibetan Buddhist form of meditation in which one's mind is merged with "the wisdom mind of the master." For details, consult *The Tibetan Book of Living and Dying* by Sogyal Rinpoche, or visit your local Dzogchen meditation center.

Zazen—the Zen Buddhist practice of "sitting in absorption" employs a variety of techniques, including *susoku-kan* ("contemplation of counting the breath"), a beginning technique of counting one's inhalation and exhalation; pondering koans, the paradoxical "riddles" made famous by the Rinzai school; and *shikantaza*, "nothing but precisely sitting," a technique of the Soto school in which one sits facing a wall with no specific goal in mind, or anything else in mind, for that matter. Make sure you don't nod off; during your sesshin (a day of intensive zazen meditation under the guidance of a Zen master), your teacher will patrol the ranks with a *kyosaku* or "wake-up stick," a flat rod used by masters to strike zazen practitioners in order to "encourage" and "stimulate" them (i.e., keep them from falling asleep). The stick symbolizes the sword of the boddhisattva of wisdom, but it still hurts like hell.—M.G.L., D.G., J.Y.

BUDDHISM BY THE NUMBERS

THE THREE TREASURES
(to be revered by the faithful)

The Buddha (the revealer)

The Dhamma (the teachings)

The Sangha (the priesthood)

THE FOUR NOBLE TRUTHS
(to be learned and accepted)

1. Nothing is permanent; satisfaction is temporary, and its loss is painful. Thus, life is permeated with suffering.
2. The cause of suffering is the desire for existence in the world.
3. Suffering ceases when people are freed of their desires.
4. To eliminate desire, one must follow the Eightfold Path.

THE EIGHTFOLD PATH
(to be followed)

1. Right view (understand the Buddha's teachings)
2. Right thought (be unselfish)
3. Right speech (speak kindly and truthfully)
4. Right action (behave well)
5. Right work (do good and avoid harm in your job)
6. Right effort (self-improvement)
7. Right mindedness (develop self-awareness)
8. Right concentration (focus in meditation)

THE FIVE PRECEPTS
(to be obeyed)

1. No killing of living creatures
2. No stealing
3. No acting unchastely
4. No lies, speaking falsely
5. No drinking alcohol to cause intoxicatedness or carelessness

Chinese

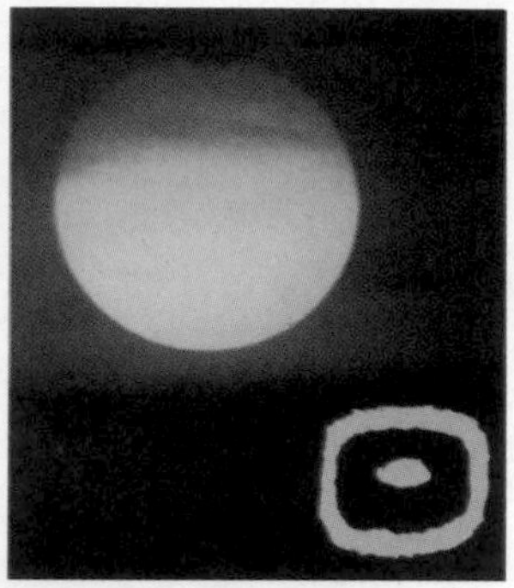

With evidence of its existence dating back 4,000 years to around 1700 B.C., Chinese is one of the world's oldest living languages. Although it isn't an international language of trade, as are English or French, it is one of of the United Nations' five official languages, and more people speak it than any other language—in large part because of China's huge population.

LEARNING IT

Chinese has a simple, logical grammar, no verb conjugations, and no verb tenses. However, Chinese does have intonations, with spoken words conveying wildly different meanings depending on whether they are spoken in flat, rising, or dropping tones. For example, in Mandarin, which has four tones, the syllable *ma* can mean "mother," "hemp," "horse," or "to scold," depending on tone; it should be clear that an errant tone can easily produce confusion. (You think Mandarin is bad; Cantonese has *nine* tones.) As for the written word, looking at a Chinese character may give the initiated an indication of what it means; it won't give any indication of how it should be spoken. And—worse yet—literacy requires a minimum vocabulary of about 3,000 written characters, just to do something as simple as reading the paper.

DIAL D FOR DIALECTS

There are seven major Chinese dialects. The most widely spoken is Mandarin—also known as *putonghua*—which is based on Beijing dialect, and has been the official Chinese of the People's Republic since 1949. It's spoken by two-thirds of the Chinese population, and understood by most Chinese immigrant communities, though the earliest Chinese Americans were most likely to have spoken Cantonese (*Yue*), which is the predominant dialect in the South of China and in Hong Kong. Shanghainese are likely to speak *Wu*, residents of Jiangxi speak *Kejia*, *Hakka*, or *Gan*, Hunanese to speak *Xiang* (or *Gan*, in the North), and residents of northern Beijing to speak Pekinese.

WRITE THIS WAY

Chinese script employs more than 40,000 symbols, which to the untrained eye may well resemble chicken scratch. It isn't. Basic written chinese is composed of stylized drawings of items and ideas that have evolved into standardized form (see illustrations). These ideographs and pictographs, called radicals, are combined into rebus-like compound characters to signify more complex concepts: For example, the word for "good," *hau,* consists of two radicals—the pictographs for woman and child—side by side, the rationale being that a woman and child together is synonymous with goodness. (A rather patriarchal idea, though at least the radicals for "barefoot" and "kitchen" aren't included.) Even more complex concepts are represented with multiple-character compound words: "telephone" is translated as dien hua, which literally means "electric speech." Foreign loanwords are usually expressed phonetically as compound words. Two of the best such phonetic translations refer to beverages. The Chinese transliteration of "martini" is the brilliant pun *ma ti ni*, or "a horse kicked you." And Coca-Cola researched hard and long before coming up with *ke kou ke le*: "Makes your mouth happy"! —D.G.

WHEN IN THE WEST, DO AS THE ROMANIZERS DO...

A scholar named Sir Thomas Francis Wade created the first standard for phoneticizing Chinese in 1859, which, after revision by Herbert A. Giles in 1892, was adopted as the first widespread romanization system. Today, however, Wade-Giles is similar to the old English system of measures—still in use, but clearly not as efficient as its later official replacement, pinyin. Meanwhile, in 1906, a romanization for place names was developed by the Chinese Post Office. This incorporated many common usages (like "Peking" for Beijing), but had no logical consistency, and was thus unusable as a standard. In 1920, Chinese academics made a stab at a standard called Gwoyeu Romatzyh, which translates as "country-language roman characters." Its difficulty in representing sounds that are unique to Chinese meant that it shared Wade Giles's worst problems, while offering no real improvements; though it still has limited use in Taiwan, it was abandoned by the mainland government. During World War II, Yale University linguists developed a system called, naturally, "Yale"—an improvement on Wade-Giles, but not much of one. Finally, the PRC made a last attempt at creating a standard: Called pinyin, it was officially adopted in 1958, then embraced by the U.N. in 1979. It is now the most widely accepted system. As a result, Mao Tse-tung became Mao Zedong and Peking (Post Office) became Beijing (pinyin). Westerners still haven't gotten the hang of converting their Chinese geographical terms into pinyin, and may never do so. Szechwan (Post Office) may now be commonly spelled Sichaun (pinyin), and Canton is Guangdong. But will Hong Kong ever become Xianggang?

Confucianism

Though he's known in the U.S. as the alleged source of quotations for fortune cookies, in Asia Confucius (K'ung Fu-tzu) is revered as China's greatest political philosopher, and his teachings continue to influence heads of state today, notably in Malaysia and Singapore. Born in 551 B.C. in the state of Lu in China's Shantung Province, Confucius was raised in humble circumstances. The period during which he lived, the Chou dynasty (1027-256 B.C.), was a less than auspicious era in Chinese history. The central government was weak. The arts weren't flourishing like they used to. The country was fractioning into a conglomeration of hostile states vying for power. Like cranky old men today, Confucius believed that things must have been better in the good old days, when men were men, emperors were fathers, and feudal dukes were sons in an extended family. Unlike cranky old men today, Confucius wrote down his beliefs, and spent much of his life wandering throughout China trying to influence rulers to follow his counsel.

Confucius found a patron in Duke Ting of Lu, who in 501 B.C. appointed the sage to the governorship of a district in his home state. As governor, Confucius practiced what he had preached, guided by his own belief that "maldistribution is a greater evil than scarce resources." His management was heralded for its efficiency, and he found himself elevated to Minister of Public Works for the state of Lu, and then Minister of Justice. As Justice Minister, Confucius sought to eradicate the lack of social discipline and ethical upbringing that he saw as the cause of crime, rather than simply pass sentence on the guilty.

Alas, Confucius's attempt at molding the ideal society came to a premature end when Confucius had a falling out with the Duke, a weak man who lacked the backbone necessary to support such a reformer. "Rotten wood cannot be carved," remarked the sage, leaving government to wander once more, expounding his teachings to a growing community of disciples. He died in 479 B.C., having edited works that became the core of the Confucian tradition—which today is perceived as the bedrock of the Chinese value system [👁210].

THE BASIC PHILOSOPHY

The central doctrine of Confucianism is the idea of *jen*—"benevolence" or "altruism." In preaching the need for jen, Confucius sought to cultivate the basic sense of moral correctness and concern for others that distinguishes man from beast.

The keys to jen can be found in *hsiao* ("filial piety") and *li* ("proper behavior"). Filial piety was manifested through loyalty not just to one's parents but to a just ruler, who, like the head of a household, is responsible for setting a pristine ethical example to gain the respect and obedience of his subjects. Li, which corresponds to duty to brothers or peers, could be manifested through the proper performance of responsibilities and rituals. However, loyalty is inherently hierarchical: Lord and parents must always come before friends, siblings, and countrymen.

Jen is seen as the basis for all ethical actions; it provides a sense of well-being regardless of one's circumstances. "Without jen, a man cannot long endure adversity, nor can he long endure prosperity," said Confucius. "A man of jen rests in jen; a man of wisdom finds it beneficial." By cultivating jen, one lives up to the full potential of the human condition in all areas of life. Note that Confucius did not proclaim supernatural rewards for virtuous living; there is no "Confucian paradise" or heaven. In his mind, virtue was its own reward. —K.P.

CONFUCIUS SAID...

Some real sayings of Confucius

"The essence of knowledge is, having it, to apply it; and not having it, to confess your ignorance."

"Study the past if you would divine the future."

"In a country well-governed, power is something to be ashamed of. In a country badly governed, wealth is something to be ashamed of."

"He who wishes to secure the good of others has already secured his own."

"He who will not economize will have to agonize."

The "Works" of Confucius

The following texts have traditionally been ascribed to Confucius, probably in error; however, regardless of their origin, together they form the basis of Confucian philosophy.

THE SIX CLASSICS

I Ching ("Book of Changes," a manual of divination; [👁224])

Shu Ching ("Book of Documents," a historical anthology)

Shih Ching ("Book of Poetry")

Ch'un Ch'iu ("Spring and Autumn Annals," a history of Lu)

Li Chi ("Record of Ritual")

Yueh Ching ("Book of Music"; no surviving copies)

ALSO:

Lun Yu ("The Analects," a collection of Confucian sayings)

Hsiao Ching ("Classic of Filial Piety")

Creation Myths

The radiant sun, the lucent moon, the velvet expanse of space—from whence did it all come? Well...science tells us that the universe sprang into being on its own, and expanded in all directions at phenomenal speeds; after this primordial explosion, over the course of billions of years, matter clumped together to form clouds, which further clumped to form stars, which eventually spun out planets. It's not a very convincing explanation on the face of it, and—even worse—it's as boring as hell. The job of adding color to the cosmos has always been left up to myth and legend. Folk tradition tells us that our origin isn't simply the result of a quantum accident of massive proportions; rather, we and our world exist due to the sacrifice of gods, the quelling of demons, and the glory of heroes. Quirky, inspirational, tragic, or absurd, these stories enliven an existence that often seems all too mundane, and expand our awareness beyond the curved boundaries of the scientific universe, into the limitless domain of imagination. And after all, what's more interesting to believe—the tired old tale of the "Big Bang," or the Indonesian legend that the universe was the offspring of Manuk Manuk, the blue cosmic chicken?

Our bet's on the chicken. —J.Y.

THE WORLD ACCORDING TO CHINA

In the beginning, Pan Gu—the Cosmos—gestated within an enormous egg that floated in the darkness. Pan Gu awoke within his egg shocked to see that all was without form. He broke the egg apart and began to bring order to the void: the lighter *yang* portion of the egg floated up and became the heavens, and the heavier *yin* portion drifted down and became the earth. *Not bad,* thought Pan Gu, except that Heaven and Earth were resting on top of one another—a rather cramped condition. Frustrated, Pan Gu decided that, since he was the only other thing in the universe, he had to solve the problem himself, by standing on the Earth and lifting up the sky. For 18,000 years, Pan Gu pushed the heavens higher, consuming nothing but vapor and never daring to sleep; every day, the foundation and the firmament moved 10 feet farther apart, until Pan Gu could stand fully upright with his arms and legs outstretched. Looking down at his feet, he realized that the Earth and Heaven were far apart enough for him to take a rest without fear that the skies would come crashing down. And so Pan Gu lay down...and died. Some good came of this tragedy, however, because various parts of his body transformed into everything that exists in the universe: His head, left and right arm, and feet became the four pillars of the compass (with his torso becoming the fifth, the Center); his hair became the planets and stars, and his eyes the sun and moon; his flesh became the soil, his blood the running waters, his bones the gems and minerals; his body hair grew into the plants, and his lice became the animals, birds, and fish. Once the Earth had form, Nu Gua the mother goddess descended from the heavens to examine the new world. But with the Earth inhabited only by animals, Nu Gua was lonely, and so she decided to create beings to provide her with company. Traveling to the banks of the Yellow River, she took handfuls of clay and created tiny figures, into which she breathed life. Some of them she infused with yang, making them male; others she infused with yin, making them female. Pleased with her creations, she decided to cover the world with them, and so she dipped the end of a rope in the clay and spun it around her body; wherever a spatter of mud fell, a human arose. But of course, the original humans, crafted by hand on the banks of the Yellow River, were superior to the mud-splotch barbarians who appeared elsewhere—in the north, west, and across the oceans.

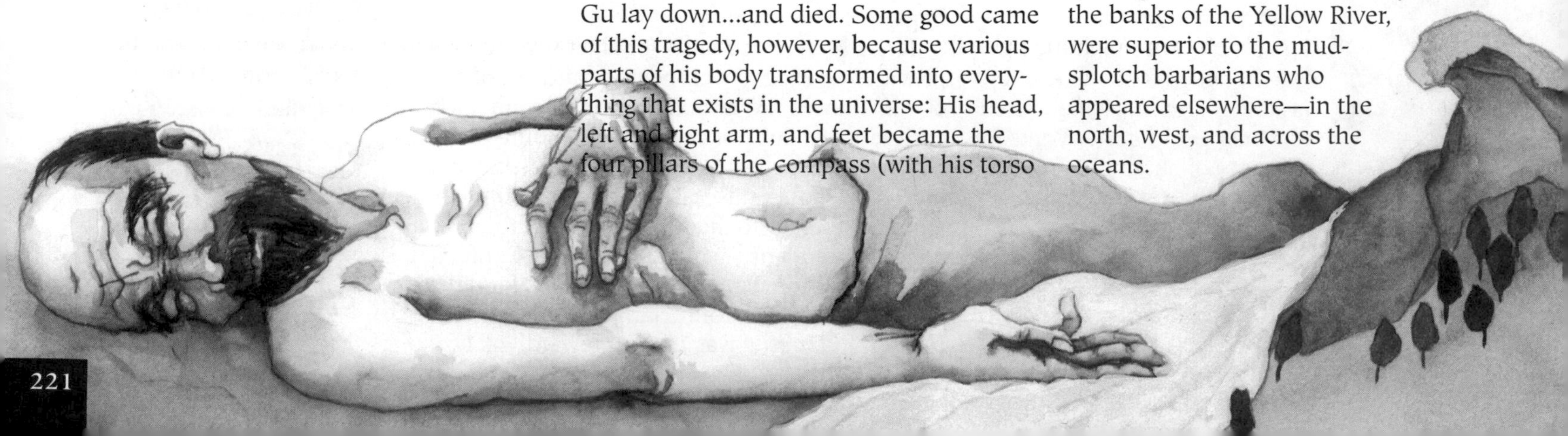

THE WORLD ACCORDING TO JAPAN

The cosmos began as a formless void. This cosmic void slowly began to separate, dividing into the light and the heavy; that which was light became the heavens, and that which was heavy coalesced slowly into clumps of matter floating within the waters beneath the sky. As this division occurred within the void, a set of primordial entities sprang into existence—five enigmatic beings known as the Separate Heavenly Deities. The three most potent of these, Amanominakanushi-no-kami (the "Lord of the Center of Heaven") and his two attendants Takamimusubi-no-kami ("High Wondrous Exalted Creator") and Kamimusubi-no-kami ("Wondrous Divine Creator") then engendered two younger gods, to embody the active-yang and passive-yin essences of the cosmos: Izanagi no Mikoto ("Exalted Male") and Izanami no Mikoto ("Exalted Female"). After being created, Izanagi and Izanami climbed up to the Bridge of Heaven to look down at the waters below, seeking solid land. In order to uncover what their eyes could not, the two sibling deities took a jeweled spear and stirred the depths; when they pulled the spear from the roiling current, the salty water that dripped from its head formed an island, which Izanagi and Izanami claimed for their own. Alighting upon the isle, they erected a beautiful palace and a heavenly pillar to honor the Separate Heavenly Deities. Then they decided to explore the pleasures of their new creation, each taking opposite courses around the island. When they had completed their circuits and met one another once more, Izanami exclaimed, "How wonderful to have found a handsome young man!" The two came together and had divine sex. But when Izanami gave birth to their first child, it was a horrible mutant leech-baby, which so dismayed its parents that they set it adrift on the ocean in a boat of reeds. The elder Separate Heavenly Deities tsked at the misfortune of their children, and informed them that Izanami's lack of manners was the reason for the misbirth: A woman should never speak prior to a man. Shamed, Izanagi and Izanami promptly repeated their ritual, this time with Izanagi speaking first. The divine couple then produced eight perfect offspring, who became the islands of the Japanese archipelago. Over time, the two joyfully created many more deity-children, who became the gods of the mountains, the rivers, and the trees, as well as the three most potent gods: Amaterasu the goddess of the sun, Tsukiyomi the god of the moon, and Susano the god of storms and disorder. The beauty of Amaterasu was such that her parents proudly urged her to climb the Ladder of Heaven, so that she might shine from the heights of the firmament and rule the entire universe. (Their sons Tsukiyomi and Susano, on the other hand, would prove to be more disappointing. The former would kill Ogetsu-no-hime, the Goddess of Food, in a fit of pique; the latter would grow to be so rebellious, temperamental, and ill-mannered that he would bring the universe to the brink of catastrophe and be exiled to the Underworld. Boy-gods will be boy-gods.) Curiously, there is no explicit description of the creation of mankind in Japanese folk mythology; however, it is assumed that men and women were among the creatures who were created by Izanagi and Izanami.

THE WORLD ACCORDING TO INDIA

Indian mythic tradition changed rapidly as Hinduism, the nation's prevailing religion, evolved. An early Vedic legend accorded the origin of the cosmos to the thousand-headed primordial deity Purusa, who engendered Viraj, the goddess of creation; she, in a quirk of paradox, then gave birth to her father Purusa. In the presence of their generative cycle, other great gods appeared, who then sacrificed Purusa to himself, dismembering him, anointing him, and burning him in a tremendous pyre. From the pieces of his body sprang all animate and inanimate things, while the sun emanated from his burning eyes and the moon from his mind; out of his mouth came Indra, the original warrior king of the gods, and Agni, god of fire. Later Indian stories ascribed a sophisticated cyclical nature to the cosmos, while raising new gods into the position of primordial deity—in particular Vishnu, the greatest of the three deities at the center of classical Hinduism.

According to later Hindu texts, the universe has no origin or final end; it instead wheels through a constant and eternal series of creations and destructions, with each creation and destruction comprising a single "day" in the life of the cosmos. At the beginning of each cosmic day, a lotus flower springs from the navel of Vishnu, still fast asleep until his time commences. The flower blossoms, and Brahma, the creator, emerges to break open the egg of the universe and create all that exists within it out of the void.

When Brahma has emerged from Vishnu's navel-lotus, he creates all that exists within the universe, first the inanimate and then living beings. He brings forth the demon hordes from his anus, and then discards his body, which transforms into the darkness we know as night; this is the realm of demons. He forms a second body and draws the immortal deities from his face, then discards that body as well, which becomes the lightness we call day; this is the domain of gods. Brahma continues to create and cast away bodies, producing humanity, Rakshasas, and every kind of animal in successive incorporations, until all the cosmos is populated for the new cosmic day.

Once the universe is created and populated, Vishnu awakes, and serves as the preserver of the universe for 4.32 billion years; then, at the end of that term, he sleeps once more, and Shiva the destroyer wipes the slate clean, as the cosmic night of 4.32 billion years begins. When night is complete, once more the lotus flower blossoms, and the cycle continues.

Yet another Hindu creation myth exists regarding Vishnu, in this case incarnated as his fifth avatar, Vamana the dwarf. It's not clear how this story fits into the greater cycle of cosmic regenesis, but it's a cute tale nevertheless. The universe has been subjugated under the iron thumb of the demon Bali, who rules over it in a state of primal chaos. Vishnu the preserver, realizing that life and growth are impossible in such a cosmos, approaches the horrific fiend in his dwarfen form, asking for a small plot of earth on which to meditate. Amused, the contemptuous demon agrees to Vamana's request, granting him a space exactly three paces wide. Vamana thanks the demon, instantly returns to his immense Vishnu proportions, and takes his steps; with the first, he divides and separates the earth; with the second, he defines the region of heaven; and with the third, marks out the world of all living creatures, thus banishing Bali from the cosmos.

Divination and Fortune Telling

Since ancient times, men have been obsessed with attempting to lift the veil of time—to peer forwards into the dusky future to get the merest glimpse of what might occur, in minutes or millennia to come. Some of the earliest evidence of ritual divination is found in Northern China, where more than 4,000 years ago, ancient mystics chose to slaughter innocent tortoises for use in fortunetelling rituals. The unsuspecting beasts were rudely ejected from their shells, which were then subjected to the heat of red-hot pokers; the cracks that resulted were analyzed, and a prophecy of the future somehow derived. It may be that tortoises were chosen due to the traditional belief that the reptile is an auspicious beast, bearing the load of the cosmos upon its back [👁237]; it may simply be that tortoises were slow-moving enough even for slightly addled ancients to catch and torture. Either way, plastromancy, as this process has been named, was practiced in Asia for thousands of years, until it was largely replaced by the techniques elaborated below.

Is plastromancy any less accurate than astrology, the I Ching, or palmistry? Only the spirit world knows. But the following methods are, at the very least, less messy. —J.Y., D.Y., Je.C.

CHINESE ASTROLOGY

Fortunetelling by the stars originated in China as early as 1111 B.C., during the Western Zhou Dynasty. Unlike Western astrology, which is based on 12 horoscopic signs corresponding to months of the year, the Chinese zodiac is based on animals corresponding to the 12 years in the lunar cycle. Chinese astrological tradition has it that one possesses the traits of the animal under whose sign one was born (*see sidebar*). For example, tigers are powerful and ferocious; as a result, those born in the Year of the Tiger are likely to be aggressive, temperamental, and independent. One unfortunate side effect is that, in China, women born in "strong" years once faced the danger of spinsterhood—as men feared the temperament of a Tiger woman, preferring more docile Rabbits or Oxen instead. Another effect is what could be called the Dragon Boom: Every 12 years, in the Year of the Dragon, there's a sharp rise in childbirth—since the dragon is the most potent and auspicious of beasts to be born under, for either boys or girls. [👁237]

THE I CHING

Blending aspects of religion, philosophy, and mysticism, the I Ching is perhaps most easily understood as a staggeringly complex advice column. Imagine Ann Landers manipulating 50 thin yarrow sticks into hexagrams and then consulting a dense text for a corresponding prophecy—which is ambiguous at best, and utterly cryptic at worst. However, if interpreted properly, the I Ching can reward its follower with the answers to questions ranging from the soul-searching to the shallow: Should I sign the contract? Return my lover's letter? Get fitted for contacts?

The term I Ching can refer to the method of seeking advice; the method's underlying Taoist philosophy, which embraces the concepts of chance and change; or the book that holds the keys to reading the castings themselves. This book, perhaps one of the earliest texts in history, is said to have been written by King Wen and his son the Duke of Zhou in 1150 B.C., but its origins may go back as far as 3000 B.C. Since then, commentary that is now integral to

The 12 Animals and Their Characteristics

The corresponding year for each animal cycle can be calculated beginning with 1900, which was the Year of the Rat. (Keep in mind that Chinese new years start in late January or February, so if you were born in the early part of the year, you probably fall under the preceding year's animal sign.)

1 RAT—sociable, persistent, intellectual, manipulative

2 OX—patient, hardworking, loners, stubborn

3 TIGER—courageous, self-assured, authoritative, rash

4 RABBIT—discreet, ambitious, forgiving, devious, squeamish

5 DRAGON—scrupulous, sentimental, influential, demanding, judgmental

6 SNAKE—wise, elegant, decisive, ostentatious, possessive

7 HORSE—amiable, skillful, independent, weak, hot-headed

8 SHEEP—creative, sweet-natured, persevering, pessimistic, undisciplined

9 MONKEY—intelligent, achievers, passionate, opportunistic, unscrupulous

10 ROOSTER—frank, resourceful, generous, braggarts, short-sighted

11 DOG—loyal, modest, prosperous, introverted, cynical

12 PIG—obliging, impartial, sensitive, profound, naive, insecure

DREAM SYMBOLS AND WHAT THEY MEAN

ANCESTORS: Dreaming about your ancestors means there's money in your future.

BLOOD: Don't be worried if you dream of being covered in blood; this is actually a good omen, though it's admittedly a scary dream.

CRYING: Tears in a dream are a sign that illness will come to the person seen crying.

DANCING: A dream of dancing means that you'll argue with your dancing partner.

DOORS: If it's open, good luck will come your way. If it's hanging on a hinge, watch out.

FIGHTING: Dreaming of fighting is fortunate, and means that any problems you might have with the person you've dreamed of will soon go away.

KILLING: Strangely, if you dream of killing someone or of being killed, you will have great fortune soon.

MOON: If you dream of moonlight, you're due for a positive career change in the near future.

SUN: Dreaming of dawn can mean either an improvement in business prospects or longevity; dreaming of a sunbeam that comes into your home, however, is an indication that you will be investigated by the government. Dreaming of a sunny day means that your child will be famous and rich.

WATER: Dreaming of pure water in any form is always lucky and a sign of wealth.

WOMEN: As sexist as it may seem, dreaming of walking with a woman is an omen that you'll lose money, although dreaming of a naked woman is a sign of good fortune. Or simply a sign that you're male.

the main text has been added by numerous scholars, including Confucius. The great teacher once said that if he had 50 years of his life to spare, he would devote them all to studying the I Ching. The I Ching has seen some unusual usage in this century. Japanese officers in World War II attributed their early victories to the I Ching; the psychologist C.G. Jung championed it as a means to manifest the unconscious; cancer researchers have used it in their quest for a cure. Today, Buddhist monks across Asia incorporate the I Ching into rituals and ceremonies. In this country, numerous English translations have made the I Ching accessible to the general public, ensuring that it will continue to pop up in the unlikeliest places.

PHYSIOGOMY

The next time you outsmart your arch-enemy or stand up to your boss, you might want to take a moment to thank your long ears and your uneven eyebrows. These are just a few of the traits that face readers, or physiogomists, claim are written in the folds, flaps, and features of your face.

There are many ways to read a face, each involving dividing the face into sections corresponding to traits or destinies. One of the most common methods is known as "six storehouses, three powers, three stops." The storehouses, or elements, are metal, wood, water, fire, earth, and grain; the three powers are Heaven (the forehead), Earth (the nose) and Man (the chin); the three stops are the three thirds of your face, as divided vertically, with the upper third representing intelligence, relationships, and life force. If you're curious as to what a physiogomist might think of your mug, note that in general, larger features portend good fortune, but overall balance and harmony is the final indicator, so if you have big ears that are ill-defined or a big mouth with drooping corners, poverty and misery will likely be your lot (although someone should probably inform Ross Perot, Clark Gable, and Alicia Silverstone). Face readers also look for animal characteristics, linking specific traits in your personality to similarities to the 12 animals of the Chinese zodiac.

A skilled face reader can examine the shape and placement of your facial features within these locations to give an astoundingly accurate analysis of your character, though Western scientists, ever the party poopers, have attributed face-reading accuracies to psychosomatic factors rather than any kind of mystical forces; still, out of the many possible means of divination, physiogomy has the advantage at least of "reading" something that bears a direct relationship to one's identity—and enough people take it seriously that it shouldn't be dismissed out of hand. Physiogomy was accorded extreme social importance in ancient China, where facial characteristics might help to make or break a bureaucrat's career. And even today, employment agencies in France often narrow their lists by analyzing candidates' photographs for promising traits, while in Hong Kong, companies hire face readers to sit in on job interviews.

PALMISTRY

In the world of palm reading, there's fast food and health food. The first costs about $5, and can be found in dingy stores where your reader will quickly tell you about your happy, prosperous, and lengthy future, and then forsee a tall, dark stranger in your life. Entertaining, but not very substantial. Then there are cheirologists—scientific-minded folks who scorn the cheap, schlocky stuff, and use the art to divine temperament, longevity, wealth, intellect, character, and destiny—which may involve tall, dark strangers after all.

Experts trace the origins of palm reading back to about 2000 B.C. in India. The clue? The hands of Indian statues from that period, which were often carefully marked with lines relevant to palmistry. From India, palm reading is thought to have spread to China and Japan; Egypt; and eventually, the West, where mention of the subject appears in Aristotle's notes. Indeed, for centuries, up through the Victorian era, the principles of palm reading were mainly derived from the ancient Asian practice, diverging only in relatively recent times. As to whether it works, in 1990, British scientists examining the hands of 100 corpses found a correlation between the length of the "life line" and longevity, while modern practitioners of holistic medicine, drawing from traditional Chinese principles, have developed elaborate rationales for correspondence between aspects of the mind and body, and marks on the palm. The answer: as with most divinatory arts, it works if you think it does.

Your Future Is in the Palm of Your Hand

If you're curious about what a Chinese palm reader might say about your hand, note that he or she will likely pay close attention to "the three wonders, or the bumps at the base of the the three middle fingers. The "virtue peak" (under the index finger) is an indicator of wealth, as well as the first 25 years of your life; the "emolument peak" (under the middle finger) is an indicator of official position and the second 25 years; the "blessings peak" (under the ring finger) is an indicator of longevity, as well as of the third 25 years. (Presumably, those who outlive the age of 75 record their fortunes somewhere in the pinky area.) Another characteristic he or she will analyze are palm lines, examining their depth, length, and refinement. Different readers may also look for messages in the joints, in the fingers, or in lines that seem to form Chinese characters—for example, those owning lines forming the character for "ten," shaped like a cross, will likely gain assistance from someone wealthy.

CHAN MENG: CHINESE DREAM ANALYSIS

In psychoanalysis, the vivid illusions we experience at night are held to contain secrets about our waking lives; in the ancient Chinese art of chan meng, our dreams are believed to be coded glimpses of the future. Dream analysis and prophecy have been practiced in virtually every culture in the world, but rarely with the thoroughness and complexity of the Chinese system. The rationale behind chan meng is convincing, in a pseudoscientific way: In traditional Chinese belief, the human soul has two parts—one that drives the body, the other that commands the intellect; dreams are the wanderings of the higher soul through space and time, released by sleep and guided by the hands of higher beings. Though chan meng had many disciplines, perhaps the most prominent was known as the "dialectical school," said to have been popularized by the legendary Duke of Zhou, compiler of the massive dream guide known as the *Zhou gong jie meng*. In this school, dream-symbols are (with some exceptions) assumed to be representative of their real-life opposites: Misfortunes experienced while dreaming indicate good luck to come, and vice versa.

Feng Shui

It has been said that the night before Bruce Lee died, a typhoon hit Hong Kong, knocking down the kung fu star's *pa kua* mirrors. This altered Lee's *feng shui*, leaving him unprotected, and resulting in his untimely demise. What's a pa kua mirror? For that matter, what's feng shui? Pa kua mirrors are traditionally used by Chinese to protect homes, offices, and buildings from evil. When yin and yang **[👁241]** energy form stagnant eddies or flows the wrong way, locations can be vulnerable to misfortune, disharmony, or ill-health; these special mirrors deflect the adverse energy that causes them. This is feng shui, an art of environmental design used to improve fortunes by directing qi **[👁241]**, the cosmic flow of life and energy, in beneficial and advantageous ways.

Feng shui, literally "wind and water," originated at least 3,000 years ago, and its age-old concepts are still practiced by many Chinese (and increasing numbers of Westerners) today. Of course, to adhere exactly to the principles of feng shui is nearly impossible. Ideally, you would live in a perfectly shaped house (rectangular, square, or circular) located on a hill, facing the proper direction, and surrounded by an acceptable configuration of houses, trees, rivers, and other factors largely out of your control. That done, you would have to arrange your furniture and decorations precisely according to the day and time of your birth—and shift it regularly according to changes in the seasons, the environment, or your health.

One of the few examples of a structure built precisely with principles of feng shui in mind is Beijing's Summer Palace, constructed between 1886 and 1891. From the rectangular plot overlooking a lake, the Empress Dowager could pull political strings without worrying about cosmic winds blowing misfortune her way (never mind would-be assassins). Since you probably don't have the millions of peasants required for such a task, you'll have to make do with simpler efforts maximizing your current situation. Even the most hapless of houses can be tuned with relative ease: One can hang chimes, get rid of disharmonious objects, and rearrange furniture. One can place an odd number of goldfish in strategic locations. And one can, as noted above, hang mirrors to turn away malign influences (but don't redirect them toward someone else; this could start a mirror war, with unfortunate consequences for all).

Trump International Hotel & Tower, NYC

Is feng shui a skill to live by or a scam preying on the spiritually and architecturally naive? Urban and not-so-urban legends abound regarding the successes of those who follow feng shui and the tragedies of those who don't. Chiang Kai-shek's political ascent has been linked to the ideal placement of his mother's grave site; his fall, to Mao Zedong's digging it up. There may not be a connection, but why take chances? Shrewd millionaire Donald Trump didn't when he broke ground for the new Trump Hotel in Manhattan in the summer of 1995. Trump and his business-suited colleagues were led by traditionally garbed Chinese geomancers, who properly assessed and blessed the site, giving it the Good Feng Shui Seal of Approval. Has that done anything for the former billionaire's fortunes? Time will tell. And anyway, at least he's still a *millionaire*. —M.W.

FENG SHUI-ING THE WHITE HOUSE

How can the hot seat in the Executive Office be cooled down? According to the ancient system, 16th Street stabs the White House right in its doorway, piercing the President's ch'i and symbolically dividing the country. Installing a fountain or windmill is one way to disperse and distribute the energy. Such neutralization of the "killing ch'i" would improve the mansion's feng shui, allowing the President to act more wisely and, in turn, help the country to flourish.

DO-IT-YOURSELF FENG SHUI

If you're down on your luck or just want more of it, but don't want to pay a geomancer big bucks (at least $200 an hour) to improve your environmental harmony, adhere to the following rules:

Bathroom

- One's bathroom can be anywhere in the house except for the center, since it's unpleasant when foul odors spread throughout the house. Also, as water flows down the drain through the center of the household, so will fortunes.

Kitchen

- In the kitchen, it's important for the oven and rice cooker to be out in the open, so the cook's qi can circulate. If you have a small kitchen, mirrors can help. It's also a good idea to hang a picture of the kitchen god above the oven. If you smear honey on his mouth before the New Year, he'll have nothing but sweet things to say about your household when he makes his annual trip to heaven.

Color

- The colors in your home affect your destiny. **Red**, associated with fire, warmth, happiness, and strength, is ideal. **Green**, the color of spring, connotes freshness. **Yellow**, like the sun, symbolizes longevity. Because **white** is worn by mourners in China, it should be avoided where possible. Besides, according to some, the lack of color dulls the senses.

Your Bedroom

- If you live in a boot-shaped house or apartment, the bedroom must not go where the toe would be. This dead-end arrangement stifles fate and career opportunities, especially if your bed is against the furthermost wall.
- The bed should never face directly towards the door. All your energy will flow out the door. This arrangement also resembles a funeral parlor's, inviting premature death. However, you should always be able to see the door from your bed.
- Don't place your bed beneath a visible beam. A beam that goes directly over a bed can cause headaches, drain creativity, and promote mental disorder in the person who sleeps below. If the beam runs perpendicular to the bed, it will cause stomachaches and problems in your career.

Decoration

- The patterns on your wallpaper, table linens, tile, or carpet, can be beneficial. Patterns that resemble chrysanthemums and other long-lived plants symbolize eternity and patience. Similarly, patterns that look like tortoise shells represent the longevity that is associated with the revered animal. Water and cloud patterns bring blessings from the heavens (read: cash money).
- If you have paintings, they should be hung in pairs to maintain balance. Scrolls should be equal length, and frames should be circular or fan-shaped for purposes of balance, as well. The paintings themselves should include plants that represent longevity, landscapes with yin and yang elements, or gods or deities to guard the household from evil. Often, depictions of god and demons are placed on doors for protection.
- Negative energy can be converted into good with goldfish, as the Chinese word for fish resembles the word for prosperity. To maximize your luck, stock your aquarium with an odd number of fish and place it in your unluckiest spot. The fish bring fortune and the water absorbs evil energies.

Windows

- The windows of a house are directly related to its residents' orifices. So, if your windows are dirty or blocked, your eyes, ears, and mouth may not function well. Likewise, if you're pregnant, childbirth will also be more difficult. Windows that only open halfway only let in half the qi; make sure you can open them wide, and let the sun shine in.

GURUS: The Good, Bad, and Frankly Scary

The term "guru" simply means "teacher" in Sanskrit; it was used by Hindus as a term of respect for a spiritual leader, and later by the Sikhs to refer to the ten great leaders who founded and built their religion. In the West, it has since acquired a more troubling definition, denoting a Svengaliesque "holy" person whose honesty is suspect. Unfortunately, some Asian religious leaders have been tarred with the darker side of the guru brush—even those with devout faith and unimpeachable values. Here are some of the many who've been called spiritual gurus in recent history, both good and less good. —H.K., J.Y.

THE GURU HALL OF FAME

Name:
Mahad Prasad Varma
Better known as:
Maharishi Mahesh Yogi
Religious Organization:
The Spiritual Regeneration Movement
Phenomenon Most Associated With:
Transcendental Meditation
Origin:
Born October 18, 1911, in Uttar Pradesh, India.
Star Groupies:
The Beatles, Mia Farrow, Shirley MacLaine, Doug Henning
Rise to Guruosity:
In 1958, the man who would be called Maharishi established his Spriritual Regeneration Movement in Madras. He soon acquired a following that included some of that era's most famous individuals—most prominently the Beatles, who were responsible for introducing the hitherto-unknown spiritual leader and his message of Transcendental Meditation to the Western world. Once he'd broken through, the Maharishi quickly wound his way into the Western psyche, by regaling audiences with homilies about the ecstasy that springs from twisting one's legs into pretzels and contemplating nothingness. The spread of TM led to the creation of a tightly organized syndicate of practitioners, supported by a massive web of local TM centers throughout the world. Meanwhile, the glassy-eyed devotion with which thousands of disciples have embraced his teachings has invited charges of cultism. It's not entirely difficult to see why: According to the tenets of the Maharishi, world peace, natural harmony, and even the Dow Jones Industrial Average are directly linked to the number of people meditating in the world. The chorus of skeptics has led to attack by anti-cult groups, as well as TM-EX, a group of ex-Transcendentalists, mobilized expressly to work against the spread of the Maharishi's teachings. Still, despite these nattering nabobs of non-belief, the Maharishi, who currently resides quietly in the Netherlands, soldiers on. The Maharishi University of Management in Fairfield, Iowa—created as a learning annex to further spiritual evolution—still operates. The Maharishi Ayurveda Health Center in Lancaster, Massachusetts, a mind-body health spa, offers a comprehensive prevention and healing program.

Name:
Dr. Deepak Chopra
Better known as:
The "Doc of Ages" (just kidding)
Origin:
Born in 1946 in New Delhi, India
Star Groupies: George Harrison, Country & Western star Wynonna Judd, New Age luminary Marianne Williamson, filmmaker David Lynch
Rise to Guruosity:
After earning a medical degree from the All India Institute of Medical Sciences with residencies in Internal Medicine and Endocrinology, and then becoming chief of staff at the New England Memorial Hospital, Chopra's life and career took a mystical turn when he became enamored with the teachings and philosophy of the Maharishi Mahesh Yogi. He consequently immersed himself in the study of

Ayurveda, the ancient system of holistic (mind-body) healing from India [212]. "Private practice had become extremely frustrating," Chopra has said. "The main thing I did was hand out pills. I felt like a legalized drug pusher." Chopra became the Maharishi's point man at the Maharishi Ayurveda Health Center; later, after a hostile split with the Maharishi, he left the center and established the American Association of Ayurvedic Medicine. The literate and telegenic Chopra has since put his holistic wizardry into overdrive, with dozens of bestselling books and programs, including blockbusters like *Return of the Rishi, Quantum Healing, Ageless Body, Timeless Mind* and *The Seven Spiritual Laws of Success.* While devotees claim that his writings have enriched their lives enormously, there's no doubt that they've at the very least enriched their author.

Name:
Bikram Choudhury
Better known as: The Yogi to the Stars
Origin:
Born 1946 in Calcutta, India
Star Groupies: Kareem Abdul-Jabbar, Jerry Seinfeld, Carol Lynley, Candice Bergen, Quincy Jones, and (of course) Shirley Maclaine
Rise to Guruosity:
At the age of 12, Choudhury became the youngest national yogic master in India; six years later, he helped open a number of schools, and developed an enthusiastic expatriate American following in Bombay by the mid 1960s. Ultimately, this led to a trip across the waters, where he started the Yoga College of India in Beverly Hills, California, catering to the needs of a star-studded community looking to escape the centrifuge of modern life. Choudhury doesn't mollycoddle his rich and powerful clientele, instead demanding total submission to a strict, painful regimen. In return, he promises a robust life filled with great sex and gobs of money. And, since many of his followers are big celebrities, wouldn't you know it, his promises often come true.

Name:
Kamala Reddy
Better known as:
Mother Meera
Origin:
Born 1961 in India
Star Groupie: Madonna
Rise to Guruosity:
Mother Meera is a Hindu philosopher living in Germany, whose wisdom is bestowed upon seekers with a simple (and silent) laying on of hands. Mystic and author Andrew Harvey's 1990 book *Hidden Journey* provided a literary forum for Mother Meera's voice, instantly creating a worldwide following for the tight-lipped giver of peace. Even pop deity Madonna, a Catholic (well, sorta), knelt before her for her manual blessing. Since then, however, Harvey has completely divorced himself from Mother Meera's movement, citing sinister attempts at spiritual manipulation. Harvey alleges that Mother Meera cajoled him, to no avail, to write a book about how she'd "cured" him of his homosexuality.

Name:
Chinmoy Kumar Ghose
Better known as:
Sri Chinmoy
Origin:
Born 1931 in Bangladesh
Star Groupies:
Carlos Santana, Sheena Easton, Carl Lewis; plus, the following who aren't groupies per se, but people who've received Chinmoy's unusual "honor" (he's lifted them above his head with one arm): Reverend Jesse Jackson, Eddie Murphy, Roberta Flack, former Chicago Bulls coach Doug Collins. He's also had pictures of himself taken conversing with Muhammad Ali, Mikhail Gorbachev, and two Popes.
Rise to Guruosity:
One of modern spiritualities most engaging and peculiar figures, Chinmoy entered an ashram in India at the age of 12, and spent his adolescent years meditating 11 hours a day. At age 32, he decided that the strange skills and inner peace he'd developed through his meditative training needed to be shared with the world, beginning with New York City, where he arrived a year later in 1964. The skills in question aren't just spiritual: Chinmoy, if you believe his assertions, is also one of the world's greatest poets and authors, as well as a world-class sprinter and power weightlifter. Chinmoy's teachings, which he explicitly states are not religious, advocate that inner peace can be found through "self-transcendence"—a feat that can be achieved through massive amounts of meditation, plus extreme physical activity. As a result, his thousands of followers often dedicate themselves to excelling in athletic competition,

or more often in somewhat more bizarre physical feats, like setting world records for underwater pogo-stick jumping. Chinmoy and his followers are also known for scouring the globe for prominent locations on which to stick a Chinmoy "Peace Plaque," a metal memorial bearing a somewhat surreal poem about global harmony penned by the guru himself. Recently, an uproar arose when the keepers of the Statue of Liberty allowed one to be bestowed upon the statue's base—only to hastily rescind permission after people questioned its appropriateness. Chinmoy currently lives in a small house in Queens, New York, and is proud of the fact that he drives not a vast limousine (as some other spiritual leaders have transported themselves) but a 1972 Ford Maverick.

Name:
Yogi Amrit Desai
Better known as:
"Gurudev," or
"Blessed Teacher"
Origin:
Born in 1933 in India

Star Groupies:
Tony Goldwyn, Woody Harrelson, Isabella Rossellini, and Olympia Dukakis
Rise to Guruosity:
Desai learned his hybrid blend of mediation from a teacher named Swami Kripalvanandji as a young man, but gave no thought to becoming a guru himself until, with business sense at least as keen as his spiritual insight, he recognized that there was great potential in proffering meditation as a relaxation medium for harried and disenchanted yuppies—a revelation he came to while giving yoga classes to fellow students at the Philadelphia College of Art. Abandoning his original goal of becoming a graphic designer, he began teaching yoga full time, and eventually drew enough followers to set up his own center in 1972 in Sumneytown, Pennsylvania, which he named the Kripalu Center for Yoga and Health after his former mentor. In 1983, the Kripalu Fellowship had grown enough to purchase a former Jesuit seminary in the town of Stockbridge, Massachusetts, transforming it into a new world-class headquarters. Thousands of new adherents were drawn to the center. In October 1994, however, the fellowship was thrust into crisis when it was revealed that the then 61-year-old Desai—whose central dogma was the necessity of celibacy—had been having long-term affairs with at least three of his woman devotees. While Desai's downfall was a stunning blow to the Kripalu fellowship, it wasn't deadly; the center continues on, though without its charismatic leader, it has had less cachet. Meanwhile, Desai has expressed his sorrow, both publicly and privately.

Name:
Reverend Sun Myung Moon
Stage Name:
Dr. Moonbeam
Origin:
Born January 6, 1920, in Cheong-ju, Pyong-an Buk-jdo, Republic of Korea
Rise to Guruosity:
Founder of the Holy Spirit Association for the Unification of World Christianity, otherwise known simply as the Unification Church, Moon purports to have been visited on Easter Day 1936 by Jesus, who commissioned him to create Heaven on Earth. Moon set out on his mission as a full-time preacher, eventually founding his church in Seoul in 1953. His recorded epiphanies make up the crux of The Divine Principle, the abiding testament of "Moonie" life. One central facet of the Moon doctrine is the grand role that marriage plays in a person's life; Moon, the avuncular matchmaker, has performed several mass weddings over the years, marrying thousands of devotees in one fell swoop. In October 1982 in Seoul, he led 11,674 of his followers over the threshold, with most of the participants having met their betrothed just hours before the ceremony. Reviled by the press and public as a self-serving miscreant, Moon has been charged with robotizing thousands of young, vulnerable people for personal gain in Korea and through his extensive operations in the U.S., and indeed, Moon has proven to be as inspired as much by profit as he is by prophecy. Most Americans can recollect being accosted at some point in their lives by zombie-like Moonies hawking flowers and trinkets. At one time or another, Moon has also greased his palms in the media business (with his ownership of the *Washington Times* and other papers) and the movie industry (with the 1982 multimillion megaflop *Inchon*). With estate holdings estimated in the millions, Moon was hounded by the IRS for years, eventually serving 13 months in prison in the mid 1980s for tax evasion. Though no longer personally welcome in America, his empire and following remain huge—here and throughout the world. —D.G., J.Y.

Hinduism

Hinduism, the faith of 83 percent of the population in India, is perhaps the world's oldest religious tradition. While it has not spread broadly beyond its origin culture (as has, for instance, Christianity), because of the sheer size of the Indian population, it is the 3rd largest religion in the world, with over 700 million believers. Of course, Hindu beliefs are far from monolithic, and in a random sampling of a dozen faithful worshippers you'll find at least six divergent doctrinal interpretations: Some Hindus eat meat, while others are strict vegetarians. Many see the universe as governed by a staggering number of gods (330 million, at last count), while others see the Hindu pantheon as simply the many faces of the One God. Some worship objects in nature, like trees or rocks, and some worship nothing at all—it's entirely possible to be a Hindu atheist. And yet, despite these broadly disparate ideologies and approaches, the Hindu community manages to coexist in relative harmony, embracing a melting pot of religious ideas under the umbrella of Hinduism.

THE HISTORY OF THE HINDU TRADITION

Unlike other major religions such as Christianity or Islam, it is hard to date the beginning of the Hindu faith, since it has no single founder and no revelatory event; the traditions of the Hindu community are a complex amalgamation of beliefs of the original Dravidian inhabitants of the Indus Valley, and its Aryan invaders, who arrived around 1500 B.C. A few centuries after the Aryan invasion came a period that scholars call the preclassical or "Vedic" era, during which the worldviews of the invaders and their sub-

Rama, an avatar of Vishnu

jects were fused and reinterpreted, and the earliest sacred texts, or vedas, were collected. This period began around 1000 B.C., when the Brahmins (the Aryan priestly caste) compiled a volume of hymns known as the *Rig Veda*. The primary deities of the Vedic period were the warrior god Indra; the god of order Varuna; Agni, the god of fire, and Soma, the god of a hallucinatory drug taken by Brahmins during their rituals. Standing in the shadow of these mighty deities were minor gods Vishnu and Rudra. The former would later move to a central position in the Hindu pantheon, as the lord and preserver of the cosmos, while the latter, renamed Shiva, would similarly rise in importance, becoming the cosmic destroyer.

Around 500 B.C., several important developments occurred. The first was the emergence of two religious traditions in India that broke from the main body of Brahmin tradition: Buddhism, as taught by Siddhartha Gautama, and Jainism, founded by the ascetic Mahavira. The second was the distillation of Brahman thought and doctrine into a series of sacred texts known as the *Upanishads* ("secret teachings"), which sought to clearly explain the purpose and meaning of Brahmin sacred rituals.

It was at this point in Indian history that Hinduism as a distinct set of religious beliefs began to emerge. The *Upanishads* provided a skeleton upon which Brahmin teaching could grow: they framed a religious philosophy in which the rituals performed by the Brahmins were merely external manifestations of the sacrifices that must be made within, in one's internal quest to achieve oneness with brahman, the divine power. Meditation, sacrifice, and holy living bring one closer to brahman; evil deeds and unclean living push one farther away, creating *karma* that must be redeemed through *samsara,* the cycle of transmigration and rebirth. The ultimate goal of existence is thus the complete elimination of negative karma, so as to win freedom from samsara's wheel of suffering.

The revelations of the *Upanishads* ushered in the classical period of Hinduism, which added complexity to the basic doctrine set forth in those texts (collectively, with the earlier vedas, called the *sruti*) by binding to them a devotional aspect known as *bhakti* (literally, "warm devotion toward god"). While the *Upanishads* suggested that worship was an external manifestation of one's inner quest, the idea behind bhakti was that fervent, devotional worship of a god (or, if one prefers, an aspect of God) would release the faithful from the suffering of samsara more quickly than mere meditation. The key inspirational text of bhakti was the *Bhagavad Gita*, or the "Song of the Lord" **[👁32]**—an epic poem composed some time between 300 B.C. and 300 A.D. that tells the story of Krishna, an avatar (human incarnation) of Vishnu. In it Krishna declares quite clearly that those who worship him with complete discipline and faith will be saved from samsara. (The contemporary ISKCON or "Hare Krishna" movement, which takes this declaration quite literally, is an example of a bhakti branch of Hinduism.)

SACRED TEXTS

The Four Vedas—Earliest Hindu texts, but believed to have been passed on orally for centuries before they were transcribed. Includes the *Rig Veda* (the veda of poetry), the *Samaveda* (the veda of songs), the *Yajurveda* (the veda of sacrificial texts), and the *Atharvaveda* (the veda of Atharvan, a mystical fire ceremony priest). Of the four, the *Rig Veda* is the oldest and the most extensive.

Mahabharata—One of the two great Indian epics, written between 300 B.C. and 300 A.D. Contains over 100,000 verses describing myths and dynastic histories. Also contains the *Bhagavad Gita*, a religious story that expounds Hindu attitudes toward life, action, and purpose in the cosmos. **[👁32]**

Ramayana—The second great Hindu epic, it tells the exploits of the hero Rama (like Krishna, an avatar of Vishnu) and incorporates a variety of Hindu myths. Written between 200 B.C. and 200 A.D. **[👁32]**

Puranas—A collection of ancient myths transmitted orally and written down between 250 A.D. and 1550 A.D.

Upanishads—Dialogues between guru and student, many of which are related through stories of great sages who become the courtly teachers of kings desiring instruction in the ultimate truth. The principal *Upanishads*, which laid the foundation of the Hindu faith, were composed between 800 and 400 B.C., though additional *Upanishads* were composed as late as the 16th century A.D.

BASIC CONCEPTS

dharma—the proper way to behave according to social norms, which themselves are merely reflections of the overall cosmic pattern.

karma—the doctrine that one's actions determine one's fate.

samsara—the doctrine of the cycle of transmigration. One's soul (*atman*) is reborn after death, and its new incarnation depends on the karma it has accrued in previous states of existence.

caste—everyone is born into one of four varnas, or social groups. Brahmins or priests, unsurprisingly, are at the top, followed by the Kshatriya class (warriors and administrators), the Vaishya class (cultivators and merchants), and the Sudra class (artisans and laborers). The four castes are further split up into more than 3,000 jatis, or occupational groups, each with its own rules and regulations, such as arranged marriages. Beneath the caste system are the "untouchables," or outcastes who have no social status. Mahatma Gandhi called them *Harijans*, "children of God," in his Hindu reform movement. Unfortunately, the laws of karma don't permit social climbing on the earthly plane, essentially because you deserve to be where you are: to advance in caste one has to advance in samsara.

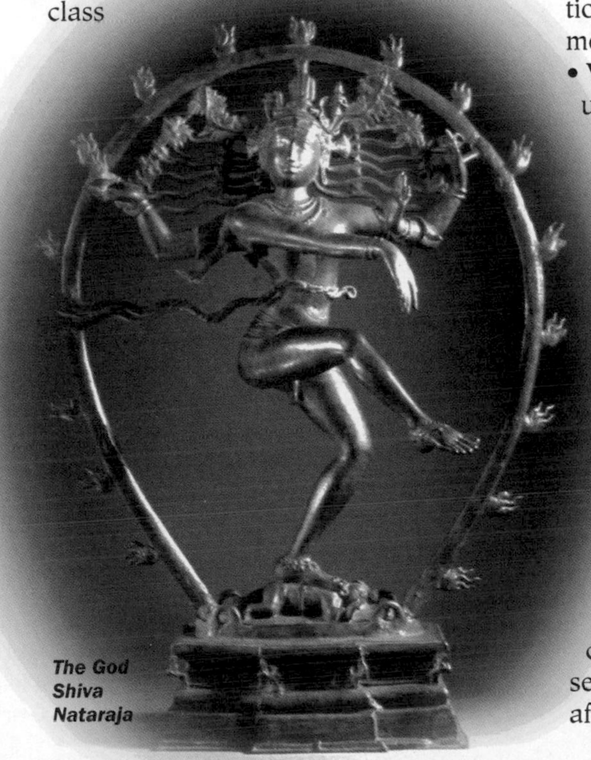

The God Shiva Nataraja

THE CENTRAL TRINITY

- **Brahma** is the creator of the universe, who brings into being life and order from the cosmic chaos. Though in other faiths the creator is usually revered as the highest of divinities, because of the cyclical nature of the Hindu universe **[👁223]**, "creation" takes a back seat to preservation. In modern times, Brahma is given more lip service than full-scale devotion.
- **Vishnu** is the lord and preserver of the universe. Throughout the cycles of cosmic creation and extinction, Vishnu is the stable force that keeps the wheel of existence turning. Through his many avatars, Vishnu also takes a direct interest in human events. All of this makes Vishnu the most popular of Indian deities.
- **Shiva**, the destroyer, rules over death and transformation, of endings that lead to new beginnings; he also represents healing and medicine. Highly feared and respected in the Hindu pantheon, Shiva is responsible for destroying the universe, sweeping up, and turning out the lights at the end of a cosmic cycle. As a result, he has perhaps the second greatest number of worshippers after Vishnu. —K.P, J.Y.

Great Inventions of Asia

While the primordial geniuses responsible for technological innovations like fire and the wheel have gone unsung through time, history has noted that many of the world's other great inventions had their origin in China. Chinese inventors improved on fire by blending saltpeter and sulfur to make gunpowder, leading to a slew of destructive devices, including bombs, grenades, land and sea mines, guns, cannons, and mortars. More peaceable innovators took the wheel and adapted it into devices like the spinning wheel and the water clock. And still other Chinese prodigies developed such necessities as the stem-post rudder, playing cards, paper money, cast iron, and silk. While China's innovative streak has seemingly run down in the modern era, its industrialized Asian neighbors have picked up the slack. Today, Japan is neck and neck with America as the world's leader in innovation, judging by the number of U.S. patents Japanese companies and individuals are granted every year—an average of about 22,913 between 1991 and 1994, nearly half of the total granted to all foreign countries. China, it seems, was simply before its time. Can you imagine what the world would be like today if China had managed to secure a patent on gunpowder—and folding currency?

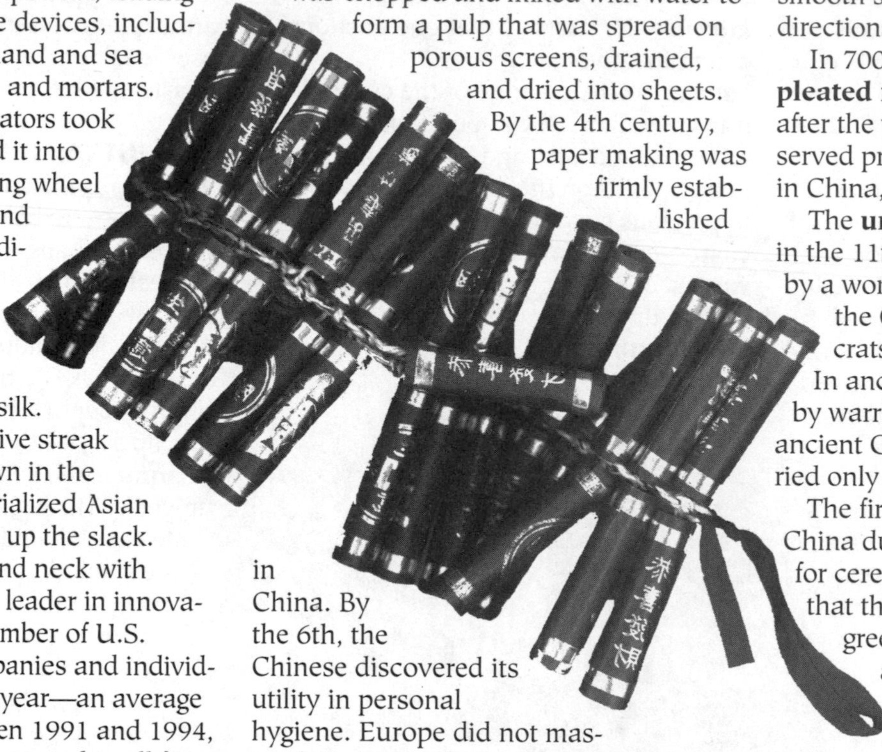

AN ASIAN INNOVATION HALL OF FAME

Paper was invented by Cai Lun, a Minister of Public Works under Emperor He Di during China's Han Dynasty (202 B.C. to 202 A.D.). In 105 A.D. Cai Lun told the emperor, "Bamboo tablets are so heavy and silk so expensive that I sought ways of mixing together fragments of bark, bamboo, and fishnets and I have made a very thin material which is suitable for writing on." The raw material was chopped and mixed with water to form a pulp that was spread on porous screens, drained, and dried into sheets. By the 4th century, paper making was firmly established in China. By the 6th, the Chinese discovered its utility in personal hygiene. Europe did not master the science of papermaking until the 12th century.

Though it is often believed that German printer Johannes Gutenberg developed **movable type**, it was actually invented in China by Pi Sheng in 1045, to equip printers with permanent raised characters. Pi Sheng's original characters were made out of heat-fired clay; in 1234, Korea developed metal type, which was widely used by the 1400s.

During the 1st century B.C., the Chinese observed that pieces of lodestone, an iron-containing ore, always pointed north when placed on a surface where it was free to spin. This curious discovery eventually led to the modern **compass**. The first Chinese compass was a spoon made of lodestone that rested on a smooth surface marked with the four directions.

In 700 A.D. the Japanese invented the **pleated fan [👁7]**. Probably modeled after the way a bat folds its wings, the fan served practical and ceremonial purposes in China, Japan, and Korea.

The **umbrella** first appeared in China in the 11th century, reportedly invented by a woman. Originally, only members of the Chinese royal family and aristocrats were allowed to use umbrellas. In ancient Egypt, they were even used by warriors during battle, while in ancient Greece and Rome they were carried only by women.

The first **fireworks** were created in China during the 10th century and used for ceremonial functions. Legend has it that the first firecrackers were stalks of green bamboo, which exploded with a bang when set aflame. The earliest records of **gunpowder** use in fireworks, cannons, and guns, are in Chinese and Indian manuscripts dating back to the 9th and 10th centuries. Ironically, the Chinese inventors of gunpowder were said to have been seeking an alchemical elixir of eternal life. Obviously, they failed.

The first recorded account of a **suspension bridge** dates back to 25 B.C., from a Chinese dynastic text. These early bridges were made of bamboo. In 1638, Major Li Fang-hsien built a suspension bridge made out of metal chains. —C.Y.

Japanese

Compared to other Asian tongues, Westerners may find the sound of Japanese relatively familiar; it uses sounds that are similar to those found in English and Romance languages, with vowels pronounced more or less as they are in Spanish or Italian. But instead of an alphabet, Japanese uses a syllabary of 46 vowels and consonant-vowel units. Japanese grammar is also significantly different from Western tongues; the basic sentence structure is subject-object-verb (for example, "Johnny Japanese speaks"). Instead of prepositions, there are *post*positions, and there are particles that go after words to indicate part of speech. In addition, conversing without causing offense requires mastery of a hideously complex system of "conjugation" to indicate levels of politeness, gender, and social status. Meanwhile, writing Japanese requires memorizing two separate sets of characters representing the syllabary, as well as a minimum of 3,000 out of the 50,000 or so Chinese characters that have been incorporated into the Japanese written language.

日本語

アカサタナ

あかさたな

RISING SUN SIGNS

The modern Japanese written language uses a combination of *kanji,* Chinese characters, and *kana,* the two sets of symbols used to represent the syllabary. This rather awkward hybrid system emerged from a series of innovations added after Japan's original adoption of the Chinese writing system in the 6th century A.D. Chinese characters were deemed eminently capable of conveying meaning, but they offered little indication of pronunciation; as a result, the phonetic kana (originally meaning "temporary writing") were invented.

Hiragana, the 46 rounded, cursive kana used to write native Japanese words, verb and adjective endings, and particles, was said to have been invented by the Buddhist priest Kukai (774-835). Meanwhile, the angular symbols of *katakana* ("side writing") were said to have been created by Kibi no Makibi (693-755) around the same time. Katakana is generally used for foreign terms.

Kanji are used for most words with substance, and the proper use of kanji is a requirement for any educated individual. Though kanji are Chinese characters, they aren't pronounced as they are in Chinese, and in some cases the meaning of characters has changed over time. Some 3,000 kanji characters are commonly used Japanese, a daunting total that the government of Japan has tried to streamline several times.

Reading kanji out loud presents yet another dimension of complexity in the Japanese system: each kanji character can be read in two ways, depending on whether it is pronounced using Japanese pronunciation (*kunyomi*) or a pronunciation derived from the root Chinese (*onyomi*). No one said learning Japanese was going to be easy.

SPELLING IT OUT

In addition to the systems noted above, Japanese also commonly uses *romaji,* or romanized writing. Romaji are transliterations of Japanese words written out using the English alphabet; the names of Japanese companies—"Sanyo" or "Honda," for instance—are instances of romaji. Americans commonly use the modified Hepburn (or Hyojun) system, developed in 1885 and named after the American missionary James Curtis Hepburn, who used it for his Japanese-English dictionary in 1886. In Japan, however, the Kunrei system, which originated in the 1880s, is widely used.

Still, the differences are minor; for example, where Kunrei uses a "z," modified Hepburn uses a "j." —D.G., J.Y.

KANSAI-BEN, THE DEALER'S DIALECT

While standard Japanese (Hyojun-go) is based on the dialect spoken in Tokyo, there are dozens of regional dialects, differing both in word usage and accent. One of the more popular nonstandard dialects is Kansai-ben ("Western dialect"), spoken in Japan's Osaka region. Since Osaka has long been a primary center of commerce, Osakans are stereotyped as being thrifty, hard-dealing, and money-minded, and the Kansai dialect reflects this cultural strain: it's clipped and direct, with many words contracted and syllables dropped. Drawn-out vowels are also typically trimmed off: "ikou" means "let's go" in standard Japanese; an Osakan would say "iko" instead, cutting the word short. There are also minor word substitutions, such as the use of word "ya" for "desu" and its variations. All of these changes make Kansai-ben a colorful variant to the standard dialect, particularly for situations like street haggling. Here are some sample Kansai-ben phrases, in case you find yourself in a dealmaking position with an Osakan native:

MOKARIMAKKA: "How's business?" This isn't just a polite term or use in commerce; it's a daily greeting in Osaka.

BOCHI BOCHI DENNA: "Not bad." This is an appropriate response to "Mokarimakka."

OOKINI: "Thanks."

NANNBO?: "How much?"

MAKETE: "Make it cheaper." A key word for tourists in Kansai—since negotiating is considered the norm, all prices are "adjusted" for haggling purposes.

CHAU CHAU: "Chau" ("Chigau" in Hyojun-go) means "That's wrong"; the word is often repeated for emphasis.

NAMETONNOKA!: "Don't make a fool of me!"

THE CORRECT SOUNDS FOR THE INSTRUCTION OF THE PEOPLE

The letterforms in Hunmin chong-um were inspired by observation of human speech, as well as natural phenomena: consonants were crafted to mimic the shape one's mouth should form in speaking them, with additional strokes added to indicate the strength or "aspiration" of the sound; vowels were adapted from stylized images of the sky, land, and mankind. Over time, four of the original 28 letterforms were dropped, leaving 14 basic consonants and ten vowels: From these 24 easy pieces, grouped into syllable units for ease of reading, Koreans compose nearly 3,000 syllables (even though only a few hundred are used with any regularity). Ironically, the strongest proof of Hangul's ease of use came from its earliest critics: Contemptuous scholars called it Amk'ul ("women's letters") or Ach'imgul ("morning letters," since the system could be learned in a single morning).

CONSONANTS:

g	n	d	r or l	m	b
ㄱ	ㄴ	ㄷ	ㄹ	ㅁ	ㅂ

s or sh	voiceless	j
ㅅ	ㅇ	ㅈ

ch'	k'	t'	p'	h
ㅊ	ㅋ	ㅌ	ㅍ	ㅎ

VOWELS:

a	ya	uh	yuh	o	yo
ㅏ	ㅑ	ㅓ	ㅕ	ㅗ	ㅛ

u	yu	eu	ee
ㅜ	ㅠ	ㅡ	ㅣ

Korean

한국말이 어렵습니까, 쉽습니까?

Is Korean difficult or easy?

Koreans immigrated Westward in large numbers only in the latter part of the 20th century, and as such Korean is still perceived as something of a novelty by most Americans, with relatively few institutions offering programs of Korean study. Still, it's one of the top 15 most spoken languages in the world, with more speakers than Italian. Besides the 70 million or so inhabitants of North Korea and South Korea, another million speak the language in the People's Republic of China, along with half a million each in the former Soviet republics and the U.S. In ease of study, it's somewhat less difficult to learn than Chinese and Japanese (which still doesn't make it easy). And Hangul, the writing system used in Korean, has long been lauded for its simplicity and logic, having been called the "the most scientific system of writing in general use in any country" by the late Edwin O. Reischauer, Harvard professor and former U.S. ambassador to Japan.

WRITING KOREAN

Like the Japanese, Koreans initially borrowed their writing system from Chinese, and then later made vast changes when they realized the shortcomings of that language for their particular polysyllabic spoken tongue. The period of Korea's usage of written Chinese lasted until the 13th century, during which many Chinese words were incorporated into the local vocabulary (about half of the words in a standard Korean dictionary are of Chinese origin). Unfortunately, the use of Chinese characters made widespread literacy all but impossible, and in 1446, during the Choson Dynasty (1393-1910), the great king Sejong determined that broad access to the written word was essential for the welfare of his people. King Sejong envisioned a uniquely Korean writing system using a phonetic letterset, making it easily learnable and usable even by those without full education. Thus was born the *Hunmin chong-um* (literally, "the correct sounds for the instruction of people")—the root of modern Hangul. In the proclamation he delivered announcing its creation in 1446, King Sejong said: "Being of foreign origin, Chinese characters are incapable of capturing uniquely Korean meanings. Therefore, many common people have no way to express their thoughts and feelings. Out of my sympathy for their difficulties, I have created a set of 28 letters. The letters are very easy to learn, and it is my fervent hope that they improve the quality of life of all people."

DIALECTS

Although many regional dialects exist, such as the Pusan dialect of the south, the dialect spoken in Seoul, South Korea's capital, is considered the national and international standard.

ROMANIZATION

The predominant method of Korean transliteration was devised in the 1930s by George M. McCune, an American scholar, and Edwin Reischauer. The McCune-Reischauer system was adopted by the Library of Congress in 1991. —D.G. & J.Y.

The Cult of Mao

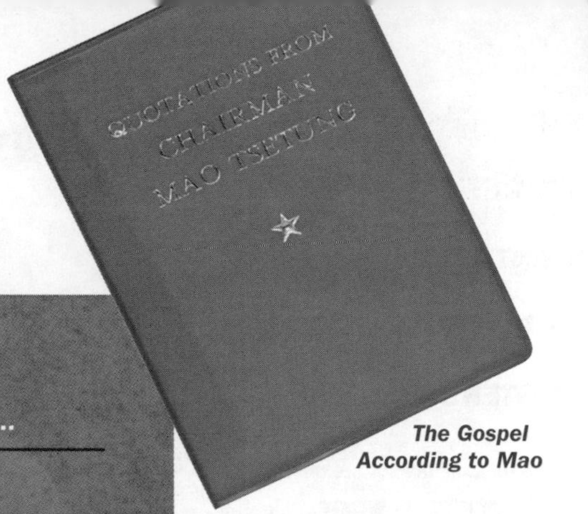

The Gospel According to Mao

He was the leader of the greatest social revolution in history, credited with unifying a country as vast as the territories of Europe. To the Chinese, he's a figure who has alternately been revered and feared, whose power during his life rivalled any of the ancient emperors; to Westerners, Mao Zedong was an iconic stand-in for the Communist threat in China—the face of evil. (Though, to be sure, the counterculture in America admired him as much as the establishment despised him.) Was he a good guy or a bad guy? Like most great leaders in history, it's hard to say for sure.

On the one hand...	On the other hand...
He had the soul of a peasant.	He was a tyrant.
He was a teenage rebel, just like James Dean. ("I graduated from the University of Outlaws.")	He was a control freak.
His Red Army's "Norms of Conduct" included things like "Speak politely" and "Do not hit or swear at people."	More people died under his regime than under Hitler or Stalin.
He stood up for women's rights (Mao married for love and passed laws giving women equal rights to own land and to get divorced).	He had no regard for fidelity in marriage and, as Chairman of the People's Republic of China, slept with dozens of young females from the Cultural Work Troupes.
The "Little Red Book" is the world's second best seller, next to the Holy Bible.	His ideology of constant revolution felt more like having one's own vomit every night for dinner; then again, he did say, "A revolution is not a dinner party."
The Cultural Revolution seemed to make workers feel better about themselves. Until they died, anyway.	All work and no play made China a dull country.
He had that cute mole on his cheek.	He was a bit whacked in the head.
Billions of Chinese can't be wrong.	According to Mao, they often were.

THE POP CULT OF MAO

Once upon a time, people took Mao very, very seriously. During the Cultural Revolution of the 1960s and 1970s, Mao's image and ideology saturated the People's Republic of China. Statues of him were everywhere, people clutched his "Little Red Book" as though it were the Bible, newspapers ran columns of his daily thoughts, and airline flights began with a Mao recitation conducted by a stewardess.

Then Mao died. For a while, a reverent silence fell upon the land; then, in 1981, the Chinese Communist Party said that, on second thought, maybe Mao wasn't right about everything. By the mid 1980s, most of the Mao statues had been removed. No longer a political messiah, people began to look at him as a man. By the late 1980s, a slew of biographies had been written, exposing the Chairman's health problems, his mental state, and his sexual habits. This, of course, fostered a brand new fascination for Mao. By 1990, with the 100th anniversary of his birth looming in 1993, Mao-Maoing had become a popular fad. Karaoke clubgoers sang songs about Mao; the number of annual visitors to his birthplace quintupled. And, with the loosening of China's markets, entrepreneurs began cashing in on Mao commercially. Street peddlers hawked key chains with Mao's photo. Street markets sold old Mao posters, Mao badges, Mao caps, Mao cigarette lighters, and even glow-in-the-dark Mao busts. Today, Beijing cab drivers still hang Mao portraits off their rearview mirrors as a talisman against accidents. Some liken the contemporary pop cult of Mao to a kind of religious iconography in a nation of state-imposed atheism. Some credit the fad to a mood of nostalgia for the uncorrupted 1950s, when Communism was a force for good instead of evil. In any case, Mao kitsch sells, from posters to Pop Art—and the red trade winds are wafting westward. —D.G.

THE SECRET IDENTITIES OF REGULAR CRITTERS

Not all magical beasts are many-headed monsters or bizarre amalgamations; according to Asian myth, many more common animals have secret identities as magical heroes...or villains. Here are a few whom you shouldn't (if you know what's good for you) overlook:

THE FOX—In Chinese and Japanese folk myth, the fox is more than just good eatin' for a pack of hounds; this sharp-witted forest animal is also considered to be a kind of fairy, which can change its shape and possess the unwary.

THE RABBIT—Throughout Asia, the rabbit is identified with the moon; although Westerners see a man in the moon, Chinese and Japanese legend place a rabbit there instead, which is either grinding out the Elixir of Immortality in a sacred pestle or pounding out rice cakes (mochi). In Buddhism, the hare represents complete self-sacrifice, since the rabbit is said to have thrown itself on a burning fire in order to provide food for the Buddha when he was hungry. Rabbits generally represent longevity, since they are supposed to live (if they aren't killed and eaten) a thousand years, turning white at age 500.

Mythical Beasts

The legends of Asia are populated with strange creatures; sometimes they bring fortune, and other times, mischief—but always they lend life and animation to the surroundings of those who have imagined them, turning a walk in the woods into a possible encounter with tengu, or a sudden downpour into the passage of a dragon overhead. What would the world be without them?

THE CHINESE DRAGON (China and Japan)

The dragon has the head of a camel, the eyes of a demon, the ears of a bull, the antlers of a stag, the neck of a snake, the paws of a tiger, and the belly of a clam. This whole monstrosity is covered with 117 scales, which are those of a carp. Despite this description, dragons are generally depicted as being snakelike. The dragon is the greatest of the Four Auspicious Beasts, which include the Phoenix and Unicorn, as well as the Great Tortoise. Emperors throughout Chinese history have claimed descent from dragons, notably Liu Bang, founder of the Han (207 B.C.-220 A.D.), who claimed that he was the son of a dragon who had descended upon his mother in secret—an announcement that must have come as a shock to his father. **LEGEND OF THE DRAGON:** One day in the 4th century B.C., a fortuneteller named Kuei-ku-tzu was visited by a stranger who asked him to predict the weather. Kuei-ku-tzu made a prediction, not knowing that the visitor was actually a dragon in disguise. The dragon proceeded to cause devastating rain throughout the kingdom; many people drowned, and the Jade Emperor of Heaven banished the dragon from the earth. From then on, the dragon provided gentle rains; in return, the people memorialized the exile with a large dragon-banner made of bamboo and paper. This evolved into the dragon dance, which people perform when they want rain or other blessings to arrive. Besides being the spiritual mascot of the Chinese people, the dragon is the symbol of yang, the masculine essence. **[👁241]**

THE PHOENIX (China and Japan)

A heron-like bird with the head of a cock, the shimmering feathers of a golden pheasant and the tail of a peacock, the phoenix is considered by the Chinese to be the second of the Four Auspicious Beasts, and the complement to the dragon. The phoenix was a representation of the Empress, and thus appeared often in company with the Emperor-Dragon symbol—the two beasts together signifying unity, wholeness, and power over the universe. It was also seen as the representation of noble virtues; as one ancient text states, "its color delights the eye, its comb expresses righteousness, its tongue utters sincerity, its voice chants melody, its ear enjoys music, its heart conforms to regulations, its breast contains the treasures of literature, and its spurs are powerful against transgressors." **LEGEND OF THE PHOENIX:** The phoenix embodies yin, the feminine principle of the cosmos **[👁241]**, thus symbolizing beauty, delicacy, and goodness—all of the traits most appreciated in a new bride; in this context, the phoenix is a common design on the clothing and belongings of newlywed women.

THE NAGA (Indian)

Godlike creatures with the bodies of serpents and the heads of humans, these fearsome-looking monsters are imperious and vain, but not always malevolent. Nagas occasionally roam among human folk; female nagas have even intermarried with mortal men. They are the children of Kadru the Mother of Snakes, and their mortal enemy is the Garuda, the giant human-headed bird upon whom Vishnu rides—a case of rivalry among cousins, since Garuda's mother Vinata is the sister of Kadru. **LEGEND OF THE NAGA:** Since nagas were seen as the guardians of the precious (both in terms of material treasure and sacred knowledge), they were often placed at the gates of temples. Hindu myth is full of legends of the naga, some good, some ill. The god Krishna (eighth avatar of Vishnu) defeated the many-headed naga Kaliya by dancing on its heads. The naga king Vasuki was used as a giant spinning-belt to turn Mount Mandara in the great churning of the ocean, which gave rise to Lakshmi the goddess of fortune, as well as other great treasures. Finally, Vishnu **[👁223]** is said to rest on the back of another giant naga, Ananta, during each Cosmic Night.

THE TENGU (Japan)

Tengu have long red noses, birdlike talons and wings, and large round eyes. These mountain goblins can assume the shape of human beings and possess the bodies of the unwary. They love to play tricks on mortals; sometimes these tricks can be dangerous or fatal. Tengu are vain, boastful, and arrogant by nature, and they are said to hate Buddhists—perhaps because of the legend that a lapsed Buddhist priest transforms into a tengu. When Europeans first arrived in Japan, they were often mocked as tengu, due to their large noses. **LEGEND OF THE TENGU:** Official belief in tengu (the magical kind) continued well into the 19th century; in 1860, government officials issued and posted an edict banning tengu and other demons from the Nikko region, where the Shogun had decided to visit.

THE KAPPA (Japan)

A peculiar water goblin with a hairy body, the shell of a turtle, and an apelike head with a concave depression in its forehead, the kappa lurks in streams and near bridges, awaiting passersby. When a mortal attempts to pass its domain, the

kappa challenges him or her to combat; those who choose to fight are generally pulled into the water, drowned, and drained of blood. But those who treat the kappa with courtesy can defeat it, since the source of its great strength is the pool of liquid in the depression in its forehead; bowing politely to the kappa causes it to bow in return, spilling out the liquid, and forcing it to retreat beneath the waters. **LEGEND OF THE KAPPA:** Supposed victims of the kappa who are not killed are marked by a terrible disease, caused by the sucking away of their blood; their skin turns pale, and they waste away. Though this is more probably due to a river-borne disease than the effects of any aquatic goblin, in certain regions of Japan, as many as two deaths per year are ascribed to kappa attack.

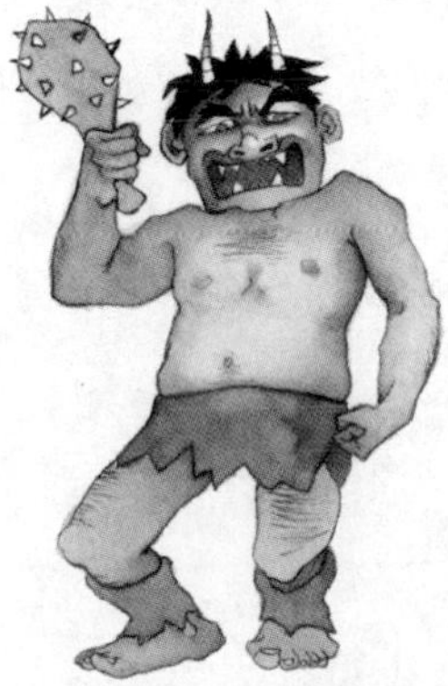

THE ONI (Japan)

The real demons of Japanese legend, oni are terrible, ogreish creatures with wide, tusked mouths, horns, and talons on their hands and feet. They serve Enma, the king of hell, and they are generally depicted as carrying large spiked clubs. Unlike rural loners like the tengu and kappa, oni are organized, martial creatures of evil, who often gather in bands or great armies to challenge gods and human heroes. They occasionally cause changelings to be born in the place of human infants, known as *onikko*; these demon children can be identified by the fact that they are born with a full head of hair or a mouth containing teeth. **LEGEND OF THE ONI:** Oni are woven throughout Japanese myth and legend, and as a result they've resulted in numerous traditions, taboos, and colloquialisms. The Japanese variant of hide and seek is called *onigokko,* and the seeker is known as the oni. A protruding front tooth is referred to as an *oniba,* after the tusks of the oni, but as fearsome as this might be in a demon, in Japanese girls, this is considered to be cute. —J.Y.

THE TORTOISE—The tortoise is often represented as either the supporter of the world or the supporter of the heavens. It is one of the Four Auspicious Beasts of Chinese tradition, and it represents divine wisdom, strength, and immortality.

THE LION—Although the lion is not native to East Asia, it still managed to become central to Chinese and Japanese myth as the defender of just rule and the guardian of the sacred. Over time, the image of the lion converged with that of the Pekingese "lion dog," thus replacing its toothy, ferocious visage with a somewhat more cuddly one; its responsibility as guardian against evil did not dissipate, and lion dances became traditional as a way to drive out demonic forces.

THE MONKEY—One of the most popular and paradoxical beasts in Asian folk tradition is the monkey, who is variously seen as a hero, a trickster, a thief, and a loyal aide. In Hindu myth, Hanuman the monkey god was one of the most important retainers of Rama, the seventh avatar of Vishnu; without Hanuman's help, Rama could not have defeated the demon king Ravana. His East Asian counterpart, Sun Wu K'ung (Son Goku in Japan) is hardly as consistent: Born from a piece of mystical stone, the Monkey King won himself some terrible weapons, stormed heaven, stole the peaches of immortality, and finally was sentenced to protect a travelling monk from harm, which he did, though not without lapses.

South Asian Languages

One out of every four people walking the earth speaks a South Asian language. This shouldn't be a surprise, since the South Asian region is one of the most populous in the world. It's also one of the most linguistically byzantine, with as many as 2,000 languages reported to exist in the region encompassing India, Pakistan, Nepal, Bangladesh, and Sri Lanka. Because of this incredible diversity, South Asia is often called "the linguistic laboratory of the world"; however, many of these so-called languages may actually be dialects, and some may even be the same language, reported under alternative names because of varying social, religious, or ethnic reasons. For example, South Asian Muslims may report their native language as Urdu, but the tongue they speak is perfectly intelligible to Hindus and non-Muslims who speak Hindi. Still, even with this taken into account, the territory offers an enormous verbal spectrum—one that at its best represents a world of cultural richness and variety, and at its worst a world of discrimination, hostility, and contempt.

বাংলা জানেন ?

Do you know Bengali?

The four main South Asian language families are Indo-European, Dravidian, Mundam, and Tibeto-Burman. The Indo-European family includes Hindi/Urdu, Bengali, and Punjabi, as well as most of the European languages. —D.G., N.R.

Hindi is one of the five most widely spoken languages in the world, used by 600 million people in India, Pakistan, Nepal, and—outside Asia—in Mauritius, Trinidad, Fiji, Surinam, Guyana, and South Africa. Along with English, it's the official language of India, and, in fact, the literal translation of "Hindi" is as an adjective meaning "Indian." Written in the Devanagari script of Sanskrit, it reads from left to right, as are Western languages; in its spoken form, Hindi is more or less the same language that Muslims call Urdu.

Urdu is spoken by about 50 million people in Pakistan, where it is the national language, and in India. Its primary difference from Hindi is in its written script, which uses the Perso-Arabic script, and reads from right to left.

Hindustani is the common and standardized form of Hindi and Urdu, adopted as a symbol of national identity by Mahatma Gandhi and the Indian National Congress during the nation's struggle for independence from England.

Bengali is one of the 10 most widely spoken languages in the world, spoken by 150 million people, mainly in India and Bangladesh; it is the national language of Bangladesh and the official language of the Bengal state in India.

Punjabi is the official language of the Punjab in Northern India. Defined by five rivers, the state's name comes from the Persian words for "five" (*Panj*) and "water" (*Aab*); its population is mostly Sikh, particularly since the state was partitioned in 1947, 1948, and 1966, each cut creating subregions of distinct language or faith.

Sanskrit is called the "language of the gods," and the name it carries translates alternately as "purified," "adorned," "cultured," "perfect," "complete," and "ultimate." No wonder; for want of a better comparison, Sanskrit is the Latin of India, the primordial ancestor of all of the dozens of tongues used in modern South Asia. It is also the sacred tongue of the Hindu faith, since all Hindu religious texts were originally composed in Sanskrit. This early, entirely oral form, Vedic Sanskrit, dates back to before 2000 B.C.; it evolved into what is known as "classical" Sanskrit centuries later, developing an alphabet and script forms known as *Devanagari,* derived from the words *deva,* "God," and *nagari,* "city", denoting that the language serves as the home for the words of the gods.

Like Latin, Sanskrit today is considered a "dead" language, since no modern community speaks it as a native tongue. Even in its heyday, however, Sanskrit was never a colloquial language, since it was reserved by the Brahmins, or priestly caste, for devotional purposes, to preserve the sanctity of the sacred word. As a result, Indian language divided into a cultural language, Sanskrit, and a vernacular, Prakrit. As Sanskrit was not used in trade or other forms of foreign contact, it remained more or less homogeneous; Prakrit, on the other hand, diversified quickly to reflect the changing nature of India.

Southeast Asian Languages

Would-be omniglots beware: More than 800 different languages are spoken in the Southeast Asian region, which includes Myanmar (formerly known as Burma), Cambodia, Laos, Thailand, Vietnam, Malaysia, Singapore, Indonesia, and the Philippines.

ผม(ฉัน)พูดภาษาไทยไม่เป็น

I don't speak Thai.

Indeed, most of these regions actually boast multiple distinct regional tongues, spoken in parallel with the country's official language; the Philippines, for instance, had more than 159 regional languages from which to choose a national standard when the islands became independent in 1946. Though, because of the American occupation, English was among the country's most-spoken languages, Tagalog, the language used in and around the capital of Manila, was chosen in an attempt to avoid the lingering shadow of colonialism. In the 1970s, the Philippines officially adopted Pilipino, a standardized version of Tagalog, as its official tongue; more than 25 million people speak Pilipino today.

Indonesia, which became independent three years after the Philippines, had an even more dramatic linguistic problem, with over 500 indigenous dialects used within its borders. Its innovative solution was to dump them all and standardize on the neutral language Malay, which most Indonesians were familiar with from their trading activities with Malaysia. As a result, all across Indonesia's 30,000 islands, the country's citizens—Javanese and Balinese alike—were required to learn Malay as their second, and official, tongue. —D.G.

TONGUES THAI (AND VIETNAMESE, AND SO FORTH)

The many languages of the Southeast Asian region can be classified into four major groups:

Austroasiatic: Encompasses as many as 150 languages falling into the following groups—the Munda languages, spoken in eastern India, and the Mon-Khmer, which includes Vietnamese and Cambodian, which are the national languages of Vietnam and Cambodia respectively.

Sino-Tibetan: Sinitic (Chinese) languages are spoken mostly in Singapore and in parts of Malaysia. The Burman branch includes Burmese, the official language of Myanmar, which is spoken by over 25 million people. Other major languages in this category are Karen, Chin, and Kachin, as well as Hmong (Miao), spoken by the tribal Hmong peoples who live in Cambodia, Thailand, and elsewhere throughout Southeast Asia; many Hmong sought refuge in the U.S. following the Vietnam War.

Tai: Includes standard or Central Thai, the national language of Thailand, and the related minority languages of Red, White, and Black Tai (named after the colors of the dresses worn by the local women of these groups). The national language of Laos is also related to Thai, although Thai speakers claim to find Laotian linguistically unintelligible, perhaps due to cultural differences and the fact that many Thai people regard Lao people as country bumpkins.

Austronesian: More than 200 million people speak languages in the Austronesian group. The six main branches are Sundic (Javanese, Balinese, Sumatran, Malay), Bornean, Moluccan (found on the Celebes Islands), Northern Philippine, Central Philippine, and Southern Philippine.

Taoism

The Pa-Kua

Taoism is a philosophy and a religion. It's both. It's neither. It is a way of thinking as well as a way of not thinking, a way of being, or simply a way. In fact, the surest way to not receive an intelligible answer regarding a definition for Taoism is to ask a Taoist—because to a Taoist, simply asking the question renders the answer nonsensical.

For something indefinable, it has been spoken of, written of, and practiced in China for over 2,000 years. The goal (or non-goal) of Taoists is the pursuit of the Tao (the "Way"). In philosophical Taoism, the Tao is what the German philosopher Immanuel Kant called a "noumenon," a concept one knows exists but cannot be experienced, and to which no properties can be intelligibly ascribed. It represents the cosmic state of constant change, in which all things are at any given point in time destroying or being destroyed, creating or being created, in a seamless, eternal, and harmonious process. Taoism can thus be defined as a means of thinking and behaving that is in keeping with that state, though—because the universe is in a state of unending flux—this means must also be in constant flux. Being at one with the universe is thus like playing a game in which the only rule is that the game must be played, whatever the rules.

The quasi-legendary founder of Taoism was Lao-tzu, whose name literally means "old child"; one legend has it that while still in the womb, Lao-tzu was so suspicious of human civilization that he delayed his birth until he was already an old man, which must have come as a considerable shock and inconvenience to his mother. He was a scholar who lived sometime during the Chou Dynasty (1027-256 B.C.), perhaps during the 6th or 7th century B.C. He is said to have scribbled the *Tao Te Ching* just before he left China for points west. Philosophical Taoism, as defined by Lao-tzu in the *Tao Te Ching*, is the root of all Taoist belief; later writings by Chuang-tzu (369 B.C.-286 B.C.) expanded upon the *Tao Te Ching*, elaborating on the Taoist doctrines of serenity and passivity, while advising that followers cease their embrace of dualities such as health and sickness, pleasure and pain, brightness and darkness, and so on. Such dualities are illusory, since each concept contains its opposing concept, and is thus an aspect of its other.

Chuang-tzu's esoteric extension of Taoist doctrine opened the door to mystical experience, a door entered in great hordes both by occultists and those seeking spiritual faith. Over the centuries, Taoism evolved from a philosophy into a religion—people began to worship Lao-tzu as a god, calling him *Tai Shang Lao Jun* ("The Most Exalted Venerable Lord"), and invoking other traditional

YIN AND YANG

The fundamental concept of the complementarity of all things, expressed as yin and yang, is at least as old as the 8th century. Originally, yin was the term for the northern slope of a mountain, which faced away from the sun and was associated with cold waters and a cloudy sky. Yang was the side of the mountain facing the sun, associated with warmth and a bright sky. Eventually the two terms came to describe the vital, complementary, yet opposing cosmic forces that create all things and events. They also came to symbolize the Tao as natural order: Yin was the feminine, passive, receptive, dark, or soft. Yang was the masculine, active, creative, bright, or hard. These concepts have played a vital role in Chinese philosophical, scientific, and religious thought, and are fundamental concepts in the practice of Chinese medicine [👁243], feng shui [👁226], and divination [👁224]. From the interrelation of yin and yang arise the five elements, which are in turn the basis of the "10,000 things," that is to say, everything. All phenomena contains yin and yang, which are two poles of the same energy. In the Chinese symbol for this relationship, each holds within it the seed of the other. For example, women, traditionally yin, are said to be yang on the inside. Likewise, men are yang on the outside but yin on the inside.

YIN—even numbers, moon, water, clouds, the phoenix, the color black, the north, the west

YANG—odd numbers, sun, fire, stars, the dragon, the color red, the south, the east

THE FIVE ELEMENTS

Taoists believe that the wu hsing, or five elements—earth, wood, metal, fire and water—control every event in the natural

cosmological deities, all in the name of the Way. Even later, during the Song dynasty (960-1279 A.D.), Taoism infused itself into Buddhism to result in the particular strain known as ch'an or Zen [216]. However, as those who truly seek the Tao know that it must not be sought, religious Taoism can only be seen as a perversion of Lao-tzu's original ideas.

"The Tao that can be told of is not the eternal Tao."
—from the *Tao Te Ching*

THE TAO GOES WEST

The *Tao Te Ching* was first translated into English by Jesuit missionaries in China in the late 18th century. In 1788, the text was introduced at the Royal Society in England, and has attracted increasing attention ever since, particularly in the middle of the 20th century, when it became a counterculture classic. "The *Tao Te Ching* was widely read in the '60s," says Harold Netlend, philosophy of religion professor at Trinity International University. "It fit in very nicely with the whole back-to-nature movement, the reaction against technology and modernization." Along with the Bible and the *Bhagavad Gita,* the *Tao Te Ching* is one of the most frequently translated works in literature: More than a hundred English translations of the text currently exist.

Taoism was brought to the U.S. in the 1850s, by Cantonese immigrants who came to work on the railroads; it Taoism remained more or less the concern of Chinese communities until after World War II, when affluent Chinese intellectuals began coming to America to escape communism. These intellectuals brought the philosophical aspects of Taoism into American academia, where colleges began teaching Taoist classics in their religion departments. During the Vietnam War (1965-1973), the teachings of Chuang-tzu in particular struck a chord with the antiwar sentiments of many young Americans, who produced a uniquely hippiefied brand of Taoism. By 1976, there were reportedly over 100,000 avowed Taoists in California; national figures are unavailable because the U.S. Census Bureau does not include Asian religions in its statistics, and because of Taoism's freestyle spiritual nature.

—D.G., J.Y., C.H.H.

world. Rather than actual substances, the five elements are abstract forces of energy that affect all aspects of life. Every phenomenon is thus related to one of the five elements:

WATER: the planet Mercury, the direction north, the color black, the numbers one and six, the kidneys, the emotion of fear

FIRE: Mars, south, red, two and seven, heart, joy

WOOD: Jupiter, east, green, three and eight, liver, anger

METAL: Venus, west, white, four and nine, lungs, sadness

EARTH: Saturn, the center, yellow, five and 10, pancreas, worry

COSMIC CYCLES

As the Tao teaches, the cosmos, and thus the Five Elements, is not static, but in a constant and eternal state of change:

DESTRUCTION AND PRODUCTION

Water destroys Fire; Wood produces Fire

Fire destroys Metal; Fire produces Earth

Metal destroys Wood; Earth produces Metal

Wood destroys Earth; Metal produces Water

Earth destroys Water; Water produces Wood

CONTROL AND DISSOLUTION

Wood destroys Earth; Metal controls Wood; Fire dissolves Wood

Metal destroys Wood; Fire controls Metal; Water dissolves Metal

Fire destroys Metal; Water controls Fire; Earth dissolves Fire

Water destroys Fire; Earth controls Water; Wood dissolves Water

Earth destroys Water; Wood controls Earth; Metal dissolves Earth

TCM THEORY BY THE NUMBERS

THE ONE GOAl: TCM's essence is balance; it's not really about curing illness, but about preserving well-being. As the saying goes, "Taoists do not study disease; they study life and health and how to maintain them."

THE TWO COMPLEMENTS: A basic aspect of the TCM system, which is dependent on Taoist fundamentals, is the concept of the complementary opposites yin and yang [241]. The feminine polarity of yin is associated with darkness, moistness, coolness, and rest, while the masculine polarity of yang is associated with light, dryness, heat, and activity; passive-yin and active-yang traits are found in parts of the body, in different ailments, and in possible treatments.

THE THREE TREASURES: Also known as the "three fundamental substances," the treasures are qi, jing, and shen; the flow and action of these three substances drive the operation of the human body. Qi is the body's vital energy; while there are different kinds of qi, ranging from protective qi (which provides resistance to external causes of illness) to organ qi (which maintains the strength of individual body parts) to meridian qi (which links the network of organs, while giving animation to our bodies). Qi is ingested

Ancient Chinese Secrets: Traditional Chinese Medicine

Acupuncture. Acupressure. Herbal and dietary therapy. The common root of all of these diverse healing arts, collectively known as "Traditional Chinese Medicine" (TCM), is the ancient *Huang Ti Nei Ching Su Wen* ("The Yellow Emperor's Classic of Internal Medicine"). This seminal text was composed by seven Han Dynasty scholars some time during the 2nd century B.C.; two millennia later, it's still referred to regularly by practitioners around the world.

Although each of the techniques that comprise TCM are learned and practiced discretely, their original compilers intended them for use together; the TCM system offers a complete health regimen in its different parts, with food cures, *tai ch'i*, and *qi gong* serving as preventive aspects and herbal therapies, acupuncture, and acupressure as forms of treatment. Binding together the different elements is a comprehensive physiological theory that, beneath its wilder mystical aspects, seems to have some empirical basis.

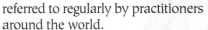

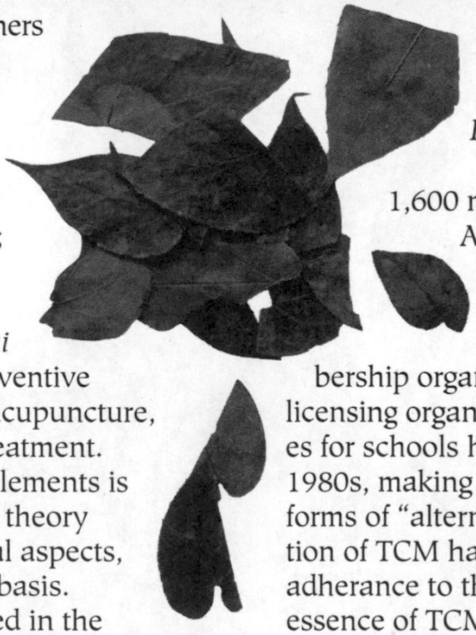

Chinese medicine first arrived in the U.S. in the 1700s, via physicians who were trained in the techniques in France; in the 1800s, Asian immigrant practitioners arrived on the scene, bringing firsthand skills, as well as original TCM texts and formularies, to the New World. Though Chinese medicine only began to show signs of widespread acceptance in the early 1990s, acupuncture was mentioned, as early as the late 1800s, as a successful treatment for the back ailments sciatica and lumbago in two mainstream American medical texts—the 1901 edition of H. Gray's *Anatomy, Descriptive and Surgical,* and in the 1892 through 1947 editions of W. Osler's *The Principles and Practice of Medicine.*

By 1995, there were more than 1,600 member practitioners of the American Association of Acupuncture and Oriental Medicine, which was founded in 1981, and remains the largest membership organization of its kind. Meanwhile, licensing organizations and accreditation processes for schools have been in place since the mid 1980s, making TCM one of the most accepted forms of "alternative" medicine. Part of the attraction of TCM has been its elegant cohesiveness and adherance to the principles of moderation: The essence of TCM is the abjuration of excess in all of its forms. And whether or not you believe in the specific techniques involved, this underlying philosophy is one even Western physicians would surely recommend.

A TRIP TO THE CHINESE MEDICINE DOCTOR

Welcome to the office of **Dr. Jessica Yu, D.O.M.** (she's a **Doctor of Oriental Medicine**). Take a seat; the doctor will be with you shortly...

1. Instead of the tongue-depressing and knee-tapping you might find in a Western physicians office, expect Dr. Yu to ask you **a battery of questions**, while examining your skin, complexion, bones, smells, sounds, mental state, spirits, preferences, emotions, "outlets" (tongue, eyes, lips, nose, ears), pulse, and body build. Some practitioners derive this information through physical examination and little verbal exchange; others conduct an extensive interview; some may even ask you to fill out a written questionnaire. This process is known as **"Eight-Condition Diagnosis,"** because its result will place you into one or more of eight diagnostic categories. Only after thoroughly assessing your case will Dr. Yu determine a treatment. She won't assign a specific name to your illness or syndrome, or define an empirical cause; rather, she, like other TCM practitioners, will assess the imbalances in your ailing body and prescribe a treatment that equilibrates them.

Some possible questions from Dr. Yu:

- *Do you feel hot or cold?*
- *How often do you get up at night to urinate?*
- *Are you thirsty?*
- *Describe your bowel movements.*
- *If you're a woman, how is your menstrual cycle? Is it regular? Is the flow thick or thin? If you're having any discharge, what color is it and is there any odor?*

2. The first matter that Dr. Yu might consider is whether your imbalance is **"external"** or **"internal."** Disharmony from "external" causes includes diseases of infection by bacteria or viruses (which she might refer to as an "evil wind"); "internal" causes might include nutrient deficiencies, stress, drug or alcohol dependency, or even emotional problems. If the ailment is from an external source, it might be either "damp" or "dry," "cold" or "hot"; each of these distinctions will warrant a different treatment.

3. A separate category of ailment is a **qi** (or ch'i) **deficiency**, which might be isolated to a single organ or be comprehensive, throughout the body; symptoms of a global qi deficiency are paleness, weakness, and fluttery pulse. In an insufficient-qi case, Dr. Yu will likely prescribe some sort of dietary change, herbal tonic, or perhaps acupuncture stimulus if the problem is localized.

Qi excess is also possible, with symptoms including redness in the face, headaches, nervousness, and heavy breathing. Again, herbs, dietary change, or acupuncture are likely treatments.

4. Dr. Yu will also consider whether your illness is **"cold"** or **"hot."** Chills, clear or pale secretions, and diarrhea are all symptoms of a cold ailment, while fever, swelling, redness in the face or eyes, thirst, and thick or yellow secretions are symptoms of a hot ailment. She will simultaneously decide if your problem is **yin** in nature or **yang**; yin illnesses reside in the blood and are associated with inactivity, while yang ailments are externally oriented and associated with motion and restlessness.

5. A Western practitioner's route to treatment is simple—he'll generally attempt to find the single cause for a disease, and attack that cause. But Dr. Yu has the more complex and in some ways more sophisticated task of determining the **holistic causes** behind illness, and placing them in a context that includes your background, current environment, and even the time of year.

6. Once Dr. Yu arrives at her diagnosis, it's sure to sound somewhat peculiar—it'll be something like "deficient kidney yin" or "spleen invading liver."

through breathing and eating, and can thus be increased or decreased based on breathing exercises (qi gong) or changing eating habits. Jing, or "essence," can be seen as a special variant of qi—it's inherited qi, which we receive from our parents when we're first conceived. If one or both of our parents were unhealthy at the time of our conception, we're born with bad jing, and will be predisposed toward illness. Jing regulates, growth, the hormones and reproductive systems, and the brain and nerves. Unlike qi, jing is a limited resource, and once it's been expended in life, it's gone for good, which is how TCM explains why otherwise healthy young people die suddenly of causes like strokes and heart attacks. Jing is stored in the kidneys, which the ancient Chinese thought to be the warehouse of sexual energy; the reason why we age is due to the gradual expenditure of jing. This is why celibacy, particularly for males, is a healthy pursuit, because every male ejaculation results in a small but measurable loss of jing. The final treasure is shen, or "spirit." It can be described as the transcendent element in the human body—the consciousness; it resides in the heart, and can be observed through the eyes, which are after all the windows of the soul. Mental prowess, memory, and cognition are all driven by shen; like qi and unlike jing, it replenishes itself, generally with rest and sleep.

"FOUR" TO AVOID: While western buildings skip the 13th floor to avoid the misfortune that that

numeral is said to bring, the corresponding unlucky number in Chinese tradition is the number four—and for a good reason: In Chinese, the word for "death" and the word for the number four are pronounced the same, si, so using one is considered an invitation to the other. As a result, you'll never see a TCM practitioner with an office on the fourth floor, and if you do, avoid it like the plague.

THE FIVE PHASES, also known as **THE "QUINARY":** Chinese Taoist belief holds that there are five elements [👁241]: fire, earth, metal, water, and wood. These are also called the "five phases" or "five quintessential processes," since each of these elements is seen as being constantly in flux, changing from one into the next, destroying its predecessor or producing its successor. All of the major bodily organs are assigned to one of the phases, as are the five elemental colors, the five tastes, the five primary emotions, and so forth; a TCM practitioner's choice of treatment for an imbalance in an organ can involve either affecting that organ directly, or possibly its "mother organ." For example, water is said to produce wood in the "birth cycle" of elements (in the "control cycle" it controls fire); the liver is associated with the wood element, and the kidneys are associated with the water element. If there is a deficiency in the liver, a TCM treatment might either treat the liver itself or the kidneys, "strengthening the mother to treat the child."

Treatment may range from **acupuncture** to **dietary restrictions** to **herbal remedies**, but all are designed to address imbalances in the body, in order to allow it to cure itself. Whatever Dr. Yu decides to prescribe, it is attuned to your individual situation—someone walking in with the same basic symptoms will not necessarily receive the same prescription. This, of course, goes against the grain of Western medicine, which sees both the source of disease and its cure as being standardized and thus generically treatable.

7. At the end of the visit, Dr. Yu may schedule future appointments—it's unlikely that a TCM treatment will involve something as glib as the popping of a set of pills. The whole thing will set you back between $150 and $250, with future visits at $100 or so each. Will you come out ahead, compared to Western treatment? Maybe not monetarily (although it depends on the severity of your ailment). But, by taking the holistic TCM approach, you'll likely at least get a better sense for both your body and its surroundings—which by any assessment is a plus.

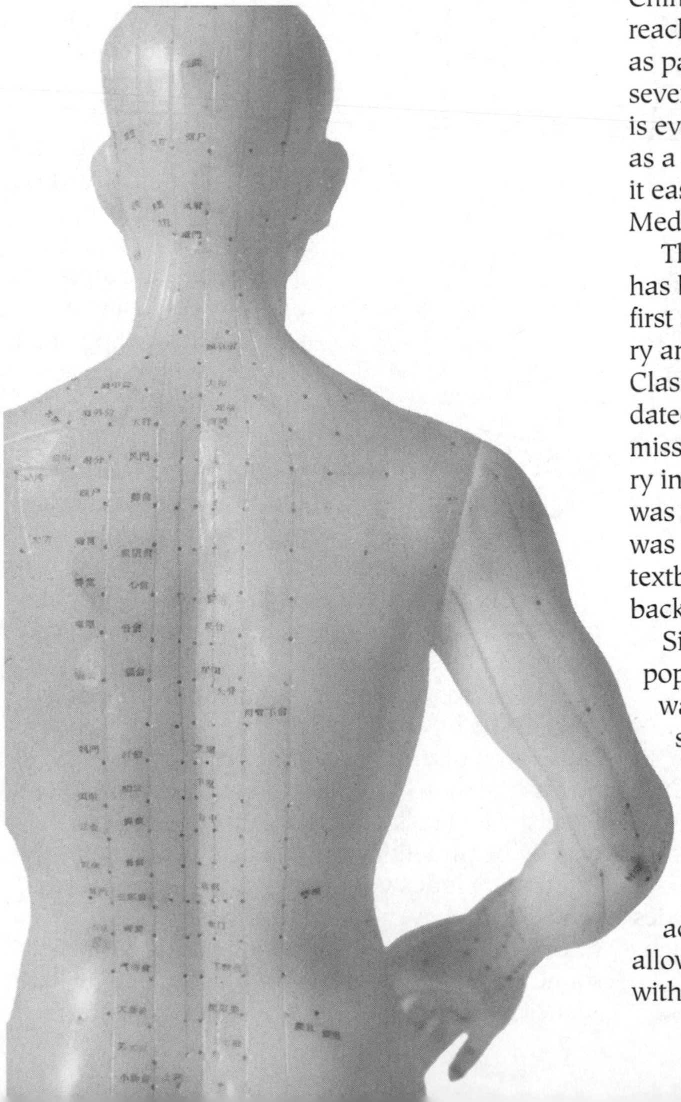

ACUPUNCTURE: POINTED FACTS

In 1994, more than half a million Americans paid good money for the privilege of lying on a table and having dozens of tiny needles inserted into their bodies—all in hopes of curing a variety of conditions, ranging from arthritis to impotence. Crazy? Crazy like a fox, perhaps. Once derided as "quackupuncture," the 2,000-year-old form of Chinese medicine known as acupuncture has now reached respectability. Acupuncture can be found as part of mandatory drug treatment programs in several states, and the Food and Drug Association is even considering a ruling that would recognize it as a legitimate form of medical treatment, making it easier for patients to get reimbursed through Medicare, Medicaid, and private insurers.

Throughout East Asia, of course, acupuncture has been a legitimate treatment for centuries; the first systematic compendium of acupuncture theory and techniques was the "The Yellow Emperor's Classic of Internal Medicine," which has been dated back to about 200 B.C. Meanwhile, Jesuit missionaries stationed in Beijing in the 17th century introduced the therapy to the West, where it was first used in the U.S. in the 19th century, and was described in Osler's seminal 1892 medical textbook as a recommended treatment for lower back pain.

Since then, numerous efforts have been made to popularize the technique in the West, but it wasn't until 1971, when *New York Times* correspondent James Reston wrote an account of how acupuncture was used to reduce his pain after an emergency appendectomy in China, that popular interest in the procedure was raised. Now there are more than 6,000 active licensed acupuncturists in the U.S. and 50 acupuncture schools. Although most states allow certified physicians to practice acupuncture without getting special certification, 31 states plus

Washington, D.C., have specific licensing requirements for nonphysicians to practice acupuncture. "Fifteen years ago, if you mentioned acupuncture people would stare at you and have no idea what you were talking about," says Barbara Mitchell, chairwoman of the National Commission for the Certification of Acupuncturists in Washington, D.C. "Now everyone has tried it themselves or at least knows someone who has." You could say—pardon the pun—that people are finally getting the point.

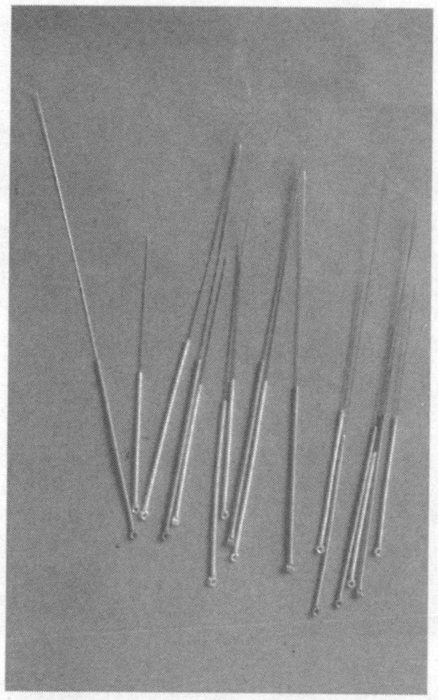

How It Works

Like other traditional Chinese therapies, acupuncture is based on the idea that illness results from an imbalance of bodily energy, or qi, which flows through channels called meridians along the body; there are 12 "major" meridians, each of which is associated with a major organ, and eight "extra" meridians, plus numerous secondary meridians with more obscure special purposes. The meridians are more than just abstractions; acupuncturists believe that they actually connect the outer surface of the body with its inner structure, forming a kind of living map.

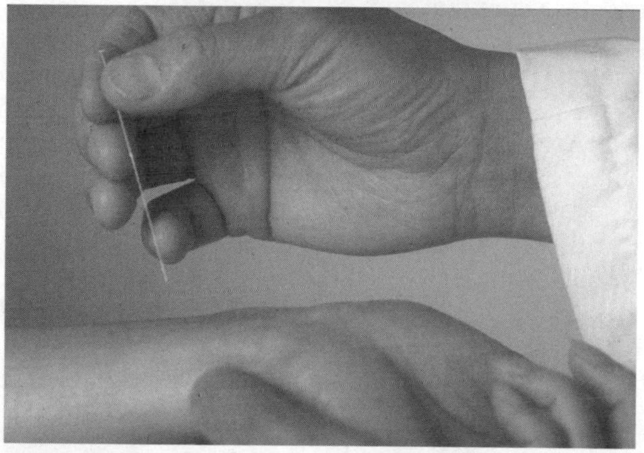

By stimulating any of 365 different junctures with tiny needles (about one-tenth the diameter of those used to draw blood), the flow of qi along the meridians is thought to be rerouted, restoring the body's balance of energy, in order to "reduce what is excessive, increase what is deficient, warm what is cold, cool what is hot, circulate what is stagnant, move what is congealed, stabilize what is reckless, raise what is falling and lower what is rising." Sometimes acupuncture is combined with acupressure (applying physical pressure to acupuncture points, a principle element in shiatsu massage), or with moxibustion, a procedure in which the leaves of certain plants are burned above vital points on the body to add further therapeutic stimulus.

Why It Works

Western science requires a rationale for any phenomenon, and the rather counterintuitive practice of sticking needles into someone to make them feel less pain simply begs for explanation. Theories for how acupuncture works tend to fall into three major categories: the first is that the needles somehow stimulate the body to release its own pain-relieving chemicals, called endorphins, thereby achieving a therapeutic effect; the second is that that stimulating specific areas of the body blocks sensations coming from other areas of the body whose nerves are located lower on the spinal cord; lastly, there are skeptics who invoke the placebo effect, stating that acupuncture is effective because those undergoing the technique naively believe it to be. However it works, acupuncture has been shown to be an effective treatment for many disorders—in particular, as a pain reliever, a treatment for arthritis and allergies, and as a treatment for substance addictions. As a result, Western medicine is starting to pay close attention to this Eastern tradition. Who knows? Someday soon, at your next visit to the doctor, she might tell you to take two needles and call your acupuncturist in the morning.

What to Pay, Who to See

An initial diagnostic visit should cost around $200 to $300 if your therapist is a physician/ acupuncturist; expect to pay between $80 and $150 for

THE SIX EXTERNAL PATHOGENS (also called THE SIX EVILS): These are, in turn, wind, cold, heat, dampness, dryness, and fire. These external "climatic changes" affect the human body and can cause disease. For example, "injurious wind" is the ailment otherwise known as the common cold.

THE SEVEN EMOTIONS are joy, anger, anxiety, concentration, grief, fear, and shock. The seven emotions can cause internal disease, and vice versa.

THE EIGHT CONDITIONS (also known as the EIGHT INDICATORS or EIGHT PRINCIPLES) are pairs of complementary conditions that describe patterns of imbalance in the patient. The yin/yang principle [241] is the "commander of the Eight Indicators" because each of the other indicators is also associated with either yin or yang. Yin diseases are treated by boosting yang; yang diseases are treated by boosting yin. The interior/exterior principle refers to the location of the ailment in the body (internal organs, as opposed to skin or bones). Cold/hot refers to the nature of an illness as manifested by variations in qualities such as fever versus chills or flushed versus pale complexion. Empty/full indicates whether the condition is chronic or acute, and whether the body's responses are weak or strong. And dry/moist illnesses can be manifested, for instance, by thirst in the case of the former and diarrhea in the case of the latter.

TCM VS. WESTERN MEDICINE

CHINESE—Its strength is preventive medicine, skin and internal diseases, and chronic ailments; it also does well with acute conditions like the common cold, flu, allergies, and headache

WESTERN—Its strengths are surgery, emergency medicine, and trauma care

CHINESE—Focuses on achieving bodily homeostasis

WESTERN—Focuses on treating symptoms of disease

CHINESE—Treatment is relatively inexpensive, but is often not covered by insurance

WESTERN—Treatment is costly, but covered by insurance

CHINESE—Treatments are person-specific

WESTERN—Treatments are standardized, symptom-specific, and disease-specific

CHINESE—Pulse is measured in six locations on the body and assessed by 28 different qualities, such as slippery, tight, soft, drumming, empty, and so forth

WESTERN—Pulse is measured in number of beats per minute, though irregularities are noted

CHINESE—The tongue provides a world of information about the rest of the body; the tongue is evaluated by qualities such as "tender," "shiny," and so on

WESTERN—The doctor sticks a tongue-depressor in your mouth and you say "Ahh."

each successive treatment (some of which may be covered by insurance). Non-physician acupuncturists charge between $70 to $100 for initial visits and $45 to $65 for each successive treatment. Acute minor ailments should be treatable in fewer than four sessions, but chronic problems may need ten or more. In any case, you should always make sure that your therapist is an accredited one. Most acupuncturists worth their pins and needles will have one of the following certificates:

Dipl.Ac.—The **Diplomate in Acupuncture** is granted by the National Commission for the Certification of Acupuncturists.

M.Ac./M.O.M.—The **Master of Acupuncture/ Master of Oriental Medicine** is granted by schools recognized by the National Accreditation Commission for Schools and Colleges of Acupuncture and Oriental Medicine.

L.Ac./L.A.C.—Licensed Acupuncturist; this certification is required for nonphysicians to practice acupuncture therapy in 13 states.

O.M.D./D.O.M.—Oriental Medical Doctor/Doctor of Oriental Medicine. This certification is granted via a number of programs; therapists with O.M.D./ D.O.M. certificates from outside of the U.S. must pass an American qualification test before they can practice domestically.

AN APOTHECARY OF OVER-THE-COUNTER CHINESE CURES

While none of the following remedies are FDA approved, they are widely available in Chinese communities throughout the world, and reputedly effective. Self-dosing is always dangerous, but these formulas are generally not potentially toxic—and they might well cure what ails you.

Gan Mao Ling ("Common Cold Tablet")—remedies symptoms of cold and flu, such as chills, fever, sore throat, and stiff neck. (Ilex root, Evodia fruit, Isatis root, chrysanthemum, Vietx fruit, Lonerica flower, menthol)

Fargelin for Piles ("Potent Hemorrhoid Dissolving Remedy")—provides quick relief from hemorrhoidal pain and swelling (psuedoginseng root, Succinum resin, Sophora, Scutelleria, Callicarpa root, Sanguisorba root, Corydalis, bear gallbladder)

Yunnan Paiyao ("Yunnan White Medicine")—stops internal or external bleeding on contact; effective for both excessive menstrual bleeding and gunshot wounds (psuedoginseng, various secret ingredients)

Po Chai Pills ("Protect and Benefit Pill")—remedies nausea, cramps, gas, and indigestion. (Gastrodia elata, Poria cocos, mint, tangerine peel, Halloysite, Pueraria lobata, Trichosanthes root, Coix seed, Saussurea root, chrysanthemum, angelica, Lophanthus rugosus, Atractylodes, Oryza malt, magnolia)

Resources

Members of the American Academy of Medical Acupuncture are physicians with at least 200 hours of continuing education training in acupuncture; the AAMA will provides referrals to qualified members in your area. (800) 521-2262

More information is also available from the American Association of Acupuncture and Oriental Medicine, which has a library on conditions for which acupuncture is effective; it provides referrals to accredited therapists on request. Finally, a list of Dipl.Ac holders in your area is available for $3 from the National Commission for the Certification of Acupuncturists, P.O. Box 97075, Washington, DC 20090-7075.

CHINESE HERBAL MEDICINE

As a form of TCM, herbal medicine has been in use for at least 2,500 years. The Taoist sages who developed the fundamental systems of TCM were adept empirical observers; they determined the effectiveness of herbs simply by observing what animals ate when they were injured or ill. It was the legendary Emperor Shen Nung, whose reign was in the prerecorded period 5,000 years in the past, who allegedly took the next step of experimenting with herbal formulas, discovering many new effects by ingesting them himself—a courageous act, but not the most sensible activity for a nation's ruler.

Unlike Western herbal medicine, Chinese herbal remedies were originally prepared as food, to be consumed as a part of daily meals; ancient Taoist herbal texts spoke of "soups" rather than potions, and medicinal elixirs were simply special cases of the body-strengthening dietary regime.

This is, in some ways, the greatest strength of Chinese traditional medicine: It isn't about curing disease, but enhancing and preserving life. Ancient Chinese practitioners were paid regularly when patients were well; they were considered to have done their job improperly if their patients ailed, at which point they would provide treatment at no charge (assuming, of course, that the patient had been following doctor's orders).

This inverted orientation is part of why Chinese herbal medicine has had relatively little acceptance in the West; it's only in the last decade or so that Chinese herbal techniques have begun to be embraced as a legitimate alternative therapy. Many Americans now report success with Chinese herbal remedies, especially when conventional treatments prove ineffective; enthusiasts claim that herbs are a gentler way to cure or tonify the body. Skeptics, on the other hand, say that, at best, herbs are placebos, and, at worst, pure poison.

Still, researchers in the U.S. and Europe have scrambled to harvest pharmaceuticals from traditional Chinese cures. The stumbling block they've run into is that Chinese cures are not prescribed according to the relationship of chemical constituents with specific effects, but rather as a part of a broad-spectrum, holistic therapy; Western doctors are thus often frustrated in their attempts to isolate "active principles" of Chinese cures.

Chinese herbal remedies are widely available in the traditional pharmacies of Chinese communities in the U.S., and several American companies also market herbal extracts based on classical formulas through mainstream health food stores. Not quite food and not quite drug, herbal remedies have been criticized by the Food and Drug Administration, which does not yet have the resources or methodology to put these products through its standard battery of tests. However, the Dietary Supplement Health and Education Act of 1994 allows the sale of products making claims to health "maintenance," so long as manufacturers also label them with disclaimers that they are not FDA-approved. The lack of regulation hasn't weakened the market: Americans are buying into herbal remedies to the tune of nearly $1 billion a year.

This isn't to say that Chinese herbal medicine, which includes in its formulary some 20,000 herbal concoctions, doesn't have its controversies. First among them are reported cases of death or illness as a result of improper use of Chinese medicines. For instance, the unregulated adoption of one traditional Chinese herb, ma huang, in American concoctions like "herbal ecstasy" has led to several deaths, since the herb is a potent stimulant that should not be taken recreationally. There's also the issue of the use of animal parts from endangered species, such as rhinoceros horn and Siberian tiger bone (in TCM, "herbs" can mean any organic substance or mineral).

Still, no accredited D.O.M. will use any products from an endangered species, and—as with Western medicine—consulting a licensed practitioner will also prevent dangerous misuses of herbal remedies. The peril in adopting Chinese medicine as a therapy lies in relying on it for the wrong things, in attempting "do-it-yourself" cures, and in taking it less than seriously; users who take a whimsical approach to its principles and prescriptions may pay a tragic price. —D.G., J.Y.

GINSENG, THE WONDER ROOT

The virtues of this root have been extolled by Chinese for thousands of years. More recently, ginseng has been discovered by the West—consumed as a part of New Age elixirs, candies, and even carbonated soft drinks. Ginseng is said to relieve stress and build energy; Western scientists have confirmed that the active ingredients in ginseng have stimulant, immune-building, and anti-cancer properties. Ginseng comes from the roots of two shrubs, Panax ginseng, native to China, and Panax quinquefolium, native to North America). Chinese ginseng, which is more potent than the North American variety, is available in two forms: red and white, of which the red is stronger. All types of ginseng are available whole—dried and powdered—or in liquid extracts and capsules. And, of course, you could always simply slug down a six-pack of Ginseng-Up.

EATING THE EMPEROR'S WAY

Those wishing to enjoy the full benefit Emperor Shen Nung's regimen should visit Singapore, where Wang-Lee Tee Eng owns the Imperial Herbal Restaurant. There, herbalist Li Lian Xing and chefs Bian Jian Nian and Shi Lian Yong cook a menu of traditional herbal recipes, with ingredients ranging from ordinary (meats and vegetables) to frightening (scorpions, deer penis). Lunch for two is around $40, while dinner costs $60 for a health (and taste) conscious couple.

SOUND AND STAGE

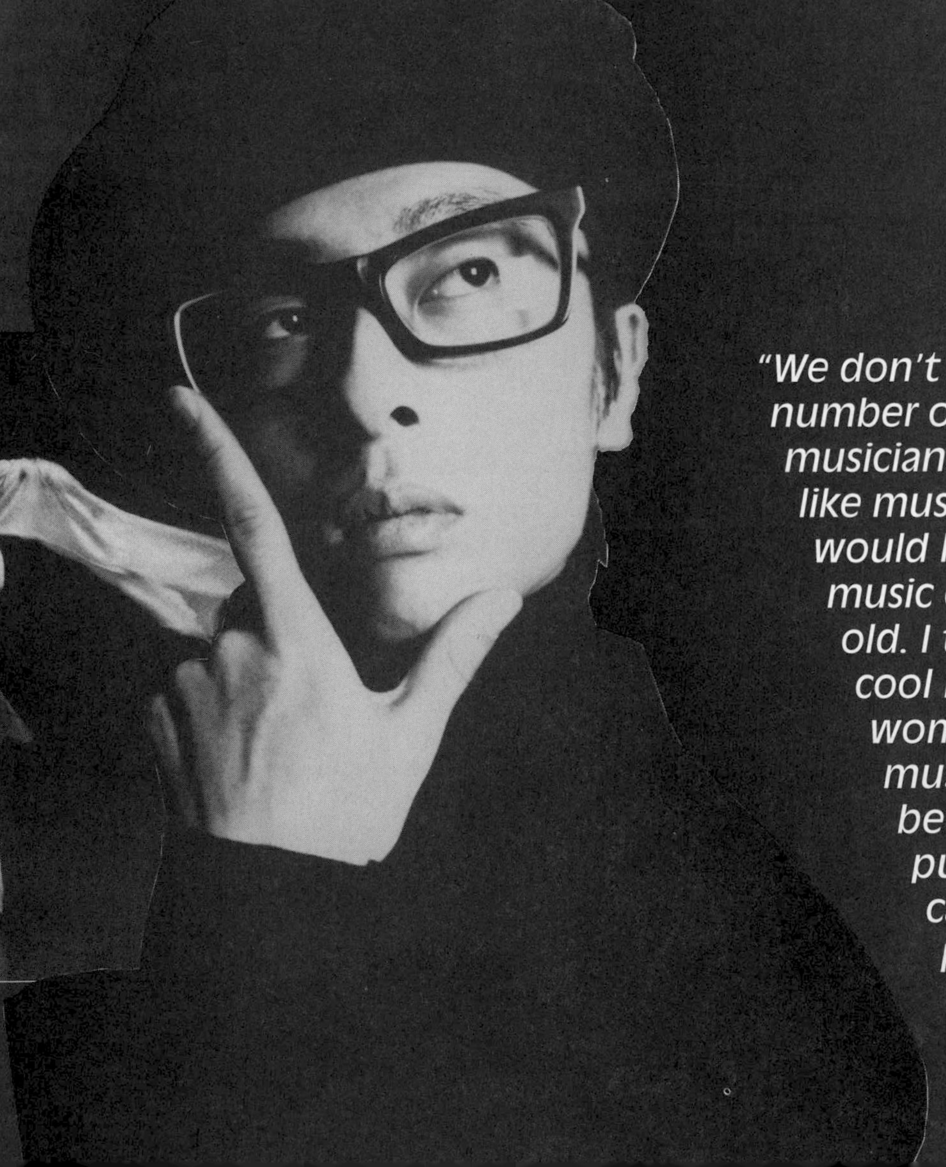

"We don't care if our songs are number one, two, or 10. We are musicians, and we are happy. I like music very much, so I would like to continue to do music even when I'm very old. I think it would be very cool if old Japanese women could play rock music. We would like to be the world's oldest punk-rock band. If we can, we would like to play into our eighties."

—Naoko Yamano of Shonen Knife

Asian Classical Musicians

Yo Yo Ma. Sarah Chang. Midori. These household names are just droplets from the flood of young, popular, and devastatingly talented Asian performers who have burst onto the classical music world over the past two decades. And the floodwaters keep on rising: At prestigious musical institutions like the Juilliard School in New York and the Walnut Hill School in Natick, Massachusetts, Asians and Asian Americans make up over half of the student population, while the number of Asians in American orchestras—particularly in string sections—continues to increase every year. "Asians are the Jews of the future," says violinist Yehudi Menuhin, noting the past legacy of Jewish classical luminaries, including Jascha Heifetz, Vladimir Horowitz, and Arthur Rubinstein.

What's the reason for this burgeoning rise in Asian classical musicians? According to conductor Seiji Ozawa, it's because "Asians love to study; it's in our blood." Violinist Cho-Liang Lin agrees: "I think it's a work ethic—the notion that hard work pays off," he says. But hard work alone doesn't make for artistry, and while Lin notes that some people feel that Asian musicians produce music that's "too analytical, too clean, and not terribly warm," fellow violinist Kyung-Wha Chung vehemently disagrees: "Western music, you see, is an art form that's learnable—it's simply a language," she says. "One is not born with a talent for Western music or Eastern music; one is born with a sensitivity for music in general, and then it's a question of what you do with it. I think Asian children have the drive to succeed very early—they work with tremendous discipline. Maybe it's because Asian society is based on teachings and philosophies of Confucius, which stress the beauty of living up to the expectations of your elders and your society."

Lin himself says that "People keep asking how I can play and understand Brahms, since I have slanted eyes. I want to scream, 'I can play Western music as well as the next guy; and, after all, Brahms was German, not American.' For all my American ways, deep down it's clear that I have to know my music better than the next guy. And that, for the rest of my life, even if I become famous, someone will ask me how I can possibly understand Mozart." —C.K.

Kyung-Wha Chung: Born 1948 in Seoul, Korea, Chung is a world-class female violinist and a musical prodigy who comes from a family of six brothers and sisters—all of whom are musicians. (Her family had 20 music and language tutors.) Chung started playing piano at age four and a half, but "hated it." At seven, she discovered the violin, and played in the Korean National Symphony Orchestra and the Seoul Philharmonic; by the age of eight, she was already renowned throughout Korea. At 13 years, she left Korea to study at Juilliard on scholarship. After four years in New York, she went to California to study with Gregor Piatagorsky, and entered the Edgar M. Leventritt competition at Carnegie Hall in 1967, which launched her career. At the tender age of 23, she was recognized as one of the great violinists of her age.

Yo-Yo Ma: Born 1955 in Paris, France, he's considered by many to be the best cellist in the entire world. He began playing at such a young age that there were no cellos small enough to fit the four-year-old Ma. His father, an instructor for musically gifted children, attached a cello's end pin onto a viola, and had the young boy sit on a stack of telephone

books to play; his first recital was at age six. A year later, his family moved to New York, and he began studying at Juilliard in 1962 with Leonard Rose. After high school, instead of entering musical competition, he enrolled at Columbia University, then majored in humanities at Harvard. He made his debut at the Salzburg Festival in 1978, and the rest is history. He plays a 1733 Montagna made in Venice, as well as a 1712 Davidoff Stradivarius.

Zubin Mehta: Born 1936 in Bombay, India, he's one of the world's most renowned conductors and music directors. Like many of his peers, he was born into a musical family; his father, Mehla Mehta, was co-founder of the Bombay Symphony. By age 16, the young Mehta was conducting concerto accompaniments, and leading the orchestra when his father was away on concert tours. He left his medical studies to study at the Vienna State Academy of Music from 1954 to 1957, and made his American debut conducting the Philadelphia Orchestra in 1960. Later, he was music director for the Montreal Symphony Orchestra from 1961 to 1967; music director for the Los Angeles Philharmonic Orchestra from 1978 to 1991; music director for the New York Philharmonic from 1978 to 1991; and Music Director for the Israel Philharmonic Orchestra from 1977 to the present. In 1981, Mehta led the New York Philharmonic in a concerto for sitar and orchestra with world renowned sitarist/composer Ravi Shankar as soloist [@ **305**]: "I have never really believed that Indian music can be played by a Western symphony orchestra....Ravi feels that at this point he has done so much of it that he can write for us. His problem is that he cannot read our nota-

tion, and I cannot read his—I mean, there is hardly any Indian notation." On a side note, Mehta loves spicy food, and carries around a box of peppers wherever he goes.

Kent Nagano: Born 1951 in Morro Bay, California, Nagano is the grandson of first-generation Japanese American farmers who were interned along with his parents during World War II. Nagano is an internationally renowned conductor specializing in contemporary music and 20th century classics, and "music's next superstar, a baby-boomer Bernstein," or so he's been hailed by *New York* magazine. Nagano's mother, an amateur cellist, introduced music to the family. (A multifaceted musician herself, Mrs. Nagano plays the piano, viola, clarinet, and koto.) Following in her footsteps, Nagano studied conducting at San Francisco State University, sang with the San Francisco Opera, and then joined Sarah Caldwell's Opera Company of Boston as apprentice conductor. He returned to the San Francisco Bay Area in 1979, and led the Berkeley Promenade Orchestra, which later became the Berkeley Symphony. Simultaneously, since 1989, Nagano has been music director of the Lyons Opera and Ballet in Lyons, France; leader of the Hallé Orchestra in Manchester, England; and associate principal guest conductor of the London Symphony Orchestra.

Midori: Born Midori Goto in 1971 in Osaka, Japan; she dropped her surname when her parents divorced in 1983. A violin virtuoso and musical prodigy, since debuting at age 15, she has "gained Madonna-size popularity within the genre," according to the *New York Daily News*, working with other classical music stars as Leonard Bernstein, Isaac Stern, and Yo-Yo Ma. By the age of two, she could hum Bach concertos. She began her first music lessons at age three

with her mother, Setsu Goto. At 10, she moved to New York with her mother to further her career. She studied on full scholarship at Juilliard in the pre-college division until she was 15, when it was decided she no longer needed lessons. Throughout her teen years, she practiced seven hours a day. Conductor Zubin Mehta invited her to give a surprise performance at the 1982 New York Philharmonic gala. Her skill garnered her a standing ovation, not to mention international renown as a child prodigy. Sadly, in September 1994, Midori dropped off the touring circuit for several months due to health problems (officially described as "a digestive disorder"), and what she later revealed to be reactions to the pressures of being a prodigy in the public eye. Among the rumors that floated around were that she suffered from an eating disorder and had had a nervous breakdown. She has since returned to her career, older and wiser. Midori plays a 1735 Guarnerius del Gesu; she 's 5' 1", she reads "a lot," and she crochets. Since 1992, she's headed a non-profit cultural organization for children called Midori & Friends.

Seiji Ozawa: Born 1935 in Shenyang, China (Manchuria) to Japanese parents, Ozawa has been maestro for the Boston Symphony Orchestra since 1973, and the San Francisco Symphony from 1969 to 1976, making him the first East Asian ever to lead a major symphony orchestra. Ozawa studied composition and conducting at Tokyo's Toho Gakuen School of Music. After graduating, he won a scholarship to study in Berlin with the legendary Herbert von Karajan, who emphasized the importance of opera in the development of the conductor. He worked with Leonard Bernstein as assistant conductor with the New York Philharmonic during the 1961-'62 season, and made his first professional North American concert appearance in January 1962 with the San Francisco Symphony. He was music director for the Chicago Symphony Orchestra's Ravinia Festival for five summers beginning in 1964, as well as the Toronto Symphony

from 1965 to 1969, and the San Francisco Symphony from 1970 to 1976. He began conducting opera in 1969 at Vienna's Salzburg Festival, debuting with Mozart's *Cosi Fan Tutti.* Ozawa and the Boston Symphony have had the longest relationship of any active conductor and American orchestra. He was the youngest-ever conductor (of any ethnicity) of the Boston Symphony Orchestra, and was the first East Asian to lead one of America's Big Five.

Sarah Chang: Born 1981 in Philadelphia to Korean parents, Chang emerged as a charismatic violin prodigy, notable for her signature stage outfit: A shocking pink party dress worn with patent leather Mary Janes. At age two, Chang began to pick out cartoon tunes on the piano, started studying violin at four, and was performing in public within a year. She's studied at

Juilliard since age six, under the instruction of Dorothy Delay. When she auditioned for conductor Zubin Mehta at the age of eight, he was so impressed with her playing ability that he invited her to play the Paganini violin concerto with the New York Philharmonic two days later as a surprise guest soloist. Since then, Chang has played all over the U.S., in the Far East, and Europe. She plays a borrowed Guarnerius del Gesu, of which she says, "I'm not grown up yet; my hand is small and the violin's sound is very big. I would like to own it, but violins are very expensive these days."

Asian Musicals

The great musical-makers Richard Rodgers and Oscar Hammerstein II could be seen as both problematic and prescient. Though they returned several times to the "exotic Orient" for source material, they were also the first dramatists to realize Asians and Asian Americans as fully three-dimensional characters on the stage—as 3-D as was possible for their time, that is. They also actively confronted issues like racism and intolerance, though they were held by the singsong on-with-the-show limits of their genre. Even so, many of their musicals proved to be pretty contentious stuff: Social issues, particularly those dealing with race, were simply not "appropriate" for the musical stage. For instance, many theater people, along with a few Georgia legislators, tried to suppress or purge "Carefully Taught" from *South Pacific,* a song condemning prejudice and racist attitudes. R & H stood their ground.

In today's more enlightened times, the "revolutionary" attitudes of R & H don't stand up quite as well: The Liat-Cable relationship from *South Pacific* is typical of doomed interracial romances, for example, as is that of the King of Siam and Anna from *The King and I,* ending in death and misery. Meanwhile, Anna herself is a "civilizing" force, a kind of missionary charged with saving barbaric Thailand. And the enigmatic Pacific paradise Bali-Ha'i is seen as a stereotypical land of limitless fantasy and danger. And finally, the glorious flowering of Euro-American civilization is not only most desirable but inevitable in both the Chinese American environs of *Flower Drum Song* and the totalitarian Thai court of *The King and I.* Still, though the "Orient" of these musicals doesn't depart too radically from the usual images and ideas, R & H deserve to be lauded for being more aware than most of their contemporaries about racial politics and European colonialism—particularly when more contemporary efforts, like *Miss Saigon,* are considered. Here's a rundown of the Asian-themed shows that have made it before the footlights: —G.C.M.

Name of Musical/ Original run	Synopsis	Notable for...
The King and I (3/29/51 -3/29/54) based on *Anna and the King of Siam* (Margaret Langdon)	Set in Siam, 1862. An Englishwoman comes to teach some of the Thai king's 106 (!!!) children, setting the stage for (unresolved) interracial attraction between a European woman and an Asian man.	The Broadway show ran for more than a thousand performances. Yul Brynner won an Oscar for the 1956 film version; it also won Oscars for Best Score Adaptation, Costume Design, and Art Direction.
South Pacific (4/7/49 - 1/16/54) Based on *Tales of the South Pacific* (James Michener)	Interracial/interethnic/intergenerational love and lust between the natives, the ex-pats, and U.S. Naval forces on a South Pacific island in wartime. A hundred and one pounds of fun, but those color filters...ohhhh!	The 1958 film version shot on Kauai, Hawai'i, and won an Oscar for sound recording. Breathtaking cinematography in stunning technicolor.
Flower Drum Song (12/1/58 - 5/7/60) based on *Flower Drum Song* (C.Y. Lee)	F.O.B. Chinese woman is arranged to be married to an "Americanized" San Francisco playboy, who is otherwise embroiled, and the fireworks begin...	The first Chinese American musical—with an all-Asian American cast—based in San Francisco's Chinatown in the '50s. Ran for 600 performances. 1961 film version garnered five Oscar nominations, no awards.
Shogun (1990-1991) based on *Shogun* (James Clavell)	Englishman searching for loot crashes in feudal Japan with his crew; he rises to advise the military governor while bedding the governor's wife, and eventually is made a samurai.	Production marred during previews, when a piece of scenery beaned the actor playing Blackthorne. Great costumes, but the critics panned it. It didn't last long.
Miss Saigon (1990-) based on *Madama Butterfly* (Puccini)	American G.I. fathers Vietnamese prostitute's child; after they're separated, he marries a white woman, she suicides. A doomed interracial lust story with a typical sick ending.	Won Tonys galore, but became center of controversy during the 1990 Actors' Equity protest against the casting of Caucasian Jonathan Pryce as a "Eurasian" pimp.

H A N G R A

BREAKING BHANGRA

The following performers have pioneered the bhangra beat to mainstream audiences, fusing Indian melodies and words with video-friendly packaging.

APACHE INDIAN

Born Steven Kapur, the toaster/rapper known as Apache Indian almost singlehandedly popularized the bhangra/ragga blend called "bhangra-muffin." His 1993 debut on Island Records, No Reservations, featured a hit duet with dancehall king Maxi Priest, as well as the single "Arranged Marriage," which went to number 16 on the British pop charts. Sales for No Reservations have been estimated at over 160,000 units worldwide; since then, Kapur has hosted his own bhangra music show on BBC Radio One and served as a guest VJ on MTV U.K.

BALLY SAGOO

While Apache made his name as a toaster or MC, Baljit "Bally" Sagoo took his turn for glory behind the steel wheels, remixing Indian film music with pounding club-ready beats, and inspiring a dance subgenre called "bhangle"—a blend of bhangra and jungle house. The Birmingham-born DJ's debut album Star Crazy is said to have inspired more aspiring bhangra spinners than any other, and his pyramiding sales have prompted Sony Music International to market Sagoo's most recent disc, Rising from the East, in international markets, including the U.S.

Bhangra

Bally Sagoo

Warriors from the Northern Indian province of Punjab would sing and dance to bhangra for hours at harvest ceremonies and other celebrations; today, their remixed offspring dance to bhangra in the wee hours at dancehalls throughout the U.K., the U.S., and Canada—and increasingly, so are non-Indian beat enthusiasts.

The percussion-heavy folk music known as bhangra, featuring lilting vocals, dhol and dholak drums, and the keening of the one-stringed instrument known as the tumbi, first arrived in the West in the 1950s, gaining a foothold in England as immigration from the former crown colony of India boomed. By the mid 1970s, bhangra instrumentation had evolved, incorporating new technology like the synthesizer, the drum machine, and the electronic keyboard. Meanwhile, a bhangra performance circuit had begun to develop, as diasporic Indian communities became entrenched, and celebrations ranging from weddings to holiday festivals became more frequent. Popular bhangra ensembles became stars, with fan followings that even reached back to the homeland of the bhangra beat, India.

It was into this fertile creative environment that Pran Gohil, former head of Phonogram's Far East division, returned in 1979. Recognizing that bhangra had emerged into a fully fledged musical niche with a ripe and lucrative potential audience, he founded Multitone Records, now the dominant player in the Asian Indian music industry in the U.K. But the enterprising Gohil wasn't satisfied with targeting traditional bhangra audiences; he also recognized a second budding phenomenon—a rediscovery (and reinvention) by second and third generation Anglo-Indians of the form.

Apache Indian

Many young British Asians, growing up alongside Afro-Caribbean communities in areas like Southhall and Birmingham, identified themselves with the black British experience—listening to black music, and speaking in transplanted Jamaican patois; as a result, the first infusions of bhangra into popular music were reggae/dancehall hybridizations that took the instrumentation and language of bhangra and spot-welded them to island melodies and rhythms. And bhangra's influence soon spread into other musical milieux, such as techno and house (with bhangra house dominating club scenes in London, Birmingham, and Manchester in the late 1980s), and even being heard on radios around the world in remixes of M/A/R/R/S's dance hit "Pump Up the Volume." Multitone's artist list includes bhangra rappers, bhangra/R&B crooners, and other hybrids, some of whom have toured internationally and sold over 100,000 records—a stunning number for an independent label. In 1994, Multitone formed a partnership with BMG's U.K. subsidiary, and opened its office in the U.S. with an eye toward launching a new British Invasion—this time to the thumping beat of the dhol. Multitone's artists, like Bhangra/R&B diva Sasha, are hopeful. "Reggae was very underground at first and was restricted to the black community," she says. "Eventually it became the sound that everybody liked, and it will be the same with bhangra. But we need to be careful. The music can't be too alien for Western ears, but it's vital to keep the Indian elements. I don't want anything taken away from pure bhangra; I want something added to it. I always want people to know this girl is Asian." —N.G.,J.Y.

Hype and Glory: The Hitmakers of Hong Kong

Nowhere in the world is the art of packaging better practiced than in the Hong Kong music industry: a universe in which stars are made, not born, and where a pretty face and marginal talent can add up to nearly improbable fame and fortune...at least until the next flash appears in the musical pan.

Still, despite its adherence to formula and its flair for promotion, or maybe because of it, Cantopop is nothing to scoff at. Indeed, Hong Kong's hit factories are a very big business. Like Hong Kong cinema, Cantopop is a commodity consumed eagerly in Taiwan, on the mainland, and throughout Asia. Cantopop's biggest star, Jacky Cheung Hok Yau, is among the most popular artists in the world, with over a hundred platinum discs to his name and millions of fans around the globe. (Not bad for a former Cathay Pacific airline reservations clerk.) A 1994 sociological survey found that, among mainland Chinese 20 and under, Cheung's fellow "Heavenly King" Andy Lau Tak Wah was better known than Mao Zedong. And even in the United States, where Cantopop performers regularly tour the casino-hotel circuit, a show by a top star will draw enough screaming admirers to require the intervention of riot police.

Million-selling records. Mountains of souvenir merchandise. Sold-out concerts, and groupies who devote their lives to "supporting" their idols. All centering around performers whose saccharine ballads and bouncy dance jingles are generally dismissed as artistically mundane by critics—and even by many devotees. Outsiders may find the Cantopop phenomenon inexplicable, but those in the know recognize that the success of this intensely profitable industry is due to textbook marketing brilliance.

"Our niche is to establish an image and mature the artists. That way we develop confidence among current and future consumers," says Phillip Chan, general manager of Capital Artists, one of a half-dozen or so independent Hong Kong record companies. He keeps behind his desk a plaque bearing the graphic of a triangle, in each corner of which is a word: "Good," "Cheap," and "Fast"—a three-word slogan as appropriate for a fast-food franchise as for a Cantopop label. "You can only have two [out of the three]," says Chan. "Usually we try for good and fast, although sometimes it is good and cheap." And, though Chan doesn't openly admit it, sometimes Cantopop releases are simply fast and cheap—since "good," after all, is in the ear of the listener.

Cantopop songs are product, and so are the singers; the starmaking process has been honed to an exact science. Labels like Capital scout out likely proteges by the dozens, in open talent searches and from the ranks of models, actors, and beauty pageant winners. They groom them carefully—"maturing" artists being a euphemistic term for coaching them on how to sing mostly on key, restyling their coifs or wardrobes, and pairing them with other artists in PR-invented rivalries or romances. Then they set them loose amidst a barrage of publicity, having them appear at store openings, do television commercials, and lip-synch endlessly in variety programs and showcase concerts, all the while tweaking public interest with carefully released leaks to the gossip rags.

A Canto-label can break even on an album with as few as 40,000 unit sales, and declare a performer a star if he or she sells 100,000 records. A 200,000-plus seller has entered into the airy heights of the Cantopop aristocracy. A performer who produces sales in the 500,000 to a million range is dubbed a "king" or "queen"—with all of the attendant privileges of reigning royalty. Still,

A CANTOPOP PANTHEON

JACKY CHEUNG HOK YAU—Known as the most (some say the only) talented singer among the Heavenly Kings of Cantopop. Consequently, he's called the King of Songs, or, when people are being particularly effusive, the God of Songs. Born in Hong Kong on July 10, 1961, Cheung began his career as a reservations clerk for Cathay Pacific airlines. Urged on by friends and family, in 1984, he entered a local radio contest, the 18th District Singing Competition, and won. Smile, his debut with Polygram, sold a smashing 200,000 records; in 1992, he was named one of the four Heavenly Kings of Cantopop. A year later, he scored his biggest breakout success, <u>Kiss and Goodbye</u>, whose 3 million in sales throughout Asia tripled the previous Hong Kong sales record. Without a doubt, Cheung is Hong Kong's biggest musical star—and the only Asian singer whose sales rank among the top 10 globally.

LESLIE CHEUNG KWOK-WING—His transcendently boyish good looks and very real acting talent more than make up for any failings in the adequate, silky voice of this crooner-turned-marquee-idol. Born in Hong Kong in 1956, Cheung was

sent to school in London as a boy. Upon his return to the island, he decided to forgo college in pursuit of a career in entertainment. After winning runner-up in a major singing contest, he acted in small roles on Hong Kong's TVB while pursuing a vocal career with Capital Artists, a TVB subsidiary and the island's biggest independent label. By 1983, he was a star, and within several years, he'd replaced reigning king Alan Tam as idol of choice among the island's adolescent female population. Cheung eventually began to focus on his acting, delivering a string of solid hits. In 1989, Cheung announced he was tired of the teen-idol scene and that he was retiring "permanently" from singing to concentrate on acting. That didn't last long: in 1996, he released a comeback album, humbly titled <u>The King of Movies and Songs</u>.

AARON KWOK FU SHING—Kwok's big-eyed, boyish looks, and dancing ability have made him a figure of worship for millions of girls throughout Asia, as the Heavenly King of Dance. Born on October 26, 1965, Kwok finished high school and was preparing to work at his family's jewelry business when in 1986 a friend convinced him to attend the TVB Dance Team tryouts. Ironically, Kwok was selected; the friend was not. Kwok began a new career as a dancer for pop stars on TVB variety shows. After unsuccessfully trying to

while there are a handful of idols whose imperial status seems all but permanent, even the kings and queens of the Cantopop world mostly fade into quick obscurity. "Like the price of seafood, the commercial worth of entertainers fluctuates," jokes Jacky Cheung. "We are all lobsters. Our only difference is in size." If that's the case, the hit kitchens of Hong Kong have cooked up a sure-fire recipe for pop success.

POP EXPLOSION: THE ROOTS OF CANTOPOP

Despite Hong Kong's status as a British colony since the turn of the 20th century, the island's predominant popular music continued to be songs inspired by Beijing Opera until the late '60s, when performers from Taiwan brought over their Western-inspired, Mandarin-language ballads. But while the Hong Kong listening audience initially embraced Taiwanese singers, they soon demanded popular music in their own dialect, Cantonese. They got what they wanted from an unusual source: television. TVB, the network owned by cinematic pioneer Sir Run Run Shaw, began hiring songwriters like Joseph Koo to compose Cantonese-language theme songs in the pop vein for hit drama serials like *Sorrow Of Forbidden City*. The songs soon outstripped the shows in popularity, planting the seeds for a new genre of music. Those seeds came to fruition in the early '70s, when a performer emerged who has since been called the Father of Cantopop: Sam Hui Koon Kit.

In collaboration with composer and producer Koo, Hui wrote songs with lyrics that spoke of everyday matters—like worker exploitation and the rising costs of living—set to Western-style melodies and instrumentation. When Hui made his acting debut in the film *Games Gamblers Play* in 1973, he sang the title song himself. The film was a box office smash; the theme song, meanwhile, was the first real Cantopop hit.

In Hui's wake came other singers mimicking and elaborating upon his successful formula.

Jackie Cheung Hok Yau

Foremost among them were a band who called themselves the Wynners, led by a young man named Alan Tam Wai Lun. The five-man combo—which included Danny Yip, Bennett Pang, Anthony Chan, and Kenny Bee—would go on to dominate the Hong Kong music scene throughout the '70s, ruling the burgeoning world of Cantopop as the Beatles had ruled the West. The Wynners broke up when Bee left to make movies in Taiwan, but the end of the Wynners only gave Tam the opportunity to begin a phenomenal solo career, in which he replaced Sam Hui as the reigning King of Cantopop. Other top acts of the '70s and early '80s included the moustachioed former spokesman for Guinness Stout ale, George Lam Chi Cheung, who began singing Cantonese songs in 1976, and the flamboyant Roman Tam Law Mun, who got his start as a lounge singer. Both continue to perform, though their audiences are largely driven by nostalgia.

At the end of the '70s, the Cantopop boom hit unexpected resistance, as Hong Kong teenagers turned their attention to Japanese pop idols, whose peppy, electronic music was more fun and danceable than the melodramatic love songs of the local Canto-minstrels. The J-pop fad ultimately faded, but only because the Hong Kong music industry had learned to assimilate and adapt to this new challenge: The '80s saw the emergence of a crop of artists who combined the teen-idol appeal and kitschy dance groove of Japanese popsters with a feel for traditional romantic ballads. Among the biggest stars of this era were Danny Chan Pak Keung, who would die of a tragic drug overdose at the tender age of 35, and Leslie Cheung Kwok Wing—the first modern Cantopop icon.

Cheung had launched his career by winning a singing contest with a cover of Don McLean's "American Pie" in the late '70s; in 1984, he catapulted to the top of the Canto-heap with a Japanese-language cover version of the song "Monica." Cheung laid the blueprints for today's

Hong Kong idols, attracting a bevy of female fans with his boyish, drop-dead-handsome looks and his melodramatic songs of desire and loss. His instant popularity and domination of the charts soon locked him into fierce competition with Alan Tam, though both stars disavowed any rivalry. Still, their respective fan clubs waged a war that ranged from heckling at "enemy" concerts to actual physical violence between Cheung-lovers and Tam-fans—the first major Hong Kong "fan wars," though far from the last.

Sick of the commotion, Cheung announced his retirement from singing in 1989, devoting his energies to acting (he has since, as expected, emerged from retirement). Tam, meanwhile, declared that he would no longer accept any major musical awards, so as to give "new voices" a chance. Though neither performer actually disappeared, new voices certainly did emerge—in spades. Most prominent among them: the four male idols who would be dubbed the *Sei Tai Tien Wang,* the "Four Great Heavenly Kings" of Cantopop.

WE FOUR KINGS OF CANTOPOP ARE:
Hong Kong's "Heavenly Kings"

"The press loves it. Why have one Elvis when you can have two? Look in your files, you'll see things were set up exactly the same 10 years ago when Alan Tam and Leslie Cheung were the big rivals. Once, the fans started fighting together so badly they both had to go on stage and tell them to cool it."
—U.S.-educated Hong Kong record executive.

Even in an industry chock-full of promotional genius, there's never been a marketing coup like this one. As both Alan Tam and Leslie Cheung cut back their musical output in the late '80s, the Hong Kong music world hungered for new idols. Unfortunately, no single superstar had attained a level of popularity worthy of mentioning in the same breath as the legendary Tam and Cheung, and some in the industry feared a crippling loss of momentum for a business driven by fan-worship. Then, in 1992, the Hong Kong celebrity machine came upon the idea of crowning not one, but four new pop emperors, a complete set of Canto-kings. Suddenly, the gossip pages and star magazines blossomed with pictures and pop propaganda touting the Sei Tai Tien Wang—the Four Heavenly Kings of Cantopop. They were a motley lot: Jacky Cheung Hok Yau, a former airline employee; Leon Lai Ming, an aspiring policeman; Andy Lau Tak Wah, a television actor; and Aaron Kwok Fu Sing, an ex–jewelry store clerk. Respectively, they were known as the Kings of Singing, Fan Support, Acting, and Dancing, and despite singing ability that ranged from abysmal to acceptable to pretty darn good, they captivated the world of Hong Kong pop as no other performers had before, or have ever since.

Andy Lau Tak Wah

Without a doubt, the most popular and successful of the Four Kings is Jacky Cheung. Cheung, who boasts the biggest global following of any Hong Kong pop star, rebounded from a dismal series of albums in the '80s to score Hong Kong's biggest record to date—his 1993 *Kiss and Goodbye,* which moved over 3 million units. Cheung continues to expand his audience overseas, and, in 1995, toured North American arenas like New York's Madison Square Garden, achieving sellout crowds, the biggest concert series to date by a Cantopop performer.

The second-ranked Canto-king is generally considered to be Andy Lau, whose singing is at best mediocre, but whose marquee looks and popularity as a cinema star as well as a musical performer have enabled him to overcome a shaky talent. With more than 60 platinum discs to his credit, Lau is nearly as profitable for his label BMG (a recent entrant into the Hong Kong market) as Cheung is for Polygram.

Third amongst the Heavenly Kings is Leon Lai, whose title, the King of Fan Support, is due to the

jump over to drama, Kwok left Hong Kong in 1990 to try his luck in Taiwan. There he filmed a commercial for a bicycle company, leading to his "discovery" by Taiwanese independent label Era International. In 1993, Kwok—an established heartthrob—jumped ship to sign with Warner Hong Kong, whose global clout he coveted. Now finally receiving recognition as a "legit" pop idol, Kwok has also ramped up his acting career, using his dance-derived athleticism to spin a role for himself as action-hero heir apparent.

LEON LAI MING—Despite his rather bland good looks and minimal vocal talents, Lai's mostly female fans have thrown themselves under cars to gain his attention. As a result, he's been dubbed the Heavenly King of Fan Support—a nice enough distinction. Lai was born in Beijing on December 11, 1966, moving with his family to Hong Kong as a toddler. He aspired to become a policeman, but, while exiting the station one day, he was discovered by a passing talent agent, and broke into acting with a TVB contract in 1986. Stardom awaited: by 1990, he'd become one of Hong Kong's most popular romantic actors. Meanwhile, Lai made the requisite move to singing (after working tirelessly to learn fluent Cantonese), and managed to score enough success with his first release, Leon, to be accorded the title of Heavenly King.

ANDY LAU TAK WAH— Nicknamed "Wah Chai" by his fans, meaning "Andy Boy," Lau's distinctive looks—scupted cheekbones and a prominent, aquiline nose—have helped him as much as his line-reading ability in garnering the official title of "Heavenly King of Acting." Lau was born in 1962 in a rural village in Hong Kong's New Territories, a middle child in a family with six children. Growing up in poverty made the young Lau determined to succeed, and, banking on his striking looks, he joined TVB's drama training program in 1981. In 1982, he received a break when Chow Yun-Fat turned down the lead role in director Ann Hui's Boat People, allowing Lau to launch his acting career. Then, in 1985, Lau joined Capital Artists, though his initial releases were greeted with disdain. He didn't achieve commercial and critical respect until his fifth album in 1990, Can It Be Possible—which scored triple-platinum sales, garnered him a Most Popular Singer award in Taiwan, and placed him on the fast track to Heavenly success.

ANITA MUI YIM-FONG— Nicknamed "The Hong Kong Madonna" for her outrageous antics in younger days, Mui's enigmatic past has led to many unfounded allegations about her life before she became

rabid nature of his groupies: the "Leon Family" dresses in "Leon Uniform" (red baseball caps and "I Love Leon" T-shirts), gathers in huge crowds at his concerts and other appearances, and occasionally gets into frenzied, purse-swinging, eye-gouging brawls with members of the Andy World Club. "Leon Family is not just a fan club, it is a way of life," says club organizer Ann Chan. "Through Leon we have a whole social world." The Family's nearly 5,000 members regularly gather with their god for fundraisers, dances, barbecues, and other glorious highlights of a life spent in devotion. Lai hardly discourages his admirers, who range from 13-year-old middle-school girls to 60-year-old grandmothers; indeed, the unmarried performer has said to the papers that, should he decide to tie the knot, he will probably marry one of his fans.

The fourth Heavenly King—occasionally seen as something of an afterthought to the Big Three—is Aaron Kwok, a baby-faced pretty boy who has long been dismissed as a teen idol with a girlish voice. However, a diligent attempt at improving his singing seems to have recently paid off: He went from being regularly shut out from Hong Kong's music awards to receiving numerous accolades in 1995, and has since become Warner's top-selling Cantopop artist, now that Andy Lau has moved to BMG. Kwok has also been the subject of rumors that he's being groomed as an action actor to replace departed kung-fu king Jackie Chan, whose journey to the West has left a notable void in the ranks of longtime Chan-studio Golden Harvest.

In recent years, Hong Kong pundits have begun a kind of Heavenly King deathwatch—counting out the months until one or more of Cantopop's royal quartet falls by the commercial wayside. Releases in 1995 by the pre-fab four fell considerably short of expectations, and the Kings are all in their thirties—longish in the tooth for teen idols. The ever-fickle celebrity media has even noted that *shi li pai* stars, or "singers with substance," whose talent actually outstrips their aesthetic value, are becoming increasingly popular. Still, the Heavenly Kings have ruled Cantopop for half a decade, and their appeal abroad may be just beginning. Lau has flirted with coming to America, retaining top agency ICM to search out potential roles for him in Hollywood. And Cheung is preparing to record his first English-language album. In short, while the kings may eventually be dethroned in their native domain, there are still new worlds to conquer.

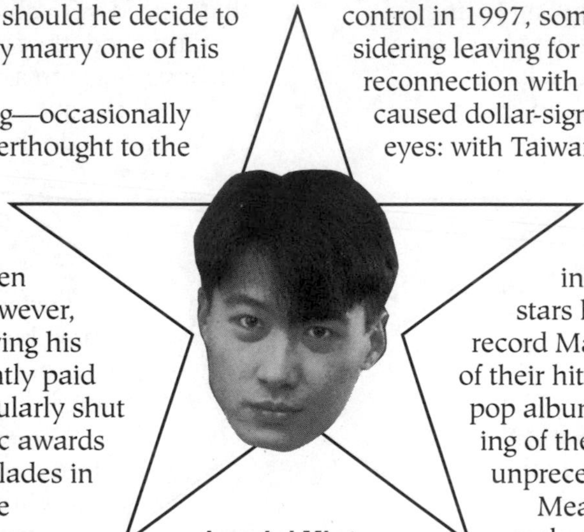

Leon Lai Ming

CANTOPOP NOW

As with most things in hyperactive Hong Kong, the sands beneath Cantopop's feet is constantly shifting. With the turnover of the island to Chinese control in 1997, some top-drawer stars are considering leaving for parts west. The official reconnection with the mainland has also caused dollar-signs to flash in music-mogul eyes: with Taiwan and China already accounting for a healthy percentage of the Hong Kong recording industry's revenues, Canto-stars have made it a practice to record Mandarin-language versions of their hits and even whole Mando-pop albums, and the full-scale opening of the China market presents an unprecedented opportunity.

Meanwhile, the traditionally male-vocalist-dominated industry has seen the emergence of some credible female superstars: joining Anita Mui Yim Fong and Sally Yeh Chen-Wen in the ranks of Canto-queens are Faye Wong Ching-Man, Cass Phang Ling, and Sandy Lam Yik-Lien, each of whom has managed to consistently sell records in the hundreds of thousands, sometimes even topping the results of their Heavenly male counterparts.

The opening of the Cantopop market to new voices—female and male—can be ascribed in part to the raging popularity of karaoke **[👁328]**, which has made it possible for an artist to be viable with sales as low as 25,000 units. Most Cantopop songs, with their simple ABABA structure and less-than-challenging range, are almost perfectly tuned for karaoke success; indeed, some jokers claim that nearly every karaoke house contains an amateur capable of singing the hits of the Heavenly Kings better than they can themselves.

Because of this secondary market, Cantopop has been given something of an artistic lease on life; so long as Faye Wong, for instance, churns out a few snappy singalong staples on each of her albums, she has freedom to also include more challenging and experimental work, including covers of Western obscurantia, like the songs of Brit mood-pop crooners the Cocteau Twins. As a result, singers are finally breaking out of the idol mode, and demanding musical respect in addition to worshipful awe. And who knows? Perhaps someday soon, Westerners will join their Hong Kong brethren and sistren in snapping their fingers and kissing their lovers to the tunes of Cantopop balladeers.

HOW TO BE A CANTOPOP STAR

Want to be big in Hong Kong's hectic hit parade? It isn't easy—but it *is* possible, if you've got the look (and maybe even a little bit of talent). A trio of Chinese American rappers with slick dance moves and indifferent skills launched themselves into the pop stratosphere, by bringing their Sino-hip hop act to Taiwan and then throughout Asia as the L.A. Boys. Canadian Christy Chung became an actress and Cantostar after winning a beauty pageant for overseas Chinese. So...what's stopping you? Here's a step by step primer on how to join the Cantopop constellation.

Aaron Kwok Fu Sing

1. Be beautiful. Or hunky. This is more a matter of genes than choice, but it's unfortunately a basic requirement if you're going to be a Hong Kong pop idol. If you don't have matinee looks, an outrageous sense of personal style helps—though not too outrageous: Cantopop prefers its sensationalism packaged in juicy little niblets, and Madonna-esque flights of erotic fancy will be more likely to provoke horror than fascination.

2. Get discovered. This isn't really as hard as it seems: if you're stunningly gorgeous, entering a beauty pageant guarantees you a talent scout's attention, as does simply walking around in downtown Hong Kong. You might try applying for one of TVB's "apprenticeship programs"—the equivalent of indentured labor for creative types; this will get you in the back door if you're accepted, but you'll probably spend a lot of time as a backup dancer or soap-opera bimbo before you get your shot at the real deal. TVB and other radio and TV stations also sponsor singing contests, and winning an award (or even an honorable mention) is a virtual guarantee that you'll be offered a singing contract. This, of course, is just the beginning.

3. Let yourself be groomed. Becoming a pop idol in Hong Kong is more a function of image control than just about anything—bad singing can be fixed in the remix, bad dancing can be saved by good lighting and backup hoofers, but if your look and attitude aren't exactly right, you're doomed to be just another one of the hundreds of file-and-forget singers generated by the Hong Kong hit machine. At any given time, there's only room for about a dozen top stars in the Cantopop cosmos, and if you don't let your handlers take control, you won't be one of them. They'll change your name, pay for your singing lessons, buy your wardrobe, arrange your personal appearances, hire fans to scream when you take strolls in the nabe, and be your best friend—for a healthy cut, if not the majority, of what you'll earn in your budding career years.

If it works out, it'll all be worth it—top stars make millions, not just from record sales, but from ribbon-cuttings at store openings, concerts, special appearances, and movie and television performances.

And if it doesn't, don't worry—you'll have plenty of company in the record-store bargain bins... —J.Y., Y.K.C.

a star. Some rumormongers claim she was affiliated with the Triads, or even a high-priced call girl; that she'd had an abortion; that she'd been a drug addict. Whatever the truth, it's clear that Mui has not had an easy climb to the top. Born to a family of entertainers, she was raised by her mother—her father having died when she was still an infant. In order to help support the family, she became a professional singer at age 8, performing as a novelty act in local nightclubs. In 1981, she won the first-ever Hong Kong Talent Quest Singing Awards, and became the island's biggest female star. Since then, Mui has parlayed her singing success into an equally successful acting career.

ALAN TAM WING-LUN—Tam is the Dean of Cantopop—the man who more than any other popularized the saccharine formula concocted by Canto-godfather Sam Hui. He was born August 23, 1950, in Hong Kong, the second of five children and the only son. After high school, Tam left Hong Kong for Singapore to study economics, but grew bored with college and returned to Hong Kong with the idea of starting a band. The group, which Tam named the Wynners in homage to the Beatles (another pop band with a misspelled name), first performed together in 1973. Their first album, entitled Listen to the Wynners, was a breakout hit; all told, the band released 10

albums together and starred in four movies. In 1978, however, the Wynners broke up, and Tam embarked on an even higher-flying solo career as Hong Kong's first pop idol. In 1987, Tam announced that he was semi-retiring; these days, while he continues to release albums, he tours less frequently, and spends more of his time managing his considerable business empire.

FAYE WONG CHING-MAN—Wong's quirky and inimitable vocal style, tempestuous personality, and gamine looks have made her Hong Kong's biggest current female star. Born in Beijing, the daughter of a businessman father and a mother who was trained in classical Chinese opera, she moved to Hong Kong at the age of 18 and began taking vocal lessons from Tai See-Chong—a well-known starmaker who also taught Jacky Cheung, Andy Lau, and Leon Lai. Shortly thereafter, she was scouted by record execs, and—even though she claims to have learned her Cantonese from TV shows—quickly became Hong Kong's biggest-selling female artist. She divides her time between Hong Kong and the mainland, where she makes her residence with fellow China-rocker Dou Wei.

THE MAINLAND ROCKS!

China isn't just the world's biggest unexplored market; it's also, to the dismay of Beijing's gerontocrats, a hotbed of rock and roll rebellion, boasting artists whose lyrics and vocals are as brash and biting as any to emerge from the decadent, capitalist West. The most popular of China's rockers outside of the mainland's environs is probably pop queen Faye Wong, but singer-songwriters and guitar heroes also abound. Bands like Three Princes (featuring Wong's longtime boyfriend Dou Wei) and Tang Dynasty are among the 500 or so rock bands to have achieved noticeable success. Early rocker Cui Jian, whose music inspired and emboldened the protestors at Tiananmen Square, even toured the United States in 1996, as did the all-girl rock quartet Cobra—and eccentric musical pastiche artist Dadawa released a critically acclaimed American album in 1995.

Pop music on the mainland began with imports from Hong Kong and Taiwan, particularly the songs of beloved pop crooner Teresa Teng, but the glib ballads of the islands didn't tap into more quintessentially Mainlander concerns and issues. It wasn't long before indigenous pop stars began to emerge—first Cui Jian, whose 1986 "I Have Nothing" is generally accorded the status of the first Mainland rock hit. The music of Mainland China tends to be more spirited and experimental than its syrupy counterparts in Hong Kong and Taiwan, an apt reaction to China's oppressive atmosphere. But Tiananmen proved that both music and rebellion can survive the most crushing of attacks. Cui Jian has taken up touring in his native land once more, now that the three-year ban against his concerts has finally been lifted. And rock 'n' roll continues to thrive, despite concert ticket prices equal to five times an average worker's salary, and warnings from authorities that rock can lead to "excessive drinking, drug-taking, gang fights, and homosexuality." The music is hated by the government but allowed to exist regardless, becoming a part of the counterculture known as "hui se wen hua," or the "grey culture." After all, when students are rocking out, they're distracted from organizing a revolution. —J.Y.

Chungking Express

Chinese Opera

Like the traditional arts of any culture, the form of musical theater that the West has labeled "Chinese Opera" tends to divide onlookers into two sharply drawn categories. The uninformed will find its exaggerated poses and inflections, its boinging musical accompaniment, and its over-done costumes annoying, obscure, and ridiculous. Devotees, on the other hand, point to its dramatic richness, the remarkable acrobatic choreography of its performers, and its visual splendor. They call it sublime.

Either way, Chinese Opera, known as *xiqu* in its native Mandarin, is a sight to behold—at least once. And even those who don't immediately fall in love will probably appreciate the extraordinary leaps, somersaults, and contortions that expert performers engage in on the tiny stage; they might also recognize the seeds of modern kung fu film choreography within the elaborate opera dance, and indeed, some of Hong Kong cinema's greatest began their careers in the Chinese Opera **[👁74]**.

Over 2000 different regional subgenres of xiqu exist, each shaped by regional preferences and dialects; the form most familiar to the West is probably the one native to Beijing. Each region's form of opera is distinct, though they share themes, characteristics of movement and staging, and some conventions of costume and makeup.

IN THE BEGINNING

The Chinese dramatic tradition began in the Hubei and Anhui provinces of China, with roots going back to the Shang Dynasty (1523-1028 B,C.), when performances involving music and theater were part of rituals practiced by ancient seers. Gradually, the mystical element of the performances were subordinated to their entertainment value, and the nascent theatre grew in popularity and extravagance.

One early high point for Chinese theatre occurred during the Han Dynasty (202 B.C.-220 A.D.), when a performance before Emperor Wu Ti (140-87 B.C.) featured clowns, wrestlers, and musicians disguised as gods, fairies, warriors, tigers, leopards, bears, dragons, divine turtles, white elephants, and dragons, together with armies of acrobats and singers, enacting stories drawn from ancient mythology. From 712 to 54 A.D., the

HOW TO BE AN OPERA MAN

Traditional opera training began early, and discipline was harsh; opera masters had the right to punish students in any fashion, "even to death." If you had had the fortune (or is that misfortune?) of living in those times, and if you wanted to pursue a career in this enigmatic art, here's what you would've had to do:

1. BE A GUY. Remember, first and foremost, that this is a male-only art; those lacking Y chromosomes need not apply.

2. BE A KID. A young one. Since the apprenticeship lasts a minimum of seven grueling years, the traditional age at which a student was accepted into training was six years old.

3. BE PATIENT. And be ready for the worst time of your life. A typical day might begin with students rising at dawn to "shout at the sun" for an hour to develop vocal endurance, then a light breakfast of gruel, then several hours of exercise and practice in forms; after an equally light lunch, tumbling, weapons training, and singing lessons. In the late afternoons, students might be sent out to beg for food. Household chores might occupy the evening, after which students would flop down in a spartan communal bunk room to sleep until dawn arose once more. Reading, writing, and arithmetic weren't part of the routine; as a result, for all of their carefully cultivated air of culture and sophistication, most opera singers remained woefully

ignorant into adulthood.

4. BE LUCKY. After a few years of training, a student's destiny as an actor was determined. Slighter boys with higher vocal ranges would find themselves training exclusively for female roles; heavy-set, deep-voiced boys were allotted warrior and emperor roles. By late adolescence, students would have been segregated into stars and supporting players, a division as swift as it is permanent. For those who'd excelled, however, the world was their oyster—mass acclaim, mobs of screaming fans, generous patrons, and all the luxuries denied in a childhood of penury.

genre found a patron in Emperor Ming Huang, who established the "Academy of the Pear Orchard" to train young singers and actors to perform for the court.

Still, the highly formalized mode of theater that would evolve into xiqu didn't emerge until the mid 19th century, when *qing xi,* the direct predecessor to modern Chinese opera, replaced *kun ch'u* (Cantonese), a type of musical theater which had reigned as the national entertainment since the middle of the Ming Dynasty (1368-1644). Qing xi was well received, granted Imperial patronage, and continued to develop and expand its audience well into the 20th century.

Out of the roots of qing xi came xiqu, a stylized, elaborate art whose skills required a lifetime to master. A broad system of schools that trained orphan, foundling, and otherwise underprivileged young boys (always boys) grew up in the cities, indoctrinating them through rigid discipline and demanding, in return for training, shelter, and sustenance, what amounted to indentured servitude.

Still, during the height of the opera, a well-trained xiqu performer was guaranteed a living, either as part of a touring troupe roaming the countryside and performing well-worn favorites, or—if he was good enough—as part of a permanent resident company in a large city. The best performers became stars, adored by the masses and given grand gifts by patrons.

During the Cultural Revolution, traditional opera pieces reflecting old, decadent societies were banned; only a style called "Eight Model Plays"—featuring officially endorsed Communist heroes, events, and activities—could be created and performed. Predictably, this had a stultifying effect on the opera, as audiences failed to thrill to such Communist Party favorites as *The Great Oppressor Landlord Is Ground Under the Heel of the Victorious Proletariat*.

Even after the post-Revolution return of more traditional opera in 1978, the form's popularity continued to dwindle. Today, because of the lack of historical and theatrical knowledge among contemporary Chinese youth, the opera has taken a back seat to less cultivated forms of entertainment, such as imported Western movies and karaoke bars. Farewell, indeed, my concubine. —C.K.

ANATOMY OF THE CHINESE OPERA

THE ACTOR: He's the opera's all-important presence, dominating the stage in high platform shoes, padded clothes, extended sleeves, heavy make-up, headdress, and wig—all adding to the illusion of almost an extra yard of height.

MAKEUP AND COSTUMES: The intricate style of an actor's makeup and dress is meant to reveal elements of the character's temper, level of honesty, and intellect, not to mention whether he's a historical or mythical character; as a result, actors are trained to put on their own makeup, since it is an intimate part of their persona and performance. All details of costuming, even the most minute, are significant. For example, the way the actor strokes his beard can show his wealth, the level of his health, how socially refined the character is, and his present state of sobriety—or drunkenness. Meanwhile, young heroes or heroines rely on rouge and red powder to give them the "flush of youth" (though an excess of red produces instead the "flush of rage" attributed to generals and warlords).

VOICE: Voice training for Chinese opera, as for Western opera singers, varies depending on which role the person is playing. The most typical timbre, however, is a rather nasal falsetto, which allows for the most resonance in large venues. Female characters will twitter in the upper range of the falsetto, while male characters will swing from throaty rumbling to high-pitched but masculine keening.

THE PLOTS: Two basic storylines dominate: 1) The "civilian" plot, about two star-crossed lovers, or poor, but noble officials and 2) The "military" opera with more action-oriented scenes, such as Robin Hood–like stealing from the rich to give to the poor, heroes trying to save besieged kingdoms, or good versus evil, usually involving mythical creatures like the Monkey King or the White Snake. Before the curtain goes up, the audience is expected to be familiar with the story of an opera, so as to appreciate the nuances of the performances.

INSTRUMENTS: The orchestra, unlike in Western opera, usually sits to the side of the stage, and is comprised of only about eight members. The hu qin (a bowed string instrument comparable to the Western violin) is played by the leader of the orchestra, who usually works closely with the opera soloist; the hu qin must reinforce the vocal line discreetly, following every inflection minutely. Meanwhile, the percussion section follows every movement of the actor, making a beat with the bamboo clapper on every step or important gesture. During more exciting action sequences, gongs, cymbals, and drums bring up the level of intensity.

Japanese DJs

The evolution of Japanese DJs is an example of how imitation can transform into innovation when people truly love an art form. There are those who claim that the impetus for the entire Japanese DJ community came when old-school hip hop cinema classix like *Krush Groove* and *Wild Style* were imported into Japan in the mid 1980s. Though they made a minimal box-office and cultural dent in the U.S., they hit Japanese youth like the New Testament hit the Torah, prompting them to invent a hip hop–homage underground—complete with break dancers, graffiti artists, DJs, and MCs—that has continued to thrive even as American rap has slipped into gangsta mode.

While Japanese breakers and scribes have kept a relatively low profile, like their brethren around the world, Japanese MCs are starting to make some noise, and Japanese DJs have become potent enough to score hits across the Pacific. The rise and globalization of club music has led to a resurgence of J-DJs in the dance genre, working as remixers and producers. And, in the bebop/hip hop fusion world of acid jazz and the sonic fog of trip hop, Japanese DJs have reigned supreme—going far beyond duplication of the latest U.S. and U.K. grooves to set inventive trends of their own. The mainstay of Mo Wax, for instance, a U.K. label specializing in abstract/deep hip hop, has been Japan's DJ Krush, who's worked with artists worldwide, especially in the U.S. And Towa Tei, long seen as just one of the DJs for the club-pop group, Deee-lite, has gone on to critical success with his own solo sound, an "easy listening" blend of diverse musical genres. "Japanese DJs have now reached the level of international DJs," says Japanese producer Dr. Tommy. "They're not copying techniques from overseas anymore—there's an original Japanese style now."

Most Japanese DJs, however, still fall into two main categories: producers and scratchers. The former category is musically diverse, and many of these DJs are highly respected in their respective genres. The latter remain strictly true to the hip hop vein, never having strayed from their beginnings as turntable technicians. Most scratchers gain their fame as competitors in the DJ battle arena; with each new contest, Japanese DJs are consistently gaining prominence, and inspiring a growing category of "turntabilists"—DJs who make music (as opposed to simply spinning records or providing background beats) by scratching. Pioneers in this field (including Filipino American DJs from California like the Invisible Skratch Picklez) represent a new movement to make DJs into serious musicians, crafting an entirely new sonic dimension. —O.W.

J-DJ, WON'T YOU PLAY THAT SONG

Name	Best Known As	Sound	Selected Discs
DJ Krush	Perhaps one of Japan's best known DJs/producers. His early efforts have been derided as somewhat mediocre, but in more recent times, he's won over a lot of converts.	His sound falls into an amorphous zone that goes by various names, including: trip hop, down tempo, and abstract or deep hip hop. Interpreted, this means that his sound is characterized by jazzy aesthetics, eerie samples that float in and out of the track instead of dominating it, subtle scratching that doesn't overpower, and slow-tempo beats that combine for a moody and rather dark effect.	*Meiso* (Mo Wax) 
DJ Honda 	Honda shocked the world battle DJ community by making the semis at the 1992 World DJ Championship. He's Japan's best known scratcher/battler, who recently has gotten into producing music.	Honda's production sound shares sonic similarities with American hip hop, though few feel it is yet on par with the best producers the States have to offer, like DJ Premier or Diamond D. Still, his beats are hot and accessible.	*DJ Honda* (Sony)
Tadashi Yabe and **Toshio Matsuura** of UFO	Along with the third UFO pilot, Raphael Sebbag, they began their career as event promoters. In 1991, they decided to infuse their club nights with original material; they eventually fueled the Japanese acid-jazz explosion.	Funk, jazz, R&B, and more, smoothed out over cool beats and presented in cooler neo-beatnik style. 	*United Future Organization; No Sound Is Too Taboo* (both on Polygram)
Towa Tei 	The funky groovester who gave the trippy post-hippie trio Deee-Lite their mellowed-out cosmic dance-beats, under the stage name Jungle DJ Towa Towa.	With Deee-lite, a groovy, peaced-out funk; after a stage accident in Brazil, however, Towa Tei took a leave from the band, and emerged from the hospital with a yen for bossa nova and Rio beat, which have infused his subsequent solo output.	With Deee-Lite: *World Clique; Infinity Within;* Solo: *Future Listening* (all Elektra)

Japanese Girl Bands

Savor for a moment the title of the Cibo Matto song: "White Pepper Ice Cream": Imagine the sweet coolness of ice cream, blended with the shocking kick of pepper, and you get an idea of the paradoxical joys offered by many of the Japanese all-female bands who've landed on American shores, and grabbed hold of the American rock imagination. Shonen Knife's naive lyrics and matching A-line pink, blue, and yellow dresses suggest that they're the musical equivalent of ice cream—cute, campy, and harmless. But once they slam into one of their thumping guitar-driven sets: white pepper. Then there's the duo Cibo Matto, who take the stage wearing baggy, layered clothes, sneakers, and shy smiles, only to rip through breathy acid-jazz raps that seem to burst directly from the id—twisted odes to consumption, compulsion, and appetite. For most Western ears, their appeal—like that of white pepper ice cream—might unfortunately begin as novelty. But those with more refined tastes might recognize their music as a delicacy to be prized. Dig in. Eat up. It's good. —G.L., J.Y.

IN THE BEGINNING: Pink Lady

Despite limited musical abilities, teen duo Pink Lady hit number one on the Japanese pop charts in the late '70s, propelling them to a pioneering (and blissfully temporary) crossover career in the United States. Mitsuyo "Mie" Nemoto and Keiko "Kei" Masuda were schoolgirls and best friends in 1976 when they were spotted by talent scout Kazuhiko Soma, who thought their looks and above-average height (for a Japanese woman, anyway; Mie is 5'5" and Kei 5'3") gave them star potential. Soma was no dummy; with their disco sound and go-go dance moves Pink Lady was an instant hit. But conquering Japan was just the beginning. Teaching Mie and Kei enough phonetic English for an album's worth of songs, Soma had the pair release an American record, titled *Pink Lady* (1979, Elektra/Curb; *Rolling Stone* dubbed it "a pop sound rooted in the Archies, with touches of Abba and the Supremes"). He then hooked them up with U.S. TV producers Sid and Marty Krofft. The result was the appalling and short-lived NBC variety show *Pink Lady & Jeff*, which showcased Mie and Kei's childlike innocence and obvious linguistic handicap. The album fared no better than the show, and Pink Lady quickly faded into obscurity.

Shonen Knife

For anyone who's counting, the J-Grrrl revolution began in 1981, when Michie Nakatani and Naoko Yamano—college chums with a common love for '70s punk like the Ramones and Gang of Four—decided to start their own band. Recruiting Naoko's sister Atsuko, the fledgling rockers named themselves (after a brand of pocketknife) and then got down to the business of learning how to play their instruments. "We had no experience," says Michie. "We just went to the music store and bought guitars and a book to study." The trio then began to lead a double life: "office ladies" by day, and guitar heroines by night, soon attracting a cult audience playing in Osaka clubs; by the mid-'80s, they'd garnered a

record deal with a Japanese indie label, and word about the band had begun to spread through the underground grapevine. Then, in 1986, the trio's big break arrived: Jeff McDonald, lead singer for seminal L.A. punk band Redd Kross, saw a bootleg videotape of a Shonen Knife concert. He was instantly hooked, and wrote the band a letter, which became a mutual correspondence. In 1988, McDonald booked the band into a concert in Los Angeles, and watched the crowd go wild. He subsequently dedicated himself to Knife evangelism, organizing a 1989 tribute album, *Every Band Has a Shonen Knife That Loves Them*, that featured a string of Ameri-punk notables, including Sonic Youth, L7, and the Reverb Motherfuckers. The late Kurt Cobain became a fan and invited Shonen Knife to open for Nirvana in Britain. Knife's Japanese material was re-released in the U.S. in 1990 as *Shonen Knife* (Gasatanka/Giant) and *Pretty Little Baka Guy* (Dutch East India Trading). And then, after hitting number one on the British indie charts with a cover of the Irving Berlin classic "White Christmas," the band was signed to Virgin for their major-label debut, *Let's Knife* (1992). The trio was finally able to quit their day jobs, dedicate themselves to music—and slam their way into punk-pop history.

Cibo Matto

Trippy lyrics over acid-etched beats. Moody, handlebar hooks. A stage presence that veers from schoolgirl innocent to diva-abrasive. Even if they weren't being packaged as part of the J-grrrl explosion, Cibo Matto would be, well, unique. Although Miho Hatori and Yuka Honda attended the same high school in Tokyo, they first met while both were living in New York's East Village, several years later. Recruited to join a band called Leitoh Lychee ("frozen lychee nut"), they discovered a mutual appetite for food and sound. On impulse, the pair went on stage together during an improv night in 1993, with Miho reading a stream-of-consciousness rap from her journal and Yuka laying down background beats with her synthesizer. When asked for the name of their "band," they came up with Cibo Matto, a name-check to the '70s Italian sex comedy *Seso Matto* ("Sex Madness") that roughly means "crazy for food." Since then their distinctively minimalist food-funk has resulted in a major-label record deal with Warner Brothers and a legacy of samplatronic cult-hits from "Beef Jerky" and "Know Your Chicken" (1995, El Diablo), followed by the eponymous *Cibo Matto*, (1995, El Diablo) and *Viva! La Woman* (1995, Warner Bros.); it's also produced a spinoff group called Butter, featuring Cibo Matto and members of Jon Spencer Blues Explosion. Watch this band.

Buffalo Daughter

Are these Japanese cowgirls the next big thing? The Beastie Boys, who've signed BD to their label Grand Royal, sure seem to think so. Daughters Sugar Yoshinaga and Yumiko Ohno originally served as half of the four-girl band Havana Exotica, which released three albums in Japan before breaking up in 1993. After the split, guitarist Yoshinaga and bassist Ohno decided to go it on their own, recruiting DJ Moog Yamamoto to provide turntable support. After touring the club circuit, the trio cut their first demo in July 1993, then spent the next few years refining their noise, producing other bands, cutting soundtrack songs, and finishing their debut album, *Shaggy Head Dressers*, and a followup, *Amoebae Sound System*. In March 1996, BD signed to Grand Royal, went on its first U.S. tour, and released its American debut, *Captain Vapour Athletes*. The Buffalo stampede is about to begin.

Japanese Heavy Metal

With the twang of busted strings and the buzz of long, permed hair being shorn, glam metal died in the early '90s, crushed under the triple juggernauts of alternative, industrial, and skate-core. The appeal of grown men wearing Spandex, studded leather, and too much makeup while fellating microphones and abusing Stratocasters ultimately proved to be as ephemeral as the equally embarrassing postures of disco. But at glam metal's peak, American bands like Mötley Crüe and Poison, Brit-crunchers like Ozzy Osbourne and Judas Priest, and Teutonic titans like the Scorpions ruled the arenas and the airwaves. And—after the U.S., U.K., and Germany—glam metal's biggest market was Japan.

It was almost inevitable that shrieking Pacific feedback would lead to J-metal groups crossing back into the West. By the mid-'80s, the Japanese glam-band Loudness had signed to Atco, a subsidiary of Atlantic Records, making them the first Japanese heavy metal act signed in the U.S., followed shortly thereafter by EZO. The latter released two U.S. albums, EZO (produced by glam godfather Gene Simmons of Kiss) and Fire Fire. Made up in full-face paint (just like Kiss) and residing in Hoboken, New Jersey, EZO was moderately successful, and has even been named as a seminal influence by such artists as Steve McDonald of Redd Kross and Michael Steele of the Bangles.

While amps that go to 11 have been drowned out in the States by the distorted drone of garage-chic alterna-rockers, glam metal still has a wide following in Japan. The band X, renamed "X Japan" so as not to be confused with America's home-brew Angeleno punkers, was signed to Warner Music International in 1992, and has had success touring as a kind of retro-glam flashback—in full Kabuki makeup. Crediting Crüe and Van Halen among their influences, they've released a cult-hit concert film entitled *Kogeki Saikai* ("Renewed Attack") that features live smoke effects and a light show in theaters where it's been released; their indie debut *Vanishing Vision,* released only in Japan, sold over 800,000 copies.

Glam may be dead in the U.S., but it's still alive—bigger and badder than ever—in Japan. —N.G., J.Y.

ANATOMY OF A J-METAL BAND: LOUDNESS

In the early '80s, lead singer Minoru Niihara, Akira Takasaki, drummer Munetaka Higuchi, and bassist Masayoshi Yamashita released five albums in the U.S., before succumbing to the Great Metal Fadeout. They had the hair, the crunch, the costumes, and the cosmetics, and they sounded like a cross between Mötley Crüe and Ozzy Osbourne. They toured with major acts like Stryper and Iron Maiden. And their debut U.S. release, *Thunder from the East,* actually broke into the Billboard Top 100—a rarity for a Japanese band at the time.

The group's four members grew up in Tokyo, where they spent their childhoods listening to Western rock. "I loved everything from the Beatles and the Rolling Stones to heavy metal bands like Led Zeppelin, Black Sabbath, and Kiss," says drummer Munetaka Higuchi. "And all of those groups used to come and tour, so we got to know them really well."

The onslaught of metal monsters from the U.S. and the U.K. inspired the quartet to form their own band in 1981—against, of course, the wishes of their parents. "Japan is a very traditional country, and the older people don't like changes," says guitar hero Takasaki. "Especially something like heavy metal."

Loudness began playing in local clubs, and soon acquired fame—or infamy—for their hard-hitting attack and Western-style image. They were quickly signed to a Japanese rock label, and released two successful albums, while touring constantly. "We toured all over Japan and played every possible place," says bassist Yamashita, "but it's a very small country, and in the end we just got sick of playing the same old places and realized it was time to expand our horizons."

In 1983, Loudness made its first U.S. tour, playing club dates on the West Coast. They followed the U.S. gigs with a tour in Europe, where they were embraced like conquering heroes. "We just didn't expect anything like it," says Takasaki, referring to sold-out concerts in Britain, Holland, Germany, and Belgium. In Germany, Takasaki was even voted "Top Player of the Year," beating out American axemen like Eddie Van Halen.

Returning to Japan, Loudness released a hugely successful live album—*Live-Loud-Alive*—and an hour-long concert home video, then headed to L.A., where they recorded an all-English album produced by Max Norman, who had adjusted levels for acts like Ozzy Osbourne and Y&T. The result was their first U.S. label release, *Thunder in the East* from Atlantic Records' Atco division. which reached as high as 82 on the Billboard charts, and scored a hot-playing video on MTV, "Crazy Nights." They also got a nickname—the Kamikaze Kids. Five albums later, they've fallen into obscurity. But who knows? In these post-modern times, retro is always nuevo, and glam metal—and Loudness—could one day rise again.

Idolsingers

L-R: Seiko! Noriko!

She's cute. She's sweet. She's just a little bit sexy. Can she sing? Does it matter? Not in the world of the *idoru kashu*. While every culture can boast its own version of the teenybopper idol, Japan has raised the creation of instant pop sensations into a science—and a multi-million-dollar industry. The phenomenon of the idoru kashu emerged during Japan's first post–World War II generation, who grew up fascinated with things American—including American teen idols like Fabian, Pat Boone, and Connie Francis. Typically resourceful Japanese promoters soon decided to coin their own pop currency, "inventing" teen idol acts with squeaky-clean good looks and machine-stamped music. In America, as rock rolled its way into pop domination, the teen idol paradigm quickly morphed from button-cute to rebellious and sexy; in Japan, even today the idol ideal remains schoolgirl-innocent, saccharine sweet, and as virginal as the driven snow. "Idoru are little assembly-line girl singers who are just turned out in lots of 20 a month," says science fiction author William Gibson, whose book *Idoru* extrapolates on the idoru kashu phenomenon. "The Milli Vanilli factor is really high—everybody knows that when you hear the record, it's probably not the girl actually singing."

Idoru don't need to know how to write music, play instruments, or even sing on key; so long as they're sufficiently *kawaii* ("cute"), the idolmakers can shape them into stars. "Talent doesn't make a difference," says Yukiko Nakajima, a Japanese journalist and the West Coast editor for the Japanese fanzine *Roadshow*: "It's not about singing, it's about image. It's an independent form of art—the art of celebrity."

It's an art, however, that has an expiration date: The life span of an idol can be as short-lived as teen acne. When idoru can no longer pass for teens, they find themselves replaced by fresher faces. Each year, dozens of idols appear at the top of the charts; as quickly as they rise, they disappear, sometimes forever. An idol's star can be ignited by a catchy advertising jingle, a hit TV theme song, or a successful appearance on a variety show (and as a result, over half of all songs that chart in Japan—the world's second largest music market—have their origin in TV commercials or series).

Not all idols in Japan are Japanese; for example, Alyssa Milano (formerly of the sitcom *Who's the Boss*) has four gold albums in Japan, while Edward Furlong (*Terminator 2*) has two. Sherman Oaks, California–based idolmaker Joey Carbone specializes in transforming American stars into Japanese idols. "People with real talent often do nothing," says Carbone. "But projects that are well-marketed and merchandised can do very, very well."

Unfortunately, the few times that Japanese idols have attempted to cross over into the U.S. market have resulted in pop-chart disaster. Seiko Matsuda, perhaps Japan's greatest idoru ever, has twice attempted to seduce American ears—the first time in 1990, with the eponymous *Seiko*, featuring a duet with Danny Wahlberg of the then-hot New Kids on the Block, and most recently with 1996's *Was It the Future*, an album intended to re-spin her image in a more street-friendly, urban-dance direction. Both albums had limp sales. "The grand failure of Seiko in the U.S. shows that cute doesn't get the same kind of mileage here as it does in Japan," says Keith Cahoon, Far East Managing Director for Tower Records. —J.Y., C.K.

IDOLS WITH LEGS

Here are a pair of idoru who've seemingly stood the test of time:

SEIKO MATSUDA: In 1980, a pretty 18-year-old discovery named Noriko Kamachi was renamed Seiko Matsuda, given a bubbly confection titled "Aoi Sangosho" to sing, and unleashed on an unwitting Japan. The results exceeded anyone's expectations. "Aoi Sangosho" became a blockbuster hit, and Noriko—now Seiko—became Japan's biggest and most adored idol of all time. She's had 15 number-one albums and 25 consecutive number-one songs on the Japan hit charts; the total revenue generated by her sales is quickly approaching 1 billion dollars—with no forseeable limit in sight. Despite being married, a mother (her nickname is mamaidoru, or "mama idol"), and approaching middle age, she continues to be one of Japan's top stars—a stunning achievement in an industry where puberty is grounds for retirement.

NORIKO SAKAI: It's no coincidence that Sakai, whose face graces the walls of boys' bedrooms throughout Asia, was born on Valentine's Day, 1971. The eternally waifish Sakai, who began her career by winning a beauty pageant in 1986, at the age of 16, is called Nori-P by her fans. She's survived beyond an idol's mayfly existence primarily because she's established a burgeoning trans-Asian career, releasing an album in Mandarin Chinese and starring in a Taiwanese serial melodrama.

Japanese Jazz Musicians

More than any other musical form, jazz is *American*. You could even say that jazz—with its blend of the earthy and eclectic, the black, white, brown, yellow, and other—is America. That's why it may come as a surprise that some of jazz's most distinctive performers are of Japanese origin, where this transplanted American musical form has taken deep and dynamic root. Japanese jazz audiences are enthusiastic, yet diverse in taste: If it's improvised, swings, or grooves, then someone in Tokyo will be snappin' away on 2 and 4. Often U.S.-born artists will tour Japan, to greater success than in their homeland. Here's a list of Japanese musicians who have returned the favor, bringing their groove to the land where jazz was born. —N.G.

Name	Instrument(s)	Selected Recordings	Best known for
Kei Akagi	Contemporary jazz keyboards	*Playroom, Mirror Puzzle*	Has performed with Miles Davis.
Toshiko Akiyoshi	Piano, composer, bandleader	*At Top of the Gate, Desert-Lady Fantasy, The Toshiko Akiyoshi/Tabalkin Big Band, Toshiko & Modern Jazz*	Married to saxophonist/bandleader Lew Tabackin; incorporates Japanese chordal structure in her compositions. Struggled until signing with Sony in late '80s.
Tatsu Aoki	Bass	*If It Wasn't for Paul...*	Mostly records cool jazz and solo bass.
Motohiko Hino	Drums	*Sailing Stone*	Included Mick Jagger compositions on solo album.
Terumasa Hino	Trumpet/cornet	*Acoustic Boogie, Alone Together, Bluestruck, Hinology, Taro's Mood, Unforgettable*	Led "Asian All-Stars" tour.
George Kawaguchi	Drums	*Sticks 'n' Skins*	Also led the George Kawaguchi Big Band.
Magabumi Kokuchi	Keyboards	*Tethered Moon, Kikuchi, Peacock & Mo*	Some of his works performed by Gil Evans.
Eiji Kitamura	Clarinet	*Seven Stars, Swinging Age Part II*	Benny Goodmanesque clarinetist of the early '50s.
Hiroko Kokubu	Keyboards	*Moments, More Than You Know, Pure Heart.*	Plays in contemporary jazz, funk, and fusion styles.
Keiko Matsui	Keyboards	*A Drop of Water, Cherry Blossom, Doll, Night*	Has toured extensively in the U.S. Husband Kazu has produced all her records.
Hidehiko "Sleepy" Matsumoto	Tenor saxophone	*Papillon*	Be-bop style sax player of late 1940s who has managed to keep up with contemporary changes in jazz.
Tiger Okoshi	Trumpet	*Echoes of a Note: A Tribute to Louis, That Was Then, This is Now, Two Sides to Every Story*	Played with David Grusin, Buddy Rich, Tony Bennett, and David Sanborn.
Junko Onishi	Piano	*Cruisin, Live at the Village Vanguard*	Plays in straight-ahead jazz style.
Makoto Ozone	Keyboards	*Now You Know Starlight*	Straight-ahead stylist.
Sharps and Flats	Band		Japan's most popular jazz Big Band of the '50s.
Aki Takase	Keyboards	*ABC, Blue Monk, Close Up of Japan, Shima Shoka*	European/Japanese jazz blend.
Kazumi Watanabe	Guitar	*Best Pogatana, Kilowatt, Kylyn, Lonesome Cat, Mobo Club, Mobo I & II, Mobo Splash, To Chi Ka*	Fusion-style guitar with funk, rock, Latin, and be-bop roots; no references to Asian music—but that's OK.
Sadao Watanabe →	Saxophone	*A Night with Strings, Birds of Passage, Dedicated to Charlie Parker, Good Time for Love*	Moved from be-bop to contemporary jazz; popularized bossa nova in Japan in mid '60s.
Yosuke Yamashita	Piano, composer	*Kurdish Dance, Asian Games, Sakura*	Sakura is an assembly of Japanese folk songs. Compared to pianist Cecil Taylor.

Japanese Noise Bands

As Asian American performance artist Lane Nishikawa once noted, everything in Tokyo is either huge (skyscrapers, neon signs) or tiny (automobiles, food portions, condoms).

It runs both ways with Japanese noise bands; their following is tiny, but the sound emitted is huge. No country has been quite as successful in utilizing and shaping noise into pure pandemonium than Japan. The country's leading noise offenders include such mysteriously named groups as Merzbow, CCCP, Volume Dealers, the Copass Grinderz, Bloodthirsty Butchers, and the Ruins. There's absolutely nothing you can do with this product, which one might hesitate to call music: You can't think, write or dance to it, and you certainly can't make love to it. On wax, the only thing J-noise regularly succeeds at is annoying surprised neighbors or making door-to-door solicitors nervous. In America, however—where sonic disruption is a way of life—J-noise bands are making a cult breakthrough. Industrially damaged elder statesmen the Boredoms even crashed the Lollapalooza party in 1994, levying tinnitis upon X'ers who braved the aural threat of the Land of the Rising Pain Threshold. With Boredoms gigs selling out from coast to coast, watch for more parent-antagonizing J-noise product to arrive Stateside soon. —T.I., E.N., J.Y.

ANATOMY OF A J-NOISE BAND: THE BOREDOMS

The foremost purveyors of the dissonant, patently insane genre known as J-noise, this Osaka-based band have become cult sensations in the U.S. for their unpredictable and incomparable live concerts. The Boredoms' lineup currently consists of lead singer Eye Yamatsuka, bassist Hira, guitarist Yamamoto, vocalist Toyohito Yoshikawa and drummers Yoshimi P-We and ATR (also known as "Atari"). On stage, the Boredoms wear outrageous gear—combining bondage gear, football helmets, and all manner of campy apparel drawn from the Japanese and American pop consciousnesses—and fling themselves around the stage, at each other, and into the crowd. First-timers react with horror, or (most frequently) utter confusion; vet Boreheads swoon in near-religious ecstasy. The ear-shattering, discombobulated music is arbitrary and almost secondary—songs can be as short as 10 seconds or as long as half an hour—to the overall bizarreness of the effect. Yamatsuka calls the Boredoms' music "acid punk," while critics have compared them to everything from Black Sabbath to Frank Zappa to the Butthole Surfers. Who knows? Who cares? The typical Boredom song—screamed Japanese lyrics over a conflux of popping bubbles, tin whistles, guitar thrashes, Cookie Monster gobbles, and incessant quacking—won't make the *American Bandstand* hall of fame, but, in contrast to the band's name it definitely isn't boring.

There aren't many success stories more unlikely than that of the Boredoms, whose sonic product has been heaped with adjectives ranging from "obnoxious" to "unlistenable." Yet the sextet from Osaka is one of the very few Japanese bands to have crossed over into a major-label American record deal, having been signed to Warner Bros., in what must have been a fit of inspired lunacy on the part of Warners. (It helped that alt-rock deities Sonic Youth are among their biggest fans.)

Yamatsuka takes their unexpected success in stride; after forming the band in 1986, he says that his goal was originally just "to be able to put out a seven-inch single," he says. "I didn't have a full-time job at the time. If I needed money, I would work at 7- Eleven sometimes."

Gathering members as time went along, the Boredoms began as a more or less standard free-jazz combo, and evolved as it built momentum and audience. "In the beginning, the Boredoms was just me," says Yamatsuka. "Then it was me and Yoshikawa. Then Hira and Yamamoto joined. Later, when Yoshimi joined, it became similar to the Boredoms now." Other members came and left, including a female video artist named God Mama, who was featured on the Boredoms' first two albums. *Soul Discharge*, the Boredoms' second record, was the first to hit Stateside, with a re-release on the indie hipster labelette Shimmy Disk. It registered negligible sales, but—with songs like "J.B. Dick + Tin Turner Pussy Badsmell"—built enough of a buzz that, in 1992, they garnered a deal with Warners' Reprise division. Reprise's first release, *Pop Tatari* (1993), sold under 3,000 copies in the U.S., and about 14,500 in Japan—hardly blockbuster numbers. Not that this has given Yamatsuka and his mates any inhibitions. He describes his latest effort as "Japanese primitive meets Space Age," and promises that it adheres loyally to the Boredom magic formula: one part industrial clatter, one part untranslatable gibberish, one part random sound effects, one part jazz improv, and four parts straight-ahead J-punk energy. Time for a recitation of the Bored's Prayer: Thy Boredom come, thy ears be stung, in America as it is in Osaka—forever and ever, Amen.

BRINGING THE NOISE

Where to get J-Noise in the U.S.

Charnel House Records
(P.O. Box 170277, San Francisco, CA 94117-0277)

Public Bath Records
(P.O. Box 884162, San Francisco, CA 94188)

Skin Graft Records
(P.O. Box 257546, Chicago, IL 60625)

Japanese Stage Traditions

It's spectacle, it's spectacular! Masks, lavish costumes, musical instruments, screeching characters, twanging instruments...the traditions of the Japanese stage outdo most every culture's dramatic creations in their vivid formalism—from the noisy opulence of Kabuki to the odd austerity of No. Here's a bluffer's guide to Japan's three primary traditional dramatic arts. Read up and be in the No. —T.L.

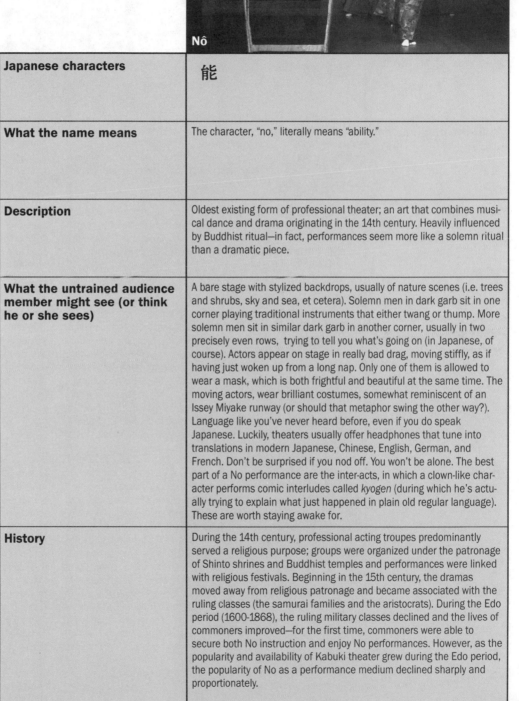

Nô

Japanese characters	能
What the name means	The character, "no," literally means "ability."
Description	Oldest existing form of professional theater; an art that combines musical dance and drama originating in the 14th century. Heavily influenced by Buddhist ritual—in fact, performances seem more like a solemn ritual than a dramatic piece.
What the untrained audience member might see (or think he or she sees)	A bare stage with stylized backdrops, usually of nature scenes (i.e. trees and shrubs, sky and sea, et cetera). Solemn men in dark garb sit in one corner playing traditional instruments that either twang or thump. More solemn men sit in similar dark garb in another corner, usually in two precisely even rows, trying to tell you what's going on (in Japanese, of course). Actors appear on stage in really bad drag, moving stiffly, as if having just woken up from a long nap. Only one of them is allowed to wear a mask, which is both frightful and beautiful at the same time. The moving actors, wear brilliant costumes, somewhat reminiscent of an Issey Miyake runway (or should that metaphor swing the other way?). Language like you've never heard before, even if you do speak Japanese. Luckily, theaters usually offer headphones that tune into translations in modern Japanese, Chinese, English, German, and French. Don't be surprised if you nod off. You won't be alone. The best part of a No performance are the inter-acts, in which a clown-like character performs comic interludes called *kyogen* (during which he's actually trying to explain what just happened in plain old regular language). These are worth staying awake for.
History	During the 14th century, professional acting troupes predominantly served a religious purpose; groups were organized under the patronage of Shinto shrines and Buddhist temples and performances were linked with religious festivals. Beginning in the 15th century, the dramas moved away from religious patronage and became associated with the ruling classes (the samurai families and the aristocrats). During the Edo period (1600-1868), the ruling military classes declined and the lives of commoners improved—for the first time, commoners were able to secure both No instruction and enjoy No performances. However, as the popularity and availability of Kabuki theater grew during the Edo period, the popularity of No as a performance medium declined sharply and proportionately.

	Kabuki	Bunraku
Japanese characters	歌舞伎	文京区
What the name means	Three-character compound, meaning "song," "dance," and "ability." The word "kabuki" is derived from the verb *kabuku,* meaning "to incline," "to tilt," "to lean to one side"; the implication is that "kabuki" signified the "unusual" and "unconventional," and eventually came to mean "fashionable" and "faddish," even "avant-garde."	Two-character compound, literally meaning "culture" and "enjoyment." Although the widely used term is indeed "Bunraku," the more correct description is *ayatsui joruri: ayatsui* means "puppetry," and *joruri* refers to the text and the art of chanting it. So Bunraku is actually the combination of two different art forms: puppetry and dramatic chanting.
Description	Classical theater form combining acting, dance, and music. Unlike the more somber No, Kabuki performances are a spectacle of color and sound, filled with exaggerated, sweeping movement, and a variety of vocal and/or instrumental musics.	The national puppet theater of Japan. Bunraku drama can be either serious or entertaining (or both), and includes elaborately choreographed movements and dance. The puppets (which are one-half to two-thirds of actual life-size) are but a part of the Bunraku stage set: other elements include the puppet operators, the *tayu* who provides the chanting, and the lone shamisen-playing musician.
What the untrained audience member might see (or think he or she sees)	It's big, it's loud, it's colorful, it's action-packed. Unlike the more sedate, ritualistic No performance, Kabuki is an all-out, no-holds-barred Theater Event. Dressed to the nines with faces lost in garish make-up are characters who leap, dance, fight, twirl, and even change shape and costumes right on stage before your very eyes. There is much yelling, sword-clanking, and eerie music to set the scene. And if you don't know what's going on, that's okay—it's probably because you aren't seeing things quite in sequence since they leave the boring parts out. Those helpful headphones will fill you in, telling you what action is occurring and what action occurred while you weren't looking. What's most important is the spectacle...and this is as lavish as it gets.	These puppets look awfully realistic—even the eyebrows move. Dark-robed people, two or three to a puppet, provide the motive force. They're completely visible and they know it. The stage is big, and the sets are elaborate, if downsized. A single shamisen-plucking musician adds to the atmosphere. But the puppet operators remain silent (seen but not heard), and all the sounds come from a narrator who sits to the side next to the shamisen player, with what looks like an open book on a pedestal, chanting away.
History	Legend has it that Kabuki was first created by a female attendant at the Izumo Shrine, who led a mostly female group in light comic and dancing performances in Kyoto as early as 1603. These entertainers (who were also prostitutes) were the cause of endless fights whenever they were in town. In 1629, the Tokugawa shogunate banned female performers and replaced them with young males; however, authorities still grumbled, since these young men also sold their sexual favors. Not until 1652 was the problem solved, when both women and young men were forbidden to perform Kabuki in favor of "mature" men, who had to prove to the authorities that there was nothing provocative about the way they used their bodies on stage. Thus Kabuki as a theater form was allowed to mature during the Genroku era (1688-1704). Having rid the stage of women, the roles played by *onnagata* (female impersonators) grew in importance; the most accomplished onnagata were greatly revered. Kabuki developed from a kind of variety show cabaret into a true dramatic form, adapting and borrowing from the more established No stage.	Like its cousin Kabuki, Bunraku owes its inception to the common folks living in cities during the Edo period (1600-1868). Bunraku is the marriage of two distinct art forms with separate roots: The first Japanese work of puppetry dates back to the 11th century, although an oral tradition exists of itinerant entertainers who presented episodic plays with small puppets. Eventually, a number of these performers settled on the island of Awaji, considered to be the birthplace of professional puppetry. In an unrelated development, the joruri tradition had its origins in the 15th and 16th centuries when *biwa hoshi* (blind bards) dressed in Buddhist robes chanted historic episodes from the *Heike monogatari* ("The Tale of Heike"), a 13th century text, self-accompanied by the *biwa* (lute). During the 16th century, the biwa was replaced by the shamisen, imported to Japan from the island of Okinawa. During the Edo period, commoners—denied access to the higher art form of No (which were limited to samurai and aristocratic audiences)—welcomed the birth of the lively, colorful Bunraku tradition. As commoners rose in economic status and gained control of the changing culture, Bunraku, too, grew in popularity.

Kitaro

One of the greatest gurus of so-called New Age music, the composer and musician known as Kitaro was born Masanori Takahashi in 1953 in Japan's Aichi Prefecture. Takahashi's love of music began early; after a brief post-grad flirtation with rock, he took the pseudonym Kitaro and launched a solo career as an instrumentalist, releasing his debut album, *Tenkai* (English name: *Astral Voyage*) in 1978.

In 1980, Kitaro completed the score for the popular TV documentary series *Silk Road,* broadcast on NHK, Japan's national broadcasting company. Heard by millions, his music and his name quickly became staples in households throughout Japan. Kitaro then produced a succession of recordings that took him from national to international acclaim as a "New Age" icon, joining such musicians as pianist George Winston and Swiss electrocoustic harpist Andreas Vollenweider.

While some criticize the New Age genre as being composed of saccharine, predictable melodies anchored by spacey, meditative harmonies, others assert that these are assets, not liabilities: New Age music offers a musical respite from the storm of modern life.

Kitaro's own music stands toward the grandiose end of the spectrum of styles that have been lumped together under that banner. He says that his synthesizer compositions are inspired by nature and the cosmos, all of which are in plain view from his home in the mountain village of Yasaka in Nagano Prefecture. However, he also cites 1970s English progressive rock bands, such as the Moody Blues, as among his musical influences, which explains the roots of the Kitarô formula: simple tunes married to crunchy, melodramatic chord progressions. Like it or hate it, the formula works: Kitaro continues to be among the most successful non-classical instrumentalists around. And who can argue with success?

Now living in Boulder, Colorado (on a mountaintop, of course), Kitaro is likely to keep putting brains on pause for decades to come. One demonstration of his staying power: Although most listeners might think of his music as mood-setting background sound, Kitaro does play concerts—to sold-out audiences around the world. Critics say that Kitarô's live act, in which he performs on both guitar and synthesizer, consists of unabashed bombast with little artistic flesh. But the crowds just keep on coming. Maybe there's something to that purification ritual after all. —H.K.

Selected Discography:

Tenku (*The Firmament*, 1986), *Kojiki* (*Record of Ancient Matters*, 1990), *Mandala* (1996)

Overlooked Facts

ROCK OF (NEW) AGES—Although today Kitaro is best known for swoony, atmospheric instrumentals, like many teens with sonic dreams, his first love was rock and roll: upon graduating from high school, he formed a rock group called the Far East Family Band, which, fortunately for New Age enthusiasts everywhere, broke up in 1976.

PURIFY ME—Every year, Kitaro performs a solitary "cleansing ritual," in which he and a set of his favorite drums abandon civilization for the barrens of a remote mountain peak. Alone with the wilderness, he pounds out rhythms for hours until his hands bleed, and drenches himself with icy cold water until he feels ready to rejoin humanity.

Kodo

One of the world's greatest taiko drumming companies, Kodo was originally formed by rebel members of taiko master Tagayasu Den's Ondekoza ("Demon Drummer") troupe. Den had moved his troupe to Sado Island in 1969 for intensive taiko training; in 1980, a faction within Ondekoza broke away from Den, finding his tyrannical style and rigid training methods to be excessive. Den left and eventually reformed Ondekoza in Nagasaki, where they continue to this day. The members who remained renamed themselves Kodo, and dedicated themselves to a more holistic means of training—which, while kinder and gentler, was no less rigorous.

In 1981, the group made its world debut as Kodo at the Berlin Festival, where they received encore calls for a record-setting hour at the Berlin Symphony Hall. By 1988, the Kodo collective had moved out of the converted schoolhouse where they had been living for a decade (it now serves them as a training hall for apprentices), bought 25 acres of thick forest on the island's south peninsula, and built a village near the town of Ogi where all 40 of Kodo's members and their families live and work. The collective also entertains the world's artists there during their yearly Earth Celebration, a massive three-day percussion and arts festival held each summer.

Since their founding, Kodo has released numerous albums and movie soundtracks. However, those who have had the fortune to be among their audiences know that the only real way to experience Kodo is live: Fans today continue to marvel at the rich, sonorous rhythms, the crisp, flamboyant choreography, and the rather skimpy, thong-like loincloth (*funodoshi*) worn by the wire-muscled players working up a sweat at the huge *o-daiko*. No recording can substitute for the awe-inspiring performances of these master musician-athletes, who use their art to bridge the gap between the ancient popular traditions of Japan and those of the modern world. —G.C.M.

Selected Discography:

Ubu-suna (1988); *Blessing of the Earth* (1989); *Irodori* (1990); *Gathering* (1991); *Kodo* (1992); *Best of Kodo* (1993); *Nasca Fantasy* (1995). (All on Sony Records)

SONS OF THE DRUM: How to Join Kodo

1 First of all, you must be healthy and between 18 and 25 years of age; playing the taiko is as much a workout as a rhythmic experience. The training demands tremendous physical stamina in order to play with the requisite spirit and endurance. It probably helps to be male, as well; there are just three female drummers in the company.

2 Travel to Sado Island, Japan. There are usually 20 to 30 applicants to the apprenticeship program, from whom a dozen or fewer are selected. Make sure you're comfortable in a loincloth. And make sure you have no habits you're not willing to break—no smoking, no alcohol, and no TV are allowed during the apprenticeship, which lasts for two years, and takes place in an unheated former schoolhouse in Iwakubi, about a 40-minute drive from Ryotsu, Sado's main city.

3 Train rigorously for two years. Kodo's taikoka (taiko players) usually run at least five miles, do a few hours of calisthenics, then practice for six hours—six days a week. "We start with breakfast at 7:15," says Kodo's manager. "We take turns cooking. After the meal we clean, and then from 9 a.m. to 6 p.m. we practice, with one lunch break. Dinner is at 6:30, and then there is free time in which you can continue to practice, or do whatever you want." You should probably continue to practice. Meanwhile, you'll be given extensive training in Kodo's instruments, which include:

- bachi—drumsticks, used with any of the drums below or struck against one another
- miyadaiko—drums carved from a single block of wood
- odaiko—the largest drum in the ensemble, carved from a single tree trunk, about four feet wide, weighs 900 pounds
- okeidaiko—drums constructed like barrels
- shimadaiko—a double-headed drum, made like a snare drum
- "wooden fish"—an instrument with a hollow "tock-tock" sound
- atari gane—a small hanging metal gong struck to keep time

4 Cross your fingers and hope. Out of 12 apprentices, only four will be chosen for the 40-member group. If you're one of them, expect to spend one-third of each year touring Japan, one-third performing overseas, and one-third preparing new material on Sado Island, where you'll have to live as long as you're a member of the group.

5 If this seems too insanely difficult for you, you can still get involved with Kodo on a less committed basis by joining its fan club, taking any of its workshops (which are held both at Sado and throughout the world), or even clicking on its home page on the World Wide Web on Sony Music's server in Japan. Or, if you have the time and money, join Kodo in their annual three-day Earth Celebration in Ogi on Sado Island; the event draws some of the world's top musicians and percussionists for a weekend-long jam session.

Nusrat Fateh Ali Khan

Nicknamed *shahen-shah*, or "king of kings," Khan is universally acclaimed as the world's greatest *qawwal*, or "singer of *qawwali*"—a melodic, intoxicating musical form native to the Sufi Muslim faith. Similar in sound to the Indian raga, which is performed on the harplike sitar, the instrument used in qawwali is the human voice—and qawwals must have immense range and improvisational talent, not to mention endurance; qawwali songs can be half an hour in length and must be performed without a break.

Khan was born October 13, 1948, in Faisalabad, Pakistan, the son of Ustad Fateh Ali Khan, a qawwal whose ability was renowned throughout Pakistan and beyond. (Indeed, when the Shah of Iran visited the singer and was treated to a qawwali chant sung in impeccable Persian, he was so moved that he instantly gave Ustad his car, a Chevrolet.) Despite the elder Khan's success, he discouraged Nusrat from pursuing music, preferring his son to be a doctor or some such practical professional, so as not to have to face the hardships of making a living at music—not unlike many typical Asian fathers. Nusrat was forced to listen to his father's classes in secret, practicing qawwali on the sly. When Ustad discovered his son singing, he was at first angry, but then recognized a budding talent. Unfortunately, Ustad died before being able to teach his son as he might have wished.

As a result, Nusrat learned his first classical music in 1965, a year after his father's death, by joining his uncle Ustad Mubarik Ali Khan's qawwali group. Six years later, after Ustad Mubarik died, Nusrat went solo with his own remixed brand of qawwali. Sufi religious music, like gospel, is meant to bring listeners closer to God (or, in this case, Allah) through ecstatic vocals and rhythm. To bring qawwali up to date, Nusrat sped it up and made it more accessible. Suddenly, an esoteric art form attained mass recognition. "My music is for all because it is the same message for every person in every nation," said Khan. "It is a message of peace and love and tells that people must love one another as well as their God." —N.G., J.Y.

Performing Qawwali

When preparing for a concert, Khan and his 12-person backing group, who go by the name Party, select a poem in Urdu or Punjabi, then pick a *taal*, or time measure, and a *raag*, or scale pattern. The tabla players pound out the beat, while harmonium players provide fill-in harmonies; everything else is left up to Khan and his magnificent voice. Each piece is an improvisation: The song is essentially invented by the musicians as they play. Khan or any of the musicians may choose to vamp a phrase or even a single syllable until the audience is lifted to a higher state of consciousness—though when he performs in his native Pakistan, Khan tends to stick more closely to rigid classical tradition, to allow his audiences to sing along.

Overlooked facts

DREAM INTO ACTION—One of the most repeated stories about the fabled qawwali singer is that Nusrat was motivated to perform in public for the first time by a dream of his father, Ustad Fateh Ali Khan—himself one of the greatest qawwali vocalists of all time. At the time, Nusrat was just 16 years old, and still mourning his father's death, which had occurred 10 days earlier. "I dreamed that he came to me and asked me to sing," says Nusrat. "I said I could not, but he told me to try. He touched my throat, I started to sing, and then I woke up singing." Nusrat was convinced that he had been told that his first live performance would be at his father's chilla funeral ceremony, which would occur on the 40th day after his death. And, indeed, Nusrat sang at the ceremony—thus beginning his legendary career.

NUSRAT LOVE—Numerous Western musicians have declared themselves Khan fans—and become his collaborators. Pearl Jam's Eddie Vedder dueted with Khan on the soundtrack to Dead Man Walking. And Peter Gabriel has long been a fan and recording partner. His popularity among his fellow artists may explain why he's has recently experienced a pop revival—with his music appearing, in addition to Dead Man, in such films as The Last Temptation of Christ (an odd juxtaposition for a devout Muslim) and Natural Born Killers.

Orientalism in Music

When a music critic describes an artist's work as "orientalist," it's not a compliment. Whether the artist is guilty of the hypnotic repetition of a pentatonic motif, or the plucking of a jazz standard on the strings of a sitar or koto, orientalism in music has become something to avoid like the Asian flu. Indeed, the virus of cheap exoticism has stricken many a Western musician. But a century before Orientalism became an insult, it was an integral part of musical modernity.

Western interest in Asian music began in the late 18th century, when European and especially French musicologists began to research, write, and publish treatises on the techniques and styles of African, Middle Eastern, and Asian music in earnest. But Asian music did not exert a noticeable influence on European composition until the end of the 19th century and the beginning of the 20th, when Asian musicians traveled to Europe to perform at world's fairs and colonial expositions. When a Javanese gamelan orchestra performed at the World Exhibition in Paris in 1889, the music—a melody sung by a bamboo flute, a bowed string instrument, or a human voice, riding over a complex texture of melodic patterns played on gongs, kettles, and xylophones—made a deep impression on visitors. Among the many listeners were two music students who would soon become titans of the Impressionist movement in French composition, and, into the 20th century, forefathers of musical modernism: Claude Débussy and Maurice Ravel.

Another contingent at the Exhibition which made a lasting impact on the young French innovators came from Russia. Russian music of the period—by Alexander Borodin, Modest Mussorgsky, and Nicolai Rimsky Korsakov—celebrated the vast diversity of Russian folk music, reaching far into central Asia, and strived to create a proud, national musical identity, independent of the previously dominating influences of French and German music.

The exposure to Asian music couldn't have happened at a riper time. Young French composers, tiring of the rather tenacious influence of German composers on French composition, undertook radical innovations in harmony, rhythm, and instrumentation which would pave the way, in the 20th century, for Modernism. And while German and Eastern European masters looked to popular folk tunes and nationalist sentiment for their inspiration, French composers sought to escape, looking to the world of dreams, the animal kingdom, the world of myths and fairy tales. When the gamelan came along, it was perhaps inevitable that, as in French painting and sculpture, the non-West would become a reference for musical material as well. Moreover, the gamelan's five-tone scale, its complexity of rhythm, and its rich timbres provided Impressionists with even more ideas in their assault on tonal and harmonic conventions.

Just as they embarked on radical experimentation with composition, French composers were also inspired by the experimentation with color and composition undertaken by Impressionist painters, who, in turn, were deeply influenced by Japanese painting—especially the works of Hokusai and Hiroshige [👁24], both of whom were fashionable in Paris in Debussy's day [👁14].

While some orientalisms can be heard in Ravel's work, in the work of Debussy—who was, arguably, the more innovative and influential of the two—an Asian influence is decidedly more pronounced. For instance, gamelan-like inflections can be heard in the symphonic tone poems of *Les Nuages* (*The Clouds*). In the 20th century, references to Asian music in European composition became audibly more literal. Belgian composer Olivier Messiaen and American composer John Cage, both deeply influenced in their thinking by Asian philosophy and mysticism, also borrowed heavily from Indonesian gamelan music and from the melodic-rhythmic proportions employed in Indian music. —A.R.

ASIA THROUGH OPERA GLASSES

European fascination with the exotic has its supreme expression in the colorful, exaggerated spectacle of grand opera. Numerous operas take place in the "Orient"—which, for Europeans, stretched from Morocco in the West, to Japan in the East, to Sri Lanka in the South. But the extent to which they provide a faithful representation of Asian people, culture, and beliefs range from slightly off-base to downright execrable. A European opera about Asia can generally be categorized as one of the following:

Musical versions of non-Asian stories which were transplanted to Asia:

Turandot, composed by Giacomo Puccini (1858-1924), debuted in Milan, Italy, in 1926, is set in ancient Peking, but it's based on a 1761 play by Carlo Gozzi (1720-1808), who, in turn, had lifted the story from a Persian fairy tale and simply reset it in China. Its title character, an outwardly man-hating Chinese princess who summarily executes any man who falls in love with her, is probably the West's first "Dragon Lady." (She's finally won over by a Tartar prince who manages to solve three riddles.) When Chinese theater director Xu Xiaozhong mounted *Turandot* for Beijing's Central Opera Theater in 1995, he was appalled at the opera's depiction of China as a barbarous culture with barbarous practices. He took special offense at its apparently sadistic princess, noting that a real Chinese princess would have been taught to behave with obedience and kindness. Moreover, she would never have enjoyed the privilege of choosing a husband, nor of executing suitors who failed to pass her muster. For his audience, Xu took *Turandot* out of Peking, set it in "an unnamed place in the East," and removed all references to China in the libretto.

Les Pecheurs de Perles (*The Pearl Fishers*), composed by Georges Bizet (1838-1875), debuted in Paris in 1863, is set in Sri Lanka, also in "ancient times." In *Les Pecheurs,* whicn Bizet (best known for *Carmen*) composed at 25, love for a Brahmin priestess threatens to wreck the friendship between two fishermen. Strangely, its librettists, E. Cormon and M. Carre, took much of the material from an libretto for earlier opera, *Les Pecheurs de Catane*—which was set in Mexico!

An opera which pays no mind whatsoever to cultural and musical authenticity:

The Mikado, by Sir William Gilbert (1836-1911) and Sir Arthur Sullivan (1842-1900), is a witty, tuneful bit of fluff about a prince trying to dodge an arranged marriage. It was a smashing success when it debuted in London in 1885, and it's perhaps the best known and loved English operetta to this day. Its depiction of Japan is meant to be farcical, but it's riddled with characters with names like Nanki-Poo, Katisha, Yum Yum, and Pooh-Bah. It's also set in a town called Titipu, where a man can be beheaded for flirting. Fun as a tunefest, but as a glimpse of Japanese culture, *The Mikado* is utter crap.

An opera whose cultural and historical values are acceptable, but whose music is indifferent to Asian tradition:

Lakme, composed by Leo Délibes (1836-1891) and debuted in Paris in 1883, is a Brahmin priestess in British-occupied India who falls in love with a British soldier and suffers unhappy consequences (she's one in a long line of women of color in opera who fall for white men and suffer unhappy consequences, including Dido in *Dido and Aeneas, L'Africaine, Madame Chrysantheme, Madama Butterfly,* and Cleopatra in *Antony and Cleopatra*). In what was to be his masterpiece, Délibes deployed oriental color in religious scenes, for prayers and dances, and in the riotous market scene. But while the music, characteristic of French composition of the time, is inventive and evocative, it can't be said to bear any true reference to Indian musical tradition. Its greatest hit, a sensuous female duet, "*Dome epais,*" was used as background music for Susan Sarandon and Catherine Deneuve's lesbian seduction scene in *The Hunger.* Since then it's also been used in countless television commercials.

An opera whose cultural and historical representations are passable and whose music actually strives for authenticity:

Regardless of what one may think about the stereotypes it engendered, in composing *Madama Butterfly* (debuted in Milan in 1904), Puccini actually did some homework, consulting a well-known Japanese actress who lived in Milan at the time, as well as sheet music for folk songs provided by the wife of the Japanese ambassador to Italy. The result is a striking hybrid of believably Asian melody and Puccini's lush, daring harmonies.

Madama Butterfly, about a 15-year-old ex-geisha who marries an American naval officer only to be abandoned by him, had quite a pedigree. The opera was based on a one-act play by Broadway impresario David Belasco, which in turn was adapted from a popular 1897 short story "Madame Butterfly" by Philadelphia lawyer John Luther Long. Long said he got the story from his sister, a missionary stationed in Japan. But English musicologist Charles Osborne asserts that Long practically stole the characters from *Madame Chrysntheme,* an 1887 novel by Pierre Loti. A French naval officer whose career took him throughout the Middle East and Asia, Loti wrote popular novels which took place in exotic locales (his novel Rarahu provided the story for Délibes's *Lakmé*).

Language is another of *Madama Butterfly*'s virtues. In Belasco and Long's work, *Butterfly* speaks English in an execrable pidgin ("Wael, twenty, mebby; an' sa-ey, w'en we see him comin quick up path...to look for liddle wive, me jus' goin' hide behind shoji an' watch an' make believe me gone 'way.") But in the opera, *Butterfly*'s Italian is as standard as her Japanese, as a young woman of samurai descent, would have been. The result is a character who is far more articulate, dignified, and believable than her American predecessors.

Perhaps the most controversial aspect of *Butterfly*'s story is her suicide. Anyone who understands the samurai concept of dying with honor rather than living in shame would understand it. Without family, fortune, or any other means of survival, Butterfly kills herself out of pride, not self-pity. But the interpretation of her death as a supreme rite of Caucasian male worship (and as the submission of Asian civilization to Western dominance) has also led to some of the most tenacious and harmful stereotypes about Asian women. Nor does it help that the Japanese men in *Butterfly* are either pimps, fey buffoons, ghouls, or all of the above.

Of course, modern Asian women resemble *Butterfly* about as much as women of any culture resemble their predecessors from the turn of the century. But Western audiences love to feel sorry for *Butterfly,* and it's unlikely that her story will lose its box office power anytime soon. After being a real person (allegedly), two fictional characters, a role in a play, and the subject of an opera, Butterfly has had countless incarnations: in film (*Love is a Many Splendored Thing*, 1955), on stage (David Henry Hwang's *M. Butterfly*, 1988 and Alain Boublil and Claude-Michel Schönberg's *Miss Saigon*, 1989), and on radio ("Poor Butterfly," by John Golden and Raymond Hubbel, which became a hit in the 1950s for Sarah Vaughan, and "Madam Butterfly," a 1984 dance hit by Malcolm McClaren). As for the opera, it's remained in standard repertory since its debut, and ranks among the most frequently performed operas of all time.

Overlooked Facts

LOVE, HATE, AND THE LENNON LEGACY—Ono blames much of the hostility she's faced on racism. "I was a scapegoat. When Asians are attacked, they don't hit back," says Ono. Critics like John Perreault of the Village Voice agreed, writing "Isn't it clear that a good part of the hostility to Yoko Ono was racist, sexist, anti-adult and anti-avant-garde?" More progressive authorities also credit her for keeping her husband's memory alive by posthumously releasing his music, writings, and recently, his art and calligraphy. And meanwhile, after Lennon's death, she successfully invested his fortune in art, real estate, and even livestock. Today the Lennon holdings are worth between $500 million and $1 billion.

A WOMAN OF INFLUENCE—While her music of the '60s and '70s—before, during, and after John—has been viciously attacked by the more acerbic critics as "music nobody listened to," her adventurous albums have influenced artists as unrelated as Sonic Youth, Chrissie Hynde, former Sugarcubes lead singer Björk, and the B-52's. In fact, the B-52's 1979 hit "Rock Lobster" was an homage to Ono's stuttering, verbal-collage vocal style. In 1992, a six-CD career retrospective of Ono's indescribable music was released by Rykodisc; suddenly, Ono was being heralded as a brave innovator whose work was a precursor to many of contemporary alterna-pop's musical trends.

Yoko Ono

Yoko Ono was born February 18, 1933, in Tokyo. Her father Eisuke was the head of the Bank of Japan; her mother Isoko was a frustrated artist, and the granddaughter of one of Japan's richest merchant princes. She was educated at a series of exclusive Japanese private schools, then taught by private tutors, and she spent two semesters at a Japanese university, before immigrating to the U.S. with her mother, brother, and sister to join their world-traveling father in Scarsdale, New York.

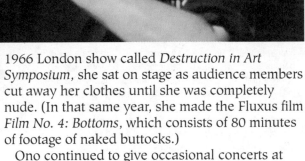

Upon coming to America, Ono studied briefly at Sarah Lawrence College, but dropped out to elope with her first husband, Anthony Cox, a jazz musician and film producer. Through Cox, Ono entered into the world of art, music, and performance that she'd longed to belong to ever since she was a girl. In 1958, she first started displaying her interactive conceptual art pieces; in the early '60s, she began holding concerts at her loft on 112 Chambers Street in Greenwich Village. Ono and her collaborators called themselves the Fluxus movement, defining their form of art as an interactive and participatory medium—one in which the audience was as important as the artist in producing the final product or performance, which could convey a meaningful message, a random one, or none at all. By way of example, in Ono's first public concert in 1961, at the now defunct Village Gate, she peeled grapefruit, squeezed lemons, and counted the hairs on a dead child. In another performance, a 1966 London show called *Destruction in Art Symposium*, she sat on stage as audience members cut away her clothes until she was completely nude. (In that same year, she made the Fluxus film *Film No. 4: Bottoms*, which consists of 80 minutes of footage of naked buttocks.)

Ono continued to give occasional concerts at Carnegie Hall and other venues until 1968, when she gave birth to her first child, Kyoko. But it was another event that same year that would change her life completely. Two years earlier, Ono had met a superstar rock musician at a London art gallery—and come away utterly unimpressed. "I didn't even remember him," she says. But a second meeting that year, when John Lennon showed up and reintroduced himself at an exhibition of Ono's art in a London West End gallery, the two exchanged playful banter over one of her interactive pieces—and this time, they connected. In May 1968, despite their existing matrimonial entanglements, the two rendezvoused at Lennon's country house in Weybridge, England. There they made music all night—literally and figuratively—and the fruit of their labor was the album Two Virgins, featuring a controversial cover with the couple photographed entirely naked.

The world had been served notice that Lennon and Ono were a pair, but the couple had no intentions of returning to a quiet, private life. They appeared together on stage at the Royal Albert Hall for a Christmas party in December that year, where they writhed around completely enclosed in a giant white bag—"bagism," Ono called it. After getting divorces from their respective spouses—Cynthia Lennon and Anthony Cox—they were married on March 20, 1969; their honeymoon, spent entirely in a Montreal hotel bed, became the legendary "Bed-In for Peace," where the couple promoted the cessation of world hostilities (by giving anti-Vietnam interviews) and sang "Give Peace a Chance."

Ono and Lennon's collaborations extended beyond performance art and pajama-protest. In December 1970, Ono and Lennon put together two feature films: *Up Your Legs Forever,* 75 minutes worth of people's legs, and the similarly avant-garde *Fly*. In the early '70s, Lennon and Ono formed the Plastic Ono Band, which some Lennon fans mark as a creative low-water-mark and others see as a period of intense, if incoherent, inventiveness.

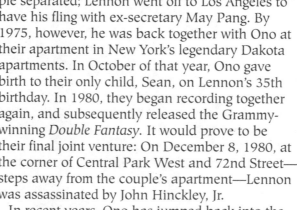

Life with John wasn't all wine and roses, of course. In 1973, the famous couple separated; Lennon went off to Los Angeles to have his fling with ex-secretary May Pang. By 1975, however, he was back together with Ono at their apartment in New York's legendary Dakota apartments. In October of that year, Ono gave birth to their only child, Sean, on Lennon's 35th birthday. In 1980, they began recording together again, and subsequently released the Grammy-winning *Double Fantasy*. It would prove to be their final joint venture: On December 8, 1980, at the corner of Central Park West and 72nd Street—steps away from the couple's apartment—Lennon was assassinated by John Hinckley, Jr.

In recent years, Ono has jumped back into the media limelight, doing a variety of unexpected and surprising things. She made a cameo appearance on primetime TV, appearing in an episode of the ABC hit series, *Mad About You*. (Ads for the episode showed Yoko nestled under the covers between the series' two costars—a comic throwback to that other popular "Bed-In" scene.) In 1995, she also released her first album of new songs in over 10 years, called *Rising,* in which she was backed by her son Sean's band, IMA. Despite a legacy of tragedy, controversy, and creativity that has spanned decades and generations, Ono has made it clear that she's not going to go quietly into the night—and nor does she intend to be remembered forever as a grieving widow or a rock Jezebel.

—Am.W., T.H.

LIFE AFTER JOHN

Ono has kept busy since her husband's death. In 1981, she completed *Season of Glass*, a controversial album that included a song ending with gunshots and moaning. In 1989, the Whitney Museum of American Art staged a career retrospective of her art, "Yoko Ono: Objects, Films," which focused on her work from her '60s Fluxus days. Not that her recent work hasn't been equally worthy of interest: In 1991, Ono called New York bohemians to a Greenwich Village gallery, where she shattered a rare Ming vase with a hammer; she distributed the pieces to members of the audience and told them to come back in 10 years, when she would glue the pieces back together. Two year later, she was back in the limelight for displaying collages using Lennon's bloodstained shirt (the one he was shot and died in) and his shattered glasses. She maintains that her most recent 1995 show, "Blood Objects," was actually not related to Lennon's death. Instead, Ono insists that the nine sculptures in the show were inspired by her own birth, which she refers to as a person's first violent experience. In 1994, New York's Off-Broadway WPA Theater debuted Ono's rock opera *New York Rock*, which interwove 30 of her songs. A semi-autobiographical musical drama, *Rock* featured key scenes showing the effects of a father's disappearance on a young child's life, and a woman's reactions to the shooting murder of her husband. Critical reception was kind.

Pizzicato 5

The dynamic team of diva extraordinaire Maki Nomiya and musical mastermind Yasuharu Konishi, P5, as they're known for short, are an innovative, outrageous, and delightfully post-modern pop group whose sound changes, Maki claims, based on what she's wearing at any given time. Their eclectic sound encompasses '60s soul, lounge, disco, and '70s TV theme songs—think *Love, American Style*. Although they've had a huge cult following in Japan since the mid 1980s, they didn't break through in the U.S. until 1994, on the heels of the popularity of Japanese pop rockers Shonen Knife.

The lovely and talented Nomiya was born on March 12 sometime within the last three decades (the exact year is a closely guarded secret); her P5 partner Konishi came into this world on February 3, 1959—the day that Buddy Holly and Richie Valens died in an airplane crash, a fact he's always careful to emphasize. And clearly, Konishi sees himself as an innovator in the mold of those two departed rock pioneers—though his influences are hardly limited to '50s pop.

Konishi formed P5 with K-Taro Takanami in 1985 while both were still in college, drawing on their common love of the Monkees, the B-52s, and seminal Japanese technopop band the Plastics, as well as a mix of kitschy cultural swipes: lounge-king Esquivel, Andy Warhol, the film *Breakfast at Tiffany's* (one of their Japanese releases is entitled *Audrey Hepburn Complex*), Burt Bacharach, Donovan, and the Steve Miller Band, and the soundtrack of *Bye Bye Birdie*.

Maki, a former fashion model who had been a part of J-pop scenesters Portable Rock and who'd delivered one solo album, joined P5 in 1990. After Takanami left the band, the P5's current dynamic-duo lineup was forged—and began to score hit album after hit album in their native Japan. Their crossover into American hips and lips began in 1992, when New York's New Music Seminar hosted a show at church-turned-nightclub Limelight called "Psycho Nite: Musical Madness from Japan," featuring original flash-from-Japan Shonen Knife and a cluster of other bands of the Rising Sun. But P5 might as well have been headlining the show: When Maki appeared in a black-and-white, skin-tight harlequin outfit and delivered a murderously stylish, finger-popping, heart-stopping set, the audience was entranced. The band from Shibuya was primed for Stateside success.

Since then, P5 has signed to Matador/Arista records and released several albums; their music became the beat of choice for style scenesters, providing background sound for Fashion Week runway turns and soundtrack cuts for films like Robert Altman's *Ready to Wear* and the Isaac Mizrahi biodoc *Unzipped*.

P5 has accomplished all this with a rudimentary grasp of English; their lyrics stand on the fine line between bilingual and incomprehensible. And guess what? When they toured the U.S., Konishi was amazed to find fans singing along in Japanese. —G.L.

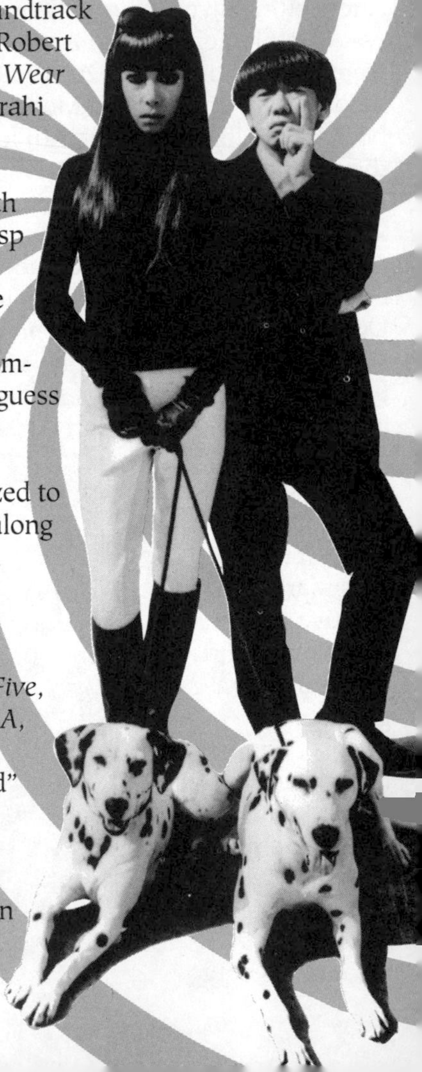

Selected Discography:

Five by Pizzicato Five, 1994; *Made in USA*, 1994; *Quickie EP*, 1995; "Happy Sad" single (from *Unzipped*), 1995; *The Sound of Music*, 1995; all on Matador Records. —T.H.

Overlooked Facts:

ORIGINAL SPINS—Konishi formed his first band (while still a schoolboy) based on his admiration for the Monkees' Davy Jones. All four of the band's members played the tambourine. Meanwhile, Maki had her pop start when she shelled out $500 for a guitar and amp once used by Kiss's Ace Frehley. Later, when she performed at her high school graduation party, she became addicted to rock. The rest was destiny.

THE STYLE COUNCIL—P5 has been known to set up their concerts in Japan like fashion shows, complete with catwalk, P5 signs designed like the Chanel logo, and leggy models. Like any committed fashion victim, Maki understands that successful style combines haute and baisse. On a recent trip to New York, Maki patronized both the House of Gucci (for black, patent-leather thigh-highs) and some flea markets (in search of '50s-era vinyl airline bags).

Quirks:

I WANT MY MTV (TO HAVE A SENSE OF HUMOR)—When any band is as ironic, silly, and brilliant as P5, there's always the danger of misinterpretation. Take MTV, who censored the words "Buy Japanese" from the end of P5's "Twiggy Twiggy/Twiggy vs. James Bond" video. MTV should've taken a cue from Konishi, who says, "Don't take us seriously. We are a joke."

Ryuichi Sakamoto

The founder of the seminal synth-fusion group Yellow Magic Orchestra, Ryuichi Sakamoto is one of Japan's most influential and best known musicians, as well as a prolific composer of soundtracks (winning an Oscar for his score for Bernardo Bertolucci's *The Last Emperor*). Born in 1952 in Tokyo, Sakamoto began studying classical music composition as a child. Then, of couse, like everybody else, he discovered the Beatles. That, plus early exposure to jazz great John Coltrane and avant-garde composer John Cage, put a definite spin on Sakamoto's brand of music—a quirky synthopop-jazz fusion that defies easy categorization. Sakamoto released his debut album in 1978, entitled *Thousand Knives,* while paying his dues as a composer and arranger of other people's music, and as a studio musician. Soon after its release however, he formed the band Yellow Magic Orchestra with Haruomi Hosono and Yukihiro Takahashi. Their self-titled debut album came out the same year. Yellow Magic Orchestra shattered preconceptions of electronic music as weird, bleepy, and incomprehensible, combining jazzy grooves with unprecedented synthesized hooks. Musicians throughout the world took notice, as fans as diverse as Kitaro, Jan Hammer, Chick Corea, and Herbie Hancock added it to their collections. After this auspicious debut, the group stayed busy, producing its second album *B-2 Unit* in 1980, then *Left Hand Dream* the following year. In 1983, however, YMO disbanded, as Sakamoto determined to pursue other projects.

The first of these was film, as Sakamoto composed the score to and acted in Nagisa Oshima's *Merry Christmas Mr. Lawrence* **[👁99]**. He also established his own music publishing company, Honhondo, and put out a fourth solo album, *Music Encyclopedia*. His collaborators during this period included Thomas Dolby (on the album *Field Work*) and former Stooge Iggy Pop, who did guest vocals on *Neo Geo*. Meanwhile, he was also the subject of a documentary, *Tokyo Melody*.

In 1988, Sakamoto composed the score to Bernardo Bertolucci's *The Last Emperor,* which went on to win an Oscar, a Golden Globe, and the Los Angeles Film Critics Association Award for Best Original Score. (Sakamoto also appeared in the film itself in a cameo role.) In 1990, Sakamoto wrote the haunting soundtrack to another Bertolucci film, *The Sheltering Sky,* racking up another Golden Globe. Then, in 1991, Sakamoto scored Pedro Almodovar's *High Heels,* wrote the theme to the World Athletic Championships, and released the solo album *Heartbeat,* which featured guest vocals by David Sylvian and Ingrid Chavez.

Sakamoto shows no signs of slowing down. In 1992, he conducted his own compositions for the opening ceremonies of the Barcelona Olympics. He's produced albums for the group Aztec Camera, composed and performed the score for Oliver Stone's dark television miniseries *Wild Palms,* and reunited with Bertolucci again in 1994, providing the score for the film *Little Buddha.* After that experience, however, Sakamoto decided that the partnership needed time apart. "Bertolucci is difficult to work with," says the composer. "He's Italian and he's a filmmaker—that's two times difficult.'"

Perhaps the most anticipated event in Sakamoto's recent history, however, was the reunion of Yellow Magic Orchestra in 1993 with the release of *Technodon.* YMO's return was most welcome in Japan, where they sold out two dates at the Tokyo Dome, playing to crowds of over 100,000. Still, Sakamoto has no plans to end his solo career: In 1996, he released a new album, also called *1996,* and showcased its classically oriented sound in his first world tour in years. —E.G.

Overlooked Facts:

ACTING OUT—While Sakamoto is justifiably best known for his music, he's also proven talented as an actor as well, with his brooding, impassive charisma lending him unmistakable screen presence in films like Nagisa Oshima's 1983 Merry Christmas, Mr. Lawrence [👁92], in which he costarred with the man some call his western counterpart: English rocker David Bowie. "The most inspirational moment was when I saw the rough edit of the film," says Sakamoto. "My first view of my acting, it was so bad, I almost fainted." Luckily, most critics disagreed—particularly one very blonde, very popular singer. After seeing his chiseled good looks on the big screen, Madonna cast him in her video for the hit song "Rain."

AND MARY ANN?—Sakamoto, who earned an MFA from the Tokyo University of Fine Arts and Music, is as much a music scholar as a musician. Indeed, he's been nicknamed "Professor" by his peers and fans—a tag that's stuck.

Overlooked Facts:

GEORGE AND RAVI, 2GETHER 4EVER—Although Shankar was long known in South Asia as one of the world's greatest raga performers and sitar composers, his discovery by the West came not through classical channels but through his Fab following: The Beatles' George Harrison made a musical pilgrimate to learn the secrets of the sitar from Shankar, and then introduced its sound in "Norwegian Wood." After the Beatles' breakup, Harrison continued to work with Shankar, performing with him at the charity Concert for Bangladesh and touring with him in 1974. In 1995, the occasion of Shankar's 75th birthday led to the release of In Celebration, a four-CD retrospective of Shankar's work with Harrison. "He regards me as his father, I regard him as my son," says Shankar. "I love him, and it is a very special relationship."

TAKING HIS DAUGHTER TO WORK—Unlike his fellow South Asian superstar Nusrat Fateh Ali Khan [👁272], Shankar has decided to pass on his sitar skills to his daughter Anoushka, who has already performed with him on several tours. As to whether she will rise to his lofty heights, "That only time will tell," says Shankar. "It depends on how much she is willing to do sadhna—dedication to music. Love for music is one thing, and sadhna is another. Classical music is more of sadhna."

Ravi Shankar

Ravi Shankar has been deemed the greatest sitar virtuoso and composer this planet has ever produced. He's also one of the most internationally well known of 20th century classical musicians—and something of a pop icon as well, due to his longtime association with the Beatles.

Shankar was born April 7, 1920, in Varanasi, in Utta Pradesh, India, the son of a Bengali statesman. At the age of 10, he joined a performing arts troupe headed by his older brother, Uday. Shankar traveled throughout Europe, Canada, and the United States with the company, learning the basics of several traditional instruments, as well as classical dance forms. After eight years on the road, Shankar spent six years in rigorous training with Allauddin Khan, studying the traditions of North Indian classical music. The teacher-student relationship proved especially fruitful for Shankar, who developed lifelong relationships with Khan's son, sarod player Ali Akbar, and marrying his daughter, Annapurna (though they eventually divorced). In 1948, Shankar began working at All-India Radio as a composer and performer, and soon became the brightest star in the world of traditional Indian music. But Shankar had higher goals in mind—bringing Indian music beyond the borders of South Asia—and to that end, began collaborations with such luminaries of Western classical music as Andre Previn, Philip Glass, Yehudi Menuhin (who compared him to Mozart), and countryman Zubin Mehta, much to the chagrin of purists. He also began creating music for film scores, including soundtracks for Satyajit Ray's legendary "Apu Trilogy" **[👁89]**. Of course, most Westerners know him not through his classical achievements but for the embrace of his music by the '60s counterculture. After his work was introduced to the pop world by George Harrison, Shankar made appearances at the Monterey Pop Festival and Woodstock. People like Timothy Leary and Allen Ginsberg irresponsibly linked their theme of "Turn On, Tune In & Drop Out" with his sinuous harmonics. Shankar has long repudiated the drug connection, and spoken out fiercely against this misappropriation of his music.

While Shankar has reduced the number of his concert performances after having twice undergone heart surgery, nearly half a century after he first debuted, listeners continue to be enthralled by his ethereal melodies. And though nearing the magic age of 80, he still has no plans to retire. "There are new things," Shankar says, "new ideas all the time, in my head." —H.K., J.Y.

The "Sukiyaki" Phenomenon

In 1963, when Hachidai Nakamura and Rokusuke Ei wrote "Iu O Muite Aruko" ("I Look Up When I Walk"), little did they know that they'd be unleashing a phenomenon. Their song—retitled "Sukiyaki"—became the only Japanese-language song ever to hit number one on the Billboard charts, and the only foreign-language song to see itself remade into an English-lyric smash hit...twice.

After pop balladeer Kyu Sakamoto took the song to the top of the Japanese charts, American DJs somehow managed to acquire copies of it, breaking the song across the Pacific in America, where it also became a number one single, staying on the charts for 14 weeks—despite the fact that none of its listeners could understand its lyrics. This proved to be just the beginning of the song's U.S. invasion. Later that year, when British jazz musician Kenny Ball did an instrumental version of the song, executives at his label Pye Records idiotically decided to change the song's title to "Sukiyaki," assuming that that was the only Japanese word that white people might have a vague awareness of in those unenlightened times. (Never mind that naming the ballad "Sukiyaki" was akin to changing the name of "Always and Forever" to "Beef Stew." [147])

Soon thereafter, the close harmony group The Four Preps managed to release their own cover of the song—sung in the original Japanese. "One of the fellas in the group had a house in Toluca Lake at the time with a crew of three or four Japanese gardeners," says Bruce Belland, tenor and leader of the group. "He asked one of them to sit down and listen to the record with him, and help him write out how to say the Japanese phonetically. He just thought it was so funny listening to these four Anglos trying to pronounce these words correctly." Then, the Four Preps, in one of their many appearances on the *Ed Sullivan Show,* were asked to perform "Sukiyaki" live. "That's a funny story," says Belland. "Ed Sullivan said something like, 'Here's a great surprise for all of you fans of the Four Preps out there: They're going to sing in a language you've never heard before.' So we came out and started to sing, and got to the first solo part. And here we are on the *Ed Sullivan Show* live, and my mind went completely blank! I could not think of the first syllable of my solo. I proceeded to step forward and make up some "Japanese"; to this day, I don't know what I said. I have often wondered if Japanese-speaking people watching at home were thinking, 'What dialect of Japanese is that? I've never heard that before in my life!"

But even that day of linguistic infamy was just a prelude to what would come a few decades later.

A TASTE OF SUKIYAKI...PART DEUX

It's been said that, whenever Japanese people get their hands on a product, they'll remake it—smaller, better, and more efficient. When Americans get their hands on a product, on the other hand, they simply make it...American. So was it with "Sukiyaki." At the end of the disco era, the duo A Taste of Honey rewrote the song with new, English-language lyrics, and gave it a second Anglicized life on the charts. Honey's "Sukiyaki" went to number three on the *Billboard* charts, and became a part of camp history. Subsequently, rap artist Slick Rick crooned Honey's "Sukiyaki" lyrics on Doug E. Fresh's hip-hop classic, "La-Di-Da-Di"; and, in 1995, the R&B harmony group 4PM ("For Positive Music") became the latest to turn the tune into gold. Their a capella version debuted on September 17, 1994, at number 90, and rose steadily to peak at number eight. "I was always fond of the song, and sang it often," says 4PM lead singer Ray Peña. "And once I formed a group, I decided I wanted it to be our first hit." —R.N., J.C.

The Original Song:

"Ue O Muite Aruko"
("I Look Up When I Walk")

I look up when I walk
So the tears won't fall down
I remember that spring day
I am alone tonight

I look up when I walk
I counted the blurry starts
I remember that summer day
I am alone tonight
Happiness is in the clouds
Happiness is up in the sky

I look up when I walk
So the tears won't fall down
I cry as I walk
I am alone tonight

The English Version:

"Sukiyaki"

It's all because of you
I'm feeling sad, and blue
You went away, and now my life is just a rainy day
And I love you so, how much you'll never know,
You've gone away and left me lonely

Untouchable memories
Seem to keep haunting me
and I'm in love so true, that once turned all my grey skies blue
But you disappeared, now my eyes are filled with tears
And I'm wishing you were here with me

Soaked with love, all my thoughts, of you
Now that you're gone I just don't know what to do
If only you were here
You'd wash away my tears
The sun would shine, once again you'd be mine o mine
But in reality
You and I will never be
'Cause you took your love away from me

Traditional Asian Instruments

When asked to name traditional Asian instruments, some people might respond the piano and the violin. Don't be silly. We're talking about instruments from Asia—musical implements ranging from the koto to the gamelan, with decidedly non-Western sounds and pedigrees.

Part of the reason why many of these instruments have had meager (or nonexistent) penetration into the mind and music of the West is due to cultural and musical differences between hemispheres. The Arab musical scale is based on a 17-note structure, for instance; slightly farther east, in India, not only are there microtones in the scales—tones between tones—but songs are generally improvisations, wrapped around musical motifs called raga. Musicians consider the time of day, place, season, and the like, pick the appropriate raga, and improvise from there. And even father east, in China and Bali, five-toned scales are the standard.

Perhaps this proliferation of musical diversity, then, and the sheer differences in what each hemisphere's listeners consider to be "good music" might obviate any cross-cultural exchange of ideas. Luckily, that's simply not the case. Much musical border crossing was initiated through rock music's experiments during the sixties, for instance. An inspired George Harrison learned enough sitar to drone a few tones on the Beatles' Revolver, on songs like "Love You Too" and "Within You Without You." In doing so, they launched a quest for authentic "ethnic" sounds, of which musicians like Peter Gabriel and Paul Simon have not been able to get enough since. Nevertheless, the most progressive cross-cultural work has not been in rock but rather in experimental music and jazz.

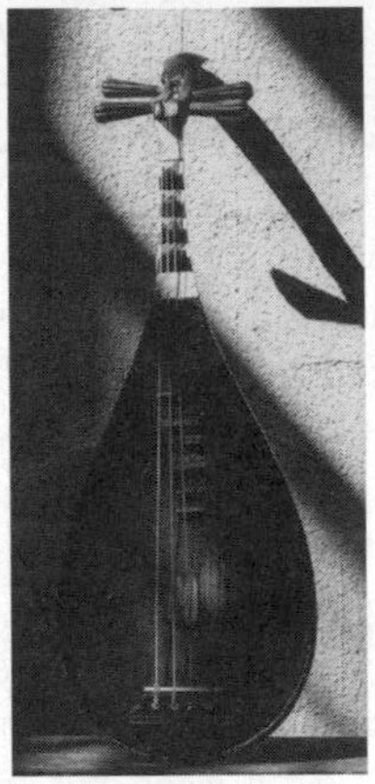

While the minds of individual instrumentalists like Ry Cooder were always open to inquiry, jazz's more free-form, progressive structure and ideology really pushed the bandwidth for new forms and instruments. The African American drummer Leon Alexander worked taiko-inspired rhythms into his trap set performances, and the James Newton Quartet put some koto in their mojo. Perhaps most significantly, Asian American jazz musicians, seeking to explore identity and culture through their music, have begun incorporating authentic instruments into their work, as well as classical Asian musical forms and motifs.

Which just goes to show: music is one thing in the world which seems to know neither race nor creed. Good taste, however, is another issue. —G.C.M.

From China
qin (zither); pipa (four-stringed lute); cheng (like the koto, below); sheng (17-pipe mouth organ); ta ku, panku (types of ku, or drum); sona (double-reed oboe); dizi (flute); erhu (two-stringed bowed fiddle); yang qin (hammer dulcimer); cheng hu qin (two-string lute)

From India
bansri (bamboo flute); vina (stick zither or fretted lute); dilruba (Punjabi fretted, bowed long-neck lute); jaltarang (porcelain bowls filled with water to different pitches and struck with sticks); pak hawaj (double-headed barrel drum); sarangi (bowed fiddle); sarod (unfretted, long-necked lute); shahnai (Hindustani oboe-like instrument; the South Indian equivalent is called the nadhaswaram); sitar (fretted long-necked lute); surbahar (bass sitar); sursringar/swarsringar (bass sarod); tabla (paired hand drums; dayan is the tuned right drum, and bayan, the untuned left drum); tanpura (four, five ,or six string unfretted droning lute); vichitr vina (South Indian unfretted stick zither)

From Indonesia
gamelan gong kebyar (modern style of Balinese metallophone orchestra; includes gongs and xylophone-type instruments called gender and gangsa); kendang (barrel drums); suling (bamboo flutes); rebab (bowed lute); jegog (bamboo gamelan; poor villages sometimes have these instead of metal ones)

From Japan
shakuhachi (bamboo flute); samisen (three-string lute); koto (zither); taiko (drum ensemble composed of several types of drums, gongs, cymbals, and sometimes string and wind instruments); odaiko (biggest drum in taiko; about seven feet tall); shimadaiko (double-headed drum, like a snare drum); atari gane (small hanging metal gong, struck to keep time in taiko)

From Korea
kayakeum, komungo (types of zither; komungo has thicker strings; haekeum (lute); changko, puk (types of drum)

From Thailand, Cambodia, Laos
pi-phat (Thai; gamelan-like orchestra); pi-nai (Thai) or sralay (Cambodian) (quad-reed oboe)

From Vietnam
tam thap luc (originally a 36-, now 82-stringed hammer dulcimer

From the Philippines
kulintang (gamelan-type orchestra)

STYLE AND FASHION

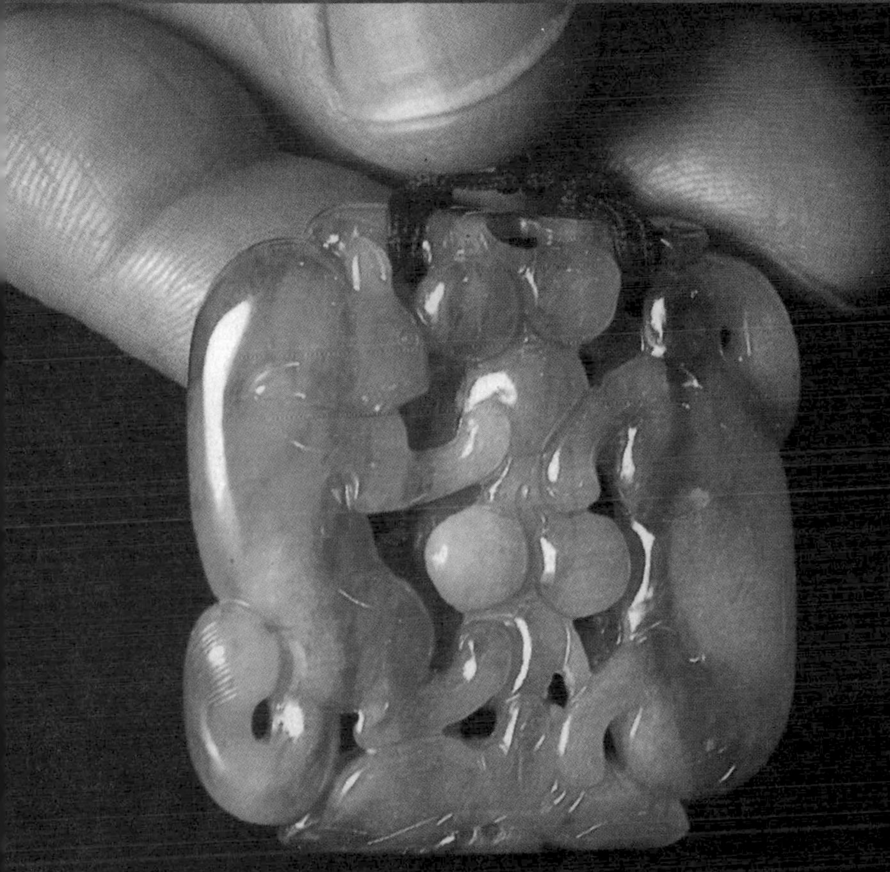

"The Asian aesthetic is about spiritualism, minimalism, and simplicity. It's easier not to have too many choices; less is more. And more comfortable. That's what Asian style is about. It's not about making someone look like an opium addict, or the Last Empress."

—Josie Natori

Asian American Designers

Some were born in America. Some were born in Asia and moved to America. All have made a unique impact on the impenetrable American fashion scene.

Tina Chow

Birth name: Bettina Louise Lutz
Born: 1951 in Cleveland, Ohio; died 1992
Why she'll live forever: Chow was a model, artist, and a cause célèbre. She was also the first famous woman to die of AIDS.
Biographical notes: After moving to Tokyo with their family, both Tina and her older sister Bonny (who later married ex–Talking Head David Byrne) were discovered by advertisers hungering for that "Eurasian" look. In 1968, she signed with Shiseido, Japan's preeminent cosmetic company. As a result, she was initiated into fashion's big leagues, meeting the likes of Issey Miyake and English designer Zandra Rhodes, who eventually introduced Tina to her future: socialite and restaurateur Michael Chow. After their inevitable divorce, Tina remained in the public eye. She was a cultural icon, photographed by the likes of Helmut Newton and Herb Ritts. Tina's spare sense of style combined with her lacquered-looking, boyish hair to give her an androgynous, otherworldly appearance. It also made her an ideal model for the Gap's celebrity-focused "pocket-T" print ads of the late '80s. Karl Lagerfeld credited Tina with inventing "minimal chic." Unfortunately, it wasn't Tina's life that put her on everyone's lips, so much as her death: a brief post-Chow fling led to her becoming infected with HIV, which sent earthquakes through the style and socialite circles she ran in (upon hearing of Chow's illness, Richard Gere, an ex-beau, reportedly took a panicked test himself). Chow was far from idle in her final days: She began designing Zen-inspired jewelry—unique crystals wrapped in bamboo, a pursuit which brought her comfort even as she lost weight and took on an ethereal, too-delicate appearance.
Life after death: In 1993, fundraising began for Tina's House Foundation, an AIDS hospice in Mexico City run by Elena Lopez, the nurse who cared for Tina until her death. —R.G.

Han Feng

Born: August 23, 1962, in Hangzhou, China
Signature look: Accordion-pleated silk scarves.
Label: Han Feng (New York)
Revolutionary statement: Revitalized the crinkled look for the '90s.
What she actually wears: Cropped hair, no makeup.
Biographical notes: Feng is one self-willed, self-starting designer. She graduated from Zhejiang Academy of Fine Arts in 1984 with a degree in graphic design, then moved to New York in 1986 with her Chinese-speaking American husband, Stuart Schonberger. In 1987, she began designing pleated scarves, and launched a line of accessories and simple separates in 1992. By the spring of 1993, she'd designed her first ready-to-wear collection. She sold her first pleated items in 1988 to a SoHo boutique for $5,000. Her 1992 ready-to-wear collection resulted from a request by the Henri Bendel store to make blouses pleated like her scarves; the blouses sold out in a matter of days. And now Han Feng sells in more than a hundred stores in the U.S. and around the world.
The secret of her success: A psychic once told her that her destiny was America. —D.G.

Josie Natori

Name: Josefina Cruz Natori
Birthdate: May 9, 1947, in Manila, The Philippines
Signature look: Beaded and embroidered bustiers, leggings, and slip dresses.
Labels: Natori (couture and lingerie); Natori II (casual); Josie (lower-priced for younger women); Natori fragrance (licensed to Avon Products). (All New York; boutiques in New York, Paris, and Manila)
Revolutionary statement: In the 1980s and '90s, Natori made it chic for women to go out in their underwear, until Madonna made it cliché.
What she actually wears: Couture (French and her own)
Biographical notes: Natori moved to New York at 17, studied economics at Manhattanville College, and in 1968 got a job at Bache Securities, and then Merrill Lynch, where she became its first female vice president. She married rival banker Kenneth Natori in 1972. In 1977, she quit the finance world and started The Natori Company, which began importing baskets and things from the Philippines. One of the "things" Natori first imported was a hand-embroidered traditional blouse, which a Bloomingdale's buyer suggested that Natori turn into a nightshirt. Within three months, $150,000 worth of Natori's nightshirts were sold to stores like Saks Fifth Avenue and Neiman-Marcus. The Natori Company has since turned into a $40 million–a-year empire.
The secret of her success: In the early days, Daddy's money financed her factory in the Philippines; now, her husband is her company's chairman (but she's president). —D.G.

Anna Sui

Born: 1955 in Dearborn, Michigan (she's a second-generation Chinese American)
Signature look: funky outfits with matching hats, bags, and shoes
Labels: Anna Sui (quirky, neo-retro couture); Sui by Anna Sui (modern classics, licensed to The Gilmar Group) (New York)
Revolutionary statement: That it's actually possible to make fun, eccentric, couture-quality clothes at below-designer prices. Her clothes have inspired a cult following among the ever-so-hip—models and celebs like Naomi Campbell, Winona Ryder, and Madonna.
What she actually wears: Black.
Biographical Notes: She was voted best-dressed student in 9th grade. Upon graduating, she went to Parsons School of Design in New York, and left after her sophomore year to work for various Seventh Avenue designers. In 1980 she launched her own firm. That same year, Macy's bought six of her Lycra designs, and used one in a New York Times ad. Fame was not long in following; Anna Sui is now a multi-million-dollar business, with Sui-wear available in over 200 department stores worldwide.
The secret of her success: She's long-time friends with top fashion photographer Steven Meisel, with whom she worked as a stylist in the early days. —D.G.

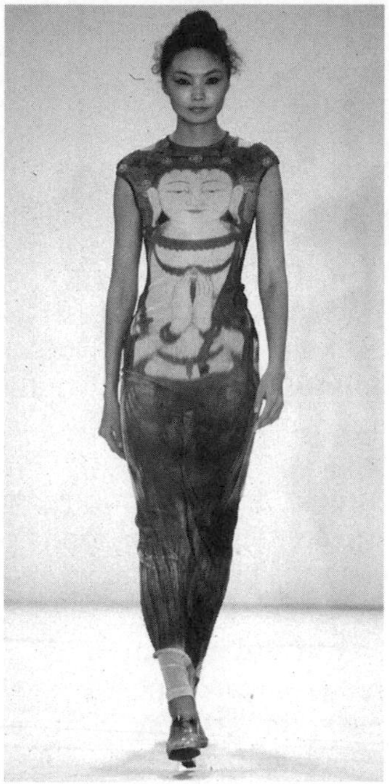

Vivienne Tam

Birthdate: 1956 in Canton, China
Signature look: Goofy Chairman Mao prints (in pigtails, with pink lips, with bumblebee on nose, and so forth; [👁223])
Labels: East Wind Code (until 1990), Vivienne Tam (1990 and after) (New York, with production and boutiques in Hong Kong)
Revolutionary statement: Tam is the grand dame of modern Sino-Western fashion.
What she actually wears: Side-parted long black hair, no makeup except lipstick. And her own designs.
Biographical notes: Tam studied design at Polytechnic in Hong Kong and worked briefly in London, before moving in 1981 to New York, where she founded East Wind Code (a literally translated Chinese expression meaning "prosperity and good fortune"). She showed her Chinese-workwear-inspired designs to department stores during "open days" for unknown designers. Henri Bendel and Charivari bought them immediately. In 1982, her first official showing at the International Fashion Boutique Show resulted in $100,000 worth of orders in four days. In 1990, she closed the Code label and began designing under her own name. Her first New York runway show in 1993 brought her an avalanche of press coverage; Vivienne Tam now sells $10 million annually, is available in 200 stores in the U.S., Europe, Asia, Australia, and South Africa, and has established a reputation for being the high-water mark of reasonably priced funky fashion.
The secret of her success: Brian Hogan, her company's VP, has adeptly handled Tam's merchandising since 1986. —D.G.

Yeohlee Teng

Born: 1951 in Penang, Malaysia
Signature look: The coat, especially the one-size-fits-all style from 1987; in 1995, the modern cheongsam.
Label: Yeohlee (New York)
Revolutionary statement: Simple, architectural clothes that women actually want to wear.
What she actually wears: Her own stuff in black, plus basics from J. Crew and the Gap.
Biographical notes: Teng is a precocious child dressmaker turned New York designer. At age nine, she took patternmaking lessons from a Javanese woman in Malaysia. At 18, she moved to New York to study at the Parsons Schools of Design, dropped out after two years, and freelanced for other designers. In 1976, she assembled her first collection—five pieces in black, off-white, and tan cotton—which were snapped up by Henri Bendel. In 1981, she founded Yeohlee; now her label grosses $10 million a year.
The secret of her success: She's a Gemini. —D.G.

Zang Toi

Born: 1952 in Kelantan, Malaysia
Signature look: Tweed suits and bustier dresses with gold orchid buttons
Labels: Zang Toi, Zee Collection (lower-priced) (New York, Malaysia)
Revolutionary statement: Yves Saint Laurent meets *The Last Emperor*: opulent, unorthodox—or, as *Vogue* said, "wake-the-dead"—color combinations (example: chartreuse and fuschia); classic styles worn by the likes of Peggy Lipton, Sharon Stone, and Patty Hearst.
What he actually wears: An oxford shirt and sarong-like batik shorts.
Biographical notes: Toi moved to New York in 1981 to study at Parsons, then worked from 1983 to 1988 for designers Mary Jane Marcasiano and Ronaldus Shamask. In 1988, he opened his own studio and became the instant darling of the fashion world. He got his big break when his first collection of sarong skirts and classic suits were sold to Saks Jandel, Okeon, and Linda Dresner.
The secret of his success: He garnered the patronage of Martha Inc.'s buyer and president Lynn Manulis, the "regal godmother of young designers." —D.G.

Vera Wang

Born: June 1949 in New York.
Signature look: The bare-back "Sheer Illusion" wedding dress.
Labels: Vera Wang, Vera Wang Bridal, Vera Wang Made to Order
Revolutionary statement: Made it possible for brides to look like they didn't just step off a wedding cake.
What she actually wears: Sophisticated, tailored things, and her own stuff (well, not the wedding dresses).
Biographical notes: As a child Wang attended private schools, studied ballet, and ice-skated competitively. She graduated from Sarah Lawrence in 1971 with an art history degree. Her first job out of college was at *Vogue*, as a sittings editor. She worked there for 16 years, then, in 1988, got a job as creative director at Ralph Lauren. When she finally decided to get married in 1989 (at the age of 40, to businessman Arthur Becker), she couldn't find a decent wedding dress. As a result, she designed her own, which led to her setting up her own shop. Two years later, she started her own company; in 1992, she designed skater Nancy Kerrigan's Olympic outfit; in 1994, she introduced her first evening ready-to-wear line. She has since cultivated a loyal following among celebs who want to look sexy and sophisticated (Mariah Carey, Sharon Stone, Marisa Tomei, Holly Hunter). Bad news: Despite the fact that her dresses cost thousands of dollars, as of 1995, her company has yet to show a profit.
The secret of her success: Having Ralph Lauren as her mentor. And having a rich daddy, who financed her business. —D.G.

Your Asian Wardrobe

If you concentrate really hard, you may be able to conjure up a few garments that you'd recognize as notably Asian—the Japanese kimono, the Chinese cheongsam, the Indian sari. Little do you realize that—within your very closet!—there are clothes whose origin is every bit as Asian as those staples of designer exotica. Take the following, for example:

Bandannas

A strange, but true fact: The bandanna—essential fashion accessory to biker, skinhead, and junkyard dog alike, and legendary symbol of the American West—originated in the East. India, to be exact. Its name derives from the Hindi *bandhani* (from Sanskrit *bandhana* or *bandhna*, "to tie"), which refers both to a technique of resist-dying cloth **[👁308]** and the textile it produces. In bandhani, small areas of cloth are pinched and bound before the cloth is dunked in dye, creating the patterns of small dots we associate with bandanna prints today. —D.G.

Jodhpurs and the Jodhpur Boot

Jodhpur the place, with a history spanning more than half a millenium, was one of the most beautiful and distinctive regions in northwest India. Famous for its beautiful sandstone palaces and majestic fortified bastions, the former state of Jodhpur also spawned two fashion classics: the eponymous jodhpur pants and the jodhpur boot. Jodhpurs, made famous in modern times by Patten and Hollywood's German film directors, are riding breeches that flare out at the hips and fit tightly from the knee to the calf. The style was adapted from breeches worn by Indian Rajput princes in the early 19th century, who wore the pants to play the game of polo against the British. The Jodhpurian passion for polo also resulted in the popularity of the jodhpur boot, also known as the chukka boot (after the chukka, a period of play in polo). The original boots, also used for riding, were made out of smooth leather, with a plain toe, an adjustable strap, and buckle. Both the pants and the boots have become something like regulation wardrobe for polo, but really have dropped from day-to-day sight since the '40s. Could this be because they make every person, no matter how svelte, look like they're storing two camels' worth of fat in their thighs? —O.P.M.

Kurta

The kurta is a traditional Indian shirt that, like many other "exotic" pieces from the Asian wardrobe, has recently found favor with purveyors of modern fashion. Originally, kurta simply referred to an undershirt, which could be of any length from tunic to gown. In the 19th century, however, the kurta evolved into an outer-garment, and developed some of the characteristic elements by which we know it today: a round neckline with a slit opening either at the middle or off to one side of the placket, and side slits at the hem.

America first spotted the kurta, made of lightweight cotton or silk, on Indian political figures like Mahatma Gandhi. A few decades later, in the mid 1980s, the Indian-inspired collections of Ralph Lauren and Calvin Klein featured slit-collared shirts which attempted to duplicate the kurta's loose, sheer charm. In the early 1990s, designers like Jean-Paul Gaultier began offering even more direct translations. Today, though not as well known as another traditional Indian garment—the sari **[👁302]**—the kurta has now become firmly entrenched in the

fashion vocabulary. —D.G.

Nehru Jacket

Let's get one thing straight right off the bat: The Nehru jacket—the five-button, hip-length, stand-up collar jacket frequented by the prime minister of India from 1947 to 1964—is only called the "Nehru" jacket in the West, where we don't know any better. In India, the jacket is called a *bandgalla*, and its knee-length version a *sherwani*; both are more or less traditional garb worn by millions of Indian men other than Jawaharlal Nehru himself; naming the bandgalla after its most famous enthusiast is something like calling the tuxedo the "Bond suit."

Whatever you call it, after its introduction on Jawaharlal's back, the bandgalla quickly became an international phenomenon. Pierre Cardin was the first to realize its fashion potential, putting one on display in his Paris boutique in the mid 1960s. By 1968, the bandgalla, as it came to be known, was a full-fledged fashion fad in Europe and the States, where it was accessorized with peace signs and hip-hugging bell-bottom pants. Although Nehru himself usually wore his jacket in white, the Beatles (who were better known) popularized the style in numerous colors and patterns. However, because the jacket was stiff and fitted at the waist, only skinny rock stars like Jimi Hendrix could really carry off the look. This quickly led to its demise.

Still, several fashion designers, including Anne Klein, Perry Ellis, Kenzo and Jean-Paul Gaultier attempted to revive the style in the mid 1980s, when Indian-inspired looks came into vogue partly as a result of movies like *Gandhi* and *A Passage to India*. Unlike the heavy fabric of the original bandgalla, the new versions were lighter in weight and more loose-fitting. Recently, the bandgalla made yet another mini-comeback, surfacing in the mid 1990s under assumed names, like "the Bombay" or the "band collar jacket," proving that bad fashion, like the living dead, can never truly be vanquished—only forced briefly back into the crypt. —D.G.

> **"In India, the Nehru jacket is called a *bandgalla*, and it's a traditional garb worn by millions of Indian men; naming the bandgalla after its most famous enthusiast is something like calling the tuxedo the 'Bond suit.'"**

The Pajama

Like the Japanese kimono, the pajama is an example of Eastern daywear evolving into Western nightwear. The English word "pajama" (alternately spelled "pyjama") comes from the Hindi words *pae* (or "leg") and *jamah* (or "garment"). The pajama was worn by Indian men (and occasionally women) as an alternative to the traditional *dhoti*, trouser-like pants made by wrapping loose cloth around and between the legs, mostly because pajamas offered better mobility for active types, like soldiers and housewives. Indeed, it was the warrior-caste Rajputs of northern India who were the first to widely adopt them.

The pajama gradually became popular among both women and men, and spawned several distinct versions. Prior to the 18th century, women tended to wear tighter styles of pajama underneath their gowns; men wore loose pajamas underneath long kurta shirts. By the 19th century, in a foreshadowing of the bell-bottoms craze of the '60s and '70s, very wide and loose pajamas became all the rage. pajama fabrics tended to be richly colored, and often were embroidered or brocaded silk.

When the winds of trade brought Indian import goods to points west, the paijama was among them. It might be seen as somewhat ironic that in the modern West, pajamas—originally the most basic of activewear—became clothing worn for sleep, or alternatively, lounging around. One of the earliest English-language references to them, in the *Oriental Sporting Magazine of 1828*, exemplifies the garment's Western application: "His chief joy smoking a cigar, in loose paeejams and native slippers." Of course, in fashion, it's only a matter of time before everything old arrives as recycled chic: In the '20s, early '40s, late '60s, and most recently in the early '90s, the "Pajama Look" for evening and casualwear took runways by storm.

But even as bedtime garb, the oh-so-luxurious silk pajama has never gone out of style: it's still a staple of women's intimates catalogs like Victoria's Secret. Word to the wise, however: As Audrey Hepburn proved in *Roman Holiday* (and Claudette Colbert in *It Happened One Night*), there's no sexier look than a woman in men's pajamas. According to industry experts, 75 percent of men's pajamas are purchased by—and for—women. —D.G.

Batik

THE BATIK PROCESS

Batik tulis, or hand-drawn batik, begins with the use of a long-spouted, pen-like tjanting (pronounced "canting") to retrace with hot wax a fabric design first composed in pencil. When the wax dries, the fabric is dipped in dye, which is absorbed only by the unwaxed portions of the cloth. After the dye sets, the fabric is dipped in boiling water to soften the wax so it can be scraped off. The process can be repeated as much as two dozen times. A swatch of batik tulis, usually made by women, takes about six months to complete and can cost hundreds of dollars.

Hand-stamped batik, meanwhile, is made using an engraved-copper stamping block called a tjap (pronounced "chap") to imprint wax in interlocking designs that appear continuous. The process, used since 1815 and usually performed by men, is less time-consuming than batik tulis. As a result, the finished product is considerably less expensive, costing as little as $5 U.S. a piece. Don't be fooled, however: The majority of batik-look fabric available today is created through modern silkscreen processes, which, while nontraditional, can be made to produce a similar effect. It's often difficult to tell whether batik has been hand-drawn, stamped, or silkscreened—stamped batik in particular can be done well enough to render it indistinguishable from batik tulis. The best batiks are rendered on cotton or silk, although today, wool, linen, and rayon are also used.

The literal meaning of batik, from the Indonesian *mbat*, "to play with," and *ntik*, "to make a dot," only hints at the complex wax-resist technique used to make the fabric's intricate designs. Although printing using wax-resist methods was known in ancient China, India, and Egypt, the process was perfected as an art form on the Indonesian island of Java. For about 700 years, only royal families could wear batik in Indonesia; creating it was a form of meditation and spiritual discipline. In the 1800s, batik spread to the common people, and is now produced in other Southeast Asian countries and all over the world. Batik came into vogue in the US between 1910 and 1920, and resurfaced in the 1960s and 1970s.

In 1972, former photojournalist Inger McCabe Elliott began importing Javanese batik through her New York-based company China Seas. Elliott transformed the batik industry by having Indonesian manufacturers make entire bolts of batik fabric, instead of just small individual swaths. Batik prints, which are now mass-produced in Indonesia, Malaysia, and Sri Lanka, have been popular ever since in both fashion and home decor.

THE UNITED COLORS OF BATIK: Pigments to Dye For

While a number of techniques exist for its creation, the key to quality batik is in the dyes. The recipes to traditional batik dyes, which might use bark, brown sugar, cassava, banana, or even shredded chicken, are hoarded as family secrets. Patterns on a brown background come from Solo or Jogja; bright designs with reds and blue come from Cheribon or Pakalongan. The oldest dye known was made from the indigo plant, and produced a deep blue hue, which, along with the dark browns produced using human blood, was a color of nobility. The cracked, feathery lines Americans usually associate with batik are actually the result of low quality waxes. Indonesian royalty generally desired smooth lines; later, less elitist Indonesians purposely crackled their batik to prove they had no such pretensions.

THE BATIK CAPITAL OF THE WORLD

Yogyakarta, or Yogya, is where most of the world's quality batik is created. Located in Java about halfway between Bali and Jakarta, Yogya claims to have almost a thousand batik "factories," but this actually includes hundreds of women who make and sell batik out of their homes. The Batik Research Insitute is located in this walled city of central Java, as is the Royal Sultanate, where descendants of the first batik-makers still live and practice traditional batik design. Just an hour north of Yogya is Solo—which, naturally, is the batik export capital of the world.

BATIK CUSTOMS

Traditionally, different patterns of batik were worn in Indonesia to indicate status, occupation, or state of health; batik was also worn to soothe volcanoes and to ward off illness and bad luck. The national costume of Indonesia is the Nehru-like *kebaya* jacket, worn with a batik cloth wrapped around the hips and secured by folding over and tucking in the fabric at the waist. —D.G.

Cheongsam

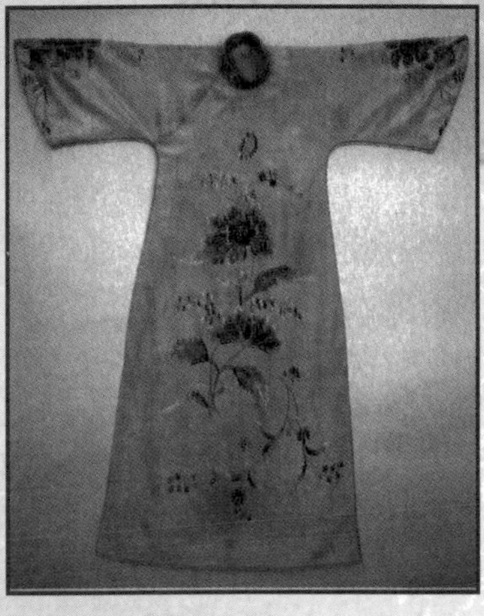

A hundred years ago, if you'd asked a Chinese tailor for a *cheongsam,* you'd have gotten a men's undershirt. Etymologically speaking, the form-fitting dress with frog closures and mandarin collar that the Western world thinks of as the traditional outfit of the Chinese woman originated as a *male* garment. In Cantonese, cheongsam (*chang shan* in Mandarin) literally translates as "long gown." For centuries, the *cheongsam ma-gua* was an outfit for Chinese men of quality, particularly scholars and merchants. It consisted of a long jacket (*ma-gua*), worn over ankle-length shirts—cheongsams—which for all intents and purposes were dresses.

These, however, were loose and billowy, not painted-on tight. Women wore a different two-piece outfit, called the *ao gun*; this consisted of a long, loose A-line jacket (the *ao*) over a simple ankle-length skirt, for married women, or straight trousers, for unmarried girls.

By the mid 1920s, in Shanghai, the "Paris of the East," the ao gun had evolved into a one-piece outfit called (in Mandarin) the *qi pao* ("banner gown.") Even then, it was hardly slinky; it fell in a straight A-line from shoulder to ankle, giving wearers a Gumbyesque profile. Common usage led Cantonese-speakers to refer to this dress by its literal description—which is to say, "long gown," or cheongsam. As for the taut, fitted qi pao which caused William Holden to flip for Nancy Kwan, that didn't appear until after World War II—mostly as a reaction to Western influences on Chinese style and libido. —K.M.L.

The Rise and Fall and Rise of the Cheongsam

1912 With the fall of the Qing dynasty, Manchu rule ends and the Republic of China is formed. Foot-binding is abolished. Suddenly, Chinese women find their bulky, embroidered robes uncomfortable, too. Women start wearing the ao gun, a simpler outfit consisting of a long, loose jacket over a skirt or pants. Unlike the West, which used the hemline as a barometer, early ao gun fashion trends mostly center on the jacket collar, which eventually rises as high as the earlobes.

EARLY 1920s The ao gun evolves—the top gets more fitted and sleeves shorten to three-quarter length. Skirt length rises to a shameful mid-calf height.

1925 In Shanghai, the ao gun becomes a one-piece dress, called a qi pao by Mandarin speakers, and eventually referred to as a cheongsam in the South. While its daring styling quickly makes it a hit in urban metropoli, it is derided as impractical by rural women, who find it unsuitable for field work.

1927 Nanjing becomes capital of the Republic, and the qi pao becomes the fashionable formalwear choice (for women, that is). The qi pao goes A-line with a just-below-knee-length hem.

EARLY 1930s The qi pao gets even more fitted, but hems drop back down to the ankle.

1931 Asian American actress Anna May Wong saunters across the big screen swathed in a silk qi pao in Daughter of the Dragon.

1932 Marlene Dietrich joins Wong in the cinematic qi pao canon, slinking her way through Shanghai Express in semi-authentic Shanghai style.

1935 Back in real-world Shanghai, dress hems go down, in some cases falling over the feet. As a result, slits rise up to the thigh to facilitate walking. Chinese women discover silk stockings and high heels. Sleeves get slimmer and shorter, rising above the bicep as cap sleeves or, sometimes, no sleeves at all.

LATE 1930s Hems go back up to mid-calf, sleeves go back down to the wrist, and narrow piping accentuates the edges of the dress, which is now cut looser overall but tighter at the waist, hips, and hem, exaggerating the female figure.

1940s The qi pao hem goes ankle-length again. Conservative women line their sleeves with fur or silk; trendy women wear cap sleeves or go sleeveless. Decorative frog closures are added at the tou jin, the qi pao's diagonal-cut front opening.

1950s Whoops! Hems rise to mid-calf again. The qi pao collar is rounded and shoulder seams are added to make the shoulders appear to slope in a gentle, "feminine" fashion.

LATE 1950s The qi pao becomes very fitted through the addition of bust and waist darts. For the first time in its history, the dress is fastened up the side with a zipper.

1960 Nancy Kwan stars as a qi pao–clad Hong Kong woman-for-rent in the British-made film The World of Suzie Wong. The outfit becomes world-famous as the "cheongsam." A member of the British royal family wears one on a visit to Hong Kong, despite the fact that, because of Suzie Wong, it is a style associated by most of the Western world with Chinese prostitutes. A non-mitigating factor: Americans decide that they like them, too.

1966 The Cultural Revolution. Wearing the qi pao is banned in China, along with other decadent Western habits, like getting permanent waves or eating regularly. Meanwhile, in the British colonies of Hong Kong and Taiwan, the cheongsam peaks in popularity.

1976 Mao dies and Chinese clothing styles on the mainland creep toward Western fashion. The qi pao is worn only for formal occasions and by older women.

1992 Madonna wears a cheongsam in Body of Evidence, but the movie still sucks.

1994 A slew of Hollywood actresses are seen socializing in cheongsams, bought cheap in Chinatown. Designers start offering their own high-priced versions. In People magazine, Los Angeles Times fashion columnist Betty Goodwin calls the cheongsam "sexy without being trashy. It's like a Chanel suit from China."

Cotton

"There are trees in which fleece grew surpassing that of sheep and from which natives made cloth."
—Greek historian Herodotus, after a trip to India circa 500 B.C.

"They came swimming toward us and brought us parrots, and balls of cotton thread...we gave them such [things] as strings of beads and little bells." —Christopher Columbus, in his journal entry of October 12, 1492, after meeting natives of Watling's Island [the Bahamas]

From cosmetic swabs to casualwear, the magical plant cotton—what the given-to-surreal-description Greeks called the "Vegetable Lamb"—is more or less ubiquitous throughout our modern world. Even the invention of "miracle fibers" like polyester hasn't killed off the popularity of this light, durable, and easily maintained fabric, thank God.

Or perhaps, as the case may be, thank the Indians. Cotton was first discovered and then cultivated in India around the year 5000 B.C.; over the next few millennia, Indians developed the textiles that came to be known as calico, chintz, madras, and seersucker [**307**], as well as advanced cotton textile processing techniques such as weaving and dyeing that Europe would later steal—er, import. From India, the cultivation of cotton spread east to China, which invented the spinning wheel and introduced the plant and its uses to Japan.

Meanwhile, an ocean away, a separate cotton culture was developing in Mexico and Peru, but Europeans wouldn't find out about that until the (uninvited) arrival there of the conquistadores.

COTTON-PICKIN' COUNTRIES

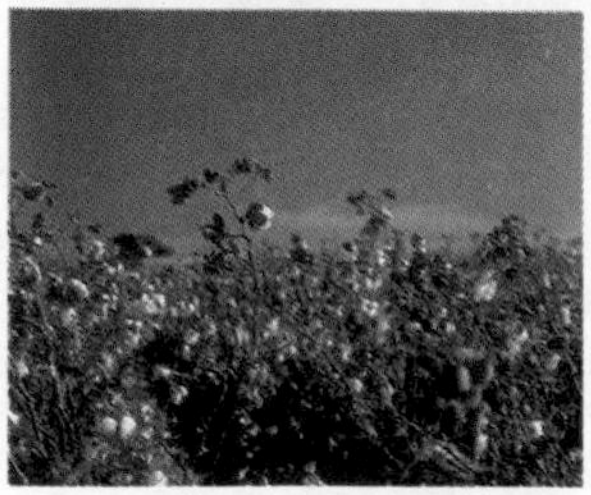

According to USDA economist Leslie Meyer, about 89.3 million bales of cotton were grown by about 50 countries in 1995. China and the U.S. are the world's top two producers, accounting for almost half the global total—enough for about 46.6 billion men's T-shirts or 9.5 billion pairs of women's jeans. (One bale = 480 pounds of cotton lint)

A COTTONBALL OF FACTS:

- *Gossypium,* the cotton plant, is a member of the mallow family. As a result, cotton's cousins include hibiscus, okra, and the marshmallow (the plant, not the puffy corn syrup and sugar confection).
- Of the dozens of cotton species, only three have commercial importance:
  - —About 88 per cent of the world's cotton and 99 per cent of U.S. cotton is *G. hirsutum,* otherwise known as "upland cotton," which produces a medium-length fiber with hundreds of variations.
  - —Egyptian, Peruvian, and pima cotton are made from *G. barbadense,* which produces fine, lightweight fibers.
  - —*G. herbaceum,* a short, coarse fiber, is produced mostly in Asian countries. —D.G.

A BRIEF HISTORY OF COTTON

336–324 B.C.: The armies of Alexander the Great bring Indian cotton to Egypt. Israeli and Phoenician traders are the first to traffic fine Egyptian cotton textiles, which soon surpass the quality of those made in India.

7TH and 8TH CENTURY A.D.: Arabs spread cotton from Egypt to Spain, which is why Columbus, when he accidentally lands in America and trades his little bells for balls of thread, knows what the thread is made of.

1588: England wrests the cotton trade from Portugal and Spain. Spreading their colonies diligently across the New World, the English decide that America's climate is perfect for establishing cotton plantations. They are surprised to discover that the little plants have already been there for ages.

1607: The first cotton plantation is established in Virginia, using seeds from the West Indies. The cotton plant is indigenous to the Americas, but it is originally harvested using the ancient Indian method of churga gin, which involves hand-cleaning the seedy, hairy bolls.

1793: Eli Whitney invents the cotton gin. This eliminates half of the horrendous chore of cotton manufacture, and is hailed as a tremendous labor-saving invention by white people, but is considered less of a boon by black slaves, who are still forced to do the back-breaking other half: picking, sorting, and baling.

THE "VEGETABLE LAMB"

- The ancient Greeks thought that cotton bolls were actually a kind of vegetable sheep, which bent down to graze until the stalks grew too high. The "sheep" would starve and their bodies would turn into "fleece."
- In 1350, English explorer Sir John Mandeville returned from India with tales of "a wonderful tree which bore tiny lambs on the ends of its branches."
- The German word for cotton is still *baumwolle,* literally "tree-wool."

Cultured Pearls

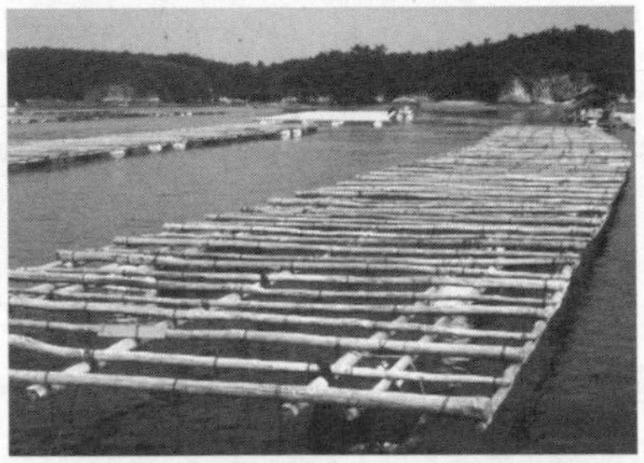

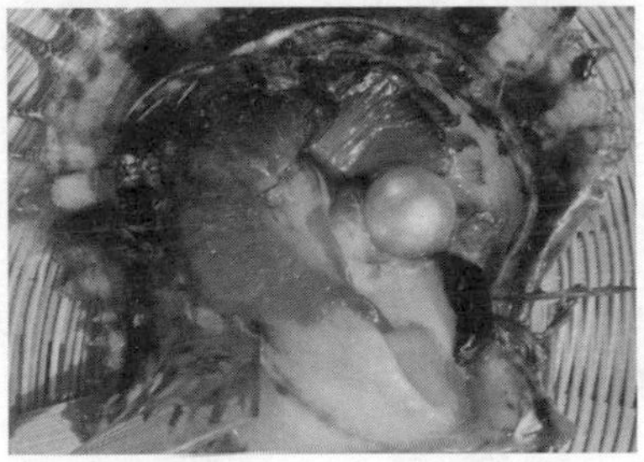

We all know the story of where pearls come from. These polished orbs begin as irritants: When a particle of offending foreign matter—sand, a shell fragment, a tiny parasite—enters the shell of a bivalve mollusk and gets lodged in its mantle tissue, the mollusk begins to isolate the object by secreting concentric coatings of nacre, or mother-of-pearl, the same lustrous substance found on the insides of the shell. Any mollusk can make pearls except the octopus. Of the 200 or so kinds of mollusks in existence, including saltwater and freshwater oysters, mussels, clams, and abalones, only six varieties make pearls of any value to humans, and each pearl requires three or more years of development before it can be harvested and fashioned into jewelry—thus transforming the pain of an innocent shellfish into the pleasure of the rich.

The Japanese have been credited as the first to make pearl cultivation commercially viable, although the Chinese have practiced it for centuries. In the 9th century, the Chinese discovered that if a mollusk were shot with a pellet of mud or a tiny piece of twig or bone and then returned to its bed for three years, a pearl would eventually form; legend has it that tiny metal Buddhas were implanted in mollusks to cultivate pearls in the Enlightened One's image. Despite this knowledge, perhaps due to the effort required, pearlmaking remained a process mostly left to nature until the late 19th century.

MIKIMOTO, THE PEARL KING

In 1888, on Japan's Shima Peninsula, a former vegetable vendor named Kokichi Mikimoto established the first pearl farm in hopes of preserving the famous local product known as "Ise Pearls," which were facing extinction from overfishing. After raising the oysters naturally for several years, Mikimoto was struck with how inefficient it was that pearls were created at a rate of only one or two per several thousand oysters, and he became obsessed with finding a better, more productive way.

In 1890, he met Kakichi Mitsukuri, a professor of marine biology, who told him about the way in which pearls are created from foreign particles lodged in oysters' shells. Though this was common knowledge in China and throughout the world, no one had cultivated pearls on a widespread scale. Mikimoto promptly set about artificially implanting oysters and cultivating them inside cages in the Shinmei Inlet and at Toba, now called "Pearl Island." After years without success, on July 11, 1893, Mikimoto finally found a semi-spherical pearl embedded against the shell of one of his oysters. He received a patent for the semi-spherical pearl on January 27, 1896, and three years late, opened the Mikimoto Pearl Store in Tokyo's Ginza district.

It took him a decade more to perfect the process for producing spherical pearls, which involved wrapping a core particle with mantle from one oyster and implanting it in another. Mikimoto received the patent for this method on February 13, 1908.

Mikimoto exhibited his cultured pearls in 1910 at the Anglo-Japanese Fair in London, and in 1926 at the Philadelphia World's Fair. By the mid 1920s, more American women were wearing Mikimoto pearls than any other women in the world.

PEARL FACTS

- **Japan produces 70 per cent of the world's saltwater pearls—more than 77 tons annually. Other saltwater pearl-producers include China, Australia, Tahiti, the Philippines, and Indonesia.**
- **China produces 90 percent of the world's freshwater pearls, though they have a lower market value ($6 per strand vs. $800 for saltwater).**
- **America is the biggest market for pearls, where nearly a quarter of the the world's export supply is sold. Hong Kong and Switzerland are the world's next largest consumers.**
- **Some of the best core beads used for nucleating oysters in Japan are made from the pig-toe clam, found in beds of the Tennessee, Wabash, and Mississippi Rivers.**

PEARL FAQS

Woe is the oyster, for whom growing a pearl is like having a golf ball lodged in one's brain!

CAN AN OYSTER PRODUCE MORE THAN ONE PEARL AT A TIME?

Yes. To make small pearls (less than 6mm in diameter), some hardy strains can be implanted with two core beads at once.

HOW MANY PEARLS CAN AN OYSTER PRODUCE IN A LIFETIME?

It depends. The tough-guy oysters of the South Seas can go through the rigorous nucleate-and-nacre routine up to four time. The dainty Akoyas can only take implanting once before giving up their shelly ghosts.

Kinds of Pearls

AKOYA PEARL: the classic 2 to 10mm saltwater pearl produced by the Akoya oyster, grown in Japan and China. The pearl is white with a spectrum of possible color tones. Akoyas account for 80 percent of all pearl sales.

BIWA PEARL: a generic term for freshwater pearls, a popular source for which used to be Japan's Lake Biwa, until pollution curbed the industry after 1980.

BLISTER PEARL: a flat-backed pearl grown against the inside shell of a mollusk.

FRESHWATER PEARL: a pearl produced with a piece of mussel tissue as its core. Recognizable by odd shapes resembling rice grains or raisins, they are cultivated in China, Japan, and the U.S. and are easily grown from any old freshwater mollusk.

IMITATION PEARL: fake pearl made from a glass, ceramic, shell or plastic bead coated with pearl essence, a liquid extracted from herring scales. Also called simulated, fashion, faux, organic, man-made, and Mallorca (a region of Spain famous for its imitation pearls).

MABE PEARL: a hemispherical pearl grown againt the inside shell of an oyster.

MOTHER-OF-PEARL: the lustrous nacre that coats the insides of the shell.

SOUTH SEA PEARL: a 10 to 20mm pearl produced by large tropical oysters grown in the warm South Seas. High-priced because of the harvesting time—up to 12 years for one necklace's worth of pearls.

MODERN CULTURED PEARL FARMING

Today, instead of depending on the biological idiosyncrasies of wild oysters, Japanese scientists have isolated certain strains of oysters with superior pearl-bearing capabilities. Following Mikimoto's patent, skilled technicians implant live oysters with a small bead of shell wrapped in mantle tissue. The process, called "nucleating," is "like doing major surgery on a human being," says Devin Macnow of the Cultured Pearl Association. The oyster is placed alongside a bunch of its oyster friends inside a special basket, which, suspended from a raft, is submerged in the nutrient-rich water of a sheltered bay. Pearl technicians carefully monitor the oysters, moving the rafts during the winter, when the water gets too cold. Over the next 10 months to three years, the oysters receive the spa treatment: Technicians periodically clean them of seaweed and barnacles, and treat them with medicinal compounds. At harvest time, if the oyster hasn't been killed by a typhoon, red tide, or a random aquatic predator, the shell is opened: an oyster shuffles off its mortal coil, and a pearl is born. Although cultured pearl farming is more efficient than nature alone, it's still not foolproof. Of the millions of oysters nucleated each year, about half survive to bear pearls; only one-fifth bear market-worthy pearls; and less than five percent produce gem-quality product. After harvesting, pearls must be sorted, drilled, strung, and blended—not an easy task, considering that artisans must sift through 10,000 pearls just to find enough matching ones for a single necklace.

THE GENUINE, THE CULTURED, AND THE FRANKLY FAKE

Diamonds are forever, but pearls only last about 400 years. Still, a strand of "genuine" pearls can be a treasured heirloom passed down for generations. Although the Federal Trade Commission classifies only natural pearls as "genuine," both natural and cultured are grown inside real oysters. Natural pearls make up less than 0.3 percent of the world's pearl supply; the only sure-fire way to tell the difference is by x-ray, although experts can sometimes tell by looking inside the drill hole to examine the core particle. Imitation pearls, which have no real gem value, can look as good as the real thing. To tell the difference, rub the pearls slowly against your front teeth; fake pearls will glide smoothly, while real ones will feel "gritty," due to the crystalline structure of the nacre that forms real pearls.

Unfortunately, since most jewelery stores will probably prosecute if you perform the "tooth test" at the counter, you'll have to buy the pearls first and do it in the privacy of your own home.

DEEP(-WATER) THOUGHTS

Before the Chinese made the critical oyster/pearl connection, any number of weird theories circulated freely:

- Malaysians once thought pearls were formed in coconuts.
- Some Chinese surmised that freshwater pearls grew inside a kind of squid. Others believed that pearls were produced by a wild pig-like animal. A few scholars claimed that they popped out of dragon brains.
- Indians believed that pearls formed in the clouds, then dropped down into open oyster shells; meanwhile, Japanese believed that they came from raindrops that fell from the mouth of a sky dragon. —D.G.

Furoshiki

Furoshiki are sturdy, ornamental square cloths that are folded and tied around objects to conceal and present them in a decorative fashion, much as wrapping paper is used in the West—though without the annoying gobs of sticky Scotch tape and environmentally unfriendly wastage associated with the latter.

A stylish example of the Japanese art of origata, or traditional gift-wrapping, furoshiki (from *furo,* "bath," and *shiki,* "spread") date back to the 17th century, when the cloths did double duty in public bathhouses: you stood on them while undressing, and you wrapped them around your bath articles to store and carry them. Over time, the bathing association faded away, and the use of furoshiki evolved into a formal tradition of wrapping—an art indicating politeness and respect in a culture that places as much emphasis on presentation as it does on content.

Furoshiki can be tied around objects in three basic ways: *Fukusa-zutsumi* (wrapping without tying), *otsukai-zutsumi* (wrapping and tying with one knot), *yotsu-musubi* (wrapping and tying with two knots). Depending on the size and thickness of the cloth, furoshiki can be used to wrap anything from a tea cup to a television, although wrapping the latter would put you into the category traditionally known as "overkill."

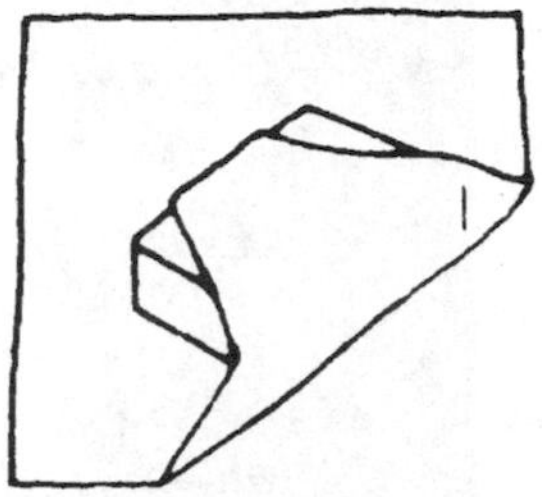

Furoshiki has sadly fallen out of favor with young Japanese in recent years, but the older generation still uses them daily in wrapping everything from documents to groceries to the occasional infant. In the U.S., a few companies are trying to bring this functional art form into the mainstream. The New York boutique Felissimo has sold furoshiki in both its retail store and its mail-order catalog, and a Connecticut company markets furoshiki as "Angel Cloth," prepackaging it with handy instructions. Will furoshiki take off in America? Now that recycling has become more or less entrenched in our society, perhaps—although it's far more likely, as teens in Japan have already demonstrated, that our own habits of material waste and disposable goods will catch on over there.

—D.G.

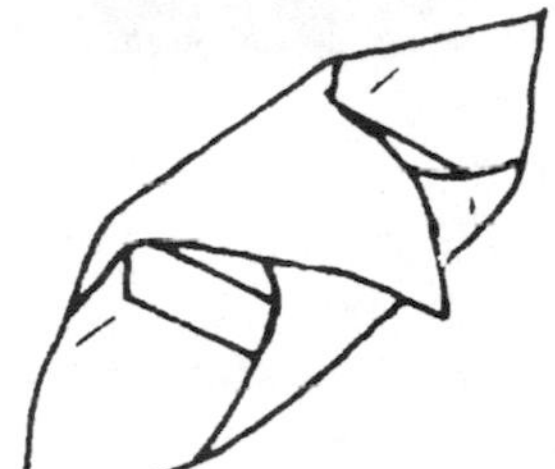

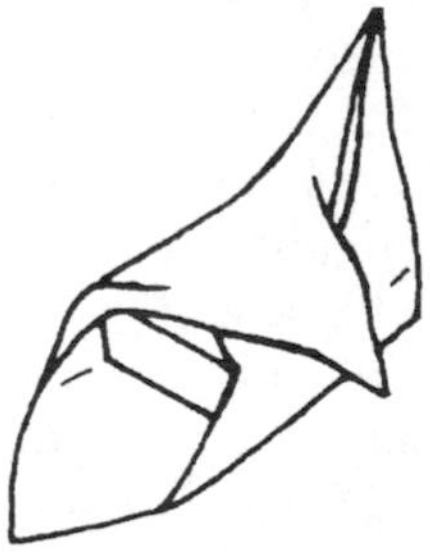

WRAPPING WITH FUROSHIKI

1 Start with a square cloth. Anything soft and fairly thin will do: You can use a bandanna, scarf, napkin, or even a tablecloth, as long as it is about four times larger than the thing you'd like to wrap.

2 Spread the cloth wrong-side down.

3 Place the object diagonally on the cloth.

4 Bring one corner over the object, tucking it under the object if necessary.

5 Fold the opposite corner over the object, letting it drape loosely over the side.

6 Bring the remaining two corners together and tie a square knot (right over left, left over right).

7 Tote the resulting bundle by holding it as if the knot were a handle. Small bundles composed of multiple objects can be slung behind the back; attaching the furoshiki to the end of a long stick and carrying it hobo-style over your shoulder is not traditional, and could put out an eye.

8 If you give the bundle to a friend, it's not polite to ask for the furoshiki back. The friend may keep it for use in wrapping another bundle—hopefully for you, since you've been such a sweetie.

Jade

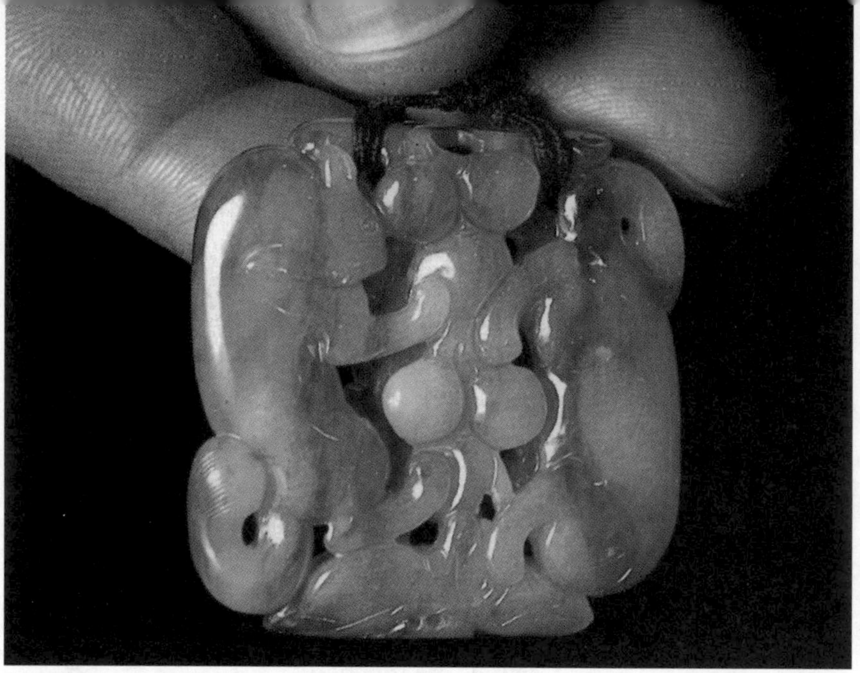

The translucent, icy-green beauty of jade has been coveted for millennia, not merely for its material value but for its subtle aura of spiritual power—that indefinable quality that has led civilizations throughout Asia (and even the Greeks and Egyptians) to declare it not merely a mineral, but a receptacle of cosmic forces, mystical energy, or the living soul itself.

The earliest use of jade as jewelry is believed to be around 4000 B.C. in China, where small earrings formed from polished jade have been discovered; from the year 3000 B.C. and onward, jade was carved and polished into ceremonial objects known as cong tubes, which were interred along with the dead as containers for the deceased's spirit. The use of jade in burial rituals continued through China's history, only waning after the Han Dynasty (206 B.C. to 220 A.D.), as the ultrahard mineral was thought to possess the essence of immortality; the highest of the immortal deities was even called the Jade Emperor of Heaven. Royalty and nobility drank from cups formed from jade, or even consumed elixirs containing powdered jade, thus partaking of its eternal nature. "Ancient superior men found the likeness of all excellent qualities in jade," goes a saying attributed to the great sage Confucius **[👁220]**. "Bright as a brilliant rainbow, like heaven; exquisite and mysterious, appearing in the hills and streams, like the earth; standing out conspicuous in the symbols of rank, like virtue; esteemed by all under the sky, like the path of truth and duty."

But the Chinese have no monopoly on the reverence of jade; the ancient civilizations of Burma, Japan, and India also held it to be sacred, and even today, wherever Asians are found, so is jade.

JADE FACTS

Though synonymous with an electric shade of green, jade can be found in colors ranging from nearly pure white to red, blue, and brown. All are valuable, though the most precious is Imperial jade, found in Burma—a translucent emerald-green variety that owes its coloration to a natural infusion of chromium. (White, red, blue, and brown varieties contain calcium, while dark green and black varieties are colored by iron.) The mineral name of jade is jadeite, though another mineral, nephrite, is similar, and is sometimes called "lesser jade."

THE POWER OF JADE

For the modern jade-wearer, there are any number of interesting and vaguely mystical uses for a piece of this green stone. Nervous about a business meeting? Hold some jade in your right hand, and try visualizing money. If your houseplants are dying, try wearing jade while gardening. Burying four pieces of jade along your garden's perimeter also helps, since it could drive up real estate values. And if the personal ads haven't been working out, attract love by wearing jade in the shape of a butterfly. (When you do find the love of your life, give them some jade to seal the bond.) Jade is also sometimes worn by older folk to ward off rheumatism and arthritis, though even those of less advanced age often sport jade pendants, called *yuk-choy* in Cantonese, to ward off misfortune and propitiate long life.

GETTING JADED

Unfortunately, even the most faithful wearing doesn't guarantee results if the jade is fake, and since 1990, the international jade market has been hit by an avalanche of doctored and fraudulent jadeite. How can you tell if you have the real thing? When making a purchase, be sure to consider the hue of the stone: The color of green jade should be an even and translucent—not too saturated or dark, and with a luminescent glow when brought into the light. Of course, the truest test is also the oldest: As your mother always told you, and her mother before her—you get what you pay for. —L.L.

Japanese Designers

A monk, a nun, a lawyer, a flower child, a doll collector, and a butterfly queen. What do they all have in common? They're the most influential Japanese designers in the international world of fashion. —D.G.

Rei Kawakubo

Born: 1942 in Tokyo, Japan
Signature look: Black, androgynous outfits featuring assymetrical cuts, uneven hemlines, unfinished edges, holes, and odd buttons, all done on purpose.
Labels: Comme des Garçons, Comme des Garçons Homme, Comme des Garçons Parfum
Revolutionary statement: Rei made it hip to look homeless.
What she actually wears: Black clothes she designed herself and black hair that looks like she cut it herself.
Biographical notes: Kawakubo graduated with a fine arts degree from Japan's Keio University in 1964, then worked in the ad department of textile maker Asahi Kasei. After a stint as a freelance stylist, she started her Comme des Garçons (French for "like the boys") label in 1969. She quickly became part of a ruling Japanese fashion triumvirate that included Issey Miyake and Yohji Yamamoto, and took the West by storm in the 1980s. Her first Paris show in 1981, according to *Time* magazine, "caused one of the biggest furors since Stravinsky introduced *The Rite of Spring*." (That's meant to be a compliment.) Kawakubo is the sole owner of her company, which, including furniture and perfume divisions, rakes in about $100 million a year, making her one of the world's richest female fashion designers. Kawakubo had a long "personal relationship" with Yohji Yamamoto. (They were known as "the Monk" and "the Nun" of fashion.) In 1992, however, Kawakubo married Adrian Joffe, who manages her European business.
The secret of her success: Fabric technologist Hiroshi Matsushita, who has been with her since the early days.

Issey Miyake

Real Name: Kazunaru "Issey" Miyake
Born: April 22, 1939, in Hiroshima, Japan
Signature look: Pleated, twisted architectural styles that never need ironing
Labels: Issey Miyake (couture), I.S. (Issey Sport), Plantation (lower-priced line)
Revolutionary statement: Sculpted, fun (if slightly alien and hideously expensive) clothes that double as works of art.
What he actually wears: Subdued versions of his own designs, and old wristwatches.
Biographical notes: After studying at Tama Art University in Tokyo and La Chambre Syndicale de la Couture Parisienne in Paris, he designed for Guy Laroche and Givenchy from 1966 to 1969, and Geoffrey Beene from 1969 to 1970, at which point he struck out on his own, establishing Miyake Design Studio, Issey Miyake & Associates, Miyake On Limits, and Issey Miyake International, all in Tokyo. He also established Issey Miyake, Europe, in Paris, and Issey Miyake, USA, in New York for good measure. His holdings gross more than $60 million annually.
The secret of his success: He's worked with the same textile designer, Makiko Minagawa, for more than two decades.

Yohji Yamamoto

Born: 1943 in Tokyo, Japan
Signature look: Black asymmetrical suits and dresses; "genius-cut" white blouses
Labels: Yohji Yamamotó, Y's (simpler and more affordable styles)
Revolutionary statement: Alternative Fashion in the '80s–stark, minimalist clothes for artsy people, or people who wanted to look artsy.
What he actually wears: Black.
Biographical notes: This would-be lawyer turned fashion designer attended French Catholic school in Tokyo and graduated from Keio University in 1966. He then entered the prestigious fashion school Bunkafukuso Gakuin, and graduated in 1969. He went to Paris and floundered, then returned to Tokyo and designed for his mother's boutique. He struck out on his own in 1972 with a company called, simply, Y's. In 1977, he showed his first couture collection in Tokyo, followed by a triumphant return to Paris in 1981, and New York in 1982. His menswear collection debuted in Paris in 1984.
Big break: The press and public went wild over his 1977 show at the Bell Commons in Tokyo. Afterwards, Yohji broke into tears.
The secret of his success: Hand-treated fabrics, broken in by the friction of tiny pebbles, or washed in the Nagara River.

Kenzo

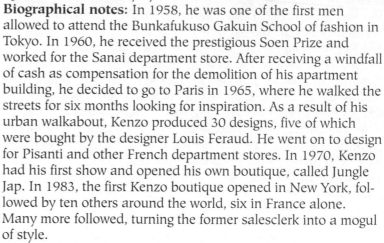

Name: Kenzo Takada
Birthdate: February 27, 1939, in Himeji, Japan
Signature look: Small flower prints.
Labels: Kenzo, Kenzo Homme, Kenzo Jeans, Kenzo Jungle, Kenzo Enfant, Kenzo Bebe, Kenzo Accessories, Kenzo Maison, Kenzo Parfum, Kenzo Studio (licensed).
Revolutionary statement: Mixing prints, like tartan plaids, stripes and flowers in one outfit.
What he actually wears: Spectacles and a Mary Tyler Moore hairdo.
Biographical notes: In 1958, he was one of the first men allowed to attend the Bunkafukuso Gakuin School of fashion in Tokyo. In 1960, he received the prestigious Soen Prize and worked for the Sanai department store. After receiving a windfall of cash as compensation for the demolition of his apartment building, he decided to go to Paris in 1965, where he walked the streets for six months looking for inspiration. As a result of his urban walkabout, Kenzo produced 30 designs, five of which were bought by the designer Louis Feraud. He went on to design for Pisanti and other French department stores. In 1970, Kenzo had his first show and opened his own boutique, called Jungle Jap. In 1983, the first Kenzo boutique opened in New York, followed by ten others around the world, six in France alone. Many more followed, turning the former salesclerk into a mogul of style.
Big break: After his very first fashion show in April 1970, Kenzo made the cover of *Elle*. He was world-famous the following year.
The secret of his success: Francois Baufume, who managed the business end of the Kenzo house of fashion from 1980 to 1992. In 1993, LVMH (Moet Hennessy Louis Vuitton) acquired Kenzo for $100 million (despite having "gone corporate," Kenzo continues to design for the brand). Clothing and perfume sales for 1995 were expected to reach $250 million.

Matsuda

Real Name: Mitsuhiro Matsuda
Born: 1934 in Tokyo, Japan
Signature look: Layers of black, and his designer eyeglasses.
Labels: Matsuda (America and Europe), Nicole, Madame Nicole, Nicole Club, Nicole Sport (Japan)
Revolutionary statement: Zenwear for the urban samurai.
What he actually wears: Black clothes and Converse All-Stars.
Biographical notes: He's an impoverished kimono merchant's son who did good. Educated at Waseda University, he graduated in 1961 from the prestigious Bunkafukuso Gakuin school of fashion (along with Kenzo). After traveling to Paris (with Kenzo), Matsuda returned to Tokyo and worked for San-Ei, a clothing manufacturer. In 1967, he opened Nicole Boutique, named after a model in *Elle* magazine. The first Nicole boutique did poorly until Matsuda decided to produce custom-made t-shirts. T-shirts remained a staple of his business for more than a decade. (Jack Nicholson reportedly loves them.) In 1971, he incorporated himself as Nicole, Ltd. and opened his first New York boutique the following year. By 1995, Matsuda's wholesale revenue was up to $228 million, although only $2.5 million of this was generated in the U.S.
The secret of his success: His designers. Yukio Kobayashi joined Nicole in 1974, became the head designer of men's clothing in 1983, then head of women's in 1995. Istuko Nakashima joined the company in 1976, and designed the entire women's collection from 1983 until her death in 1988 at the age of 38.

Hanae Mori

Born: 1926, in Shimane Prefecture, Japan
Signature look: Butterflies. Lots of butterflies.
Labels: Hanae Mori
Revolutionary statement: Known as "the First Lady of Tokyo fashion," she was the first Japanese designer to make a name in the international fashion world.
What she actually wears: Prim, dark outfits; poofy hair.
Biographical notes: She's a country doctor's daughter turned big-city artist. As a student during the Second World War, she studied Japanese literature and worked in a factory. After the war ended, she met her future husband, who had inherited a textile business. Mori decided to study design (to better make use of her husband's textiles, of course). In 1955, she set up a shop in Tokyo and designed for a private clientele. She then began designing costumes for movies (more than 500 in all). In 1960, she took time off and went to Paris, where she was inspired by Coco Chanel to become a Paris-based designer of haute couture. In 1965, she staged her first New York show, which was very well-received. Prince Rainier of Monaco saw a Hanae Mori dress in a Neiman Marcus store in Dallas and ordered one for his wife, Grace Kelly, who became a steady client. Since then, she has designed for the wives of political figures, such as Nancy Reagan and Imelda Marcos, as well as for the Japanese royal family. Three decades later, the Hanae Mori empire, with 70 boutiques worldwide, is worth $450 million.
The secret of her success: Her husband, Ken—and her butterflies.

TYING THE OBI (Women Only)

Men can get away with tying their slender, simple obi sashes in a basic tucked-in or half-bow fashion; for women (as usual) a much more intricate process is required. The obi is considered to be far more important than the kimono itself, and a good one is likely to cost many times that of the garment it decorates.

1 Try to get someone to help you. Tying an obi for the first time is not easy, and doing it alone is akin to wrestling with a 12-foot anaconda with both hands bound behind your back. Plus, if you do it wrong, you'll look stupid.

2 Throw one short end of the obi over one shoulder (to temporarily keep it out of the way)and bring the long end around to the front of your body.

3 Making sure that the short end stays on your shoulder, wrap the long end around your waist. Insert a stiff obi support in front to prevent wrinkles from showing in the fabric.

4 Tie the obi-age around the waist, to cover the small pad which will prop up the obi knot. The pad should go on your back. (Married women used to put their obi knots in front to indicate their status; this tradition has since gone the way of the whooping crane, and now everyone wears the obi-knot in back where it's out of the way.)

5 "Arrange" the obi over the pad in a decorative knot or bow. There are a zillion intricate (and symbolic) ways to do this;

Kimono

The Japanese say that the virtue of the kimono is its capacity to reveal the "inner nature" of its wearer. Perhaps this is because of its subtle and refined elegance; perhaps this is because it used to be worn as underwear. Either way, the kimono is the among the most resonant of Asian traditional clothing—synonymous with Japan in the way that, say, the sari [👁302] is synonymous with India. Indeed, these days, many Japanese use the term kimono (from *ki,* "to wear," and *mono,* "thing") simply to describe native Japanese clothing, as opposed to *yofuku,* or Western-style clothing.

In particular, however, kimono refers to the traditional Japanese robe with large rectangular sleeves and a wide sash, worn (with variations) by both sexes. Its origins are in the archetypal Japanese robe known as the *kosode* (literally "small sleeves"). The kosode was worn as an undergarment beneath more elaborate robe styles ever since the Nara period (710-794 A.D.), and as an everyday outergarment since the mid-16th century. By the 18th century, the kosode had evolved into the kimono, which continued to be worn as the average Japanese person's daily wardrobe until the 1920s, when the aftereffects of the Meiji Restoration's opening of trade doors to the West led to the entrenchment of yofuku's popularity among professional and educated women.

After World War II, of course, Western clothing became the norm for everybody, and the kimono became generally reserved for formal or special

occasions in Japan. The teaching of how to wear one was once traditionally an art passed on from mother to daughter. Nowadays special schools exist to teach young women the proper techniques. While most women can boast at least one "festival" kimono for such occasions as Tanabata and Obon, these days geisha are the biggest kimono-buyers, spending up to $10,000 to buy their basic wardrobe of ten kimonos, plus accessories. Among fashion-conscious Westerners in the late 19th century, informally tied kimonos became popular as dressing gowns and loungewear, and European artists like Klimt, Monet, and Toulouse-Lautrec did portraits of women dressed *a la japonaise.* The kimono has continued to be an influential shape in Western style, though few Americans have worn kimonos of authentic cut and material, preferring instead cheap cotton prints with cheesy rising sun patterns.

IT'S ALL IN THE SLEEVES

Some historians maintain that the kimono evolved from the Chinese robes that influenced Japanese dress in the 7th century. However, the Japanese insist somewhat nationalistically that the kimono was a direct descendent of the kosode instead—the small-sleeved undergarment (of Japanese origin) worn under as many as 12 layers of Chinese courtly robes. The rationale: the kimono's sleeves resemble the kosode's—not those of the wide-wristed Chinese robe.

HOW TO WEAR A KIMONO
Japanese Method #1 (The Hard Way)

This is a guideline for wearing a full kimono outfit in traditional fashion; the rules here differ only slightly for men (more grunting is involved).

What you'll need

Two-piece kimono underwear
An underkimono (*nagajuban*)
Two wide under-sashes (*date-obi*)
A very wide oversash (*obi*)
A thin silk cord (*obi-jime*)
A stiff, flat obi support
A thick, also flat obi pad.
A dyed silk sash (*obi-age*)
A pair of two-toed kimono socks (*tabi*)
Wooden sandals (*geta* for summer, *zori* for winter)

1. Put on your kimono underwear, which consists of a half-slip and an undershirt, belted at the waist. Both are made of silk.
2. Over this goes your nagajuban. This, too, should be tied just above the waist. The nagajuban should extend just above the ankles.
3. Tie your first under-sash so that it covers the first tie.
4. Now you can don your actual kimono, lapping the left side over the right in front, unless you're dead, in which case lap it right over left. (This is perhaps the most common kimono faux pas, having produced numerous titters over Gaijin of the Living Dead who carelessly appear in public dressed for their own funerals.)
5. Suck in that gut.
6. Tie the kimono with a sash, the date-obi.
7. Don't worry if the kimono seems to have yards of excess material dangling around your feet: All kimonos are the same length. Any overhang should be pulled up to hang over the under-sash. This may create giant, odd-looking dewlaps that hang to hip level or below. Again, don't worry—this will all be covered by other stuff.
8. Secure the dewlap-fabric by tying on another date-obi.
9. Suck it in again. Deeper.
10. Now, finally, you can tie the obi. This is a whole exercise in itself (*see sidebar*).
11. Don the white two-toed socks that make you look like Sylvester the Cat (maybe that's why the Japanese call them tabi). Actually, you really should have donned the tabi first, before the kimono; the stiff, multi-layered fabric of your outfit will make putting anything on your feet, not to mention bending over, a tiresome process.
12. Slip into a pair of sandals. In summer, you'll wear geta, with their front-and-back platform risers. For winter, wear zori, which are basically wooden thongs. Your toes will be cold.

Japanese Method #2

1. Attend a kimono school. This will cost you many yen, but you'll get it right at least once.

Western Method

If you're not strict about tradition, you might consider the following more casual kimono technique:
1. Pull the kimono over your shoulders, inserting your arms in the sleeves.
2. If desired, tie it at the waist with a scarf, silk sash, or stray necktie.
3. Fold the obi carefully and put it away in a drawer. Make a note about trying to figure out what to do with it. Someday. —D.G.

the most common is the square otaiko knot.

6 It's time for the obi-jime, which further secures the knot and obi. It should be slipped through the knot in back and tied with a square knot in front; the loose ends can be tucked into the sides of the obi.

7 The loose ends of the obi-age, which should be sticking up at the front of the obi, are then tied in a single knot and tucked away into the obi's top edge. A certain amount of the obi-age should remain visible for accent; young girls tend to leave more obi-age showing than older women.

8 At this point, you've come about as close as you're going to get to dressing like a traditional Japanese woman. You probably feel a bit like a tree trunk, enveloped in hundreds of concentric rings of fabric. Wearing a kimono does not encourage brisk activity; it's meant to make you elegant, decorative—and slow-moving.

KIMONO-A-GO GO!

SHIROMUKU: the all-white kimono worn by the traditional Japanese bride to signify her role as a pure maidservant to the gods.

FURISODE: the bright-colored formal kimono worn only by young unmarried women.

YUKATA: the summer kimono made of lightweight cotton, usually in a blue-and-white stenciled design. Prior to the Edo period, yukata were worn only by the upper class going to and from the bath. Nowadays, everyone wears them going to and from the bath.

"Oriental" Fragrance

Scent of an Oriental

The first perfume classified as "oriental" was Jicky by Guerlain, a women's fragrance which dates back to 1889. Old Spice was the first oriental scent for men, released in 1937, and still being purchased as a default Father's Day present today. In the 1960s hippie culture, consumers began to prefer aromas evocative of a natural earthiness, such as patchouli and sandalwood, and oriental fragrances became especially popular. The 1970s saw a shift toward fruity scents, although Opium, released in 1977, was a bestseller throughout the 1980s.

Recently, the demand for heavy, intense oriental scents has been replaced with a new category called "floriental," which blends top-notes of lighter florals such as jasmine and rose, with bottom-notes of the traditionally "heavy" oriental scents such as musk or oak moss. Bridges, named after the hit book and movie Bridges of Madison County, is a "floriental" scent containing jasmine, ylang ylang, rose, and orange blossom top notes, along with fruit and cocoa middle notes, and woody, vanilla bottom notes. Is there any reason why this combination should bring to mind Clint Eastwood and Meryl Streep in a passionate, Midwestern-midlife menage?

We suspect the connection is in the woody, vanilla bottom notes.

So what exactly is an "oriental" fragrance? Apparently, not even the fragrance industry can tell you for sure. Elvis Costello once said that "writing about music is a bit like dancing to architecture," and the same might be said about trying to describe a perfume in words. According to fragrance researchers Haarmann & Reimer Corporation, "floral" scents comprise 65 per cent of the perfume market, "oriental" perfumes comprise 25 per cent, and "chypre" 10 per cent. But while "floral" is a fairly easy concept to grasp (just think of, well, flowers), the scent of an "oriental" is a bit more...inscrutable. (And chypre? Your first challenge is pronouncing it. Chypre, or "chai-per," is a sharp, musky Mediterranean spice.)

Some industry sources point to certain spice combinations as being the source of that oriental odor. Others describe an oriental scent as "erotic, sultry, and mysterious"—which would seem to imply that an "occidental" scent would be "frigid, obvious, and banal." Luckily, there is no "occidental" scent.

Some even say you can judge an "oriental" perfume by the color of its bottle, which tends to be deep red, gold, or black. The fact is, what makes a scent "oriental" seems to stem partly from the imagination. Annette Greene, Executive Director of the Fragrance Foundation, believes that the mysterious and sexual connotations of the "oriental" category derive partly from the image of "incense dens in China." And oriental scents tend to be intense and heavy, with a higher concentration of aromatics, which give off a warm and intimate aroma that is often perceived as sensual.

Of course, it would seem to make more sense (no pun intended) to classify fragrances by ingredients rather image. The Haarmann & Reimer *Book of Perfume* defines oriental scents as "spicy, sweet, and heavy" perfumes containing "ingredients that are reminiscent of fragrances from the East." Bob Foster, Vice President of Fine Fragrance Development at H&R, believes that the oriental category may have derived from the spice routes from the East, which delivered to the West spices such as myrhh, cinnamon, and clove, all of which are characteristic of oriental perfumes. This does not mean that oriental perfume ingredients are native to Asia, although some are. For example, sandalwood, jasmine, and patchouli and the oil of the costus root are common ingredients in oriental perfumes that are actually native to Asia. The Bulgarian rose is not.

To further add to the confusion, some perfumes which contain ingredients "reminiscent of the East" are *not* "oriental." Christian Dior's Poison, a "sweet floral," contains civetone and orange blossom, ingredients that are not only native to Asia, but have a history of ritual aphrodisiac use [👁195].

To confuse things further, the oriental category is subdivided: "Spicy orientals" are dominated by the smell of brown spices like cinnamon and nutmeg; "amber orientals" are characterized by honey or vanilla notes; and "woody orientals" mix the scents of dried wood and twigs. —A.W.

How to Tie a Sari

Before even beginning to talk about putting on a sari, it should be made clear that there is only one garment among the many clothes and styles in India with that name: A sari is not a *salwar kameez,* a *dhoti,* a *churidar,* a *lainga,* a *ghagra,* or a *kurta pajama,* all of which are pieces of clothing made by cutting and sewing clothing into two or three separate pieces. The sari is an authentic Indian dress, having existed on the subcontinent long before the invasions of the Lodis, the Mughals, and the British. Unlike the others, however, a sari is a single swath of uncut fabric about two feet wide and traditionally, nine yards long (thankfully, these days it's more like six), wrapped and pleated around the waist so that it drapes the legs like a long skirt. At the top, one can wear a close-fitting blouse or *choli*; usually, the midriff remains exposed.

Note that the sari is not a unisex garment: it is worn only by women, or men who wish they were. Moreover, there is an accepted way of wearing it, and not doing so will raise eyebrows in South Asian society. Here's a step-by-step guide on how to wear your sari properly and with pride. —A.M.

TYING A SARI: AN EXPERT TALKS

To start, you'll need: the sari itself, a petticoat—a pencil-shaped slip with a drawstring waist, preferably the same color as the sari—and a blouse, usually made to your measurements by a tailor (but a stretchy little Anna Sui top can work just as well).

1. Put on your blouse and petticoat. Being stark naked will not make any of the following easier.
2. Unfold your ironed sari on to the floor. Pick up the end of the sari that is not decorated. If you are lucky, it is a sari that has been worn by your mother and it already has a "fall" border attached at the first yard of fabric along the bottom to keep it weighted to the floor. Keeping the fall lined up slightly lower than the hem of your petticoat, tuck the top corner of the sari into the petticoat at the waist. Moving from left to right, continue tucking in the sari as you wrap it once around.
3. Now, take the top hem of the sari which you've been tucking into your waist and slide your fingers along it to the other end of the sari, so that the remaining fabric is oriented properly and you don't get it twisted up. Holding the other end of the sari in your right hand (the decorated side, or the pallu), accordion-pleat it, and hand it across the front of your body to your left hand. Moving the fabric which is around you on the floor in a sort of heap, pass the accordion pleat behind your back to your right hand and pull the sari around your hips and waist like a skirt. Pull about a yard of fabric from the decorated end in front of you and throw it over your left shoulder like a sash.
4. Pull all the remaining fabric in front of you so that you have a single long fold of excess fabric. Straighten the front and the back section of the sari so that it becomes an even skirt, with all the hems lined up at the bottom. Again, slide your fingers along the top of the remaining fabric to orient it. Holding the section closest to your right in your right hand, begin to accordion pleat it, like the front of a kilt, putting each pleat on top of the next so that you end up with a flat section of fabric which you'll tuck into your petticoat at the top.
5. At this point, you could put a big safety pin through the pleats and sari beneath to hold it all in place while you're dancing—"safety" being the operative word here—but traditionally, any kind of fastening is frowned upon. You should now also make any necessary adjustments to the sash-portion on your shoulder. Here, too, you might consider the judicious use of a safety pin—pinning it to the blouse to keep it from falling down or getting stuck in the door of the car. However, be careful here: I once pinned a too-large blouse to my bra and the sari pallu to that, and reached gracefully across a dinner table only to have all three pieces of clothing fall off at once.

Other methods of sari-tying involve having the pallu at the front rather than the back, and clever tying of the pallu. You might also consider taking the last bit of sari and pulling it between your legs so that the sari becomes a sort of trouser, a style favored on the docks in Bombay. For modern wearers, well-placed pins are a must. They will keep your clothing from fluttering to the floor—embarassing, no matter how ethereal it might look. And please note: If your sari gets caught in a subway door, the pleats and petticoat reassure that you will not spin around like a top and end up naked on the platform. That is a myth. —A.M.

SO YOU WANT TO BE A SILK FARMER...

Here's a quick and easy 12-step program for getting started.

WHAT YOU'LL NEED

One (1) pregnant moth of the cultivated silkworm, *Bombyx mori*.

One (1) or more mulberry trees, as a source of fresh mulberry leaves. These are the only thing silkworms eat.

Spinning equipment

A warm climate, approximating China in the springtime.

DIRECTIONS

1 Place your knocked-up moth on a tray in a temperature-controlled, antiseptically clean environment.

2 Let the moth lay its eggs. There should be 500 to 700.

3 Remove the moth from the tray. Kill the moth if desired.

4 Incubate the eggs under a heat source and let them hatch. This will take a while.

Silk

According to Chinese legend, the mysteries of silk were unraveled by a 14-year-old girl. In 2640 BC, the "Yellow Emperor" Huang Di instructed his favorite teenage wife, Empress Xi Ling Shi, to do something productive with the empty cocoons of moths that were ruining mulberry trees on the palace grounds. The young Empress dutifully studied the life-cycle of the moth, watching in wonder as it went from worm to cocoon. On the day that the moth emerged from its wrappings, the Empress took the cocoon inside to show to her ladies-in-waiting, who were calling her for her bath.

In her excitement, the Empress accidentally dropped the cocoon into the hot tub water, and watched in amazement as the gummy substance holding the cocoon together dissolved, revealing delicate strands of fiber. (Another version of this legend had the ladies calling the Empress to tea, whereupon she dropped the cocoon into her teacup. Xi Ling Shi was smart and beautiful, but apparently not the most graceful woman in China.) She brought the damp fiber to the attention of the Emperor, noting that it could be spun into thread; the Emperor gave her a pat on the head and the run of the palace grounds, whereupon she began cultivating silkworms and making the Emperor new clothes out of fine silk fabric.

Of course, for the more literal of mindset, *The Chronicles of Chou-King,* compiled in 2200 B.C., describes a gift of silk garments made to the Emperor Qin Tian by the people of the "Sacred Province" of Shandong. The *Chronicle* incidentally states that silk culture originated there on the banks of the Huang He, or Yellow River. Whether you accept the *Chronicle*'s chronicle or the more picturesque story of Xi Ling Shi and Huang Di, one undisputed fact is that the secrets of silk production remained a closely kept secret in China for nearly 2,500 years. Chinese imperial law prohibited the export of silkworm moth eggs and mulberry

SCARFING THE SECRETS OF SILK

So how did sericulture's secrets get out to the rest of Asia, and then the world? A number of competing myths exist:

- **According to Japanese legend, around 300 A.D., the Japanese nobility hired a couple of Korean thugs to kidnap four Chinese maidens who subsequently—under coercion—revealed all.**
- **A slightly more palatable, if duller, version of the silk-export legend has Chinese refugees bringing sericulture to Korea circa 200 B.C. Five hunded years later, Korean nobles traded silkworms to Japan in exchange for military aid.**
- **Around 200 BC, the sly Prince of Khotan, an ancient Mongolian territory in eastern Turkestan, coveted the secrets of silk. In order to wrest them from the hands off the Han, he arranged to marry a daughter of the Chinese emperor. In secret, the prince convinced his bride-to-be to smuggle some silkmoth eggs and mulberry seeds in the lining of her headdress so that she would be able to continue her pasttime of making silk in her new home. (As a member of the Imperial family, the princesswas immune to such indelicacies as customs searches.) Once established in Khotan, sericulture spread throughout Central Asia, and then to India.**
- **Meanwhile, Chinese legend has it that silk was brought to the West in 552 A.D. by two expatriate Persian monks, who smuggled silkworm eggs and mulberry seeds out of China in the hollows of their bamboo walking canes. Once back in their native Constantinople, they established the city as Western world's center of sericulture and China's primary competitor in the production of raw silk.**

tree seeds under penalty of death; until 1150 B.C., no one except Chinese royals could even wear silk. The trade of silk to foreigners was initiated by the Qin emperor, Qin Shi Huang Di (not to be confused with the original Yellow Emperor, although his adoption of the title was an unhumble reference to that legendary monarch); in fact, he initiated the building of the Great Wall as an attempt to protect silk caravans from the ravenous Hun tribes. By the time of the subsequent Han Dynasty (206 B.C. to 220 A.D.), the "Silk Road," or overland caravan route of the silk trade, was firmly established, and silk export had developed into a full-scale industry.

> **"One undisputed fact is that the secrets of silk production remained a closely kept secret in China for nearly 2,500 years. This is because Chinese imperial law prohibited the export of silkworm moth eggs and mulberry tree seeds, under penalty of death."**

SILK COMING AND GOING

Once the ancient Chinese secret was out, silk production flourished in countries the world over. China, of course, continued to be the world's biggest producer of silk, due to the lucrative trade of the caravans of the Silk Road, which extended through India to Baghdad, Damascus, and other Middle Eastern trade centers. From there, silk textiles and raw silk were re-exported to Europe.

By the 12th century A.D., Italy had mastered the production of silk, and Italian Renaissance silk is still regarded as some of the finest ever made. The French city of Lyon also became a silk textiles center, assisted by government subsidies on mulberry orchards, and was a major silk power by the 17th century. French Huguenots and other emigres to England established a native silk industry there as well, though one which never competed with Italy or China for quality or fineness of work.

In Asia, the Japanese silk industry had been firmly established by 600 A.D., and the careful breeding and development of Japanese silkworms soon led to a product of incomparable quality. Japanese production peaked in 1934; until 1941 (when the War eliminated trading ties between the two nations), 85 percent of Japanese silk was exported to the U.S. India, which was producing wild, or tussah, silk as early as 1400 B.C., never developed a prosperous cultivated silk industry; however, tussah silk, though inferior in quality, is also popular, and India remains its largest producer.

In the United States, although the climate for raising silkworms is excellent, the high cost of labor and lack of suitable mulberry trees has prevented American sericulture from becoming a commercially viable industry. —D.G.

SILK FABRICS

BROADSILK: silk wider than 18"

CHARMEUSE: satin, shiny on one side and dull one on the other

CHINA SILK: a lightweight, plain-weave silk or silk-rayon blend

DUPPIONI: irregularly slubbed fabric woven from silk reeled from two cocoons spun by adjacent worms peau de soie—a thin, soft satin

PONGEE: a wild, or tussah, silk

SARI SILK: a very lightweight silk handwoven in India for saris

SATIN: a smooth, lustrous fabric woven by allowing warp threads to "float" over weft threads

SHANTUNG: a tussah silk named for the Chinese province where it originated

5 Once they've hatched, feed the silkworms fresh mulberry leaves every few hours.

6 In five weeks, the worms will be fully grown and three inches long.

7 Place the worms on a bed of clean straw and watch them spin their cocoons. The silk filament come out of the worm's butt in a series of delicate figure eights—truly a fascinating sight.

8 Now that the worms have finished spinning their cocoons, you can kill them, too. Heating the cocoons in an oven will do.

9 Drench the cocoons in hot water to soften the gelatinous protein called sericin, which binds the cocoons together.

10 Remove the soaked filaments and wind them on a reel. Each filament is extremely fine, so the filaments from five to ten cocoons should be twisted together into a single fiber. A machine called a "filature" comes in handy here.

11 This raw twisted silk is still very thin, so twist it some more, and then ply it with another strand of silk yarn and twist it again. This step is called "throwing," and usually requires expensive machinery.

12 Go ahead and weave something. Silk fabric is used for parachutes, due to its lightness and tensile strength. If you have no use for a parachute, silk is also a fine fabric for clothing—light, durable, and warm.

JAPANESE TATTOO TYPES

Japanese tattoo artists don't ink "originals." They choose from a selection of classic symbols:

FLORA • PEONY: wealth and good fortune; often inked onto gamblers. CHRYSANTHEMUM: long life and health. CHERRY BLOSSOMS: the impermanence of life. MAPLE LEAVES: very popular as a pattern for fleshing out a full-body design.

FAUNA • LIONS AND TIGERS: Popular because they were featured in the tattoos of traditional Chinese heroes. CARP: Famous for their masculine qualities: They swim upstream, and when caught, sit stoically while waiting to be cut. DRAGONS: Can symbolize a number of things depending on the number of their claws (for example, an imperial dragon has five); position (in a coil, stretched out, or running); and color (different hues suggest different elements). In general, however, they symbolize wisdom and power **[👁236]**

MYSTICAL • PRAYERS: Messages to Buddha may be the oldest subject matter for Asian tattoos; the Chinese were tattooing characters on their backs 7,000 years ago. FUDO, THE GUARDIAN OF HELL: Fudo wields a flaming sword in one hand and rope in the other; he appears scary, but really, he's a good guy. THE DEVA KINGS: These two guardians of Buddhism always appear as a pair.

A Body of Work

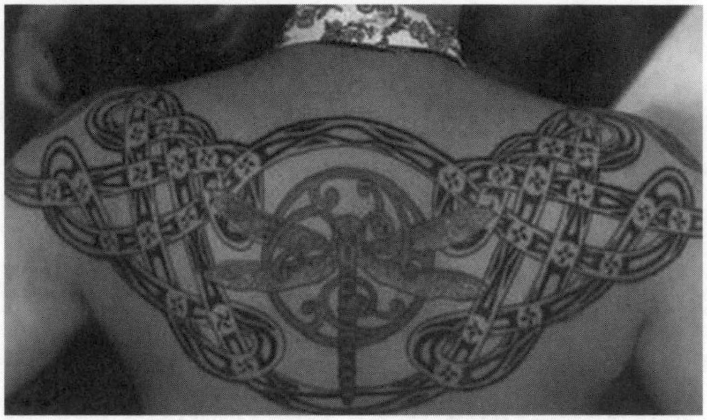

Anchors, flags, hearts, Mom. Here in the States, the word "tattoo" has traditionally conjured up visions of drunk frat boys going under the needle on a dare, or military types inking a traditional American icon or the name of a girl back home on a spare bicep. Today, however, Modern Primitives throughout the world are exploring tattooing—or "body art"—as an aesthetic, and even stimulating experience. This tattooing vogue has led to a broadening of the art's horizons here in the States as well, meaning that those looking for a tattoo no longer have to wear their hearts on their sleeves, so to speak: Common options for a contemporary tat-enthusiast include many with origins in Asia, where the art of tattooing has thrived and evolved through thousands of years of tradition, and Micronesia, where tattooing is central to the maturity rites of many cultures.

TATTOOING IN JAPAN

Like many art forms we consider quintessentially Japanese, the Japanese art of tattooing probably originated in China. Seven thousand years ago, it was customary to mark the backs of Chinese generals with characters reading "Loyalty to the Emperor." The Japanese took this practice and inverted it to indicate social unacceptability: Criminals and lawbreakers were marked as such by tattoos. By the 1600s, this system had become so precise that carefully placed symbols indicated exactly what crime a person had committed and where it happened. Eventually, the wearers of such markings either hid or embellished their tattoos with illustrations, and the practice of marking criminals faded away.

Pictorial tattoos made a brief comeback in the late 18th century, perhaps due to factors such as the banning of fancy kimonos during those austere times and the popularity of the Chinese novel *The Water Margin*, which featured tattooed rebels as underground heroes. Full-body tattoos became especially popular among lower-class workers such as firefighters and carpenters. Then, almost a hundred years later when Japan was opened to the West, tattooing was banned as bad for business. Fortunately for tattoo fans, the artistry managed to survive: Japanese tattoos, which are traditionally created with a sharpened bamboo needle, are amongst the most richly detailed and vividly colorful of any in the world.

Today, tattooing in Japan, like in America, is largely an underground art, catering mostly to insiders and criminals. To get an appointment with a tattoo master, connections are required; only a small handful of tattooers still wield the customary tools and style, and they can choose their canvasses selectively, demanding nearly any price they like. In contrast, American tattoo artists such as Don Ed Hardy and Bill Salmon (who studied with Japanese masters Horihide and Horyoshi II and III) will give anyone with the time, money, and commitment a full-body tattoo of the same approximate quality.

THE MARKS OF MICRONESIA

The dark, slashlike tattoo designs of Pacific cultures such as Borneo and Samoa also have a rich past. Indeed, the word "tattoo" descends from the Samoan word tatao, which, as Captain James Cook discovered in 1769, refers to the all-black skin markings used to indicate the social status of adult males. These days, tattooing as a rite of passage in the Pacific is less common, and traditional designs can usually only be seen on older men.
—E.N., M.W.

A Quilt of Asian Textiles

"From 1600 to 1800, India was the greatest exporter of textiles the world has ever known, and her fabrics penetrated almost every market of the civilized world."
—from *Origins of Chintz* (London: Her Majesty's Stationery Office, 1970)

American culture is draped in Indian cloth, and many words in our lexicon of fabric derive from Hindi. Beginning with basic cotton, textiles were a major export from India aboard the ships of Europe's various East India Companies—first the Portuguese, followed by the Dutch, the English, the Danes, and the French. Indeed, if you inspect the label of this traditional American quilt closely, it actually reads "Made in India." —D.G.

MADRAS

Madras, that peculiarly preppie fabric, is associated with "plaid" the way tweed is associated with "itchy brown wool." Originally, however, "madras" was a general term referring to any coarse-spun, hand-woven cotton produced in the former state of Madras in southeastern India. The British East India Company founded a trading post at Madras in 1640, and distributed madras throughout Europe in white, solid, striped, and checked patterns. However, in the 19th century, after observing festive colonials prancing around in Scottish tartan kilts, local weavers were inspired to create the design by which madras became famous—the madras plaid.

In the late 19th century, Brooks Brothers made madras synonymous with golf; in 1937, the fashion quotient of the colorful fabric took another leap with a bold spread in the pages of Esquire, featuring madras swim trunks as worn by the snooty locals of Southampton and Newport.

The fact that vegetable-dyed madras textiles had a tendency to bleed wasn't a problem for swimwear, but it did prove upsetting to customers who bought madras shirts sold by the Hathaway company a few years later. Marketing wunderkind David Ogilvy helped reverse customer attitude by proclaiming the bleeding effect to be a positive—even "magical"—thing; fading, announced his ad copy, was "guaranteed."

In the late 1940s, madras sport jackets were all the rage, followed by madras Bermuda shorts in the 1950s, and a general madness for madras of all kinds in the 1960s. In the 1970s, weavers in India changed the dyeing process to stanch the fabric's bleeding, which made it even more appealing to designers the world over.

Today, madras has entered the canon of style classicism as an essential element in the closets of buttoned-down traditional dressers. Lord knows what country clubs would look like today had the weavers of madras taken a more local model for their ultimate pattern—say, a stray leopard.

PAISLEY

The mention of paisley—the weird decorative design that seems, to the uninitiated, to swarm with colorful bacteria—is likely to bring many contradictory things to mind: Preppie power-tie prints. Hippies on acid trips. The Artist Formerly Known as Prince.

None of these, of course, give any indication of the pattern's true origins, which link a small region in northern India, Kashmir, with an even smaller town in Scotland—the village of Paisley.

Those Squiggly Things—What Gives?

When examined closely by those with an appropriate background in Indian history and textile design, the paisley print's distinctive protozoan shape reveals itself instead to be the *boteh,* a stylized Indian symbol of the "Tree of Life." Originally,

OTHER FAR-EAST FABRICS

CALICO
Originally the term for any cotton cloth from Calicut, India, but eventually denoting textiles with insipid, small-scale floral designs of the "bread-and-butter" variety, known as such because they always sell. By the 1850s, every general store in the U.S. carried these cheesy cotton prints. Laura Ashley and the costume designer for Little House on the Prairie made them momentarily fashionable in the early '80s.

CHINTZ
From the Anglicized plural of Hindi chint, meaning "variegated or spotted," it's calico with a dust-defying sheen. In India, the waxy glaze was rubbed onto the cotton textile by hand, using shells or smooth stones. By the mid 17th century, Dutch and English traders began ordering fabric makers in India to produce chintz with the large floral designs that now characterize this shiny, happy fabric, making it popular for upholstery and curtains.

CASHMERE
The fine wool from the undercoat of the Kashmir goat, found in that region of India, as well as in Asia and the Middle East. Most cashmere now comes from Inner Mongolia. Once a year in June, the goats molt, which yields only around four ounces of usable

fleece—enough, perhaps, for one pricey mitten. Cashmere is called pashmina in India and first caught the world's attention when it was made into highly coveted "paisley" shawls (see PAISLEY).

SEERSUCKER

From Hindi sirsaker (derived from Persian shir-o-shaker, literally meaning "milk and sugar"), this summerweight fabric of cotton, linen, or rayon is distinctively puckered and usually striped in thin bands of blue.

GUNNY

From Hindi gani, "sack." Gunny cloth, gunnysack, and gunny-bag are all words derived from this coarse, jute-fiber fabric. It was used in India to make sacks to hold, ship, and store trade goods; fortunately for the fashion victimized, no designer has yet discovered a wearable means of incorporating this rough and scratchy textile into their couture lines, though R&D teams are probably working to solve this problem as we speak.

these were the traditional design embroidered on woolen shawls in Northern India's Kashmir region. Woven from the downy underfleece of the Kashmir goat—thus their later, corrupted name "cashmere"—the shawls were reputedly worn by the more fashion-forward of ancient Rome, and, in subsequent centuries, found their way to Persia, Russia, and China.

By the end of the 16th century, the Mogul emperor of India, Akbar the Great, decided that the paisley shawls were a terrific export concept, and stepped up their production. (That is, as much as one can step up production of a handwoven item that takes up to five years to complete.) In the 1770s, the English East India Company was the first major importer of the shawls, but the paisley shawl didn't come into real vogue in Europe until Napoleon mistakenly gave one to his Empress Josephine (the shawls were meant to be worn strictly by men). Regardless of her conquering hubby's faux pas, Josephine was delighted, and collected many more. The Empress's taste became the taste of the empire. By the early 1800s, surging demand had transformed the cashmere paisley shawl into a fashion statement available only to the extremely wealthy, and a well-crafted specimen could cost as much as a Parisian townhouse.

Naturally, something so desirable was bound to be copied in a lower quality, yet more affordable fashion. (On such were Hong Kong commercial empires built, not to mention The Limited.) Weavers in Scotland, England, and France began making imitations of the shawls almost as soon as they became popular. By the 1830s, Paisley, Scotland, had become famous for its Indian shawl knock-offs, mass-produced in silk and wool on mechanical Jacquard looms, which, having just been invented, were all the rage—capable of duplicating the entire five-year effort of a master Kashmiri artisan in a matter of minutes. Or close enough, anyway.

But rock bottom in the affordability-for-quality exchange had not yet been hit: An even cheaper method than mechanical weaving was the printing of the paisley pattern onto plain woven cloth. Soon enough, other items of clothing, such as dresses and skirts, were appearing in the paisley print. By the late 1860s, printed paisley shawls were available to the most budget-conscious women of the working classes. Naturally, this made them completely superfluous for upper-class snobs to own. In 1869, the paisley shawl (imitation or otherwise) got the final boot, when a new fashion must arrived: the bustle. Since this artificial booty-enhancing chaser interfered with the drape of the shawl, the paisley fad soon dropped dead in its tracks. Still, like the tree it symbolizes, the print is perennial. To this day it remains a popular one—worn, once again, mostly by men.

INDIGO

Nowadays, you can pick your denim from a spectrum of colors broader than the rainbow, and nearly as broad as Calvin Klein's ego. Without indigo, however, cowboys and construction workers may have been stuck with "blackjeans" from the very beginning. Indigo, the dye that put the blue in blue jeans, has as its source plants of the genus *Indigofera,* which have been harvested in India since 4000 B.C. for use as a paint, cosmetic, and a permanent, deep-blue dye for textiles.

It wasn't until world-traveller Marco Polo took his 13th century jaunts to India that tales of this bright blue marvel came to the West; then, in the 14th century, merchants from Venice and Genoa began importing the dye from Muslim territories in the Mediterranean, coining the name "indigo" in reference to its place of origin: The word, derived from an Italian dialect, is based on the Latin term *indicum,* meaning "from India."

Italy maintained control of indigo distribution, petering it slowly out to the rest of Europe, which at first was less than enthusiastic. Why? Simple economics. For centuries, Europeans had been dying things blue with a plant called woad, which produces the same colorant in indigo—indigotin—except in a concentration 30 times weaker.

In order to protect domestic woad production, in the late 16th century, Germany and France banned the use of indigo, even going so far as to nickname indigo the "devil's dye." However, indigo, which can produce blue-tones ranging from cobalt to midnight, was clearly superior, and England and Holland, which had no home-grown woad industry, soon told the lesser dye to hit the, er, woad, and embraced the new, truer blue.

Indeed, by the 18th century, England had monopolized trade of the dye through its indigo plantations in colonial India, and begun to rake in profits as demand for indigo blue–printed fabrics increased in Europe and the New World. In 1740, Indigofera crops were planted in the Caribbean and the southern U.S., where the climate was sultry enough for its cultivation. Indigo became one of the first American colonial exports, and by the 1770s, a million pounds a year were being shipped back to England from Georgia and the Carolinas alone. Slaves harvested the crop; a common feature of most colonial homes was an indigo dye pot by the hearth. Then, in 1873, a dry goods salesman named Levi Strauss used the dye for his first pair of Double X Blue Denim 501s, and the rest, as they say, is history.

KHAKIS

Second only to jeans in ubiquity, America's most versatile pants—khakis—first arose in the battlefields of the Indian desert. Khaki, touted by Gap ads as worn by everyone from the Bhagwan Shree Rajneesh to Marcel Marceau, began simply as a color designed to camouflage sniper-shy British troops stationed on the sub-continent. Alternately spelled "khakee," "kharkee," or "kharki," khaki is the Hindi word for "dust-colored," derived from the Persian *khak,* meaning "dust." The blue denim of jeans is associated with working-class utility; khaki, on the other hand, is identified with safaris, expeditions, and the smug colonial elegance of the British Raj. Just take a look at the ads of Banana Republic or Polo by Ralph Lauren.

TIE-DYE

You know it as an earmark of American hippiedom, and a low-water-mark in American style. But—like incense, TM, and Yoko Ono—this quintessential '60s fashion statement may have its origins in Asia.

Those in the know know that tie-dyeing began as two separate textile techniques, called *plangi* and *ikat*. The former process creates the ugly rainbow-colored sunburst patterns you may still find on the chests of California surf hounds. The latter, a much more complex technique that involves tying together the threads of a fabric before they are woven together, can create more subtle—and often very beautiful—detailed designs.

Both forms involve binding parts of textiles prior to dyeing them; the sealed-off tied portions remain white against the colored background of the dye. Early examples of tie-dyeing were depicted on the walls of the Ajanta caves in India, as early as the 6th century A.D.—long before the birth and death of Jerry Garcia.

The earliest samples of actual plangi and ikat textiles, dating back to the 7th and 8th centuries, have been found in Japan, although evidence suggests that these textiles were brought to Japan from China, and may have been woven in India. Anthropologists now say that tie-dyeing either originated in Asia and spread to other continents, or developed independently and more or less simultaneously in Asia, Africa, and the Americas.

Still, whatever its precise origins, tie-dyeing is now found in all parts of the world—though, thankfully, not as frequently today as in decades past.

A KHAKI HISTORY

1846—A moonlighting British Army officer named Sir Harry Lumsden creates a new outfit for his soldiers: a light smock and wide pants, stained with mulberry juice to produce a yellow-brown color called "khaki."

1856—The Magistrate of Meerut forms the infamous Khaki Risala ("Dusty Squadron") to patrol the Delhi Road and keep it free of Indian mutineers.

1857—Recognizing that khaki-wearers get shot less frequently, all British regiments begin dyeing their white linen uniforms with tea, tobacco juice, or mud to produce the khaki hue.

1884—The first khaki uniforms are mass-produced in England, for use by troops in India.

1898—During the Spanish American War, khaki is adopted as an official color for summer dress by the American military. Fabric to make the pants is purchased in bulk from China; the baggy work pants are nicknamed "chinos"—a pan-Asian connection.

1949—Khaki pants make the transition to civilian life after WWII, when G.I.s wear their uniforms home and decide their khakis are too comfortable to take off.

1953—Levi Strauss & Co. debuts its first line of khaki pants. The new khakis become popular among college students.

1989—Aging Baby Boomers begin a trend of dressing more casually at work, which helps fuel the demand for khakis. The second American khaki revolution is in full swing.

TRENDS AND PHENOMENA

"In 1953, 'Made in Japan' was regarded as meaning very cheap, poor quality. When we started up our exports, the regulations said we had to put 'Made in Japan' on them. But we were ashamed, so we made the label as small as possible. Later, when we announced that we intended to build factories in the U.S. and in Britain to make televisions, we saw a very odd reaction. Our customers preferred to buy Sony television sets labeled 'Made in Japan'."

—Sony co-founder and former chairman Akio Morita

Asian Adoptees

"If you love your own children, love those of others."
—ancient Korean proverb

Since the 1940s, many Americans have taken the above proverb to heart, adopting children from abroad whose families have been lost or displaced by war or poverty; the vast majority of these adoptees have been Asian. According to the Immigration and Naturalization Service, in 1994 Americans adopted 8,200 children from other countries, 39 percent of them from East Asia. The earliest Asian intercountry adoptions involved Eurasian children fathered by American soldiers after the end of World War II in Japan (1945) and the Korean War (1953); soon, however, the placement of Asian children in Western homes became an institution. China's Communist Revolution in 1949 resulted in large numbers of orphans, many of whom were placed abroad. Similarly, the Vietnam War also resulted in many orphans, as well as abandoned children fathered by occupying G.I.'s; over two weeks in April 1975, the U.S.—evacuating from a miserable defeat in Vietnam—attempted one of the most phenomenal rescue efforts in history, "Operation Babylift," evacuating 3,303 orphans to new homes and families in America and in Europe. Rampant poverty in Thailand, the Philippines, India, and Bangladesh has also prompted the beginning of intercountry adoptions by would-be parents in the U.S. Meanwhile, due to economic struggles following the Korean War and Korea's tradition of patrilineage (which made children with unknown fathers unadoptable), by the 1980s, Korea was the leader in Asian adoptions, providing the U.S. with an average of 4,440 children each year.

Jeffery and Elizabeth Spring with their children Jonathan and Kirstin

William Pierce, president of the National Council on Adoption, says that the popularity of Korean adoptees may have been the result of "whiz kid" stereotypes [👁**331**]. "Parents think 'Korean' equals 'high achiever' kids," he says. "As if adopting a Korean kid means you automatically have a computer scientist." During the 1988 Seoul Olympics, however, North Korean critics and the American media joked that children had become South Korea's largest export. Embarrassed, the Korean government enforced stricter restrictions on overseas adoptions.

The American demand for children didn't abate, however, and the slack was quickly taken up by adoptees from mainland China; the number of Chinese children adopted by Americans rose from 27 in 1990 to 2,049 in 1995—the highest number of U.S. adoptions from any country, according to Debra Smith, director of the National Adoption Information Clearinghouse, and a number that continues to increase. Because of the Chinese traditional preference for sons, many of the children provided for overseas adoption are female, a factor which matters far less to American parents.

RESOURCES FOR ADOPTIVE PARENTS

Adoptive Families of America is a nonprofit support group for adoptive parents. 3333 Highway 100 North, Minneapolis, MN 55422. (612) 535-4829. The **National Council for Adoption** is a nonprofit research and education center. If you write to them, they'll provide you with a free packet of information on adoption. 1930 17th St. Northwest, Washington, D.C. 20009. —C.Y.

ADOPTING IN ASIA

While one adoptive mother likens the process to "buying a new car—the paperwork is a pain, but you go over there for 10 days, spend $15,000 and come home with a baby," remember, a baby can't be returned. If you're still set on intercountry adoption, here's a brief primer:

1 First, consider all available alternatives. Most intercountry adopters are unable to adopt domestically, often because they're over 45, the maximum age for domestic adoption. In addition, many intracountry adoptive parents are single women, who are not restricted from adopting in China.

2 Be prepared to pay. The average cost of an overseas adoption is between $10,000 and $20,000; $5,000 of this goes to the U.S. agency that arranges the referral, and $3,000 or so goes to the foreign orphanage (Chinese orphanages demand that the fee be paid in new U.S. $100 bills). The remainder goes toward travelling to pick up the child.

3 Contact a private adoption agency or an adoption attorney. (Public agencies don't perform foreign adoptions.) Immigration law requires that a child be orphaned, abandoned, or have a single surviving parent in order receive an "orphan visa" to be adopted into an American family. Legal counsel is advised.

4 And, as you raise your child, remember: Cultural sensitivity is everything. Love, of course, is essential, but regardless of the adage, it doesn't conquer all.

Asian Pets

Over the decades, lonely folks looking for animal companionship have flung their arms out to increasingly remote regions of the globe; many of the world's most popular pets originate from Asia (though, regrettably, private ownership of the most beloved cuddly beasts of the East, giant pandas **[👁335]**, is utterly illegal. Break it to the kids gently). —J. R.

THE STANDARD GOLDFISH (*Cyprinidae*)
Once a gray, bland-colored variety of carp from China and Japan, the Chinese bred goldfish to produce miniature varieties with beautiful colorings and feathery fins. Goldfish first became a U.S. novelty in 1878, and have been a staple amusement park prize (not to mention an unwilling participant in fraternity hazings) ever since. Goldfish farms all over the country breed fish in colors including red, gold, orange, bronze, white, black, gray, and brown.

THE CARP (Koi fish, *Cyprinidae*)
The bubble-nosed koi carp, originally native to Chinese lakes and streams, quickly became key elements in Japanese gardens; though edible (the U.S. Fish Commission brought the koi's garden-variety cousins to America in 1877, and now they've propagated everywhere, especially the Mississippi River), their beautiful colors make them more appropriate as aesthetic, rather than culinary objects.

SIAMESE FIGHTING FISH (discus fish, bettas)
A popular American pet fish since the 1970s, this commercially produced and exported Singapore piscine breed often come with certificates proving their unusual pedigree. More colorful and easier to maintain than goldfish, the males of the species build nests made of tiny bubbles on the water's surface to hold the eggs of their mates. Their name derives from the fact that males placed together in an enclosed tank will fight to the death; yes, betta duels were historically held, but it's a nasty, cruel sport. Don't submit to the temptation.

MINIATURE TURTLES
These tiny turtles (usually under four inches long)—smuggled in from mainland China—were outlawed in 1985, because children would put the turtles or their turtle-tainted fingers inside their mouths, resulting in outbreaks of salmonella poisoning. Popular in America since the early 1980s, mini-turtles can be purchased legally if bred in the States in captivity. In China, turtle blood is believed to soothe insomnia and painful childbirth, turtle meat is thought to prolong life, and turtle eggs are esteemed as an aphrodisiac. In the U.S., turtle anything is more likely to cause uncontrollable diarrhea.

VIETNAMESE POT-BELLIED PIGS
The average price for one of these adorable beasts is about $500, though show piglets go for $1000, with some fancy breeds selling for as much as $12,000. As baby piglets, they're silky, small, and cute; note, however, that they quickly grow into 100-pound-plus beasts with enormous stomachs. The American pot-bellied pig craze peaked in the early to mid-1980s, necessitating the brief existence of a National Committee on Pot-Bellied Pigs in Southern California. Born in the wild rather than bred in captivity, the pot-bellied pig must literally be domesticated before it can be owned as a pet; nevertheless, the breed is highly intelligent, and can be housebroken in a matter of days. Municipal zoning has made the ownership of pot-bellied pig illegal in many areas of the country. Also note that pig urine has a pungent, extremely penetrating odor. Think twice before buying your own pet Babe.

SIAMESE CATS

These royal cats from Siam (today's Thailand) originally graced palaces and temples in the 1600s; imported to England and then brought to the in 1865, they've graced many an American lap and armchair ever since. Male Siamese cats are rare in that they're not deadbeat dads: They'll stick around to protect their newborn kittens, rather than abandoning them to the care of their exhausted mother.

AKITA (*Canis Japonicus*)
Originally used for dogfighting in Japan, this breed is best for people experienced in teaching dogs obedience. These fierce and aggressive dogs may attack other dogs during walks; some will automatically hold strangers at bay; still others are prone to biting owners and strangers alike—hard. Despite these personality foibles, the American Kennel Club reports that the popularity of the Akita has surged over the last 10 years. They can weigh up to 100 pounds but don't let them near the kids unless they've been raised around them since puppyhood.

LHASA APSO

These small canines originated in Tibet about 1,000 years ago as palace guard dogs because of their sharp hearing and almost manic state of hyperalertness. Because they're clean, kind to children, obedient, and affectionate, they're very good as household pets. Not surprisingly, their popularity has continued to increase, according to the American Kennel Club.

PEKINESE

This scrunchy-faced toy breed dates back to the 8th century in China, where it was called the "Lion Dog." Sacred to the people of Peking (today's Beijing), the dog was kept away from foreign fur-hungry hands until 1860, when the British military claimed four of the dogs as booty. Pekineses are now available throughout the world.

SHAR-PEI

In the 1970s, this breed was brought back from near extinction by a few Hong Kong and Taiwanese breeders. The shar-pei's distinctive wrinkled skin usually doesn't survive puppyhood, but the breed is loyal, protective, aloof towards strangers, and housebroken virtually from birth (always a plus). Shar-peis are high-priced, but good for city apartments because they're small, alert, and low-maintenance, making them the ideal yuppie accoutrement.

SHIH-TZU

Similar in appearance to the Pekinese, the Shih-tzu was introduced from Tibet into China in the 16th century, when it was customary to present visiting Chinese officials with a pair of these toy dogs. However, they were virtually unknown in the West, until a small number were imported to England in the 1930s. Mainstream American caught on in the late 1970s, and they've been a popular domestic pet ever since.

Movin' on Up: Asian Suburbs

Historically, Asian ethnic enclaves—America's Chinatowns, Koreatowns, and Little Tokyos—arose because Asians weren't readily able to assimilate into mainstream culture. Language and culture barriers made hanging together preferable to hanging separately, while racial discrimination inhibited suburban homeowners from selling to those Asians who wished to move on up and out. In the mid 1960s, however, a new breed of immigrants arrived in the States—young, educated professionals, recruited by a nation eager for fresh blood in engineering, medicine, and other skilled fields. Many of these new immigrants migrated out to affluent neighborhoods in the suburbs. And, as political uncertainty increased in places like Hong Kong and Taiwan, they were joined by migrants motivated by the protection of their economic interests.

By 1990, 25 urban areas in the U.S. had at least 25,000 Asian Americans living in their surrounding suburbs. The average income of these households is $56,300, 23 percent higher than that of urban Asian American households, and these upscale enclaves reflect a strongly middle-class sensibility. Suburban towns with high percentages of Asians are marked by a proliferation of Asian-language publications, Asian-owned businesses catering to Asian tastes, Asian restaurants, and even Asian-language movie theaters. The difference, however, is that—unlike the residents of urban enclaves—suburban Asians preserve their culture out of personal preference, rather than out of necessity.

A LOOK AT MONTEREY PARK

The *Los Angeles Times* called it "the first suburban Chinatown." In the 1960s, Monterey Park, east of Los Angeles, had 38,000 residents, 3 percent of them Asian, mostly Japanese American. Then, in the mid 1970s, Taiwanese developer Frederic Hsieh bought up large tracts of land in the community, and put the word out in Taiwan and Hong Kong that the town was an ideal destination for affluent Chinese immigrants seeking to escape economic and political concerns generated by Mainland Chinese expansion. Monterey Park became known as the "Chinese Beverly Hills"; by the late 1980s, Monterey Park became the second most common settling ground for Asian immigrants in the U.S., second only to New York's Chinatown. Indeed, more Asian immigrants settled in Monterey Park than in the Chinatowns of Los Angeles and San Francisco (the oldest Chinatown in America). By 1994, Monterey Park had 60,000 residents, 56 percent of whom were Asian. Today, Asians own more than half of the community's property and businesses, and most classes at its elementary schools—of which Asian kids are the majority—are taught in both English and Chinese. The town has not been without racial tension, however, as whites and other racial groups have expressed feelings of disenfranchisement. In the mid 1980s, for instance, the Monterey Park city council—which at that time had never had an Asian American member—passed a resolution making English the city's official language. Other city officials proposed decrees banning the use of any foreign language on public signs, and removing foreign-language books from the local library. One leading advocate of this anti-immigrant backlash was resident Frank Arcuri, who said in a radio interview that he'd always "avoided ethnic communities. I never would have felt comfortable.... Now all of a sudden, to have a group come to our city, which in this case is Chinese people, with enough money so they can buy our city, buy our economy, and force their language and culture down our throats. This is what is disturbing to people in Monterey Park." As with most ugly clouds, there was a silver lining: Out of the turmoil came Monterey Park's first Asian American councillor—Judy Chu, a psychologist and second-generation Chinese American, who was elected in 1988. —D.G.

THE MOST ASIAN SUBURBAN AREAS

(Metropolitan areas, followed by the percentage of suburban population that was Asian American in 1990)

- Honolulu, HI, 57.1 percent
- San Jose, CA, 15.6
- San Francisco, CA, 13.5
- Oakland, CA, 12.7
- Los Angeles–Long Beach, CA, 11.5
- Anaheim–Santa Ana, CA, 10.6
- Washington, DC, 5.8
- Middlesex-Somerset, NJ, 5.8
- Bergen-Passaic, NJ, 5.7
- Seattle, WA, 5.2
- Sacramento, CA, 5.1
- San Diego, CA, 5.0
- Chicago, IL, 3.8
- Riverside–San Bernardino, CA, 3.8
- Houston, TX, 3.7
- New York, NY, 3.6
- Newark, NJ, 3.2

SUBURBAN TOWNS WHERE ASIANS ARE AT LEAST 30 PERCENT OF THE POPULATION

- Walnut, CA
- Alhambra, CA
- Rosemead, CA
- South San Gabriel, CA
- San Marino, CA
- San Gabriel, CA
- Daly City, CA

A R S

ON A ROLL

1939—Ford Motors—which overwhelmingly dominates carmaking in Japan, producing 75 percent of all cars sold in that market—is forced to shut down its Yokohama factory. This gives Japanese automakers a chance to build its domestic market, and from there, launch an export-focused growth strategy.

1957—Toyota arrives in the U.S.

1958—Nissan, then selling its cars under the Datsun label, joins Toyota stateside.

1968—Subaru becomes the third Japanese company to enter the U.S. market.

1970—In roll Honda...

1973—...and Mazda.

1973—Arab oil producers shut off the spigot, and the world feels the effects of the gasoline crunch. Japan's small economy cars receive a huge bounce in sales; U.S. car companies dither and lose market share.

1981—Isuzu, a truck manufacturer that entered the market by building cars for GM, decides to sell cars under its own name.

1982—Mitsubishi, which built cars for Chrysler, also goes solo.

1985—Motorcycle manufacturer Suzuki jumps into the market.

1986—A South Korean company joins the ranks of Asian import carmakers: Hyundai's affordable, compact Excel sells 170,000 units in the company's first year.

1994—South Korea's Kia, which began by making the hit econobox Festiva for Ford, makes its small but firm solo debut in the U.S.

Engines from the East
Asian Automobiles

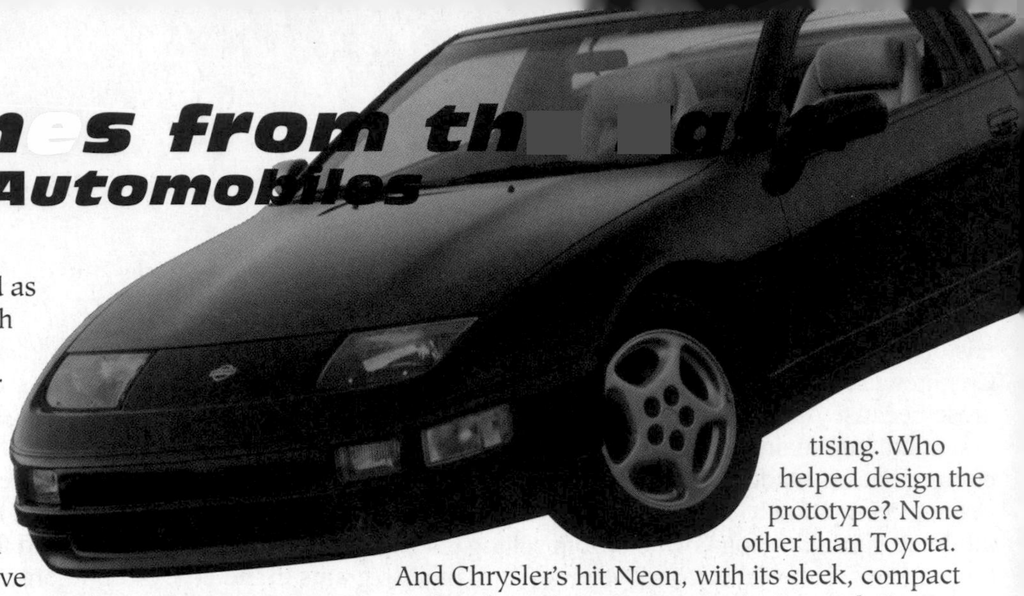

Originally perceived as boxy Tinkertoys with performance as abominable as their prices were cheap, in recent decades, high production standards, positive word of mouth, and clever marketing have helped make Japanese imports a dominant force in the automotive industry. For most of the 1980s, buying a Japanese car was considered downright unpatriotic by those sympathetic to the American auto industry; by the early 1990s, however, polls showed that most American consumers believed Japanese cars are better engineered and more reliable than American cars. Indeed, after two decades of improvement (and lack of real competition from Detroit), Japanese cars have become the new benchmark for quality and affordability.

And meanwhile, Japanese automakers have proven they have more to offer than just economy cars. In 1990, Toyota and Nissan stormed into the high-end land-yacht market with their Lexus and Infiniti marques respectively, offering the same plush interiors and advanced "standard options" previously available only in high-end European and American sedans—at a competitive price. Both were immediate hits, as was Honda's Acura line of upper-crust autos, selling more than 138,000 units in 1990 alone. Meanwhile, Japanese carmakers also charged into another market segment in which Detroit's Big Three once held a monopoly, trucks and sport utility vehicles, with hot-selling models like the Nissan Pathfinder, the Toyota Landcruiser and 4Runner, and the Isuzu Trooper and Rodeo.

American car companies now look to Japan for technological and marketing inspiration. General Motors' Saturn is a popular American car which has captured a huge fan base through its reasonable prices and "different-kind-of-company" advertising. Who helped design the prototype? None other than Toyota. And Chrysler's hit Neon, with its sleek, compact styling, has obvious roots in Japanese design, while the car's ad campaign, in which the car says "Hi!," hearkens back to the fun spirit of the old "Oh what a feeling!" Toyota ads.

These days, the auto industry is still a political sore spot for some, but with many Japanese manufacturers cutting deals with the Big Three, it's often almost impossible to tell whether a car is American or Japanese. But one thing's for sure: more competition means better cars for consumers. —J.Y., L.P.

MULTICULTURAL MOTORS

While car manufacturers are still fond of presenting the auto market as a kind of patriotic battle, the truth is that national distinctions in the auto industry have virtually been erased over the last few decades. Many popular makes of cars have near-identical siblings sold by a transnational counterpart. So what does "Buy American" mean today? Not much: by the turn of the century fewer than half of all cars made in the U.S. will contain enough American-made parts to qualify as "domestic." Here are some examples of auto-crossing that have occurred in recent years:

AMERICAN CARS, MADE BY JAPAN

South Korea's Daewoo Motor Company, which is half-owned by General Motors, produced the Pontiac LeMans subcompact, which peaked in sales in 1988, with 64,000 units sold. Korea's Kia Motors supplied Ford with the Festiva subcompact, which sold 69,000 units each year in 1988 and 1989; after the Festiva was discontinued, Kia built Ford's disastrous Aspire subcompact.

JAPANESE CARS, MADE IN AMERICA

Between 1982 and 1989, Asian auto makers spent $5.5 billion to build new plants in North America.

Honda was the first to set down roots in the U.S., planting itself in Marysville, Ohio. An engine plant sprouted four years later, in 1986, and in 1989 Honda added a second U.S. assembly plant. In 1983, Nissan began making pickup trucks in Smyrna, Tennessee, adding production of the Nissan Sentra to the plant in 1985. In 1984, GM and Toyota embarked on a 12-year joint venture called NUMMI (New United Motor Manufacturing, Inc.), setting up production in Fremont, California. With labor costs low in the U.S. compared to Japan, this made economic sense; it also proved to be a public relations coup, as Japanese companies reaped praise for saving auto worker jobs eliminated by Detroit's Big Three.

BUT WOULD YOU BUY A BONGO FRIENDEE?

In Japan, where English is recognized but not particularly well spoken, car names have a bizarre flavor that often demands renaming of marques and models before they reach American shores. "The use of foreign words is part of the overall trend in Japanese advertising to give a young and exciting image," says industry analyst Steve Usher. "The word itself doesn't have to have any meaning." The following examples certainly make that clear.

Nissan Fairlady—Back in 1970, Nissan—then Datsun—considered calling its new sports car by this decidedly feminine name; the company's U.S. division was appalled, and the car was released under its production code, 240Z. Note that the later 300ZX was actually sold in Japan as the Fairlady, to great success.

Nissan Leopard J. Ferie—Who knows what Nissan was thinking when they thought up this name? In the U.S., consumers know this sedan as the Infiniti J30.

Nissan Sunny—A cute—too cute—name for the middle-sized car known in the U.S. as the Sentra.

Nissan S-Cargo—The quirky automaker also created a microtruck that it sold domestically with a name that sounds like the French word for snail. Japanese consumers didn't care; American purchasers might have shied away from purchasing a slow-moving vehicle that leaves a trail of slime behind it.

Mitsubishi Lettuce—In a kind of zen haze, Mitsubishi created a tiny car named after a salad green and sold it, appropriately enough, in supermarkets. No word on how many Lettuces were eaten by neighboring S-Cargos.

Mazda Bongo Friendee—Had this van only been exported to the U.S. in the 1960s, it would surely have challenged the Volkswagen Van for hippie popularity on the strength of its acid-damaged name alone.

SEPARATED AT BIRTH?

A red-blooded Ford Explorer sport-ute passes by in a cloud of dust, followed shortly thereafter by an imported Mazda Navajo. You do a double-take as you realize that the two cars look and drive exactly the same. No wonder; they're the same car, differing only in label and marketing. Here's a list of similar cars "manufactured" by the Big Three that are actually Asian to the core, with the only distinctions being minor cosmetic differences—or the nameplate.

- **Geo Metro and Suzuki Swift**
- **Geo Prizm and Toyota Corolla**
- **Geo Tracker and Suzuki Sidekick**
- **Chevrolet S Pickup and Isuzu Hombre**
- **Chrysler's Dodge Stealth and Mitsubishi 3000GT (similar engine, slightly different body)**
- **Chrysler's Eagle Talon, Plymouth Laser, and the Mitsubishi Eclipse**
- **Ford Explorer and Mazda Navajo (strangely enough, the Navajo, not the Explorer, was named Motor Trend "Truck of the Year.")**
- **Ford Ranger and Mazda B-series Pickup**
- **Ford Probe and Mazda MX-6 (similar engine and chassis, different body)**
- **Mercury Villager and Nissan Quest (created by Ford/Nissan joint venture)**

THE SECRET MEANINGS OF CAR NAMES

There's an art to creating the perfect name for a new auto, and as imports have become a major segment of the American car market, that art has become increasingly surreal. Part of the reason is language barriers; while international marketers agree that English has proven to be the best tongue in which to name global brands, a poor grasp of the meanings behind nifty-sounding Anglo words has led to some brand-name stumbles for European and particularly Asian manufacturers. Luckily, help has arrived on the scene, with agencies like London's Interbrand and America's Name Lab (famous for naming Honda's Acura line) offering assistance at a price for tongue-tangled marketers. The agencies rely on "brainstorming committees" to come up with possible monikers, or use software programs to assemble random nonsense words from basic phonemes. These potential names are checked against existing trademark databases and researched for possible linguistic shortcomings; names that are already being used within the general motor vehicle category or that have unfortunate secondary meanings are dropped. A promising selection of a few dozen that clear these hurdles are submitted to the client, who then submits them to focus groups. The name with the most positive customer reaction ends up as the winning selection. Not that the process is anywhere near perfect, as the following list of marques currently in manufacture shows:

CAR/COMPANY NAME	WHAT IT MAKES YOU THINK OF	WHAT IT REALLY MEANS
TOYOTA  The company is named after its founder, Kiichiro Toyoda...sort of. The superstitious entrepreneur changed it to "Toyota" because a fortuneteller told him that a name comprised of eight brushstrokes (as Toyota is, in Japanese) would be luckier than one made up of 10. That same fortuneteller also told him that names starting with "C" would sell better—and thus the Toyota Camry, Celica, Corolla, Cressida, and so forth. Hey, it worked—Toyota is one of the best-known (and respected) auto nameplates in the world.		
Avalon (Medium car over $25,000)	A quiet, peaceful place where, ironically, there aren't any cars	The name of the final resting place of King Arthur in British legend.
Camry (Medium car under $25,000)	A Southern tourist's Kodak ("Look at the camry and say cheese!")	Derived from the Japanese *kanmuri* or "crown."
Celica (Sporty car under $25,000)	Breast implants	Derived from the Spanish word for "heavenly" or "celestial."
Cressida (Medium car under $25,000)	Funky salad greens	From one of Shakespeare's lesser plays, *Troilus and Cressida.*
Tercel (Small car)	Absolutely nothing	The Latin word for "one-third"; a member of the falcon family whose males are one-third the size of the females.
LEXUS (Toyota's name for its luxomobile line)	A research database, which is why Mead Data Corporation sued Toyota over infringement of its Lexis-Nexis tradename	A meaningless term (name-generators call them "neologisms") conveying luxury and, presumably, sexiness.
 **HONDA** Named after the its founder, Soichiro Honda, who founded the company after World War II to make motorcycles; the company made its first automobile in the early 1970s.		
Passport (Sport utility vehicle, also the Isuzu Rodeo)	An official travel document	Supposed to convey an absence of borders, but it sounds as if the vehicle is small and flat enough to fit in your pocket.
Prelude (Sporty car under $25,000)	An introduction	Sounds as if this car is an appetizer for something much better and cooler yet to come. So why buy it?
ACURA (Honda's luxury car line)	One of Godzilla's giant rubber foes	Neologism conveying "precision and technological progress."
ISUZU Founded in 1916, Isuzu was Japan's first motor vehicle manufacturer; it achieved its early successes mostly in the truck market, and it continues to be Japan's biggest diesel truck manufacturer and exporter. The company's name means "50 bells"; it is now 34.2 percent owned by GM.		
Oasis (Minivan; also **Honda Odyssey**)	A desert spring, surrounded by vultures and skeletons	Since oases are stationary features of the landscape, this doesn't seem to be the best choice for a moving vehicle.

<table>
<tr><th>CAR/COMPANY NAME</th><th>WHAT IT MAKES YOU THINK OF</th><th>WHAT IT REALLY MEANS</th></tr>
<tr><td colspan="3">MITSUBISHI
The company's zen-infused name literally translates as "three pebbles," but Mitsubishi has spun it to mean "three diamonds." One of Japan's superconglomerates, its parent company Mitsubishi Heavy Industries began building cars in 1917, and later, during World War II, it made the infamous Zero fighter plane.</td></tr>
<tr><td>Galant (Medium car under $25,000)</td><td>A pretentious pronunciation of "gallant"</td><td>A pretentious, misspelled pronunciation of "gallant."</td></tr>
<tr><td>Mirage (Small car)</td><td>A Vegas casino</td><td>Something false or illusionary. Why do you want to buy a car that advertises itself as a fraud?</td></tr>
<tr><td colspan="3">MAZDA
While "Mazda" is the Zoroastrian God of Light, the company actually derived its name from a bastardization of the name—Matsuda—of corporate parent Toyo Kogo's first president. Toyo Kogo began as a bottle cork manufacturer, and began building trucks in the 1930s; it created its first passenger autos in the 1960s. It is now majority-owned and controlled by Ford Motors.</td></tr>
<tr><td>Protege (Small car)</td><td>An apprentice or student</td><td>Why would anyone want to buy a car that makes you think of a someone who's still learning the fundamentals of a trade? Bring me the Maestro.</td></tr>
<tr><td colspan="3">NISSAN

The Nissan Motor Company began in 1911 as the Kwaishinsha Company, founded by engineer Masujiro Hashimoto. The company's first car was 1914's DAT, whose name came from the initials of Hashimoto's partners, Den, Aoyama and Takeuchi. In 1932, the company marketed its first Datsun—originally called the "Datson," for "son of DAT." (The name was altered to make it sound less like the Japanese word for "ruin.") In 1934, after a number of major mergers, Kwaishinsha's name was changed to Nissan, which comes from the phrase Nissan sangyo, meaning "Japanese industry." Big, prestige cars were labeled Nissans; smaller cars continued to be called Datsuns—until 1981, when the Datsun nameplate was dropped entirely. This has proven to be a disaster from which the company still hasn't fully recovered.</td></tr>
<tr><td>Maxima (Medium car under $25,000)</td><td>The absolute most...</td><td>...Except the Maxima isn't (Nissan has saved its best for its Infiniti line); the name sets unrealistic expectations.</td></tr>
<tr><td colspan="3">SUBARU
A subsidiary of Japan's Fuji Heavy Industries conglomerate, the name Subaru means "to unite"; it's also the Japanese name for the group of stars known as the Pleiades, of which six stars are visible to the naked eye. Fuji was formed after World War II by the union of six smaller companies—thus the name and logo, a six-star constellation.</td></tr>
<tr><td>Impreza (Small car)</td><td>An unsightly skin condition</td><td>Another neologism, attempting to suggest "impressive" with a European flair.</td></tr>
<tr><td colspan="3">SUZUKI
Founded by Michio Suzuki as the Suzuki Loom Company in 1909, the company made its first motorcycle engine in 1937 and began producing vehicles in 1952.</td></tr>
<tr><td>Swift (Small car, sold by Chevrolet as the Geo Metro)</td><td>Something really fast</td><td>Named for speed, this buggy doesn't deliver, maxing out at about 70 m.p.h., at which point its chassis disintegrates.</td></tr>
<tr><td colspan="3">HYUNDAI
Founded in 1967, Hyundai Motor Company is a key part of Korea's largest conglomerate, the Chung-family owned Hyundai Business Group. Hyundai made its first car in 1974, and it's currently the undisputed leader of Korean auto manufacturing and the largest non-Japanese car exporter. The literal translation of Hyundai is something like "current century."</td></tr>
<tr><td>Elantra (Small car)</td><td>A synthetic fat substitute</td><td>A neologism meant to convey "elegance" and "class."</td></tr>
<tr><td colspan="3">KIA
Kia Motors Corporation began in 1944 as a bicycle manufacturer, building its (and Korea's) first passenger car, the Brisa, in 1974. According to the company, "Kia" apparently means something like "to rise in Asia."</td></tr>
<tr><td>Sephia (Small car)</td><td>A sexually transmitted disease</td><td>A typically unintelligible neologism from a company known for its bizarre automotive names: among its other offerings (not yet available in the U.S.) are the Avella, the Besta, the Clarus, the Credos, and the Pregio.</td></tr>
</table>

Chinatowns, Etc.

You're walking in a major urban metropolis, when suddenly the signs you see are no longer in English; groceries unknown at the local A&P—shiny brown-skinned roast ducks and goggle-eyed, wriggling eels—are hung in glass windows or piled high in wooden crates. You guessed it: You've wandered into an Asian enclave—one of the many Chinatowns, Little Tokyos, or Koreatowns that dot America's urban landscape.

When out-of-town travelers walk through these gates, words like "exotic," "unusual," and "exciting" inevitably tumble from their lips (not unlike the rice from their quivering chopsticks). But for the Asian immigrants who live or work in these districts, ethnic enclaves offer the culinary, linguistic and social comforts of their native countries, giving them (or their children) a secure base from which to acculturate into their new and second home. Some of these districts are strictly business, existing mostly to cater to the tourist trade. Others are virtually self-sufficient communities, comprised of large residential populations, factories, banks, clinics, and more. In either case, ethnic enclaves provide more than just quaint "local color": For immigrants of any origin, the ethnic neighborhood is a necessary bridge that makes their transition to a new country possible.

CHINATOWN, U.S.A.

A Chinatown, or some semblance of one, can be found in just about any major U.S. city. Some, like San Francisco's, have been around since the late 1800s, when lonely Chinese laborers—barred from bringing their families into America—formed bachelor communities where they could socialize in their native tongue and eat the food they missed. Meanwhile, as Anglo Americans came to resent the growing influx of Chinese immigrants, Chinatowns offered them a haven from labor and housing discrimination.

Today, exclusionary barriers have been lifted and such discrimination is illegal, but the notion of Chinatown as the first station on the American Express is still prominent in the minds of many new immigrants form China. Not surprisingly, Chinatowns in cities heavily populated by newer immigrants—New York City and Los Angeles, for example—are thriving. But those in cities with declining Chinese immigrant populations, like Washington, D.C., are struggling to survive.

Outsiders know Chinatown mostly for "authentic" restaurants and cheesy souvenir stands. But major Chinatowns also offer supermarkets, herbal pharmacies, senior citizen centers, churches, bakeries, butchers, bookstores, and music stores, all catering to local populations, as well as Chinese immigrants from miles around. The most festive—and most tourist-crowded—day in any Chinatown is Chinese New Year [👁206], when fireworks continuously explode in a spray of red paper and martial artists cavort in lion and dragon dances. But Chinatown continues to exist when the sun goes down—and there's far more to these communities than meets the eye.

OTHER ASIAN ENCLAVES

For the most part, other Asian groups have been either too few, too assimilated, or too diverse to segregate themselves into urban enclaves. Still, there are stretches of restaurants, shops, and other businesses all over the country that help recent immigrants feel more at home—and give tourists a taste of trans-Pacific culture. Here's a quick rundown of some of them.

Little Indias

It wasn't the language barrier that spawned the original Little India in New York City. Rather, it was the immigrants' search for spice in their lives—traditional cooking spices, that is. They found them in a Middle Eastern shop on Manhattan's East Side, on 28th Street. Not long afterward, an entrepreurial Indian immigrant opened an authentically South Asian spice shop nearby. Soon, he was joined by other shops and restaurants, and the entire area around 28th Street and Lexington Avenue became a favorite pit stop among Indians of every social background. Meantime, in Jackson Heights, Queens, New York's newest and biggest Little India emerged in the area around 74th Street and Broadway. Smaller Little Indias are erupting across the nation. Most of them are in the Northeast, where as many as 34 percent of Indians in the United States reside. Some larger ones can be found on 6th Street in New York's East Village; in Edison, New Jersey; in Pasadena, California; and in Jersey City, New Jersey.

Little Saigons

Many Vietnamese restaurants have sprung up in and around Chinatowns throughout the country, but only the Los Angeles enclave has a large enough concentration of Vietnamese businesses to be officially designated Little Saigon. This area, North and South of Balsa Avenue in Westminster, is home to the largest Vietnamese population outside of Vietnam. The overwhelming majority arrived as the result of the 1980 Refugee Act, which opened the doors to Southeast Asians fleeing their war-torn countries–including Vietnamese, Cambodians, and Laotians (some of them ethnic Chinese). The closest thing to Little Saigon elsewhere in the United States is Chicago's New Chinatown on Argyle Street between Broadway, West, and Sheridan Roads.

Japantowns and Little Tokyos

Only two official Japanese neighborhoods exist in the country: Japantown in San Francisco and Little Tokyo in Los Angeles. Due to Japan's modern economic success, in recent decades, few Japanese have chosen to permanently immigrate to the United States, says Pyong Gap Min, Ph.D., professor of sociology at New York's Queens College. As a result, the Japanese population in the States tends to be assimilated second or third generation Americans, who don't generally require the social and economic security blanket of a Japanese neighborhood. Today, Japantown and Little Tokyo are places where few reside, but thousands will converge for cultural events. Note that communities of expatriate Japanese do exist on the East Coast, mostly due to executive rotations by Japanese companies; cities like Scarsdale, New York, and Fort Lee, New Jersey, have particularly large Japanese populations.

Koreatowns

Los Angeles's Koreatown emerged in 1975, along Olympic Boulevard between Vermont and Western Avenue. The majority of the residents in Koreatown are Hispanic, according to 1990 Census figures; only 15 percent are Korean, most of them recent immigrants—who require Korean-speaking businesses nearby—and the elderly, who need access to Korean healthcare and support services. The remainder of the 260,000 Koreans living in California (the so-called Korean capital of America) reside in more affluent neighborhoods outside of Koreatown proper or in suburbs outside of Los Angeles. The New York–New Jersey region has the next largest concentration of Korean Americans, with 18.8 percent of the total population. Not surprisingly, a number of ethnic business enclaves have emerged to serve those living in the area—a strip around Broadway and 31st Street in Manhattan; in Flushing, Queens; and in Fort Lee, New Jersey.

Little Manilas

More Filipinos live in America than any other Asian ethnic group—1.4 million in all—and yet there aren't any discernible urban Filipino enclaves. Los Angeles's designated Manilatown is little more than a few storefronts, and declining in size. Because almost all Filipinos are English-speaking and the bulk are professionals, they don't depend on the services of a full-fledged ethnic enclave. Recent arrivals, especially in California make their homes together, but usually in the suburbs. Besides California, relatively large gatherings of Filipino Americans exist in New York, New Jersey, and Seattle—but not in the colorful format patented by Chinese immigrant enclaves.

International Districts

Seattle's International District is a third Chinese and a third Filipino, with the rest a mix of immigrants of various Asian origins, including Vietnamese and Japanese. It's also home to many African Americans. Flushing, Queens in New York has also emerged as one of the largest—and most dynamic—multiethnic and multicultural centers in the United States. In addition to being home to the largest community of Chinese Americans in the East Coast (outstripping in size even Manhattan's Chinatown), Flushing also boasts large South Asian, Southeast Asian, and Korean populations. Down South, a multiethnic Asian community has sprung up on the outskirts of Atlanta, Georgia, in a region now known as the International Village; many Southeast Asian, Korean, and Chinese immigrants now live in the area, commingled with a large Latino and Caribbean American community. —J.C.

The Connie Chung Syndrome: Asian Female Television Journalists Everywhere!

Soon after Constance Yu-Hua Chung (a.k.a. Connie Chung) became the first Asian anchor on a major network evening news show on June 1, 1993, she transformed into a phenomenon. Suddenly it became apparent that Asian female anchors were everywhere. In 1995, the Asian American Journalists Association listed more than 100 Asian American female anchors and broadcast reporters in its membership file. By contrast, the number of Asian American male anchors and reporters was about one-fourth that total. That's the Connie Chung Syndrome at work.

So what *is* the Connie Chung Syndrome? As it's been variously defined in the press, the Connie Chung Syndrome is:

- the practice of pairing an Asian American female anchor with an Anglo American male anchor
- the phenomenon of Asian American female anchor or reporters on at least one news show (and occasionally, on all of them) in every major U.S. city
- the phenomenon of individual networks feeling compelled to have at least one Asian American female anchor or reporter on staff
- the media stereotype of the broadcast reporter as an attractive Asian female, as regularly depicted in movies, television shows, and commercials.
- the syndrome experienced by young, Asian American females who aspire to TV news stardom—known to their sniggering peers as "Connie Wannabes."

More recently, and for a different reason, the term "Connie Chung Syndrome" has been applied to the phenomenon of women in their forties deciding to have babies, after Chung's sensational announcement at age 44 that she would temporarily set aside her career in an attempt to become pregnant by her husband, Maury Povich. While the couple did not succeed, they did adopt an infant together (Povich has other children by a previous marriage); currently, the happily married pair are preparing to launch a career together, in a new news magazine show called the *The Connie and Maury Show*. Time for another definition of the Connie Chung Syndrome: Women who work with their husbands? —D.G.

Connie and her broadcast sisters

After the Fall:
The Legacy of Hiroshima and Nagasaki

It was the terrible beginning of a new age of warfare. On August 6, 1945. 8:15:17 a.m., the *Enola Gay,* a U.S. B-29 bomber named after the mother of its pilot, Lieutenant Colonel Paul Tibbets, dropped an 8,900-pound atom bomb, nicknamed "Little Boy," on Hiroshima, Japan, a city of approximately 350,000 citizens. Never in history had the atomic bomb was used against human targets; three days later, at 11:02 a.m., it would be used again, when a bomb called "Fat Man" was detonated over Nagasaki, a city with a population of 270,000.

The force of the first bomb, which exploded over a Hiroshima hospital, was estimated to be equal to 20,000 tons of dynamite. The explosion's core temperature was estimated to be 4,000 degrees Celsius (7,200 degrees Fahrenheit), incinerating anything in its immediate radius. Nearly all of the victims exposed to the heat within one kilometer of the blast died within a week from ruptured skin and organs. Those as far as 3.5 kilometers suffered severe skin burns. Even people who entered either city within 100 hours of the bombings suffered from considerable levels of residual radiation poisoning. Approximately 125,000 people died on August 6 or soon thereafter. In Nagasaki, the initial death toll was estimated between 60,000 and 70,000.

The bombs had their desired effect: On August 15, 1945, Japan gave its unconditional surrender. The Pacific War was over, and America had, with a single act, put a decisive stamp on victory. But what was the price?

The bomb's survivors, who were called *hibakusha* (literally, "explosion-affected persons"), suffered from a terrible range of radiation-related illnesses. Those who received heavy doses of radiation died within 10 days of exposure. Those who survived beyond the initial period developed such symptoms as hair loss, hemorrhaging, declining white-cell and platelet counts, and oral and pharyngeal lesions. In some survival cases, illness did not become apparent for years: hibakusha developed much higher incidences of leukemia, multiple myeloma, and cancers of the blood, compared to the general population. And several thousand unborn

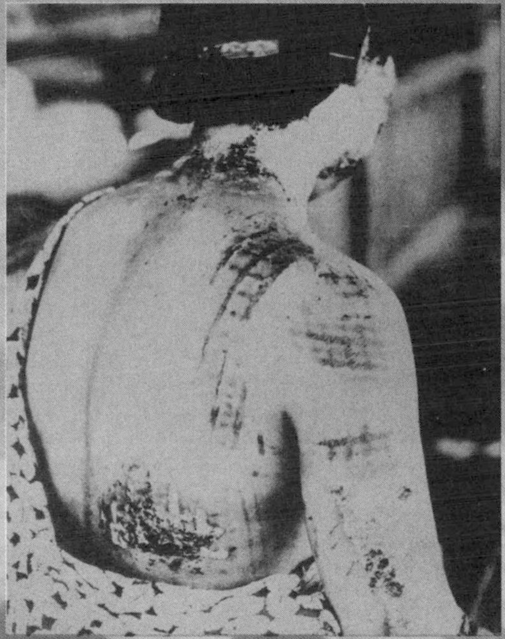

children who were exposed in utero in both Hiroshima and Nagasaki suffered extreme developmental and congenital malformations.

Then-president Harry Truman had reasoned that dropping the bomb would spare as many as a million American lives. However, modern historians argue that with the death toll already above 500,000 from massive firebombings, and 13 million citizens homeless by the summer of 1945, Japan had clearly already lost the war; it was merely a matter of when they would surrender.

Whatever one may believe regarding their necessity, the bombings of Hiroshima and Nagasaki were acts that deserve remembrance throughout the world, as examples of the ultimate terror of modern warfare. Every year since 1946, a commemorative ceremony has been held in Hiroshima at the site that was the epicenter of the bomb, where the Peace Memorial Park is located. The ceremony has becomc the city's most important annual cvent. Hiroshima's Peace Memorial Museum, which opened in 1955, houses some 6,000 grim relics of the explosion, including twisted roof tiles and melted bottles; it draws 1.2 million visitors annually.

Hiroshima is also the home of a more gentle memorial: In 1955, when a young hibakusha named Sadako developed leukemia, she decided to follow a tradition that said that if she folded a thousand paper cranes, she would be granted her wish to live. Sadly, the wish did not come true, but her schoolmates raised money to build her a monument: a life-size statue of Sadako holding a golden crane over her head, dedicated to the children of Hiroshima who died as a result of the bomb. Another memorial came in the form of the Paper Crane Club, organized by girls in Sadako's school. Each year, children from all over the world send folded paper cranes to Hiroshima—as many as 400 million cranes annually, which are strung together and hung beneath Sadako's statue, as a memorial to the atomic bomb's youngest victims. —A.W.

Climbing Gold Mountain: Immigration from Asia

"Give me your tired, your poor, your huddled masses yearning to breathe free..." Those immortal words, penned by Emma Lazarus in 1883 and slapped on the Statue of Liberty three years later, never rang true. By 1875, America's free immigration policy, based on the principle of universal religious, political, and economic asylum, was already twisting itself in circles. From that year's first immigration restriction act until America's elimination of national immigration quotas in 1965, U.S. immigration policy has essentially been governed by three basic principles: keeping out undesirables, discriminating against certain races, and protecting the domestic work force from having to compete with cheap labor. After 1965's reforms, an immigration preference system was created guided by the principles of family reunification, access to needed skills, and accommodation of refugees. Unfortunately, the pendulum has swung back in the other direction—towards exclusion and xenophobia. Candidates of both political parties have called for measures to stem or even halt immigration, while using immigrants as scapegoats for American economic woes. Will the pendulum swing back, or will the huddled masses be pushed, finally, into the pit? Whatever the case, it's certainly seemed in recent years like Liberty's "golden lamp" has dimmed—perhaps for good. —D.G.

Asian Immigration Through the Ages

In the 1990s:

- About 600,000 immigrants come to America per year. Nearly 50 percent of them are Asian. The 7.3 million people of Asian ancestry in America today comprise 2.9 percent of the population. (Whites are 76 percent, blacks 12 percent, Latinos 9 percent.)
- Asians are America's fastest growing minority group, increasing in size by 95 percent since 1980. (The white population increased only 6 percent; blacks 13.2 percent; and Hispanics 53 percent.)
- Annual levels of Asian immigration: Filipinos 60,000; Chinese 55,000; Koreans 30,000; Indians 30,000; Pakistani 9,700; Thai 8,900.
- 64 percent of Asians are foreign-born.

By the year 2020:

- 54 percent of Asians in America will be foreign-born.
- Asians will number more than 20 million, up 177 percent from 1990.

By 2050:

- Asians will be 10 percent of the U.S. population. (Whites 52 percent, blacks 16 percent, Latinos 22 percent).

Angel Island

CHINESE: The first three Chinese docked in Baltimore in 1785. Before the Gold Rush of 1849, there were only about 359 living in the U.S. By 1852, there were more than 25,000, mostly in gold-mining regions. By 1880, there were more than 100,000 Chinese in the continental US, 71 percent of whom were concentrated in California, forming about 10 percent of the state's population, and 25 percent of its labor force. They were a major force in building the transcontinental railroad, and by 1890 Chinese lived in every state in the Union. Between 1882 and 1943, Chinese immigration was curtailed due to labor pressures. Existing Chinese in America were segregated and discriminated against. Until 1965, their immigration was further restricted because Cold War fear of the "Communist threat." After 1965, immigration from Hong Kong and Taiwan increased dramatically. When the U.S. normalized relations with the People's Republic in the late 1970s, immigration from mainland China also increased. Chinese in New York became as numerous as those in San Francisco. From 1970 to 1980, the Chinese population almost doubled from 382,795 to 749,246. By 1990, more than a million Indochinese refugees, mostly ethnic Chinese, arrived, along with the mass exodus of Vietnamese, Cambodians, and Laotians following the Vietnam War. New York, San Francisco, and Los Angeles were centers of the Chinese in America, but new immigrants also changed the face of some suburban towns [👁311]. By the 1990s, 40 percent of the Chinese in America lived in California, and 70 percent of all Chinese Americans were foreign-born.

JAPANESE: Japanese first arrived in 1868 as contract laborers working in Hawaiian sugar plantations. Between 1885 and 1894, about 29,000 Japanese (20 percent of whom were women), overcome with the romantic notion of emigrating to the U.S. as agricultural laborers, were sent by the Meiji government to Hawaii. By the end of the century, they were 80 percent of the

Hawaiian plantation labor force. Between 1901 and 1910, about 130,000 Japanese immigrated to the States. In 1907, via the Gentlemen's Agreement, Japan agreed to limit its immigration to the U.S. After that, immigration decreased by a third; during World War II, it came to a halt. Still, in 1960, Japanese comprised 52 percent of America's Asian population, though that percentage has declined sharply with the influx of other Asian groups. Between 1965 and 1984, only about 94,000 Japanese immigrated to the U.S.—just 3 percent of total Asian immigration. Japanese economic expansion has led to a trend in Japanese wanting to stay home. In 1990, only 17 percent of the Japanese population in America were foreign-born who had arrived since 1980, while fully 68 percent were born here.

KOREANS: Political upheavals at home motivated Koreans to leave for America beginning in 1903. Like the Japanese, they came to Hawaii to work the plantations. About 40 percent were Christian and had already been converted by American missionaries by the time they got here. About 7,700 Koreans arrived by 1910, declining to just over 1,000 by 1920, and only 600 more by 1940. From World War II to 1950, Korean immigration fell to zero. The following decade, however, Koreans began to arrive in the thousands. After 1965, record levels of Koreans began immigrating, (nearly 272,000 in the 1970s, and 339,000 in the 1980s), peaking between 1985 and 1987, at about 35,000 people a year. By 1990, 660,000 Koreans had come to the States as permanent residents. The post-1965 wave of Korean immigrants consisted largely of urban, white-collar, middle-class families motivated primarily by better educational opportunities for the kids.

FILIPINOS: Aside from the poorly documented settlements of "Manila Men" who cultivated rice in what would become the Louisiana lowlands before the Revolutionary War, formal immigration from the Philippines began after the U.S. took possession of the islands after the Spanish American War of 1898. In 1903, the Pensionado Act allowed the immigration of hundreds of select Filipino students until the 1930s. By 1930, there were 108,424 Filipinos counted in the census. Although exclusion of Filipinos, as U.S. protectorates, was unconstitutional, the Tydings-McDuffie Act of 1934 limited immigration of Filipinos to just 50 per year. The Filipino Repatriation Act of 1935 even encouraged them to go back by providing free transportation home. Only about 2,100 accepted the offer. After 1946, when the Philippines became independent, Congress passed the Filipino Naturalization Act, which made Filipinos eligible for citizenship. Filipino immigration, especially of women, has steadily risen since then. From 1966 to 1970, more than 62 percent of Hawaiian Filipino immigrants came to join family members, while mainland immigration was driven by the occupational selectivity of the new immigration policy. More than half of the Filipinos in America today live in California and Hawaii, followed by large numbers in Illinois, New York, and New Jersey, and then West Virginia, Florida, and Maryland. A high proportion of Filipino healthcare professionals have settled in the New York-New Jersey area. Filipino immigration nearly tripled from 1960 to more than 350,000 in the 1970s. In the 1980s, more than half a million Filipinos arrived in the U.S., and that number has continued to rise, despite political and economic improvements in the Philippines.

SOUTH ASIANS: The first wave of South Asian immigration lasted from 1907 to 1924, mostly consisting of Sikhs from the Punjabi region; until the 1960s, only about 5,000 per decade arrived on America's West Coast, most having stopped first in Canada. In 1923, a man named Bhagat Singh Thind took on the U.S. Supreme Court to see if he could get Asian Indians classified as whites, and therefore eligible for citizenship. Thind lost. The 1965 immigration reforms greatly affected South Asian immigration, which transformed itself into a wave of mostly Hindu, educated professionals and their families. Between 1965 and 1974, immigration from India increased 2,000 percent, while Pakistani immigration leapt 1,000 percent. By 1990, South Asians had become the fourth-largest group of Asian Americans, with Indians numbering 815,447, Pakistani 81,371, Bangladeshi, 11,838, and Sri Lankans 19,970.

A Brief History of Immigration

1864 — **First federal immigration law created—"An Act to Encourage Immigration." However, WASPs were already calling for limits on German, Irish Catholic, and southern and eastern European immigrants.**

The first immigration restriction barred criminals and prostitutes from entering the country. This didn't mean, of course, that an immigrant couldn't become a criminal or prostitute after entering the country.

1882 — **The Chinese Exclusion Act of 1882 banned Chinese laborers from entering the U.S. until 1892. This was the first time the U.S. denied a group entry on the basis of race, ethnicity, or national origin, though not the last; free immigration comes to an end.**

The Immigration Act of 1882 barred convicts and the insane from entering the country. It also tried to ban the mentally retarded and the socially dependent, but, apparently, wasn't very successful. Every incoming immigrant was now charged a head tax of 50 cents.

1907 — **The Immigration Act of 1907 basically extended the restrictions of earlier acts by using synonyms for criminals and the insane, just in case there was any question. In practice, few immigrants were actually excluded on these principles because it's tough to tell who's insane. However, it's pretty easy to tell who's Japanese or Korean, the groups at whom Section One of the Act was really aimed.**

1917 — **The Immigration Act of 1917 was also called the Barred Zone Act, because it barred immigration from a zone consisting of a broad range of Asian regions.**

1921 — **The Immigration Act of 1921 introduced a quota system into the immigration system. Based on the census of 1910, each nation was allowed an annual quota of 3 percent of that nationality's U.S. population. The net result was to keep majority groups majority, and minority groups minority.**

1924 — **The Immigration Act of 1924, also called the National Origins Act or the Johnson-Reed Act of 1924, demanded a 2 percent rather than 3 percent quota. The Act greatly favored immigrants from Northern and Western Europe, since they constituted the vast percentage of the existing American population. It also included a clause barring entry to any "alien ineligible to citizenship." Since U.S. naturalization laws granted citizenship only to whites and those of African descent, this legislation pretty much ended Asian immigration until after World War II.**

1943 — **The Immigration Act of 1943, also known as the**

IMMIGRANT PROFESSIONS

When immigrants arrive in the United States, they're often faced with a dilemma: How does one survive in a new culture, restricted by barriers of language, prejudice, and occasionally, education? The answer is often to rely on the example of other immigrants from the Old Country, who have found success in niches left open by more established Americans. It's no coincidence that thousands of Greek immigrants opened diners and coffee shops, while similar numbers of Irish immigrants became policemen. Here are the roots and reasons for some typical Asian immigrant professions:

CHINESE LAUNDRIES: In 1849, the Chinese were lured to America by the California Gold Rush, making a long and painful journey to a land that was touted as being a "mountain of gold." For many, it was more like a mountain of dirty underwear. As laundry legend goes, Wah Lee, one of many unsuccessful miners, opened up the first Chinese laundry in San Francisco in 1851. By 1900, there were about 4,800 Chinese laundrymen in California. By 1940, the phenomenon had spread across the nation, with New York City boasting more than 5,000 Chinese laundries. In fact, at one point, 60 percent of the Chinese population in New York worked in laundries. The Chinese latched onto the laundry trade for practical reasons: It allowed them to earn capital without causing hostility among white workers and hand laundries had small startup costs. Very few Chinese became rich from the laundry business, but the laundries gave immigrants a tenuous foothold in a country they discovered was far more mountainous than golden. Then, beginning in the 1950s, the number of laundry stores decreased, due to new conveniences like washing machines and coin-operated laundromats. By the 1970s, for better and for worse, the hand laundry had finally ceased being the economic lifeline for the Chinese immigrant.

KOREAN GROCERS: The rise of Korean-owned groceries in this country has been nothing less than astonishing. In Southern California, Korean Americans own 46 percent of all small grocery stores. In Manhattan, the ownership level is 85 percent. But Korean grocery ownership is really part of a larger phenomenon; it's one of many small, labor-intensive businesses to which Korean immigrants have turned in droves, unable to find employment opportunities commensurate with their education and ability. It's not unusual to find that a Korean storeowner has a Ph.D., or is a former engineer. But a degree earned in a foreign language all too often isn't worth much more than the paper it's printed on. And thus, the seeming flood of Korean American liquor stores, nail salons, and 24-hour green groceries. But these hard-working Korean immigrant entrepreneurs have to be given credit for resourcefulness as well as perseverance. Most store owners get their financial backing from an informal money-pooling system known as *kye*, in which members—friends, relatives, or fellow churchgoers—contribute to and collect from a group pot. Most major cities also have guilds, formed by Korean immigrant owners of similar businesses, which assist new startups with establishing supplier connections and clearing administrative hurdles.

SOUTH ASIAN MOTELOWNERS: Indian hospitality may be legend, but thousands of Indian Americans have taken the myth to entrepreneurial—and profitable—heights. According to a 1995 survey conducted by the Asian American Hotel Owners Association, 4,600 Indians own nearly 7,500 properties in the economy lodging section of the hotel industry. Their numbers are expected to rise to 16,500 by the year 2000. The survey puts the payroll of the Asian American motelowners at $1 billion, and their annual contribution to taxes at $410 million. Approximately 95 percent of Asian American–owned hotels, both big and small, are owned by Indian Americans, many of whom immigrated to the U.S. in the 1960s and 1970s, primarily from the State of Gujarat in India.

SOUTH ASIAN CABDRIVERS: They may be the butt of many jokes, but South Asian drivers keep New York City in constant motion. South Asians form a vast majority of cab drivers in New York and several other major U.S. metros. According to New York's Taxi and Limousine Commission, more than 40 percent of the 12,000 licensed cabbies in New York are South Asian, most from Punjab, a North Indian state, and Bangladesh, formerly known as East Pakistan. Cab driving has always offered immigrants a means of livelihood, and before South Asians took to the taxis, Italians, Irish, Russians, Jews, and Haitians formed the bulk of the driver community. For most South Asian taxi drivers, being a cabbie is a stepping stone. Many simultaneously attend college, and strive toward white-collar futures.

Magnuson Act, finally repealed the Chinese Exclusion Act, and allowed Chinese to become naturalized citizens. This token gesture was due to China's status as a U.S. ally during World War II.

1946 **The Luce-Celler Bill of 1946, also called the Filipino Naturalization Act, allowed people to immigrate from India and the Philippines, and made both groups eligible for naturalization. Quotas were set at 100 people per country per year. By this time, the U.S. was beginning to realize how offensive its immigration policies were.**

1952 **The McCarran-Walter Act of 1952 removed all racial criteria for naturalization, and eliminated more barriers to Asian immigration. Quotas were still small (185 for the Japan alone), but additional provisions allowed for the entry of large numbers of nonquota immigrants, including the spouses and children of quota immigrants. However, Communists were barred from entering the country. At the height of the Cold War, the U.S. cared less whether immigrants were brown or yellow, and more whether they were Red.**

1965 **The Nationality Act of 1965, also called the Hart-Celler Act, abolished the quota system established by the National Origins Act and designated family reunification as the guiding principle for immigration. In reality, "skilled" immigrants exceeded quotas, and the number of refugees varied widely according to the vagaries of geopolitics.**

1968 **A cap of 120,000 was placed on immigrants from the Western hemisphere, the percentage of European, Canadian, and Central American immigrants dropped, while the number of Asian immigrants rose signficantly.**

1986 **The Immigration Reform and Control Act of 1986, also called the Simpson-Rodino Act, was designed to stem the flow of illegal immigrants from Mexico; it made employers prosecutable for the hiring of illegal immigrants. The act also upped the ceiling on immigration from Hong Kong, from 600 to 5,000, just in case any rich people wanted to flee the British colony before it reverted back to mainland China in 1997.**

1990 **In the Immigration Act of 1990, effective October 1991, total immigration was capped at 700,000, to be lowered to 675,000 in 1995, with each nation allowed 25,000 immigrants to the U.S., not including refugees. Family reunification categories were retained, allowing up to 480,000 family-based immigrants a year. Meanwhile, employment-related provisions were added, including a category allowing the entry of "employment-creating" immigrants who agree to invest $1 million in capital in a U.S. concern. Give me your wealthy, your rich, your leisure classes yearning to buy stock...**

In_ermarriag

Whoever said Asians stick together was wrong. According to Gabe Grosz, associate publisher of *Interrace* magazine, almost one third of all Asians in the U.S. marry outside their race, a trend that is expected to continue as the Asian American population grows. Outmarriage rates among Asians weren't always so high; in the late 1800s and early 1900s, only two to five percent of first-generation Asians immigrants of Chinese, Japanese, and Korean ancestry married outside their race. Part of the reason was that the first wave of immigrants were generally male, and often had wives waiting for them back home; in addition, in those days, interracial marriages were forbidden either by law or rigid social custom. There were some exceptions: Chinese immigrant men in Hawaii frequently married Native Hawaiian women, while early male Asian Indian immigrants in rural California married Mexican women at an outmarriage rate of nearly 100 percent, and early Filipino immigrants, who were treated differently than other Asians under American law due to the fact that the Philippines were a U.S. colony, outmarried at a rate of almost 90 percent.

In the 1930s and 1940s, while antimiscegenation laws were still strong, outmarriage rates increased to about 10 percent for second-generation Japanese and Chinese Americans. Still, it wasn't until World War II that interracial marriage would become a broad phenomenon, for two reasons. The first was America's wartime internment of its citizens of Japanese descent; following this appalling act, the community's dominant organization, the Japanese American Citizens League, issued a statement urging that Japanese Americans actively seek to marry Anglo-Americans, so as to eliminate perceptions of foreignness or unassimilability and prevent a future recurrence of such injustice. As a result, Japanese American outmarriage rates rose to a majority of all marriages.

Secondly, the U.S. military involvement in Asia resulted in numerous interracial marriages between G.I.'s and Asian women. The War Brides Act of 1945 granted American soldiers permission to legally bring their foreign-born wives to the United States; after 1945, U.S. troops continued to be stationed in Japan, Korea, the Philippines, and Vietnam. Between 1947 and 1975, more than 46,000 American men married Japanese women. During the period between 1951 and 1980, a total of 45,551 Korean women entered the U.S. as wives of servicemen. And in 1952 alone, 677 Filipina women came to the U.S. as war brides. The war bride phenomenon helped to make intermarriages—specifically those between white males and Asian females—legally and socially acceptable. In 1948, California was the first state to repeal its antimiscegenation laws, and by 1967, all antimiscegenation statutes had been declared unconstitutional.

As the Civil Rights movement increased racial tolerance in the 1960s, intermarriage increased sharply. The trend exploded in the 1970s and 1980s, when the Chinese, Japanese, and Filipino populations reached their third and fourth generations. Although the U.S. Census Bureau does not tally interracial marriages which are specifically Asian and non-Asian, estimates suggest that half a million or more Asians outmarry each year. In part due to the American history of war brides, the overwhelming majority of these are between Asian women and white men. Other factors cited for this phenomenon include the public perception of Asian females as more sexually desirable than Asian males, and the cultural burden on Asian males to produce offspring who will "carry on the family line," with the perception that mixed-race children are somehow not as acceptable.

It should be noted, however, that Asian/non-Asian couples of both varieties are becoming more common and high-profile—leading to the regular emergence of the "interracial" issue as a topic of heated discussion. Whatever one's opinion, it's clear that in recent decades, the boundaries of color have fallen ever more freely to the battering-ram of love. —D.G., C.Y.

INTERRACIAL MARRIAGE IN THE U.S.

Total marriages: 44,598,000 (1970); 54,251,000 (1994)

Interracial marriages: 310,000 (1974); 1,283,000 (1994)

black/white: 65,000 (1974) 296,000 (1994)

white/other: 233,000 (1974); 909,000 (1994)

black/other: 12,000 (1974); 78,000 (1994)

RATES OF ASIAN OUTMARRIAGE

Asian Indian: 98 percent (1913-1949); 18 percent (1980)

Chinese: 10 percent (1950s); 26 percent (1979)

Filipino: 90 percent (1950s); 24 percent (1980)

Japanese: less than 5 percent (1920s); 50 percent (1980s)

Korean: 18 percent (1980)

Vietnamese: 12 percent (1980)

(above: U.S. Census Bureau)

RATES OF IN-MARRIAGE

(courtesy of Interrace)

95 percent of whites marry whites

92 percent of blacks marry blacks

68 percent of Asians marry Asians

68 percent of Latinos marry Latinos

25 percent of Native Americans marry Native Americans

Learning from Rising Sun, Inc.
A guide to Japanese industrial innovation

If you happen to run a giant multinational corporation, you've probably already been exposed to one or more of the many Japanese industrial management fads that gained currency during the 1980s heyday of "Japan Inc." If you aren't a CEO, your only exposure to these highly touted techniques might be through incomprehensible newspaper articles, or worse, even more incomprehensible training seminars implemented by your company's clueless executive committee. Here's a simple guide to the methods that fueled the rise of Japan's corporate megaliths, illustrated with examples from the idealized manufacturing company, Widget Motors. —J.Y.

Revolutionary Japanese technique	Why is it called that?	What is it in ordinary English?
FMS	"Flexible Manufacturing System"—a production process utilizing sophisticated computerized machine tools to enable instant switching of assembly lines to produce any of a variety of products.	"Transformers....More than meets the eye"
hoshin kanri	Literally "policy deployment," this planning methodology involves step-by-step breakdown of strategy, execution, and process change.	"Two thousand heads are better than one"
kaizen	Kaizen means ongoing, continuous improvement.	"Little things mean a lot"
kanban	Kanban are literally small cards, sent from final assembly stations to earlier ones, requesting production of additional units. Kanban is also called JIT (for "Just in Time") or "zero inventory" techniques.	"Fresh-baked while-U-wait"
keiretsu	Literally translating as "headless groups," keiretsu are the massive networks of cross-invested companies that form the core of Japanese industry.	"I own you, you own me, we're a happy family"
Quality circles	A "QC" consists of six to 12 employees in the same workgroup, meeting regularly to discuss workplace problems and solutions.	"Wage-slaves Anonymous"
Theory Z	A theory of management offered by social psychologist Douglas McGregor and completed by William Ouchi (who wrote a book by the same name), which describes the philosophy of typical Japanese companies.	"We are family"

How do you do it?	A real life example, courtesy of the Widget Motor Ccorporation...
Spend a lot of money on computers and specialized equipment.	Give the people what they want, when they want it! If there's a run on Garbo roadsters, Widget's FMS automatically switches production lines from making Wembley four-by-fours—and vice versa.
Instead of having a high-level committee determine all aspects of organizational direction, top executives simply create broad-based "vision statements," while teams composed of executives, plant managers, foremen, and workers determine a consensual set of "core objectives" in keeping with the corporate vision.	It's Widget's annual planning time, and *everyone's* involved in determining company policy and direction. From the CEO to the assembly line workers, everyone's got an opinion. Yes, this may waste loads of time—but it promotes communication and ensures that everyone's on the same track. Teamwork is everything!
In contrast to the American emphasis on revolutionary, innovative change on an arbitrary occasional basis, kaizen looks for ongoing incremental change.	Rather than reviewing the work process and implementing quality control on an annual or seasonal basis, Widget constantly examines its production systems, noting any variations and making slight alterations to correct them, the goal being "zero defects."
Set up your plant so that units are assembled only as finished products are sent out. In essence, the shipment of products "pulls" the line along—in contrast to traditional U.S. manufacturing processes, in which units are assembled as fast as possible and "pushed" along the line, waiting for the next stage in the assembly process to begin. This not only reduces capital tied up in excess inventory, and enables tight quality control—mistakes can be caught immediately, rather than after a thousand faulty units are made	Widget's distribution chief tells its plant foreman that he's just shipped a Braggart station wagon. The foreman notifies the paint and polish assembly site to slap a coat of neon purple on another new Braggart; the painters, in turn, tell the frame welders to put a body on another Braggart chassis, and so on up the line. Just one Braggart is kept ready for shipping at any given time, so there's no need for all those extra warehouses. Go ahead and turn 'em into executive offices!
Rather than bidding out to many different suppliers and changing them at will, form ties with vendors—ideally by buying some or all of their equity. This binds them to you, providing them with security and inspiring them toward long-term investment and risk-taking Widget	Motor Holdings purchases an equity position in the Spungely Tire Company and Gearloose Gearboxes. Spungely and Gearloose pay for half of Widget's forward R&D, in exchange for guaranteed contracts. Everybody's happy!
Trained and mediated by members of management, QCs discuss and suggest solutions for improving product quality and worker efficiency. (Unfortunately, while QCs allow the line worker opportunity for feedback in the decision-making process, they have no actual authority, and worker suggestions can easily be ignored.)	Each site on each line in each of Widget's plants is organized into one or more QCs, each of which meets to discuss screwups and ways to avoid them. The Ostrich engine-block team, for instance, offers a solution to the "exploding minivan" problem. The solution is implemented, and everyone, particularly the consumer, wins.
In Theory X companies, workers are seen as lazy; to get them to perform, you have to reward or punish them. In Theory Y companies, workers are seen as genuinely interested in doing a good job, and want empowerment. Theory Z advances beyond Y to say that all people in a company are valued parts of the whole; workers are not only consulted, they actually help make decisions. Meanwhile, management commits to long-term retention of employees.	At Widget, there's a flat compensation pyramid: top executives make a fixed multiple of what the lowest-paid line worker makes; meanwhile, a profit-sharing program splits up the benefits of fiscal success. All major decisions are made by labor-management committees. There's never been a layoff, and no "early retirement"—people not only work at Widget all their lives, so do their children. It's common to see "Widget Families" working side by side.

SALARYMEN: THE FRONT LINE FORCES OF JAPAN INC.

Harried, henpecked, and hopeless, the sarariman ("salaryman") has entered into American pop culture as the stereotypical figure of the Japanese white-collar worker a salaryman. The term was originally coined during Japan's Taisho period (1912-26) to describe a swelling class of salaried, white-collar workers, in contrast to blue-collar workers who were paid hourly wages. Today, salaryman refers to managers, salesmen, executives, and office workers from private companies or government agencies, many of whom are sent "on rotation" to the U.S. to work in branch offices or corporate subsidiaries, for tenures lasting from six months to 20 years—with or without their families. A key figure in any contemporary Japanese drama, sitcom, comic book, or work of fiction, salarymen have also gained currency in the American media, which has swung from being contemptuous of their office-drone habits to being gently amused by their desperate after-work attempts to let off steam.

TROPHIES FOR SALE

With a gleeful disregard for real income potential, Japanese companies depended on brand-name value to determine the worth of their investments. Boy, did they get screwed.

• Mitsui Real Estate doled out $610 million for the Exxon building in Manhattan, even though the asking price was only $375 million. The company's president, Mitsui Fudosan, reportedly overpaid by $235 million because he wanted to beat the record price for a property of $600 million listed in the Guinness Book of World Records. Similarly, critics theorized that Matsushita bought MCA just because Sony bought Columbia Pictures, and Bridgestone bought Firestone just because its rival Sumitomo Rubber bought Dunlop. The end consequence of all this posturing? Everyone got laid out flat.

• When Mitsubishi acquired an 80 percent share of Rockefeller Center, the Rockefeller family was accused of "selling America's soul" to the Japanese. In actuality, Rockefeller Center Properties, a public trust, continued to hold a mortgage on the buildings, convertible to a 71.5 percent stake by the year 2001. In October 1989, the David Letterman Show was introduced sarcastically as "Coming from New York...a subsidiary of Mitsubishi." But, referring to the sky-high price Mitsubishi paid, a Manhattan real estate broker quipped, "John D. would have been proud of the boys."

• And, in 1992, Hiroshi Yamauchi, founder and president of Nintendo, paid $75 million for a 60 percent (silent) share in the Seattle Mariners baseball team, which, at the time, was in last place in the American League West. Yamauchi reportedly isn't terribly interested in baseball (and doesn't, for that matter, even like video games).

Sold! Japan's U.S. Investments

They came, they bought...they were fleeced. It was 1985, the start of Japan's *babaru keizai* ("bubble economy")—five years of the nation's highest levels of financial speculation and industrial expansion since World War II. Between 1985 and 1990, Japanese companies invested $3 trillion into its own plants and equipment, while becoming the world's biggest creditor nation. In short, with its stock market soaring and its cash supplies burgeoning, Japanese companies were in the money. They did what anyone would do in that situation: They decided to go shopping. In America. And not for clothes and souvenirs—they bought companies, buildings, movie studios, baseball teams...nothing was sacred if it was for sale, and where eager Americans were concerned, *everything* was for sale. All told, Japanese invested $77.3 billion in U.S. real estate between 1985 and 1995. American developers, who put up buildings on the assumption that they'd find Japanese customers even had a gag term for the phenomenon—"Tokyo takeout"—while Jay Leno joked that in Japan, the Home Shopping Network displayed a map of the U.S. Critics began to worry about U.S. "economic sovereignty."

And then...the bubble burst. Japan plunged into its worst recession since the War. Meanwhile, with U.S. real estate values plummeting, selling American commercial property was like hawking radioactive popsicles to Eskimos with pneumonia. In 1993, Japanese companies had sold $3 billion worth of their U.S. property. By the end of 1994, Japanese investors had put $6.4 billion worth on the block. As much as $10 billion more went up for sale in 1995. All of these sales socked their Japanese owners for huge losses; it has been estimated that about 40 percent of Japanese investments were bad.

As for the pundits, doomsayers, and nativists? They were unusually silent. —D.G.

Conspicuous Consumption

Year	This Japanese company	paid (in billions)	for this US property/company	and then...
1990	**Matsushita**	$6.1	MCA Inc. (including Universal Pictures)	Sold it to Canada's Seagram Co. in 1995 for $5.7 billion.
1989	**Sony**	$5.0	Columbia Pictures and TriStar Pictures	Lost more than $3 billion so far
	Mitsubishi Estate	$1.3	Rockefeller Center (80 percent share)	Went bankrupt in 1995
	Minoru Isutani	$.841	Pebble Beach Golf Club	Sold for $340 million
	Sazale Group	$.12	Hotel Bel Air	Sold for $60 million
1988	**Bridgestone Corp.**	$2.6	Firestone Tire and Rubber	Lost $850 million
1987	**Aoki Corp.**	$1.5	Westin Hotels and Resorts	Sold for $537 million
1986	**Daiichi Real Estate**	$1	Tiffany Building	Sold building in 1992

Anyone Can Be a Star!
The Karaoke Phenomenon

Be a rock star or pop idol or balladeer...in the comfort of your own home (or at least a sleazy bar). This pastime, which has quickly become a way of life for some, dates back to the early 1970s in Japan. One account says that karaoke was invented in Kobe, Japan, in a bar that couldn't afford to pay for a live band; some manager had the brilliant idea of using taped songs without vocals as backup music for hired singers. Another legend has it that an opera singer once taped an orchestra to practice along with at home, an idea that soon became a trend. This would explain the term *karaoke,* which literally means "empty orchestra" (from *kara,* short for *karappo,* "empty," and *oke* short for *okesutora,* "orchestra"). The correct pronunciation of the term is "kah-rah-oh-kay," but most Americans won't know what you're talking about unless you say "carry okee."

Not that the activity's origin or pronunciation matters. Helped along by the ritualized participation of Japanese businessmen, who use it to relax after many a stressful and demanding work day, karaoke has grown into a multi-billion-dollar industry in Japan. With about 500,000 commercial establishments and 7 million karaoke-equipped homes, the Japanese have found myriad ways to boost karaoke's economic boom. For a while there were even accounts of karaoke-equipped Japanese taxis—a nifty feature quickly outlawed because it resulted in too many accidents. According to Neal Friedman, executive director of the Karaoke International Sing-a-long Association, the Japanese karaoke market is roughly $5 billion in size, although only about 30 to 40 percent of that revenue is from "pure karaoke." (The Japanese use a holistic means of measuring karaoke sales, including every component—even the food ordered during karaoke sessions—as part of the market.)

But the Japanese aren't the only ones who are spending big bucks on the karaoke craze. Friedman says that, worldwide, the pure karaoke industry revenue is about $5.4 to $5.8 billion, with the phenomenon taking Taiwan, Korea, Philippines, Singapore, and Hong Kong by storm, and even reaching beyond China's communist borders—filling the need for karaoke versions of Party classics like "Our Great Leader Mao" and "On the Golden Mount of Beijing."

KARAOKE IN AMERICA

According to Ron Arnone, publisher/editor of *American Karaoke* magazine, karaoke really took off in the U.S. in the late 1980s when it became a "video-based entertainment." Before this, manufacturers had been making cassette tapes of songs with the vocals stripped, but they were known as sing-alongs, not karaoke software. "Full-motion video," conveyed via laserdisc, has now become the norm for karaoke format, since it allows for lyrics to scroll across the screens for easy singalong (for those who can stand watching the inane accompanying visuals). The Japanese company Pioneer (a Matsushita subsidiary) played a major role in the prominence of both laserdiscs and karaoke, creating the first laser karaoke players in 1987. And the demand is still growing, according to Laurie Anderson, a marketing specialist at Pioneer Entertainment, who reports that sales of software (i.e., laserdiscs and CD+G, a new small-disc format) were up about 5 percent in 1995 over the previous year. As new technology (like DVDs; [👁176]) appears and an avalanche of cheesy ballads swamps the Top 40, it's unlikely we'll hear the last of karaoke anytime soon. —S.T.

WORDS TO SING BY

ECHO: a standard feature on karaoke units that enhances the singer's voice by making it richer and fuller sounding. If turned to an extreme level, it causes the singer to sound like he or she is underwater of several miles beneath the surface of the earth.

CDG: also CD+G, "compact disc plus graphics." Despite its name, the CDG format shows only the lyrics onscreen, which could be something of a bonus to despisers of crappy karaoke videos.

KJ: "karaoke jockey." Arnone attributes much of karaoke's success to KJs. "KJs are the movers and pushers of karaoke," he says. "They're people who have understood and come to master the art of associating an audience—of getting people to sing when they're too embarrassed to."

MIDI: Musical Instrument Digital Interface; a set of protocols that describe in computer language the sounds played on an electronic keyboard. This gives musicians the ability to create a wide range of orchestration using only keyboards. Now used to create karaoke music in computerized formats.

MULTIPLEX: a recent feature on karaoke units, which allows one to add or remove a prerecorded lead singer's vocals from cassette tapes, CDG's, and other karaoke software.

RS MODULE: a frequency module allowing CDG players to coordinate with monitors.

SCORING: a feature found on some karaoke machines that presents singers with a numerical rating from 1 to 100, based on some arcane (and possibly random) means of determination. Note that it is virtually impossible to predict what score your performance will produce. Do not fly into a rage.

SYNCHRONIZATION RIGHTS: the rights that all "full motion video" formats must buy from song publishers, enabling them to accompany music with video footage.

Mail Order Brides

"The ultimate 'good deal' for a middle-aged, middle-class divorced white man is an 'Oriental girl'...20 years his junior who will 'gratefully' sleep with him, prepare his meals, do his laundry, clean his apartment, and serve his female guests in a maid's uniform without showing any jealousy or resentment."

—Oakland, California, newspaper columnist Bill Fiset

"Do you believe in miracles?"

—advertisement from Pacific Romance, a mail-order bride company

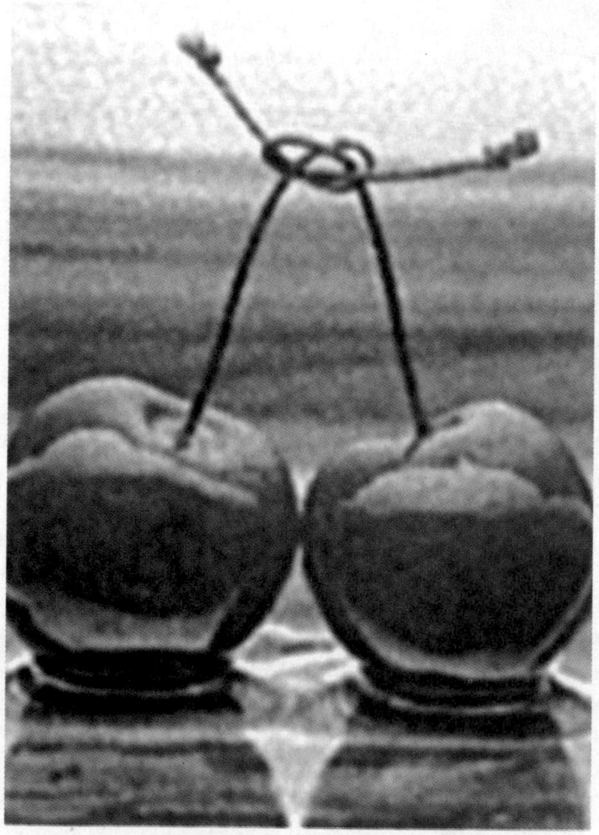

In the last decade, tens of thousands of American men have established correspondences with Asian women through mail-order bride companies such as Pacific Romance, Cherry Blossoms, Asian Experience, Simpatica, Pacific Century, and Thai-Asian Worldwide; approximately 2,000 to 3,000 find wives through such services each year. With ads appearing regularly in publications ranging from *Penthouse* to *Rolling Stone,* the popularity of these companies—which offer catalogs filled with photos and short bios of Asian women for just $30 to $80—is perhaps understandable.

Most of these companies are overt about promising love and marriage (though a few claim to simply be "pen pal" services); all of them sell men the privilege of writing to an Asian woman for as little as $4 per name and address, with the option of courting, meeting, and importing an overseas fiancee of choice.

By some accounts, the mail order bride business is as old as "them thar hills"; early American pioneers used to advertise for wives to help them settle the Old West. To others, the practice seems to be a modern perversion of the "picture bride" trend, which peaked between 1908 and 1924, in which overseas matchmakers arranged brides for Japanese and Korean male immigrants living in America using pictures and correspondence. The picture bride custom derived from the practice of arranged marriages, long a tradition in many Asian cultures, and proved to be an effective way for Japanese and Korean male immigrants without access to women in America to find wives and start families.

In the late '70s, however, after several decades of U.S. military occupation of Asia, enterprising entrepreneurs began promoting sex tourism and mail-order bride services, targeting American veterans of Asian wars who had grown accustomed to traditional Asian women, whom they perceived as less "liberated" and "more subservient" than American women. A 1983 study conducted by Dr. Davor Jedlicka at the University of Texas found that the typical mail-order client is white, middle-aged, college-educated, and had been divorced at least once. Meanwhile, Asian women abroad

began to see marriage to an American man as way to find economic security and move to the United States, despite restrictions against immigration; in particular, Filipinas, who are often fluent in English and have some familiarity with American culture, began to make up the majority of the mail-order offerings.

Japanese Picture Brides upon arrival at Angel Island in the 1920s

Critics deride the mail-order bride business as tantamount to "an international sex ring" supported by loser men (such as, for instance, the alleged Oklahoma City bomber) and economically desperate women. The Asian women, sometimes catalogued only by a number and picture, must typically fill out a detailed form divulging everything from their attitude about "women's liberation" to the kind of underwear they wear. Answers often seem coached, though the occasional heartwrenchingly innocent statement will find its way into an entry.

The "Cherry Blossoms" agency believes that its success stories discount criticisms of exploitation. "This is not slavery," says a Cherry Blossoms representative. "What we are doing is promoting world peace more than anything else; we give men choices and bring cultures together."

Still, incidents such as the 1986 discovery of an Asian mail-order bride in Hawaii who was killed and dismembered by her husband have inflamed concern over these postal courtships; the match had been arranged by Cherry Blossoms.

Despite negative press, the services continue to be popular, and have even begun to offer a new geographical spin: In addition to women from Asia, many agencies now offer matches with women from Eastern Europe and the former Soviet Union, who have similar rationales for escaping their native countries.

Do "mail-order bride" agencies exploit poverty and the plight of women in war-torn or distressed nations? The answer is often yes. Are happy matches between mail-order grooms and their overseas brides possible? The answer, again, is also yes. And so the controversy roils on... —C.Y.

Model Minority

Are we or aren't we? Only the Census Bureau can say for sure. What started out as a seemingly harmless observation has grown into a scary socio-theoretical monster, devouring all racial groups in its path. Holding up Asian Americans as paragon and proof that racial discrimination need not be a barrier to social advancement, the "Model Minority" thesis drove a wedge between racial groups trying to forge coalitions after the Civil Rights movement of the 1960s. Thirty years since its inception, the end result of the Model Minority myth has been resentment of Asian Americans by blacks, whites, and even those Asians themselves who didn't fit the stereotype of the hardworking, lots-of-money-making, good-grade-getting, all-in-the-family-keeping whiz-kid. Though the stereotype might seem to be relatively innocuous—and even positive—it has simply proved the difficulty of living up to high expectations, while giving rationales to those who would kick out support props from under "bootstrapping" Asian Americans.

PROOF OF THE MODEL MINORITY?

Median Household Income	1980	1990
Asian Americans	$22,075	$42,250
White Americans	$20,840	$36,920

Mean SAT scores, 1992	Verbal	Math
All Students	423	476
Asian Americans	413	532
African Americans	352	385
Native Americans	395	442
European Americans	442	491
Mexican Americans	372	425
Puerto Ricans	366	406

Percentage of those over 25 with four years of college	1980	1990
Asian Americans	33%	39
White Americans	17.5	22

EVIDENCE TO THE CONTRARY

Though household income is higher, Asian American families tend to be larger, with more wage-earners. Meanwhile, Asian Americans are concentrated in cities, where the cost of living is higher. The poverty rate for recent Asian immigrants is twice the national average. And even though Asian Americans tend to be more educated, this does them little good, since Asian American college grads earn less than their white counterparts. Asian American per capita income is lower than that of whites. So who's a model anyway? —D.G.

THE MEDIA AND THE MYTH

1960s: The first time the term "model minority" appears in print, on January 6, in The New York Times Magazine. In "Success Story: Japanese American Style," sociologist William Petersen compares Japanese Americans to African Americans, crediting Japanese culture, with its family values and strong work ethic, for saving Japanese Americans from becoming a "problem minority." On December 26, U.S. News & World Report prints a similar article, "Success Story of One Minority Group in the U.S.," except it uses Chinese Americans. The "Model Minority" thesis becomes a ray of hope for those wishing to discredit the Civil Rights movement and Affirmative Action.

1970s: The U.S. loses a war in Vietnam. Southeast Asian refugees come in droves to take over American jobs. The Japanese auto industry muscles in. Model Minority articles begin to include sidebars on white resentment of Asian American success. Instead of using the thesis to disparage blacks and other minorities, the media use it to accuse whites of becoming soft and express white America's fears about competing with Asians, both in America and around the world.

1980s: Model Minority articles begin to mention the breadth of Asian American diversity, but continue to treat Asian Americans as one group, lumping fourth-generation Japanese and Chinese Americans alongside immigrants from South Korea, India, and the Philippines, and refugees from Cambodia, Laos, and Vietnam. With titles like "The Drive to Excel" (Newsweek on Campus, April, 1984) and "The New Whiz Kids" (Time, August, 1987), Model Minority articles tend to focus on Asian American success in school.

1984: In February, during a White House address, President Ronald Reagan holds up Asian Americans as an example all Americans should follow, citing the fact that the median household income for Asian Americans is higher than the national average. He probably means that as a compliment, but his administration also wants to wipe out government programs for minorities. The Model Minority thesis becomes a handy tool for fiscal razor-wielders.

1990: Model Minority articles begin to focus on Asian American entrepreneurial success, throwing around phrases like "refugee mentality." Native-born Americans, both black and white, are seen as having lost the "hardworking immigrant spirit" this country was built upon and being "too spoiled" to take on tough jobs. The Model Minority thesis begins to include recent European and Latino immigrants.

1992: The Model Minority is finally exposed as a myth. In June, The Washington Post prints an article called "Myth of Model Minority Haunts Asian Americans: Stereotype Eclipses Group's Problems." In June, Reason prints University of California–Davis professor Thomas Hazlett's obnoxious response, in which he sarcastically states that anyone who marvels at the success of certain disadvantaged minority groups "must harbor the soul of a Nazi."

1994: Charles Murray and Richard Herrnstein publish the controversial nonfiction work The Bell Curve, which suggests that Asian Americans and Jews statistically measure as more intelligent than African Americans because they're genetically more intelligent than African Americans—an interesting twist on Hitler's Aryan superiority theories. Speaking of the "soul of a Nazi..."

Asian Names: A Quick Guide

You've heard the joke, "Your momma is so fat she's got more chins than a Chinese phone book." Well, the fact of the matter is, as the Asian population in America increases, Chins are becoming prolific in American phone books as well—outpacing Joneses in popularity in many major metropolitan areas. Here's a rundown of some of the most common names found among the largest Asian American ethnic populations:

Note: Most Asian Americans use the standard Western name order (first name first, surname second); if they're second generation or later, it's likely their parents have given them English first names. They may also use an "Americanized" pronunciation of their surname (i.e., Gan with the "a" like "gigantic" as opposed to the proper pronunciation, which is more like "Gahn"). The following guide to Asian names is just a basic primer. As with anyone's name, if there's any doubt, it's best to ask someone for their preference. —D.G.

Ethnicity	Name order	Helpful hints	Common last names (pronunciations provided for the non-obvious)
Chinese	surname, first name (Mainland Chinese skater Chen Lu is often mistakenly called "Chen" by people who mistake it for her first name.)	Mainland Chinese use pinyin spellings; Chinese from anywhere else (Hong Kong, Singapore, etc.) use Wade-Giles spellings. To tell the difference: if it's got hyphens (i.e. Mao Tse-tung), it's Wade-Giles. Pinyin (Mao Zedong) doesn't use hyphens, and uses x's and c's to stand for Chinese sounds that don't transliterate well into English.	Chan (chahn, jahn), Chen (chuhn), Chin (cheen), Lin, Li (lee), Wong (wahng), Huang (whong), Yang (young), Fong (fahng), Chow (choh), Chang (chahng), Chung (chahng)
Japanese	surname, first name	Women's first names often end in -ko (i.e. Asako, Natsuko, Junko). Last names are usually (but not always) longer than first names.	Yamamoto, Kawaguchi, Nakamura, Tanaka, Watanabe, Suzuki
Korean	surname, two-part first name	Married women in Korea don't take their husbands' names; Korean American women do. You know it's the first name if it has a hyphen in it (i.e., Soo-young)	Kim, Park, Lee
Asian Indian	first name, surname	Initials are important to a woman's identity. In South India, women have two initials. Women take the initial of their dad's first name as their middle initial. After marriage, they use the initial of their husband's first name.	Patel and Chowdry (or Chaudry, Chadhury, or other variant spellings) are Hindu. Khan is Muslim. And if the person's got Singh in his name, you know he's Sikh.
Vietnamese	surname, middle name, first name	In Vietnam, it's okay to refer to people as Mr. Firstname (i.e. Nguyen Dustin could be called Mr. Dustin). If the person's middle name is Van, he's probably a man; if her middle name is Thi, she's a woman.	More than half of all Vietnamese are surnamed Nguyen ("nwen," though it's occasionally pronounced "nwin" or even "nuyen" in the U.S.). Another third have one of the following: Tran (truhn), Le (lay), Pham (fam), Vu, Ngo (nwo), Do (doh), Hoang (hwang), Dao, Dang, Duong (yung), or Dinh.

Ethnicity	Name order	Helpful hints	Common last names (pronunciations provided for the non-obvious)
Cambodian	surname, first name	Married women keep their maiden name, but it's okay to address them with Mrs. followed by their husband's surname (i.e. if you called Premier Pol Pot's wife Mrs. Pol, she wouldn't have a cow).	Keo (kyoo), Muy (maw-ee), Long (lung), Nuth (newt), Oum (ohn), Phal (pahl), Phay (pah-ee), Seng (sayng), Sok (sawk), Thuy (toy-ee)
Filipino	first name, surname	Most Filipino names are Spanish from the colonial era. Use the Castillian version (i.e. say "y" when you see "ll"; say the "j" like an "h"). You can tell which are the native Tagalog names because they're a lot harder to pronounce. Also, Filipinos like cutesy nicknames like Pinky, Cherry, Baby, and Boy. This doesn't say anything about their personalities, so don't be fooled.	Cruz (kroos), de la Cruz, Santos, Reyes, Ramos, Rodriguez, Gonzales, Hernandez, Fernandez, Garcia. Some Tagalog names (not necessarily common since they tend to vary by region) include Macapuguay (mahkapoogai), Dimaano (deemahahno), Sulit (sooleet), Tagalicod (tagahlikod). Filipinos of Chinese descent have standard Chinese surnames, such as Chang.

MORE ABOUT CHINESE NAMES

Legend has it that all Chinese surnames originated from the dozen or so names of regions handed down as fiefdoms by the Yellow Emperor to his sons. There are now a hundred or so common Chinese names; traditionally, like-surnamed Chinese were forbidden to intermarry, because they supposedly shared an ancestor (though granted, in some far-distant past). As names gradually mutated according to dialects and imperial rules, however, it has become less clear who's related to whom. Today, Chinese names that are spelled and pronounced differently may actually derive from the same Chinese character, and might therefore be considered related under the above custom. For example, the character for Chen can also denote Chin, Chan, Tan, or Ting, depending on whether the dialect is Mandarin, Cantonese, Hokkien, or Hokchew. A Lin is also a Lum (Cantonese), Lam (Cantonese), Lim (Hokkien), or Ling (Hokchew). Indeed, as a Chinese saying goes, "The Chens and Lins share half the world." —D.G.

Asian Organized Crime

They're lean, mean, and the travel in packs; if stared at too long, they'd just as soon cut your throat with a butterfly knife as stare at you back. According to recent hearings conducted by the Senate Permanent Subcommittee on Investigations, Chinese gangs are allegedly the most serious emerging threat to law and order in America. The subcommittee notes that criminally influenced business organizations called tongs, along with street gangs like the Flying Dragons and the Ghost Shadows, are at the fulcrum of many illicit activities in the U.S., including extortion scams and the opiate trade.

But the flip side of the "gangster threat" is the fact that street gangs serve as a support group for culturally alienated Chinese and Southeast Asian youths, of which there is no shortage. Membership has grown tremendously, although it is difficult to estimate how many gang members actually exist. "It's hard to keep tabs on Asian street gangs in terms of membership," explains T.J. English, author of Born to Kill, a look into the lives of Southeast Asian gangmembers. "The Asian underworld is very fluid with many of these kids having multiple memberships, quitting a gang one week and joining a different one the next. Unlike the Italian mob, Asian groups don't maintain membership oaths."

Street gangs also have loose ties to Triads, which began as secret ancient societies in China and have long been the linchpins of organized crime in Asia, with many of them headquartered in Hong Kong and Taiwan. These groups feast on a multi-billion dollar smorgasbord of illegal enterprises, including extortion, prostitution, alien smuggling, money laundering, and drug trafficking, including the lucrative heroin trade, formerly under the purview of La Cosa Nostra.

MONEY, THAT'S WHAT I WANT

The impact on the local Asian communities has been demoralizing. According to a 1990 study, it was estimated that 81 percent of the restaurants and nearly 66 percent of other businesses in New York's Chinatown were required to pay monthly "protection" to gangs. Smaller merchants generally pay between $100 to $200 a month, while larger proprietors are forced to cough up $300 or more. And if you're cutting the ribbon on a new venture, you can expect to be welcomed into this odd fraternity of commerce with an exorbitant membership fee.

VIETNAMESE GANGS

A troubling offshoot from Chinese organized crime in this country has been the increase of Southeast Asian gang activities. In 1992, the US government estimated that there were more than 80 different Vietnamese gangs in Orange County, California, alone. Vietnamese street gangs have had success in recruiting large numbers of young disenfranchised immigrants, thereby expanding their influence to rivals that of Chinese gangs. In fact, the most powerful Vietnamese street gang, the Born to Kill/Canal Street Boys, have so grown in stature over the years that they have been recruited by Hong Kong's Sun Yee triad to assist in its U.S. ventures.

JAPANESE GANGS

The high-profile Japanese Yakuza—which takes its name from a bad hand in a Japanese card game, thus implying "loser" and "outsider" status, has also hooked into niches in the U.S. crime bazaar, bringing in an estimated $10 billion dollars in annual illegal revenue. This includes the wildly profitable crystal methamphetamine or "Ice" trade. A global multi-billion dollar racket, the Yakuza is considered responsible for the most of the ice trafficking in Hawaii. Referred to nowadays as the *Boryokudan* or "Violent Ones," gang members are easily recognized by their lavish tattoos and occasionally, their truncated pinkies, cut off at the joint as penance for failure or for shame brought on the organization. —H.K.

A Worldwide Web of Fear

Each of the following groups are 20,000-plus members strong, with ties to U.S. groups:

- **14 K Triad, Hong Kong-based, with ties to the Hip Sing Tong, Flying Dragons gang, On Leong Tong, Ghost Shadows gang, Chinese Freemasons (all New York), and the Wah Ching gang (San Francisco)**
- **Sun Yee Triad, Hong Kong-based, with ties to Tung On gang, Tong On Tong, Flying Dragons gang, Ghost Shadows gang, Born to Kill gang, On Leong Tong, Tsun Tsing Association (all New York), and the Wah Ching gang (San Francisco)**
- **United Bamboo gang, Taiwan-based, with ties to the Fuk Ching Gang, Flying Dragons gang, Ghost Shadows gang (all New York, and the Wah Ching gang (San Francisco)**

Pandas

PANDA FACTS, IN BLACK AND WHITE:

- In the wild, pandas eat up to 40 pounds of bamboo daily (but they also eat meat).
- Newborn cubs weigh only four ounces; adults weigh between 175 and 300 pounds.
- A full-grown panda is about five feet long and stands two feet high at the shoulder.
- Pandas have a sixth digit that acts as a thumb, similar to the opposable thumbs of humans and apes.
- The World Wildlife Fund adopted the giant panda as its logo in 1958.
- The cat-sized red panda, which is distinguished by a foxy white face and bushy tail, was known to Western scientists before the giant panda.
- Of the 40 pandas taken out of China, only eight are known to be living at zoos, including those in Paris, Mexico, London, Madrid, and Japan; there are also five giant pandas in North Korea; but it is unclear whether those pandas are still alive.

The rare giant panda is probably the most endearing of China's mascots; over the past half-century, this black-and-white raccoon-bear has transcended continental borders, to burst into the political limelight as the animal kingdom's hottest international ambassador. Sadly, with only about 1,000 giant pandas left in the world—predominantly residing in the mountainous bamboo forests of China's Sichuan province—giant pandas are in grave danger of becoming extinct, from destruction of their habitats and from pelt-hunting poachers.

Giant pandas were first brought out of China and sent to foreign zoos in 1937: Pandas were housed in the U.S. at the Brookfield Zoo in Chicago and the Bronx Zoo in New York in the 1930s and 1940s. America's most famous pandas, however, were a male and female pair named Hsing Hsing and Ling Ling, given to President Richard M. Nixon in 1972 as a sign of China's newfound friendship with the States. Housed at the National Zoo in Washington, D.C., the widower Hsing Hsing remains the only panda permanently in the United States; during many years of fumbled mating attempts before her death in 1993, Ling Ling gave birth to five cubs—none of which survived beyond infancy. The National Zoo reports that the sweet-tempered Hsing Hsing, whose name translates as "Shining Star," is doing as well as any elderly panda is expected to do. He is fed rice gruel, apples, carrots, and vitamins, in addition to its natural diet of bamboo. Michael Morgan, a public affairs officer at the zoo, says the 24-year-old Hsing Hsing is probably the oldest panda in captivity, and for all of his age, he's still, per his name, a star, visited by 3,000,000 people per year.

The San Diego Zoo has been successful in obtaining a pair of pandas, Bai Yun and Shi Shi, on a research loan beginning in 1996; however, the loan is for just 12 years, and sadly, when Hsing Hsing's star falls, America will be deprived of its most beloved friend from China, possibly for good.

PANDA ORIGINS

The earliest reference to the giant panda appears in a dictionary dating back to the Qin Dynasty (221-207 B.C.), which describes them as a "white leopard" with black and white markings that eats bamboo stems...as well as copper and iron! This is because pandas (like raccoons) sometimes scavenged food in pots left outside peasants' houses, and occasionally chewed up the pots afterwards. Long debated whether pandas are closer to bears or raccoons, most scientists now believe the panda is, indeed, a type of bear.

WHY DO PANDAS HAVE CUTESY NAMES?

Morgan says that the Chinese traditionally gave pandas double names as a term of endearment. "Like Danny for Daniel," he explains, "Ling Ling means 'Little Darling.'" (The London Zoo in the late 1930s departed from tradition, naming their pandas Grumpy and Dopey.) Morgan adds that the Chinese Embassy even supplied the National Zoo with a list of viable names to pick from, in case one of Ling Ling's cubs had survived. —C.Y.

Fightin' Words: Slurs and insults

If you're a writer, editor, reporter, or simply someone trying to avoid starting a fight, you should be aware of the painful connotations of the following words—all of which are considered slurs when applied to Asian Americans.

buddhahead: Japanese American, referring to the religious preference of many Japanese and Japanese Americans. Note that Japanese Americans use the term with abandon, particularly those from the island of Hawaii, where the term is used to contrast with "katonks," or Japanese Americans from the U.S. mainland. (The mildly derogatory "katonk," one Japanese Hawaiian suggests, is derived from the hollow sound made when a mainlander Japanese American's head is tapped.)

Chinamen: from the 19th century, when Chinese immigrants referred to themselves as "China men" (two words). This is a literal translation of the Chinese phrase for "Chinese person"; but when whites deployed taunts of "Chinaman" and "Chinamen" during violent attacks and in racist propaganda against Chinese, the terms acquired a derogatory meaning. "Chinaman's chance," for instance, means "very little or no chance"—derived from the chance of survival for a Chinese immigrant under violent racial attack.

chink: Chinese or Chinese American; also used as a catch-all term for any East or Southeast Asian. Used widely as a slur since the 1850s, derived from a shortening of "Ch'ing Dynasty," which ruled in China during the first wave of Chinese immigration to the U.S. (Ironically, the Ch'ing emperors were not themselves ethnically Chinese, but rather Manchurian invaders.)

coolie: menial laborer, originally the 19th century Chinese immigrant workers. Believed to be derived from *ku-li,* a Chinese term meaning "bitter strength" or "bitter labor."

dogeater: Asian or Asian American, derived from the belief that dogs are part of a balanced diet in Asian countries. Most used to refer to Filipinos.

dot, dot-head: Indian or Indian American, derived from the dot-like *bindi* painted on the foreheads of married Hindu women.

dragon lady: an Asian woman, stereotypically evil, ruthless, and sexually predatory. Believed to have originated from the early 1900s comic strip *Terry and the Pirates,* which has since been revived by Michael Uslan. The original comic-strip Dragon Lady was beautiful but sinister, and she was the queen of a group of Chinese pirates; since then the term has achieved currency in referring to any strong and aggressive woman, but it still has special meaning when applied to Asian women.

flip: Filipino or Filipino American, derived from abbreviating "Filipino."

gook: Korean or Korcan American, also used as a catchall slur for any Asian. Probably derived from a corruption of *Hankook,* the Korean word for "Korea," and used widely by American G.I.s during the Korean and Vietnam wars.

Jap: Japanese or Japanese American, used widely before and during World War II, when Americans first needed a hateful term for the enemy. (Note: The proper abbreviation for Japan is "Jpn.")

nip: Japanese or Japanese American, derived from Nippon, which means "Japan" in Japanese. In widespread use since the early 1900s.

slant, slant-eye: Asian or Asian American, originating in the 19th century when white cartoonists would draw caricatures of Asians as having slanted lines, with no visible pupils, for eyes. A related sexual myth suggested that Asian women had horizontally oriented vaginas, leading to heated speculation on the part of the anatomy-ignorant.

slope: Asian or Asian American. Again referring to the stereotypical shape of Asian eyes, this slur originated in the U.S. military during the 1950s.

yellow peril: Asians as a threat to Western civilization, referring to the fear that Asians would take over the earth because of their large numbers. First used by media and politicians in the 1880s to portray Asian immigrants as poised to invade the U.S.—militarily or economically; revived a century later in reference to Japan.

THEY DO, BUT YOU CAN'T Derogatory terms Asian Americans use to refer to themselves

BANANA: Like the fruit, "yellow on the outside, white on the inside"—used by Asian Americans to refer to other Asian Americans whom they perceive as denying their Asian heritage or identity.

COCONUT: Similar to "banana," "brown on the outside, white on the inside," but used by South Asian and Filipino Americans.

FOB: "Fresh Off the Boat"—pronounced either "fob" or "Eff-Oh-Bee," this acronym refers to recent immigrants who have a disoriented, disheveled, or otherwise out-of-the-acculturated-mainstream appearance. Sometimes used as the root of an adjective ("fobby" or "fobbish"); rarely, but occasionally modernized to "FOP" for "Fresh Off the Plane."

JOOK SING: A specifically Cantonese term translating as "hollow bamboo," and referring to born-in-the-U.S. Chinese Americans who have lost critical elements of their heritage, like fluency in the language or the ability to use chopsticks.

TWINKIE: A modernized, trademarked synonym for "banana." Used occasionally as an adjective: "Her clothes are so Twinkie."

WHIGGIE: A relatively new and vicious derogatory term, derived from an acronym for "White Guy Groupie"; refers to Asian women who only socialize with or date white men.

THEY DO, BUT THEY SHOULDN'T

Derogatory terms Asians occasionally use to refer to non-Asians

BAK GWAI; HAK GWAI: literally, "white ghost" or "black ghost" in Cantonese.

LO FAN: "Foreigner" in Cantonese

GWAI LO: "Foreign ghost" in Cantonese.

GAIJIN, BAKUJIN, HAKUJIN: In Japanese, "foreigner," "white person," and "black person," all with negative connotations.

ROUNDEYE: In contrast to the slur against Asians, "slant-eye"

PUTE: Filipino for "white," often with a negative connotation

HAOLE: Hawaiian for "white," sometimes with a contemptuous tone; it's been adopted widely in the West Coast as well, as has the related hapa (short for hapa haole, or half-white), referring to biracial Asian individuals.

I know you are, but what am I?!!!!?!

WHY "ORIENTAL" IS A BAD WORD

Many Asians in America find the term "oriental," when used in reference to people, to be offensive. The reasons for this sensitivity are manifold, but some of the most important ones are listed below.

1. It brings up unfortunate chapters in our global history. The terms "Orient" and "oriental" were popularized during the heyday of Western colonialism, when nations to the South and East of Europe were seen as ripe for subjugation and exploitation. As a result, usage of the term is an automatic cue for references to the British Raj, the Opium War, the occupation of the Philippines, and other events and periods in which the inhabitants of Asian countries were enslaved, victimized, or otherwise mistreated by Europeans (and later, Americans).

2. It has problematic racial and political connotations. While "Orient" translates simply as "The East," over time, an ideological paradigm emerged that spun itself around the term: The Orient was seen as the farthest point from civilization (i.e., Europe) and thus a region of barbarism, exotic custom, and strange delight. "Orientals" were conceived of as mysterious and inscrutable, with traditions and beliefs so different as to be inhuman—and thus requiring of either speculative study or religious evangelism. As social historian Edward Said detailed in his seminal book of that name, the intent and result of orientalism was the objectification of cultures in Asia and the Middle East, providing a rationale for colonial subjugation, missionary conversion, and military adventure, it later also created a context for domestic racism and xenophobia.

3. It's nonspecific. As perceived by Western Europeans, "The Orient" included all of the Turkey, the Middle East, Asia, and to a lesser extent the Pacific Islands. An Iranian was therefore just as "Oriental" as a Chinese person, though in contemporary times, the term is never used in that manner. While "Asian" is not much more specific, it at least is a term bounded by geography rather than paradigm. It would be difficult to argue that "Orientals" shared anything in common, other than in the feverish minds of European orientalists.

4. It doesn't have an appropriate counterpart. The most subtle yet invidious problem with the term "Oriental" is that it stands alone: No one refers to Europeans or Americans as "Occidentals." Consider that the term "Orient" only has meaning in the West; in the East, it is America and Europe that are foreign and "outside," and most Asian cultures have similar but inverted conceptions referring to "The West." Hemispheric definitions are always problematic, since the world is, after all, round; but at least the terms East and West don't come loaded with the imagery and history of "Orient" and "Occident."

5. It's more appropriately used for inanimate objects. The establishment of trade routes linking the nations of Asia and the Middle East (which occurred long before the opening of Asia to the West) meant that commodities and other goods were regularly transmitted between cultures. As a result, when one refers to Oriental spices or rugs, one has a stable rationale from which to speak: spices and rugs are among the only things that the mixed bag of peoples known as "Orientals" actually had in common. In general, the use of the adjective in relation to inanimate objects or abstract concepts has largely been considered acceptable, if not embraced (there are people who still prefer speaking of Asian spices, or breaking down rugs into Persian, Indian, and Chinese carpets).

6. Some people don't like it. In America, at least, many Asians find the term distasteful (mostly younger Asian Americans); the term has also been eliminated from usage in journalism and entertainment. (By contrast, many British use "Asian" to refer to Indians and other South Asians, and "Oriental" to refer to East Asians.) The rule of thumb is simple: rather than risk offending, just don't bother—the term "Asian" is neutral, widely accepted—and safe. —D.G., J.Y.

EST

END

Pi‿ture Credi‿s

ART & DESIGN

Academy of Motion Picture Arts and Sciences-8; American Film Foundation/ Sanders & Mock Productions-12*(Maya Lin at work on the Civil Rights Memorial)*; Brooklyn Botanic Garden-2*(from its 1993 bonsai exhibition)*; **Henry Chen**-7; China National Tourist Office,*l*-17; **Melissa Cooperman**-14,*r*-17; Felissimo/ Ann Stratton Photography 1995-5; Government of India Tourist Office-21; The Isamu Noguchi Foundation, Inc./Kevin Noble-13*(Akari light Sculptures, model numbers from left to right: UF3-Q, UF4-33N, UF3-S, 14A)*; Yasuhiro Ishimoto-9; Japanese National Tourist Office-3,11*(Japanese Flags celebrating New Year's Day)*,18,22,23; Kwang Hwa Publishing Company/ Taipei Gallery-4*([linear] late Ch'ing period; [painterly] Sung Dynasty period)*,18,19; New York Convention & Visitor Bureau-10; Norton Simon Museum-23; Portland Oregon Visitors Association-9; Eiichiro Sakata,*s*-9; © Sanrio, Inc.

BOOKS & LITERATURE

Shino Arihara-49-53; **Henry Chen**-34,35,36; China National Tourist Office-37; The Corsortium, Inc.-48; Kodansha International-45; National Archives-31; © 1996 Rumiko Takahashi/ Shogakukan, Inc./ Viz Communications, Inc.-47; © 1993 Sho Fumimura/ Ryoichi Ikegami/ Shogakukan, Inc./ Viz Communications, Inc.-46

FILM & TELEVISION

Artifical Eye/ Thompson/ China/ Beijing Film-103*(Farewell My Concubine)*; © Artmic/ Youmex/ AnimEigo, Inc.,*t/l*-61*(Bubblegum Crisis)*; **Michael Andre Brandt**,*l*-79; Central Park Media,*b/c*-61; **Melissa Cooperman**-86; Era International Shanghai Film Studio-104(To Live); Film Comment magazine/ Film Society of Lincoln Center-90-1,102; Funimation Productions Inc.-56,58; Gigantar © and TM Entercolor Technologies Corp., All Artwork © Mitsuteru Yokoyama, *b-56,l-70*; Golan-Golbus/ Canon-109-10; Golden Princess/ Milestone-82; Guangxi Film Studio-102*(Yellow Earth)*; Guild/A2/Giai Phong Film,l-83*(The Lover)*;Harmony Gold-60; © Kitty Films/ AnimEigo, Inc.*(Urusei Yatsura)*; Kodansha, Bandai Visual, Manga Entertainment,*l*-59; Longwick Beijing Film Studio-106*(The Blue Kite)*; composite by **Garland Lyn**-115-6; Mainline/ Central Motion Picture/ Good Machine-112; Manga Entertainment, *r*-59,*t/r*-61,*b/r*-61; Miramax,*s*-76*(Chungking Express)*,83*(CK Ex)*,85*(Bridgette Lin in CK Ex)*,*105(Chen Kaige directing Temptress Moon)*; Miramax/ Dimensions Films-74,*s*-79*(Khan in Supercop)*,80*(Jackie Chan in Supercop)*,82 *(Khan)*,84,92*(Takeshi Kitano in Sonatine)*; National Archives-117; © 1963 NBC Films, renewed 1991 Suzuki Associates International, Inc. Distributed in North America by The Right Stuf International, Inc.-65-7; New Line Home Video*(The Street Fighter)*-68; Orion Home Video-57; Palace/ Era/ China Film-104,t/s-104; Paramount Pictures-91,111*(Nancy Kwan in The World of Suzie Wong)*,*119(Mickey Rouney in Breakfast at Tiffany's)*; Pioneer Entertainment,*s*-56,*t/c*-61; © 1996 Rumiko Takahashi/ Shogakukan, Inc./ Viz Communications, Inc.,*b/l*-61; Saban Entertainment in America-108; Serene / Pandora/ Beijing Studio/ Herald Ace/ Film Four/ Berlin,*s*-102; © Toei Animation/ DIC Communications-62; Toho Productions-71-73,107*(Seven Samurai)*; TriStar Pictures-75*(Tsui Hark directing Double Team)*; 20th Century Fox-78*(John Woo directing Christian Slater in Broken Arrow)*; © Ultracom-114; Voyager Entertainment, Inc.-55,64; Warner/Concord-95-8; Xi'an Film Studio,*s*-105*(The Horse Thief)*; Zeitgeist Films Ltd.,*s*-81

FOOD & DRINK

California Pizza Kitchen, Inc.-135; **Luciana Chang**-128,133-4,*t*-160,163-4,170; **Henry Chen**-123-4,127,131,133-4,136-8,157-8,*b*-160,*b*-160,161,165-6,169; Government of India Tourist Office-141-3; Japanese National Tourist Office-145-7,*s*-167; Kwang Hwa Publishing Company/ Taipei Gallery-129,139; **Garland Lyn**-121-2,133-4,167,168; Woo Chon Restaurant-146

GAMES & LEISURE

Henry Chen-173-4,181,195; Capcom-200; Honda-192; IBM-172; The Ishi Press-180; Japanese National Tourist Office-175,193,196,198; Jhoon Rhee Seminar-186; **Mike Quon**-185-9,196; Nintendo of America Inc.-199-201; Pachinko Palace-194; Sega of America-199-201; Sony Electronics Inc.-176; Studio One/ David Behl,*t*-172; Cydney Topol, model: Sarah Margolis of Yoga Fitness-202

IDEAS & PHILOSOPHY

Shino Arihara-221-3,237-8; **Henry Chen**-204,241,245-6; **Melissa Cooperman**-220; Government of India Tourist Office,*c*-207,216; Japanese National Tourist Office,*r*-207,*b*-208; Kripalu Center-230; Kwang Hwa Publishing Company/ Taipei Gallery,*r*-206,209,*t&c*-208,219,242-3,244,247-8; New York Convention & Visitors Bureau,*l*-206; Norton Simon Museum-231,232; San Francisco Tourist Bureau-207; **Chiun-kai Shih**-218; The Trump Organization-226; **Alison Wright**-217

SOUND & STAGE

Angel/ Dark Horse Records,b-279; Artifical Eye/ Thompson/ China/ Beijing Film,*b/s*-254; Atlantic/ Atco Records-264; Columbia Records,t-253; **Melissa Cooperman**,*t*-281; Domo Records Inc.-270; Sony Classical/ J. Henry Fair,*l1st*-251; Elektra Entertainment/ Kazunari Tajima (Tajjiemax Productions),*b/l*-262; EMI Classics,c*35th*-251; EMI Classics/ Cindy Palmano-250; ICM Artisst, Ldt./ Jack Mitchell,c3rd-251; Japanese National Tourist Office-268-9,273,280; Kwang Hwa Publishing Company/ Taipei Gallery-260-1,*b*-281; **Garland Lyn**,*r*-263; Matador Records/ Gen Inaba-277; Miramax-259; Reprise Records-267; Shadow Records/ James Smocka,r/l-262; Relativity Records,l/t-262; Studio One-275, 276; Verve Records/ N. Schoerner,b/r-262; Verve Records/ Polygram Records-266*(Sadao Watanabe)*; Virgin Records/ Yuu Kamimaki,t/l-263; Warner Bros. Records Inc./ Reprise Records/ Jill Greenberg,b/l-263; Tristar Records-271;

STYLE & FASHION

Henry Chen-291,301;Cultured Pearl Association-292-3; Felissimo/ Ann Stratton Photography '95-294; Kwang Hwa Publishing Company/ Taipei Gallery-295; Japanese National Tourist Office-299-300

TRENDS & PHENOMENA

ASIA (Adoption Services Information Agency)-310; National Archives-320,r-321,330; New York Convention & Visitor Bureau-317*(NYC)*,*l*-321,327

[left=*l*,right=*r*,center=*c*,top=*t*,bottom=*b*,sidebar=*s*]

SPECIAL THANKS TO:

Angel Island Immigration Station; **Kamna Chan**; Film Comment/ Film Society of Lincoln Center; Tanya Anthony of Japanese National Tourist Office; Taipei Gallery, NYC

About the Editors

Jeff Yang, one of the most acclaimed young voices of Asian America, is the publisher and founder of *A. Magazine,* the first magazine by, for, and about Asian Americans. Yang was the youngest—and first Asian American—columnist in the history of the *Village Voice,* and has been a featured contributor in publications ranging from *Mademoiselle* to *Vibe,* writing about such topics as hiphop, identity politics, and cyberpop. Yang developed the concept of *A. Magazine* as a Harvard undergraduate, and launched it upon graduation. He lives in lower Manhattan.

Dina Gan is a contributing features editor of *A. Magazine*. Highlights among the many pieces she has written for *A.* include: a survey of the sexual proclivities of Asian American twentysomethings; a report on her experiences parading around New York City in the guise of a white woman (courtesy of theatrical effects); and a road test of bras for women who don't need them. Gan graduated from Johns Hopkins University with a B.A. in philosophy and creative writing, studying under the likes of John Barth (who told her she had no talent) and Madison Smartt Bell (who begged to differ). A native of Baltimore, Gan lives in midtown Manhattan.

Terry Hong is a contributing editor and theater columnist for *A. Magazine*. Her interviews and profiles for *A.* have included David Henry Hwang, B.D. Wong, Joan Chen, and the Pan Asian Repertory Theater ("Big Dicks, Asian Men," "Shogun Macbeth"), among many others. Hong is the co-author of *Notable Asian Americans* and the literary reference *What Do I Read Next? (Multicultural Edition)*, and she is a contributor to *The Asian American Almanac*. Hong is currently completing a Ph.D. in Japanese literature at Yale. She lives with her husband and baby daughter in Connecticut.

A. MAGAZINE

A. Magazine™: *Inside Asian America* (ISSN# 1070-9401), is published six times annually by Metro East Publications, Inc.
270 Lafayette Street
Siute 400
New York, NY 10012
tel (212) 925-2123;
fax (212) 925-2896;
amag@amagazine.com;
WWW: http://www.amagazine.com /

Subscriptions: $15 for six issues (subscription tel. only, 1-800-346-0085 x477).
POSTMASTER: Send address changes to Superior Fulfillment, 131 W. 1st St., Duluth, MN 55802-2065 Attn: A. Magazine
e-mail: fulfill@superfil.com (enter "A. Magazine" in subject line.)